Muhammad ﷺ

Man and Prophet

A Complete Study of the Life of the Prophet of Islam

Adil Salahi

THE ISLAMIC FOUNDATION

First published in the UK in 1995 by
Element Books Limited

Published by
THE ISLAMIC FOUNDATION
Markfield Conference Centre,
Ratby Lane, Markfield, Leicestershire LE67 9SY, United Kingdom
Tel: (01530) 244944, Fax: (01530) 244946
E-mail: i.foundation@islamic-foundation.org.uk
Website: www.islamic-foundation.org.uk

Quran House, PO Box 30611, Nairobi, Kenya

PMB 3193, Kano, Nigeria

British Library Cataloguing in Publication Data
Salahi, M.A., Muhammad: Man and Prophet: a complete study of the life of the
Prophet of Islam—Rev. ed.—1. Muhammad, Prophet, d. 632—Biography
2. Muhammad, Prophet, d. 632—Prophetic office 3. Islam—Origin
I. Title II. Islamic Foundation
297.6'3

ISBN 0–86037–327–4
ISBN 0–86037–322–3 pbk

Cover design by Suhaib Salahi
Typeset by Nasir Cadir and N.Qaddoura
Printed in Great Britain by Antony Rowe Ltd

Dedication

TO MY PARENTS who have taught me that loving the Prophet Muhammad could only be demonstrated by following his teachings, not by singing his praises.

To Amr, Suhaib and Zaid, my children, and to their generation of English-speaking Muslims. I hope this effort will make it easier for them to follow the Prophet's guidance.

And to Hayfa... She knows why.

Transliteration Table

Consonants. Arabic

initial: unexpressed medial and final:

ء	ʾ	د	d	ض	ḍ	ك	k
ب	b	ذ	dh	ط	ṭ	ل	l
ت	t	ر	r	ظ	ẓ	م	m
ث	th	ز	z	ع	ʿ	ن	n
ج	j	س	s	غ	gh	هـ	h
ح	ḥ	ش	sh	ف	f	و	w
خ	kh	ص	ṣ	ق	q	ي	y

Vowels, diphthongs, etc.

Short:	ـَ	a	ـِ	i	ـُ	u
Long:	ـَا	ā	ـُو	ū	ـِي	ī
Diphthongs:			ـَوْ	aw		
			ـَيْ	ay		

بسم الله الرحمن الرحيم

Contents

Preface

PERHAPS THE WORLD was never in greater need of an accurate account of Prophet Muhammad's life than it is now. Interest in Islam has soared over the last couple of decades, and the trend continues after the turn of the century, but not always for the right reasons. Events, some of which were brought about by Muslims painting themselves as advocates of Islam, tended to give this last divine religion a tarnished image. Though alien to Islam's very nature, extremism has been trying to impose its hard line attitude on Islam. It continued to play its eye-catching role, providing a fertile area for those who wish to detract from Islam and to show it in a negative light. World media, always quick to feed on sensational news, has kept Islam as a recurrent topic in its coverage of events, particularly those taking place in hot spots of the world.

The charge that is often laid at the door of Islam is 'terrorism'. This has gathered much greater force after the tragic events of 11 September 2001, but certainly did not start with them. Several months earlier, news channels reported that an audience in the US were asked to state the first word that came to their minds when Islam is mentioned, and a substantial majority of the respondents said 'terrorism'. We are reminded that when the Oklahoma City explosions occurred a few years ago, few media channels were prepared to show the willingness to wait for evidence before pointing an accusing finger at Islam. Needless to say, investigations soon proved that no Muslim had anything to do with that event. But the speed with which the media reacted and its unfounded accusations were indicative of an attitude of mind that certain quarters had helped to develop, fostering a false association between Islam and terrorism.

Nothing can be further from the truth. In fact, Islam considers terrorist action against civilians a very grave crime that must be punished. In Islamic law, punishment always looks at the nature of the offence and aims to deter offenders before they embark on a course of action leading to an offence. This deterrent element is seen, for example, in the fact that Islam requires that punishment of certain offences must be carried out in public. Thus justice is seen to be done, and prospective offenders are aware not only of the magnitude of the punishment they may have but also the publicity which their offences generate. Islam, then, deals with crime before it is committed, trying to reduce its incidence. At the same time, Islamic punishments serve a dual purpose of making the guilty pay for their crimes and deterring any future offenders. The Islamic attitude towards terrorism is an implementation of its approach to crime, aiming to achieve its dual purpose.

More recently we have been hearing louder voices speaking about a clash of civilizations, setting Islam in opposition to Western civilization and speaking about the inevitability of a destructive struggle between the two. Yet Islam does not seek to destroy any civilization. In its heyday, when Islam spread into many countries with divergent civilizations, traditions and sets of values, Islam interacted with them all, endorsing whatever was compatible with its aim of building a human society based on the central idea of God's oneness. It was thus able to take the best that these civilizations had to offer, rejecting only what was of no use to human society, and what was incompatible with its central concepts. Even in Arabia, the birthplace of Islam, where idol worship was the norm, Islam accepted all good values that prevailed in that society, adopting them as its own. Thus Islam was able to incorporate into its civilization all the sound values human societies upheld, harnessing them together in a complete whole. Its approach remains the same. It is open to the best ideas and concepts people may have, rejecting only what is oppressive and false, and what stifles man's free thought.

Nevertheless, the outcry about a clash of civilizations continues, with certain loud voices trying to pour petrol on the flames. Sweeping judgements by public figures, saying that Western civilization is superior to Islam, are often quoted in the media. Needless to say, such an outcry serves no real purpose. On the other hand, some politicians, mindful of the Muslim element in their constituencies, may try to cover up their unfavourable feelings with more diplomatic statements. Others speak in conciliatory terms and make friendly gestures, but these are often belied by their aggressive actions.

But why should there be any clash of civilizations when both Islam and Western civilization lay great emphasis on man's freedom of thought, belief and expression? To my mind, erroneous perceptions on both sides have contributed to a polarization of attitudes that is unnecessary, harmful and potentially very dangerous. Unfortunately such erroneous perceptions have marred several aspects of Islam so extensively that these are often wrongly understood by both friend and foe. This has deepened mistrust and suspicion on both sides.

It only requires that both sides live up to their basic values of freedom for friendship and mutual cooperation to replace the underlying mistrust, fear and even hostility that have characterized relations between the two camps for centuries. Sadly, in the present circumstances, this is easier said than done. The attacks of 11 September 2001 and subsequent events will inevitably harden attitudes, rather than help to promote mutual understanding. When politicians try hard to defend the indefensible and justify what, deep at heart, they know to be unjustifiable, they can hardly hope to win over anyone who respects civilized values. Similarly, when those who profess to be advocates of Islam step far beyond the role God has defined for His messenger in advocating His message, the only results they can achieve are the opposite of the goals they set for themselves.

What is needed is a genuine reappraisal of preconceived notions so that we are able to determine what is right and stick to it. The West may pride itself on occupying the high moral ground, but it can only give credence to what it professes if it continues to adhere to its moral values in times of adversity, not shed them at the slightest temptation. And when advocates of Islam seek more than freedom to address other people and explain God's message to them, they do a disservice to the very cause they want to serve.

The only task Islamic advocacy should set for itself is to deliver God's message to mankind. Whether people accept or reject it is entirely their own business. No pressure should be put on them to try to bring them into Islam. Exerting such pressure is alien to the very nature of the Islamic faith. Addressing His messenger, God says in the Qur'ān: "If they turn away from you, know that We have not sent you to be their keeper: your only task is to deliver the message entrusted to you." (42: 48)

This is the mission to which Prophet Muhammad dedicated all his efforts, from the moment when he was entrusted with God's message up to the point when his blessed life on earth was over. When studying his life, we find this clearly apparent, both at the time when his message was met with endless adversity that observed no values and when he wielded power which, had he wished, he could use to force his opponents into submission. The present work aims to present his blessed life in its true light. It covers the main events in the Prophet Muhammad's life from childhood to old age. It is only natural that we give much greater attention to the events that followed the start of the revelation of the Qur'ān, God's final message to mankind. In each event we recognize his role as a messenger entrusted with delivering a message, and we see the example he sets for us to follow. Following his example is part of the requirements of being a Muslim. To abandon his example in preference for some other practices is to negate the second part of the first article of Islamic faith, namely, the declaration that there is no deity other than God and that Muhammad is God's messenger.

When reading about the Prophet's life, one must put the military activity of the Muslim community under the Prophet's leadership in true perspective. Was Muhammad a warrior, as a cursory look at his life may suggest? If so, how does this relate to the task outlined in the above-quoted, definitive Qur'ānic verse limiting his task to delivering God's message?

In the present world climate, there are people who try to limit the scope of going to war in Islam, or for Islam, to an absolute minimum. I read recently in a British newspaper an article by a prolific Muslim author, saying that war during the lifetime of the Prophet totalled no more than one week in the 23 years period from the start of his message to the end of his life. Others try to justify going to war in Islamic history by saying that Islam approves of war only when it is defensive.

On the other hand, there are well-meaning advocates of Islam who place military means high on the list of Islamic requirements, considering *jihād* as a major Islamic duty that comes next to the five 'pillars' of Islam. Others are keen to show that Islam has a militaristic approach, pointing out that it calls for 'holy war' against unbelievers.

A proper study of the Prophet's life shows us that none of these views is correct. The Prophet was engaged in full-scale military campaigns which, for the most part, took one day of fighting each, but the preparations and pre-battle engagement, and the states of siege mounted on certain occasions, took much longer than that. The Expedition of the Moat and the Siege of the Qurayẓah which followed immediately afterwards, took nearly two months, during which the Muslim state in Madinah was in full military mobilization, even though little actual fighting took place. Yet these events were the ones that turned the balance of power in Arabia irretrievably in the Muslim community's favour.

It may be easy to describe the Islamic attitude to war as purely defensive, but there is nothing to be gained by that. Islam always takes a positive attitude and calls on its followers to adopt all necessary measures to ensure the safety of the Muslim community. If this means having to go to war, then so be it. We have to bear in mind, however, that Islam does not approve of waging war except in a situation where peaceful measures are of no use. This means that Islam does not approve of a military offensive, except to repel an aggression started or planned by an enemy. We see examples of this nature in the Prophet's own actions as he took effective measures to consolidate his state in Madinah and ensure its security. Never did he start a battle or raise an army to attack any tribe or group that was willing to live in peace with Islam. Even when the Quraysh insisted on adopting a hard line just before the Battle of Badr, turning a deaf ear to the voice of wisdom emanating from some of its own elders, the Prophet was keen to avoid a military engagement. Whenever he tried to take an enemy by surprise, his strategy was to show the enemy that starting a fight was useless. Thus, bloodshed was largely avoided in such confrontations.

On the other hand, those who lay much emphasis on the role of *jihād* in the Muslim community, which is important indeed, often limit *jihād* to military fighting, showing that Islam resorts to military force to achieve its objectives. This is again an erroneous view, whether advanced by advocates or opponents of Islam. *Jihād* is an Islamic requirement, no doubt. But this applies in the proper and broad sense of the word *jihād*, which means 'to exert one's best effort'. Every Muslim is required to work for Islam, in his or her own place in the Muslim community, trying to serve God's cause and further the interests of the Muslims throughout the world. All this is part of *jihād*, or the efforts we exert to make our belief a living reality.

The efforts we need to exert may, on occasions, take the form of a military engagement, but this is the exception, not the rule. It is to be noted that not once in the Qur'ān is the term *jihād* used in the sense of a military fight, although the Qur'ān comments on many battles that took place during the Prophet's lifetime. When it refers to war, the Qur'ān invariably uses the term *qitāl*, which means 'military combat'.

Those who claim that Islam calls for a holy war betray their ignorance of this great religion. Nowhere in the Qur'ān or the Prophet's statements or in the writings of leading Islamic jurists does this term occur. In Islamic terminology, the adjective 'holy' applies to God only.

When we say all this, people are entitled to ask about the reason for the large number of expeditions that the Prophet sent out of Madinah, particularly in the first few years of his settlement there. A proper understanding of these may be gathered from reading this book that attempts to document the main events in the Prophet's life. We may say here that a new state established in one city in the middle of a vast, hostile area where tribal warfare was an everyday event could only expect to be attacked. Indeed, attacks were expected from several quarters. Hence, it was necessary for the Prophet and the Muslim community to take every possible precaution, so as to be fully prepared to face any danger that could threaten its existence at any time. Such danger was indeed imminent, culminating in an alliance of all hostile forces moving forward with the declared aim of exterminating the entire Muslim community. That Islam could overcome all this danger was due to God's help and mercy in the first place, the wise policy of the Prophet and the solid commitment of the Muslims to their cause.

It is impossible to document the Prophet's life without giving due prominence to such military activities. Indeed, early historians who wrote about Prophet Muhammad felt that these were the most important events, because they involved hostile forces. Hence, they called their histories, *Al-Maghāzī*, or *The Expeditions.* They might have felt that it was easy to gather the social and human dimensions of the society the Prophet had built, because these could still be seen in the Muslim community and the way it conducted its life. Later, a biography of the Prophet and a history of the period which witnessed the rise of the first Muslim community could not overlook the importance of the military aspect, because it was through such military events that the community could establish its right to exist and prosper.

For Muslims, studying the life of the Prophet Muhammad (peace be upon him) is a duty that gives them an insight into how Islam is to be implemented in practice. Hence, putting the military element into proper perspective acquires, particularly in the present day, added importance. Is it possible to bring about a complete Islamic revival without waging war against existing society? Which society is to be considered hostile? Could a revivalist movement resort to a pre-emptive strike against an unfriendly society? What restrictions apply to the use of military force in the context of Islamic revival? The proper answers to these questions, and similar ones, are to be deduced from studying the Prophet's life, as it provides the model to be followed in putting Qur'ānic teachings into practice. Such a study is bound to show that when the Prophet preached his message in Makkah and the Muslims suffered persecution, no military activity was allowed. Later, when the Muslims established their new state in the midst of hostile forces, war was allowed as the situation demanded. A few years later, when the Muslim community was able to wrest the initiative, war was avoided by all means. Even when the chance to wreak vengeance against those who for many years persecuted the Muslims and turned the Prophet out of his home town was there to grasp, every effort was made to shed no blood, and to make yesterday's enemies today's friends. The building of a closely-knit community based on faith, in which all maintain a bond of brotherhood, was the ultimate goal.

In our modern world, advocates of Islam want to see Islam guiding humanity again, because they believe that such guidance can only bring peace and happiness to a world that has suffered much injustice. In trying to achieve this, they must be guided by the Prophet's example, realizing that their task, for the fulfilment of which they are accountable to God, does not go beyond delivering the message of Islam to mankind. If they try to go beyond that, they run the very real risk of making their efforts counterproductive. They should always remember that God has limited the Prophet's role to this because He knows that it is the role that brings about the best results. It is not for them to try to extend their role beyond this point.

For the rest of mankind, a proper understanding of the nature of Islamic advocacy is most helpful in shaping their attitudes to Islam and Islamic revivalist movements. Such an understanding will tell them that all they need to do in order to live in peace with the advocates of Islam is to ensure that freedom of belief and expression is part of the real, not the ideal, world. After all, such freedom is an inalienable right of every human being. Islam gives it the highest rank among all human rights. It takes precedence over the right to life. Evidence in support of this is found in two Qur'ānic verses: "Persecution is even worse than killing." (2: 191) "Persecution is an even greater crime than killing." (2: 217) According to Dr M.H. Khayat, a contemporary scholar, "These verses give a clear principle that persecution, which means a 'denial of freedom' is a far worse and greater offence than killing, which is a 'denial of the right to life'. This principle leads to a logical conclusion that freedom is more important than life. This is by no means strange, bearing in mind that the very humanity of man is the result of such freedom."[1] With such emphasis on freedom, Islam treats its opponents with respect, provided that they respect people's rights to free choice. From its own perspective, Western civilization could find no reason to quarrel with this attitude since it takes pride in guaranteeing such freedom to all people.

London **Adil Salahi**
January 2002

Note

1. M.H. Khayat, *Health as a Human Right*, to be published by the World Health Organization, Cairo, 2002.

Introduction to the First Edition

I CANNOT REMEMBER how old I was when I completed the first book I read which gave a proper history of the life of Prophet Muhammad (peace be upon him). But I was probably 12, or a little younger, when my Arabic teacher, Mr Muhammad al-Jābī, gave me a book on the Prophet's character as a prize for being top of the class in Arabic. Although I read the book at that time, I confess I did not understand it well. Maybe its superb literary style, or its philosophical outlook, was a little too hard for me. Yet I treasured the book and kept referring to it now and then, using it to much advantage eventually.

My first job after graduation was with the Syrian Radio in Damascus. I was still receiving training when the post of Controller was given to a man with a clear vision of what a radio station being monitored in neighbouring countries should be broadcasting. In his brief spell at the post, he changed the whole outlook of Syrian Radio and gave unwavering encouragement to young talent. It took him only a few minutes to accept my proposal to write the *Life of the Prophet* in the form of a radio play, to be serialized in thirty 15-minute episodes. That proposal might have reflected a young man's enthusiasm rather than a well-considered project. I praise the

Almighty for the success of that first venture in writing about the Prophet. Those two experiences must have left a profound influence on me so as to herald a strong relationship with the events of that remarkable and unique period in the history of mankind when the Prophet moulded the first Muslim community and established the first Islamic state.

There was a period of time, during my early years in England, when I could not put down the *Life of the Prophet* by Ibn Hishām. I do not recall how many times I read that invaluable book, written over a thousand years ago, but I kept reading it again and again, feeling that each time I could learn something new. I cannot adequately describe its great appeal to me. I could see the events it related taking place in front of me. Those were the events of a period with great and everlasting influence on the area which later came to be known as the Muslim World, and indeed on the world at large. As I pictured those events, I was not a passive spectator. On the contrary, I experienced a keen sense of belonging to that community which did not only make history while it lived, but also determined the course history would follow for centuries to come.

I later diversified my sources as I tried to improve my understanding of the first generation of Muslims. My readings were instrumental in shaping my thoughts and gave me numerous ideas for my future journalistic work. There is always an example to follow, an attitude to adopt or a lesson to learn from the Prophet. Whether you are a Muslim or not, a careful study of his blessed life will enable you to have a much better understanding of Islam. Muslims find such studies immensely helpful in working out their approach to life. It should be remembered that Muslims are required to share their knowledge with others. They are duty-bound to make the faith of Islam known to non-Muslims. If they want to fulfil their duty properly, they need to have a keen insight into the life of the Prophet Muhammad (peace be upon him).

It was in April 1981 that my column 'Islam in Perspective' made its first appearance in *Arab News*, a Saudi daily paper. In those early days, with limited space at my disposal, I felt it was useful to include certain highlights from the Prophet's history. These started as no more than brief notes which hoped to introduce the Prophet of Islam to non-Muslim readers. The early response to that column was beyond my wildest dreams. Letters received by the Editor, and personal comments made to me and my colleagues, were highly encouraging. Within a few months, I decided to write the whole history of the Prophet. I began to serialize that history, attending to details and commenting on events. It took four years and a total of 200 episodes to complete. Needless to say, I had to modify my approach as the work progressed. In doing so, I benefited from comments which I regularly received from my readers. This meant, however, that there was a marked difference between early chapters and later ones. There was a need to rewrite the early part and to add a few chapters which could not have been included in the serialized form. I thought it would not be long before I could complete those chapters and have the book published. But it is a common human failing that sights are set higher than abilities. What with a total change of my circumstances, and the heavy demands on my time from different sources, a delay was inevitable. However, I praise the Almighty for enabling me to complete this work and put it in the hands of my readers.

Writing the history of the Prophet is different from anything else a writer can attempt. It is a special experience which can be shared by those who are fortunate enough to undertake this task. No other piece of work which I have attempted at any time in my life has given me similar pleasure and satisfaction. There is something in this blessed history which one can clearly perceive, although one cannot properly identify it. It imparts a blessing to one's life which enables one to enjoy most, if not all, of one's activities. The result is that your desire to have your work completed and published is accompanied by an opposite desire that the work continues indefinitely so that you continue to enjoy its blessing.

The slow progress of this work in its original serialized form has helped me understand certain aspects of the Islamic faith which are often overlooked. These are bound to have a profound influence on the thinking of the Islamic revivalist movement if they are properly studied. I have attempted to share these with my readers, in as much as the line I have followed in relating this history allows. What I can say in this introductory note is that many Muslim countries would have been spared much of the internal political conflict in which advocates of Islam were involved, had the *sīrah* (i.e. the Prophet's personal and public history) been better studied and understood by Muslims generally. To say that Islam dislikes all types of war and approves of it only as a last resort, when the very existence of Islam or its basic principles are threatened, is no more than a statement of basic facts. Islam has an even greater dislike of armed conflict, and indeed of all types of strife within its home base or in populated areas. This can be clearly seen in several main events, such as the emigration to Abyssinia and the peace agreement at al-Ḥudaybiyah. Both are related in detail in this book.

Relations between Europe and Islam have always been the opposite of what we generally associate with good neighbourliness. Even today, with the principles of democracy firmly enshrined in Europe, as well as a broad-minded understanding of human rights, there remains a sense of mistrust underlining these relations. While long drawn-out conflicts such as the Crusades and the hostility between Russia and the Ottoman Empire, as well as the European imperialism in wide areas of the Muslim World, are bound to leave lingering prejudices, increased contacts between the East and the West, brought about by the jet age, should have been enough to remove those traces and build a solid friendly relationship. Instead we find that the mistrust not only persists, but also widens in scope so as to include the whole of Europe and North America on one side and the whole Muslim World on the other. As I worked on this book, I became increasingly aware that perhaps the main reason for this mistrust has been a lingering misunderstanding of Islam by the West. Over the years, this misunderstanding has been sustained by Orientalists whose approach in their study of Islam was far from objective. Unfortunately, it is easy to quote out of context, or to utilize a particular aspect of a historical event, in order to misrepresent a great religion and a human philosophy. This has been characteristic of numerous writings on Islam by Western authors. When such writings happen to touch on the Prophet personally, Muslims find them greatly offensive and totally indefensible.

My long stay in England, stretching over 22 years, has given me a feeling that the West's misunderstanding of Islam is due to ignorance rather than prejudice. I have met many people who had the chance to know the people of the Middle East at close range, and consequently to know about Islam. Invariably, these people are ready to express their profound respect for the Islamic faith. It is unfortunate that nowadays, we in the Middle East, and in the Muslim World generally, have a very good chance of getting to know the West and its culture, but seem to be content with this one-way traffic. There is little serious attempt to redress the balance so that we can be better understood in the West. Moreover, the fact that the Western culture enjoys a position of great strength gives it an understandable feeling of self-sufficiency and an air of superiority. Hence the seemingly arrogant attitude that the West could gain little by understanding the East, while the East will benefit immensely by understanding the West. However, most educated people in the West would not approve of such an attitude, because it is contrary to many of their professed principles. Hence, a serious and sustained effort to clarify all aspects of misunderstanding of Islam by the West is needed. When the serialization of this book was still in progress in *Arab News*, I became increasingly aware that many misunderstandings of Islam by the West could be cleared up if the West could get to know the personality and the life of Prophet Muhammad better. That strengthened my feeling that an in-depth study of the Prophet's personality, lifestyle, message, work, actions and the state he established, should be made available to Western readers. This book is a humble attempt to make such a task easier. It makes no pretence of being 'objective', or trying to evaluate events in a detached manner. I do not think that such an 'objective' study serves that purpose. This book is written by a committed author who does not see that there is anything to be gained by such detachment. On the contrary, I believe that there is much that the West could learn about Islam if it is able to look at it through the eyes of a Muslim. If Western readers feel after reading this book that they have a better understanding of Islam and have acquired an insight into how Muslims formulate their ideas and arrive at their conclusions, then my purpose is achieved. If not, the fault is entirely mine.

Keeping this objective in mind, I have made no attempt to reply to specific claims or views advanced by Orientalist scholars. I am sure that much needs to be done in this area, but I feel that it is more important to present the Islamic point of view, without being entangled in side issues or disputes. However, I have fully discussed events which have aroused recurring historical controversy. Many of these were the cause of dispute at the time of the Prophet. Others were manipulated by people hostile to Islam, belonging to all shades of the religious and the political spectrum. In all these, I state the standard Islamic view in detail, trying to elucidate it as much as possible.

This book also aims at another, totally different type of reader. For several decades, Muslims have been coming to Europe seeking work and a better standard of living. Thus, new Muslim communities have established themselves in several European countries. As time passes and new generations of Muslims grow up, these Muslim communities find their contacts growing steadily weaker with the places from where their parents came. These Muslim communities are fast becoming ethnic European minority communities. As they try to preserve their Islamic identity, they feel the need to read about Islam in their native, European languages. I sincerely hope that this book goes part of the way in meeting a definite need to have a reference work in English on the life of the Prophet elucidating the Islamic point of view.

There was a persistent thought in my mind as I wrote and reviewed successive drafts of this book. As readers will realize, there were events in which the Prophet took certain measures and adopted certain attitudes which are at variance with the standards of what we call 'modern civilization'. Some of these were indeed criticized by the enemies of Islam at that time. We find that in many of these events, the Qur'ān defends or supports the Prophet's action with absolute clarity. As is well known, the Qur'ān is God's word, revealed part after part to the Prophet as and when God deemed fit. Its revelation took the whole of the 23 years from the time when Muhammad (peace be upon him) was told that God had chosen him as His Messenger to mankind to the time when he completed his mission and passed away to be in the companionship of his Lord. A clear statement of support to the Prophet in the Qur'ān means that God Himself gives him His backing. It is not difficult for anyone who wishes to criticize Islam, or the Prophet who conveyed its message to mankind, to pinpoint such events and then refer to the Qur'ānic support the Prophet received over them and insinuate that such support was particularly convenient to the Prophet, implying that he finds the idea of Divine revelation unconvincing. Such a view may be understandable if it can be shown that Qur'ānic revelations consistently supported the Prophet in all events and over all issues. The fact is that such support was given only when it was merited. There were other events and other measures adopted by the Prophet which earned criticism, disapproval or even censure in the Qur'ān. Some of these are not related in this history because they are rather personal in nature. Others, like the strong criticism of the Prophet's policy over the captives at the Battle of Badr are explained in detail.

Moreover, we find that at times, Qur'ānic revelations demanded that the Prophet should do certain things which he found extremely difficult. His marriage to Zaynab bint Jaḥsh provides the clearest example. At times, we find the Prophet adopting attitudes in his personal and family life that are dictated by his faith. His own personal preferences do not appear to be a factor influencing his decisions. A clear example of these events is that which relates to his eldest daughter, Zaynab, and how she was allowed to stay with her non-Muslim husband after the Prophet and most Muslims had emigrated to Madinah. The events of her recall and subsequent protection of her husband should also be considered in this context. At other times, we find the Prophet doing what is dictated by his faith, regardless of its likely effects on him personally. A clear example is seen in the way the Prophet went about publicizing the events of his night journey from Makkah to Jerusalem and subsequent ascension to heaven and then back to Makkah in the same night. Although he was aware of the abuse which was likely to be showered on him for such publicity, he went ahead with making his announcement, simply because he was required to do so.

It is universally accepted that justice requires that no verdict may be made in any case on the basis of partial information. It is necessary to consider every relevant issue before passing judgement. Hence we cannot accept criticism of the Qur'ānic support of actions taken by the Prophet without looking at the other aspects of the Qur'ānic comments on his other actions. We should also consider the Prophet's attitude in fulfilling the tasks assigned to him, even though it was inevitable that he would be criticized for them.

Finally, I hope that this humble attempt to give an account of the life of the most noble soul that ever walked on the face of this planet shows a glimpse of his character. We should remember here that God has made it clear that in the Prophet we have an example to follow if we truly aim to please God and win the ultimate prize of admission into heaven in the life to come. When we study his character and his life, the Prophet Muhammad (peace be upon him) appears to us as a noble, dedicated, human leader who takes good care of his followers. But he is, above all, a model believer to whom we should always turn in order to determine what course to follow and what action to take. We should always remember his last reminder to us: "I have left with you what should provide you with sound guidance and immunity from error if you would only adhere to them: God's Book and my example."

London **Adil Salahi**
February 1995

1

A Glance Back in History

WHEN EARLY PROPHETS are mentioned, one often thinks of Abraham – not because he was the first Prophet, for according to Islamic tradition he was not, but because God honoured him by placing prophethood in his seed. Yet when Abraham was advanced in years he was still childless and his wife Sarah, whom he loved and cherished, was beyond the age of childbearing. With unshakeable faith that God was always able to do what He willed, Abraham still hoped that one day he would have a child who would give him pleasure and happiness in his old age.

Sarah had a maid called Hagar whom she had brought from Egypt. She gave that bondswoman to Abraham and said: "I am now an old woman, well beyond the age of childbearing. I am giving you my bondswoman, Hagar, and hope that God may give you a child through her." Before long Hagar was pregnant. She gave birth to a son, who was named Ishmael.

Abraham's joy was great, and so was Hagar's. She felt now that her position in the house was no longer that of a bondswoman. She was the mother of the only child of the family. As Sarah watched Hagar looking after her newborn son, her feeling of jealousy grew stronger every day, especially when she noticed that Abraham was now looking after Hagar and Ishmael, showing them great love and tenderness.

Yet Abraham was very eager to keep Sarah happy. After all, she was his wife with whom he had shared his life for many years. He felt that the only way to keep both women happy was to separate them. While pondering how to do that, he received Divine orders which settled matters for him. A perfect model of a believer who was always ready to carry out God's orders, Abraham travelled with Hagar and Ishmael, along unfamiliar routes and deep inside the Arabian peninsula, until he arrived in the area where Makkah now stands. At that time the place was barren, with no vegetation or water. Nobody lived there. But Abraham was commanded by God to leave his son Ishmael with Hagar in that place. Since Abraham never disobeyed a command from God, he left his son there with his mother, giving them a sack of dates and whatever little water he had with him. He started on his way back to Palestine where he had left Sarah.

Hagar asked him how he could leave them in that barren valley. Abraham did not answer. He could not even look back, for he was so sorry to leave them there. It is easy to imagine that his eyes were full of tears as he moved away and left them alone. Desperate to be reassured, Hagar shouted to him: was he abandoning them there on God's orders? When he answered in the affirmative, she said: "He who has ordered you to do that will not abandon us."

Travelling back on his long, lonely journey, Abraham must have experienced all the feelings of an old father abandoning his only child, very young, alone with his young mother in the desert. As a firm believer in God's wisdom, however, he felt that he could nevertheless entrust them to the care of God. He raised his hands and repeated this heartfelt prayer: "Our Lord, I have settled some of my offspring in a valley where there is no vegetation, close to Your sanctified House, so that, Our Lord, they might devote themselves to prayer. Cause You, therefore, people's hearts to incline towards them and provide them with all sorts of fruit, so that they may have cause to be grateful." (14: 37) With the feeling that God would not abandon those two helpless souls who were so dear to Him, Abraham continued his journey with a new sense of relief.

A Lonely Mother with Her Child

Back in the barren valley, Hagar devoted herself to her young child, reassured that God must have a purpose for their arrival in that lifeless desert. She felt no need to despair. For a few days she and her son survived on the dates and water Abraham had left. She praised God for His bounty and prayed Him to be merciful to her and to her son. Soon, however, her supply of dates and water was exhausted. She had nothing to feed herself or her young boy. The two were soon very hungry and thirsty. With the cries of the little boy sharp in her ears, Hagar felt desperate, helpless. She was running here and there, hoping that she would find something to quieten Ishmael. She climbed the nearest hill to try to observe the area around her. That hill was al-Ṣafā. But she could see no one. She came down and climbed the next hill, al-Marwah. Again, there was no sign of life around. She went back to the first hill and kept going to and fro between the two hills. Each time she thought she heard voices from the other direction. When she had run between the two hills seven times, and was on the top of al-Marwah, she heard a voice very close to her, but she could not see anyone. She said: "Whoever you are, help us if you can." Turning towards her child in the bottom of the valley, she saw him rubbing the earth with his leg. She then heard the angel asking her who she was. She answered: "I am Hagar, the mother of Abraham's son." He asked her: "To whom has he entrusted you in this barren place?" She replied: "He entrusted us to the care of God." The angel rejoined: "He has then trusted you to the All-Merciful, the Compassionate."

At this point, while the boy was still rubbing his leg against the earth, water gushed forth between his feet. Hagar shouted: "God is Supreme." She rushed back to her son and began to form a barrier around the new-found spring so that the water would not run into the valley. She filled her water container and the water continued to gush forth. After giving her child enough to drink, she drank herself and prostrated herself in a gesture of thankfulness to God for His grace. She felt that she had been brought into that area in order that a definite purpose of God be accomplished.

The water continued to gush forth and attracted birds. It so happened that an Arabian tribe called the Jurhum was travelling north across the desert when they saw a bird flying nearby. They realized that there must be a spring in the area for birds would only fly across an area where they saw water. Keen to replenish their stock of water, they tried to determine the exact position of the spring. Their emissaries soon came back with the happy news and they moved over to wash and drink. When they saw Hagar, they realized that the spring was hers. She, however, was more than pleased to see them and said that they were welcome to encamp.

The Jurhum liked the place, and Hagar was very happy to have them. They felt that they could settle there without the need to travel any further north. This was the beginning of settled life in the valley of Makkah. Ishmael grew up among the Jurhum tribe, learning their language, Arabic, and mixing with their children. When he was a young man, he married a Jurhum girl who gave him a number of sons and daughters. Ishmael was in effect one of the Jurhum. He and his children lived in that valley, and many generations later Muhammad, God's Messenger and a direct descendant of Ishmael, was born in that very place.

Abraham did not just abandon his young child with his lonely mother and forget about them. Prophets do not abandon their families in that manner. Despite the long distance between Palestine and the place where Ishmael had been left, Abraham visited Hagar and Ishmael every now and then. He recognized God's grace, which was manifest in the fact that the Jurhum came to settle in that valley, so that Ishmael could grow up among them.

The Great Sacrifice

On one of his visits, Abraham saw in a dream that he was commanded to sacrifice his son, Ishmael, for God's sake. At that time Ishmael was in his teens, able to understand the fact that Prophets like his father did not see any 'false' dreams. It is the first mark of prophethood that the dreams a Prophet sees are as true as anything he sees in real life. The dream was repeated on three consecutive nights and Abraham realized that he had no choice but to carry out the Divine order. He put the matter as gently as he could to his son, who was still in the prime of youth, and asked him: "What do you say, son?"

Since Ishmael was brought up by a mother whose firm belief in God did not forsake her even at the moment when she was abandoned alone with her young boy in the middle of the desert, and by a father who was a Prophet, faith had been instilled in him ever since he was very young. He therefore faced the problem squarely and announced his readiness to submit himself to God's will: "Father, do as you are bid. You will find me, God willing, patient and able to face death with fortitude." (37: 102)

Both father and son went some distance out of the city, to the place known today as Minā, where they prepared to obey God's command. Satan tried to dissuade Abraham from sacrificing his son. He tried to arouse fatherly love in him. Abraham's submission to God's will, however, showed no sign of weakness whatsoever. He stoned Satan in three different spots. His action is commemorated by pilgrims when they stone the Jamrahs as one of the duties of their pilgrimage. At the point when Abraham was about to cut his son's throat in complete submission to the Divine will, an angel came to him and bade him stop. He was told that God had accepted his offering and was pleased with his obedience. He had spared Ishmael for the sake of his elderly father. The angel gave Abraham a fully grown sheep to sacrifice instead.

Building the Kaʿbah

On another visit, perhaps when Ishmael was already married and had some children, Abraham told him that God had ordered him to erect a House in that place, to serve as a consecrated temple. Ishmael expressed his readiness to help his father build the desired structure. Both father and son worked hard to lay the foundations and erect the building. Ishmael carried the stones and put each one in its place while Abraham made sure that the building was firm and well established. When the building was higher than Abraham's reach, Ishmael brought a large stone for his father to stand on and continue the work. As father and son laboured to complete the building, they prayed God to accept their work and bless their seed. The Qur'ān quotes their prayers:

> When Abraham and Ishmael were raising the foundations of the House, they prayed: "Our Lord, accept You this from us, for You are indeed the One Who hears all and knows all. Our Lord, make us submit ourselves to You, and make out of our offspring a community which will submit itself to You, and show us our ways of worship, and accept our repentance. You are indeed the One Who accepts repentance, the Merciful. Our Lord, raise up in the midst of our offspring a messenger from among themselves, who shall convey to them Your revelations, and instruct them in the Book and in the wisdom, and cause them to grow in purity. You alone are the Almighty, the truly Wise." (2: 127-129)

God accepted the work done by Abraham and Ishmael, and answered their prayers. He made the building they erected a centre of worship to which people from all over the world came on pilgrimage. God instructed Abraham to announce to mankind that God required them to make the pilgrimage to that House. Abraham asked: "How far can my voice reach, my Lord?" God told him that it was his task to make the announcement and God Himself would ensure that it was heard all over the world. Abraham complied, and God caused his announcement to be heard far and wide. People started coming to the House, which was called the Ka'bah, from the time of that announcement. Abraham taught them the rituals of pilgrimage, as he was taught them by God through an angel. God told Abraham that it was His will that Makkah should be a consecrated city where fighting was forbidden. Its animals were to move about safely without fear of being hunted. It was forbidden to cut down its trees. People were secure and safe there. Such has been the status of Makkah ever since Abraham built that House which was the first ever to be erected as a centre of worship for mankind.

Abraham was instructed by God to build the Ka'bah so that it could serve as a focal point for those who worshipped God alone and ascribed no partners or equals to Him. It was also meant to be a refuge, where everyone felt secure. The Ka'bah was always a structure of dark stones which had no special significance of their own. The ceiling was raised over pillars made of the best wood. The sanctity the Ka'bah has come to acquire is the result of the memories with which it has been associated. More importantly, its sanctity is due to the concept for whose propagation it is a symbol: the oneness of God, the only deity worthy of worship. Anyone who assumes that the Ka'bah itself, or any part of it, can have any beneficial or harmful effect of its own accord is guilty of idolatry, which Islam will always fight with all its might to eradicate.

The Ka'bah continued to be revered and sanctified by the Arabs, even at the height of their polytheism. Indeed, the Arabs who lived far from Makkah used to make the trip to visit the holy place. The Quraysh derived much of their prestige as the master tribe in Arabia from the fact that they were the custodians of the Ka'bah.

God also answered Abraham's and Ishmael's prayer to send among their offspring a messenger to instruct them in the pure faith based on total submission to God. That messenger was Muhammad, the last of all Prophets.[1]

The building of the Ka'bah and the regular pilgrimage to it gave Makkah a special importance in Arabia. In time, other tribes came to settle there. The authority in Makkah, however, belonged to the tribe which looked after the Ka'bah and held its custody. They held the keys to it and led the pilgrimage, showing the pilgrims how to perform their rituals. That was a position of great honour and the Arabian tribes competed among themselves to win over the custody of the Ka'bah. When any tribe had the upper hand in Makkah, its nobility enjoyed that honour for as long as they could keep it in the face of constant opposition from other tribes.

Naturally, the custody of the Ka'bah belonged at first to Ishmael and his offspring. It continued in their hands until it was later taken over by the Jurhum tribe. The takeover was completed without violence, since the Jurhum were considered the 'maternal uncles' of the Ishmaelites, because Ishmael was married to a Jurhum woman. The Jurhum continued to be custodians of the Ka'bah for a long while. As time passed, however, they allowed changes to creep into the rituals of pilgrimage and their rule became tyrannical. Always, in the history of Makkah, whenever the custodians of the Consecrated Mosque, that is, the Kaʿbah, allowed corruption to spread, God would cause them to lose the honour of the custody of the Kaʿbah to some other tribe. Thus the Jurhum ceded to the Khuzāʿah the supreme honour of holding the custody of the Kaʿbah. The Jurhum, however, did not surrender willingly. When they realized that they were unable to defend their position, they collected all the treasures which were dedicated to the Kaʿbah and buried them in the well of Zamzam, the spring which had gushed forth between Ishmael's feet when he was a very young boy. They levelled the well and removed all traces of its position. When they had made sure that no one would be able to discover the position of the well, they left Makkah for some other place.[2]

For a long time the Khuzāʿah continued to be the custodians of the Kaʿbah. They were the rulers in Makkah until the Quraysh took over. The Quraysh enjoyed the noblest lineage in Arabia because they were the direct descendants of Ishmael and Abraham (peace be upon them both). The man who gained that honour for the Quraysh was Quṣayy ibn Kilāb,[3] the fifth grandfather of our Prophet Muhammad ibn ʿAbdullāh.

It is important to mention here that these political changes were matched by far-reaching changes in the beliefs of the people of Arabia. Over the years, the concept of God's oneness weakened its hold on people's minds. The introduction of a physical symbol of the Divine power was the beginning of idolatry. As symbols increased in number, they came to be viewed as deities and partners with God. By the time Quṣayy was master in Makkah, pagan beliefs had spread throughout Arabia.

Quṣayy Assumes Leadership in Makkah

The story of Quṣayy's ascendancy is worth telling. His father died when he was very young. His mother married a man from the tribe of Quḍāʿah, called Rabīʿah ibn Ḥarām. Rabīʿah took his wife and her young son to live with his tribe in the north of Arabia, close to the border with Palestine. Quṣayy lived there thinking that he was Rabīʿah's own child. When he was a young man he learned that he belonged to the Quraysh and that his brother Zuhrah was the chief of the Quraysh. He therefore travelled to Makkah, where he joined his brother.

It was not long before the whole of Makkah recognized that Quṣayy was a young man of great promise. He combined a serious character with great sagacity and a noble heart. He made many friends. When he wanted to marry, his choice was none other than Ḥubbā, daughter of Ḥulayl ibn Ḥubshiyyah, chief of the Khuzāʿah and Master of Makkah who held the position of the custodian of the Kaʿbah. Ḥulayl recognized the qualities of leadership in Quṣayy and was very fond of him. He treated him like his own son. On his deathbed, Ḥulayl made it known that Quṣayy was his choice to succeed him as custodian of the Kaʿbah and ruler of Makkah. The transfer, however, was not completed without resistance from the Khuzāʿah. Quṣayy sought help from his brothers in the tribe of Quḍāʿah and they came over with speed and a large army to support him. He soon subdued the Khuzāʿah and was Master of Makkah.

Fighting broke out between the two sides, leading to much bloodshed. Arbitration was then agreed and the arbiter, Yaʿmur ibn ʿAwf, ruled in Quṣayy's favour. When Quṣayy was the undisputed leader of Makkah, he called in all the clans of the Quraysh, which were scattered all over the place, to come and resettle there. He assigned to each clan their district so that they were in complete control of the whole city. All the Quraysh were extremely happy with Quṣayy's leadership. They called him the Assembler because he had caused the Quraysh to regroup. They felt that he was a man of good omen. They honoured him to the extent that no man or woman from the Quraysh would be married, no consultation in any public matter and no declaration of war could be made unless it was done in his home. His request was an order and his word was a religion to them. He built a big hall close to the mosque to serve as a meeting-place for the Quraysh and called it Dār al-Nadwah. They assembled there for any occasion of joy or distress, held their consultations and arranged their parties and social events. Dār al-Nadwah was associated with Quṣayy and continued to serve its purpose after his death.

One of Quṣayy's noble acts was the initiation of a practice which came to be known as Rifādah. He noted that pilgrims were always coming to Makkah from distant places. By the time they arrived they were weary, their camels or horses in a state of utter exhaustion. They were ill-fed and ill-clothed, especially those who were of limited means. He recognized that Makkah must be much more hospitable to them. He therefore called in the Quraysh notables and said to them:

> People of Quraysh, you are God's neighbours and the custodians of His House who live in this consecrated city. God has chosen you for this honour. In the pilgrimage season you welcome those pilgrims who have come to visit God's House, revering its sanctity and performing its rituals. They are God's guests in His House. The guests most worthy of hospitality are God's guests. You must be hospitable to them. Let us, then, provide them with food and drink in the days of pilgrimage until they have left our city to return to their homes and families.

The Quraysh responded well to Quṣayy's appeal and approved his suggestion. Every family subscribed a specific quantity of food and drink according to their means. They put it all at Quṣayy's disposal and he supervised the arrangements by which all pilgrims were given enough to eat and drink. Quṣayy himself took part in the work and offered the pilgrims whatever the Quraysh prepared for them – bread, meat and various dishes. This increased the Quraysh's prestige and enhanced Quṣayy's honour. He in effect combined all the symbols of honour and leadership. No one could enter the Kaʿbah unless Quṣayy himself opened the door for him. During the pilgrimage season no one ate or drank anything except what Quṣayy provided. His honour was the Quraysh's honour; they loved and revered their leader.

When Quṣayy died, the institutions he had established continued to prosper. The leader of the Quraysh was the most respected chief in Arabia. The Quraysh itself commanded a position of great respect.[4]

Quṣayy was succeeded by a number of able chiefs from his own offspring. They continued his traditions of looking after the tribe and taking care of pilgrims. That latter concern and the custody of the Ka'bah were matters of great honour for the Quraysh. Hāshim, Quṣayy's grandson, put hospitality to pilgrims on an unprecedented level. He was very wealthy and his hospitality was commensurate with his wealth. He told the Quraysh that he would not have asked them to contribute anything to the feeding of pilgrims had his own resources been sufficient for the purpose. That was great encouragement for his people to make generous contributions. Hāshim got his wealth through trade. When he was the chief of Makkah, he was eager that all the Quraysh should benefit from his commercial expertise. He started the biannual commercial trips which soon became a well-established tradition in the life of the Makkans. In the summer a large commercial caravan went from Makkah to Syria, and a similar one went to Yemen in winter. Each caravan was a joint enterprise in which all Makkan people shared. It brought profit to the people and prosperity to the city.[5]

'Abd al-Muṭṭalib's Leadership

Hāshim was succeeded by his brothers before his son, 'Abd al-Muṭṭalib, took over. 'Abd al-Muṭṭalib was the Prophet's grandfather. He continued the traditions of the Makkan chiefs and proved himself a man of great integrity and an exceptional leader. His popularity in Makkah and in the whole of Arabia was unequalled by any of his predecessors.

'Abd al-Muṭṭalib continued the institution of Rifādah, which meant supplying pilgrims with food during their stay in Makkah and their fulfilment of the rites of pilgrimage. Providing them with water to drink, however, was exceptionally difficult. There were only a few scattered wells in Makkah which hardly sufficed for the needs of its own population. Fetching the water from these wells and carrying it in leather sacks and containers was a hard task. 'Abd al-Muṭṭalib thought carefully about a solution to the problem. He would have given anything for any method which would guarantee the provision of enough water for the pilgrims.[6]

One night, as ʿAbd al-Muṭṭalib was concentrating his thoughts on this problem, he was overtaken by sleep. In a dream, he heard someone saying to him: "ʿAbd al-Muṭṭalib, dig the good one." He asked: "What is the good one?" but received no answer. The following night he heard the same voice telling him: "ʿAbd al-Muṭṭalib, dig the blessed one." He asked: "What is the blessed one?" Again he received no answer. The third night the same voice told him to dig "the treasured one". Again he received no answer to his question about what he was supposed to dig. All day long he thought about those cryptic messages. He felt very uneasy about the whole thing, which was becoming an enigma to him. He was reluctant to go to sleep the next night lest he should hear more of these mysterious words. He prayed that the whole question should be resolved one way or another.

In his sleep that night, ʿAbd al-Muṭṭalib heard the same voice telling him "Dig Zamzam". He shouted angrily: "What is Zamzam?" This time he received the answer he was seeking. The voice told him that it was the water spring which would be sufficient for the needs of pilgrims, and gave him enough signs to determine its exact position. ʿAbd al-Muṭṭalib woke up very happy. He was full of hope.

The place was between the two hills of al-Ṣafā and al-Marwah, where pilgrims did their walking duty. In those pagan days, the Arabs had an idol placed on each hill. Isāf was the idol on top of al-Ṣafā and Nā'ilah was placed on top of al-Marwah. In pre-Islamic days, the Arabs made their sacrifice at that particular spot.

That morning, ʿAbd al-Muṭṭalib went to the place with al-Ḥārith, his only son. They brought all the digging equipment they needed and ʿAbd al-Muṭṭalib began to dig while al-Ḥārith helped him with clearing the sand.

Alarmed by the digging, many people from the Quraysh came over. They told ʿAbd al-Muṭṭalib that he could not dig in that spot, so close to the Kaʿbah and to their two idols, Isāf and Nā'ilah. He explained to them that he was only doing what he was bid. They did not accept his pleadings, and indicated that they were prepared to prevent him physically. Some of them told him that he had only the one son, while they had many children. This was very painful to ʿAbd al-Muṭṭalib. He prayed God to give him ten sons to support him and give him the protection he needed. He even pledged that should he be given ten sons, he would sacrifice one of them for God's sake. ʿAbd al-Muṭṭalib's position, his earnest pleadings and his apparent distress moved those Qurayshī people to change their attitude. They let ʿAbd al-Muṭṭalib continue his digging, but no one helped him. He continued to dig for three days before he began to sense a feeling of despair. He even began to doubt whether the voice he had heard on those four nights was a voice of truth. When thoughts of stopping the whole enterprise began to press on his mind, one shovel stroke hit something metallic. That renewed ʿAbd al-Muṭṭalib's hopes. He went on removing the sand around the metallic object, and soon he discovered two gold deer and a quantity of shields, swords and weapons. He recognized that these were the stuff buried in Zamzam by the Jurhum when they left Makkah. He continued his digging with renewed strength, and soon he found the well. He shouted: "God is supreme. This is indeed Ishmael's well. This is Zamzam, the drinking water of pilgrims." When the Quraysh heard ʿAbd al-Muṭṭalib's shout, they realized that he had found the water and rushed to him, claiming a share in everything he had discovered.

ʿAbd al-Muṭṭalib told them that the gold and the weapons did not belong to anyone. They were offered as gifts to the Kaʿbah and they would remain so. No one was to have anything. The water, however, was his and nobody else had any share in it. After all, he was the one given the information which determined its exact spot and selected to dig it. The Quraysh told him that it was the well of their grandfather, Ishmael. It belonged to them all. He could not claim it all for himself. There was much argument on this point. Being a man with a keen sense of justice, ʿAbd al-Muṭṭalib suggested that they should choose an arbiter. If the arbiter ruled that the water belonged to them, he would relinquish his claim. If the arbiter ruled in his favour, they would do likewise. They felt that this was fair and accepted arbitration.

Dispute Referred for Arbitration

It was customary at that time to refer such disputes to fortune-tellers and people who claimed supernatural abilities. A report exists by ʿAlī ibn Abī Ṭālib who, like the Prophet, was ʿAbd al-Muṭṭalib's grandson. This report indicates that they all agreed to refer the matter to a woman fortune-teller from the tribe of Saʿd Hudhaym who lived near Syria.

The Quraysh chose a delegation of twenty men from different clans. ʿAbd al-Muṭṭalib also had a twenty-man delegation from his clan, ʿAbd Manāf. They travelled together through some well-known routes and desert areas where there was no established track. While they were travelling in one such desert area, they lost their way. Soon, all the water ʿAbd al-Muṭṭalib and his delegation had was finished. They were extremely thirsty and were certain of death unless they could find some water. They asked the other delegation to share their water with them, but they refused. Their excuse was that they were all in a desert area and they feared the same fate for themselves. In his desperation, ʿAbd al-Muṭṭalib asked his men what they thought they should do. One man said: "We are certain of death. If we were to continue travelling we should die one by one and we shall be lost without trace in this desert. Let us stay here, and let every one of us dig his own grave. When any one of us dies we will push him to his grave. In this way, only the last one may be lost. This is better than all of us being lost. Who knows, our people may find our graves one day."

They accepted this suggestion, and started to dig their graves, awaiting their death. ʿAbd al-Muṭṭalib, however, told them: "To await death so passively, without doing anything to try to avert it, is indeed the worst option we have. Who knows, God may give us water in some place or another. Let us move on and hope to be rescued." They picked up their belongings and prepared their camels, with the other delegation looking at them. ʿAbd al-Muṭṭalib mounted his camel and signalled her to rise. As she started to move, a spring of water gushed forth from under one of her hoofs. ʿAbd al-Muṭṭalib and his kinsmen shouted: "God is supreme." They dismounted and drank their fill, then filled all their containers. ʿAbd al-Muṭṭalib then called on the Quraysh people to drink and take all the water they needed. He said to them: "God has given us this water. Come along and drink." When they had done so, they said to him: "God has given His verdict in your favour, ʿAbd al-Muṭṭalib. We will never dispute your rights to Zamzam. The One Who has given you this water in this desert is the One Who has given you Zamzam. Let us go back, and we pledge to honour your rights to Zamzam."[7]

They turned back without continuing their journey to meet the fortune-teller. Zamzam remained the sole property of ʿAbd al-Muṭṭalib and his offspring. They in turn continued to use it to provide water for pilgrims.

Many years passed and ʿAbd al-Muṭṭalib had his dearest wish fulfilled: he now had ten sons, all of them adults. In addition, he had six daughters. In all, ʿAbd al-Muṭṭalib had five wives.

One day, ʿAbd al-Muṭṭalib summoned all his sons to tell them about his pledge to God, which he had made while he was digging Zamzam. He said it was time he fulfilled this pledge by sacrificing one of them to God next to the Kaʿbah. They all expressed their readiness to submit themselves to be sacrificed. It was then a matter of choosing one of them. He suggested that they followed the Arab custom: have a toss between them administered by the man in charge of the Kaʿbah. They all went to him for the toss.

ʿAbdullāh was the youngest of ʿAbd al-Muṭṭalib's sons. He was also the dearest one to him. He was a young man of great promise, mild temperament, very sociable, not given to wild practices and, at the same time, he was a man of high moral values. All these qualities endeared him even more to his father. The old man therefore thought that if ʿAbdullāh could be spared, the pain of sacrificing one of his other children would be a little less.

The toss, however, came out against ʿAbd al-Muṭṭalib's desire: it was ʿAbdullāh who had to be sacrificed. By that time, ʿAbd al-Muṭṭalib was a very old man and had been the chief of Makkah for a great many years. He had no hesitation in fulfilling his pledge. He took his son by the hand, and took his knife and went to the mosque to sacrifice him. One of ʿAbdullāh's sisters tried to pull him away. She was shouting and screaming, appealing to the Quraysh to save him. She cried and screamed and appealed. A number of Quraysh men were moved to act. They went straight to ʿAbd al-Muṭṭalib and said to him: "You shall not slaughter him until all alternatives have been explored." When ʿAbd al-Muṭṭalib protested that it was a pledge he had made to God and there was no choice for him in the matter, they pointed out the serious danger which they saw his action would bring. They told him: "You are our leader. You are well respected in the whole of Arabia. If you were to sacrifice your son now, your action would be imitated by others. Many a man would bring his son here to slaughter him. That is bound to weaken us and cause havoc in our society." Al-Mughīrah ibn ʿAbdullāh, who belonged to the same clan as ʿAbdullāh's mother, said to ʿAbd al-Muṭṭalib: "Only when we have determined that there is absolutely no alternative may you sacrifice him. If it is possible to pay a large ransom for him we will certainly pay it, no matter how large it is." Some men from the Quraysh counselled ʿAbd al-Muṭṭalib to wait until he had seen a woman fortune-teller in Yathrib who was known to have contacts with the *jinn*. If she could find a way out of the problem, he would spare his son. If not, he could still fulfil his pledge.

When the fortune-teller was well apprised of the story she asked ʿAbd al-Muṭṭalib and his companions to wait for a while until she had referred to her *jinni*. ʿAbd al-Muṭṭalib was praying God all the time to spare his son. Although he could not see how that might be done, he still held to his faint hope that a solution could be found. It was not long before the woman found that solution for him. She asked him how much they paid as blood money for someone who was killed accidentally. They replied that they gave ten camels. She said to them: "Go back to your town and arrange a draw to be made between your man [meaning ʿAbdullāh] and ten camels. If the draw comes out against the man, add ten more camels. Continue to do so as long as the draw comes out against him. When the draw shows that the camels are accepted, this means that your God has accepted the offering and spared your man. You slaughter those camels as a ransom for him."

One Life Spared

ʿAbd al-Muṭṭalib and his companions went back to Makkah happy with this solution. When the draw was made, ʿAbd al-Muṭṭalib stood up praying God to spare his son. Every time the draw was made, it came out against ʿAbdullāh, but they increased the camels ten by ten. When there were a hundred camels, the draw indicated that the camels should be slaughtered. All this time ʿAbd al-Muṭṭalib was praying and appealing to God to spare his son. When he was told the news, he wanted to make sure. He asked the man who supervised the draw to repeat it three times. Each time it came out with the same result. The camels were brought forward and slaughtered, and left for everybody to come and take what they needed of their meat.[8]

ʿAbd al-Muṭṭalib was extremely happy when his son's life was spared. He felt that his youngest son was reborn. Like every loving father, he wanted to do his best to make his son happy. He therefore took immediate steps to arrange ʿAbdullāh's marriage. He went to Wahb ibn ʿAbd Manāf, chief of the clan of Zuhrah, and proposed that ʿAbdullāh should be married to his daughter, Āminah. The proposal was accepted, and only a few days later the marriage was celebrated.[9]

It was a happy marriage; both partners soon became very fond of each other. They seemed to have hit the right note from the first day and suited each other extremely well. ʿAbd al-Muṭṭalib wanted his children to acquire all the practical experience which was available in their society. He advised his youngest son to join the trade caravan which was about to travel to Syria that summer. Although Āminah did not like the idea of being separated from her husband so soon after their marriage, she realized that ʿAbd al-Muṭṭalib wanted only what was good for his son. As ʿAbdullāh was about to start on his journey, Āminah broke to him the happy news that she was pregnant. He then set off on his journey with his thoughts firmly centred around his wife, cherishing the hope of a bright and a happy future.

The trip was very hard on the young man. Travelling in the desert in the blazing summer sun did not suit his constitution. Although he was still a young man in his early twenties, full of vigour, he contracted some sort of disease which sapped his strength, yet he had no choice but to travel with the caravan. On the way back, his illness gradually got worse. His condition cried out for proper treatment. When the caravan arrived in Yathrib (later to be known as Madinah) it was obvious to all that ʿAbdullāh needed to be nursed. He therefore stayed behind to be looked after by his cousins of the clan of al-Najjār.

When the caravan arrived in Makkah, ʿAbd al-Muṭṭalib was alarmed not to see his son with them. Informed that he had been left to spend a few days in Yathrib to regain his strength before continuing his journey, ʿAbd al-Muṭṭalib dispatched his eldest son, al-Ḥārith, to help his brother on the journey home. On arrival in Yathrib, al-Ḥārith was given the sad news that ʿAbdullāh was dead.[10]

The tragic news was too much for ʿAbd al-Muṭṭalib in his extreme old age, and for Āminah, the youthful bride now expecting her fatherless baby. Yet ʿAbd al-Muṭṭalib could not but reflect that ʿAbdullāh was spared only for his life to be prolonged by a few months. It seemed that it was his destiny to live only for Āminah's pregnancy to take place. Little did he know that Āminah's baby was to be the last Messenger God would send to mankind.

A Campaign to Destroy the Kaʿbah

Meanwhile, a very serious event took place in Arabia that year. It affected all the Arabs and their faith, and remained so vivid in their minds that they used to date other events by reference to it. At that time, the Arabs had no specific calendar to date their events. When something very serious took place in their lives, they referred to it as a date mark.

The various reports on this event which have come to us mention that after the Abyssinians had expelled the Persians from Yemen and established their own rule there, the Abyssinian governor of Yemen, Abrahah, built a superbly luxurious church in this area, giving it the name of the Abyssinian emperor at the time. He did this after he had witnessed the love and enthusiasm of Yemeni Arabs – the same as those felt all over the Arab land – for the Kaʿbah, the sacred mosque at Makkah. His aim in building it was to make the Arabs forsake their attachment to the mosque of Makkah and turn instead to this new luxurious church.

But the Arabs did not turn away from their sacred House, the Kaʿbah. They believed themselves to be the descendants of Abraham and Ishmael who built the House. For them, this fact was a source of pride in line with their tradition of taking pride in their forefathers. The whole idea of directing their affection and respect towards this new church built by an ordinary army commander who followed a religion which they considered inferior to theirs was totally absurd. Abrahah's whole enterprise was a subject of ridicule among them. One of them went so far as to use the most splendid spot in that church for doing his toilet, to emphasize the contempt with which the Arabs viewed Abrahah's idea.[11]

When Abrahah was informed of this, he decided to pull down the Kaʿbah in order to achieve his objective of turning the Arabs away from it. He therefore marched at the head of a great army, equipped with elephants. At the front was a very big elephant which enjoyed special fame among Abrahah's men. The news of Abrahah's march and his objective spread throughout the Arab land and among the Arabs very strong feelings arose against the destruction of their sacred House. A nobleman of the royal family of Yemen, Dhū Nafar, tried to stop the Abyssinian governor, calling on his people and other Arabs to fight Abrahah and defend the Kaʿbah. Some Arab tribes joined him in a battle against Abrahah which Dhū Nafar lost, and he was then taken prisoner. Later, as Abrahah travelled on, he was attacked by Nufayl ibn Ḥabīb al-Khathʿamī, who had mobilized two Arab tribes as well as troops from other supporting tribes, but Abrahah won the battle again and captured Nufayl. Nufayl then agreed to act as guide to show Abrahah his way in the Arab land. When the Abyssinian governor approached Ṭā'if, a number of its leaders went to him to say that the House he wanted to pull down was in Makkah, not at Ṭā'if. They did this so that he would not destroy the house they had built for their idol, al-Lāt. They also provided him with a guide to show him the way to the Kaʿbah.[12]

On arrival at al-Mughammas (a valley midway between Ṭā'if and Makkah) Abrahah dispatched one of his commanders to Makkah where he looted some possessions from the Quraysh and other Arabs, including 200 camels which belonged to ʿAbd al-Muṭṭalib.The Quraysh, Kinānah, Hudhayl and neighbouring Arab tribes gathered to fight Abrahah, but realized that they stood no chance of winning, so they did not proceed. Then Abrahah sent a messenger to Makkah to meet its chief and convey to him that the governor of Yemen had come not to fight the Makkans but simply to pull down the House; if they left him to accomplish his purpose, he would be pleased not to cause any bloodshed. Abrahah also ordered his messenger to bring with him the Makkan chief if the latter did not propose to fight. When the messenger communicated his master's message to ʿAbd al-Muṭṭalib, the latter said: "By God, we do not want to fight him, and we have no power to resist him. This is God's sacred House, built by His chosen friend, Abraham. If He protects it against him, it is because the House is His, and if He leaves it to him to destroy, we cannot defend it." ʿAbd al-Muṭṭalib then went with the messenger to Abrahah.

Despite his very advanced age, ʿAbd al-Muṭṭalib was a most handsome, charming and attractive person. When Abrahah saw him he felt much respect for him. He felt that ʿAbd al-Muṭṭalib was too noble to sit beneath his royal couch, but at the same time Abrahah did not wish to be seen by the Abyssinians sitting with him on his couch, so he came down and sat with ʿAbd al-Muṭṭalib on the carpet. Then Abrahah ordered his interpreter to ask his guest what he wanted. ʿAbd al-Muṭṭalib said he wanted to request 'the king' to give him back his two hundred camels which had been looted by his commander. Abrahah ordered his interpreter to tell ʿAbd al-Muṭṭalib on his behalf: "I admired you when I first saw you, but when I spoke to you I was disappointed. Do you come to talk to me about two hundred looted camels and forget about the House which is the embodiment of the religion in which you believe, as did your forefathers, and which I have come to destroy? You did not even say a word to persuade me to spare it."

ʿAbd al-Muṭṭalib replied: "I am only the master of my camels, but the House has its own Lord who is sure to protect it." Abrahah snapped: "It cannot be defended against me." The Makkan chief said: "You take your chance!" Abrahah returned his camels.

One report suggests that a number of Arab chiefs went with ʿAbd al-Muṭṭalib to meet Abrahah. They offered to give the Abyssinian commander one-third of all the revenue of their land if he would go back without destroying the Kaʿbah. He refused their proposal. ʿAbd al-Muṭṭalib went back to the Quraysh and told them of his encounter with Abrahah. He ordered them to leave Makkah and seek shelter in the surrounding mountains. Then he went with a few important members of the Quraysh to the Kaʿbah, where they all prayed hard to God for His help and protection for the House. ʿAbd al-Muṭṭalib is reported to have held the door ring in his hand in a gesture of a most earnest plea. He is said to have recited the following lines of poetry in his prayers:

> Our Lord, a creature protects his property, so protect Yours.
> Let not their cross and their might ever overcome Your might.
> If You are leaving them to destroy our House of worship, then You surely have something in mind.

In the morning, Abrahah gave orders to his army to prepare to march with the elephants to complete their mission. While they were making their preparations, Nufayl went to the elephant and whispered in his ear: "Sit down, elephant, or go back where you came from. This is God's sacred city." The big elephant sat down when the army was just outside Makkah, and refused to go any further. The soldiers exerted every effort to persuade the elephant to enter the city, but their efforts were in vain. This particular incident is a fact acknowledged by the Prophet. When his she-camel, al-Qaṣwā', sat down some distance away from Makkah, on the day when the al-Ḥudaybiyah peace agreement was concluded, the Prophet said to those of his companions who claimed that she had become mulish, that she had not, and that mulishness was not in her nature. "But", the Prophet added, "she has been prevented by the same will which debarred the elephant from entering Makkah." (Related by al-Bukhārī.)

Then God's will to destroy the Abyssinian army and its commander was fulfilled. He sent flights of birds to bombard the attackers with stones of sand and clay, leaving them like dry and torn leaves, as the

Qur'ān tells. The majority – but not all – of the soldiers were hit by these stones. Whoever was hit was sure to die quickly. Abrahah suffered physical injuries. Those of his soldiers who were spared carried him back to Yemen, but his limbs began to separate from the rest of his body, and he started to lose one finger after another, until he arrived at Ṣanʿā'. According to various reports, Abrahah died after his chest was broken apart.

Thus God foiled Abrahah's scheme to destroy the Kaʿbah. In their way, the Arabs were very thankful to God for saving His House from destruction at Abrahah's hands. When God sent His Messenger with His final message, He reminded the Arabs of this event in a short *sūrah* in the Qur'ān which carries the title 'The Elephant', by way of recounting aspects of His favours to the Arabs. This *sūrah* was revealed as an endorsement of the Prophet's call to the Arabs to accept Islam. It says: "Have you not seen how your Lord dealt with the people of the Elephant? Did He not cause their treacherous plan to be futile, and sent against them flights of birds, which pelted them with stones of sand and clay? Thus He made them like devoured dry leaves."[13]

Notes

1. Ismāʿīl ibn Kathīr, *al-Bidāyah wal-Nihāyah*, Maktabat al-Maʿārif, Beirut, Vol. 1, pp. 153-167. [All the details of Abraham's family history given here are based on Ibn Kathīr's account.]
2. ʿAbd al-Malik ibn Hishām, *al-Sīrah al-Nabawiyyah*, Dār al-Qalam, Beirut, Vol. 1, pp. 116-118.
3. Ibid., pp. 119-123 and 130-137.
4. Ibid., pp. 123-124.
5. Ibid., pp. 138-140.
6. Ibid.
7. Ibid., pp. 150-153.
8. Ibid., pp. 160-164.
9. Ibid., pp. 164-165.
10. Ibn Sayyid al-Nās, *ʿUyūn al-Athar*, Dār al-Turāth, Madinah, 1996, pp. 78-79.
11. Ibn Hisham, op.cit., pp. 43-47.
12. Ibid., pp. 47-49.
13. Ibid., pp. 49-56.

2

The Early Years

IT IS SAID that Āminah, the Prophet's mother, had no great trouble with her pregnancy. Everything went right for her. She heard a great deal about other women having all sorts of trouble when they were pregnant. Hers, however, was a very easy pregnancy, associated with the hope that the coming child would brighten her life after the totally unexpected tragedy of her husband's death.

There was nothing unusual about the birth of Muhammad. The only thing worth mentioning is that his mother reported later that she had an easy delivery. Historians could not determine for certain the exact year of his birth. Most reports, however, suggest that it was in AD 570, the year when Abrahah, the Abyssinian ruler of Yemen, launched his attack against Makkah. As for the date, it was most probably on the 12th of Rabīʿ al-Awwāl in the year 53 BH.[1] There is nothing particularly significant about determining the exact date of Muhammad's birth. Whatever celebrations are held nowadays on that date have no Islamic basis. They are merely traditional celebrations which have no religious significance.[2]

There are some reports about certain happenings which pointed to the forthcoming destruction of the Persian Empire and its pagan faith. Other incidents suggesting the eclipse of other religions are also reported to have taken place on the day Muhammad was born. While Muhammad's birth heralded the imminent collapse of all erring beliefs, such reports cannot be taken seriously. We have no solid evidence to prove them. Moreover, no importance is attached to them from the Islamic viewpoint, even if one assumes them to be true.[3]

When Āminah delivered her baby, she sent for his grandfather, ʿAbd al-Muṭṭalib, to come and have a look at him. He was very happy when he saw him. ʿAbd al-Muṭṭalib was still very sad at the loss of his son, ʿAbdullāh, but the birth of Muhammad assuaged his sadness as he looked forward to a bright future for the newborn child. He took the baby and went to the Kaʿbah where he prayed for him at length. He thanked God for giving him a boy to bear the name of his deceased son. Then he took him back to his mother, who told him that she heard voices commanding her to call her child Muhammad.[4]

Muhammad means 'often praised', or 'worthy of praise'. It was a totally unfamiliar name in Arabia. Nevertheless, ʿAbd al-Muṭṭalib had no hesitation in calling his grandson by that name. He could never dismiss the thought that the events which led to the birth of this child suggested that he was certain to have great influence on the life of his community. When he was questioned by the notables of Makkah about this unfamiliar name he had given to his grandchild, he answered that he wished the boy to be praised by human beings on earth and by God in heaven.[5]

Muhammad was given to Thuwaybah, a servant of his uncle, Abū Lahab, to breastfeed him for a few days until long-term arrangements for his nursing were made.

Infancy in the Desert

It was the tradition of the noblemen of Makkah to send their children to be breastfed by Bedouin wet nurses. They felt that the open space of the desert was far better for the children in their early years than the close atmosphere in the city. They thought that when a child was nursed in the desert he was certain to grow up physically strong and healthy.

Every now and then, Bedouin women came to Makkah to seek newborn babies. They were prepared to wet-nurse them for the wages and gifts which were certain to be given to them by the babies' parents. There was no set fee for the task: it was left to the generosity of the father.

A group of such Bedouin women arrived in Makkah shortly after Muhammad was born. Each of them looked at Muhammad but declined to take him when she realized that his father was dead. Apparently, none of them thought the grandfather would do as well for them as the boy's own father.

Each one of them managed to get a child to nurse, except Ḥalīmah bint Abī Dhu'ayb. She later reported what she did that day:

> I travelled with my husband and our young boy along with a number of women from our tribe, Saʿd ibn Bakr, to seek babies to nurse. It was a bad year in our area of the desert. We had nothing to survive on. I was riding a mule and we had with us an old she-camel which gave us not a drop of milk. We spent many a sleepless night because our little boy was always crying of hunger. I did not have enough milk to satisfy him. Our camel was hopeless, but we still hoped for rain and better days.
>
> Because my mule was also weak, I kept falling behind my companions. I gave them so much trouble because of our weakness. When we arrived in Makkah every woman of us was offered Muhammad to nurse. When she learnt that he was an orphan, she declined. We simply hoped for gifts and presents from the baby's father. Hence, we always replied when we were offered him: "An orphan! What could his mother or grandfather do for us!"
>
> Every woman in the party was able to obtain a child to nurse except me. When we were about to set out on our journey back home, I said to my husband: "I hate to be the only one to go back empty-handed. I am going to take that orphan." He said: "It is a good idea. He may bring us some blessings." I went back and brought him. As soon as I put him to my breast, I felt that both my breasts were full of milk. He had his fill, and so did his brother, my own son. Both went to sleep immediately afterwards: we had not had much sleep in the preceding nights because of our boy's crying.[6]

It is also reported that in those days the Prophet always sucked the same breast: he never accepted the other one. It is as if he was made to feel that he had a partner and he left him his share.[7]

Ḥalīmah said: "My husband thought that it was worth trying to milk our old camel. He soon discovered that she had full breasts. He milked enough for both of us to have our fill. It was our best night for a long while. My husband said to me in the morning: 'You know, Ḥalīmah, you have taken a blessed child.' I said: 'I sincerely hope so.'"

> We started our journey that morning and I rode the same mule and carried Muhammad with me. She was now moving fast, ahead of all my friends. They were amazed, and asked me whether it was the same mule I was riding on the way to Makkah. When I affirmed that it was, they were very surprised.
>
> When we arrived at our quarters, it was hit by severe drought. Nevertheless, my sheep were always full of milk. We had more than we needed, while no one else had enough. Most of their sheep had no milk at all. People would tell their shepherds to keep their sheep alongside mine, hoping to have some milk. It was only my sheep which had their breasts bursting with milk every evening. We continued to have this Divine blessing until he was two years of age, when I weaned him. He was growing like no other child did. When he was two he was very strong for his age. I took him back to his mother, forming in my mind the best argument I could muster to persuade her to allow me to keep him for a while longer. I said to her: "I wish you would leave my child with me for a little longer until he gets stronger. I fear that he may catch an infection of some sort or another in Makkah." I tried hard until she was persuaded to send him back with me.[8]

A Very Strange Event

Muhammad stayed with Ḥalīmah, his suckling mother, in the desert for nearly four years altogether. Nothing eventful normally happens to a child at such an early age; hence nothing much is recorded by historians. An event which happened at the end of that period, however, caused Ḥalīmah to be so disturbed that she preferred to go back to Makkah and return the young child to Āminah, his mother.

While Muhammad was playing with other children, the Angel Gabriel came and took him by the hand. He laid Muhammad down and opened his chest and abdomen, took out his heart and removed from it a black clot, which he threw away. As he did so, he said: "This is what Satan has in you." He then washed Muhammad's heart in a gold bowl full of iced water before putting it back in its place. He then sealed the incision and left him.

His suckling brother, Ḥalīmah's son, ran to his mother to report that Muhammad was dead. She rushed to see him. She found him standing up but pale-faced. She asked him what had happened and he related what had been done to him by "two unknown men wearing white dresses".

This incident disturbed Ḥalīmah a great deal. She sat several nights thinking about Muhammad and what had happened to him. Some reports suggest that she took him to a fortune-teller to find out the significance of what had happened. The authenticity of these reports is not beyond question. What is certain, however, is that Ḥalīmah felt that the safest course for her was to return the child to his mother. It was her husband who suggested this, expressing his fear that the boy might have been attacked by an evil spirit. "It is wiser to return him to his people now, before any bad consequences appear."

Āminah was surprised to see Ḥalīmah bringing Muhammad back. She asked why, pointing out that Ḥalīmah had been so keen to keep him. Ḥalīmah said: "There is nothing wrong with him or us. We have discharged our task to the best of our ability. We thought he would be better off with you lest something should happen to him." Āminah said that was not the full story, there must be something else. She kept pressing Ḥalīmah until the latter told her the story. Āminah said to her: "Do not fear Satan for this boy, for he is protected against him. This boy of mine will have a renowned future. I tell you that my pregnancy was the easiest ever experienced by any woman. One night when I was pregnant it seemed in my dream as if a light came out of me to light up the palaces of Syria. When I gave birth, he lifted his head to heaven. Leave him with me and go back to your people."[9]

An authentic tradition points out that the same thing happened to the Prophet when he was fifty years old, one night while he was half-asleep. The angel made a long incision from the top of his chest right down to the end of his abdomen. He took out his heart and washed it in a gold bowl 'full of faith'. He then put his heart back in its place.[10]

It is not easy to explain these two events in ordinary terms – the event itself was extraordinary. Moreover, the question of good and evil has nothing to do with the function of any part of the human body. It is clear that a spiritual interpretation of this question is much more relevant. Its understanding is beyond human ability.

A contemporary scholar, Shaykh Muhammad al-Ghazālī, suggests that Divine care would not leave a person like Muhammad to experience the petty temptations to which all human beings are liable. If we suppose that there are 'waves' of evil all around us and that the hearts of certain people pick up these waves very easily and are influenced by them, the hearts of Prophets, who are favoured with God's care, do not receive these waves and are therefore not influenced by them. Hence, Prophets do not have to resist any downward tendency to sink into evil; they try to strengthen an upward tendency to purify themselves and their nations of evil.

In support of his argument, al-Ghazālī relates two authentic *ḥadīths* said by the Prophet on two different occasions, with more or less the same import. One *ḥadīth* was related by ʿĀ'ishah: the Prophet told her after she admitted that she was jealous of the Prophet's other wives: "Your evil spirit has influenced you." When she asked whether an evil spirit was always with her, the Prophet said: "Every human being has an evil spirit." She asked whether this applied to him also. He said: "Yes, but God has helped me against him and he has accepted Islam." That is, the evil spirit within the Prophet became an obedient one, and could not suggest any evil thought.[11]

It seems that the whole incident of opening the chest of the Prophet in his early childhood and again when he was fifty years old is indicative of the immunity God gave His chosen servant to keep him away from worldly temptations ever since he was a young boy.

A New Tragedy

Muhammad lived with his mother, who doted on him and looked after him as the most loving mother could look after the dearest of her children. It is worth noting that Āminah did not marry another man after her young husband died. This was quite unusual in Makkan society, where marriage to widows and divorcees was commonplace. Āminah had several qualities which recommended her to any suitor. Prominent among these was her noble birth, which was a very important factor in that society. Nevertheless, Āminah did not marry again. Perhaps she could not remove from her mind the thoughts of the events which preceded the tragedy of losing her husband. She had enough signs to indicate to her that her son was certain to play a great role. She probably thought that devoting herself to the upbringing of her child would give her all the satisfaction she needed.

It is in this light that we view her trip to Yathrib with her son, now six years of age, and his nurse, Umm Ayman. She wanted him to visit the clan of al-Najjār, his maternal uncles. When a man married into another tribe or clan, everyone in that clan or tribe would be considered an uncle to his children and grandchildren for the rest of time. ʿAbd al-Muṭṭalib's mother belonged to the clan of al-Najjār and this is the reason for counting them as the Prophet's uncles. More importantly, Āminah wanted her son to visit his father's grave. Perhaps she thought that it was time for him to realize that his father was buried in Yathrib, a long way from Makkah.[12]

Muhammad and his mother stayed for a month in Yathrib, before starting their journey back. It was a very sad journey for the young boy. They had not travelled far before his mother fell ill. It was a quick and fatal illness. Although she had covered only a short distance from Yathrib, she could not return there, nor could she continue her journey back home. So the six-year-old Muhammad was now without both his parents. After Āminah had been buried where she died, at al-Abwā', Muhammad continued his journey to Makkah with his nurse, Umm Ayman, his heart full of sorrow. He felt that nothing could replace for him the love and tenderness of his mother. To his last days he continued to remember Āminah, and to feel the pain of losing her.[13]

The Prophet continued to show his gratitude to all those women who took care of him in his childhood to the end of his days. He was so grateful to Thuwaybah, the first woman to suckle him immediately after he was born. When he conquered Makkah over sixty years later, he asked for her. When he learnt that she had died, he also enquired after her son whom she was suckling when he himself was born. He wanted to extend his kindness to him. But he was told that he also had died. Ḥalīmah visited him in Madinah. When she arrived he rose to receive her, shouting: "My mother! My mother!" He showed her all the gratitude of a loving and dutiful son. He was also kind to al-Shaymā', Ḥalīmah's daughter and his suckling sister. After the battle of Ḥunayn, in which the tribe of Hawāzin was defeated, al-Shaymā' was taken prisoner by the Muslim soldiers. She made her relationship with the Prophet known to them, so they took her to him. He received her well and extended extra kindness to her before sending her back to her people with honour after giving her the opportunity to stay with him. It was her choice to go back.

Umm Ayman continued to be close to the Prophet for the rest of his life. He married her later to Zayd ibn Ḥārithah, the first man to become a Muslim, whom the Prophet loved more than anyone else. She gave birth to Usāmah, whom the Prophet loved as he loved no child besides his own.

After his mother's death, Muhammad was in the care of his grandfather, ʿAbd al-Muṭṭalib. Umm Ayman, a slave girl whose real name was Barakah, continued to look after him. She had belonged to his father and now she was his own. She loved him dearly – perhaps more so because she was fully aware of the fact that he had lost both his parents before his sixth birthday. Muhammad's grandfather indulged him more than was customary in Arabian society, where the emphasis was on strict discipline in the upbringing of young ones. No child was admitted to a room where his father was meeting other men. Yet ʿAbd al-Muṭṭalib, chief of Makkah, allowed his young grandson to sit on his couch when he was in a meeting with Makkan notables. His own children, now all grown up, remained standing, but Muhammad was allowed to sit on his grandfather's couch. If

Muhammad's uncles tried to stop him, ʿAbd al-Muṭṭalib would tell them not to do so. On one occasion he told them: "Leave my child alone. He senses that he will one day acquire a kingdom." At another time he said: "He will certainly have a great future."[14]

A Transfer of Care

ʿAbd al-Muṭṭalib realized that his own death would not be long in coming. The future of the orphan child was one of his most immediate concerns. He therefore called in his son Abū Ṭālib and asked him specifically to look after Muhammad, his nephew, when he himself had died. It was good that he did so, because ʿAbd al-Muṭṭalib died within two years of Muhammad coming into his care. It is said that ʿAbd al-Muṭṭalib was a hundred and twenty when he died, but his grandchild was only eight. Again, death snatched away a loving soul from Muhammad's life. He was extremely distressed to lose his grandfather. He felt he had lost the man whose kindness to him could not be equalled by any other. He grieved for his loss as only a loving child could grieve when he realized that he would not be seeing his beloved one any more. Perhaps ʿAbd al-Muṭṭalib chose to trust Muhammad to the care of Abū Ṭālib because the latter had the same mother as ʿAbdullāh, Muhammad's father. He might also have realized that Abū Ṭālib was the kindest and most caring of his children. This explains why Abū Ṭālib was chosen for this task, despite the fact that he had many children of his own and was a man of little means. Many of Muhammad's other uncles were better placed to look after him, from a financial point of view. Yet ʿAbd al-Muṭṭalib chose Abū Ṭālib, and what an appropriate choice it proved to be.

Abū Ṭālib continued to look after Muhammad until he became a man. Even then, he continued to show him the loving care a father shows to his adult son. He was never slow in giving him sound advice and guidance. When Muhammad started to receive his message and convey it to people, Abū Ṭālib supported him in the face of strong opposition from the Quraysh. He never failed him even when the pressures were too strong to bear for an old man, as Abū Ṭālib was at that time. There was a relationship of mutual love and respect between uncle and orphan nephew. Indeed, Abū Ṭālib loved Muhammad as much as he loved his dearest child, if not more.

Again when he was in the care of his uncle, there were signs that God's blessings were associated with the presence of Muhammad. While there was no sudden influx of riches into the house of Abū Ṭālib, there always seemed to be enough when Muhammad was there. If dinner was served and Muhammad was not present, Abū Ṭālib would order his children to wait for him. He had noticed that when Muhammad was eating with them, the food seemed plentiful and everybody had his fill. If he was absent, the food seemed not to be sufficient and everybody asked for more. On the whole, Muhammad's childhood was very pleasant. He radiated happiness to all around him. Hence it was not surprising that he was loved dearly by all those close to him.[15]

We have several reports of that period in the life of Muhammad which suggest that various people recognized him as the future Prophet. Many suggest that the people recognizing him tried to get him killed. The first reports speak of Ḥalīmah taking Muhammad to a fortune-teller to divine his future. None of these reports, however, attains a sufficient degree of authenticity to make it of any great value. Such things might have happened. Their effect either on the boy himself or on those looking after him was limited indeed.

Nor can the story of Muhammad's encounter with the Christian monk of the town of Buṣrā in southern Syria be of great importance. This story suggests that Muhammad clung to his uncle, Abū Ṭālib, when he was about to depart on a trade journey to Syria, and would not let him go without him. Abū Ṭālib then decided to take his twelve-year-old nephew with him. It is said that on their way back home after finishing their business in Syria, this monk, Baḥīrā, invited the whole caravan to a dinner. This was a marked departure from his past habit. He insisted that everybody in the party should attend. He recognized Muhammad and spoke to him, questioning him on many aspects of his life. He also recognized a mark on Muhammad's shoulder which indicated that he was to be the last Prophet. When he was certain of that fact, Baḥīrā asked Abū Ṭālib what relation the boy was to him. When Abū Ṭālib said that he was his son – as the

Arabs considered that an uncle was in the same position as a father – Baḥīrā said: "He is not your son. This boy's father should not be alive." Abū Ṭālib told him that Muhammad was his nephew and that his father had died before his birth. Baḥīrā said: "That is right. Take your nephew back to his home town, and watch him carefully. Should the Jews recognize him as I have done they would try to harm him. This nephew of yours is certain to have a great future."[16]

Whatever the truth about this story and the other reports to which we have referred, it is certain that they did not influence Muhammad in any way. We have to remember that he was still a child, and he could not have aspired to any distinction as a result of Baḥīrā's discourse. Moreover, it seems that the men who heard Baḥīrā's conversation with Abū Ṭālib did not bother to relate it to other people. The only value of these reports is that they confirm the fact that learned men of other religions were aware of the imminent appearance of a Prophet in Arabia. Their knowledge is based on what is definitely contained in their scriptures.

Muhammad was only twelve when he went on this trip with his uncle, Abū Ṭālib. Some reports suggest that he was even younger. Not long after he came back to Makkah he realized that he had to do something in order to help his poor uncle, who had a large family to support. Although from the time of his birth Muhammad brought his blessings to his immediate environment, wherever it happened to be – as clearly related by Ḥalīmah, his wet nurse – he was not meant to enjoy a life of affluence. There always seemed to be enough for everyone around, but there was little to spare. Muhammad himself needed very little: he was content with whatever was available to him. But he always had a keen sense of what was going on around him. His uncle's situation cried out for help, and Muhammad was aware of that.

First Employment

In the Makkan society of that time there was little a young boy of Muhammad's age could do. The life of the whole community depended largely on trade, which thrived through the regular trips to Syria and Yemen. These trips meant that the Makkan trade was essentially what we call nowadays 'foreign trade', depending on export and import. To be successful in such a field required multifaceted experience which could not have been acquired by a young boy in his early teens. Moreover, travelling at such a tender age through a difficult terrain like that of Arabia was too much of an adventure for a young boy. There was little or no agriculture in Makkah or the area around it. Few, if any, industrial occupations were available. The Arabs actually looked down upon anyone engaged in such employment. The only occupation worthy of the Arabs of Makkah was trade. Hence there was nothing Muhammad could do to help his uncle except to work as a shepherd.

The life of a shepherd is associated with contemplation and patience. A shepherd has long periods of time when there is little for him to do, except watch his animals grazing. As he sits alone, his thoughts must inevitably turn to the universe around him. He thinks of its creation, and its limitless expanse. He thinks how different varieties of creatures share their lives in a little corner of it, and of what lies beyond the realm of human perception. He thinks of the great variety of plants that come from the earth, each with its distinctive characteristics and widely different fruits. Yet they all come out of the same type of soil and feed on the same water. His thoughts are bound to lead him to think of the great power that controls everything in the universe.

A shepherd needs patience, and as he goes about his work he is bound to develop that quality without which he cannot really tend his sheep. Perhaps it is for these two qualities, along with other less important ones, that God has chosen this type of work for His messengers and Prophets. It is well known that Moses and David were given prophethood when they were actually engaged in tending sheep. The Prophet was once asked whether he also tended sheep, and he answered: "Yes, indeed. Every Prophet tended sheep at one time or another." When we think carefully about it, we are bound to conclude that Prophets, who in the latter part of their lives look after human beings and shepherd them, receive their early training when they begin their practical life as shepherds. This particular occupation is a form of education. It helps the shepherd to acquire a keen sense of what is around him and develop his ability to attend to detail. He also develops another quality which is essential in his later career – an ability to work consistently towards the achievement of a definite goal set in advance, and to persevere with it until it is achieved.

Muhammad was not the only boy who worked as a shepherd in Makkah – this was the job which noble families in Makkah did not despise. Other boys of similar age also tended camels and sheep. Sometimes some of them met and developed friendships. They talked about what they did at night. On many occasions, parties and social events were organized in Makkah. Boys of Muhammad's age frequented these. When they met during their long days, they talked about the fun they had at these parties. It was natural, therefore, that Muhammad should think of doing as other boys did. He is quoted by ʿAlī ibn Abī Ṭālib, his cousin, to have said:

> I never thought about taking part in what the people who lived in ignorance were organizing in the way of entertainment except on two nights. On both occasions, God protected me against evil. One night I said to one of my fellow shepherds: "Would you kindly look after my sheep to give me a chance to go down to Makkah and attend a social function like other boys do?" He was willing to do that. I went to Makkah. As I entered, I heard music and singing in the first house. I asked what the occasion was and I was told that it was a wedding party. I sat down to look. Soon my head was heavy and I slept. I was awoken only next morning by the heat of the sun. I went back to my friend and reported to him what had happened. I did it again, and the same thing happened to me. I never again thought or did anything of this sort, until God honoured me with prophethood.[17]

In this way Muhammad was protected by God against indulging in any form of entertainment which was unbecoming of the one who would become the last of His Messengers to mankind.

Other reports exist which suggest that Muhammad was 'protected' against any moral slip from the time when he was a young boy.

Certain values introduced by Islam were unheard of in the Makkan society in which he grew up, as indeed they have always been unfamiliar in societies that do not observe a strict moral code. For instance, to appear in the nude in front of people of the same sex is acceptable in most non-Islamic societies. Some communities go even further. In our modern times the 'naturist' idea has found many supporters, and naturist clubs which promote communal nudity have been established in many places in Europe. This is contrary to the Islamic idea of propriety. In his youth, Muhammad was totally unaware of the Islamic values of propriety. Nevertheless, he was made to abide by them.[18]

A few years before the beginning of Qur'ānic revelations, the Quraysh decided to repair the building of the Kaʿbah (which we shall discuss in more detail later on). The Prophet helped in the repair work along with many Makkans. Those who carried the stones and went to and fro took off their lower garments and put them on their shoulders as cushions on which to place the stones. Since the Arabs had no underwear at that time, those who did this were working in the nude. Only Muhammad carried the stones with his lower garment on. His uncle, al-ʿAbbās, who was working with him, suggested to him that he should use his garment to protect his shoulder. When Muhammad did this he fell to the ground unconscious. A moment later he regained consciousness, searched for his garment and tightened it round his waist. He then resumed work.

A very similar report suggests that the same thing happened to him much earlier. The Prophet is quoted to have said that when he was a young boy he was playing with boys of his own age, carrying stones from one place to another. He said: "We were all undressed. We took our garments and placed them on our shoulders to put the stones on them. I was moving around with the other children when someone I did not see levelled at me a very hard punch. He said: 'Put on your garment.' I wrapped myself with it and made it tight. I continued to carry the stones on my shoulder, but I was the only one wearing my garment."[19]

Both reports are clear examples of how essential moral values of undistorted human nature were applied to Muhammad even before he became a Prophet. This was part of the 'education' he received. Although Muhammad was not educated in a formal school or by any particular tutor, he was placed in the thick of many events which gave him a keen sense of the values which needed to be preserved in any morally healthy society. Personal education was also given to him so that he could develop a code of behaviour which made all types of frivolity alien to his nature. Such an education is far more effective and longer lasting than any formal schooling. As we shall see in the next chapters, Muhammad's understanding of all aspects of life was much more profound than that of any philosopher or man of wisdom.

Notes

1. BH signifies 'prior to the start of the Islamic Calendar', which dates from the Prophet's settlement in Madinah.
2. Ibn Hishām, *al-Sīrah al-Nabawiyyah*, Dār al-Qalam, Beirut, Vol. 1, pp. 167-168. Also, Ibn Sayyid al-Nās, *ʿUyūn al-Athar*, Dār al-Turāth, Madinah, 1996, pp. 79-81.
3. Muhammad al-Ghazālī, *Fiqh al-Sīrah*, Dār al-Daʿwah, Egypt, 6th edition, 2000, pp. 51-52. Also, Ibn Sayyid al-Nās, op.cit., pp. 83-85.
4. Ibn Hishām, op.cit., pp. 168-169.
5. Ibn Sayyid al-Nās, op.cit., p. 90.
6. Ibid., pp. 91-92.
7. Ibid., p. 94.
8. Ibid., pp. 92-93.
9. Ibid., pp. 93-94.
10. ʿAbd al-Raḥmān al-Suhaylī, *al-Rawḍ al-Unuf*, Dār al-Kutub al-ʿIlmiyyah, Beirut, pp. 290-291. Also, al-Bukhārī, *Ṣaḥīḥ*, Dār ʿĀlam al-Kutub, Vol. 1, Riyadh, 1996, p. 91, and Muslim, *Ṣaḥīḥ*, Dār ʿĀlam al-Kutub, Vol. 1, Riyadh, 1996, pp. 103-104.
11. Muhammad al-Ghazālī, op.cit., pp. 54-55.
12. Ibn Hishām, op.cit., p. 177. Also, al-Suhaylī, op.cit., pp. 297-298; Ibn Sayyid al-Nās, op.cit., p. 90 and Muhammad al-Ghazālī, op.cit., p. 56.
13. Ibn Sayyid al-Nās, op.cit., p. 100. Also, Amīn Duwaydār, *Ṣuwar Min Ḥayāt al-Rasūl*, Dār al-Maʿārif, 4th edition, Cairo, pp. 63-65.
14. Ibn Hishām, op.cit., p. 178. Also, Ibn Sayyid al-Nās, op.cit., p. 99.
15. Ibn Hishām, op.cit., p. 189. Also, Ibn Sayyid al-Nās, op.cit., p. 103.
16. Ibn Hishām, op.cit., pp. 191-194.
17. Ibn Sayyid al-Nās, op.cit., pp. 110-111.
18. Ibid., p. 109.
19. Ibn Hishām, op.cit., pp. 194-195.

3

From Youth to Maturity

THE REPORTS WE have of the early years of Muhammad's life are not numerous. This is not surprising because, for one thing, illiteracy was the norm in Arabia at the time, and no one could have imagined the great role that Muhammad was destined to play in human life generally. The reports we have, however, are sufficient to indicate to us that from his early years Muhammad was distinguished by his honesty, kindness, patience, humility and readiness to help others. He was also known to be a youth who did not indulge in any of the vices which were widely practised in the Makkan society, such as drinking, gambling or promiscuity.

We cannot fail to notice, with hindsight, that Muhammad was being prepared for his great role. One aspect of this preparation was the fact that he never had anything to do with the idols worshipped by his people. He never revered any of those idols or bowed to them, nor did he ever give any offerings to the idols, as was the custom of his people, or attend any of the festivities which were organized as part of idol worship.

His nurse, Umm Ayman, reports that the Quraysh used to pay homage to an idol called Buwābah. On a particular day each year they organized a special festival in its honour. They stayed near the idol all day long and shaved their heads. Abū Ṭālib, the Prophet's uncle, did not fail to attend the festival. Every year he asked his orphan nephew to attend, but Muhammad declined. Abū Ṭālib was angry with him, and even his aunts spoke to Muhammad about his apparent lack of respect for the idols. They tried to persuade him not to remain the odd one out in his family. In their representation, they touched on a young man's duty to show his loyalty to his family. They said: "You seem not to wish to share any festival with your people, and not to be counted as one of their number."

Ultimately Muhammad yielded to his aunts' pleading and went to the festival. He came back in a state of fear. He told his aunts that he feared he might be possessed by an evil spirit. They assured him that God would never let him suffer such a thing, considering his numerous good qualities. Relating his experience to them, he said: "Every time I came near to an idol, I saw a tall white man telling me to hold back and not to touch the idol." Umm Ayman stresses that that was the first and the last idol festival Muhammad attended until he began to receive his Qur'ānic revelations.[1]

This is just one of several reports we have about Muhammad's attitude towards pagan worship long before the beginning of his prophethood. Taken together, these reports point to the fact that Muhammad was being deliberately kept away from pagan worship. It was only to be expected that God would protect the man He had chosen to be His last Messenger to mankind – bringing them the final message based on the absolute oneness of God – against paying the slightest homage to any idol even in his youth.

Participation in What Serves Justice

Nevertheless, Muhammad lived a normal life among his people. He was sociable, well loved and highly respected. The fact that he did not indulge in any vice earned him greater respect. Moreover, he never failed to take part in any important matter which was of concern to his tribe or his society.

One example was his participation in the war known as 'al-Fijār'. The name suggests violation of sanctity. It was so called because the war started with a treacherous murder, committed by a man from the Quraysh in one of the four sacred months. Those four months were traditionally sanctified by the Arabs and war was totally forbidden during them. For a treacherous murder to be committed in these months was a violation of sanctities of the worst type. Hence it was not surprising that a war should break out between the Quraysh and the Hawāzin, the tribes to which the murderer and his victim belonged.[2]

Muhammad was only fifteen when this war broke out. It lasted four years. He took part in it, but according to the more reliable reports he did not participate in the actual fighting. He helped his uncles, however, by shielding them against the arrows directed at them by their enemies, collecting these arrows and preparing them for use by his fighting uncles.

Shortly after the end of this war, when Muhammad was nearly twenty, he took part in forging an alliance between the different clans of the Quraysh. This was a noble alliance which the Prophet continued to praise long after prophethood. The alliance was called 'al-Fuḍūl' after three of the main participants, each of whom was named al-Faḍl. It is also suggested that this alliance was called al-Fuḍūl because it was made for such a noble goal: the name suggests maintaining honour.[3]

The immediate reason for forging this alliance was that a man from the clan of Zubayd arrived in Makkah with some goods to sell. An important man of Makkah, al-ʿĀṣ ibn Wā'il, bought them all from him, but did not pay him. When the man realized that he was about to lose everything, he appealed to several clans of the Quraysh to support him. They all declined to stand against al-ʿĀṣ ibn Wā'il and rebuked the man for his attitude. In his desperation, the man stood on top of a hill immediately overlooking the Kaʿbah at sunrise, when the men of the Quraysh met in groups around the Kaʿbah. He made his appeal to them, stating his case in a passionate and desperate manner. He reminded them of their position as the custodians of the Sacred House of Worship. Al-Zubayr ibn ʿAbd al-Muṭṭalib, an uncle of the Prophet, was the first to be moved to act. He stood up and said that injustice must not be allowed.

A meeting was organized in the house of ʿAbdullāh ibn Judʿān, a man of honour well respected in Makkah. Representatives of many clans of the Quraysh were present. The terms of the alliance were agreed at that meeting. Those who attended gave their most solemn pledges, swearing by God that they would stand united, supporting anyone in Makkah who suffered any injustice, whether he was a Makkan or an alien, and that they would stand firm against the perpetrator of that injustice until right and justice were restored.

When they had made their alliance, those people went to al-ʿĀṣ ibn Wāʾil and forced him to return to the man from Zubayd the goods he had taken from him.

Knowing the nature of this alliance, we can understand why the Prophet continued to express his support for the ideals which this covenant endorsed. Long after prophethood he said: "I attended in ʿAbdullāh ibn Judʿān's home the forming of a covenant which I would not exchange for any material gain. If now after Islam I am called upon to honour it, I would certainly do so." This shows how Islam endorses any action or covenant made for the purpose of ensuring justice for all.[4]

When the al-Fuḍūl covenant was made, Muhammad, now a young man of twenty, was opening a new stage in his life. His noble birth, strong character and physical strength would surely have put him on the road to prosperity. We have reports suggesting that in his old age Muhammad was endowed with exceptional strength. In his youth, he must have been full of vigour and ability. Combining this with his well-known honesty and wisdom which belied his years in addition to his fine character, it was only to be expected that if he aspired to any material achievement in his society he would have been certain to achieve it.

Muhammad, however, continued to set for himself a high code of honour. The strength of his character and his keen sense of morality provided a balancing factor for his physical desire. He was able to control that desire with his wisdom and spiritual strength.

Moreover, he was fast acquiring a reputation for meticulous honesty. Indeed, he was called by his society *al-amīn*, which meant 'trustworthy and honest'. Material gain did not seem to tempt him in any way. He did not despise wealth, nor did he seek any vain ideals. He only had a fine sense of proportion. He realized that wealth was not an end in itself. It was a means to a higher end. Hence he approached the task of searching for a new occupation with seriousness and dignity. It was soon decided that he should try to find employment in trade and business.

Muhammad had no money of his own to establish a business; nor was Abū Ṭālib, his uncle, a man of affluence to provide him with a good start. The only option left for him, therefore, was to prove himself as an agent, trading on someone else's behalf. Apparently, he had no difficulty in securing such a position, because of his rapidly growing reputation for honesty and sound character. We have some reports which suggest that he was trading in different markets and bazaars. He entered into partnership with a fellow agent called al-Sā'ib ibn Abī al-Sā'ib, whom he praised later for his integrity and honesty. When, many years later, the Prophet met al-Sā'ib on the day he conquered Makkah, he welcomed him warmly, saying: "Welcome to my brother and partner, an honest and straightforward man."[5]

It is not absolutely certain for whom Muhammad was working as agent in those early years. It is reasonable, however, to assume that it was Khadījah bint Khuwaylid, a rich widow, who had the benefit of his valuable services. She was later to send him on a trade mission to Syria with a great quantity of goods. Probably she would not have done that without trying him first in the local markets. He is reported to have said later that she was a very kind employer. Every time he and his partner went to see her, she offered them something to eat.

Muhammad gained a great deal of experience in business in his early twenties. He was working on commission. Khadījah, however, paid him more than she paid her other agents. She realized that she had working for her a man who combined honesty and integrity with a keen eye for business. Her admiration for Muhammad was increasing all the time. She wanted to retain his services, and she felt that the only way to do that was to increase his income. He, however, showed no sign of the greed normally shown by people in his position.

Business Travel

Things were becoming very difficult in Makkah. Business was at a low ebb after a couple of years of drought. It was important for the Makkan business people to concentrate on their traditional trips to Syria and Yemen. One year, as preparations for the trip to Syria were getting under way, Abū Ṭālib spoke to his nephew about travelling as agent of Khadījah.

Deep down in his heart, Abū Ṭālib did not wish his nephew to travel to Syria because he feared for his safety. But the situation was deteriorating and such a trip held the best promise for the family. Abū Ṭālib heard that Khadījah was planning to send someone on her trade in return for two camels. He felt that if he were to speak to her, she would be glad to send Muhammad at double that commission. Muhammad, however, was against approaching her. Soon he received the news that she wanted him to travel on her business trip. Some reports suggest that it was Khadījah who approached Abū Ṭālib first. She knew that he was not keen on his nephew travelling away from Makkah. She, however, wanted to send a man whom she could trust. Abū Ṭālib yielded to her pressure after Khadījah agreed to pay Muhammad double the normal commission. Her servant, Maysarah, was to travel with him.

It was a successful trip. Muhammad managed to sell all the goods he took out with him to Syria at a profit, and bought Syrian goods to sell in Makkah. Again, he made a handsome profit for Khadījah. One report suggests that she actually made twice as much as she hoped for. She was so grateful to Muhammad that she doubled his commission.

Maysarah gave his mistress a detailed report on the trip. He was full of praise for Muhammad, whom he came to know as a most pleasant man to be with – honest, kind and truthful. He never tried to burden others with his needs, yet he was most helpful to others. He did not wait for them to ask for help, he was always ready to oblige.[6]

Khadījah, being a wealthy widow, received one marriage proposal after another. She realized, however, that it was her money that tempted her suitors. Hence she declined as many proposals as she received. Her business association with Muhammad, however, made her recognize that there was a man for whom money was not the greatest priority. She began to think of him in a different light. Khadījah was a woman of great intelligence and noble birth. She had a strong character and she liked to act in any matter only after she had looked at it carefully from all angles. Apparently, she consulted one or two of her trusted relatives, who praised Muhammad highly. One of those was Waraqah ibn Nawfal, an old uncle of hers, who recognized that Muhammad was destined to have a very important future. Khadījah had long resolved that she would choose her future husband when she was absolutely certain of his character. Looking at her dealings with Muhammad, she felt that it was now up to her to take the next step.

Khadījah sent a close friend of hers, Nufaysah bint Munyah, to make an indirect approach to Muhammad. When she met him she said: "Muhammad, what is keeping you from getting married?" He answered: "I do not have enough to meet the expense of my marriage." She said: "What if you are not called upon to meet such expenses? What would you say to a woman of beauty, wealth and position who is willing to marry you? Would you marry her?" He said: "Who is that woman?" She answered: "Khadījah." He asked: "Who can arrange such a marriage for me?" She said: "Leave that to me." His response was: "I will do it, willingly."

The First Marriage

When Khadījah was sure of Muhammad's reaction, she sent him a message asking him to come and see her. She said to him: "Cousin, [she used this term in the widest sense, since she was a very distant cousin of Muhammad. Their ancestry did not join until the fifth grandparent.] I admire you because of your good position among your people, your honesty and good manners, and because you are a man of your word." She then made her proposal that they should get married. Muhammad was very pleased and went to inform his uncles, who were also very pleased with such a marriage.

Muhammad went with his uncles to meet Khadījah's uncle, ʿAmr ibn Asad. Abū Ṭālib spoke on behalf of his nephew. He said: "This nephew of mine, Muhammad ibn ʿAbdullāh, is without peers in his nobility of character and descent. If he is not wealthy, wealth is only something accidental. Money comes and goes, and many a wealthy man becomes poor. He will certainly have a great future. He is proposing marriage to your honourable daughter, Khadījah. He is giving her a dowry of such-and-such." ʿAmr ibn Asad did not hesitate to make his acceptance clear. The marriage was then concluded at a dowry of 20 young camels.

It was a happy marriage. Most biographers of the Prophet put his age at 25, saying that Khadījah was 40. Some reports suggest that the Prophet was nearer 30. Khadījah, on the other hand, was reported to have been 35, or even 25. In view of the fact that she gave Muhammad six children, the report which allots her a younger age seems more accurate. ʿAbdullāh ibn ʿAbbās, the Prophet's cousin, who is considered to have been the most learned among the companions of the Prophet, states that she was 28 and not a day older.[7]

Whatever their respective ages, Muhammad was to spend 25 happy years with Khadījah. The marriage gave Khadījah a man whom she could love, respect and trust. He was a most caring and loving husband who attended to his family duties with his customary seriousness. She gave him four daughters and two sons. Although polygamy was the normal practice in Arabia, Muhammad did not have a second wife while Khadījah was alive. The marriage gave Muhammad a settled life, but the real benefit of marrying Khadījah was not fully apparent until after he began to receive his revelations and face opposition to his message from all quarters. At that time, Khadījah's support was most valuable to Muhammad. She stood by his side, reassuring him and giving him all the comfort he needed. No matter how great his troubles when he called on his people to accept Islam, the moment he went home he was certain of a comforting welcome from his wife. Long after her death, and when he had married several other wives, the Prophet continued to cherish Khadījah's memory.

Khadījah gave birth first to a boy who was named al-Qāsim. Four daughters then followed, named Zaynab, Ruqayyah, Umm Kulthūm and Fāṭimah. ʿAbdullāh was the last child to be born to Khadījah. Only one of his later wives gave the Prophet a child: Maria, the Coptic slave who was sent to him as a present by the ruler of Egypt. She gave birth to a boy, Ibrahīm. Al-Qāsim lived only a few years while ʿAbdullāh died before it was time for him to be weaned. Ibrahīm, on the other hand, lived only 18 months. All four daughters of the Prophet lived until after Islamic revelations started. They all accepted Islam. The first three, however, died in Madinah, while Fāṭimah was the only daughter of the Prophet to survive him. She died six months after his death.[8]

Rebuilding the Kaʿbah

When Muhammad was 35, the Quraysh realized that it was absolutely necessary for them to rebuild the Kaʿbah: it is only natural that such an old place should suffer some structural deterioration with the passage of time. The old structure needed to be pulled down and built anew. Repair work was woefully inadequate. Makkah had suffered major flooding a short time earlier and the walls of the Kaʿbah were cracked as a result. It was not easy for the chiefs of Makkah to take this decision. They were very reluctant to pull the Kaʿbah down, yet they could not see how they could achieve their goal of preserving the building if they limited their activity to patchy repair work. Eventually they made up their minds and set a time for starting.

It was ʿĀ'idh ibn ʿImrān ibn Makhzūm, a maternal uncle of the Prophet's father, who started the work. He removed one of the stones, only to find it flying back to its original position. Apparently, he was a man of wisdom. When he saw the stone flying back, he said: "People of Quraysh, select the best of your money for building the Kaʿbah. Do not include in the building fund any money earned by a whore or from usury, or anything taken by force from any person." This shows that even in the darkest days of paganism, the Arabs recognized that adultery and usury were evil. A place built for the worship of God should not be financed by any earnings from such evil sources.

The chiefs of Makkah themselves and the noblemen in all the clans of the Quraysh were personally involved in the building work. They considered this an honour not to be missed. They organized the work so that each pair of men would work together, removing stones and relaying them in their proper positions. Women also shared in the work and carried the mortar which would hold the stones together. The Prophet himself shared in the building work, joining his uncle, al-ʿAbbās, in his shifts.

It is also said that when the men of the Quraysh met to start the demolition in order to rebuild the Kaʿbah, nobody was prepared to begin. They were extremely reluctant to pull the building down, fearing that something would happen to them. Al-Walīd ibn al-Mughīrah, one of their chiefs, volunteered to start. He took his axe and moved forward, repeating these words: "My Lord, we mean no offence. My Lord, we are only working for a good purpose." He then began to work, pulling down part of the building, near the corner of the Black Stone. No one joined him. They felt it was better for them to wait that night. They said to one another: "We will wait for tonight. If something happens to al-Walīd, then we will not continue with our project, but will put the part he has removed back as it was. If he is still all right, then God has accepted what we are doing and we will proceed."

Al-Walīd was among the first to report for his work shift the following morning. He continued with the demolition and others joined him. When they reached the foundation laid down by Abraham, they found sharp green stones held tightly together. One report suggests that one man inserted a lever between two of these stones to pull them apart. When the stone gave way, the whole town was shaken. They immediately stopped the demolition work and started rebuilding.

At the time, the Kaʿbah was much lower than it is now. Its height was equal to the length of nine arms. The Quraysh decided to double it. When the Kaʿbah was rebuilt about 90 years later by ʿAbdullāh ibn al-Zubayr, he increased its height to the present one, which is equal to the length of 27 arms. The increased height meant that many more stones were needed. All the Quraysh clans were working hard at that task. Each clan worked on its own. When they thought they had gathered enough stones, they put up the building, taking great pride in their work. Apparently, each clan wanted to have more of the honour of building the Kaʿbah for itself. Old jealousies were coming to the surface and disagreements frequently flared up. It was when the time came to restore the Black Stone[9] to its position that the dispute among the clans was at its fiercest. Each clan wanted that honour for itself. Tempers were high and people started to call for a resolution of the dispute by the sword. In no time, they were ready to engage in battle.

Four or five nights passed, with tension at its highest. An alliance was formed by the clans of ʿAbd al-Dār and ʿAdiy ibn Kaʿb to fight to the bitter end. The alliance was sealed with blood. Some wise men, however, tried to resolve the dispute. A meeting was called in the mosque itself and discussions were held on how to resolve the dispute amicably. That, however, was not easy to achieve. Finally, the eldest man in the Quraysh, Abū Umayyah ibn al-Mughīrah, made a suggestion which was met with unanimous approval. He suggested that the first man to enter the mosque be asked to arbitrate in the dispute, and whatever judgement he made was to be honoured by all.

The first man to enter was none other than Muhammad. He had not yet received his revelations and he knew nothing about prophethood. Nevertheless, he was well respected for his integrity and fairness. When they saw him, all of them expressed their pleasure. They said: "This is the man of trust, *al-amīn*, and we accept him as arbitrator." They put the matter in dispute to him. He immediately recognized that it was a very sensitive issue which needed to be approached with a great deal of tact. He asked them to bring a garment and to select a representative from each clan. When they had done so, he placed the Black Stone on the garment and asked those clan representatives to lift the garment jointly, with the Black Stone on it, and move it to its position. When they had lifted it to its exact spot he himself placed it there and secured it in position. Everyone was satisfied with this solution, which ensured that no clan could boast of monopolizing the honour of restoring the Black Stone to its position. They all had a share in that honourable task. Moreover, this solution enhanced Muhammad's standing among his people.[10]

Notes

1. Amīn Duwaydār, *Ṣuwar Min Ḥayāt al-Rasūl*, Dar al-Maʿārif, 4th edition, Cairo, pp. 80-81.
2. Ibn Hishām, *al-Sīrah al-Nabawiyyah*, Dār al-Qalam, Beirut, Vol. 1, pp. 197-198.
3. Ibid., pp. 140-141. Also, Ibn Sayyid al-Nās, *ʿUyūn al-Athar*, Dār al-Turāth, Madinah, 1996, pp. 113-114.
4. Ibn Hishām, op.cit., pp. 141-142.
5. Amīn Duwaydār, op.cit., p. 84.
6. Ibn Hishām, op.cit., pp. 198-200. Also Ibn Sayyid al-Nās, op.cit., pp. 115-117 and Amīn Duwaydār, op.cit., pp. 85-87.
7. Ibn Hishām, op.cit., pp. 200-201. Also, Ibn Sayyid al-Nās, op.cit., p. 118.
8. Ibn Hishām, op.cit., p. 202.
9. The Black Stone is an easily distinguished stone, placed a little below shoulder level at one corner of the Kaʿbah. The act of worship which is particularly associated with the Kaʿbah, and never stops except when congregational prayer is held, is *ṭawāf*, which means walking round the Kaʿbah seven times in an anti-clockwise direction. *Ṭawāf* is one of the duties of Islamic pilgrimage and *ʿUmrah* (mini-pilgrimage). It is also a recommended act of worship at all times. Moreover, it is the way to offer greetings to the Kaʿbah.

   It is said that when Abraham completed the building of the Kaʿbah, with the help of his son, Ishmael, God commanded him to do the *ṭawāf*. He was not able to keep a correct count of the rounds he made. He felt that other worshippers would be similarly confused. He prayed God to give him a sign to be used for counting rounds. The Angel Gabriel brought him the Black Stone.

   When one starts *ṭawāf*, and at the completion of each round, one should kiss the Black Stone or touch it with one's hand, if it is possible, or signal to it from a distance, if the place is too crowded. As one does so, one should repeat this declaration: "There is no deity save God, God is supreme." The significance of this particular action is best expressed by ʿUmar ibn al-Khaṭṭāb, the second greatest figure among the companions of Prophet Muhammad and his second successor as ruler of the Islamic state, and a distinguished scholar. He addressed the Black Stone in these words: "I know that you are a stone which can cause no harm or benefit. Had it not been for the fact that I saw God's Messenger (peace be upon him) kissing you, I would not have kissed you."
10. Ibn Hishām, op.cit., pp., 204-211. Also, Ibn Sayyid al-Nās, op.cit., pp. 121-124.

4

The Makkan Scene at the Start of Prophethood

IT HAS BEEN explained how the tribe of the Quraysh came to gain ascendancy in Arabia as they won supremacy in Makkah. It was Quṣayy ibn Kilāb, an ancestor of the Prophet, who established their rule in Makkah and many of the institutions of government which were still in operation when the Prophet began to receive his message. By the standards of the time, that was quite an advanced standard of government which helped Makkah to undergo a significant transition from a semi-Bedouin town to a civilized city. The system of government provided for a balanced distribution of responsibilities and functions, as well as government by consensus, which is normally achieved after an open consultation. In his scholarly work on the life of the Prophet, Shaykh Abū al-Ḥasan ʿAlī al-Ḥasanī Nadwī devotes a full chapter to setting the scene at Makkah in the period immediately preceding the start of the Islamic message.[1] He mentions that the ascendancy of the Quraysh in Makkah attracted a number of smaller Arabian tribes to move to Makkah, where they could live in the neighbourhood of the Kaʿbah and the Sacred Mosque. That led to a flourishing building industry and the expansion of Makkah in all directions. At first, the Makkans avoided building their houses in a square shape in order to keep them different from the Kaʿbah.

Gradually, however, they relaxed that restriction but continued not to raise their buildings higher than the Kaʿbah.

As mentioned earlier, the Quraysh organized two commercial trips every year: to Syria in summer and to the Yemen in winter. These two trips provided the backbone of the city's economy. In addition to that, Professor Nadwī points out, a number of seasonal bazaars and markets were organized in Makkah, as well as specialized markets which were in business throughout the year. Makkan merchants travelled to many parts of Africa and Asia. This encouraged a highly active foreign trade. That flourishing trade ensured for many people in Makkah a life of affluence. With wealth normally come several aspects of luxurious life. The wealthy Makkans had their gatherings close to the Kaʿbah; poets attended and read their poems. Poetry was the most respected form of literature, considering that the overwhelming majority of Arabs at that time could not read or write. However, poetry was a highly valued national and individual talent. In a tribal society, it is highly important for every individual to know his tribe and where he belongs because the tribe affords protection to every individual member. An individual would suffer a great deal if he could not enjoy such protection. Hence, everyone was keen to know his ancestry. This importance of lineage and ancestry continued in Makkah, and there were people who monitored the ancestry and lineage of every tribe. Most prominent among these was Abū Bakr, the closest companion of the Prophet.

Many elements of civilization were recognizable in Makkah and several aspects of science began to develop, such as astronomy and elementary medicine. People valued their horses highly and were able to learn a great deal about them. Few industries, however, developed in Makkah because its inhabitants did not like to work with their hands. Only such crafts as were absolutely necessary managed to develop, such as the manufacture of swords and spears which were needed for fighting, and the construction industry for housing. Most building workers, however, were either Persians or Byzantines.

From the military point of view, the Quraysh could muster a force strong enough to repel any would-be attacker. For this they did not rely merely on their own numbers, but forged alliances with many of the Arabian tribes which lived close to Makkah. In addition, the Quraysh had a large number of slaves and individuals who were allied to the various clans, branching out of the Quraysh. They were expected to side with the Quraysh in any battle it found itself fighting. The army raised by the Quraysh and its allies in the Battle of the Moat was 10,000 strong, the largest military force ever known in the Arabian Peninsula. The Quraysh, however, tended to prefer a settled, peaceful life. It was always prepared to live peacefully with its neighbours, provided that there was no challenge to its position or religious beliefs. When it encountered a challenge, it was always ready to take it up, relying on its superior strength.

Makkah enjoyed its position as the largest city in Arabia, serving as a religious and economic capital, eclipsing other cities, such as Ṣan'ā' in the Yemen and northern centres which were subject to Byzantine or Persian rule.

However, morally speaking, life in Makkah left much to be desired. The affluence of the Makkan people tempted them to indulge in all sorts of vice. Gambling and drinking parties and other sorts of organized entertainment, where all inhibitions were thrown to the wind, were common practice. Coupled with that, the Makkan people were not very scrupulous in their dealings with others. Cruelty, unjust practices and depriving others of their rights by force went unpunished. This inevitably led to tension, which was bound to undermine the fabric of the Makkan society.

The wealth which Makkah enjoyed and the fact that this wealth came mainly from foreign trade gave its people a pattern of life which allowed them ample spare time. As mentioned above, few of the people of Makkah were engaged in any type of work other than trade, much of which was done through organizing trade caravans and missions on which only those who had valuable experience in the conduct of such trade travelled, together with an adequate number of assistants, porters and camel drivers. Perhaps the largest trade caravan the Makkans dispatched was the one which the Muslims in Madinah tried to intercept, shortly after the Prophet had settled there. It was that attempted interception which led to the Battle of Badr, in which the Muslims achieved a great victory. That caravan consisted of something like 1,000 camel loads, while all in all only 300 people travelled on that mission. Many of the Makkan notables travelled on these caravans when they were young, because such trips gave them a great deal of experience. When they had had enough, they entrusted the task to their children or some of their assistants who had distinguished themselves in business. An example of such able people acting for Makkan notables on their trade was Ṣuhayb, who travelled on behalf of ʿAbdullāh ibn Judʿān, one of the wealthiest people in Makkah. Ṣuhayb, a former slave, acquired considerable wealth from commission, which he later began to use as capital of his own.

With such a relaxed and easy life in Makkah, it was inevitable that social vices would spread and become commonplace. Much time was devoted to the pursuit of pleasure in different ways and forms. Religious concepts and moral values were at a low ebb. Deviation from the pure faith of Abraham and Ishmael started long before the birth of the Prophet. With time, that deviation ensured that the religious beliefs of the Arabs bore very little resemblance to the faith preached by prophets. The Arabs borrowed idolatrous worship from other nations and forgot about their monotheistic faith, taught to them by Ishmael and Abraham. Idols were everywhere and in every tribe. Certain idols were revered by all the Arabs, while others were considered as special gods for special tribes. Certain families had idols of their own, and sometimes when a person travelled he took his idol with him to grant him its blessings. Although those idols were no more than inarticulate objects, the Arabs would worship them, offer sacrifice to them, consult them in their affairs and assign to them a portion of their cattle and agricultural produce. They assigned certain tasks to certain idols: some of them specialized in bringing rain or blowing wind, some in giving parents their offspring, curing illnesses, sparing the community from famine or other social evils, and so on. In order to overcome the obvious fact that those idols were no more than objects of their own making, the Arabs allocated their idols a middle position between them and God. The idols acted as intermediaries, appealing to God on their behalf, so that He did not punish them severely for their sins.

There were 360 idols in and around the Kaʿbah. Most prominent of all were Hubal, al-Lāt and al-ʿUzzā, which were considered the chiefs of all Arabian idols. Hubal was made of red carnelian, in the shape of a man. When the Quraysh gained supremacy in Makkah, Hubal was found to have one arm broken. The Quraysh replaced it with an arm of gold. It was the supreme idol. Al-Lāt was in Ṭā'if, while al-ʿUzzā had a place of its own near ʿArafāt.

When the Arabs wanted to embark on any important venture, they went to the Kaʿbah and offered a certain man who drew lots an amount of money and a camel to draw lots with the assistance of Hubal. They would accept the outcome as final. If a crime was committed and they could not determine who the criminal was, they drew lots. If the result accused a certain person, he was believed to be the criminal and there was no way he could prove his innocence.

One of their most absurd beliefs was their claim that God had married the *jinn* and begot angels as His daughters through that marriage. They therefore worshipped the angels, whom they considered God's daughters, and the *jinn*, whom they claimed to be related to God by marriage. They feared the *jinn* a great deal, because they considered them to be evil spirits whose main object was to cause harm. They tried to spare themselves that harm by wearing charms and appealing to the masters of the *jinn* for protection. To them, madness and mental diseases were caused by the *jinn*, and each fortune-teller had a *jinni* companion who gave him news from the world beyond. According to them, every poet had a *jinni* who inspired him with poetry.

They further believed in all sorts of superstition, for example, that when a person was murdered, his spirit would be embodied in a certain type of bird, named al-Hāmah, which flew round his grave, calling to people to give it a drink, until his murder was avenged.

Women were treated as far inferior to men. They were not allowed any share of inheritance. Indeed, they were treated as part of the inheritance of the deceased. The heir disposed of the wife of the deceased as he pleased. He married her without even consulting her, if he so wished. Alternatively, he gave her in marriage to anyone he liked, without even asking her whether she wanted to marry or not. A man could marry any number of women, divorcing them at will and even placing them, at times, in a state of no marriage and no divorce. The birth of a girl was received with a feeling of gloom. A father considered the birth of a daughter to him as nothing less than outright disaster. This was because women did not fight in tribal wars and could not earn their living. Some of them would even hide away for a number of days because of their shame at begetting daughters. Young girls were buried alive by their parents because they were a financial burden. Indeed, such burial was occasionally agreed upon at the time the marriage contract was made.

It is not surprising, therefore, that the pleasures of this world counted for everything with the Arabs at that time. They viewed death as bringing the absolute end of life. Resurrection was considered absolutely impossible. For anyone to suggest that people come back to life after death was interpreted as outright madness.

Yet the Arabs were not without virtues. They rated bravery, faithfulness, truthfulness and hospitality very highly. These virtues, however, were not consolidated well enough to create a noble social order. Indeed, they were overshadowed by the petty concerns and the pursuit of pleasure which were characteristic of that society.[2]

The absurd religious beliefs led to confusion and innovations in different aspects of worship. It is known, for example, that pilgrimage to the Kaʿbah continued to be observed ever since Abraham made his declaration to mankind, on orders he received from God, that pilgrimage to the Kaʿbah was a duty incumbent on them all. Although other nations might have been totally oblivious to this duty, it continued to be observed in Arabia, despite the change that crept into their religious beliefs which made them polytheists after they had been believers in God's oneness. Nevertheless, the Quraysh introduced certain innovations in the duty of pilgrimage. Although we cannot determine the exact date these innovations were introduced, it must have been approximately half a century before the start of Qur'ānic revelations.

It is well known that certain duties of pilgrimage are done outside the boundaries of the Ḥaram area, which extends in a circle of about a 20-kilometre radius around Makkah. Attendance at ʿArafāt, which is the main duty of pilgrimage, is one of these, since ʿArafāt lies outside the Ḥaram area. It is common knowledge that no pilgrimage is valid unless the pilgrim is present at ʿArafāt on the 9th of Dhul-Ḥijjah, the last month of the lunar year. The Quraysh, however, declared that they themselves were exempt from such attendance at ʿArafāt. To justify their claim, they argued that the Kaʿbah was the most sacred spot on earth. The Ḥaram area, which surrounds the Kaʿbah, derived its sanctity from the fact that the Kaʿbah was its centre point. It was not logical, they argued, for people living in the most sacred area in the world to go to an area which is less sacred in order to offer their worship, when other people covered hundreds of miles to come to the Ḥaram area for no purpose other than offering worship. They therefore decided not to attend at ʿArafāt when they did their pilgrimage, although they acknowledged that such attendance at ʿArafāt was part of pilgrimage for all other people. They called themselves the Ḥums, which meant, linguistically, 'puritanical', and included under that title the people of the Ḥaram area and their offspring, whether they lived inside or outside its boundaries. That meant a classification of pilgrims into two groups, giving unwarranted privileges to the people of Makkah, for no reason except the fact that they lived in the neighbourhood of the Kaʿbah. This is contrary to the very essence of Divine Faith as preached by Abraham, Ishmael and all Prophets, ending with Muhammad (peace be upon them all). Divine faith makes all people equal and they can achieve distinction only through their deeds, not through any coincidental factor such as birth, nationality or race.

Usually, when the notion of a privileged class takes hold in a certain society, that class manages to add to its privileges as time passes. The Quraysh did exactly that, but imposed on themselves certain restrictions which might have been introduced by way of compensation for their unwarranted privileges. They claimed that they were not allowed to produce cooking fat from milk or butter when they were in the state of consecration, or *iḥrām*. Nor were they allowed to enter any dwelling made of animal hair during their *iḥrām*. They were allowed only to stay in dwellings or tents made of animal hide. No specific reason was advanced for these restrictions except to emphasize that the Ḥums were a class apart. More stringent restrictions were imposed by the Quraysh on pilgrims from outside the Ḥaram area. Pilgrims and other visitors to Makkah were not allowed to eat any food which they might have brought with them from outside the Ḥaram area. They could eat only what they were given by the people of Makkah or what they bought in the sacred city. Moreover, they were not allowed to do their *ṭawāf* when they arrived in Makkah unless they had garments made or bought in Makkah itself. If they could not find or buy any, they had to do their *ṭawāf* in the nude. Men could wear nothing, while women were allowed to have a single garment provided that it was cut in several places in order to make their private parts visible. The idea of nakedness when practising an act of worship in a sacred place seems extremely perverted. One wonders how the Quraysh could justify it and persuade the Arabs to accept it. One has only to remember that those people accepted that wooden figures and stone statues which they themselves made were their gods, to whom they prayed and from whom they sought help. Their justification for imposing nakedness on visitors to the Kaʿbah was that people were not allowed to do the *ṭawāf* in the clothes which they wore when they committed sins. Nobody was there to tell them that purification from sin applied to the individual, not his clothes.

If a person from outside Makkah could not buy garments made in Makkah for his first *ṭawāf* and he did not wish to do the *ṭawāf* in the nude, he was allowed to proceed with his *ṭawāf* in his ordinary clothes, provided that he took them off and threw them away as soon as he finished. Neither he nor anyone else could use those garments.

These absurdities continued until the Prophet abrogated them. He sent one of his companions to declare their abrogation in the pilgrimage season of the 9th year of the Islamic calendar. This will be discussed in detail in its appropriate place in this book.[3]

In such a society, it was only natural that there were people of sound mind who rejected such absurd beliefs and practices. It only takes a person to think rationally of what he is doing and what worship he is offering to know that idolatrous worship cannot be a satisfactory religion. There are at least four people we know who took such a conscious decision in the period before the prophethood of Muhammad (peace be upon him). These were Waraqah ibn Nawfal, ʿAbdullāh ibn Jaḥsh, ʿUthmān ibn al-Ḥuwayrith and Zayd ibn ʿAmr. There were others here and there in Arabia, but little is known of them. These four were better known because they were Makkans. Moreover, they knew of each other's dissatisfaction with pagan worship. It seems that they met during a festival which the Quraysh held annually as a celebration dedicated to one of their idols. The Quraysh offered sacrifice to that idol and organized dances and other rituals. Those four were very unhappy about what they saw of their people's practices. They said to one another: "Let us be frank about it. Our people do not follow any proper religion. They have distorted the faith of Abraham, their father. What is this stone which neither hears nor sees, and we are here celebrating its festival with offerings and dances? It certainly cannot cause us any benefit or harm."

When each of them was sure that the others were not happy with idolatrous worship either, they began to think what they should do to ensure that they followed a proper religion. They eventually decided to travel separately to meet priests and other scholars in the hope of learning the original version of the faith of Abraham.[4]

Waraqah ibn Nawfal soon adopted Christianity and studied the Bible thoroughly. He became a fully-fledged Christian scholar. ʿAbdullāh ibn Jaḥsh could not make up his mind to follow Christianity or any other religion. When the Prophet began to convey his message, he accepted Islam. He was later to travel with those Muslims who emigrated to Abyssinia. There, however, he became a Christian convert and lived as a Christian until he died. ʿUthmān ibn al-Ḥuwayrith was able to meet the Byzantine Emperor and became a Christian. He apparently enjoyed a good position with the Byzantine Emperor, who wanted to make him King of Makkah. The Quraysh would not stand for that. He was nicknamed 'the Cardinal'. ʿAmr ibn Jafnah, King of Ghassān, the Arabian tribe which lived in Syria under the domination of the Byzantine Empire, apparently poisoned him. Zayd ibn ʿAmr, the last of the four, travelled widely in Syria and Iraq. He considered becoming a Jew or a Christian. An aged Christian priest, however, told him that the time was ripe for the appearance of a new Prophet in the land of the Arabs. Zayd therefore went back to Makkah to wait for this new Prophet. He took no part in idol worship and refused to partake of any animal which was slaughtered as an offering to idols. He tried to save every young girl who was about to be buried alive by her father, as the Arabs used to do. He told his people that he was the only one who followed the faith of Abraham. He used to address God, saying: "Had I known which way of worship is acceptable to You, I would have followed it. But I am ignorant of that." He would then prostrate himself, putting his forehead over his palm in a gesture of submission to God.[5]

Zayd was perhaps the most outspoken of the four. He criticized idolatrous worship, urging his people to abandon it. That prompted some of his relatives, notably his uncle, al-Khaṭṭāb, to try to bring him back to the fold. Al-Khaṭṭāb counselled him repeatedly against abandoning the faith of his people. He also tried to prevent him going abroad in pursuit of religious learning. Al-Khaṭṭāb asked a woman in their household to keep an eye on Zayd, and to report to him Zayd's intentions. Whenever she felt that Zayd was planning to travel abroad, she would tell al-Khaṭṭāb, who took measures to prevent him from leaving. When Zayd grew more outspoken in his criticism of idolatrous worship, al-Khaṭṭāb managed to banish him to an area outside Makkah in order that he should keep his ideas to himself. Al-Khaṭṭāb further assigned a number of young men from the Quraysh to report Zayd's movements to him. If Zayd came into the city, which he always tried to do in secret, they would report that to al-Khaṭṭāb and he would make sure he was turned out again. Zayd was made to suffer very bad treatment in the process. What al-Khaṭṭāb feared was that Zayd might be able to win over other people to his way of thinking; this might lead to division within Arabian society.

Zayd, however, managed to travel in secret, and he went again to Syria. Apparently, it was on this trip, and after he had travelled extensively in Syria and Iraq, that he was told by a learned Christian priest of the imminent appearance in Arabia of a new Prophet. When he learned that, he immediately decided to go back to Makkah. Unfortunately, he was murdered on his way home.[6]

It was noteworthy that his son, Saʿīd, was one of the first people to accept the message of Islam when the Prophet started preaching it in secret. Al-Khaṭṭāb's son, ʿUmar, was to become one of the strongest advocates of Islam, and the second ruler of the Muslim state after the Prophet. Saʿīd and ʿUmar once asked the Prophet whether it was permissible to pray God to grant mercy and forgiveness to Zayd. The Prophet answered in the affirmative and told them that on the Day of Resurrection, Zayd would be in a class of his own. What we understand from the Prophet's statement is that Zayd had no equal as a person who genuinely and conscientiously sought the truth with the determination to follow it once he learnt it.[7]

It is noteworthy that Zayd was told by a learned Christian priest of the message of Prophet Muhammad (peace be upon him) and that it was imminent. Indeed, learned theologians of both Christianity and Judaism were aware of the fact.[8] Salmān, the Prophet's Persian companion, was also informed of the message of Islam by one such Christian theologian. His story will be reported in detail later in this book. On the other hand, the Jews in Madinah used to tell the polytheist Arabs there that a Prophet would soon be appearing in Arabia and that they would be the first to follow him. Every time trouble arose between the Jewish and Arab communities in Madinah, the Jews would make threatening noises to the effect that the new Prophet, whose appearance they asserted to be imminent, would not hesitate to fight and inflict heavy defeats on his opponents. Indeed, the Arabs of Madinah were quick to embrace Islam when they first learnt of it, because of those threats the Jews used to make. They did not want the Jews to be allied with the Prophet against them.[9]

A more detailed story is reported by Salāmah ibn Waqsh, a companion of the Prophet from the Anṣār, who attended the Battle of Badr with him:

> We had a Jewish neighbour who one day came to speak to the men of our clan when I was still a young boy. He mentioned the Day of Resurrection and that all people would have to face the reckoning and that they would be taken either to heaven or to hell. Our people were polytheists who did not

> believe in resurrection or a second life. They asked him whether he genuinely believed that people would come to life again after they had died, and whether he genuinely believed in heaven and hell. He answered: "Yes indeed, I swear to the truth of that. I would even be prepared to barter my share of that hell with the largest furnace you have in your community. I am willing that you should light up that furnace and put me inside it and close it on me, if that would ensure that I would be spared the torment of hell in the life to come." They asked him what evidence he had in support of his claim. He said: "There will come to you a prophet from those parts" (pointing with his hand towards Makkah and Yemen). They asked how long it would take before he actually appeared. He looked at me, as I was one of the youngest in the group, and said: "If this boy lives until he reaches old age, he will be sure to see him."
>
> It was not long before God sent His messenger, Muhammad (peace be upon him). The Jew was still alive among us. We believed in the Prophet and he denied the truth of his message. When we rebuked him for his attitude and reminded him of what he told us, he said: "What I told you is true, but your man is not the one I meant."[10]

Another story involves the arrival of a Jewish scholar from Syria in Madinah a few years before the advent of Islam. This man, who was called Ibn al-Hayyabān, was a very devout person. When rain was scarce, the Jews would ask him to pray for rain. He would refuse unless they paid something for charity. They would join him in his prayer outside the town. He would hardly finish before the sky would be cloudy and rain would pour down. He did that many times.

Not long after his arrival, he fell ill and was certain to die. He spoke to his fellow Jews and started by asking them what they felt was his reason for emigrating from a land of prosperity to one of poverty and hardship. He then explained that he came to Madinah only because it was time for a new Prophet to appear and that Madinah would be the place to which he would emigrate. "I hoped", he said, "that he would appear before I died so that I could follow him. His appearance is very imminent, so let no one follow him ahead of you. He will be given power to shed blood and take the women and children of his opponents prisoner, but that should not deter you from following him, fellow Jews."

When the Prophet emigrated to Madinah and had his battle with the Jews of Qurayẓah (which will be described later) a few young men from that tribe reminded their people that Muhammad was the Prophet that Ibn al-Hayyabān had told them about. Their people disagreed with them, but those young men were determined that he was indeed the Prophet about whose appearance they had been informed. They therefore came out of the fort of Quraithah and declared their acceptance of Islam, thereby sparing themselves and their families the fate of the people of Qurayẓah. Among these were Thaʿlabah ibn Saʿyah, Usayd ibn Saʿyah and Asʿad ibn ʿUbayd.[11] That Christian and Jewish theologians should know in advance of the coming of the Prophet is not surprising, because both the Gospel and the Torah include references to Muhammad as the last of God's messengers and Prophets.

Notes

1. Abū al-Ḥasan ʿAlī al-Ḥasanī Nadwī, *Muhammad Rasulallah,* (English translation by Muhiuddin Ahmad), Academy of Islamic Research and Publications, Lucknow, India, 1979, pp. 78-79.
2. Amīn Duwaydār, *Ṣuwar Min Ḥayāt al-Rasūl*, Dār al-Maʿārif, 4th Edition, Cairo, pp. 106-113.
3. Ibn Hishām, *al-Sīrah al-Nabawiyyah*, Dār al-Qalam, Beirut, Vol. 1, pp. 214-216.
4. Ibid., pp. 237-240.
5. Amīn Duwaydār, op.cit., pp. 106-115.
6. Ibn Hishām, op.cit., pp. 244-247.
7. Ibid., p. 240.
8. Ibid., pp. 246-247.
9. Ibid., p. 217.
10. Ibid., pp. 225-226.
11. Ibid., pp. 226-228.

5

Up There in the Mountain

LITTLE IS REPORTED about how Muhammad lived after his marriage, up to the time when he started to receive Divine revelations. It is certain, however, that his marriage was a very happy one. Moreover, his marriage provided him with a comfortable life. Although there is no direct reference to the type of work Muhammad did in this period, it is reasonable to assume that he continued to manage his wife's business. Since the work was mainly done through the caravan trade, the work itself was not very demanding. None of the old biographers of the Prophet mentioned that he travelled on Khadījah's trade missions after their marriage but, most probably, he spared her the need to attend to the business herself. He might have selected the men to travel on her behalf and supervised the preparations of the shipment before the caravan set off and the sale of the imported goods when it came back.

Nor are there detailed reports on Muhammad's social activity in Makkah. It is known that the Arabs of Makkah had their meeting places round the Kaʿbah where they spent some time in the morning and the afternoon in a pleasant atmosphere. Although Muhammad had a likeable personality and everyone seemed to enjoy his company, he did not appear to care much for such gatherings, most probably because the chatting would inevitably have turned to the worship of idols and promiscuous pursuits. These were normal topics of conversation, unless something more serious imposed itself on such meetings. But neither topic interested Muhammad. He had disliked idols since childhood. Moreover, he was protected by God against indulging in wanton pleasures. Indeed there was clearly a wide intellectual gap between Muhammad and the people of Makkah. This gap continued to increase as the years went by. It did not deprive him, however, of enjoying his people's respect for his honest, serious and amiable character.[1]

It was probably because of this gap that Muhammad began to take himself away from Makkah for a period of total seclusion. In the month of Ramaḍān, each year, he went to a mountain called Ḥirā', which was only a few miles away, but offered him complete seclusion. Up there in the mountain there was a little cave where Muhammad stayed for several days at a time. When his supply of food and drink was exhausted he would go back home for a fresh supply and come back for another few days. When the month was over, he went back home, starting with a visit to the Kaʿbah, where he did the *ṭawāf*, walking round the Kaʿbah seven times before he went home to his wife.

To get to the cave, Muhammad had to climb right to the top of the mountain and descend a short distance down the other side. The cave is a small one with an entrance that is wide enough to admit one person comfortably, but does not easily accommodate two people standing to pray. The entrance narrows at the top and is just about two metres high. Although the ground of the cave is flat, the ceiling slopes down as you go inside until it becomes very low towards the end, where there is a little opening which ensures good ventilation. There is not much space in the cave altogether. It has just about enough room to accommodate one person to sit, stand or sleep. What is worth mentioning is that if one stands to offer prayers at the entrance of the cave and looks through the opening at its end, one can see the Kaʿbah on the far horizon. Just before the entrance there are two great rocks shielding the cave and giving the place an air of complete isolation. Alongside it, the great rocks form a little open space looking over an almost vertical side of the mountain. Only mountaineering experts with full equipment can attempt to climb that side. That little space next to the cave must have given Muhammad all that he needed to be absorbed in contemplating human life nearby and the universal expanse all around him.

Muhammad spent his days and nights in contemplation and worship. He addressed his worship to the Creator of the universe. He did not follow any particular method of worship because he was not aware of any, but he realized that the beliefs of his people were absurd. In those days of seclusion, Muhammad found comfort which lasted him through the rest of the year. He realized that there is a force of truth beyond this world which must have power and control over the whole universe. The world around him could not have come into being by coincidence. But how that truth manifested itself, he could not tell.[2]

It is easy to read too much into Muhammad's period of seclusion and his contemplation. Modern authors and biographers in particular have tried to show him trying to find a way out of the total darkness that enshrouded his people. This may bring us very close to saying that Muhammad was in search of an idea or a belief. This is true only in as much as it means that Muhammad rejected all beliefs which were known to him and were practised in Makkan society. He certainly did not aspire to the role that was later assigned to him. Addressing the Prophet, God says in the Qur'ān: "You had not entertained any hope that Scriptures would be given you, but this was an act of grace by Your Lord." (28: 86) Nevertheless, this regular period of seclusion helped to prepare Muhammad for receiving God's revelations.

There were other aspects of preparation. It was necessary that Muhammad should understand and realized that the unique relationship which was soon to be established between him and the Angel Gabriel is both real and truthful. He was soon to realized that every dream in his sleep was soon to come true exactly. When he was alone, he might see a light or hear a sound, someone invisible might address him by his name. Yet these matters did not worry him much. When he felt such worry, he told his wife Khadījah, expressing his fears to her. She would reassure him and say that God would not allow anything evil to happen to him. "By God," she said, "you are faithful to your trust, kind to your kinsfolk and you always tell the truth." She, however, went to her cousin, Waraqah ibn Nawfal, the old Christian scholar, asking him about what Muhammad saw and heard. He also reassured her and sent Muhammad word telling him to be reassured.

The First Revelation

Then the moment had to come. It was in the month of Ramaḍān, in the year AD 610 when Muhammad was 40 years old, spending the month in the mountain of Ḥirā', as had been his habit for several years. Suddenly, Muhammad had a most fascinating experience, an account of which is given by his future wife ʿĀ'ishah.

> The first aspect of revelation to God's Messenger was that his dreams came true. Whatever vision he might have had in his sleep would occur as he had seen. Then, he began to enjoy seclusion. He used to retreat alone into the cave of Ḥirā', where he would spend several days in devotion before going back to his family. He used to take some food with him, and when he came back he would take a fresh supply for another period. He continued to do so until he received the truth while in the cave of Ḥirā'. The angel came to him and said: "Read". He replied: "I am not a reader." The Prophet says: "He held me and pressed hard until I was exhausted, then he released me and said: 'Read', and I replied: 'I am not a reader.' So he held me and pressed me hard a second time until I was exhausted, then he released me and said: 'Read'. I replied: 'I am not a reader.' He then held me and pressed hard for a third time. Then he said: 'Read, in the name of Your Lord Who created. It is He Who created man from clots of blood. Read! Your Lord is the most bounteous, Who has taught the use of the pen. He has taught man what he did not know.'" The Prophet returned home to Khadījah, trembling, and said: "Wrap me! Wrap me!" They wrapped him and his fear subsided. He turned to Khadījah and exclaimed: "What has happened to me?" He related to her what happened and said: "I fear for myself," and Khadījah replied: "You have nothing to fear; be calm and relax.

> God will not let you suffer humiliation, because you are kind to your relatives, you speak the truth, you assist anyone in need, you are hospitable to your guest and you help in every just cause." Then she took him to Waraqah ibn Nawfal, her paternal cousin who was a Christian convert and a scholar with good knowledge of Arabic, Hebrew and the Bible. He had lost his eyesight, as he had grown very old. Khadījah said to Waraqah: "Cousin, would you like to hear what your nephew has to say?" [Waraqah was not, in fact, the Prophet's uncle. Khadījah's reference to Muhammad as his nephew was in accordance with the standards of politeness which prevailed in Arabia at the time.] Waraqah said: "Well, nephew, what have you seen?" The Prophet related to him what he saw. When he had finished, Waraqah said: "It is the same revelation as was sent down to Moses. I wish I was a young man so that I might be alive when your people turn you away from this city." The Prophet exclaimed: "Would they turn me away?" Waraqah answered: "Yes! No man has ever preached a message like yours and was not met with enmity. If I live till that day, I will certainly give you all my support." But Waraqah died soon after that...[3]

This *ḥadīth* is related in both of the two most authentic collections of the Prophet's traditions prepared by al-Bukhārī and Muslim, and also related by Imām Aḥmad in his collection.

Al-Ṭabarī also relates the following *ḥadīth*, on the authority of ʿAbdullāh ibn al-Zubayr:

> The Prophet said: "While I was asleep he came to me carrying a case of a very rich material in which there was a book. He said: 'Read'. I replied: 'I am not a reader.' He pressed me so hard that I felt that I was about to die. Then he released me and said, 'Read'. I asked: 'What shall I read?' (I said this only out of fear that he might repeat what he had done to me before.) He said: 'Read: in the name of Your Lord Who created. It is He Who created man from clots of blood. Read! Your Lord is the Most Bounteous, Who has taught the use of the pen. He has taught man what he did not know.' I read it. He

stopped. Then he left me and went away. I woke up feeling that it was actually written in my heart."

The Prophet went on to say: "No man was ever more loathsome to me than poets or deranged persons. I could not bear even looking at either. I thought: 'The man [meaning himself] is undoubtedly a poet or deranged. This shall not be said about me amongst the Quraysh. Let me climb higher up the mountain and throw myself down and get rid of it all.' I went to carry out this intention. When I was halfway up the mountain, I heard a voice coming from the heavens saying: 'Muhammad, you are the Messenger of God and I am Gabriel.' I raised my head up to the sky and I saw Gabriel in the image of a man with his feet next to one another up on the horizon. He said again: 'Muhammad, you are the Messenger of God and I am Gabriel.' I stood in my place looking up at him; this distracted me from my intention. I was standing there unable to move. I tried to turn my face away from him and to look up at the sky, but wherever I looked I saw him in front of me. I stood still, moving, neither forward nor backward. Khadījah sent her messengers looking for me and I remained standing in my place all the while until they went back to her. He then left me and I went back to my family..."[4]

An Address from Heaven

Before continuing with the narrative to see what the Prophet did when he arrived home, it is necessary to say a word or two about the significance of the relationship which was established at that point in time when Muhammad received the Angel Gabriel, who brought him his revelations. One cannot do much better than quote one of the leading twentieth-century scholars. Sayyid Quṭb (may God bless his soul) writes in his priceless work *In the Shade of the Qur'ān*:

> The true nature of this event is that God, the Great, the Compeller, the Almighty, the Supreme, the Sovereign of the whole universe, out of His benevolence has turned to that creation of His which is called 'man', and which takes its abode

in a barely visible corner of the universe, the name of which is 'earth'. He has honoured this species of His creation by choosing one of its numbers to be the recipient of His Divine light and guardian of His wisdom.

This is something infinitely great. Some aspects of this greatness become apparent when man tries, as much as he can, to perceive the essential qualities of God: absolute power, freedom from all limitations and everlastingness; and when he reflects in comparison on the basic qualities of God's servants who are subject to certain limitations of power and life duration. One may then perceive the significance of this Divine care for man. He may realize the sweetness of this feeling and manifest his appreciation with thanksgiving, prayers and devotion. He feels that the whole universe shares in the general happiness spread by the revelation of Divine words to man in his obscure corner of the universe.

What is the significance of this event? With reference to God it signifies that He is the source of all the great bounties and unfailing compassion. He is the benevolent, the loving, who bestows His mercy and benefaction for no reason except that benevolence is one of His Divine attributes. As for man, this event signifies that God has bestowed on him an honour, the greatness of which he can hardly ever appreciate and for which he can never show enough gratitude, not even if he spends all his life in devotion and prostration. This honour is that God has taken notice and care of him, established contact with him and chosen one of the human race as His messenger to reveal to him His words; that the earth, man's abode, has become the recipient of these Divine words which the whole universe echoes with submission and devotion.

This great event began to bear on the life of humanity as a whole right from the first moment. It marked a change in the course of history, following the change it brought about in the course followed by human conscience. It specified the source man should look up to in order to derive his ideas, values and criteria. The source is heaven and the Divine revelations, not this world and man's own desires. When this great event took place, the people who recognized its true nature and adapted their lives accordingly enjoyed God's protection and manifest care. They looked up to Him directly for guidance in all their affairs, big and small. They lived and moved under His supervision. They expected that He would guide them along the road, step by step, stopping them from error, leading them to the right. Every night they expected to receive some Divine revelations concerning what they had on their minds, providing solutions for their problems and saying to them, 'do this and leave that'.

The period which followed the event was certainly remarkable: twenty-three years of direct contact between the human race and the Supreme Society [Supreme Society refers to the angels]. The true nature of this period cannot be recognized except by those who lived in it and went through its experience, witnessed its start and its end, relished the sweet flavour of that contact and felt the Divine hand guiding them along the road. The distance which separates us from that reality is too great to be defined by any measure of length this world has known. It is a distance in the spiritual world incomparable to any distance in the material world, not even when we think of gaps separating the stars or galaxies. It is a gap that separates the earth and the heavens; a gap between human desires and Divine revelations as sources from which concepts and values are derived; a gap between ignorance and Islam, the human and the Divine.

The people who lived in that period were fully aware of its uniqueness, recognized its special place in history and felt the great loss when the Prophet passed away to be in the company of the Supreme Companion [The Supreme Companion is an Islamic term which refers to God]. This marked the end of this remarkable period which our minds can hardly imagine, but for its actual occurrence.

Anas related that Abū Bakr said to ʿUmar after the death of the Prophet: "Let us go and visit Umm Ayman (the nurse who took care of the Prophet in his childhood) as the Prophet used to do." When they went to her she burst into tears. They said: "What are you crying for? Do you not realize that God's company is far better for the Prophet?" She replied: "This is true, I am sure. I am only crying because revelation has ceased with his death." This made tears spring to their eyes and the three of them cried together. (Related by Muslim.)

The impact of that period has been in evidence in the life of humanity from its beginning up to this moment, and it will remain in evidence until the day when God inherits the earth and all that walks on it. Man was reborn when he started to derive his values from heaven rather than earth and his laws from Divine revelations instead of his own desires. The course of history underwent a change the like of which has never been experienced before or since. That event, the commencement of revelation, was the point at which the roads crossed. Clear and permanent guidelines were established which cannot be changed by the passage of time or effaced by events. Human conscience developed a concept of existence, human life and its values unsurpassed in comprehensiveness, clarity and purity of all worldly considerations, as well as its realism and practicability in human society. The foundations of this Divine code have been firmly established in the world and its various aspects and essential standards have been made clear "so that he who perishes may perish after having received a clear sign and he who lives may live after having received a clear sign". (8: 42)

The beginning of revelation was a unique event at a unique moment marking the end of one era and the start of another. It is the demarcation line in the history of mankind, not merely in the history of a certain nation or a particular generation. It has been recorded in the universe and echoed in all its corners. It has also been recorded in the conscience of man, which today needs to be guided by what God has revealed and never to lose sight of it. It needs to remember that this event was a rebirth of humanity which can take place only once in history.[5]

A Test for Reassurance

When the Prophet reached home after his sojourn in the mountain cave, his wife noticed that he was off-colour, which was natural after all the excitement of his first encounter with the Angel Gabriel. She asked him what was the matter as she started to wipe his face. She asked whether he had seen or heard anything new. He told her: "You remember what I told you about my dreams and the voice I used to hear when I awoke, which caused me some fear! It was Gabriel who appeared and talked to me and made me read words which left me worried. He then told me that I am the Prophet of this nation. As I was coming back, I heard trees and stones saying: "Peace be to you, Messenger of God." Khadījah said: "Rejoice! By God, I was certain that God would bring you only what is good. I certainly hope that you are the Prophet of this nation."

She continued to encourage him until he relaxed and ate. She then went to her cousin, Waraqah ibn Nawfal, who reassured her. He then promised her most solemnly that if Muhammad was truly the Prophet who is mentioned in the Torah and the Gospel, "and he calls people to believe in his message while I am still alive, I will do my best in obedience to God's Messenger and will support him to the end."

There are several reports about the encouragement Waraqah gave to Khadījah and the Prophet. If we take them together, there were probably two or three meetings between the Prophet and Waraqah, one of which occurred when they met at the Kaʿbah as both of them were doing the *ṭawāf*. Waraqah reassured Muhammad and kissed his head. Then Waraqah died within a few days. The Prophet said of him: "I have seen in my dream the priest wearing silk clothes in heaven, because he believed in me."[6]

The first few days must have been full of worry in the Prophet's home. He needed every possible reassurance. It seems that Gabriel appeared to him more than once. His wife Khadījah was certain that nothing evil could come to him. Her logical thinking led her to that conclusion. What she knew of the Prophet's character made her absolutely certain that what he saw and heard was genuine and came from a good source. Her thoughtful mind led her to try to get more reassurance. She said to the Prophet: "Cousin, can you tell me when this companion of yours comes to you next time?" He agreed to do so.

Informed of Gabriel's presence on his next visit, Khadījah said to the Prophet: "Cousin, sit on my left thigh." When he did so, she asked him whether he still saw him. The Prophet said: "Yes." She told the Prophet to move over and sit on her right thigh. As he did so, the Prophet confirmed that he could still see Gabriel. She asked him to sit on her lap and he did so, again confirming that he could still see him. She then took off her head-covering, while the Prophet still sat on her lap. At that moment, he told her he could see him no more. She said, "Rejoice, Cousin, and be firm. This is certainly an angel, not a devil." It was her clear thinking that led her to try this method, realizing that an angel would not stay in a room where a man and his wife were in a closely intimate position.[7]

Then followed a period during which the Angel Gabriel stopped coming to the Prophet. It seemed that it all stopped as suddenly as it had started. Now, no more visits by Gabriel and no more revelations. This worried the Prophet and he needed reassurance again.

There are no confirmed reports of the duration of this period during which the Prophet received no new revelations. One report puts it at two and a half years, but it is more likely that it was much shorter than that, lasting perhaps about a month or a few weeks.[8] The purpose was to allow the Prophet to have some time to himself, during which his new experience would sink in and he would be able to evaluate the new situation and its implications for his future role. What he was embarking on was by no means easy. It required strength, fortitude and perseverance. Of all these he had plenty, but his task needed even more. The history related in this book will give only a glimpse of the sort of strength and perseverance the Prophet needed to summon up in order to fulfil his task. Moreover, the process of receiving revelation was by no means easy. No human being can tell what it meant, simply because no human being has ever experienced it, apart from those chosen elite whom God has honoured so highly to make them prophets. What it is important to remember, however, is that the receipt of revelation was an actual contact between the Prophet, Muhammad, the human being, and an angel God sent specially to him to give him His own words. The process itself took several forms.

From the two *ḥadīths*, quoted earlier in this chapter, relating the first encounter between the Prophet and the Angel Gabriel, one can realize that revelation could be given to the Prophet while he was asleep or while he was awake. In that particular instance, both types might have occurred, first during the Prophet's sleep, and then confirmed when he was awake.

Alternatively, it could come through direct inspiration. In an authentic *ḥadīth*, the Prophet is quoted to have said: "The Holy Spirit has given me this inspiration that no soul shall die until it has completed its life duration and received all its provisions. Be mindful, therefore, of your duty towards God and maintain propriety when you ask Him for what you want."

Or the revelation could be given to him while a ringing noise was heard. That was the most difficult form. It is suggested that with that ringing sound, his mind was at its most alert.

Or the angel could come to him in human form. In particular, he appeared in the form of one of the Prophet's companions, Diḥyah ibn Khalīfah, who was exceptionally handsome.

Or the Angel Gabriel could appear to Muhammad in his own shape, as an angel with wings.

Or finally, God could speak to him directly from behind a screen, either when he was awake, as on his night journey, or during his sleep as the Prophet has once reported: "My Lord appeared to me in the most splendid form, and said: 'Over what do the Supreme Society dispute?' I said I do not know. He put his palm on my chest and I felt its coolness and knowledge of everything became clear to me. He said: 'Muhammad, over what do the Supreme Society dispute?' I said: 'Over atonements.' He said: 'What are they?' I said: 'Ablution after what is disliked, moving forward to do what is good and watching for the time of prayer, one after the other. If a person does this, he is praised during his life and at his death. His sins will be wiped out and he will be like a newborn child.'" (Related by al-Tirmidhī.)

'Ā'ishah reported that when the Prophet received revelations, he always sweated, even on the coldest of days.

All this meant that the Prophet had to go through a transitional period during which he would taste part of the complete transformation that was going to take place in his life. During this transitional period, there was no need for new revelations. Only reassurance was needed that what he had seen and heard was true and real. He was a Prophet chosen by God for a great task.

When the transitional period was over, revelations resumed. Jābir ibn ʿAbdullāh quotes the Prophet as saying: "As I was walking, I heard a voice from heaven. I lifted my eyes to the sky and I saw the angel who had come to me in Ḥirā' sitting on a chair raised between heaven and earth. I sat down in terror and fell. I then rushed home and said to my wife: 'Wrap me! Wrap me!' God revealed to me: 'O you enfolded [in your coverings] arise and warn . . . etc.'" (74: 1-7) From now on, Muhammad was not only a Prophet, he was also a Messenger. From now on, he was to receive revelations without worrying interruptions.

Notes

1. Ibn Hishām, *al-Sīrah al-Nabawiyyah*, Dār al-Qalam, Beirut, Vol. 1, pp. 252-254. Also, Amīn Duwaydār, *Ṣuwar Min Ḥayāt al-Rasūl*, Dār al-Maʿārif, 4th edition, Cairo, p. 119.
2. Amīn Duwaydār, op.cit., pp. 118-119.
3. Ibn Hishām, op.cit., pp. 249-254.
4. Al-Ṭabarī, *Tārīkh al-Rusul wa al-Mulūk*, Dār al-Maʿārif, 4th edition, Vol. 2, pp. 300-301.
5. Sayyid Quṭb, *Fī Ẓilal al-Qur'ān*, Dār al-Shurūq, Beirut, Vol. 6, pp. 3396-3398. English edition, *In the Shade of the Qur'ān*, Vol. 30, MWH London Publishers, London, 1979, pp. 220-222.
6. Ibn Hishām, op.cit., pp. 249-254. Also, Amīn Duwaydār, op.cit., pp. 121-122.
7. Ibn Hishām, op.cit., p. 255.
8. Ibid., p. 257. Also, Ibn Sayyid al-Nās, *ʿUyūn al-Athar*, Dār al-Turāth, Madinah, 1996, p. 170 and p. 176.

6

A Community in the Making

AS ESTABLISHED IN the preceding chapter, Muhammad was now a Prophet receiving revelations from God, through the Angel Gabriel, and a messenger required to convey God's message to mankind. He was fully aware of the magnitude of the change which this message would bring about in the life of Arabian society at the time, and human life in general. He was also aware that when he had to make his message known to people, he was bound to meet opposition. He himself, however, accepted the new faith and declared his belief in God's oneness, fully reassured that his was the true Divine Faith.

The enormous difficulty of the task ahead did not deter him from attempting it. The fact that opposition was bound to be fierce was not to stop him from dedicating all his energy and efforts to calling on people to abandon their erroneous beliefs in favour of the new message God was addressing to mankind through him. He was, however, directed by God to keep his message secret for the time being, and only to approach those whom he thought would give a favourable response. The first to accept the new faith was his wife, Khadījah. She already knew him to be a man of noble heart and upright nature. She trusted that her husband, who had never said something which he knew to be untrue, would have never contemplated making a claim to prophethood if it was not absolutely true. Knowing her husband to be exemplary in his honesty and truthfulness, she realized that he was the man God would have chosen as His Messenger to mankind. She willingly and assuredly declared that she believed in God's oneness, and that Muhammad was God's Messenger.

It was indeed a blessing that Khadījah should readily accept the new faith. She was to give the Prophet her unwavering support, and comfort him in the years to come when opposition to his message was to increase in ferocity and wickedness. When he went out to discharge his duty as a messenger, he might receive insults, ridicule and physical assault. He would return home sad and downhearted, but she would always be ready with her encouragement and support. She did her best to comfort him and he would soon regain his cheerful, optimistic attitude. For this unwavering support, Gabriel once came to the Prophet telling him to convey God's greeting to Khadījah and give her the happy news that she had a special home in heaven where she would enjoy total bliss and happiness. An authentic *ḥadīth* related by Muslim quotes the Prophet as saying: "The best woman in it [meaning heaven] is Mary, daughter of ʿImrān, and the best woman on it [meaning the earth] is Khadījah."[1]

The first male to accept Islam was a ten-year-old boy named ʿAlī ibn Abī Ṭālib. He was the Prophet's cousin, reared in the Prophet's home. Some years earlier, the Quraysh had been through hard times. Although Abū Ṭālib, the Prophet's uncle, was the chief of his clan which also enjoyed a position of honour in Makkah, he was a man of limited means and large family. In those hard times, Muhammad wanted to do something to help his uncle. He therefore went to speak to another uncle of his, al-ʿAbbās ibn ʿAbd al-Muṭṭalib, saying: "You know that your brother Abū Ṭālib has a large family, and everyone is going through very difficult times. I suggest that you and I go to him with a proposal of help: you take one of his sons and I take one to rear in order to reduce his burden." Al-ʿAbbās agreed and they went and spoke to Abū Ṭālib, proposing that they should have two of his children for as long as the difficult period continued. Abū Ṭālib agreed, provided that they left his eldest son, Ṭālib, with him. The Prophet took ʿAlī to his home and al-ʿAbbās took Jaʿfar. ʿAlī continued to be with the Prophet until he received his message, and he was in the fortunate position of accepting Islam in its very early days. Jaʿfar was also to become one of the early Muslims.[2]

The First Muslim Man

The first man to accept Islam after the Prophet was his servant, Zayd ibn Ḥārithah. The fact that Zayd should not have a moment's hesitation before accepting Islam comes as no surprise when one remembers his history with the Prophet. When Zayd was eight years old, his mother, Suʿdā bint Thaʿlabah, took him on a journey to visit her people. On the way, a group of horsemen attacked them and kidnapped Zayd, and subsequently sold him as a slave child in one of the Arabian bazaars called Ḥubbāshah. Apparently Zayd was sold once or twice before he ended up in Syria. Some time later, a man from the Quraysh called Ḥakīm ibn Ḥizām bought him and took him to Makkah. Ḥakīm, who was a nephew of Khadījah, brought with him several young slaves. His aunt went to visit him after his return. He said to her: "Aunt, look at these slaves and choose whoever you like." She chose Zayd and took him home. This happened when she was already married to the Prophet, but long before he started to receive his revelations. When the Prophet saw Zayd, he liked him and asked Khadījah to give him Zayd as a present. She willingly complied.

Zayd's father felt his loss very painfully. He could not forget his son because he realized that the boy would have been sold as a slave. As was the habit with the Arabs, he expressed his sorrow in highly moving poetry: "I wonder would you ever come back? My dearest wish would then have come true. I am reminded of him by the sun when it rises; and his memory comes back to me when the sun goes down. When the wind blows, I am also reminded of him. Long is my sorrow, little is my hope."

Reciting such poetry at gatherings and bazaars was the surest method for news to travel in Arabia at that time. Travellers memorized such poetry as they heard it, and probably chanted it as they travelled. When they encamped somewhere, reciting that poetry would be the means through which the news was transmitted. It was not surprising, therefore, that in his new dwelling place in Makkah, Zayd should hear his father's poetry. He replied to his message, reciting several lines of poetry in which he mentioned that he was living in Makkah. Before long, his father got wind of this and resolved to travel with his brother, looking for Zayd in Makkah.

It was some time before Muhammad's prophethood when Ḥārithah and Kaʿb, sons of Sharāḥīl, arrived in Makkah to learn that Ḥārithah's son, Zayd, was in Muhammad's household. Therefore, they went to him and made this passionate appeal: "You are the grandson of ʿAbd al-Muṭṭalib, the old master of this city; you are the son of the great master of his people. You and your people are neighbours of God in this blessed city. Your reputation has been established for a long while that you feed the hungry and help those who are in need. We have come to you on account of our son, your slave, to request you to be benevolent and to agree to sell him to us." Muhammad replied: "What would you say if I made you a better offer?" They asked: "What sort of proposal?" He said: "I will call Zayd and give him a choice. If he chooses to go with you, that will be it. But if he chooses to stay with me, then, by God, I would not disappoint someone who chooses me." They said: "Your proposal is more than fair."

Muhammad called Zayd and asked him: "Who are these two?" Zayd said: "This man is my father, Ḥārithah ibn Sharāḥīl, and this is my uncle, Kaʿb ibn Sharāḥīl." Muhammad said: "I am giving you the choice: if you wish, you may go with them, or if you wish, you may stay with me." Zayd unhesitatingly said: "I will stay with you." This came as a shock to the two men. His father said: "Zayd, do you prefer to remain a slave to rejoining your parents, your home and your tribe?" Zayd replied: "I have seen certain things with this man and I will never leave him to go anywhere."

At this point Muhammad took Zayd by his hand and together they went to where the people of the Quraysh used to meet near the Kaʿbah where Muhammad declared: "Bear witness that this chap is my son: he inherits me and I inherit him." That was the formal method of adoption practised in Arabia. Zayd's father was pleased by this outcome of his mission, because he was sure that Zayd would come to no harm in the company of Muhammad. From that day, Zayd used to be known as Zayd ibn Muhammad. People continued to call him by this name for many years, until adoption was totally forbidden some years after the Prophet's settlement in Madinah. It was then that God ordered Muslims to call their adopted children by their own parents' names. Adoption was totally forbidden. Zayd then reverted to his name, Zayd ibn Ḥārithah.[3]

It was some time before prophethood that Zayd realized that there was something special about Muhammad. He loved him, and his feelings were reciprocated by Muhammad before and after he became a Prophet. Two or three years after Zayd's death, the Prophet mentioned him and said that "he was one of the people I loved most". Over the years, Zayd learnt enough of Muhammad's integrity and kindness to prompt him to accept his message and believe in him without hesitation.

The Early Believers

Thus the first Muslim family came into existence. There was a man and his wife, a ten-year-old child and an adult servant, all believing in the new message which proclaimed the eternal truth of God's oneness.

The first person to become a Muslim outside the Prophet's immediate family was his close friend Abū Bakr. It is well known that Abū Bakr was not his real name. A person is rarely called Abū — when he is born. He gains this title after his first son is born, because the word 'Abū' means 'father of'. However, the title Abū Bakr has become so well known that his real name is not known for certain. Some reports suggest that he was called ʿAtīq; some say that he was called ʿAbd al-Kaʿbah. One report suggests that his mother had several children before him, none of whom lived long. She pledged that should she have another son, she would call him ʿAbd al-Kaʿbah and would make of him a servant of the Kaʿbah. When the boy reached a certain age he came to be known as ʿAtīq, as if he was freed from death by that pledge of his mother. The Prophet, however, changed his name to ʿAbdullāh because no Muslim could be called servant of anyone or anything other than God.[4]

When the Prophet spoke to his childhood friend about Islam, Abū Bakr did not hesitate for a moment: he accepted Islam immediately. The very close friendship between the two men was enough to make Abū Bakr realize that Muhammad said nothing but the truth. There is also a report which suggests that one reason why he accepted Islam without hesitation was that a short while earlier he saw in his dream that the moon descended over Makkah and was split into small pieces, with each piece going into a different home. Then it was reassembled as a moon in his lap. He mentioned his dream to some people who followed Christianity or Judaism and they interpreted the dream to him, saying that he would follow the Prophet who was soon to appear. He would be the happiest of people for following him. Therefore, when the Prophet called on him to become a Muslim, he had no hesitation.[5]

How authentic this report is one cannot tell. There was, however, a better reason for Abū Bakr not to hesitate before accepting Islam. Abū Bakr was one of the most distinguished authorities in Arabia on the tracing of people's lineage. He knew how every person descended in his tribe. This was a branch of study which was of great importance to the Arabs. In their tribal society, everyone took pride in his lineage. There was a strict hierarchy which distinguished clans and tribes from one another. To maintain their relative positions, this study of lineage was very important. A person well versed in it was a sort of historian. He knew not only the lineage but also the history of the people of each clan and tribe. He knew the weak points in everyone's history. Later, when the Quraysh launched a determined campaign of abusive poetry against the Prophet and Islam, Muslim poets, particularly Ḥassān ibn Thābit, were quick to respond. The Prophet told Hassān to go to Abū Bakr in order to learn about the weaknesses and shortcomings of every clan of the Quraysh.[6]

His knowledge and his long-standing friendship with Muhammad gave Abū Bakr an insight into his character. He knew that Muhammad was always truthful. There was no reason why he should not be telling the truth now that he was speaking of a relationship with God, the Lord and the Creator. To Abū Bakr, the most logical thing was that Muhammad was telling the truth. Therefore, as Muhammad called on him to accept a message which he stressed would bring him, the Arabs and all mankind happiness, his attitude was one of immediate acceptance.

Abū Bakr realized that it was not enough that he himself should become a Muslim. Since God had sent a new message and a messenger to convey it to mankind, it was necessary that people should hear of it and learn that God wanted them to believe in this message. Therefore, he started to speak to some people whom he knew well. Abū Bakr was very well respected in his community. He was a merchant, well known for his kindly and gentle character. People loved to come to him and listen to him talking about the history of Arabian tribes and Arabs in general. Moreover, he was very kind to everybody. Hence, people of all ages came to see him and frequented his home. It was therefore easy for him to select some of the most intelligent and promising of the young people who came to him, to explain to them the message of Islam and to call on them to believe in God and His Messenger.

Abū Bakr realized that a new faith needs advocates. As a new believer, he set out to speak to people whom he trusted to be intelligent and judicious and explained to them the essence of the new message of Islam. Soon some of them responded favourably. The first one to become a Muslim as a result of Abū Bakr's efforts was ʿUthmān ibn ʿAffān, who belonged to the Umayyad clan of the Quraysh. Four others were soon to follow: al-Zubayr ibn al-ʿAwwām, who was Khadījah's nephew, ʿAbd al-Raḥmān ibn-ʿAwf, Saʿd ibn Abī Waqqāṣ and Ṭalḥah ibn ʿUbaydellāh. When all five had accepted Islam, Abū Bakr brought them together to see the Prophet and they declared before him that they believed in God's oneness and in the message of his Prophet, Muhammad ibn ʿAbdullāh. All five, together with Abū Bakr, were among the ten persons to whom the Prophet gave, towards the end of his blessed life, the happy news that they were sure of admission into heaven. The other four were ʿAlī, his cousin, whom we mentioned as the first boy to become a Muslim after the Prophet, ʿUmar, who became a Muslim several years later, Abū ʿUbaydah ʿAmir ibn al-Jarrāḥ and Saʿīd ibn Zayd. These last two also became Muslims in the very early days of Islam. Abū ʿUbaydah was later to be given by the Prophet the title of 'the trusted one' of the nation of Islam. Sa'īd was the son of Zayd ibn 'Amr ibn Nufā , who was mentioned earlier as travelling in search of the truth and following the religion of Abraham. We also mentioned that the Prophet said that on the Day of Judgement, Zayd "would be resurrected as a nation on his own". Sa'īd, his son, was among the first people who accepted Islam in its early days.

Others followed, such as Abū Salamah, 'Abdullāh ibn 'Abd al-Asad, al-Arqam ibn Abī al-Arqam, 'Uthmān ibn Maẓ'ūn and his two brothers Qudāmah and 'Abdullāh, 'Ubaydah ibn al-Ḥārith, Asmā' and 'Ā'ishah, the two daughters of Abū Bakr, Khabbāb ibn al-Aratt, 'Umayr ibn Abī Waqqāṣ, Sa'd's brother, and 'Abdullāh ibn Mas'ūd and Mas'ūd ibn al-Qārī. Biographers of the Prophet also mention, among the people who accepted Islam in those early days, Salīṭ ibn 'Amr, 'Ayyāsh ibn Abī Rabī'ah and his wife, Asmā' bint Salamah, Khulayṣ ibn Hudhāfah, 'Āmir ibn Abī Rabī'ah, 'Abdullāh and Abū Aḥmad, the two sons of Jaḥsh ibn Dhi'āb; Ja'far ibn Abī Ṭālib and his wife, Asmā' bint 'Umays, Ḥāṭib ibn al-Ḥārith and his brothers Khaṭṭāb and Mu'ammar, as well as the wives of the first two, al-Sā'ib ibn 'Uthmān ibn Maẓ'ūn, al-Muṭṭalib ibn Azhar and his wife Ramlah, Na'īm ibn 'Abdullāh, 'Āmir ibn Fuhayrah, a servant of Abū Bakr, Khālid ibn Sa'īd and his wife, Āminah bint Khalaf, Ḥāṭib ibn 'Amr, Abū Ḥudhayfah Mahsham ibn 'Utbah, Wāqid ibn 'Abdullāh, Khālid ibn al-Bakīr ibn 'Abd Yālīl and his three brothers 'Āmir, 'Āqīl and Iyās, 'Ammār ibn Yāsir and Suhayb ibn Sinān.[7]

That makes about 40 people altogether who accepted Islam in a period of three years when the Prophet was preaching his message in secret. However, what the early converts to Islam lacked in numbers, they compensated for in calibre. Most of these people possessed qualities of leadership and vision which distinguished them and made the new call stronger than the mere number of its advocates suggests.

When one looks closely at those people who accepted the call of Islam, one finds that many of them were still very young – many were not yet 20 years old. A new message which advocates a total change in the social order often attracts young people whose vision of a better life gives them a strong motive to work hard for their beliefs. Among those in their teens were al-Zubayr ibn al-ʿAwwām, Saʿd ibn Abū Waqqāṣ, Ṭalḥah ibn ʿUbaydellāh, ʿAbd al-Raḥmān ibn ʿAwf, al-Arqam, ʿAbdullāh ibn Masʿūd and Saʿīd ibn Zayd. But it is a mistake to think that the idealism of youth was the only motive for such people to become Muslims. Islam has a simple message which appeals directly to the human mind and strongly appeals to human nature. Many of these young people were of excellent character.

ʿAbdullāh ibn Masʿūd first learnt about Islam when he was tending his sheep, since he worked as a shepherd. The Prophet and Abū Bakr saw him as they were crossing over to some place outside Makkah. They were thirsty, so the Prophet asked ʿAbdullāh ibn Masʿūd: "Have you got any milk?" ʿAbdullāh said; "Yes, but I am in a position of trust." The Prophet asked him: "Have you a female sheep which has not yet mated?" ʿAbdullāh brought a sheep whose breasts had not yet appeared. The Prophet rubbed her at the position of the breast and soon she had breasts full of milk. ʿAbdullāh brought a piece of rock which looked like a bowl. The Prophet milked the sheep and gave Abū Bakr and ʿAbdullāh milk, then he drank. He then said to the breast: "Return to your position", and it did. When he saw this, ʿAbdullāh wondered and asked questions. The Prophet told him about Islam and he accepted it. He reports: "I said, 'Messenger of God, teach me.' He went with his hand over my head and said: 'May God bless you, you are an educated fellow.' Later, I went to meet the Prophet and as we were with him, over the mount of Ḥirā', the *sūrah* entitled al-Mursalāt was revealed to him and I learnt it as he was reciting it for the first time. I learnt twenty *sūrahs* direct from him over the years. The rest of the Qur'ān I learnt from some of his companions."[8]

There were others who were not so young, like ʿUthmān ibn ʿAffān and Abū ʿUbaydah, who were in their late twenties. Such people were normally of temperate character and sound intellect. ʿUthmān ibn Maẓʿūn was probably in his early thirties when he became a Muslim. Before Islam, he declared that he would never drink intoxicants. Alcoholic drinks were very much a part of the social life of Makkah. His sound judgement, however, led him to feel that a drink which caused a man to lose his ability to think properly and judge things accurately was unbecoming of any self-respecting man.

There were others in this group of early Muslims who were a little older. The best example was Abū Bakr, who was of the same age as the Prophet, or a year or two younger. These were mostly people who knew the Prophet closely. They knew his integrity and his noble character. Therefore, they were absolutely certain that he told the truth. They followed him as a logical consequence of their conviction.

One thing to be stressed about the composition of this distinguished community is the fact that those early Muslims did not belong to any single clan or tribe or social class. They came from all strata of Makkan society at the time. They included people of distinction who commanded high esteem in their community, such as ʿUthmān and Abū ʿUbaydah. Among them there were some former slaves, like Ṣuhayb, who was probably not even an Arab. Indeed, some were still in the bonds of slavery. As Muslims, however, they all enjoyed equality and a brotherhood that was so real that it eclipsed all blood relationships. Hence the universality of Islam was established and practised right from the outset.

Those early Muslims formed the nucleus of the community of believers which was soon to create the most noble society humanity had ever known in its long history. As headquarters they used the house of one of their number, al-Arqam, in a central position close to the hill known as al-Ṣafā. It became the first Islamic school where the followers of the new religion received their instruction in the principles of their faith directly from the Prophet.[9] Indeed, al-Arqam's house was a mosque, a school and a meeting-place where the new community discussed its affairs. The Prophet spent a considerable amount of time in that house looking after his companions, educating them and guiding them in their new mission.[10]

In those early days, the Muslims were instructed by God to attend to their prayers. The Angel Gabriel taught the Prophet Muhammad the form of prayer which was to become the mark of all Muslims. There are varying reports on the number and length of prayers the Muslims were asked to offer in those days. What is certain is that these were not five obligatory prayers every day. Probably these were only two, one in the morning and one at dusk. They were to be increased later. A report exists by a man called ʿAfīf al-Kindī, who was a friend of al-ʿAbbās ibn ʿAbd al-Muṭṭalib, the Prophet's uncle. Al-ʿAbbās used to visit him in Yemen when he went on his trade missions. ʿAfīf also visited him in Makkah. He reports:

> When I was at al-ʿAbbās's place in Minā, a respectable man came along and had his ablution and stood up to pray. A woman followed him and had her ablution and joined him in prayer. Then a boy close to adolescence did his ablution and stood next to the man praying. I said: "ʿAbbās, what is this religion?" He replied: "This is the faith of Muhammad ibn ʿAbdullāh, my nephew, who claims that God has sent him as a Messenger. This boy is my nephew, ʿAlī ibn Abī Ṭālib, who has followed his faith and this woman is his wife Khadījah, who also believes in his religion.

Many years later, after he became a firm believer in Islam, ʿAfīf said: "I wish I was fourth of that little group."[11]

Notes

1. Ibn Hishām, *al-Sīrah al-Nabawiyyah*, Dār al-Qalam, Beirut, Vol. 1, p. 257. Also, A. al-Suhaylī, *al-Rawḍ al-Unuf*, Dār al-Kutub al-ʿIlmiyyah, Beirut, p. 415.
2. Ibn Sayyid al-Nās, *ʿUyūn al-Athar*, Dār al-Turāth, Madinah, 1996, pp. 179-180.
3. Ibn Hishām, op.cit., pp. 264-266.
4. Ibid., pp. 266-267.
5. A. al-Suhaylī, op.cit., p. 431.
6. Ibn Hishām, op.cit., p. 267.
7. Ibid., pp. 267-280.
8. Ibn Sayyid al-Nās, op.cit., pp. 187-188.
9. Ibn Hishām, op.cit., pp. 259-262.
10. Ibid., p. 270.
11. Ibn Sayyid al-Nās, op.cit., p. 181.

7

The Call to Islam Goes Public

FOR THREE YEARS, or perhaps a little longer, Prophet Muhammad continued his efforts to propagate Islam, maintaining secrecy as he was commanded by God, but it was now time to move into a new phase. He was given the order to go public. This order is mentioned in the Qur'ān: "And say: I am indeed the plain warner." (15: 89) "Proclaim openly all that you have been bidden [to say], and leave alone all those who continue to associate partners with God." (15: 94) He was also told: "Warn your immediate kinsfolk and spread the wings of your tenderness over all the believers who may follow you." (26: 214-15) These were plain orders, and his response was soon forthcoming.

As he was to show throughout his years of prophethood, Muhammad (peace be upon him) was never to hesitate in carrying out, in letter and in spirit, every commandment he received from God. He therefore stood on al-Ṣafā, a small hill in the centre of Makkah, close to the Ka'bah, and called out as loudly as he could every Arab clan of Makkah, mentioning them by name and asking them to come over to him. At that particular time and in that particular city, this was the surest way of getting the news to everyone. In no time, the word spread all over Makkah that Muhammad had something important to announce. People were rushing to him from all quarters of the city. When they gathered around the hill,

Muhammad put to them this question: "If I were to tell you that armed horsemen are beyond this valley heading towards Makkah to attack you, would you believe me?" "You are trustworthy, and we have never known you to tell lies," they answered. "Well, then," he said, "I am sent to you to warn you against grievous suffering."[1]

Shaykh Abū al-Ḥasan ʿAlī al-Ḥasanī Nadwī says that the Arabs' first answer in Makkah was evidence of their realistic and practical approach. They were responding to a man whom they had known to be honest and truthful and always to give sincere advice. He was standing on top of a hill where he could see what was beyond. In their position, they could not see anything beyond what was in their valley. They had no reason not to believe him, whatever he said. This was a natural opening which secured a testimony from the audience – in other words, it established Muhammad's credentials, which were well known to his audience.[2]

Commenting on the Prophet's statement that he is a warner of a grievous suffering, Shaykh Nadwī says that it outlines the position of a prophet who knows the truth which lies beyond what ordinary people can see or understand. It was a warning which combined perfect intelligence with maximum lucidity and clarity of purpose. It was the shortest way to address the minds of the Prophet's audience.

The Prophet continued his warning, addressing each clan of the Quraysh by name and said, "God has ordered me to warn my immediate kinsfolk. It is not in my power to secure any benefit for you in this life, or any blessing in the life to come, unless you believe in the Oneness of God. People of Quraysh, save yourselves from hell, because I cannot be of any help to you. My position is like one who, seeing the enemy, ran to warn his people before they were taken by surprise, shouting as he ran: 'Beware! Beware!'"

The people of Makkah were taken aback. They did not expect such a direct and clear warning. It was left, however, to the Prophet's own uncle, Abū Lahab, to give him a most hostile and harsh reply. "Confound you!" he said. "Is this what you called us here for?"[3]

This encouraged others to adopt a hostile attitude. Some dismissed the Prophet's warning as insincere, while others were quick with their insults. No single voice was raised in approval as they began to disperse.

A Forthright Challenge

One can imagine how distressing this incident was to the Prophet. As the people left, he stood alone on the hill, realizing that he now faced the whole world with no human support apart from the three dozen or so people who had responded favourably to the new call. He realized that the path ahead was an uphill struggle which might involve a conflict with his nearest and dearest. Taken in the context of the tribal Arabian society at the time, this must have been very hard for Muhammad (peace be upon him). He realized, however, that an advocate of a great message must not look for friendships or social ties if he is to put his message, as he must, above all considerations and above all human values.

Yet what happened in those few moments at the hill of al-Ṣafā was a historic event with great significance. It should be remembered that although the Prophet was making his first public announcement of his mission, the people of Makkah were aware that a new philosophy was being propagated in their midst. They were not, however, aware of the aims and intentions of the Prophet and his early followers. The declaration on the hill of al-Ṣafā brought home to them the scope of the new call. The aim was to bring about a total change in the life of Arab society: its values and standards, its sense of purpose, its practices and its whole direction. The Prophet, in effect, told his townspeople that they would have to change the whole set-up of their society if they wished to win God's pleasure. That is why the opposition which met his declaration was so fierce.

It takes great courage to challenge an established idea or a social tradition. People normally do not like to be told that they are wrong, especially when it comes to long established habits and traditions. Hence any call for a change is bound to be met, at least initially, with opposition. It is for this reason that many of those who call for social change find it judicious to make the change they advocate appear moderate and gradual.

Yet here was the Prophet (peace be upon him) standing on the hill, calling all people, warning them and asking them to accept a total and comprehensive change which embraced all aspects of human life, practices, values, ideology. His courageous action deserves much more than our admiration. One looks to the Prophet for guidance. From him one learns how to play the role of an advocate of Islam, and how to convey its message to others. His action shows that one should not compromise when it comes to explaining what sort of social change the adoption of the Islamic way of life will involve.

This accounts for the accusation of 'extremism' or 'fanaticism' which is usually laid at the door of the advocates of Islam. Nothing is more erroneous than such a charge. Muslims generally – and in particular those among them who take upon themselves the propagation of Islam – are very tolerant, compassionate, honest, frank. Frequently, however, their frankness is mistaken for rigidity; their honesty for fanaticism. The true advocates of Islam are neither rigid nor fanatical; they simply state their case with honesty and clarity. Their message does not accept compromises; hence they insist on maintaining its purity.

The Prophet also wanted to approach his immediate relatives with his message. As already mentioned, he always implemented God's orders in letter and in spirit. When he called all clans in Makkah and addressed them from the top of the hill of al-Ṣafā, he actually implemented this order taking the words 'your immediate kinsfolk' to mean all the Quraysh. As this phrase could be understood in a narrower sense, the Prophet thought of a way to speak to his immediate relatives about his new faith, which represented the only way for humans to save themselves from misery in this life and even greater misery in the life to come. However, he feared that his uncle, Abū Lahab, would do everything possible to spoil his efforts. Abū Lahab, whose real name was ʿAbd al-ʿUzzā ibn ʿAbd al-Muṭṭalib, was known by his title, which meant 'the father of a flame', because he had a bright face with reddish cheeks. He was very rich and narrow-minded, feeling that the traditions of Arabia must always be accepted by everyone. He could easily lose his temper when anyone suggested that fathers and grandfathers were mistaken in their practices or traditions. A criticism of pagan beliefs was sure to be treated by Abū Lahab as an intolerable outrage.

A Gentle Approach to Relatives

Faced with the probability that Abū Lahab might spoil the occasion, the Prophet felt that it was best to have a special gathering when he could speak to his immediate relatives in a relaxed atmosphere. He therefore invited them to a meal which was attended by over 40 of his uncles, cousins and second or third cousins. When they had finished eating, the Prophet was beginning to prepare himself to talk when the initiative was taken away from him by none other than Abū Lahab who said to him:

> These are your uncles and cousins. You may speak to them, but you have to leave off apostasy. Do not turn away from the faith of your people, and do not expose them to the anger of the Arabs. Your people cannot face up to opposition by the whole of the Arab nation, and they cannot be expected to face them all in war. Your people are aware of what you intend to invent in their faith. They have not been heedless of what you are doing and what you advocate: rebellion against religion and against the traditions inherited from our forefathers. Take care, then, of yourself and your father's offspring. To be certain, the Arabs will not leave you alone, and it will not be difficult for them to kill you. It is better for you that you revert to the religion of your fathers and grandfathers. Otherwise, we will have to put you in confinement until you are cured of the illness you are suffering so that we can spare you an attack by the Arabs. It is better that we deal with you until you have regained your mind and recovered from your illness. It is certainly better that your father's offspring take you to task and put you in confinement if you persist with what you are doing. This is easier for you and them than an attack by other clans of Quraysh supported by other Arabs. I have never heard of anyone who caused his father's offspring anything worse than you have done.[4]

As he said this, Abū Lahab was very excited, firing his words like serious threats. His cheeks were red with anger and when he finished he trembled because he could not control himself. The Prophet looked around. Everyone was silent and an air of depression and gloom prevailed. He, therefore, said nothing.

The usage of the phrase 'your father's offspring' by Abū Lahab was a common usage in Arabia's tribal society. The Prophet's father, ʿAbdullāh, did not have any children other than him. It should be remembered that ʿAbdullāh was married for only a couple of months before he travelled on a journey to Syria and died on the way back. 'Father' in this sense does not mean the immediate father; in fact, it means the grandfather or great-grandfather after whom the clan is called. Therefore, 'your father's offspring' means the whole clan, including cousins and second or third cousins.

Appeal Resumed

The Prophet allowed things to cool down for a few days before he invited his uncles and cousins to dinner again. One or two of the Prophet's aunts suggested that he need not invite his uncle Abū Lahab but, having considered the matter carefully, the Prophet did invite him. For one thing, Abū Lahab was his next-door neighbour and he could not leave him out when he was inviting second or third cousins. For another, Abū Lahab might have been tempted to create trouble if he was left out. More importantly, however, the Prophet never despaired of a change of heart taking place, even in the case of a determined enemy. So Abū Lahab was among the Prophet's guests. This time, however, the Prophet took the initiative and spoke to his relatives immediately after they finished eating. He said:

> Praise be to God! I praise Him, seek His support, believe in Him and rely on Him. I bear witness that there is no deity other than God, the only God who has no partners. A forerunner does not tell lies to his own people. If I were to tell lies to all mankind, I would not tell one to you. By God who is the only deity, I am God's Messenger to you in particular and to mankind in general. He has commanded me to call on you to believe in Him, saying: "Warn your immediate kinsfolk." I am calling on you to say two words which are easily

> pronounced but weighty in God's scale: to bear witness that there is no deity other than God and that I am His Messenger. By God, you will die as you sleep, and will be resurrected as you wake up, and you will be held to account for what you do, and you will be rewarded well for your good actions and suffer retribution for your bad ones. It will be either heaven forever or hell forever. Children of ʿAbd al-Muṭṭalib, by God, I know no one who has brought his people anything better than I am bringing you. I am offering you the happiness of this world and of the life to come. Who will accept my call and support me in furthering it?

Abū Ṭālib, the Prophet's uncle who had taken care of him ever since he was a child, the grand old man of the Hāshimite clan, said: "We dearly love to help you and we certainly accept your advice and believe what you have said. Assembled here are your father's offspring and I am but one of them, although I am the quickest with my favourable response. Go ahead with what you have been bidden and I pledge to continue to give you my support and protection. I find it hard, however, to abandon the faith of ʿAbd al-Muṭṭalib."

It was perhaps this answer by Abū Ṭālib that infuriated Abū Lahab more than the Prophet's own words. In a burst of temper, he said, "What shame! Stop him before he is stopped by someone else. If it comes to that and you abandon him, then you will be overwhelmed with shame; and if you try to protect him you will all be killed." There were apparently further heated remarks by Abū Lahab, who could not control his temper. Abū Ṭālib, however, maintained his positive attitude. All those who were present inclined towards Abū Ṭālib's view, realizing that it was their duty to protect Muhammad and that they could not put their clan to the shame of abandoning him. Abū Lahab, on the other hand, went out, still furious, threatening and pledging to do everything in his power to stop his nephew from accomplishing his mission and changing the religion of the Quraysh.[5]

These incidents help us to understand the forces that were at play in Arabian society. Abū Lahab, the conservative, hot-headed dignitary, did not stop for one minute to consider the merits of what his nephew,

Prophet Muhammad, said. He looked at the whole issue only from the narrow angle of what was likely to happen as a result of it to the clan of Hāshim and more narrowly to its sub-clan of ʿAbd al-Muṭṭalib. Viewed from this very narrow angle, Muhammad's call spelled disaster for his people. Abū Lahab was not even prepared to look further than that. He considered it his duty, and the duty of the children and the grandchildren of ʿAbd al-Muṭṭalib, to stop Muhammad from pressing ahead with his call.

On the other hand, the wiser and older brother, Abū Ṭālib, looked at his tribal duty from a different angle. His nephew, Muhammad, did not mean any harm and did not call for anything wrong. He was only advocating an idea. If it transpired that the idea was met with opposition, then so be it. The Hāshimites and, more particularly, the smaller clan of ʿAbd al-Muṭṭalib had no option but to extend their support to their man, Muhammad. After all, Arabian tribes fought fierce and long wars to protect or avenge their sons for matters which were much less important than that. Indeed, even when a tribesman committed a crime, his tribe gave him protection.

Abū Lahab continued with his hostility. He took immediate action to demonstrate his disavowal of his nephew. His two sons, ʿUtbah and ʿUtaybah, were married to the Prophet's two daughters, Ruqayyah and Umm Kulthūm. He ordered his sons to divorce the Prophet's daughters and they complied. These two daughters of the Prophet were then married, one after the other, to ʿUthmān ibn ʿAffān.

In his hostility to the Prophet and to Islam, Abū Lahab was supported by his wife, Umm Jamīl Arwa bint Ḥarb, the sister of Abū Sufyān, who was later to become the leader of the Quraysh in its determined opposition to Islam until Makkah fell to the Prophet and its population accepted the new faith. Umm Jamīl was perhaps even more hostile to the Prophet than her husband. She would ridicule him and throw dust and harmful objects in his path; she composed songs abusing him and sang them on occasions.[6]

The hostility of Abū Lahab and his wife to the cause of Islam and their active opposition to it, and abuse of the Prophet, brought them denunciation by God Himself, who revealed a powerful short *sūrah* of the Qur'ān, mentioning Abū Lahab by name and warning him and his wife of their approaching doom. The *sūrah* may be rendered in translation as follows: "May the hands of Abū Lahab perish: doomed he is. His wealth and his gains shall not avail him. He shall be plunged in a flaming fire, and his wife, the carrier of firewood, shall have a rope of palm fibre round her neck." (111: 1-5)

It may be true that the Prophet encountered some hostility when he proclaimed his message on the top of the hill of al-Ṣafā. He might have been confronted by an arrogant uncle who could not see further than the end of his nose. But the effect of that proclamation was tremendous. Every household in Makkah was talking about the new message and what change it would bring about in the lives of the Arabs. The fact that there was a nucleus of a community of believers made it easy for the Makkan people to take a reasonably correct measure of the implications of the new call. They realized that the change it was sure to bring about would be total. Hence, the elders of Makkah were soon in council discussing what steps they needed to take.

The Quraysh's Complaint

It should be said in fairness that the chiefs of Makkah did not take any action worth noting against the Prophet in the early stages. When he started to criticize their pagan faith and ridicule their idols, however, they began to think that the matter was much too serious to ignore. Yet, they could not do much about it because Abū Ṭālib protected his nephew against all threats. To ignore such protection by the Makkan chiefs would contravene one of the basic conventions of their social set-up. Therefore a small delegation composed of a number of the most influential people in Makkah went to Abū Ṭālib complaining about his nephew's behaviour. The delegation included the two brothers ʿUtbah and Shaybah, sons of Rabīʿah from the clan of ʿAbd Shams; Abū Sufyān Sakhr ibn Ḥarb from Ummayah; Abū al-Bakhtarī al-ʿĀṣ ibn Hishām and al-Aswad ibn al-Muṭṭalib from Asad, Abū Jahl ʿAmr ibn Hishām and al-Walīd ibn al-Mughīrah from Makhzūm; the two brothers Nabīh and Munabbih sons of al-Ḥajjāj from Sahm and al-ʿĀṣ ibn Wā'il, also from Sahm. They made their complaint clear to Abū Ṭālib and they offered him the choice between telling Muhammad not to criticize their ways and ridicule their idols or allowing them to take such effective measures as they might deem necessary to end the trouble. Abū Ṭālib, who continued to follow the religion of his people, spoke to them gently and calmed them down. He did not promise them much.[7]

The Prophet continued to preach his message regardless. The crisis with his people increased in intensity. Feelings of hostility spread. So the delegation went again to Abū Ṭālib and said to him: "Abū Ṭālib, you enjoy a position of honour and respect among us. We have requested you to stop your nephew, but you have not taken any action. We certainly cannot just sit and do nothing when he continues to speak ill of our forefathers and to ridicule us and our gods. You have to stop him or we will fight him and you over this question until one of the two parties is destroyed."

Abū Ṭālib was in a dilemma. He did not like to quarrel with his people, yet he could not bear to let his nephew down. So he called Muhammad and explained to him what had taken place between him and his visitors. He then said to him: "You see the difficulty of my situation. Do not put my life and your life at risk, and do not burden me with what I cannot bear."

The Prophet felt that his uncle might be contemplating withdrawing his protection so he stated his own position with the greatest emphasis he could muster: "Uncle, should they give me the sun in my right hand and the moon in my left hand in return for abandoning my call, I would not do anything of the sort until God has brought this message to triumph or until I have perished." The Prophet was under the pressure of such strong emotions that tears sprang to his eyes. He started to walk away, but his uncle called him back, saying reassuringly: "My nephew, you may go and say whatever you like. I will never withdraw my protection from you, and never will I let you down."[8]

The Prophet was happy with his uncle's support and continued to preach his message undeterred by the Quraysh's opposition. They, however, felt that their opening approaches to Abū Ṭālib had brought no positive results. They had to contemplate other measures. The hardliners among the chiefs of Makkah were gaining the upper hand.

NOTES

1. Ibn Hishām, *al-Sīrah al-Nabawiyyah*, Dār al-Qalam, Beirut, Vol. 1, pp. 280-281. Also, Amīn Duwaydār, *Ṣuwar Min Ḥayāt al-Rasūl*, Dār al-Maʿārif, 4th edition, Cairo, pp. 144-145; al-Bukhārī, *Ṣaḥīḥ*, al-Maktabah al-Raḥīmiyyah, India, Vol. 2, pp. 702-703.
2. Abū al-Ḥasan ʿAlī al-Ḥasanī Nadwī, *Muhammad Rasulallah* (The Life of the Prophet Muhammad) Academy of Islamic Research and Publications, Lucknow, India, p. 111.
3. Amīn Duwaydār, op.cit., p. 144.
4. Ibid., pp. 138-139.
5. Ibid., pp. 139-141.
6. Ibn Hishām, op.cit., p. 380.
7. Ibid., pp. 282-284.
8. Ibid., pp. 284-285.

8

Objective Containment

WHEN MUHAMMAD, GOD'S Messenger, declared his message in public and called upon the people of Makkah to adopt it as a faith and a way of life, in submission to God and fulfilment of His commandments, he in effect went on the offensive in a struggle which was to dominate the rest of his life. Up till that moment, the Prophet and his early followers confined themselves to a secret approach made to a limited number of people on a private and individual basis. These efforts won for the new message of Islam a hard core of advocates whose dedication would never slacken. The Prophet's public declaration of his message, however, changed the whole picture as the target of his efforts changed. The whole society was called upon to accept a total change in the basis upon which it was built, and of the principles and values it upheld.

The change meant much more than the mere substitution of one god for a collection of idols made of dates, stone, gold, wood or mud. The Arabs of Makkah were not just asked to pay homage to God instead of their idols; they were asked to accept His rule regarding all aspects of their social, cultural and political life. In other words, the change would also include their social practices and economic and commercial interests, as well as their political power and influence.

The response of those who wielded power in the Makkan society was therefore hostile, as was only to be expected. They realized that unless they met the new call with stiff and determined opposition, it was bound to win acceptance with a large section of the population – especially among the poor, the slaves and the deprived, but also among open-minded and liberal-thinking individuals from the powerful classes. Hence, a campaign of persecution was launched against the followers of the new calling.

The early Muslims did not belong to any particular class or social group, but were drawn from all clans and all levels of the tribal structure of Makkan society. Tribal considerations dictated that a member of a tribe should be defended by the whole tribe against any outside harassment or injustice. Indeed, as has been seen, a tribe would defend an individual member even when he was at fault. Hence, some of the early Muslims escaped physical persecution as they were protected by their tribes. Many, however, were less fortunate, for they belonged to the lower classes of slaves or 'allies', i.e. individuals attached to different clans and tribes by a verbal covenant of 'alliance'. Although they enjoyed tribal protection in normal circumstances as a result of that covenant, their status within their tribes was ambivalent. They were therefore vulnerable to stern punishment when their dispute was with the powerful leaders of their tribes.

It was indeed only natural that the brunt of the campaign of persecution would be borne by Muslims who belonged to these classes. After all, the Makkan tribal society was defending its very system which classified people according to their birth and circumstances. The privileged class would not relinquish its privileges easily. It was unable, however, to disregard those privileges or to deny them to those companions of the Prophet who were entitled to enjoy them by virtue of their birth and lineage.

A Campaign of Terror

One of the early tactics of the chiefs of Makkah to try to suppress Islam altogether was a campaign of terror which varied according to the status of the recipient. Those who belonged to the higher classes were subjected to taunts and ridicule. The most determined opponent of Islam at that time was a man called ʿAmr ibn Hishām, who belonged to the clan of Makhzūm. He was soon to be nicknamed Abū Jahl, which meant 'father of ignorance'. Abū Jahl masterminded the campaign of opposition in its two distinct forms: ridiculing those Muslims who had good connections with their tribes to ensure their protection, and persecution of the weaker ones. When he heard of a noble person who accepted the faith of Islam, he reproached and ridiculed him. He would tell him: "You have deserted the faith of your father, who was a better man than you. We will disregard any good opinion you may have, oppose your views and treat you with contempt." If the man was a merchant, Abū Jahl would threaten a boycott so that the business of the new Muslim would suffer. If the new Muslim belonged to the weaker class, then physical abuse was soon forthcoming from Abū Jahl.[1]

Abū Jahl, however, was not the only enemy of Islam; he was only the most uncompromising. Others tried to outbid him in the campaign of terror. What happened to Bilāl and Khabbāb provides good examples of the ferocity of the terror campaign.

Bilāl was born in slavery to an Abyssinian father. His master, Umayyah ibn Khalaf, the chief of the clan of Jumaḥ, wanted to show to everyone in Makkah that he was just as keen as Abū Jahl to defend the established order. Hence Bilāl was taken out to the open desert, day after day, where he was severely beaten. At midday, when the sun was at its hottest, he was made to lie on the sand without any clothes to protect his back from the burning sand. A large stone was put on his chest to increase the torture. He was dragged with ropes over the burning sand. Repeatedly he was asked to renounce Islam and to declare that he believed in the idols. Just as often he repeated: "He is One! He is One."[2]

Bilāl's ordeal lasted a long time, until one day Abū Bakr passed by while he was being tortured. He tried to soften Umayyah's heart, without much success. Umayyah, however, accused Abū Bakr of being responsible for Bilāl's transgression and challenged him to save him. Abū Bakr immediately took up the challenge and offered Umayyah an exchange deal: Bilāl would become his in return for a more youthful and vigorous slave who was not a Muslim. Umayyah accepted the deal and Bilāl joined Abū Bakr, who immediately set him free because he knew Islam disliked slavery and promised great reward from God to those who freed slaves.

Abū Bakr's Noble Heart

Indeed, Abū Bakr repeated his noble action several times. ʿĀmir ibn Fuhayrah was a slave who belonged to al-Ṭufayl ibn ʿAbdullāh al-Asdī, who was related to Abū Bakr through his wife, Umm Rūman, ʿĀ'ishah's mother. ʿĀmir ibn Fuhayrah was among the very early Muslims. For this, he suffered a great deal; he was one of the victims of the campaign of terror. Abū Bakr, however, bought him from his master and set him free. ʿĀmir continued to work for Abū Bakr as a shepherd. Later he was to play an important role in helping the Prophet and Abū Bakr to emigrate from Makkah to Madinah.[3]

The Prophet was very pleased with Abū Bakr's action with those two slaves. He encouraged him to do what he could in order to help those victims of the campaign of torture. Abū Bakr responded, as he always did, without any hesitation. He chose the most helpless and those who showed a great determination to defy the prosecutors. Zunayrah was a slave who belonged to the Makhzūm clan. As such, it was left to Abū Jahl to torture her. He gave her so much of his venom that she lost her sight. Then he told her: "It is the two gods al-Lāt and al-ʿUzzā who have done this to you." She replied: "How can al-Lāt and al-ʿUzzā know who worship them? This is simply the will of God and my Lord is able to give me back my sight." When she woke up the following day, she had regained her sight. People of the Quraysh said: "This is part of Muhammad's magic." Abū Bakr moved swiftly to rescue this woman slave and set her free.[4]

A woman called al-Nahdiyah and her daughter were slaves belonging to a woman from the clan of ʿAbd al-Dār. Both became Muslims and their mistress ordered them to be tortured. One day she gave them a quantity of flour to bake, but as she set them to their task, she threatened them: "You will remain my slaves for ever. By God, I will never set you free." Abū Bakr was nearby, and he heard the woman. He said to her: "Why don't you release yourself from your oath?" She replied, "Release myself! It was you who spoiled them, so you set them free if you wish." Abū Bakr asked her what price she wanted for them, and he paid her the price. Immediately, he declared that they were free and told the two women to give their former mistress her flour. They asked him whether he would mind if they finished it for her. He said that was up to them.[5]

Another woman slave, called Umm ʿUbays, belonged to al-Aswad ibn ʿAbd Yaghūth from the clan of Zuhrah. As Abū Bakr saw her one day being tortured by her master, he bought her and set her free. He did the same with a woman slave who belonged to the clan of ʿAdiy, in which ʿUmar ibn al-Khaṭṭāb was the tormentor of Muslims as he was still an unbeliever then. ʿUmar used to beat up this woman as frequently and as painfully as he could. One day he stopped beating her, saying: "I apologize to you! I am only stopping beating you up because I am bored." She said, "It is God who does this to you." Then Abū Bakr bought her and set her free.[6]

All in all Abū Bakr freed seven slaves to save them from the campaign of terror launched by the Quraysh. His father, who was not a Muslim, could not understand his action. He said to him: "Son, I see that you are setting free weak slaves. If you want to do this, why don't you set free some strong men slaves who will be able to protect you?" Abū Bakr explained that he wanted only to be rewarded by God for his action.[7]

Abū Bakr's action was the best example of how closely knit the new Muslim community was. Those who were able to help their brothers and sisters did not hesitate to render any assistance they could. Nevertheless, Abū Bakr's actions were exemplary. Neither he nor the other Muslims who enjoyed tribal lineage were able to stop the campaign of terror. Although he was reasonably wealthy, he could not buy all the victims of the Quraysh's persecution. Not all of them were slaves anyway, and those who were could not have been bought because their masters refused to sell them. Abū Bakr's action demonstrated the new bond that was established among the followers of the new religion. There was another aspect to what he did: it emphasized that the followers of the new religion were all equal, slaves and masters alike. Much later, when ʿUmar became one of the leading figures among the Muslims, he stated this fact in the clearest of terms when he said of Abū Bakr and what he did for Bilāl: "Abū Bakr is our master, and he has freed our master."[8]

The Great Suffering

These efforts by Abū Bakr and other Muslims to help those of their brethren who were subjected to brutal torture by the young men who belonged to the most privileged families in the Quraysh could not significantly reduce the pressure on the Muslims. Indeed, the reverse was true. With every victim released by Abū Bakr a new turn of the screw was made in order to increase the pressure on those who were still captive. With every new recruit Islam gained, the venom of torture increased.

Khabbāb ibn al-Aratt was kidnapped from his clan's area while he was still young. He was brought to Makkah, where he was sold to a man from the clan of the Khuzāʿah. He was one of the very early Muslims; therefore, he suffered more than most. The unbelievers experimented with all kinds of torture. They put him in a fire and beat him severely. They kicked him and punished him and flogged him, but he was as firm as a mountain. Once they tore off his clothes and laid him over stones heated with fire and twisted his neck all at the same time. They caused him permanent injuries to his back, but he was prepared to die for his faith. He survived the torture and lived to fight the unbelievers with the Prophet in all his wars.

Abū Fukayhah was a slave who belonged to Ṣafwān ibn Umayyah, the son of Bilāl's former master. When Bilāl was freed by Abū Bakr, Abū Fukayhah had to bear all the brutality of the Jumaḥ master. He was dragged over the burning sand and tortured until he could hardly speak. A beetle passed close to him and Umayyah pointed to it and said to him: "This is your Lord, isn't it?" He replied: "God is my Lord and your Lord and the Lord of this creature." He was nearly strangled for saying that.

Umayyah's brother, Ubay, encouraged him to increase the torture, saying: "Let Muhammad come and use his sorcery to release him." They left him only when they thought that he was dead. It is said that Abū Bakr also bought him and set him free, but this is not absolutely confirmed since most reports suggest that the total number of slaves released by Abū Bakr was seven and seven have already been mentioned.

Those who suffered most as a result of the campaign of terror mounted by the Quraysh were a family composed of two elderly parents and their only son who was about 35. Yāsir, the father, was originally of a Yemeni tribe. He came to Makkah in his youth looking for his brother. He loved Makkah and felt a strong desire to stay. He, therefore, entered into an 'alliance' with his host, a notable personality of the clan of Makhzūm, to which Abū Jahl belonged. This type of alliance meant, as far as Yāsir was concerned, a firm attachment to the tribe of his ally which burdened him with all the duties of the weaker members of the tribe and accorded him tribal protection. Without such a bond, no individual could hope to survive in the Arabian society at that time.

Yāsir married Sumayyah, a servant of his ally, and she gave birth to their only son, ʿAmmār. Yāsir never regretted his decision to stay in Makkah. He led a happy life there, although he instinctively disliked idolatry. When the Prophet started to preach his new message, ʿAmmār was among the first to respond favourably. He joined the small number of Muslims who began to gather around the Prophet in the house of al-Arqam. ʿAmmār soon persuaded his parents to embrace Islam.

Their happy family life was soon disrupted by Abū Jahl, who gathered an effective force of youths and slaves to help him in his efforts of terrorization. He wanted to make Yāsir and his family an example for anyone who might be thinking of responding to the new message of Islam. He supervised a progressive type of torture of parents and son to make them renounce Islam. As the volume of torture increased, the three afflicted victims showed a growing determination to stick to their faith.

The Prophet passed by one day while they were being tortured. He could not do anything to release them. However, he gave them the most encouraging words when he said to them: "Yāsir and family, persevere. Heaven is our meeting-place."

After weeks of varied types of torture, Sumayyah gave her tormentor a piece of her mind, telling him what she thought of him and his methods. Infuriated, Abū Jahl stabbed her in her private parts with a spear he was carrying. Then he turned to her husband, who was laid on the burning sand. He kicked him in his chest until he died. Thus Sumayyah and Yāsir were the first two martyrs in the history of Islam.

Pressure Too Strong to Bear

After the death of both of his parents, ʿAmmār was released, but only for a while. Time and again they would come to him with increased venom. After inflicting untold torture on him, they would say: "We will never release you until you abuse Muhammad and praise al-Lāt and al-ʿUzzā." One day he was in such a state that he could bear the torture no longer. He did what he was told. They let him alone and went away. When he managed to pull himself together, he went to the Prophet with tears in his eyes. The Prophet asked him what was troubling him. He answered: "It is bad news, Messenger of God." He told him what had happened. The Prophet asked him how he felt deep in his heart. ʿAmmār answered that his faith was as firm as ever. The Prophet said to him that if the unbelievers did the same to him again, he could tell them the words they wanted to hear, provided that deep in his heart he was absolutely certain of his faith.[9]

When the pressure increased so much and the torture became unbearable, some of those victims complained to the Prophet. Khabbāb reports:

> We complained to God's Messenger (peace be upon him) when he was reclining in the shade of the Kaʿbah saying, "Will you not pray God to help us?" He said, "Among believers who lived before you there were many who were placed in a hole dug in the ground and were sawn in halves, from head to foot; and there were some whose flesh was torn with combs of iron which also broke their bones. They did not turn away from their faith. By God, your Lord will certainly accomplish

> His purpose until an individual traveller can travel from Ṣanʿāʾ to Haḍramout fearing no one but God and guarding against the wolf getting away with one of his sheep. You are only precipitating events."[10]

What could the Prophet do for those companions of his who were weak, vulnerable and subjected to brutal torture. He himself was subjected to ridicule and physical abuse from the unbelievers who would throw dirt over his head as he prayed in the Ḥaram. They also threw impurities in front of his house. He had made it clear to his companions that they were not seeking any immediate gain. All that he promised them was a hard struggle for which God would reward them with heaven. It was enough for them that he had shown them the way and given them Divine guidance. Their life was transformed; they were given noble preoccupations to replace the low pleasures which were still sought after by the unbelievers. He could only reassure them as to the truthfulness of their message, and that their way was the right way. They were seeking God's pleasure, and that was the only way to earn it.

The Prophet continued to make a determined stand, despite the Quraysh's campaign of terror. He called on people to renounce the worship of idols and turn back to God, the Creator, who has honoured man and placed him in charge of the earth. Realizing that the persecution of a few helpless individuals was not deterring anyone from accepting the new faith, the Quraysh chiefs thought of making another attempt at negotiating a settlement.

Offer Too Absurd

A new delegation went to Abū Ṭālib, the Prophet's uncle and protector. All those who had tried earlier to persuade Abū Ṭālib to stop his nephew went along this time, taking with them a few more notables and a young man called ʿImārah ibn al-Walīd, whose father was a well-known figure in Makkah. They made this proposal to Abū Ṭālib: "We have brought with us ʿImārah, the smartest and most vigorous young man in the Quraysh, to offer him to you as a son. He will benefit you, with his courage and sound mind. In exchange, you give us your nephew who has rebelled against the religion you and your forefathers have followed, and has sown the seeds of discord among your people and ridiculed their practices. We would take him and kill him while you would take a man for a man.

Abū Ṭālib replied: "What a raw deal you are offering me! You want to give me your son to feed while I give you my son to kill! This will never be." Al-Muṭʿim ibn ʿAdiy, who was among the delegation, said to Abū Ṭālib: "Your people have offered you a fair deal indeed. They are doing their best to appease you, but you seem unwilling to accept any offer they make."

Abū Ṭālib rejoined: "They certainly have not been fair to me. I see that you have joined them in letting me down." The discussion became more heated before the Quraysh delegation left, with everyone feeling extremely angry.[11]

If the proposal the Quraysh put to Abū Ṭālib sounds preposterous today, the Quraysh delegation saw in it an honest attempt to achieve a solution to the satisfaction of all concerned. In the society of Arabia, where tribal ties transcended all other ties and where a man's position was determined by the number of children he had and the support he could muster, Abū Ṭālib would not be sacrificing much if he exchanged his nephew for an able and intelligent young man. It is noteworthy that the proposal was described as fair by a man like al-Muṭʿim, who would show over the years a friendly and compassionate attitude towards the Prophet and the Muslims in general. Furthermore, he was a distant cousin of Abū Ṭālib. ʿAbd Manāf was the great-grandfather of both men; hence he was expected to look at the affair from a standpoint closer to that of Abū Ṭālib. Indeed, Abū Ṭālib's remark about al-Muṭʿim's letting him down acquires a stronger sense when it is considered in this light.

The negotiations thus ended in total failure. This was only to be expected since the issue touched on basic principles. So, the Quraysh felt it had no option but to widen its campaign of persecution to all Muslims. Each clan took vengeance against any of its sons who adopted Islam. Now even free and young noble men were at the receiving end of the Quraysh's campaign. Maltreatment was much more widespread.

Maltreatment of the Honourable

Muṣʿab ibn ʿUmayr belonged to a rich family. His mother provided him with everything he wanted. He was perhaps the most handsome, elegant and smartest young man in Makkah. Yet when he became a Muslim, he was imprisoned by his people and his mother turned against him.

ʿUthmān ibn ʿAffān, who belonged to the Umayyad clan, was of a noble family. Nevertheless, his uncle al-Ḥakam ibn Abū al-ʿĀṣ tied him to a post and swore that he would never release him until he renounced Islam. ʿUthmān replied that he would never do that no matter what the pressure brought to bear on him was like. Saʿd ibn Abū Waqqāṣ, a very dutiful son, was pressurized by his mother, who thought that she would be able to use his love to turn him away from Islam. She made some threatening noises which availed her nothing. Finally, Saʿd told her point blank: "Mother, if you had one hundred souls and they came out one after the other, I would not turn away from Islam to spare you."

Not even Abū Bakr was safe. One day he addressed the people, calling on them to believe in God and His Messenger. Some of them abused him. Soon there was some confusion and Abū Bakr was bound up by several people including ʿUtbah ibn Rabīʿah, who used his shoes to beat Abū Bakr's face. When he was rescued by his own tribesmen, they thought that he was dead. Towards the evening, he came round. The first thing he did was to enquire how God's Messenger was. He would not rest until he had been taken to the Prophet. They took him after nightfall, and he walked, supported by his mother and a Muslim woman, until he arrived at the Prophet's home. The Prophet felt very sorry about what had happened to Abū Bakr. He spoke to his mother and she embraced Islam which made Abū Bakr rejoice.

Abū Ṭālib was keeping a close watch on developments in Makkah. He was increasingly worried about his nephew Muhammad (peace be upon him), and so he called upon his clan to give him their firm pledges of support in protecting Muhammad against any maltreatment to which he might be subjected. They responded favourably to his call, with only one exception – Abū Lahab. Although he was the

Prophet's own uncle, he continued his fierce opposition to Islam, joining the rest of the Quraysh in their campaign of persecution. Abū Ṭālib, however, was extremely pleased by this support. He expressed his feelings in a long, powerful poem in which he praised his clan and reminded the people of the Quraysh of their noble history. Thus, the Prophet was able to preach his message enjoying full protection.

Notes

1. Ibn Hishām, *al-Sīrah al-Nabawiyyah*, Dār al-Qalam, Beirut, Vol. 1, p. 342. Also, Amīn Duwaydār, *Ṣuwar Min Ḥayāt al-Rasūl*, Dār al-Ma'ārif, 4th edition, Cairo, p. 156.
2. Ibn Hishām, op.cit., pp. 339-340. Also, Amīn Duwaydār, op.cit., p. 153.
3. Ibn Hishām, op.cit., p. 340. Also, Amīn Duwaydār, op.cit., p. 154.
4. Ibn Hishām, op.cit., p. 340. Also, Amīn Duwaydār, op.cit., p. 155.
5. Ibn Hishām, op.cit., p. 341. Also, Amīn Duwaydār, op.cit., p. 155.
6. Amīn Duwaydār, op.cit., p. 155.
7. Ibid., p. 154.
8. Ibid.
9. Ibid., p. 153.
10. Ibid., p. 156.
11. Ibn Hishām, op.cit., pp. 285-286.

9

Misrepresentation

WHEN THE PROPHET carried out God's commandment to declare His message in public, he moved into a new stage in the history of the Islamic message concluding the first period of secrecy. The message itself was now preached publicly, but the identity of its followers, its numerical strength and its organization were not fully known to the people of Makkah who remained hostile to Islam. There are no accurate records of the numbers of those who adopted the faith of Islam at any particular time, especially in the early period. One can only guess that at the end of the first three years when the stage of secrecy was over, there were barely more than 60 Muslims. By the time of the first emigration to Abyssinia, in the fifth year of the beginning of Islamic revelations, there were more than twice this number of Muslims in Makkah. Right from the early days, the Prophet was keen to mould his companions into a closely-knit community in which everyone was ready to help others. The unifying bond of that community was faith. Hence it was very important that every single Muslim should realize that the adoption of the new faith meant a radical transformation in his life. It is in this light that we find Abū Bakr buying those slaves whom he saw being tortured and setting them free. Abū Bakr could simply have bought them and allowed them to live with him in safety, providing them with full protection against any of the persecutors. However, he did not stop at that. He immediately set them free to demonstrate that the bond of faith superseded all values and considerations which were thought to be of great importance in the Arabian society of Makkah. Abū Bakr's actions were an early indication of a basic characteristic of the Muslim community which was united by the bond of brotherhood in faith.

One of the very important features of this new community was prayer. That was the act of worship which provided the new Muslims with a sense of their link with God as they offered their worship. Prayer was made a duty binding on Muslims from the very early days of Islam. The Prophet passed on to his followers the instructions he received through the Angel Gabriel to have ablution before prayer and to offer two prayers a day, one in the morning and one before sunset. Each prayer was two *rakʿahs* in the same form as the Muslims have always adopted. The new Muslims were keen to offer their prayers either individually or in small groups. They went out of the built-up area of Makkah to pray where they could not be seen. Sometimes they were discovered by non-Muslims, as indeed happened one day with the Prophet who was offering his prayers with his young cousin ʿAlī. Abū Ṭālib was passing by and it was the first time he saw Islamic prayer. He asked his nephew, the Prophet, about his prayer and asked ʿAlī why he was joining him. ʿAlī told him that he had accepted the faith of Islam and that he believed in Muhammad as a Prophet and a messenger of God. Abū Ṭālib simply said to his son: "Since he has called you to something that is good, then follow him."[1]

Group prayer is characteristic of the Islamic faith. Congregational prayer is so important that many scholars consider it a duty. In the early days of Islam, it gave the new Muslims a sense of identity. Therefore, they were keen to go out in groups to offer their prayers. One day, a group of Muslims were discovered by unbelievers who insulted them and ridiculed their prayer. The two groups were soon involved in a heated argument, since the Muslims felt they could face up to them. Saʿd ibn Abū Waqqāṣ, who was not yet twenty, took a camel bone and hit one of the unbelievers with it, injuring him. This was the first time blood was ever spilled in defence of Islam.

But the incident indicated the readiness and willingness of the Muslims to defend themselves. However, they were restrained by God from getting involved in a fight with the unbelievers.

The First Islamic School

The Prophet's efforts to mould his followers into a closely-knit community prompted him to establish a centre for the Muslims. Obviously, in those early days, it was not possible for the Muslims to hold their meetings in public. Therefore, the Prophet chose the house of one of his companions, al-Arqam, to be the meeting-place. At that time al-Arqam was about 20 years old; he belonged to the clan of Makhzūm, to which Abū Jahl also belonged. His house was near al-Ṣafā, in the centre of Makkah. In other words, the Prophet chose a house which was right in the midst of the concentration of unbelievers. That was a very strategic spot, since the Quraysh could not have expected that such a meeting-place would be chosen in that central area under the very nose of Abū Jahl, the archenemy of Islam. Nevertheless, the Prophet was able to meet his companions there, teach them the basic principles of their faith, strengthen their bond of brotherhood, and shape their community in the true Islamic mould so that it could serve as an example for future generations, whenever a Muslim community came into existence.[2]

As days went by and the Quraysh increased its opposition to Islam, it became more and more aware that the followers of Muhammad were setting themselves apart as a community. Therefore, it was important for the Quraysh to try to establish a counter-bond. They wanted their faith to override all considerations of family and tribal ties. But how could pagan idolatry give any person an ideal for which a family tie could be sacrificed? A group of the Makhzūm clan decided that they would use strong tactics against those of their members who became Muslims. There were quite a few young men from the clan who adopted Islam, including Salamah ibn Hishām and ʿAyyāsh ibn Abū Rabīʿah. But in order for their plan to succeed, they also wanted to include with them a man who belonged to their best families, al-Walīd ibn al-Walīd. They went to his brother Hishām and told him that they wanted to punish those young men, so they would appreciate it if he turned his brother over to them. They said that in this way, they could be certain that no other men from their clan would contemplate joining the followers of Muhammad. Hishām told them that they could speak to his brother, but warned them against causing him any bodily harm. He said: "Take care, because if you kill him, then by God I will kill the most honourable among you." Thus al-Walīd was spared the punishment, and the attempt of those men from Makhzūm was foiled.

Which Approach to Follow: Moderate or Hard Line?

When a protracted problem of the kind Makkah witnessed in those early years of Islam (in the early seventh century) faces any human society, there will be no shortage of suggestions on how it may be solved. The methods suggested, however, will simply alternate between the moderate and conciliatory approach, which aims at reaching some sort of accommodation with the other side, and militant, hard-line proposals which advocate a radical solution.

When the chiefs of Makkah took stock of their longstanding dispute with Muhammad and realized that despite their opposition, the followers of Muhammad were increasing and moulding themselves into a separate community, the far-sighted among them recognized that the problem they faced was unlikely to fade away or disappear. One of the first to realize that Islam was getting stronger, despite all the Quraysh's attempts to stop its advance, was ʿUtbah ibn Rabīʿah, one of the leading figures in Makkah.

One day, as ʿUtbah was sitting with a group of the Quraysh notables, he noticed the Prophet sitting alone close to the Kaʿbah. ʿUtbah suggested to his friends: "Shall we go to Muhammad and make him some offers? He may accept one or the other. If he does we will give him that and put an end to our problem with him."

This idea was greeted with unanimous approval. As ʿUtbah sat with the Prophet he addressed him: "My nephew, you know you command a position of high esteem and noble birth among us. You have brought into the life of your community something very serious indeed. You have thus caused disunity to creep into their ranks; you have belittled their ideals, ridiculed their gods and their religion and spoken ill of their forefathers. Now listen to me. I am making you some offers which I would like you to consider. You may, perhaps, find some of them acceptable."

The Prophet asked him to make his proposals, and listened attentively. ʿUtbah said: "My nephew, if you have started this affair hoping to make money out of it, we are all willing to give you some of our own wealth so that you would be the richest among us. If it is honour and position you want, we will make you our master and seek your advice in all matters. If it is a throne you are after, we will make you our king. If, on the other hand, you are possessed and are unable to resist what overwhelms you, we will spare no expense in seeking a medical cure for you."

When ʿUtbah stopped, the Prophet asked him whether he had finished. As ʿUtbah affirmed that he had, the Prophet asked him to listen to what he had to say. The Prophet then recited the first 38 verses of *Sūrah* 41 of the Qur'ān. ʿUtbah listened attentively. When the Prophet finished his recitation, he prostrated himself in humble devotion to God, before saying to ʿUtbah: "You have heard what I have to say and you can make up your own mind."

ʿUtbah left quietly and went to his people, who realized as they saw him approaching that a change had come over him. They looked up at him curiously, listening to his words: "I have heard something the like of which I have never heard in my life. It is neither poetry nor sorcery. Take up the suggestion I am making to you, and lay the blame for the outcome at my door. Leave this man alone. What I have heard from him will certainly bring about great events. Should the rest of the Arabs kill him, you would have been spared the trouble. If he wins, whatever glory he achieves will be yours." They retorted: "He has certainly bewitched you." He said: "I have stated my opinion, and you can do as you wish."[3]

Once again the Quraysh seemed totally unable to listen to words of wisdom. ʿUtbah was known among them as a man of objective views, balanced temperament and moderate approach. What he was suggesting to them was simply to adopt a wait-and-see policy. They would lose nothing by doing that. Indeed, they would stand to gain if the Prophet were successful with his efforts. But they preferred to suppress the new call, wasting in the process all chances of prospective gain.

A Tilt Towards the Hard Line

As the days passed and week followed week, with no hint of *rapprochement* between the Prophet and the Quraysh, an atmosphere of polarization infiltrated life in Makkah. This polarization was so real that it occasionally transcended tribal loyalties. This meant that no Muslim, whatever his position or his tribal affiliation, was immune from harassment by the Makkans, should the opportunity for such harassment arise. To torment Muslims and subject them to physical torture or mental pressure became the favourite pastime for the Quraysh hardliners. Their victims were numerous and of various tribes and positions.

The Prophet himself was not immune to this, despite the protection afforded him by his uncle and his clan. Rather than violate their own tribal standards, the Makkan leaders made their henchmen abuse the Prophet by word, gesture and action. They accused him of being a magician, a poet, and a fortune-teller, and told him to his face that he was mad. All this, however, did not affect the Prophet or weaken his resolve to carry on with his mission, conveying the word of God to his people. He continued to defy the Makkans in matters of faith, stating his case openly and calling on everyone to abandon pagan worship and accept Islam.

One day, a group of the Quraysh elders met at the Kaʿbah. Their conversation inevitably touched upon their continuing problem with Muhammad and his message. Some of them said: "Our patience with this man and our tolerance of what he does are unbelievable. He has ridiculed our elders, abused our forefathers and our gods, looked with contempt on our religion and caused disunity to creep into our ranks. We have certainly suffered a great deal from him."

As they said that, the Prophet (peace be upon him) appeared. He walked to the Kaʿbah and started his *ṭawāf*. When he passed by them, a nasty taunt was directed at him. His colour changed but he went on with his *ṭawāf.* When he passed by them the second time, they repeated their taunt and his face changed colour again. They repeated the same taunt again as he went past the third time. At this point, he stopped and addressed them, saying: "Do you hear me, people of Quraysh? By Him who holds my soul in His hand, I am threatening you with throat-cutting."

They were all taken aback by what he said. Even the hardest of them was quick to pacify him. Conciliatory words came from everywhere: "Go about your business, Abū al-Qāsim. You were never known to lose control of yourself." He left them and went away.

The following day, they met in the same place. They started to blame one another for their meekness. As they were encouraging one another to show more firmness with him, he appeared. They jumped at him and started to maul him. He stood firm, defiant, resolute. Everyone was asking him whether he maintained his position that their idols were false and he said time and again: "Yes, indeed I say that."

One of them took him by the collar and others pushed him around. Then Abū Bakr tried to defend him, shouting at them: "Do you kill a man for merely saying God is my Lord?" They then left him, having savagely manhandled him. But that did not weaken his resolve to carry on with his mission.[4]

More Physical Abuse

Perhaps that was the worst physical assault against the Prophet. Hitherto, the Quraysh had respected, to varying degrees, the protection Abū Ṭālib and the Hāshimite clan afforded him. To the Prophet, however, the worst thing he could face from his people was spending all morning talking to them without a good word from anyone. This was worse than physical abuse, because he was so keen that his people should follow Divine guidance, knowing that it would bring them happiness in both this life and the life to come. But that particular event was rather significant. Apparently, it needed such a collective first assault for the Makkans to realize that they could get away with something worse. Abū Jahl was quick to realize that he could always rely on the support of the Quraysh if he wished to abuse Muhammad (peace be upon him). He therefore looked for a chance to do so.

One day Abū Jahl passed the Prophet near the hill of al-Ṣafā, a short distance from the Ka'bah. Realizing that the Prophet was alone, Abū Jahl assaulted and abused him. He also ridiculed Islam and talked about the Prophet's message with contempt. The Prophet did not say a single word in reply. The incident was witnessed, however, by a maid looking through a window of a house in which she worked. When Abū Jahl finished his repugnant exercise, he went to join a group of his folk sitting near the Ka'bah.

Soon afterwards, Ḥamzah, an uncle of the Prophet who was about the same age as the Prophet or a little older, was returning from a hunting trip. Ḥamzah enjoyed his hunting. It was his habit, whenever he returned from hunting, to go first to the Ka'bah and do a *ṭawāf*. He then greeted every group of people who sat there, as was the Makkan habit. He was well respected and everyone enjoyed his company.

This time, the maid stopped him as he passed by her. She related to him what she saw Abū Jahl doing to his nephew, Muhammad, and told him that the Prophet did not return any insult.

Ḥamzah was furious with Abū Jahl. He went straight to the mosque in search of him. When he saw him with his kinsfolk, he went up to him with his bow in his hand. As he stood over Abū Jahl's head, he struck him with the bow with all his might, causing a long cut in his forehead. He then said: "Do you abuse him when I follow his religion? I say the same as he says. Try to stop me if you can." As Abū Jahl's wound started to bleed, his comrades tried to avenge him. He, however, realized that the situation could deteriorate, so he told them, "Leave Abū 'Imārah [Ḥamzah] alone. I have indeed abused his nephew badly."[5]

This incident is laden with tribal overtones. Ḥamzah's fury and retaliation were motivated by tribal loyalties. Similarly, Abū Jahl's conciliatory remark after he was punished by Ḥamzah aimed to avoid any tribal clash over the matter. Had Ḥamzah been overcome by the sheer number of his opponents, his tribe would have had to avenge his humiliation. Matters could have got out of hand. Ḥamzah's declaration that he was a follower of Muhammad was made in a moment of great anger, so it might have had no real foundation and he might still be persuaded to forget the matter - or so Abū Jahl might have thought.

On this last point he was totally mistaken. Ḥamzah might have said what he did on the spur of the moment and without realizing its implications; however, he went to his nephew and learnt from him about Islam. As he listened, a feeling of reassurance grew stronger and stronger within him. He had no regrets. His decision gave the Prophet and the Muslims a feeling of strength, because he was one of the most courageous fighters in Arabia. The Quraysh realized that Ḥamzah was a significant recruit to Islam. It was not simply that the number of Muslims increased by one, but that now the community of Muslims had within its ranks a man of immense power who commanded great respect and imparted much confidence to them. To the last day of his life Ḥamzah continued to be one of the main stalwarts of the new call to Islam.

A Hostile Conference

People have continued to come to Makkah for pilgrimage ever since the Prophets Abraham and Ishmael built the Kaʿbah. God has ensured that successive generations have continued to revere 'the House' as it was generally called by the Arabs, and to travel to it to offer their devotion to the Creator. It was Abraham who called upon people, in fulfilment of God's instructions, to visit the Kaʿbah for pilgrimage. At the time when the Prophet Muhammad started preaching the message of Islam in Makkah, pilgrimage was well established in the traditions of the city. People from all over Arabia came to Makkah at a specific time every year to do their pilgrimage rituals. This, of course, enhanced the position of the Quraysh, who resided in Makkah as the leading tribe in Arabia. One should add here, however, that pre-Islamic pilgrimage included many practices which could not be described as 'religious', or even 'moral'. These were introduced over the years by the Quraysh as the overseers of pilgrimage. Thus, a great institution of worship was distorted and forced out of its religious nature. The fact remained, however, that people from the four corners of Arabia travelled to Makkah every year and stayed there for some time before returning home.

The Quraysh enjoyed the advantages it reaped from pilgrimage and tried to protect them against any threat. Now, however, it was waking up to the fact that the pilgrimage might produce some unwelcome results. This recognition manifested itself in various preventive measures taken by the Quraysh. At a meeting attended by a large number of Makkans and chaired, as it were, by al-Walīd ibn al-Mughīrah, a well-defined strategy was agreed.

In his opening address, al-Walīd said: "Now that the pilgrimage season is approaching, people will start arriving from all over the place. They must have heard about your friend [meaning the Prophet]. So you had better agree what to say when you are asked about him. We must guard against having too many opinions, particularly if they are mutually contradictory."

When his audience asked his advice as to what they should say, he preferred to listen to their suggestions first. What concerned al-Walīd most was that the opinion they would come out with should take account of the fact that Muhammad was asking people to listen to the Qur'ān, God's message, expressed in beautiful language and a powerful style. The description they would attach to Muhammad should also account for his persuasive, eloquent argument.

Descriptions like 'fortune-teller', 'madman', 'poet' and 'magician' were proposed. None was considered convincing by al-Walīd, who pointed out weaknesses in each, one after the other. He told his people that what Muhammad said was nothing like what was said by such men. When nobody could suggest anything more plausible, they asked al-Walīd if he had a better suggestion.

He said: "What Muhammad says is certainly beautiful. It is like a date tree with solid roots and rich fruit. Every one of these suggestions you have made is bound to be recognized as false. The least disputable one is to claim that he is a magician who repeats magic words which make a man fall out with his father, mother, wife and clan." They all approved of al-Walīd's suggestion and set about preparing their propaganda campaign to make the pilgrims wary of Muhammad and unwilling to meet him.[6]

This was the first conference organized by the enemies of Islam on how to distort its image and how to turn people away from it before they had a chance to realize that Islam was identical with the truth.

The Quraysh launched its smear campaign against Islam and the Prophet, charging the latter with being a magician who could only bring about discord within people's families and clans. The hard-liners of the Quraysh made a special effort to meet as many pilgrims as possible to explain to them the nature of their problem with Muhammad (peace be upon him) and to warn them against his magic. As pilgrims group themselves on tribal lines, the Quraysh's efforts often took the form of a semi-official tribal meeting in which a delegation of the Quraysh sought to meet as many as possible of the pilgrims of any one tribe to offer their advice and to warn them against the 'disastrous' effects that might arise from any person's attempt to meet Muhammad. Anyone who met him risked being bewitched, they claimed.

Evil Tactics Backfire

The Quraysh's campaign was certainly successful. Nobody wanted to learn about Islam in that pilgrimage season. All tribes pledged their support to the attitude of the elders of the Quraysh in trying to contain the problem they faced. The success, however, was short-lived. Those very people who listened to the warnings and thought they were wise to avoid Muhammad and his followers carried the news to their people as they went back. They obviously repeated the Quraysh's account and views. As news travels, it starts to change. In this instance, the venom of the Quraysh's false charges was bound to be toned down. In those days, when none of our present-day communications technology was in existence and publicity about anything was limited to word of mouth, the Quraysh did Islam an unintentional service: they allowed the whole of Arabia to learn about the existence of Islam. That was a very important first opportunity for Islam to get beyond the confines of Makkah.

An example of how the Quraysh's attempts were counter-productive can be provided by the story of Ḍammād, a man from the tribe of Azd Shanū'ah who was well known as a faith healer. Ḍammād heard some idiots in Makkah claiming that Muhammad was a madman. He asked them: "Where is this man? I hope I can cure him by God's will." He met the Prophet and told him that he was a faith healer and that God could cause him to be the medium to cure some people. He asked him whether he would like to try. The Prophet said: "Praise be to God, we glorify Him and seek His help. Whoever God guides to the truth will have none to mislead him and whoever God leaves to go astray will have no one to guide. I bear witness that there is no deity other than God, who is the only God and who has no partners."

Ḍammād said: "By God, I have listened to many fortune-tellers, astrologers, magicians and poets, but I have never heard anything like these words." He asked the Prophet to repeat what he had said, and expressed his admiration. He then said: "Let us shake hands. I pledge that I am a Muslim." The Prophet asked him whether he was willing to give his pledge on behalf of his people, and Ḍammād answered in the affirmative. He became an advocate of Islam among his people.[7]

At one point in this period, there was a very real danger of which Abū Ṭālib was keenly aware. As he watched the efforts of the Quraysh to dissuade other tribes from listening to Muhammad, he felt that the Quraysh might attempt a joint action against the Hāshimite clan to which he and his nephew, the Prophet, belonged. The Hāshimite clan would be no match for such a grouping, which could provide an effective but bloody solution to the problem. Today, one may be able to feel how delicate the situation in Makkah was at the time. To forestall any attempt, Abū Ṭālib made sure that everybody in Makkah was absolutely clear on where he stood and what would be expected should the Quraysh think of taking any collective, punitive measures against the Hāshimites or against Muhammad. In a splendid long poem, he sought to emphasize the sanctity of Makkah, outline the

Hāshimite heritage in the holy city, praise the nobility of Makkah and reassure them that he was one of them; but he also declared his determination to defend his nephew to the bitter end. This served as a warning against misadventure. None was attempted for some time to come.

Notes

1. Ibn Hishām, *al-Sīrah al-Nabawiyyah*, Dār al-Qalam, Beirut, Vol. 1, pp. 263-264.
2. Ibid., p. 270.
3. Ibid., pp. 313-314.
4. Ibid., pp. 309-310.
5. Ibid., pp. 311-312.
6. Ibid., pp. 288-289.
7. Ibn Kathīr, *al-Bidāyah wal-Nihāyah*, Maktabat al-Ma'ārif, Beirut, Vol.3, pp. 36-37.

10

Moving Out

THE SITUATION IN Makkah was growing more tense every day. The Quraysh were waking up to the realization that the new faith was establishing its roots and gaining more recruits in all clans. Its followers belonged to all sectors of society. Attempts to strike a compromise with the Prophet proved to be of little value. Persecution brought no results. The hard-line approach was gaining ground. On the other hand, the Prophet went on preaching his faith and conveying God's message. Those who responded to him were keen to make it clear to their people that their new faith had a positive influence on life as a whole. They also made it clear that they were not prepared to barter their faith for the richest of prizes. However, the Prophet realized that no amount of persuasion or negotiation would make the leaders of Makkah change their hostile attitude to Islam, or convince them that they should take an objective look at it and judge it on its merits. Indeed, the Makkans started to escalate their campaign of repression, subjecting the weaker Muslims to much torture and endless persecution. Those of the Prophet's companions who belonged to strong tribes and were assured of tribal protection were tormented by ridicule. Nevertheless, Islam was gaining more converts every day.

Always a far-sighted and well-informed leader, the Prophet advised his companions to emigrate to Abyssinia where the Christian king,

Negus, was known for his abhorrence of injustice. Although the main reason for this exodus given by most historians is that the Muslims were simply fleeing to save their lives, the move was certainly a very shrewd one, taken after a very careful consideration of the whole situation. In his choice of a possible refuge for his companions, the Prophet was keen to make sure that the Muslims would not be substituting one kind of repression for another. Since Negus had gained a wide reputation for his justice, Abyssinia was to be a second home for the Islamic call.

The first party of Muslim emigrants to Abyssinia consisted of 16 people, four of whom were women. The most notable figure among them was ʿUthmān ibn ʿAffān, who was to become the third Caliph, and his wife, Ruqayyah, daughter of the Prophet. Indeed, ʿUthmān was the first man ever to emigrate with his wife for no other reason than serving God's cause since Prophet Lot had emigrated many centuries earlier. Those sixteen people managed to find a boat which carried them to their destination. Apparently, they were chased by the Quraysh, who sought to force them to return but their pursuers arrived at the coast when the boat had already set sail. Other parties of emigrants followed at frequent intervals.[1]

About ten of those who had emigrated to Abyssinia soon returned home, not because they found their new abode unwelcome, but because they heard that the Quraysh had accepted the message of Prophet Muhammad and embraced Islam. Shortly before arriving back in Makkah, they realized that those reports which had precipitated their return were hasty and inaccurate. Therefore, they had to arrange shelter for themselves if they wanted to get safely into Makkah. They managed to get that shelter from some fair-minded personalities in Makkah.

The truth about that report was that the Prophet recited *Sūrah* 53, entitled The Star, or *al-Najm*, when a large number of people, many of whom were non-Muslims, were in the mosque. This *sūrah* has a very powerful ending, which reminds people of God's Majesty and His control of the universe, and that they will surely die and be resurrected. The *sūrah* reaches its climax with the last verse, which commands all mankind to prostrate themselves to God and to worship Him alone. Here is the ending of this *sūrah*:

> With your Lord is the end [of all that exists]; and it is He alone who causes you to laugh and to weep; and it is He alone who deals death and grants life; and it is He who creates the two kinds – the male and the female – out of a mere drop of sperm as it is brought forth, and it is within His power to bring about a second life; and it is He alone who frees from want and causes to possess; and it is He who is the Lord of Sirius; and it is He who destroyed the ancient people of ʿĀd and Thamūd, leaving no trace of them, as well as the people of Noah before them, since they all had indeed been most wilful in their evil-doing and most overweening, just as He thrust into perdition those cities that were overthrown, and then covered them from sight for ever.
>
> About which, then, of your Lord's powers can you remain in doubt? This is a warning like those warnings of old: that Last Hour which is so near, draws ever nearer, although none but God can unveil it. Do you, perchance, find this revelation strange? And do you laugh instead of weeping and divert yourselves all the while? Nay, but prostrate yourselves before God and worship Him alone! (53: 43-62)

When one considers that the Qur'ān always has a powerful rhythm which is most suitable for its subject matter, one can imagine that the powerful rhythm here makes these verses sound like very strong hammering. Those Arabs listening to this *sūrah* being recited by Muhammad, the Prophet, to whom it was revealed, knew deep at heart that He never told a falsehood. Hence, every single one of them, Muslim and non-Muslim alike, prostrated himself as commanded by God. Al-Walīd ibn al-Mughīrah, an old man and an unbeliever, took a handful of dust and put his forehead on it. As the news of this event travelled to Abyssinia, it reached those Muslims there in a distorted fashion suggesting to them that all trouble in Makkah was over and that the Quraysh decided to accept Islam. Hence their quick return.[2]

Fabricated Justification

Soon afterwards, the unbelievers realized what had happened. Others, like Abū Jahl, could not believe their ears when they heard the story. They wanted to continue to oppose the Prophet, but they had to explain their behaviour and to dismiss the whole incident as a non-event. One of their poets came up with the devilish idea that Muhammad mentioned their deities in favourable terms. They went as far as coining a couplet of verses praising their idols and claimed that these were used by the Prophet as he recited the *sūrah* to them. It was easy for them to do that, since the *sūrah* mentions three of their most famous idols, al-Lāt, al-ʿUzzā and Manāt. But what does the Qur'ān have to say about them in this particular *sūrah*?

> Have you thought of al-Lāt and al-ʿUzzā, as well as Manāt, the third and last of this trio? Why do you choose for yourselves males, whereas you assign to Him females? That is indeed an unfair division. These entities are nothing but empty names which you have invented, you and your forefathers, and for which God has bestowed no warrant from on high. They [who worship them] follow nothing but surmise and wishful thinking, although right guidance has indeed come to them from their Lord. (53: 19-23)

It was in the middle of this passage that those fabricators of the Quraysh sought to impose their invented couplet, after the names of their three idols. The fabricated couplet reads: "These are exalted birds, whose intercession is desirable." Little did they reflect that such an imposition could not be accepted by any thinking person among them. Almost every verse in the *sūrah* is in conflict with such description, or such compromise. It is sufficient to try to read the above-quoted passage together with the claimed couplet to realize that the whole thing was total fabrication. Even the Makkan unbelievers themselves were unconvinced and they dropped the report altogether, although some unscrupulous Orientalists and other people who are hostile to Islam have tried to make something out of it.

It is well known that most of the Arabs at the time could not read or write. Therefore, it is not surprising that the dates of events were not recorded accurately. One cannot be certain how many groups of emigrants to Abyssinia from among the Muslims of Makkah had already gone before the first group, or some of its members, were on their journey back to Makkah. Many of those who returned felt they had to go back to Abyssinia after finding out that nothing had changed in Makkah. If anything, the situation became worse for the Muslims. The emigrants were going out in small groups, two or three families at a time. Many young Muslims were not yet married. Therefore, the number of men among the Muslims in Abyssinia far exceeded the women. Altogether, 82 or 83 men arrived in Abyssinia with 19 women. They constituted a large section of the Muslim community. Those who were left in Makkah might have been fewer than those who emigrated. That was a shrewd tactical move by the Prophet which defused a potentially explosive situation. To all appearances, the Muslims who stayed in Makkah did not constitute any threat to its social order. That was bound to weaken the argument of the hard liners, who advocated a strong-fisted approach to the problem represented by Islam. The Quraysh, however, were utterly displeased that the Muslims should be able to escape its tyranny and find peace and security in their new place of abode. A meeting was called to discuss the situation, and it was resolved to send a delegation to Negus requesting him to deport the Muslims and send them back home. ʿAmr ibn al-ʿĀṣ and ʿAbdullāh ibn Abī Rabīʿah were chosen for the mission. ʿAmr in particular was well known for his diplomatic skills. He carried with him many gifts with which he sought to make the atmosphere at Negus's court favourable when he made his request.

An Appeal to Extradite the Fugitives

ʿAmr's plan was to present every one of the patriarchs who attended Negus's court with a fine gift of animal hide. Feeling that he could rely on their help, he explained his mission, saying:

> A few drop-outs of our people have arrived in your land. Having rebelled against our religion, they did not adopt yours. Instead, they have come up with a new trend, unknown to you or to us. We have come as representatives of our leaders to request the king to extradite these fugitives. When we make this request to the king, we hope you will counsel him to grant it without going to the trouble of calling them and speaking to them. You will undoubtedly agree that their own people are better equipped to judge them fairly and to determine whether their creed is of any use.

The patriarchs promised ʿAmr and his friend their support. Thus the ground was prepared for a quick decision by Negus in favour of ʿAmr and ʿAbdullāh.

When the two were admitted into court, they presented the king with a precious gift of superb camel hide. To him, that was the finest gift they could bring. He was so pleased with it that he immediately asked them to put their request.

Nothing was more loathsome to the Quraysh delegation than that Negus should call the Muslims in to present their case. Hence, they emphasized that the Muslims did not opt for Christianity, Negus's own religion. They also stressed that they were making their request on behalf of the fugitives' own parents and uncles, who could not be expected, particularly in the Arabian tribal society, to subject them to any harm. As they made their case, the patriarchs supported them, saying: "Certainly their people are best equipped to judge them. Extradition is the proper course for the king to take in these circumstances."

Negus was very angry. He said: "A group of people who have sought my shelter, preferring me over everyone else, will not be summarily judged. I shall call them in first and give them a chance to answer what these two have alleged about them. Should I find these allegations true, I will extradite them. Otherwise, they will certainly enjoy my protection." Thus the scene was set for a great encounter. Needless to say, the Makkan delegation were very disappointed at

Negus's decision, but they could do nothing about it. They had to attend the court when the Muslims were summoned.

The Muslims consulted with one another when the king's messenger delivered to them an order to appear at court. They were unanimous that they would answer any questions put to them truthfully. They would state the whole truth, as they had been taught by the Prophet, regardless of what results it might produce.

When they were admitted into the king's presence, he was surrounded by his patriarchs. The atmosphere was awesome. However, he came straight to the point and asked them: "What is this new religion over which you are in dispute with your own people and which is at variance with my own religion and with all other known religions?"

The Muslims had chosen Jaʿfar ibn Abī Ṭālib, the Prophet's own cousin, as their spokesman. He put their case as follows:

> In our recent past we were ignorant people: we worshipped idols, ate carrion, committed all sorts of sins, attached little value to maintaining good relations with our kinsfolk and behaved badly to our neighbours. Our overruling maxim was that might was right. This continued to be our situation until God sent us, from among ourselves, a Messenger whose good name, honesty, sincerity and integrity were well known to us. He called on us to believe in God, the one and only God, and to stop worshipping all idols which we and our forefathers used to worship alongside Him. He commanded us always to speak the truth and be honest, to be good to our relatives and neighbours, to preserve life and shed no blood, to refrain from sin, perjury, robbing the property of orphans entrusted to our care, and making false accusations against honourable women. He also commanded us to devote our worship to God alone, ascribing to Him no partners of any sort. He further commanded us to pray regularly, to give away certain purifying alms and to fast, etc. We gave him a favourable response, believed in him and gave him our full support. We followed these Divine commandments he conveyed to us. We began to

> worship God alone, refraining from what He forbade us and accepting what He made lawful for us. Our people, however, assaulted us and subjected us to physical torture to compel us to revert to idolatrous worship and to indulge in the sinful practices we used to indulge in. Having been overpowered, oppressed and denied the freedom to choose our faith and practise it, we sought refuge in your country, choosing you in preference to all other rulers, hoping that in your refuge we would suffer no injustice.

Negus asked Jaʿfar to read him a passage of the Qur'ān. Jaʿfar chose the opening of *Sūrah* 19, entitled Mary, which speaks about Prophet Zachariah and his son John before it goes on to relate the story of the virgin birth of Jesus. Negus and his patriarchs were in tears. Then he said: "What I have just heard comes from the same source as Jesus's revelations." He then dismissed the Quraysh delegation and assured the Muslims that they would have his full protection.[3]

It is not in the nature of things, however, that those who find themselves taking a stand against the truth accept defeat easily and abandon their attempts to suppress the cause they oppose. Hostility to the truth is often brutal, immoral, unyielding. If one imagines truth as a man, he would be of the honest, frank and straightforward type. Trying to make any gains, big or small, by petty or devious means, would be totally alien to his nature. Truth also has a direct, clear and logical way of putting its case to the human mind. Hence, the difficulty its opponents find in resisting it is very great. Therefore, they often find an inescapable need to resort to vile and devious means. This is a slippery road: once started, there is no stopping. The only way out of this dilemma is for the opponents of the truth to give up: they can either follow the truth or acknowledge the fact that they are at variance with it and allow it to take its course. Certainly the Quraysh delegation who tried to secure the extradition of the Muslim refugees in Abyssinia were in no such mood. Having failed in their attempt to overcome Negus's sense of justice by offering precious, personal gifts to him and his patriarchs, they began to think of some other, more devious way to achieve their purpose. As they left Negus's court, ʿAmr ibn al-ʿĀṣ, the more cunning of the two-man delegation, said to his colleague, ʿAbdullāh ibn Abū Rabīʿah: "I will come back to him tomorrow with something which would make him exterminate them all." ʿAbdullāh counselled him against such a step, protesting the fact that they were still their own kinsfolk.

The following day ʿAmr went back to Negus and said to him: "These people make a very wild claim about Jesus. You may wish to question them on that."[4]

When the Muslims realized the reason for their second summons to attend the king's court, they were very alarmed. They resolved, however, to stick to the truth and put their case frankly and clearly. They would simply state what God's Messenger had taught them, whatever the consequences.

Some people may argue that in their delicate situation the Muslims' stand might have been foolhardy. The situation called for a somewhat 'diplomatic' stance. People of faith, however, consider such an argument to be short-sighted. Truth, they argue, speaks louder and more frankly. Given a chance, it will always prevail. To the Muslim refugees in Abyssinia, the case was simply stating a fact revealed by God and conveyed by His Messenger. Evasion was unthinkable. Moreover, evasion is alien to the nature of those who follow the truth.

Jaʿfar, the Muslims' spokesman, therefore answered Negus's question about their view of Jesus without hesitation: "Our view is that taught to us by our Prophet: Jesus is God's servant and messenger. He is His spirit and His word delivered unto virgin Mary." Negus picked a little stick from the floor and said: "What you have just said about Jesus does not go beyond the truth by the width of this stick." To the jeers and sneers of the patriarchs he replied: "It is true, no matter what you say." He then said to the Muslims: "You are safe in my land. Whoever harms you will be brought to justice. I would not harm any one of you for a mountain of gold." He then ordered his patriarchs to return the gifts of the Quraysh delegation.[5]

A Shrewd Plan

The emigration of the Prophet's companions to Abyssinia was a highly significant event, which can be accurately described as the first major political move taken by the Prophet. Although people often give more prominence to the Prophet's desire to spare his companions the persecution inflicted by the Quraysh, it had some definite objectives. If one analyses the emigration and the whole situation that prevailed in Makkah at that time, one is bound to realize that there were other, far more important reasons, which made this emigration a shrewd strategic move on the part of the Prophet. A close examination of the list of people who travelled to Abyssinia shows that hardly any of the weak and vulnerable elements who were subjected to unbearable torture joined the travellers. Historians of that period are uncertain about ʿAmmār ibn Yāsir who was, together with his parents, a target for some of the most brutal types of torture. Indeed, both his parents died under torture. Historians are certain, however, that people like Khabbāb ibn al-Aratt and Bilāl ibn Rabāḥ, who were the most famous of ʿAmmār's fellow sufferers, did not travel. On the other hand, one finds that the list of travellers includes names of many prominent people who belonged to famous clans which were able to afford them protection.

In this list are the names of ʿUthmān ibn ʿAffān of the Umayyah clan, Abū Ḥudhayfah ibn ʿUtbah of ʿAbd Shams, whose father was one of the chiefs in Makkah, and his wife Sahlah bint Suhayl of the ʿĀmir clan, whose father was later to become the governor of Makkah, al-Zubayr ibn al-ʿAwwām of Asad, ʿAbd al-Raḥmān ibn ʿAwf of Zuhrah, Abū Salamah ʿAbdullāh ibn ʿAbd al-Asad of Makhzūm, Suhayl ibn Wahb of Fihr, Muṣʿab ibn ʿUmayr of ʿAbd al-Dār and Jaʿfar ibn Abī Ṭālib of the Hāshimite clan, who was the Prophet's cousin.

One need only look at these names to realize that the emigrants belonged to most, if not all, the clans of the Quraysh, and many of them belonged to highly placed families in Makkah. In the tribal set-up of Arabia, such people could not be subjected to physical torture and persecution in the same way as the slaves, the allies and other vulnerable people. Perhaps the most that such people had to endure was verbal abuse, or on occasion they might be drawn into a slanging match or met with derision and ridicule. This may hurt people immensely but its total effect is different from that of physical torture, which the tyrannical chiefs of the Quraysh inflicted on the weaker Muslims. Such verbal abuse may be painful, but it does not call for a break of ties with one's own clan and crossing the sea by desert people in order to live in a distant land among total strangers.

A point to be mentioned here is that Abū Bakr, the closest to the Prophet of all his companions, also embarked on this journey and travelled from Makkah. However, he was met some distance away from the city by Mālik ibn al-Dughunnah, who found it unacceptable that a man of the calibre of Abū Bakr should leave Makkah. Mālik persuaded him to return and extended his protection to him so that Abū Bakr would not be abused. It is impossible to imagine that Abū Bakr was subjected to any physical torture when he was the one who bought seven Muslim slaves to save them from physical persecution. Why would he travel when Bilāl, a former slave whom he had set free, did not find it necessary to do so? There cannot be a satisfactory answer to such a question unless we say that there is a much wider perspective to this emigration by the Prophet's companions than the mere escape of persecuted people.

Realignment of Loyalties

In order to do that, one must take a fresh look at the situation in Makkah just before the Prophet's decision to encourage his companions to go to Abyssinia. In the intervening period between the Prophet's proclamation of his message and this emigration, almost two years, there was much turmoil in Makkah, with the Quraysh putting up strong opposition to the new message. The Quraysh were fundamentally shaken by the call to accept Islam. All attempts to contain it were futile. But if hard-liners were to escalate the pressure, where would it lead them?

Perhaps it was necessary to answer this question before it was put, so that the Quraysh could contemplate the consequences of any decision. The emigration to Abyssinia made that clear. The emigrants included one man, Jaʿfar ibn Abī Ṭālib and one woman, Ruqayyah, daughter of the Prophet from the Hāshimite clan, one man from the clan of ʿAbd ibn Quṣayy, one man from Nawfal and two from ʿAbd Shams, two from Taym, four from Asad, five from ʿAdiy, seven each from Umayyah, Zuhrah, ʿAbd al-Dār and ʿĀmir, eight from Makhzūm and a similar number from al-Ḥārith ibn Hishām, twelve from Jumaḥ and four from Sahm.[6] This meant that an all-out confrontation would involve every clan of the Quraysh turning against some of its own people. That was totally unacceptable in that particular place at that particular time.

As the Quraysh watched all those Muslims suddenly move out, across tribal lines, and join an exodus to seek a safer place where they could worship God, the Quraysh realized that their rejection of tribal values was irrevocable and allegiance to the new faith was total. Moreover, the Quraysh realized that Islam was able to gain ground in all sectors of society. Hence, any move to mount a full strike against the Muslims must win support throughout all the clans, because there were a number of Muslims in each and every clan. To unite them all in a determined confrontation with Muslims was impracticable because several clans had not given up hope of the possibility of working out a certain kind of understanding which would be satisfactory to both sides. It was not possible at that time to persuade the chiefs of some of these clans that they must fight some of their dearest sons, particularly when a good number of them belonged to the most prominent families. However, to those hard-liners who were in the forefront of the confrontation with Islam, the collapse of tribal affiliation and blind loyalty to clan and tribe in the minds of Muslims was very clear. Hence they sought to forestall a move which was bound to emphasize their new allegiance to their faith.

The Prophet was keen to emphasize the very concept which the Quraysh wanted to block. He wanted his followers to realize that belonging to Islam meant that they no longer belonged to Hāshim, Umayyah, Sahm, ʿAdiy or any other clan. Their only tie of allegiance was to their faith. They were simply Muslims. As long as they were in Makkah, where hostile forces tried hard to play on feelings of tribal loyalty, this particular task was going to be difficult. Those companions of the Prophet also valued their tribal ties very highly until the moment they became Muslims. Living among their own people, where they needed tribal protection, would make it inevitable that they would have to seek some sort of *modus vivendi* with their own tribes who were still predominantly pagan. All that was needed was a tacit understanding of the relationship between a Muslim individual and his idolatrous tribe.

Leaving Makkah for a far away place like Abyssinia achieved the dual benefit of removing all social pressures which could be brought to bear on the Muslims and strengthening their own mutual ties, so that they could be moulded into a single, well-knit community. Those hundred or so Muslim emigrants belonged to no fewer than 15 clans of the Quraysh. Before Islam, these lines of separation could be very prominent. When they went out on their long trip to Abyssinia, every single one of them had in his mind only one tie of allegiance, which required him to give all his loyalty to the nation of Islam. When they faced the threat of extradition, their unity was complete.

These same ties of allegiance were also strengthened among those Muslims who remained in Makkah. Now that their number had been much reduced, they were even more keenly aware of their weakness. They were concerned for the safety of their brethren who went on their hazardous journey, and they were worried about their own safety. They trusted to the wisdom of the Prophet in encouraging his companions to leave for Abyssinia. They were now weaker than ever before, and it was only natural that their weakness brought them closer together. Thus the emigration to Abyssinia made the feelings of unity among Muslims even stronger, whether they were among the emigrants or those who stayed behind.

Establishing a New Muslim Community

When the first Muslim emigrants started on their journey to Abyssinia, the Prophet had been preaching the message of Islam in Makkah for five years, three of which were characterized by the secret approach. Although the new message went public with the proclamation made by the Prophet as he stood on the top of the hill of al-Ṣafā, Islam was still largely confined to Makkah, almost unknown to people outside. Only those Arab individuals who went to Makkah for pilgrimage or to visit the Kaʿbah, came to know about it. In the overwhelming majority of cases, such people could not take a decision without first referring to their own tribes. Moreover, those who heard of Islam did not pay much attention to it, considering it an internal matter which concerned only the Quraysh tribe. It was necessary, therefore, for Islam to break out of this imposed confinement and broaden the scope of its efforts of advocacy.

The emigration to Abyssinia gave the adherents to the new faith a chance to carry their message further afield. The Muslims in Abyssinia were able to establish a close community which conducted its affairs on the basis of Islamic teachings which they had learnt from the Prophet. Its life was the best advertisement for Islam on the world stage. The keen sense of unity among its members gave that Muslim community a real sense of confidence and reassured it that it followed the truth. The Muslim community in Abyssinia did not entertain any thoughts of establishing a separate entity in its new place of abode. No group of Muslims could establish such an entity when God's Messenger lived with another group of Muslims in a different city. Enjoying their life of freedom and ease, the Muslims in Abyssinia were all the time thinking of their brethren in Makkah and of the Prophet, who continued his struggle and never despaired of winning the Quraysh people over to Islam.

Moreover, it became Abundantly clear to Muslims of that generation and of all subsequent generations, that it was possible to establish a Muslim society which implemented Islam without the presence of God's Messenger to supervise that society and conduct its affairs. When the Prophet completed his mission and conveyed his message in full, establishing the model Muslim state which made submission to God its own foundation, his life on earth was over. His companions followed his guidance and continued along the road he mapped out. None of them ever entertained any thought that the absence of the Prophet could rule out the implementation of Islam, as is sometimes claimed by ignorant people or by tyrants who happen to rule over parts of the Muslim world. The Prophet's companions provided a practical example of what human life could be like when Islam was implemented, and of the magnitude of the blessings that are enjoyed by mankind when they adopt Islam as a code of living. The emigration to Abyssinia provided practical training during the Prophet's lifetime for the establishment of a Muslim society in which the Prophet does not live.

Perhaps some leaders of the Quraysh could see some of the benefits which this emigration to Abyssinia could bring to Islam. At least they realized that the emigration was bound to make Islam well known to people far beyond the boundaries of Arabia. Hence, their attempt to have the emigrants extradited.

Creating an Impression of Weakness

Important as the aforementioned reasons were, the Prophet might have preferred not to send his companions on such a trip had the atmosphere in Makkah been somewhat less hostile to Islam. He might have preferred to have all his followers near him in Makkah, had he felt that the Quraysh's hostility to Islam could weaken, or had he felt that he could widen the geographical area in which he was able to preach his message. One can see clearly that the Quraysh imposed a tight siege on Islam and effectively prevented its message from going beyond the valley of Makkah. Worse still, the Quraysh, or the hard-line elements in it, were able to heighten the conflict and increase its polarization. The struggle against Islam was the subject of every conversation in the traditional social gatherings around the Kaʿbah. As the Prophet reviewed the situation, he could clearly detect the danger that could threaten the very existence of the Muslim community. As he rejected every offer of compromise which required him to abandon some Islamic principles, the position of the hard-liners was inevitably strengthened. The voice of moderation in the Quraysh ranks was becoming weaker all the time. The question which needed a well considered answer was whether the extremists could persuade the chiefs of the different clans that an all-out strike for a final solution was necessary. It certainly was not beyond Abū Jahl to advocate that course of action. He was assured of enough supporters at the beginning to make it worth considering. If he could carry one or two of the influential chiefs with him, the balance could easily be tilted in his favour. If Islam could be seen to get stronger and stronger, Abū Jahl could plausibly argue that such a final solution was needed there and then. He was no different from many an extremist leader who lends temporary support to conciliatory efforts in order to show that moderation cannot bring the desired results. Once he had done that, he could easily win support for his extreme line.

As already mentioned, the fact that the Muslims belonged to most, if not all, the clans of the Quraysh was a negative factor working against this extremist way of thinking. Most Muslims were young men who were valued by their clans for their strength. No clan would readily sacrifice its young men to remove a danger of whose presence they were not utterly convinced. Hence, the hard-liners in Makkah were aware that they needed to work hard in order to have matters their way. They were of course able to argue that their approach of exterminating Islam altogether would weaken all clans to more or less the same degree. When these clans inflicted torture on the vulnerable elements in their ranks who followed the Prophet Muhammad (peace be upon him), their action did not strengthen any single one of them at the expense of any other. Similarly, a radical effort against those in their ranks who followed Muhammad would maintain their relative strength.

The Prophet always tried to gather intelligence of what the enemies of Islam were planning. He was also keenly aware that the early period in the life of any new faith or creed was also the most dangerous, because it would not be difficult physically to kill such a new creed when its following was small. In the fifth year of the start of Islamic revelation, Islam faced a real danger of extermination.

Forestalling such danger was perhaps paramount in the Prophet's thinking when he advised his companions to emigrate to Abyssinia. When the numbers of Muslims in Makkah were drastically reduced, the problem presented by Islam appeared to be a very simple one which could not warrant radical solutions, let alone extermination. The Prophet remained in Makkah surrounded by a small number of his companions, most of whom belonged to the weaker and more vulnerable elements in society. As such, Islam could not be seen to present a real danger to the social order in Makkah or Arabia as a whole. The Quraysh were sure to feel that they continued to hold the initiative and could strike at any moment. Moreover, the emigration of the Muslims made it clear to the Quraysh that a radical solution required unanimous support from all clans. It was not enough for two or three to agree to it, even though these might have been the strongest.

The emigration to Abyssinia was therefore a shrewd tactical move, calculated to make the Quraysh tend to dismiss Islam as representing little or no danger to its supremacy. Giving the enemy an impression of weakness could be a decisive factor in wars. Ten years later, when the Muslims fought their first major battle against the Quraysh in Badr, God Himself intervened to give the Quraysh the impression that the Muslims were a weak force: "God made you, when you met in battle, see them as small in number and made you appear few to them, so that God might accomplish a definite purpose of His." (8: 44) We may ask: did not this move by the Prophet make those Muslims who stayed in Makkah more vulnerable? It certainly did, but it was a move that was taken after weighing up all eventualities in order to avoid the worst dangers and in the hope of preventing them all. One should not forget that the Prophet was being directed by God, assured of His help.

The emigration of the Prophet's companions to Abyssinia took place in the fifth year of the start of the Qur'ānic revelations. It preceded emigration to Madinah by eight years. When the last of the Prophet's companions who went to Abyssinia came back, they joined the Prophet and his army at the conquest of Khaybar, when the battle was already over. This took place in the seventh year after the Prophet's settlement in Madinah. In other words, Ja'far ibn Abī Ṭālib and some of his companions stayed in Abyssinia for 15 years. The Prophet gave the new arrivals equal shares of the spoils of the war against the Jews in Khaybar. He did not apportion any share to any one of his companions who did not take part in the battle of Khaybar, apart from those returning emigrants from Abyssinia. The Prophet would not have given them such shares had he not considered that they were on a mission which was equal to that of those who took part in the Battle of Khaybar. He valued their contribution to the welfare of Islam and considered that their stay in Abyssinia was a part of the work to establish Islam as a Divine message for all mankind.

A Second Base for Islam

Perhaps one of the clearest indications to support this was the fact that some of the emigrants to Abyssinia stayed there for 15 years. As already mentioned, there was much more to the emigration than an attempt to spare the emigrants the verbal and physical abuse by the unbelievers in Makkah. Had this been the main reason, it might have been expected that those who went to Abyssinia would come back and join the Prophet in Madinah as soon as he settled there. The Muslim community in Madinah needed the support of every individual Muslim. There were more than a hundred in Abyssinia, and it would not have been acceptable for them to stay there at a time when the newly-founded Muslim state in Madinah was threatened by the Quraysh and the rest of the Arabian tribes. We cannot visualize the settlement of those Muslims in Abyssinia as something that was left to their own discretion. Indeed, contacts were maintained between them and the Prophet throughout their stay.

In this connection one can cite the fact that ʿAmr ibn Umayyah al-Ḍamrī, who embraced Islam in the third year after the Prophet's settlement in Madinah, went to Abyssinia three times with messages from the Prophet to Negus. The first time was to ask Negus to arrange the Prophet's marriage with one of the emigrants, Umm Ḥabībah bint Abī Sufyān. When she left Makkah on her journey to Abyssinia, she was accompanying her first husband, ʿUbaydullāh ibn Jaḥsh, who later in Abyssinia embraced Christianity and died a Christian. Her father was the leader of the Quraysh in its wars against the Prophet after the battle of Badr. She must have felt totally isolated in her place of emigration, having lost her husband and left her family and clan. To assure her of his care, the Prophet sent ʿAmr with this message.

Negus acted on behalf of the Prophet, gave her a generous dowry and arranged the marriage before sending her to the Prophet in the company of ʿAmr ibn Umayyah. ʿAmr's last trip was to request Negus to send all those emigrants living in Abyssinia. He complied with the request, sending them in two boats. Of the original 82 men and 19 women who travelled from Makkah to Abyssinia, only 16 men and a few women came with ʿAmr. A proper analysis of the emigration to Abyssinia would not be complete unless one knew what happened to the others.

Seven died in Abyssinia, while ten came back shortly after going there, as already related. Thirty-four came straight from Abyssinia to Madinah in small groups after the Battle of Badr. That leaves between 16 and 20 people, including ʿUthmān ibn ʿAffān and his wife, Ruqayyah, the Prophet's daughter, who arrived shortly after the Prophet's emigration to Madinah.[7] This suggests that the emigrants' return was dictated by the circumstances of their mission in Abyssinia. They very much wanted to join the Prophet and his companions in Madinah, but they had tasks to fulfil in their place of abode: to establish a base for Islam in that remote land and to stress the universality of its message. This view is further confirmed by the following report by Abū Mūsā ʿAbdullāh ibn Qays al-Ashʿarī, a companion of the Prophet from Yemen:

> We heard the news of the Prophet's (peace be upon him) emigration when we were in Yemen. We set out to join with two brothers of mine, both older than me, one called Abū Ruhm and the other Abū Burdah. We were in a group of our people consisting of fifty-odd men. We went on a boat, but the boat landed us in Abyssinia, ruled by Negus. We met there Jaʿfar ibn Abī Ṭālib and his companions. Jaʿfar said to us, "God's Messenger (peace be upon him) has sent us here and commanded us to stay. Why do you not stay with us?" We stayed with him until we returned, all of us, and met God's Messenger after he had conquered Khaybar. He gave us shares of the spoils of war. He did not apportion a share to anyone who had not been with him at the conquest of Khaybar, with the exception of those who were in our boat with Jaʿfar and his companions.

> Some of the Prophet's companions used to say to us, we have emigrated with the Prophet ahead of you. (Related by al-Bukhārī and Muslim.)

This report is highly significant in understanding the importance of the emigration to Abyssinia. It would have been the right thing for Abū Mūsā and his group to go on from Abyssinia to Madinah without staying there. After all, joining the Prophet was their reason for leaving Yemen. Jaʿfar would not have contemplated asking the Yemeni group to stay on in Abyssinia, had it not been for the fact that he was under specific instructions to fulfil a certain task. He told them that the Prophet had ordered them to stay. Since the order was not applicable to a specific number of people, but could include any Muslim who arrived in Abyssinia, he persuaded Abū Mūsā and his group to stay on. On their part, they recognized that the task which was to be done there was important. Otherwise, they would have either gone on and joined the Prophet or returned to their home country. There was no reason for them to leave, since they were not persecuted there. Moreover, they must have explained their situation to ʿAmr ibn Umayyah on one of his visits. Had their stay been unnecessary, he would have brought them word from the Prophet to that effect on his next visit.

It is also significant that the Prophet gave them shares of the spoils of war, which were equal to the shares of those who fought in the Battle of Khaybar. This suggests that the Prophet considered them to have been on a mission of *jihād*. Their shares were not merely a gesture of personal generosity on the Prophet's part. In later battles, the Prophet was keen not to give anyone who was not entitled to a share any portion whatsoever. After the Battle of Ḥunayn, he ordered all fighters to return any part of the spoils of war which they held. He did not allow any of his companions so much as a bunch of thread. Those emigrants to Abyssinia were entitled to their shares because they came from one mission of *jihād* and started another immediately. This is clearly indicated by the fact that they went on and joined the Prophet at Khaybar. Apparently the Prophet was aware that they did not fulfil their task in Abyssinia without problems. They must have met strong opposition. This is clear from the rest of the report quoted above:

> Asmā' bint ʿUmays, who was then Jaʿfar's wife, visited Ḥafṣah [the Prophet's wife and the daughter of ʿUmar]. While she was there, ʿUmar came in and asked who the woman was. Ḥafṣah said: "This is Asmā'." ʿUmar said: "We have had the honour of emigrating with the Prophet before you. We have a better claim than yours to the companionship of God's Messenger (peace be upon him)." Angry at what he said, Asmā' retorted: "No, by God. You were with God's Messenger (peace be upon him) who fed those of you who were hungry and admonished the ignorant, while we were in the land of hostile strangers, staying there only for the sake of God and His Messenger. By God, I shall not eat or drink until I have mentioned what you have just said to God's Messenger. We were abused and we often experienced fear. I shall mention this to God's Messenger (peace be upon him). By God. I shall not lie and shall not be guilty of distortion or exaggeration." When the Prophet came in, she said: "God's Messenger! ʿUmar has just said this and that." The Prophet asked her what she said to him and she reported it. The Prophet said: "He does not have a better claim to me than you. He and his fellow Muslims have the reward of one emigration, while you, the people of the boat, shall have the reward of two emigrations." Abū Mūsā and the people who came on the boat from Abyssinia came in groups to see Asmā' and ask her about this *ḥadīth*. Nothing in this world gave them more joy and greater happiness than what God's Messenger said to her. (Related by al-Bukhārī and Muslim.)

The emigrants' meeting with the Prophet was a joyful occasion. Jaʿfar walked on one leg when he saw the Prophet, as a gesture of respect. Apparently, this was an Abyssinian tradition. Jaʿfar wanted to show every kind of respect when he saw the Prophet. On his part, the Prophet said: "I do not know which gives me greater pleasure: the conquest of Khaybar or the arrival of Jaʿfar."[8] When one considers that the conquest of Khaybar changed the fortunes of the Muslims in Madinah, ushering in a period of affluence after they had suffered great poverty, and when one considers that this conquest meant the liquidation of all opposition from the Jewish enemies of Islam, one realizes how happy the Prophet was to see Jaʿfar and those who emigrated with him to Abyssinia.

All the foregoing confirms the view that the emigration to Abyssinia was intended to accomplish very clear and important tasks. If one wants to identify them, one can only suggest that Jaʿfar and his fellow emigrants were asked by the Prophet to propagate the faith of Islam in Abyssinia. Their efforts were clearly met with opposition, as is clear from Asmā's report. Of course, there was a favourable response from some people. Otherwise, there would have been no need for them to stay in Abyssinia when Muslim forces in Madinah needed strengthening. The question here is: how far were they successful? A report mentioned by al-Qurṭubī in his commentary on the Qur'ān states that Jaʿfar and his companions brought with them from Abyssinia 62 people who met the Prophet and believed in him. Another report mentioned by Muqātil and al-Kalbī, two prominent scholars in the early period of Islam, suggests that those who came with Jaʿfar included 40 people from Najrān, 32 from Abyssinia and 68 from Syria.[9] The very fact that such a delegation of Abyssinian Muslims came to see the Prophet is enough to clarify the nature of the mission undertaken by Jaʿfar and his group in Abyssinia.

Notes

1. Ibn Hishām, *al-Sīrah al-Nabawiyyah*, Dār al-Qalam, Beirut, Vol. 1, pp. 344-356. Also, Ibn Sayyid al-Nās, *ʿUyūn al-Athar*, Dār al-Turāth, Madinah, 1996, pp. 209-213.
2. Ibn Sayyid al-Nās, op.cit., pp. 214-215.
3. Ibn Hishām, op.cit., pp. 358-360.
4. Ibid., pp. 360-361.
5. Ibid., pp. 361-362.
6. Ibid., pp. 344-353.
7. Ibn Sayyid al-Nās, op.cit., pp. 213-214.
8. Ibn Kathīr, *al-Bidāyah wal-Nihāyah*, Maktabat al-Maʿārif, Beirut, Vol. 3, pp. 71-72 and Vol. 4, pp. 205-208.
9. Ibn Qayyim al-Jawziyyah, *Zād al-Maʿād fi Hadi Khayr al-ʿIbād*, Vol.3, Mu'assasat al-Risālah, Beirut, 1986, pp. 332-333.

11

Hope and Despair

THE EMIGRATION TO Abyssinia gave the impression that there were fewer Muslims in Makkah than their actual number. This helped to avert any all-out aggression the hard-liners of the Quraysh in Makkah might have been contemplating. Support for such an action would not be readily forthcoming if the problem was made to appear much smaller.

The emigration, however, made those who were left behind much more vulnerable. There would be many more tormentors for every Muslim left in Makkah. In that tribal society, where personal and tribal influence counted for much more than physical or numerical strength, the balance could be restored easily if people of the right calibre came forward. It was in recognition of this fact that the Prophet used to pray God in those days to support Islam by making either ʿAmr ibn Hishām, most famous for his nickname, Abū Jahl, or ʿUmar ibn al-Khaṭṭāb join the ranks of the Muslims.

The latter were very hostile to Islam. Abū Jahl was the archenemy. ʿUmar betrayed no soft feelings towards the Muslims. Indeed, he tortured a slave woman in an attempt to make her renounce Islam. It speaks volumes for the Prophet's confidence in the truth of what he was preaching that he should hope for a change of heart by either one of these two men.

It was in the nature of things that ʿUmar should be the first to want to bring the conflict in Makkah between the Quraysh and Islam to a final end. Perhaps the easiest and surest way to achieve that was to kill Muhammad, a feat which was certain to kill his message too. ʿUmar was not a man who shrank from a difficult task or pretended not to know what he could or should do. If Muhammad was to be killed, then he would be the one to kill him. He therefore went out carrying his sword in search of Muhammad.

He was soon met by a man called Nuʿaym ibn ʿAbdullāh who, like many others, hoped to escape trouble by keeping secret the fact that he was a Muslim. Nuʿaym asked ʿUmar where he was going. Unhesitatingly, ʿUmar declared his purpose. Nuʿaym then said: "Your strength has certainly fooled you. Do you imagine that the ʿAbd Manāf clan [to which the Prophet belonged] would leave you to walk these roads when you have killed Muhammad? You would be better advised if you went back to your own household and put them on the right course." ʿUmar asked: "What do you mean, and who of my household?" Nuʿaym replied: "Your cousin and brother-in-law Saʿīd ibn Zayd and your sister, Fāṭimah, have both followed Muhammad and become Muslims." Obviously Nuʿaym's purpose was to divert ʿUmar's attention. If ʿUmar was preoccupied with his own household, the Prophet would be in no imminent danger from that quarter.

Saʿīd and his wife Fāṭimah also kept secret the fact that they were Muslims. When ʿUmar approached their home, they were studying the Qur'ān with a fellow Muslim called Khabbāb. When they realized that ʿUmar was approaching, Khabbāb sought somewhere to hide, while Fāṭimah hid the sheet they were reading. In his fury, ʿUmar asked as he entered about the voices he overheard. Receiving an unsatisfactory answer from his sister, he assaulted his brother-in-law making it clear that he knew their secret. His sister rushed to push him away from her husband but he struck her, causing blood to gush from her face. She then said, with a boldness and determination which surprised ʿUmar himself: "Yes indeed, we are Muslims; we believe in God and His Messenger. You may do as you please."

The sight of blood on his sister's face made ʿUmar feel sorry for her. He said in a rather conciliatory tone: "Give me what you have been reading. Let me see what Muhammad teaches." When she hesitated, expressing her fear that he might destroy the sheet, he swore by his idols to give it back to her after he had read it. The sheet contained the opening verses of *Sūrah* 20, entitled Ṭā Hā. The meaning of these opening verses may be rendered as follows:

> We have not bestowed the Qur'ān on you from on high to make you unhappy, but only as an exhortation to all who stand in awe [of God]: a revelation from Him Who has created the earth and the high heavens, the Merciful, the One established on the throne of His almightiness. To Him belongs all that is in the heavens and all that is on earth, as well as all that is between them and all that is beneath the sod. And if you say anything aloud, well, He indeed knows even the secret thoughts as well as that which is hidden even more deeply. God, there is no deity other than Him; His alone are the attributes of perfection. (1-8)

Softening of a Hard Heart

Impressed, ʿUmar read on, and then he read the whole sheet again. He felt the powerful verses striking their notes on the strings of his heart. He looked at the floor for a moment as he repeated verse 13: "For certain, I – I alone – am God; there is no deity other than Me. Hence, worship Me alone and be constant in prayer, so as to remember Me." He then raised his head and said: "How beautiful and how noble." At this point Khabbāb came out and told ʿUmar about the Prophet's prayer for fresh support to Islam, saying: "I sincerely hope that you will come forward in answer to the Prophet's prayers."[1]

ʿUmar then declared that he wanted to be a Muslim and asked to be taken to the Prophet to declare his submission to God and his belief in the message of Muhammad. ʿUmar did not need much persuasion to tackle such a step. Indeed nobody tried to persuade him, not even his injured sister. Everybody was aware of ʿUmar's enmity towards Islam which was so fierce that no one close to him would have imagined such a change was at all possible.

Some may wonder whether ʿUmar's sense of guilt, which must have been very acute as he saw the blood gushing from his sister's face when he hit her, was the main factor in bringing about such a change. What is known of ʿUmar's personality, before and after his conversion to Islam, lends no support to this argument. What happened was that the sight of blood awakened ʿUmar's sense of justice. He decided to listen to the case of the other side. Hence he asked to look at the sheet his sister was studying. When he read it, he was overwhelmed by the power of the argument and submitted to the truth.

Although ʿUmar asked to be taken to the Prophet, it was judged that it would be better if he went alone with his sword tied to his side. He went to the house which served as a school and a hideout for the new Muslims. Someone looked through a little hole in the door when he knocked. Alarmed at the sight of ʿUmar carrying his sword, he went hurriedly to tell the Prophet. Everyone in Makkah was aware of ʿUmar's strength and courage. Ḥamzah, the Prophet's uncle and a very powerful warrior in his own right, said to the Prophet: "Shall we let him in? If he has come for something good, we will grant him that. If his motive is evil, we will kill him with his own sword."

The door was opened. ʿUmar came in. The Prophet went up to him, took him by the collar and pulled him hard and said: "What brings you here, ʿUmar? It looks to me as if you will not mend your ways until a calamity has befallen you." ʿUmar replied humbly: "Messenger of God! I have come to you to declare that I believe in God and His Messenger and accept what God has revealed." The Prophet said: "God is supreme." Everybody in the house realized that ʿUmar had joined the Islamic camp. They were so delighted because, with him, the Muslims had become infinitely stronger.[2]

It may seem illogical that one man should make such a difference, but the peculiarities of the Arabian tribal society confirm this difference. Two things ʿUmar did immediately after adopting his new religion would provide an insight into the nature of that society.

ʿUmar said: "The night when I became a Muslim I sat up thinking who was the hardest opponent of the Prophet. Abū Jahl was undoubtedly the one. So I went to his house in the morning. He welcomed me heartily and asked what I wanted. I said: 'I have come to tell you that I have embraced Islam and that I now believe in God and His Messenger, Muhammad.' Furious, Abū Jahl slammed the door in my face, saying: 'Confound you and what you have come here for.'" This incident acquires more significance when one realizes that ʿUmar's mother was Abū Jahl's own sister.[3]

That morning, ʿUmar also made the fact of his conversion known to Jamīl ibn Maʿmar, who made it his business to spread every piece of news around Makkah. Immediately, Jamīl was doing his act, telling everybody. ʿUmar was near at hand, confirming the fact with a challenging attitude. A number of men went up to him and he fought them single-handed for an hour or so. Worn out, he sat down and said: "You may do as you like. Had we been three hundred in number, I swear we would have fought it out with you to the bitter end." At that moment, a wise old man from the Quraysh came along. He reprimanded the men, reminding them that the ʿAdiy clan, to which ʿUmar belonged, would not hesitate to avenge him if he came to any harm. So they left him alone.[4]

These two incidents show the sort of strength ʿUmar brought with him to the Muslim camp; a strength which was honest, open and bold. This was to remain the character of ʿUmar's contribution to the cause of Islam throughout his life.

A Show of Strength

It did not take ʿUmar long to grasp the true nature of Islam. He was a man of keen native intelligence. Moreover, he fully appreciated what was needed to grant the small Muslim community in Makkah some sort of status. He wanted to throw a challenge to the Quraysh. Therefore, he suggested to the Prophet that Muslims should go out from their secret school to pray at the Kaʿbah as a group. He defended his view by asking rhetorically: "Are we not following the truth?" The Prophet affirmed that the Muslims were. ʿUmar then asked: "Are they [the Quraysh] not following false beliefs?" Again the Prophet answered in the affirmative. ʿUmar then asked: "Why then should we be the ones who accept humility when it comes to the question of faith?"

The Prophet himself was not against the idea of launching a demonstration of power. He chose forty of his companions who walked in double file from the house of al-Arqam to the Kaʿbah, with his uncle Ḥamzah at the head of one file and ʿUmar at the head of the other. They offered a congregational prayer at the Kaʿbah and dispersed.

That demonstration gave the Quraysh a clear signal that Islam was there to stay. Its followers might be few in number, particularly after many of them had left for Abyssinia, but they had strength of character and powerful new converts. The conflict might be prolonged, unless something was done about it quickly. Any thought of a total war against the Muslims was abandoned, at least for the time being, because the shrewd move of emigration to Abyssinia, which served as a method of thinning out the Muslim forces, ensured that such suggestions would not be met with approval, because the Muslims did not represent an imminent danger to the existing set-up in Makkah. The elders of the tribes recognized that they had a problem to solve, but final solutions were not yet called for. The idea for containment through temptation, which was started by ʿUtbah ibn Rabīʿah as reported in Chapter 9, seemed to offer the best chance of achieving some sort of accommodation. Hence a delegation from the Quraysh went to meet the Prophet, headed by two men known for their 'diplomatic talent', al-Walīd ibn al-Mughīrah and al-ʿĀṣ ibn Wā'il. The delegation made what in any circumstances could be considered a very attractive offer: "We will make you the wealthiest of us all, and we will give you the prettiest of our virgin daughters to marry. We will ask of you nothing in return except to stop abusing our gods and ridiculing our practices."

The poor Quraysh! They could not understand that they were dealing with a man of principle. Their offer did not go beyond what was sure to satisfy any person of ambition. All they came up with was wealth and women. In their small world, there could be nothing more attractive. Besides, they did not ask for anything much in return. They simply wanted Muhammad to accept the principle of compromise and to 'live and let live'. Muhammad should simply leave them alone and not criticize their beliefs or their practices.

Perhaps it is important to point out here that although the Quraysh delegation referred in their offer to a pledge by the Prophet not to 'abuse our gods or ridicule our practices', the Prophet never used any foul or obscene language, even when he criticized idolatrous practices most strongly. His manners were too refined to allow any usage of vulgar or obscene language. Moreover, Muslims are not allowed to refer in such terms to the idols or deities of the polytheists: "Do not revile those beings whom they invoke instead of God lest they revile God out of spite, and in ignorance." (6: 108) The Prophet simply stressed the fact that those false gods had no power to bring benefit or cause harm to anyone. He also criticized ignorant practices, calling for a fundamental change in beliefs, concepts, behaviour and social traditions so as to bring them in line with the basic principle of God's oneness.

Tempting Offers

Deep at heart the chiefs of the Quraysh recognized the strength of the Prophet's argument and the truthfulness of his message. They realized that their own beliefs had no solid foundation and feared that the social structure which brought them all those privileges they enjoyed would soon collapse, as it could not be expected to resist the message of Muhammad for long. Hence, they came up with the proposal of coexistence, coupled with the temptation of wealth and women, which they were ready to provide for Muhammad. God's Messenger, however, made it clear to them that he wanted nothing for himself and would not compromise any principle of his message. He meant to go on preaching it, unhindered by any opposition, hoping to save mankind from tyrannical beliefs and offer them the freedom which is enjoyed only by those who worship God alone.

That should have brought this round of negotiations to a halt, since it was clear that the Prophet was not in a compromising mood. Indeed, he never was. To compromise any principle of his faith never entered his mind, no matter what attractions were on offer. The

Quraysh, however, had a genuine desire to contain the problem. They changed direction and abandoned offers of personal temptation to make a proposal which may be described in human terms as demonstrating an exceptional degree of fairness. They offered to extend full recognition to Muhammad and his message, asking in return only that Muhammad should extend the same treatment to them. Their proposal was simply: "We will worship your God one day and you worship our gods the following day."[5]

Had Muhammad been after any material gain, or had he been a politician or a party leader, he would have jumped at this offer. The Quraysh were not making a simple offer of recognition of the rights and aspirations of their opponents, they were offering full partnership in the government of Makkah, and perhaps Arabia as a whole. One can see in this offer something similar to a grand coalition between two major parties in the political arena in modern times. But the Prophet was an advocate of the truth. He could not simply accept half the truth and sacrifice the other half. Such a sacrifice meant acceptance of half the falsehood. That was not something which could be done by a Prophet, let alone Muhammad, the last of God's messengers to mankind. He was commanded to reply to this offer in the following terms, set out in the Qur'ān: "Say: Disbelievers, I do not worship what you worship, nor do you worship what I worship. I shall never worship what you worship, neither will you worship what I worship. You have your own religion and I have mine." (109: 1-6) Thus this round of negotiations ended like previous ones with the Prophet maintaining his ground, stating that he wanted nothing except a chance to convey his message to people, so that they might accept it if they so wished.

The strained relations between the Prophet and his people continued as he went about fulfilling his task, calling on people to abandon idolatrous beliefs and practices and to worship God alone. There were new converts, but no major breakthrough was to be expected with the sort of determined opposition shown by the Quraysh. However, the hopes of arriving at some sort of accommodation was never far from the minds of at least some of the chiefs. One day, a large group of them met after sunset at the Ka'bah:

famous people like ʿUtbah and Shaybah, the two sons of Rabīʿah, Abū Sufyān ibn Ḥarb, al-Naḍr ibn al-Ḥārith, Abū al-Bakhtarī ibn Hishām, al-Aswad ibn al-Muṭṭalib, Zimʿah ibn al-Aswad, al-Walīd ibn al-Mughīrah, Abū Jahl ibn Hishām, ʿAbdullāh ibn Abī Umayyah, al-ʿĀṣ ibn Wā'il, Umayyah ibn Khalaf and Nabīh and Munbbih, the two sons of al-Ḥajjāj. Inevitably, their discussion drifted to the problem presented by the message preached by the Prophet. Some of them felt that since so many of the chiefs of Makkah were present, an attempt to achieve a compromise with Muhammad could be fruitful. They sent a messenger to tell Muhammad that the leaders of his people wished to speak to him. He came quickly, hoping that they might have started to realize the truthfulness of Islam.

Absurdity Knows No Limits

Nothing would have given him greater pleasure, since he loved his people and cared for their well-being. As he listened to their spokesman, however, he realized that he was in for another futile discussion. The spokesman started with an appraisal of the situation in Makkah and a repetition of an old offer:

> No man in the history of the Arab nation has ever caused his community a problem like the one you have caused: you have insulted our forefathers, criticized our beliefs, reviled our gods, ridiculed our sages and caused division within our community. Indeed, you have been the cause of every bad thing in the relationship between you and us. Nevertheless, we have the following offer to make to you: if you have started this matter of yours in order to become rich, we will pay you from our own money until you are the wealthiest among us. If it is honour that you are seeking, we are prepared to make you our leader and if you seek a kingdom, we will make you our king. On the other hand, if what you experience is some sort of evil spirit which you cannot control, we will seek medical treatment for you and will pay for that whatever is required of us until you have been cured or until we have done everything we can.[6]

One may observe here that these offers were more of a test than a realistic or practical offer. The chiefs of Makkah were simply hoping for the slightest indication from Muhammad that he was after some material gain. That would have given them all the justification they needed to resort to the most violent means in order to suppress his call. He, however, was clear about his priorities and objectives. He said to them:

> I am not after your money, and I do not seek a position or a crown. God has made me His messenger and revealed to me a book and instructed me to give you a message of good tidings and a warning. I have conveyed God's message to you as best as I could and I have given you good counsel. If you accept it from me, it will be good for you in this life and in the life to come. If you turn it down, I will continue to preach it until God settles the issue between us.[7]

Perhaps that should have been the end of the matter, since it was apparent that no change of attitude was possible. But the Quraysh had not brought all its chiefs, hard-liners and moderates alike, just to reiterate old attitudes. Therefore, the elders proceeded to confront Muhammad with impossible demands, making their realization a proof of the truthfulness of his message. How ill-advised and short-sighted! Their spokesman put their demands in the following terms:

> You know that our country is so hard to live in: water is scarce and we are very poor. Pray your Lord Who sent you to us, then, and ask Him to move away these mountains surrounding us and make our land an open plain with rivers similar to those in Syria and Iraq flowing through it. Ask Him also to raise for us a few of our forefathers who should include Quṣayy ibn Kilāb,[8] who was a man of his word, so that we may ask them about what you say and whether it is true or false. If you do that and if they testify for you, we will recognize your high position with God and will believe that you are His messenger.[9]

The line of argument, then, had nothing to do with the subject matter of the conflict between the Quraysh and the Prophet. They said nothing about the oneness of God, the basic principle the Prophet advocated. They did not defend their idols either. They simply wanted mountains to be moved and rivers to flow. Such are the demands of the weak who cannot address the main issue. It is worth commenting here about the request they made that Muhammad should resurrect some of their forefathers, including Quṣayy ibn Kilāb, the one they described as 'a man of his word'. None of them ever met Quṣayy, because he died long before their time. They asked for him specifically because he had earned the reputation of being truthful. Little did they reflect that they had known Muhammad himself for close on 50 years and they had never accused him of telling even the smallest of lies. They knew from their personal experience that he never told a lie. If they could not believe the man whom they knew to tell the truth would they have believed Quṣayy, about whom they had heard from their fathers and grandfathers that he was a man of his word? What if Quṣayy told them what they did not want to hear: that Muhammad was telling the truth? Would they not have turned against him in the same way as they turned against Muhammad when he told them that he was God's messenger?

The Prophet paid no attention to their demands, but simply said to them: "This is not what I was sent to you for. I have conveyed to you the message with which God has entrusted me. If you accept it, you benefit yourselves here and in the life to come. If you deny it, I will await God's judgement between us."[10]

Apparently, the Quraysh chiefs had planned in advance what line they would follow in their discussions with the Prophet and they were determined not to deviate from this predetermined line. They continued to demand acts of a miraculous nature, challenging the Prophet to prove his superiority: "Since you decline that, why do you not get something for yourself? Ask your Lord to send you an angel to endorse what you say and argue your case with us. Ask Him further to give you a palace and a garden and a great amount of gold and silver so that you do not need to work for your living. We will then realize that you are favoured by God, and we would know that your claim to be His messenger is true."[11]

In this request, the Quraysh chiefs betrayed their naïvety and ignorance. They knew Muhammad to be a man of great integrity. Before he preached his message, they always expressed their admiration for his good manners and his moral values. All that was heightened after he received his message, but all these qualities were not equal in their view to material wealth, such as a palace, a garden, and an amount of gold and silver. This, however, did not deter the Prophet from making the proper answer: "I would not ask Him anything of the sort. I am simply sent to deliver good tidings and a warning. If you accept, you benefit yourselves. If you refuse, I will await God's judgement."

All these demands were made by way of trying to exact a price before the Quraysh chiefs changed their view of the message of Prophet Muhammad (peace be upon him). Such attempts to set a price in return for conversion to Islam is often made. It betrays, however, complete ignorance and perfect delusion. Man thinks himself more important than the whole universe. Hence, if he supports an idea, then that idea is indebted to him. If he believes in a particular religion, it is the good fortune of that religion that won him as a believer! Wise human beings tend to examine the issue under discussion and make an objective judgement. This was far from the approach of the Quraysh chiefs in that meeting with the Prophet. They continued their challenge, asking the Prophet now to bring about their doom: "Make the sky break up then, and let it fall over us as you claim your Lord is capable of doing. We will not believe in you unless you do this." How misguided! God tells us in the Qur'ān that on another occasion the Quraysh prayed: "Our Lord, if this be the truth which has come from You, then rain down on us stones from the skies or inflict some other grievous suffering on us!" (8: 32) Indeed, the stupidity of disbelievers is limitless. They ask God to pour over them stones from the skies if Islam be the truth, when they should have prayed God to guide them to the truth, whatever it is.

At this point, the Prophet's answer was very simple and to the point: "That is up to God. If He decides to do that He will." By now, the mood of the Quraysh was that of someone who has deliberately turned a deaf ear to any answer that might be given. They interpreted Muhammad's attitude to their demands as an indication of weakness and powerlessness. Therefore, they said to him: "Muhammad! Was not your Lord aware that we would be meeting you and putting to you these requests and demands? Why has He not told you what answer you should give us or what He will do to us since we have rejected your message?"

Apparently, the meeting degenerated at this point into complete chaos, with each one of those chiefs saying whatever occurred to him without discipline and with a total lack of coherence. Everyone shouted as loud as he could in order to emphasize his opposition to the Prophet. One of them said: "We shall not believe in you until you have brought us God and the angels marshalled in ranks." Another said: "We worship the angels, who are God's daughters." A third said: "We have heard that all this you have been preaching has been taught you by a man from Yamāmah called Raḥmān. We will never believe in this Raḥmān, whatever happens." Yet another said: "By God, we shall not leave you alone after you have done all this to us. We shall fight you until we have destroyed you or you have destroyed us." More voices were heard, a greater lack of coherence, more chaos. The Prophet stood up and walked away, sad and overwhelmed with grief that his people deliberately rejected what they knew to be the truth.

As the Prophet walked away, a cousin of his (the son of his paternal aunt), ʿAbdullāh ibn Abū Umayyah walked by his side, not to console him but to express thoughts that proved that he was an unrivalled lunatic and an uncompromising fool. He said to the Prophet:

> Muhammad, your people made you practical proposals, but you refused them. They asked you to bring them some favours by which they would recognize your high position with God as you claim, but you refused. You even refused to take for yourself things that would prove that you enjoy a position of favour with God. By God, I shall never believe in you until you have stretched a ladder to the sky and climbed up that ladder in front of my eyes until you have reached the sky. You

> then come back here with four angels testifying to the truthfulness of what you say. By God, even if you do all this, I do not think that I will believe in you.

Absurdity knows no limits. A man specifies his own conditions but then says that he would not budge even if his conditions were met.

Was this truly an attempt to achieve compromise or an attempt to force the Prophet into a corner which offered no escape except by admission of defeat? One sees in the offers of the Quraysh only a series of demands which would prove nothing even if they were met. What difference would it have made had the Prophet been given palaces, gardens and enormous wealth, or had the valley of Makkah been transformed into a fertile expanse overnight? The real question was one of faith, which could be based only on conviction. Had the chiefs of Makkah really wanted to know whether Muhammad was a messenger of God, they only needed to look at what he was preaching and study it objectively. That would have been sufficient to reassure them that what he said could not have been invented by a human being. The Prophet tried to persuade them to do that by sticking to his argument that no worldly offer or demand was worth consideration: he was simply a messenger conveying God's message to people. Any person, in whatever station he is, should have the chance to make up his mind whether to accept or reject it.

An Opportunity for Escalation

When the discussion degenerated into the sort of chaos related, the hardliners seized their opportunity with both hands. Abū Jahl, who had said nothing throughout the exchange, tried to capitalize on the anger that was widespread among the chiefs of Makkah. He put to them the solution for which he had longed:

> People of Quraysh! You realize that Muhammad has refused to change his way of ridiculing our religion, insulting our forefathers and abusing our deities. I pledge to the Supreme Deity that I will wait for him tomorrow with a heavy rock

> which I can hardly carry. When he prostrates himself in his prayer, I will throw that rock over his head. It is up to you then to give me up to his clan or to protect me. Let the people of ʿAbd Manāf then do what they will.[12]

Considering the mood of gloom which prevailed over the meeting, Abū Jahl's suggestion held the prospect of an end to the conflict. Even those who would have argued against assassination in normal circumstances could not raise any objection. The chiefs of Makkah gave Abū Jahl the firm pledge of protection, encouraging him to carry out his plan.

The following day, Abū Jahl sat in ambush to carry out his assassination plot. He had his big rock with him. The Prophet came to the Kaʿbah to offer his prayers, as was his custom. Many disbelievers also came to the Kaʿbah and took up their usual positions, chatting as they habitually did but with a spreading air of expectation.

When the Prophet was fully occupied with his prayers and had prostrated himself, putting his forehead on the ground, Abū Jahl drew near with his rock. As he poised over the Prophet's head, his colour changed and his hands were struck motionless. He walked back, absolutely terrified, and threw his rock to the ground. His friends went up to him and asked what was the matter. He said: "You saw me going up to him, resolved to carry out my plan which I explained to you yesterday. When I drew near him, I saw a huge camel standing between me and him. Never in my life had I seen such a camel with such a big head and such big sharp teeth. Had I moved one step nearer, he would have eaten me."[13]

Thus the assassination attempt was foiled and Muhammad was protected by God from the schemes of his enemies. He was guaranteed this protection so that he would be able to convey God's final message to mankind in its entirety. God says in the Qur'ān: "Prophet, announce what is revealed to you from your Lord. If you do not, you will surely have failed to convey His message. God will protect you from all men." (5: 67) It was therefore essential that Muhammad should enjoy such protection. This did not give the Prophet any status apart from the fact that he was God's Messenger and had a role to fulfil. It is God alone who determines how to provide this protection.

Whether the camel Abū Jahl saw was a real camel, or an angel in the shape of a camel, and how it came there and how it then disappeared if it was a real camel are matters of secondary importance. The incident gives us an example of how God accomplishes what He wills in His own way, without interference from anyone. When the Prophet was told of what Abū Jahl said, he commented: "That was Gabriel (peace be to him). Had he drawn nearer, he would have taken him away."[14]

The clouds of despair thickened over the Quraysh as they saw all their attempts to contain the message of Islam rendered futile. No temptation was strong enough to make Muhammad moderate his stand, and no threats could be used against him. Moreover, the Quraysh recognized that they would not be able to assassinate Muhammad, even if they attempted to do so time after time. At no time did the moderates or hardliners of the Quraysh ask themselves what motivated Muhammad into his unshakeable resolve to carry on with his message, or why he should prefer the hard option to that of compromise, with all its promise of wealth, power and pleasure. The only question to which the Quraysh wanted an immediate answer was: how can we prevent Muhammad from exploiting our failure to win new recruits to his religion? That was the main preoccupation of the Quraysh chiefs. To achieve their purpose, they adopted a dual strategy.

More Pressure, More Torture

The Quraysh lost no time in escalating its ruthless campaign of repression. As always, the slaves, the allies and those who lacked influential support among their clans had to bear the brunt of this wicked campaign. The rest of the Muslims were not immune. Even the strongest among them were subjected to great pressure, both physical and mental. In addition, torture of intense severity was inflicted on the weak and the vulnerable.

ʿAbdullāh ibn ʿAbbās, the Prophet's cousin who achieved high scholarly renown, was once asked: "Did disbelievers in Makkah inflict on the companions of the Prophet torture intense enough to justify the latter's turning away from Islam?' He answered:

> Yes, indeed. They used to beat their victims very badly, and allow them nothing to eat or drink, until they could not even sit up. They inflicted so much pain that the victim would give or say anything he was asked just to win a short rest. The situation of some of those victims was so bad that they would answer any questions put to them by their tormentors in the way acceptable to them. The disbelievers would ask: "Are al-Lāt and al-ʿUzzā [two major idols worshipped by the pagan Arabs] your gods?" or "Is this cockroach your lord whom you worship?" In their unbearable plight, the believers might answer these questions in the affirmative.[15]

In fact, God permitted those afflicted people and others who might have found, or may find, themselves in similar situations to give in verbally to their tormentors. They may say what they are asked to say, provided they remain, deep at heart, faithful to their religion. God says in the Qur'ān: "Those who are forced to recant while their hearts remain loyal to the faith shall be absolved; but those who deny God after professing Islam and open their bosoms to unbelief shall incur the wrath of God and be sternly punished." (16: 106)

The other half of this strategy was adopted in another meeting of the Quraysh elders, but this time the Prophet was not present. A man called al-Naḍr ibn al-Ḥārith ibn ʿAlqamah took the floor. By modern standards, al-Naḍr may be described as an intellectual. He had visited Persia, one of the great empires of the day, where he studied history and learnt a great deal about the lives and times of ancient and recent kings and emperors. Al-Naḍr outlined the Quraysh's predicament in this way:

> People of Quraysh, you are confronted with a problem for which you have not been able to find a solution. When Muhammad was still a young man living among you, he won general admiration because he always spoke the truth and his honesty could not be faulted. When he had grown grey, and

> started to preach whatever he is preaching to you, you began to allege that he was a sorcerer. By God, he is no sorcerer. We have seen magicians and their tricks in the past. You also accused him of being a fortune-teller. By God, he is not one, for we have seen fortune-tellers and how they repeat their rhyming phrases. You also claimed that he was a poet. Again I say that, by God, he is not a poet, for we have seen poets and listened to all types of poetry. You claimed that he was also a madman, but he is far from being so. We have seen what madness has done to people, and how it causes them to say incoherent things. I say, people of Quraysh, you have to look at this question very carefully, for you have a big problem on your hands.[16]

That was indeed a very accurate description of what the Quraysh considered to be a disaster that it had to face. It was they who called Muhammad 'Al-Amīn' or 'the trustworthy' when he was a young man because he was, as al-Naḍr himself said, generally admired. He always spoke the truth and displayed a high standard of honesty. Would such an honest young man start lying when he grows old? And would he choose for his lying and fabrications none other than God Himself? But if one were to ask the Quraysh elders why they were so determined to oppose Muhammad when they knew that he spoke the truth, one only betrays naïvety. The Quraysh did not want to know whether Muhammad was truthful or not; they realized that he was telling the truth, as he always did. They simply wanted to find the best means to oppose him and defeat his message.

This situation was to repeat itself time after time, whenever the call to Islam found itself on a collision course with those who wielded power in the land. In history there are many incidents when special committees were formed and study groups were organized for no reason other than mapping a strategy to silence the message of Islam. Every time, those committees and study groups came out with the same results: the advocates of Islam are the best of people, most patriotic, demonstrating great resolve in resisting temptation and corruption. Every time the line to be followed was that of total liquidation.

On this particular occasion, the Quraysh decided to send two people, al-Naḍr ibn al-Ḥārith and ʿUqbah ibn Abī Muʿayṭ, to Yathrib where they would meet the Jewish rabbis and enquire from them about Muhammad and the truthfulness of his message. Without waiting for his visit, al-Naḍr started his own campaign against Islam. He set up for himself a special position in the mosque. Whenever the Prophet addressed a group of people, al-Naḍr would wait until he had left. Then al-Naḍr would say to those people: "I have something better to say to you. Come and listen to a better discourse than his." He would relate to them some of the history of ancient kings. He would then ask them: "What has Muhammad got to say that is better than what I say?" Indeed, it was al-Naḍr who used to describe the Qur'ān as 'tales of the ancients'. The Qur'ān refers to him whenever this is mentioned. The reference is also to him in the verse which speaks of a person who claims: "I shall send down something similar to that which God had sent down."

This attempt by al-Naḍr ibn al-Ḥārith was perhaps the first propaganda campaign against Islam. It was to be followed by numerous, similar campaigns which were to employ better tactics and far-reaching tools as means of communication developed. The message of Islam has always been able to counter such propaganda campaigns with the truth it declares.

When the two-man delegation prepared to set out from Makkah to Yathrib to ask the Jewish rabbis about the Prophet, their terms of reference were outlined to them. The Quraysh elders told al-Naḍr ibn al-Ḥārith and ʿUqbah ibn Abū Muʿayṭ to ask the Jewish rabbis about Muhammad, describing him in detail and reporting truthfully what he said. "The Jews", said the Quraysh elders, "are the people of early scriptures and they have a wealth of knowledge about prophets which is not available to us."

In Yathrib the two Quraysh men put their questions to the rabbis and solicited their honest opinion about Muhammad. The rabbis told them to ask Muhammad three questions. "If he gives you satisfactory answers, then he is a Prophet and a messenger of God. If he has no answer to give, then he is fabricating whatever he says. You may do what you like with him. Ask him about a group of young people who had a strange story in ancient times, and let him tell you what happened to them. Ask him also about a man who travelled all over the place and went to the far east and far west. The third question you should ask him is to tell you about the spirit." One report suggests that the Jewish rabbis told the two Quraysh men that if Muhammad were to give them a detailed answer about the spirit, then they should not believe him. If he refrained from answering this question, then that would confirm that he was a Prophet.

The Quraysh were happy with the results of this mission and wasted no time in putting those three questions to the Prophet. When he heard their questions, the Prophet told them that he would answer them the following day. Apparently he did not qualify this promise by saying: "God willing", as he should have done and as Muslims should always do. As a result, nothing was revealed to him for 15 days. Some reports suggest that it was only a three-day lull before the Angel Gabriel came down with the revelation of *Sūrah* 18, entitled The Cave or *Al-Kahf*. The *sūrah* opens with a statement of praise to God which confirms that it was He who revealed the Qur'ān to His servant and Messenger Muhammad. In other words, this is an answer to the questions the Quraysh put to the Jews. The opening also outlines the role of the messenger: giving a stern warning against Divine punishment and happy news for those who believe and do good works. It refutes the claims of the Quraysh and other disbelievers who ascribe children to God or describe the angels as daughters of God. It states categorically that all such claims are lies. It then tells the Prophet not to grieve too much for his people if they refuse to listen to him. These opening verses may be rendered in English as follows:

> In the name of God, the Merciful, the Beneficent.
>
> All praise is due to God, who has bestowed on His servant this revelation from on high and has not allowed any deviousness to obscure its meaning. It is [a revelation] that is unerringly straight, meant to warn of a severe punishment from Him, and to give to the believers who do good works the glad tidings that theirs shall be a goodly reward – [a state of bliss] which they shall enjoy for ever. Furthermore, [this revelation

> is meant] to warn all those who assert that God has taken to Himself a son. No knowledge whatever have they of Him, and neither had their forefathers: dreadful is this saying that comes out of their mouths, and nothing but falsehood do they utter. Would you, perhaps, torment yourself to death with grief over them if they are not willing to believe in this message. We have willed that all beauty on earth be a means by which We put men to a test [showing] which of them are best in conduct; and indeed We shall in time reduce all that is on it to barren dust. (18: 1-8)[17]

The *sūrah* goes on to give a detailed account of the young men whom it calls 'people of the cave.' The details it gives of what happened to those young men could never have been learnt by the Prophet from a book or a scholar. These details could be provided only by God, who knows everything. This account is outlined in verses 9-26 of the *sūrah*, which then proceeds to speak of other matters before it answers the second question suggested by the Jewish rabbis. Verses 83-98 provide a detailed account of the man named in the *sūrah* as Dhul-Qarnayn and his three trips. There is no shortage of suggestions as to the identity of this man, but perhaps Mawlānā Mawdūdī's view that the man was no other than the Persian king, Cyrus, carries most weight.

As for the third question, there is a short reference to it in verse 85 of *Sūrah* 17, entitled The Night Journey or *al-Isrā'*. This verse may be rendered in translation as follows: "They ask you about the Spirit. Say: [Knowledge of] the Spirit belongs to my Lord and you have been granted very little of real knowledge."

More Hostility, More Defiance

What change would these answers to the questions suggested by the Jews and put to the Prophet by the unbelievers bring about? Certainly not much. Al-Naḍr ibn al-Ḥārith continued with his propaganda campaign, and the Quraysh continued with its persecution of the believers, and the two camps were as far apart as ever. Something new had to be worked out. Something had to happen soon, either to break the deadlock or to pull the two parties further apart. In the particular circumstances of Makkah at that time, further polarization was more likely.

The Muslims in Makkah felt that they could not allow the Quraysh to continue their persecution campaign without asserting their own presence. They started to be more open with their challenge to the unbelievers. Some of them even prayed in congregation at the Ka'bah. Moreover, with 'Umar and Ḥamzah in the ranks of the Muslims, more and more people were joining the new religion.

By now the unbelievers realized that there could be no meeting-ground between them and the Muslims. They were also aware that the tactics they employed to check the tide of Islam were of no great use. A conference was therefore called early in the seventh year of Muhammad's prophethood to find some more effective methods for achieving that ungodly objective.

A Total Boycott

The hard-liners held sway in that conference. They advocated a total boycott of the Muslims and their supporters. Keen to see their plan implemented, they persuaded the other participants to make their resolutions binding on everyone in Makkah. Hence, they wrote down their resolutions on a scroll and posted it inside the Ka'bah. This added an air of solemnity to those resolutions which made it much harder for anyone who cared for the Muslims or wished them well to contravene them.

The terms of the boycott were so strict as to rule out any intermarriages or trade transactions between the Hāshimite clan as a whole and the rest of the Quraysh. The Hāshimites were defiant; they joined ranks. The Muslims and the unbelievers among them were unanimous in their support of their leader, Abū Ṭālib, who, in turn, did not waver in his wholehearted support of his nephew. One exception, however, was Abū Ṭālib's own brother, Abū Lahab.

Abū Lahab was hostile to Islam right from the beginning. He could not bring his tribal loyalties in line with the rest of the

Hāshimite clan. He therefore broke off relations with his own clan and joined the boycott. Although his action was so obviously out of line with the traditions of Makkan society, the Quraysh were very happy with his decision to join them, since it showed that opposition to Muhammad was so widespread that even his own kinsfolk wanted to get rid of him. Perhaps one should add here that the terms of the boycott spelled out the conditions for its termination: that the Hāshimites must give up Muhammad to the Quraysh, whereupon he would be killed.

All the Hāshimite clan, including the non-Muslims among them, along with Muslims of other tribes suffered a great deal as a result of the boycott. If a tradesman or a farmer brought some goods or provisions to sell in Makkah, he was offered much more than his asking price on condition that he would not sell anything to the Hāshimites, who were confined to their quarters. The situation became very grave indeed as month after month went by with no flicker of hope for a quick end to this harsh boycott. Starvation was the order of the day for the Muslims and the Hāshimites. Their children cried themselves to sleep every night. Occasionally there was some relief as some kind-hearted person, moved by the cries of hungry children, would smuggle relief supplies through to the Hāshimite quarters under cover of darkness.

Such very welcome relief was bound to be temporary. The hardship continued for nearly three years. While the non-Muslims among the Hāshimites suffered from the boycott, the Muslims in general were subjected to much more persecution. That, however, did not weaken their resolve to hold fast to their new religion and to try to propagate it to their fellow citizens. They continued to do so patiently and tirelessly, under the supervision of the Prophet, the perfect example of a man of perseverance and confidence that his cause was sure to triumph.

In practical terms, the boycott imposed by the Quraysh meant a great deal of hardship which was equally endured by men, women and children. For three years, the Hāshimites were practically prevented from buying anything on the open market, even food for their families. The following report by Saʿd ibn Abū Waqqāṣ provides a glimpse of the suffering of the Muslims in this period: "I went out one night to relieve myself. [The Arabs did not have toilets in their homes at that time.] The urine fell over something which crackled. I picked it up. It was a piece of camel skin which had dried. I washed it well before burning it and mixing it thoroughly with water. It was my food for three days."

Humanitarian Feelings Aroused

This moved some kind people to act to relieve the hardship of the boycotted people a little. A man called Hishām ibn ʿAmr did more than anybody else to help the Hāshimites. Hishām enjoyed a position of respect among his people. His help started by smuggling food and clothes to the Hāshimites in their quarter. He would load a camel with provisions or material and take it, under cover of darkness, to the entrance of the Hāshimite quarter, where he would release it so that it went in.

Meanwhile, God caused the writing which spelled out the covenant of boycott to disappear. He informed the Prophet of what had happened to that scroll posted inside the Kaʿbah. Moths had eaten all the writing which contributed to the injustice suffered by the Hāshimites. Whenever God's name was mentioned, it remained as it was. The Prophet informed his uncle Abū Ṭālib, who, in turn, informed his brothers. They went out together to the Kaʿbah, where Abū Ṭālib said to the chiefs of Makkah: "My nephew, who has never told a lie to me, has informed me that God has caused moths to eat up everything that contained injustice or boycott of kinsfolk in your covenant. The only thing that has remained is God's name. Let us go together and find out whether my nephew has told the truth. If what he says is true, then you give in and stop your injustice. If he has told a lie, I will give him up to you, and you may kill or spare him."

They agreed to his suggestion and said that it was fair. They sent someone to look at the covenant and it was exactly as the Prophet had described. They were at a loss and regretted their agreeing to Abū Ṭālib's suggestion. They made it clear that they would continue with their boycott. Abū Ṭālib asked them: "What have we done to deserve this state of siege imposed on us, when everything has been made clear?" He and his companions went straight to the Ka'bah and entered between its robes and its walls.[18]

They pleaded: "Our Lord, give us victory over those who have dealt unjustly with us, severed our ties and done away with what they had no title to take from us."

Abū Ṭālib and his brothers then went back to their quarters. The scene was witnessed by many a person in the Quraysh who was unhappy with the boycott. They felt that they could not just sit idle while their kinsfolk, with their women and children, suffered deprivation and hunger. Hishām ibn 'Amr was the first to recognize that whatever help he could give by smuggling supplies into the quarters of the Hāshimite clan could do very little to help them. He felt that he could not do much on his own. He needed to work out a plan which could foil any attempt by Abū Jahl to continue with the boycott.

So he went to Zuhayr ibn Abī Umayyah who belonged to the Makhzūm clan, to which Abū Jahl also belonged. Zuhayr's mother was the Prophet's own aunt. Hishām's approach was to arouse Zuhayr's feelings of loyalty. He said:

> Are you happy to sit back, enjoying your food, wearing whatever clothes you fancy, able to marry as you wish, while your uncles are confined in their quarters: no one buys from them or sells anything to them, and no one accepts any marriage contracts with them. I swear by God that had they been the uncles of Abū al-Ḥakam ibn Hishām [Abū Jahl's original name] and you made an approach to him to boycott them in the same way as he asked you to boycott your own uncles, he would never have consented to join in.

Zuhayr was overwhelmed by the strength of the argument, but said: "What can I do on my own, Hishām? If I have one man to support me, I would do all I can until I see that covenant of boycott abrogated." Hishām assured him of his own support but Zuhayr suggested that they should first try to get another man to support them.

Hishām then went to al-Muṭʿim ibn ʿAdiy, who belonged to the clan of ʿAbd Manāf from which the Hāshimites branched out. Al-Muṭʿim was a man who enjoyed a position of honour and respect among the Quraysh. Hishām appealed to his values of justice and integrity: "Are you happy to see two clans [Hāshim and ʿAbd al-Muṭṭalib] of ʿAbd Manāf starve to death before your own eyes? Do you not realize that if you remain quiet, the rest of the Quraysh will press on and get away with it?"

Al-Muṭʿim also protested his inability to do much on his own. Hishām told him of the support he could offer along with Zuhayr. Al-Muṭʿim suggested that yet more support was required. Hishām then secured the support of two others, Abū al-Bakhtarī ibn Hishām and Zamʿah ibn al-Aswad.

The five met and agreed their plan of action. The following morning, at the appointed time, Zuhayr came to the Kaʿbah wearing one of his best garments. He walked round the Kaʿbah seven times, performing the *ṭawāf*, before addressing the people there in these words: "Fellow Makkans! Are we to go on enjoying our food, and wearing the best clothes, while the Hāshimites are starving; no one dare buy from them or sell to them? By God, I shall not sit until this oppressive covenant of boycott is torn to pieces." Abū Jahl, who was sitting in a corner, said: "You are a liar. By God, no one will touch it." Zamʿah then said to Abū Jahl: "You are a worse liar! We did not approve of it when it was written." Abū al-Bakhtarī then came to his support, saying: "Zamʿah is right. We do not sanction its terms."

Further support came from al-Muṭʿim, who said: "You are right and whoever disputes what you say is a liar. We disclaim it in front of God." Hishām, who engineered the whole plan, also declared his support.

Abū Jahl was confounded. He simply said: "This has been planned somewhere else. It could not have come on the spur of the moment."

Al-Muṭʿim then rose and went to the Kaʿbah to pull the covenant out and tear it. He found that nothing of its writing remained, with the exception of the expression: 'In Your name, Our Lord.'[19]

Thus ended a period of excessive hardship which the Prophet and his companions endured with patience, confident that their cause would come out of it much stronger.

By now Muhammad had been preaching the message of Islam for close on ten years, but the overall situation could not be described as promising. The Quraysh were successful in the attempt to confine Islam to Makkah itself. Even in Makkah, Muslims were still a minority. Apart from the distant base in Abyssinia, Islam was virtually unknown outside Makkah. There seemed to be no great prospect for the final Divine message. But God accomplishes His purposes through a variety of methods some of which may be totally unexpected by human beings.

Notes

1. Ibn Hishām, *al-Sīrah al-Nabawiyyah*, Dār al-Qalam, Beirut, Vol. 1, pp. 367-370.
2. Ibid., pp. 370-371.
3. Ibid., p. 375.
4. Ibid., pp. 373-374.
5. Ibn Sayyid al-Nās, *ʿUyūn al-Athar*, Dār al-Turāth, Madinah, 1996, p. 197.
6. Ibn Hishām, op.cit., pp. 315-316.
7. Ibid., p. 316.
8. Although Quṣayy was an ancestor of the Prophet, a seventh generation grandfather, he was in the same relationship to many of the Prophet's interlocutors. He was the one who established the Quraysh's position in Makkah.
9. Ibn Hishām, op.cit., p. 316.
10. Ibid., pp. 316-317.
11. Ibid., pp. 317-318.
12. Ibid., pp. 318-319.
13. Ibid., pp. 319-320.
14. Ibid., p. 320.
15. Ibid., pp. 342-343.
16. Ibid., p. 320.
17. Ibid., pp. 321-323.
18. The Kaʿbah has always had cloth coverings, normally black. If one goes underneath this covering, that is, its robes, one's action signifies a more earnest supplication. The practice is not Islamic. A person in fear may hold the robes of the Kaʿbah to imply that he earnestly seeks God's protection.
19. Ibn Hishām, op.cit., pp. 375-380. Also, Ibn Sayyid al-Nās, op.cit., pp. 222-225.

12

Difficulties in Abundance

ALTHOUGH THE PERIOD of boycott, which lasted for three years, meant that a large section of the Makkan population endured great hardship, it was not without some benefit to Islam. For one thing, it ensured that newcomers would belong only to that breed of people who support the truth regardless of what they may have to endure as a result. Despite the boycott, new recruits to Islam continued to trickle through, albeit on a very limited scale. They were, however, of the calibre no ideology can do without.

Another benefit of the boycott could be seen in the way it was ended. The suffering of the Hāshimites moved the kind hearted among the unbelievers to take action in defiance of the hard-liners like Abū Jahl. This caused disarray in the ranks of the unbelievers. Moreover, the hard-liners appeared in a bad light, since they opposed an act of kindness to their kinsfolk.

Furthermore, the boycott was a period of relative lull in the conflict between the Muslims and the unbelievers. There was little contact between the two parties. Therefore, many of the Quraysh personalities had time to reflect on Islam, the message of the Prophet contained in the Qur'ān. To them, the Qur'ān was something wonderful. It spoke so powerfully that they could not turn away when it was recited. The hardliners who continued to hold sway felt that they must do something to stop the general public listening to the Qur'ān. Everyone was told that they should not listen to the Qur'ān when they heard it. Instead, they should raise their voices so as not to hear it. This is not much different from dictatorial regimes jamming other nations' radio stations to keep their populations ignorant of what is taking place elsewhere, or indeed of oppression in their own countries. But the Qur'ān had its attraction even to the most outspoken enemies of Islam. They realized that Muhammad spent some time every night in worship reading the Qur'ān in prayer. Therefore, protected by the cover of darkness, some of them sat just outside his house, listening to the Qur'ān being recited inside. Every one of them was on his own, thinking that no one would know about his action. One can only assume that the motivation was either to try to judge the message of Muhammad objectively, or to learn the truth about it, or to listen to the superb literary style of the Qur'ān. As the day began to break, each one of them went back so that no one could find out about his action. Soon, the three of them: Abū Jahl himself, Abū Sufyān and al-Akhnas ibn Sharīq met. There was no need to ask each other what they were doing. There was only one reason for their presence there at that particular time. Therefore, they counselled each other against such action: "Should some of your followers see you," one of them said, "you would stir doubts in their minds."

The following night they did the same, and once again they met at the break of day. Again they counselled each other against their 'irresponsible' action. Nevertheless, the third night each of them went to sit outside the Prophet's home and listen to the Qur'ān. When they met in the morning, they felt ashamed of themselves. One of them suggested that they should give each other their word of honour not to come again. They did so before going home.

Later that morning al-Akhnas ibn Sharīq went to see Abū Sufyān in his home. He asked him what he thought about what he heard Muhammad reciting. Abū Sufyān said: "I heard things which I know and recognize to be true, but I also heard things whose nature I cannot understand." Al-Akhnas said that he felt the same. He then left and went to Abū Jahl's home to put the same question to him.

Abū Jahl's answer was totally different. For once, he was candid and honest with himself and his interlocuter:

> "I will tell you about what I heard! We have competed with the clan of ʿAbd Manāf for honours: they fed the poor, and we did the same; they provided generous support to those who needed it and we did the same. When we were together on the same level, like two racehorses running neck and neck, they said that one of their number was a Prophet receiving revelations from on high! When can we attain such an honour? By God, we shall never believe in him."[1]

Last-Minute Negotiations

Shortly after that, Abū Ṭālib, the Prophet's protector, was taken ill. He was an old man, over 70 years of age. It was clear that his illness would be terminal. The Quraysh leaders conferred among themselves on what the death of Abū Ṭālib might signify in their relations with his nephew, Muhammad, the Prophet of Islam. They said to each other: "Ever since Ḥamzah and ʿUmar became Muslims, the strength of Islam has continued to grow. Now Muhammad's followers come from all clans of the Quraysh. Let us go to Abū Ṭālib so that he may work out some sort of accommodation between us and his nephew. Who could guarantee that they would not try to take power in this city of ours?"

A strong delegation, including the most distinguished among them such as ʿUtbah, Shaybah, Abū Jahl, Umayyah ibn Khalaf and Abū Sufyān, went to Abū Ṭālib, enquiring after his health. They then said to him: "You know how distinguished your position is among us, and how much we respect you. In your present condition we candidly say that we fear the worst for you. You are aware of the strained relations between your nephew and ourselves. We suggest that you call him and let both him and us give you some form of pledges so that each party will leave the other alone and we establish a peaceful relationship between him and us."

Superficially, this was a very 'innocent' approach. The Quraysh seemed to offer a fair deal which guaranteed freedom for both sides. The fact was that they wanted nothing less than a complete cessation of the new message. The Prophet should no longer speak about

God's Oneness. This is clear in the ensuing dialogue between the two sides.

Abū Ṭālib called the Prophet and said to him: "These are the leaders of your people. They have asked to see you for an arrangement of give and take." Addressing the delegation, the Prophet said: "I ask of you only one word. Should you give me that, your authority over all the Arabs will be strengthened. The non-Arabs will also submit to you."

Thinking that this signified a shift in the Prophet's position, Abū Jahl said: "Yes, indeed. We will give you that, and ten words like it. What is it you ask of us?"

Was this a blank cheque Abū Jahl was offering to the Prophet? It seemed so, but Abū Jahl was not of the compromising type.

God's Messenger, the advocate of truth and the herald of every good thing, put his request clearly: "You declare that you believe in the Oneness of God and renounce the worship of any deity beside Him." He wanted nothing for himself: no wealth, position, honour or authority. He wanted everything for his message. He required them to abandon all deities other than God, be they made of stone or of flesh and blood.

The Quraysh delegation understood clearly what Muhammad wanted. They clapped in disapproval.[2]

One of them said: "Do you, Muhammad, want to have only one God instead of all those deities? That is very strange indeed!"

Recognizing that there was no possibility of a compromise, the delegation left in disappointment.

When they had gone, Abū Ṭālib said to the Prophet: "My nephew, I do not think you asked them too much." Encouraged by this remark, the Prophet said: "Then you, Uncle, say that word. It will benefit you on the Day of Judgement." Abū Ṭālib said: "If it was not for fear that you and your clan would be abused after I had gone, and for fear that the Quraysh would think I said it because I was afraid of death, I would have certainly said it to please you."

One report suggests that al-ʿAbbās, Abū Ṭālib's brother, noticed his lips moving just before he died. He stooped to listen, then he raised his head and confirmed to the Prophet that Abū Ṭālib made that declaration which would have included him among the Muslims. In reply, the Prophet said: "I have heard nothing." It is simply not known whether Abū Ṭālib was a Muslim when he died.[3]

The Prophet was very sad to lose his uncle. Abū Ṭālib was the man who brought up Muhammad, the orphan who had lost both his parents and his grandfather by the time he was eight years old. He took him into his family and treated him like his own son, giving him extra kindness out of sympathy for the bereaved child. When Muhammad grew up, Abū Ṭālib recognized that he had a nephew of great standing, combining strength of character with high moral standards and refined manners. Moreover, Abū Ṭālib was the protector of Muhammad, the Prophet of Islam, when he needed protection. His loss meant a great deal to the Prophet. After Abū Ṭālib's death, the irresponsible characters of the Quraysh started abusing the Prophet with word and deed.

Tragedy Strikes Again

Within five weeks of Abū Ṭālib's death, the Prophet suffered another great loss: his loving wife Khadījah died. Reports are not very clear who of the two died first, but their deaths came in quick succession. To Muhammad, Khadījah was a kind, loving wife who cared deeply for her husband and for his mission. With her, he found all the comfort a man expects of an understanding wife. She shared with him all his feelings and worries. She had known his worth ever since she had proposed marriage to him. When he received his message, she was the first to believe in it. From that day on, she was his main supporter. No matter what problems he met outside, he was certain of finding comfort in his home. Her departure meant that he could no longer find the compassion with which she comforted him after the many disappointments he received from the Quraysh.[4]

In other words, the Prophet lost his internal and external support within a very brief period of time. He was now more vulnerable to the Quraysh's attacks. In later years, recalling memories of this period, the Prophet said: "The Quraysh could not cause me much harm until Abū Ṭālib died." Once Abū Ṭālib departed from the scene, the Prophet had to bear an increasing degree of the Quraysh's persecution. One day, an idiot stopped the Prophet and threw dust over his head. Some of the Quraysh leaders were delighted to see the Prophet being publicly humiliated. He went home with dust on his head. One of his daughters went up to him to clean his head, tears pouring down her cheeks. He comforted her saying: "Do not cry, young daughter, God will protect your father."[5]

In an authentic *ḥadīth*, Muslim relates on the authority of ʿAbdullāh ibn Masʿūd:

> God's Messenger was once praying at the Kaʿbah, while Abū Jahl sat with a few of his friends not far away. Some camels had been slaughtered the day before. Abū Jahl came up with a devilish suggestion, saying to his friends: "Which of you would be prepared to take the stomach of the camel slaughtered yesterday and put it on Muhammad's back when he prostrates himself?" One of them did just that, while the rest of them laughed. I was standing by, feeling my powerlessness that I could not even take that dirt off the Prophet's back. The Prophet continued in his prostration, unable to lift his head, until someone went to tell his daughter, Fāṭimah, who was just a young girl. She came and took it off his back. She went to those people of the Quraysh and abused them. When the Prophet finished his prayer, he raised his head to the sky and uttered a little prayer: "My Lord, I appeal to You against the Quraysh." He said this three times. When they heard him saying this prayer, they stopped laughing and felt afraid. He then said: "My Lord, I appeal to You against Abū Jahl ibn Hishām, ʿUtbah ibn Rabīʿah, Shaybah ibn Rabīʿah, al-Walīd ibn ʿUtbah, Umayyah ibn Khalaf, ʿUqbah ibn Abū Muʿayṭ" (and he mentioned a seventh person whose name slips my mind). By God who sent Muhammad with the message of the truth, I saw all those he named killed at Badr. They were buried there in the well which served as a mass grave for the unbelievers who died at Badr.[6]

Some of the Prophet's neighbours were tempted to cause him whatever harm they could. When his family wanted to cook something for him, they put animal dirt in his cooking pan. The Prophet took that off with a stick, stood on his own doorstep and called to his clan: "You children of ʿAbd Manāf! What sort of neighbourly kindness is this?" He then threw the dirt away.[7]

Worse was still to come, for it appeared that the death of Abū Ṭālib meant that the Hāshimites' resolve to protect the Prophet became considerably weaker. With memories still fresh in their minds of the hard times they had just gone through when they were boycotted by the Quraysh, and with Abū Lahab, the Prophet's own uncle, joining the rest of the Quraysh in their stiff opposition, the Hāshimites were keenly aware of the high price they were paying for their protection of Muhammad. Like the rest of the Quraysh clans, the majority of the Hāshimites were still holding to their pagan beliefs. Hence it was not surprising that many of them decided to cut their losses and withold their support, which they had previously extended to Muhammad on grounds of tribal loyalty.

The Trip to Ṭā'if

This new situation meant that the Prophet had to explore new avenues in his search for support. After long deliberation, he set out on foot for Ṭā'if, a mountainous town about 110 kilometres from Makkah. His only companion on this trip was his faithful servant, Zayd ibn Ḥārithah.

Ṭā'if was populated by the Thaqīf, the second largest tribe in Arabia. As he began his journey, Muhammad was full of hope. If the Thaqīf would respond favourably to the call of Islam, that would signify a new, happier phase in the history of the Divine message.

Once at Ṭā'if, the Prophet approached its leading personalities, explaining his message and calling on them to believe in God and to support him in his efforts to establish the Islamic code of living. Ṭā'if was the town where the major idol, al-Lāt, had its temple. The Thaqīf had tried to give al-Lāt a special status and to make its temple one to be visited by other Arabs, on a similar footing to the Kaʿbah. The

Thaqīf were fully aware of what the Prophet advocated. Its leaders had similar considerations to those of the Quraysh in determining their attitude to the Prophet. For ten days the Prophet spoke to one chief after another. None gave him a word of encouragement. The worst response came from three brothers, the sons of ʿAmr ibn ʿUmayr. These three brothers, ʿAbd Yālīl, Masūd and Ḥabīb, were the recognized leaders of Ṭā'if. One of them was married to a Qurayshi woman and the Prophet hoped that this relationship would work in his favour. In the event the three men were extremely rude in their rejection of the Prophet's approach.

The first one said: "I would tear the robes of the Kaʿbah if it was true that God has chosen you as His Messenger." The second said: "Has God found no one other than you to be His Messenger?" The third said: "By God, I will never speak to you. If it is true that you are God's Messenger, you are too great for me to speak to you. If, on the other hand, you are lying, you are not worth answering."

Fearing that the news of their rejection would serve to intensify the Quraysh's hostility to Islam, the Prophet requested the Thaqīf notables not to publicize his mission. They refused him even that. Instead they set on him a crowd of their teenagers and servants, who chased and stoned him. His feet were soon bleeding and he was in a very sorry state. Zayd tried hard to defend him and protect him from the stones. The Prophet then sought refuge in an orchard which belonged to two brothers from Makkah. They were in their orchard, and they saw Muhammad when he entered. At first they watched him quietly, but he did not see them.

As the Prophet sat down, he said this highly emotional and touching prayer:

> To You, My Lord, I complain of my weakness, lack of support and the humiliation I am made to receive.
>
> Most compassionate and merciful! You are the Lord of the weak, and You are my Lord. To whom do You leave me? To a distant person who receives me with hostility? Or to an enemy to whom You have given power over me?
>
> If You are not displeased with me, I do not care what I face. I would, however, be much happier with Your mercy.

> I seek refuge in the light of Your face by which all darkness is dispelled and both this life and the life to come are put on their right courses against incurring Your wrath or being the subject of Your anger. To You I submit, until I earn Your pleasure. Everything is powerless without Your support.

The owners of the orchard were none other than ʿUtbah and Shaybah, the two sons of Rabīʿah, who commanded positions of high esteem in the Quraysh. Although the two brothers were opposed to Islam and to Muhammad, they felt sorry for him in his unenviable plight. Therefore, they called a servant of theirs, named ʿAddās, and told him to take a bunch of grapes on a plate to Muhammad. ʿAddās, who was a Christian from the Iraqi town of Nineveh, complied.

As the Prophet took the grapes he said, as Muslims do before eating: 'In the name of God.' Surprised, ʿAddās said: "This is something no one in these areas says." When ʿAddās answered the Prophet's question about his religion and place of origin, the Prophet commented: "Then you come from the same place as the noble Divine Jonah." Even more surprised, ʿAddās asked: "How did you know about Jonah? When I left Nineveh, not even ten people knew anything about him. The Prophet said: "He was my brother. Like me, he was a Prophet." ʿAddās then kissed the Prophet's head, hands and feet in a gesture of genuine love and respect. As they watched, one of the two owners of the orchard said to his brother: "That man has certainly spoilt your slave."

When ʿAddās joined them they asked him the reason for his very respectful attitude to Muhammad. He said: "There can be no one on earth better than him. He has indeed told me something which no one but a Prophet would know." They said: "You should be careful, ʿAddās. He may try to convert you while your religion is better than his."[8]

It is clear from their attitude that although they might be kind to the Prophet in a situation which aroused their nobler feelings of pity and compassion, they begrudged him even the slightest gain from his unsuccessful trip. ʿAddās did not follow his masters' religion. Their opinion of Christianity was not at all flattering. Yet they would rather have their slave sticking to it than following Muhammad, so that the Islamic camp might remain weak. In this, the two Makkan chiefs were no different from others who have taken a stand of opposition to Islam throughout history. Even the slightest gain Islam achieves pains them.

The Long Journey Back Home

The Prophet then set out on his journey back to Makkah. He stopped at Nakhlah, not very far from Makkah. Considering the situation he was in from all angles, he realized that the Quraysh might prevent him from entering Makkah again. Worse, they might kill him or have him locked up. There was only one way out: to seek the protection of one of their notables.

The nature of Arabian tribal society was such that any individual coming into a town or a tribe needed to have an alliance with, or protection from, a man of good standing in that town or tribe. Normally people of such standing would extend their protection to anyone who sought it, because by doing so they enhanced their own standing and reputation. In the case of the Prophet, however, the first two people his messenger approached, al-Akhnas ibn Sharīq and Suhayl ibn ʿAmr, declined. The third, al-Muṭʿim ibn ʿAdiy, responded favourably. He and his children and nephews took up their arms and went to the mosque. He then sent word to the Prophet to enter. The Prophet came up to the mosque and walked round it seven times, guarded by his protectors.[9]

Abū Jahl, dismayed at the loss of this chance of putting an end to Muhammad, asked al-Muṭʿim: "Are you a follower or a protector?" Al-Muṭʿim confirmed that he was only protecting Muhammad. Abū Jahl then declared that there would be no intervention to threaten such protection.

The Prophet then went home safely. He had learnt, however, a very important lesson: that he must not venture outside Makkah before first completing the necessary groundwork which ensured a good reception for his message and his own safety.

This disappointing trip to Ṭā'if had a profound effect on the Prophet. He was deeply hurt by the hostility of some of those Thaqīf leaders. Several years later, ʿĀ'ishah, his wife, asked the Prophet after the defeat suffered by the Muslims in Uḥud, their second major battle against the Quraysh: "Have you ever gone through a day harder than that of Uḥud?"

He replied: "I have suffered a great deal from your people; but the worst I have been through was on the Day of al-ʿAqabah. I offered myself to ʿAbd Yalīl ibn ʿAbd Kallāl, but he rejected my offer. I left him in a very depressed mood, and I did not come to myself until I reached Qarn al-Thaʿālib. I raised my head to find a cloud over me. I looked up and saw Gabriel (peace be to him) speaking to me: 'God has heard what reply your people gave you, and He has sent you the angel in charge of the mountains to carry out your orders.' The angel of the mountains greeted me: 'God has heard what your people said in reply to you, and He has sent me to you to be at your service. If you wish, I will bring the mountains over their heads, and if you wish, I will cause the earth to swallow them.' I said to him: 'No, I hope that God will bring out from their offspring people who worship Him alone and associate no partners with Him'."[10]

When the Prophet re-entered Makkah after his disappointing journey to Ṭā'if, he must have felt that he was in a very dire situation. Within the same year he had lost his loving wife and his uncle, who afforded him unwavering support. His attempt to compensate for this dual loss with outside support not only failed to win him anything, but also compelled him to seek the protection of al-Muṭʿim, a Quraysh notable who did not believe in Islam. Muhammad was by now fully aware that he could no longer rely on his own clan, the Hāshimites, for any measure of firm support. He felt himself alone in the whole world. His few followers were no match for the forces opposing him. Yet he firmly believed in the truth of the message he was preaching. His faith in God did not waver.

Comfort on the Way

At this point something unusual happened to him. One night, as the Prophet was asleep in the home of his cousin Umm Hāni' bint Abī Ṭālib in Makkah, the Angel Gabriel came and woke him up and took him by hand to the mosque, where he found an animal smaller than a mule but slightly bigger than a donkey. The animal, which was a quadruped, also had two wings and floated easily as he moved with unimaginable speed. The Prophet's own description of his movement was that "he put his foot at the furthest point to his side".

Together, the Prophet and Gabriel rode the animal, which was called Al-Burāq, a name derived from 'Barq', meaning lightning. In no time at all they reached Jerusalem in Palestine. There the Prophet met Abraham, Moses, Jesus and other noble prophets. He led them all in prayer. He was then brought three cups: one contained milk, another contained wine, and the third contained water. He drank the milk. When he had finished, Gabriel said, "You and your nation are rightly guided."

When they had finished their business in Jerusalem, they flew up to heaven. The Prophet tells us that as they entered each of the seven heavens Gabriel would confirm to its guardian angel that Muhammad had already received his mission. In each heaven he met one or other of the prophets who preached the message of God's oneness to mankind. Among those mentioned in the authentic accounts of this very special journey were Adam, Jesus, John, Joseph, Moses and Abraham.

He also saw examples of the suffering which would be endured by certain groups of people, as they would be condemned to hell in the hereafter. The description of these groups and their suffering is so vivid that one can almost see them in their plight, yet the suffering was so horrible that one would do anything to escape it.

The Prophet was then admitted into Paradise and saw examples of the happiness to be enjoyed by those who would seek God's pleasure and do His bidding. Here the Prophet was delighted with what he saw and expressed his wish that all his followers would be able to partake of such enjoyments. While he was in Paradise he was informed of the obligatory prayers he and his followers were expected to offer.

As he passed Moses on his way back, Moses asked him about this particular point of prayer. When Muhammad informed him that Muslims would be required to pray 50 times each day, Moses counselled him to go back and pray God to reduce this requirement, commenting: "Prayers constitute a heavy burden and your nation is weak." The Prophet acted on this advice, and God reduced this obligation to 40 prayers each day.

When he stopped by Moses again, Moses repeated the same advice. Again the Prophet acted on it. The whole procedure was repeated several times until the obligatory prayers for Muslims were reduced to five daily. Moses still thought they were hard to observe and counselled the Prophet to request a further reduction. The Prophet, however, felt too shy to do that.

The Prophet then returned to Makkah, having been absent only for part of the night; he returned just before dawn. On this unique trip, he witnessed the expanse of the universe as well as the link between our life in this world and the greater and larger life of the other world. God also wanted him to see other signs and symbols which filled his blessed heart with unshakeable faith.

Since he was taken on that unique journey from the house of his cousin Umm Hānī', where he was staying that night, it was to her house that he returned. Everyone in the house soon woke up. When they had finished their dawn prayers, the Prophet told Umm Hānī' about his journey. A firm believer, she accepted what the Prophet related as true. When he was about to leave, intending to go to the mosque, she stopped him, saying: "I fear that people would not believe you if you tell them what you have just told me." The Prophet made clear his intention to tell them "even though they would not believe me".

When he was sitting in the mosque, he was totally absorbed in his thoughts. Abū Jahl, the arch-enemy of Islam, noticed that and came up to him to ask: "Any news?" The Prophet replied: "Yes. I was taken last night to Jerusalem." Making sure that he had heard him correctly, Abū Jahl asked: "To Jerusalem?" The Prophet's clear answer came in the affirmative. Realizing that there was a chance to consolidate the opposition to Muhammad and his message, Abū Jahl asked him: "If I call the others to come over, would you repeat to them what you have just told me?" Unhesitatingly, the Prophet said: "Yes."

Thus Abū Jahl did what the Prophet intended to do, that is, to gather the people so that he would tell them about his journey. When the Prophet had finished his story, everybody was expressing disbelief in one way or another. Some people clapped, some put their hands over their heads and others jeered. One of them asked about the caravan the Quraysh had sent to Syria. The Prophet gave a detailed answer on its conditions and specified its arrival time. They went out at the appointed time and, to their surprise, there was the caravan in exactly the same condition the Prophet had described. Yet that did not influence or weaken their opposition to the Prophet.

As the Prophet's account of his journey was completed, there were many unbelievers going around into every quarter in Makkah to relate what sounded to them the most incredible story ever told. Some of them went straight to Abū Bakr, the Prophet's closest friend, to tell him and to find out what his reaction would be. Abū Bakr first accused them of bringing him false stories. When they assured him that Muhammad actually claimed to have made the return journey to Jerusalem overnight, Abū Bakr's answer was: "If he has actually said this, he is telling the truth." When they expressed their amazement that he would believe such a singular story, Abū Bakr said: "What is so surprising? I believe him when he says something even more incomprehensible. He says he receives revelations from God and I believe him."

Abū Bakr then went to the mosque where people were still gathered around the Prophet expressing their disbelief. He asked the Prophet whether he made the statement that he went to Jerusalem and came back on the same night. When he heard the Prophet's affirmative reply, Abū Bakr said: "I believe you; you always tell the truth." Then he asked the Prophet to describe Jerusalem. As the Prophet went on with his description, Abū Bakr kept repeating his words: "I believe you; you always tell the truth." The Prophet was so pleased with Abū Bakr that he gave him the title Ṣiddīq, which denotes 'a true and firm believer'. This was Abū Bakr's most cherished title which he kept for the rest of his life.[11]

A small number of people rejoined the unbelievers after accepting Islam. The Prophet, however, was not influenced by their apostasy. He continued to preach his message with unshaken determination.

Direct Confrontation with Adversity

Two points need to be made here: the first concerns the example provided by the Prophet for all advocates of Islam. He faced the Quraysh with his story, fully aware that he would be accused of telling lies. That did not influence his determination to do what was required of him. The interests of his message came first. People's accusations could not weaken his resolve.

The point is that people may accept the idea of revelations but turn away from Islam for lesser reasons. In this case they found it difficult to accept the idea that God could take His Messenger on a journey like this while they believed that He would inspire him with His words, sending down His angel messenger to convey His message. In other cases people may opt for disbelief for even less important reasons. That, however, should not weaken our resolve to follow in the footsteps of the Prophet and his noble companions.

There is no doubt that the night journey was a very effective morale booster for the Prophet. He was, after all, a human being who shared in all human emotions of sorrow, grief, pleasure and delight. Only a short time earlier he had lost his wife Khadījah, who was his main source of comfort, and his uncle Abū Ṭālib, who ensured that Muhammad received all the support and protection to which he was entitled, according to the traditions of the Arabian society. Then came that disappointing trip to Ṭā'if, which was intended to broaden the base of the Islamic message.

It is only natural that Muhammad should feel downhearted after those three major jolts which affected both his personal and his public life. There was no question that his sorrow would affect his faith. Nevertheless, his losses were, by human standards, of huge proportions. Hence, a comforting gesture which gave him first-hand experience of the smallness of this world in relation to the wider universe, and the triviality of what one may experience in this life in relation to what lies in store in the next life, would, as the expression goes, do him the world of good.

There is no doubt that his night journey had a lasting effect on the Prophet. It boosted his confidence in himself and in his message;

it enhanced his aspirations and helped put his efforts in the service of his faith on a higher level. Subsequent events show that there was a marked change in his attempts to set the course for his message.

Universality of the Islamic Message

The night journey was of great significance in more ways than one. Note, for example, that at Jerusalem, Muhammad led the other Prophets in prayer. It is a well established Islamic concept that the messages of all Prophets were basically the same. They all called on mankind to believe in God, the one and only deity. With Islam, these messages were brought to their full and complete form. With Muhammad, the line of prophethood reached its end.

For the Prophets to pray together at Jerusalem signifies the continuity of their messages and their unity of rank and purpose. Jerusalem thus occupies a unique position as a sacred place for all followers of the Divine religions. That unique prayer of the Prophets, led by Muhammad, also signifies that as Islam has crowned all Divine messages and brought them to their final form, Jerusalem, the spot revered by all religions, belongs to the Muslims who follow Muhammad, the recognized leader of all Prophets.

The night journey also stresses the universality of the Islamic message. Muhammad is taken to Jerusalem which, at the time, was inhabited by non-Arabs. He is engaged there in the most religious of human activities before he is taken to heaven. It would have been just as easy for God to raise Muhammad to heaven from his home in Makkah. The fact that He chose to take him to Jerusalem first, to lead his fellow Prophets in prayer, endorses the fact that Islam is a message for mankind, not for the Arabs alone.

In those congregational prayers of the Prophets one also sees a reference to the fact that all the distortion which crept into earlier messages had been pushed aside. A fuller and more complete version of these messages has been revealed and guaranteed by God to remain intact for the rest of time. That version is Islam.

Was It a Physical Journey?

Muhammad's night journey from Makkah to Jerusalem and hence to heaven, and his return to his home town on the same night, was, to a contemporary mind, very much a miracle. Caravans took a whole month to cover the distance between the two cities. How, then, could Muhammad make a return journey overnight, and have a side excursion to heaven in the same package? Even to those accustomed to today's jet travel and to the notion of supersonic speed, the event can only be classified as supernatural. Hence questions have always been raised about the true aim of this journey and its nature. More precisely, people wonder whether it was a 'spiritual' or physical journey.

The Qur'ān answers the first question clearly. The *sūrah* entitled The Night Journey or *al-Isrā'*, opens with this verse: "Limitless in His glory is He who made His servant go by night from the Sacred Temple [of Makkah] to the further Temple [of Jerusalem] whose surroundings We have blessed that We might show him some of Our signs. He alone hears all and sees all." (17: 1)

The whole object of the journey, then, was that the Prophet would have a chance to see some of God's signs. What these were, we are not told. Seeing them, however, had a greatly reassuring effect on Muhammad, since it enabled him to experience at first hand the limitless ability of God the Creator. This was bound to put the dispute in which he had been engaged with the Makkans into perspective. It exhibited before his eyes the true nature and the real might of the two camps: his own, in which God is an active participant, and that of the unbelievers. Hence, it is not surprising that the following years of his life were free of any feelings of weakness or downheartedness. He remained to the last day of his life unaffected by adversity, certain that he would be victorious as long as he and his followers were true believers, sincere in their intentions and actions.

Here, one should emphasize that the journey was not a miracle with the aim of persuading the unbelievers to accept the faith. It was not one of the type of miracles which was given to other Prophets as evidence of their truthfulness. The unbelievers had actually challenged the Prophet to go up into heaven, but he refused their challenge, as he refused all their other challenging requests. His answer to all such requests was: "Glory be to my Lord. I am only a human Messenger." (17: 93) When he actually rose to heaven he did not portray the fact as a reply for their challenge. Hence, one needs to understand the night journey in its proper light: it was merely an act of God to reassure His Messenger at a time when such a reassurance was needed for the proper conveyance of His message.

The majority of Islamic scholars are of the opinion that the night journey was not purely 'spiritual'. They believe, as does the present author, that the Prophet did physically, in body and spirit, go on this journey. Some people may find this hard to believe because it involves preternatural powers. The answer is that whatever powers such a journey required, they were easy for God to provide.

Look back only one hundred years and imagine what would have been the reaction of people if someone had told them that anyone would be able to travel the distance between Bahrain and London in a little over four hours, in luxurious comfort. Now reflect on travelling speeds, if one maintains the rate of progress achieved in this field in the present century. Would supersonic travelling have seemed natural?

Indeed, the term 'natural' is certainly relative. What is natural today was preternatural to our ancestors and may become, in our grandchildren's view, primitive. 'Natural', in essence, signifies little more than 'familiar'. One need only look, with open eyes and mind, at the world to find that there are many miraculous facts which are readily accepted as 'natural' for no reason other than their familiarity. Every childbirth is a miracle, but it is simply overlooked because it occurs so often. One need only reflect over it a little to understand its miraculous nature.

In tackling such events as the night journey, one needs to remember only that they occur because God has willed that they should occur. To Him there is no such thing as 'natural' or 'preternatural'. He has created all the laws of nature, whether they are familiar or not. To Him the operation of all laws is equally easy. What is not understood of His actions is readily accepted, because the fact that His power is limitless is already accepted.

Notes

1. Ibn Hishām, *al-Sīrah al-Nabawiyyah*, Dār al-Qalam, Beirut, Vol. 1, pp. 337-338.
2. Apparently clapping was a gesture of disapproval in the Arabian society of the time. Contemporary reports do not mention clapping as a gesture signifying approval or appreciation.
3. Ibn Hishām, op.cit., Vol. 2, pp. 58-59.
4. Ibid., Vol. 2, p. 57. Also, Ibn Sayyid al-Nās, *'Uyūn al-Athar*, Dār al-Turāth, Madinah, 1996, pp. 226-227.
5. Ibn Hishām, op.cit., pp. 57-58. Also, al-Ṭabarī, *Tārīkh al-Rusul wa al-Mulūk*, Dār al-Ma'ārif, 4th edition, Vol. 2, p. 244.
6. Ibn Sayyid al-Nās, op.cit., pp. 193-194. Also, al-Bukhārī, *Ṣaḥīḥ*, Dār 'Ālam al-Kutub, Vol. 1, Riyadh, 1996, p. 37.
7. Ibn Hishām, op.cit., p. 57.
8. Ibid., pp. 60-63. Also, Ibn Sayyid al-Nās, op.cit., pp. 231-233.
9. Ibn Hishām, op.cit., Vol. 2, pp. 20-21.
10. Al-Bukhārī, op.cit., Vol. 1, p. 458. Also, Muslim, *Ṣaḥīḥ*, al-Maktabah al-Rashīdiyyah, Delhi, India, Vol. 2, p. 109.
11. Ibn Hishām, op.cit., pp. 36-40. Also, Ibn Sayyid al-Nās, op.cit., pp. 241-242.

13

A Major Breakthrough

IN THE SPACE of less than a year the Prophet went through a number of events which were bound to influence his thinking with regard to what line he should follow in order to bring his call to success. First, with the death of his wife Khadījah and his uncle Abū Ṭālib, he lost all the support and comfort he was certain always to receive both at home and in public life. Secondly, the failure of his trip to Ṭā'if, which aimed at soliciting outside support for his call, brought home to him the fact that, except for his few followers, he stood literally alone in opposition to the whole world. Thirdly, his night trip to Jerusalem provided him with the true perspective with which he should view all situations. It brought added clarity to his vision of where true power lay in the confrontation between true faith and its enemies.

Reviewing his situation in Makkah, the Prophet realized that he was locked in a stalemate in his own town. Although new converts to Islam were still trickling through, a major breakthrough seemed as remote as ever. Attitudes hardened and well-entrenched tribal loyalties constituted a stumbling block, preventing many people who would otherwise be expected to think clearly from making a rational and objective assessment of what Muhammad was calling for. The only alternative then was to try to achieve the breakthrough away from Makkah.

The emigration to Abyssinia and the trip to Ṭā'if may be viewed as two steps in that direction, although their immediate objectives were vastly different. Moreover, the Prophet repeatedly tried to make the most of the pilgrimage season, approaching pilgrims to explain to them the fundamental principles of Islam and invite them to accept it and convey its message to their own people. Although some of those pilgrims responded favourably they were too few to bring about any change in the Muslims' general situation. These approaches should be seen as a consistent attempt to break the deadlock. Indeed, the pilgrimage season seemed to offer the best chance to carry the message of Islam beyond the narrow boundaries of Makkah. His trip to Ṭā'if proved to the Prophet that it was too risky for him to venture outside without first securing a strong base from which to operate. Approaching individuals, however, did not seem to be the answer. A change of emphasis was apparently needed.

When the next pilgrimage season arrived, the Prophet started to implement his new approach. Pilgrimage to Makkah had been a yearly event ever since Abraham built the Kaʿbah on God's own instructions. Over the years, however, many irreligious practices and rituals had crept into the pilgrimage. These were later to be stamped out by Islam.

Making Use of the Pilgrimage Season

The Prophet now approached the pilgrims from the major tribes of Arabia. Naturally, they formed their own groups and remained together throughout their stay in the area of Makkah and ʿArafāt. The Prophet went and addressed the pilgrims from each tribe as one group. He explained that he was a Messenger from God entrusted with His message: to call on people to worship Him alone and to abandon all other forms of worship. The Prophet also asked every tribe he approached to provide him with protection so that he might be able to convey his message to mankind. Previously, the Prophet had approached individual pilgrims in the hope of winning new recruits. Now he approached tribes for an alliance which could give him freedom of action.

Obviously, the Quraysh, who begrudged the Prophet even the slightest gain he was able to make as a result of his previous efforts with the pilgrims, could not sit still now that his approaches took on a collective form. His own uncle Abū Lahab, who had always been a fierce enemy of Islam, took it upon himself to mount a counter-campaign in order to dissuade people from listening to Muhammad. The following account is from Rabīʿah ibn ʿAbbād from the Dīl, a branch of the major tribe of Kinānah:

> I was a teenager accompanying my father in Minā [where pilgrims encamp after ʿArafāt] when I saw the Messenger of God coming to the quarters of Arab tribes. He addressed each tribe by their name and said: "I am God's Messenger to you. He commands you to worship Him alone and to ascribe to Him no partners whatsoever. He also commands you to abandon all those idols you worship in preference to Him, and to believe in me and accept what I say and to protect me so that I can convey the message which God has entrusted to me." Behind him stood a cross-eyed man with a beaming face, his hair in two plaits, wearing an Adenan garment. When the Messenger of God had finished what he had to say, the other man addressed each tribe by name: "What this man is asking you to do is to abandon al-Lāt and al-ʿUzzā [their two principal idols] and to abandon your allies of the *jinn* in order to follow his craze. Never listen to him and never obey him." I asked my father about the man contradicting the Prophet and he told me that he was his own uncle, Abū Lahab.[1]

The Prophet's attempts to win support from other tribes was opposed by all the vigour the Quraysh could muster. However, he continued to address his message to every tribe which could afford him the protection he needed to carry out his task. This meant, in effect, standing up to the Quraysh and going to war with them, which was bound to happen. Hence it was not surprising that there would be no great enthusiasm among the Arab tribes to take up the Prophet's offer.

The Kindah delegation, headed by a man called Mulaiḥ, were not the only ones to give the Prophet a blunt refusal. The tribe of Banī ʿĀmir ibn Ṣaʿṣaʿh were initially less negative. One among them, called Bayḥarah ibn Firās, said to his fellow tribesmen: "If I take this Qurayshi man, I will be able, with him, to subdue the rest of Arabia." He then turned to the Prophet and asked him: "If we accept your call and give you the support you need, and if you, then, by the will of God, are victorious, would we be rulers after you?" The Prophet answered, "Power belongs to God. He gives it whomever He wills." The man said: "Are we expected to fight the whole of Arabia to support you, then when victory is achieved, we hand power over to others? We will do no business with you."

When their delegation arrived back home they related to their elders, as usual, the events of their journey. When they told them about their encounter with the Prophet and their reply to him, an old man who enjoyed much respect among them raised his hand to his head in disappointment and said: "Is there any way to rectify this mistake? By Him who holds my soul in His hands, no Ishmaelite has ever made a false claim of this type. The man is genuinely a Prophet. Where had you left your reason when you met him?" The affair, however, came to nothing.[2]

The Ḥānīfah tribe, on the other hand, gave the Prophet a very nasty reply. Rejection was also the answer of Banī Kalb.[3]

Neglecting No Individual

The Prophet, however, did not limit his approach to delegations of other tribes. Every time he heard of the arrival in Makkah of any man who enjoyed a position of respect among his people, he would approach him and explain Islam to him. In these cases he did not ask for protection. He made that request only when he spoke to a tribe collectively.

One such man was Suwaid ibn al-Ṣāmit from Madinah. When the Prophet spoke to him, he said: "Perhaps you have something similar to what I have." When, in response to the Prophet's request, he quoted some passages from a book he called 'Luqmān's magazine', the Prophet said: "This is certainly good, but I have something better." He read him a passage from the Qur'ān and invited him to become a Muslim. Suwaid made no comment other than: "What you have read is certainly good." However, he was killed shortly after his return home. His people believed that he actually embraced Islam before his death.[4]

Another group of people from Madinah led by a man called Abū al-Ḥaysar Anas ibn Rafiʿ, arrived in Makkah seeking an alliance with the Quraysh against the Khazraj tribe in Madinah. The Prophet went to them and said: "I can offer you something better than what you have come here for." In answer to their questioning, he replied: "I am God's Messenger to mankind. I call upon them to worship God alone, associating with Him no partners. He revealed to me His book containing His message." He further explained the principles of Islam and read them a passage from the Qur'ān. A member of the group, called Iyās, who was still a boy in his teens, said: "By God, this is better than what we have come here for." His leader, Abū al-Ḥaysar, took a handful of sand and threw it in Iyās's face, saying, "Leave us alone. We have come here for a different purpose." The Prophet then left them.

Soon after their return, the Battle of Buʿāth broke out between the two Arab tribes in Madinah, the Aws and the Khazraj. Iyās soon died and those who attended him at his deathbed reported that he glorified God and praised Him until he died. They had no doubt that he was a Muslim.[5]

Cases like those of Suwaid and Iyās served as encouraging signs for the Prophet. An even more encouraging one was the case of al-Ṭufail ibn ʿAmr, a leader in the Daws tribe. When he came to Makkah for pilgrimage, the Quraysh elders made sure to warn him against the Prophet. They went as far as requesting him more emphatically not to meet the Prophet or listen to what he said. Al-Ṭufail reports:

> They continued to pressurize me to the extent that I made a firm decision that I would never listen to anything he said, nor even speak to him. When I went to the mosque the following morning, I put cotton into my ears so that I did not

> accidentally hear anything he said. I simply did not want to listen to him. Nevertheless, he was praying only a short distance from me when I was in the mosque and God simply wanted me to hear his words. I recognized that what he said was certainly good. I said to myself:
>
> "You are certainly on the wrong track. You are a good poet who could distinguish good words from bad ones. What prevents you from listening to this man and judging what he says? If it was good, you would accept it; and if it was bad, you would leave it." I waited until God's Messenger went home, and followed him. I said to him: "Muhammad, your people have said to me this and that and warned me most emphatically against listening to you until I closed my ears to anything you said. Yet God wanted me to hear what you say and I found it good. Will you please explain your message to me?" The Prophet told me about Islam explaining its principles, and recited a passage from the Qur'ān to me. By God, I had never heard anything better than that. I immediately adopted Islam and declared my belief in God's oneness and the message of Muhammad.

When al-Ṭufail arrived at his tribe's quarters, his father, an elderly man, came to greet him but al-Ṭufail told him that they no longer belonged together since he had adopted Islam and followed the Prophet Muhammad. His father declared that he would follow the same religion. Al-Ṭufail told him to have a bath and wash his clothes. When he had done that he explained the principles of Islam to him and his father became a Muslim.

Al-Ṭufail did the same with his wife, who was also ready to adopt Islam as soon as its principles were outlined to her. He started calling his people to Islam but they were not ready to respond to his call. After some time, he felt downhearted and he went to the Prophet complaining of the slow response. He suggested that the Prophet curse them. Instead the Prophet prayed for their guidance and instructed al-Ṭufail to go back and call on them gently to adopt Islam. He went back to act on the Prophet's instructions. He did not see the Prophet again for several years, until the Battle of the Moat had taken place. He travelled with about 80 families of his tribe who adopted Islam. They joined the Prophet at the Battle of Khaybar and the Prophet gave them shares of the spoils of that particular expedition.[6]

The People of Madinah

The city of Yathrib, now known as Madinah (meaning 'The City'), was inhabited at the time of the Prophet by two major Arab tribes, the Aws and the Khazraj. These two tribes had a long history of bloody wars which sapped their strength. The last of these battles, named Buʿāth, took place about two years before the events we are now relating.

A large Jewish community had lived in Madinah for well over a century. All history books agree that the Jews were instrumental in keeping the two Arab tribes, the Aws and the Khazraj, at each other's throats. Historians also relate that the Jews came to Madinah because their sacred books mention it as the place where the last messenger from God was to establish his state.

Like the rest of the Arabs, the Aws and the Khazraj were idolaters. In common with all Arabs they revered the Kaʿbah and offered pilgrimage. In a pilgrimage season after the Prophet had adopted his strategy of speaking to the various Arab tribes, seeking their protection in his fulfilment of his mission, a group of six men from the Khazraj tribe were offering the pilgrimage. The Prophet met them at a place called ʿAqabah, at Minā, where pilgrims encamp for three days. When they identified themselves to the Prophet and he ascertained that they were the neighbours of the Jews, he sought to explain his message to them. They were willing to listen to what he had to say.

The Prophet outlined to them the principles of his message and read them a passage from the Qur'ān. He called on them to believe in God as the only deity to be worshipped. Some of them said to the others: "You may be sure that he is the Prophet with whom the Jews keep threatening you. Let them not be the first to follow him."

That apparently touched a sensitive nerve with them. The Arabs of Madinah used to respect the Jewish religion. They recognized that their own pagan beliefs stood no comparison with the monotheistic religion of the Jews, who professed to have better knowledge of God and man. Every time the Arabs of Madinah clashed with the Jews, the latter would say: "It will not be long before a new messenger shall be sent by God. We shall follow him and will kill you all in the same way as the peoples of ʿĀd and Iram were killed."

The six Khazrajis did not hesitate to accept what the Prophet said. They were Asʿad ibn Zurārah, ʿAwf ibn al-Ḥārith, Rāfiʿ ibn Mālik, Quṭbah ibn ʿĀmir ibn Ḥadīdah, ʿUqbah ibn ʿĀmir ibn Zayd and Jābir ibn ʿAbdullāh ibn Ri'āb. They declared their belief in God and the message of Muhammad. They also said to the Prophet: "We have left our people in an unprecedented state of mutual hostility. May God make you the cause of their unity. We shall call on them to follow you and explain to them your religion which we have accepted. Should God unite them in following you, you shall enjoy with them a position of the highest prestige."

Thus the Prophet had six emissaries who carried his message to their own people. They were apparently very active emissaries. In no time the whole of the city was speaking about the Prophet and his call. Many accepted Islam through the efforts of these six.[7]

It was clear that Madinah was the most fertile environment for Islam to spread. In the first place, it was free from any hostile feelings like those which existed in Makkah. Hence Islam, with its clear and simple logic, had a great appeal among its inhabitants. Secondly, the monotheistic idea was particularly appealing to the Arabs of Madinah, owing to their respect for the Jewish religion. Some historians see the arrogance of the Jews in Madinah as the only thing which prevented its Arab population from converting to Judaism. The Jews behaved in a condescending manner towards the Arabs and showed them that Judaism was the religion of the elite only. Moreover, the embattled Arabs of Madinah yearned for a life of peace. It was not easy for the two tribes of Aws and Khazraj to achieve a lasting reconciliation without a powerful catalyst. It is obvious from what the six said to the Prophet that they hoped he would be the catalyst of peace and unity.

With Islam making such headway very quickly in Madinah (or Yathrib), converts longed to meet the Prophet. The obvious time for such a meeting was the next pilgrimage season when the original six were joined by six more to meet the Prophet at ʿAqabah.

The Prophet was very pleased with the enthusiasm shown by this delegation for the cause of Islam. They were very keen to do their utmost for their new faith. The Prophet, however, did not ask them, at that particular stage, for protection as he used to ask other tribes. A shrewd statesman, he recognized that such a pledge would come at the right moment, without him asking for it. The immediate necessity was to consolidate the new base in Madinah. Hence, the Prophet entered into a covenant with the 12 men, ten from the Khazraj, the other two belonging to the Aws. The terms of the covenant meant that the 12 pledged themselves "to worship no deity other than God, to commit neither theft, nor adultery, nor child-murder, to utter no monstrous falsehood of their own invention, and never to disobey the Prophet over anything which was just or reasonable." This covenant came to be known later as 'the covenant of women', for its terms continued to apply to women only. Men have to add a pledge to fight the enemies of Islam.[8]

This pledge of support was a very important breakthrough in the history of Islam. The terms did not include any military provisions but the need for those was not yet pressing. It was enough, for the time being, that Islam should be able to establish its roots in Madinah by the recruitment of more people. After all, Islam does not like to go to war unless it is absolutely unavoidable. Although the Prophet realized that the Quraysh would not let Islam move freely in Arabia without trying to silence it by all the means at its disposal, such a confrontation was not yet imminent. Hence the pledge included what could be termed 'the Islamic peaceful programme'.

The Prophet sent Muṣʿab ibn ʿUmayr to Madinah with his new followers. His mission was to educate the new Muslims in Madinah in their new faith, to teach them the Qur'ān and all they needed to know about Islam. He was to call on people to adopt Islam. He also led the Muslims in Madinah in prayer.[9] As the memories of the most recent battles between the two tribes, Aws and Khazraj, were still fresh in their minds, neither group found it easy to be led in prayer by someone from the other tribe. Muṣʿab was therefore the perfect choice. He also had an additional task: to study the situation in Madinah very closely and to make an assessment of likely reactions in all eventualities. The Prophet would then be able to make the decisions he had to make on the basis of first-hand information.

Winning Influential Recruits

Muṣʿab ibn ʿUmair was a dedicated worker with the right temperament to mix with strangers and invite them to adopt Islam as a religion and a way of life. He was also to assess the general situation and the feasibility of an exodus of the Makkan Muslims to Madinah. He might also have had further instructions. It is noticeable that in the contacts that had taken place so far between the Prophet and the people of Madinah, the tribe of Khazraj figured more prominently than the Aws. This is probably due to the fact that the first six who met the Prophet and accepted Islam belonged to the Khazraj. It was only natural that they would concentrate their efforts within their own tribe. Hence it was not surprising that the 12 who entered into the covenant of support with the Prophet the following year included ten from the Khazraj and only two from the Aws. Hence, Muṣʿab might have been instructed to try to redress this imbalance. The last thing the Prophet wanted was that Islam should contribute to the division among the people of Madinah. He was eager that Islam should be a unifying force.

Muṣʿab stayed with Asʿad ibn Zurārah, a Khazraji with immediate relatives from the Aws. Asʿad supplied him with all the information he needed about the people of Madinah. One example of the main achievements made through their joint efforts is perhaps sufficient.[10]

One day Asʿad took Muṣʿab to an orchard which belonged to the clan of ʿAbd al-Ashhal, a branch of the Aws tribe. They were joined there by a few Muslims. Saʿd ibn Muʿādh and Usaid ibn Ḥuḍair, the two most prominent figures of that clan, were still following the Arabian version of paganism. Learning about the presence of Asʿad and Muṣʿab, Saʿd addressed Usaid: "Go to these two men who have come here to spread their ideas among our simple people and tell them not to come to us again. Had Asʿad not been my own cousin, I would have spared you the trouble. As it is, I feel somewhat uneasy about turning him away myself."

As Usaid approached the two men, Asʿad said to Muṣʿab: "This man is the chief of his people. Make a sincere effort with him." Muṣʿab answered: "I will certainly try if he agrees to sit down with us." Usaid adopted a tough attitude, making plain his objection to their approaches to the 'simple' people. He followed that with a threat: "Stay away from us if you care for your own safety." Muṣʿab said: "Would you like to sit down with us and listen to what we have to say? If you find it reasonable, you accept it. If not, we will not bother you with it again." Usaid said: "Fair enough."

As Muṣʿab explained the basic principles of Islam and recited a passage from the Qur'ān, Usaid's face shone with admiration. When Muṣʿab had finished, he said, "This is a fine word indeed. What do you do if you want to adopt this religion?" Muṣʿab explained and Usaid immediately made the necessary ablution and declared that he believed in the oneness of God and that Muhammad was His Messenger.

Usaid then said: "I am sending you a man who would be joined by all his people, if he decided to follow you. He is Saʿd ibn Muʿāth."

As Usaid drew nearer to Saʿd, the latter remarked that a total change had come over Usaid's face. Usaid, however, reported to him that he did not find the two men doing anything bad. He also reported that another clan were plotting to kill Asʿad in order to get at Saʿd himself.

Angry, Saʿd said: "I will go myself and tell them to keep away from us." As he drew closer to them, he suddenly realized that Usaid wanted him to speak to them. He, however, started with some harsh words. Muṣʿab made the same offer he made earlier to Usaid. Thus, Saʿd sat down to listen as Muṣʿab explained the basic principles of Islam.

Muṣʿab and Asʿad realized that they had won over their man long before he uttered a word. The expression on his face as he listened to the Qur'ān said it all. As Muṣʿab finished, Saʿd indicated his acceptance of Islam.

Going back to his people and joined by Usaid, he knew exactly what to do. He simply addressed his people, asking them: "What is your opinion of me?" They answered: "You are our master and the wisest of our men." "Then take this from me," he said. "I forbid myself all communication with you all, men and women, until you believe in God and His Messenger. That very evening, every man and woman of the ʿAbd al-Ashḥal clan became a Muslim.[11]

Innovative Ways to Win New Recruits

Needless to say, the new converts to Islam in Madinah were very enthusiastic about their new faith. They realized that as believers in the Oneness of God, they were starting a new stage in their history in which faith was the prime mover. They had a mission to fulfil. Their immediate task was to win new recruits to the new faith so as to consolidate its base. Hence they were very active in preaching the message of Islam. They were particularly keen to win new converts among those who commanded respect and were influential among their people. One such person was ʿAmr ibn al-Jamūḥ from the clan of Salamah.

A few young Muslims of his clan were keen to persuade ʿAmr to join them, but he was an old man who could not easily respond to a call which would necessitate a radical change in his life pattern. The young men of Salamah recognized that they must think of a method which would bring ʿAmr face to face with the fact that Islam was a far better religion than idolatrous beliefs.

As already discussed, throughout Arabia the worship of idols was the recognized religion. People did not stop to think that their idols, which were made of stone or wood or gold or other materials, were of no use and no benefit to them. Following in the tradition of men of honour in Arabia, ʿAmr had his own personal idol, which was made of wood. He kept the idol in his room, where he glorified and worshipped it.

The young men of Salamah decided to make ʿAmr's idol their target. When ʿAmr was fast asleep they would enter his home and take the idol away and throw it into some hole, full of dirt. In the morning, when ʿAmr woke up and discovered the loss of his idol, he would start looking for it. He took the idol out of the hole it was thrown in, cleaned and perfumed it, before putting it back in its place. The same thing happened day after day and ʿAmr was irritated, but he did not know what to do. He apologized to the idol: "Had I known who did this to you, I would certainly punish him severely."

After a few days, just before ʿAmr went to sleep, he took his sword and gave it to the idol, putting its strap round the idol's neck, and said: "I have no idea who abuses you at night. If you are of any use to yourself, then defend yourself against their assault. You have got the sword now." That night, when the young men of Salamah saw the sword with the idol, they took the idol, tied it to a dead dog, and threw it into a disused well where people threw their dirt and litter. In the morning ʿAmr looked for his idol. When he found it after a long search, he was really shaken at the sight. His son and the others who were administering this treatment to the idol spoke to him and pointed out that if the idol could not protect itself, then it could be of no use to anyone. When they outlined the message of Islam to ʿAmr, he accepted it without hesitation. He composed a fine, short poem describing the idol and its uselessness. He also praised God for enabling him to see the truth of Islam.[12]

Muṣʿab ibn ʿUmayr, the Prophet's emissary to Madinah, returned shortly before the next pilgrimage season.[13] He reported to the Prophet the good news that there was hardly an Arab household in Madinah which did not have at least one Muslim among its members. He further reported on the composition of the population of the city.

Full Assessment of the Madinah Situation

Muṣʿab's report was carefully considered in order to establish whether Madinah was a suitable place for the establishment of the first Islamic state. The first covenant the Prophet made with the people of Madinah required them simply to live as Muslims by themselves. It did not include any provisions for dealings with other communities and states. Now it was time for a decision on this aspect.

On the basis of the information supplied by Muṣʿab, the Prophet recognized that apart from the Muslims from both Makkah and Madinah, there would be two groups of people in Madinah. First, the Arabs who had not yet joined Islam. They had their own divisions but there was scope for Islam to make further inroads into their ranks. There would obviously remain a hard core of resistance to Islam but it should not pose much of a problem as time was on the Muslims' side. Secondly there were the Jews, whose attitude to the new religion was not yet known. Muslims must be prepared for all eventualities on that front but they should not be the first to take a hostile attitude. They should strive to establish good neighbourly relations.

The Muslim community would also have an economic problem which would need urgent attention: the immigrants from Makkah would arrive in Madinah without any money. They would need housing and jobs. Moreover, the Prophet also recognized that the new state to be established in Madinah was bound to face an immediate external threat. The Quraysh in Makkah were not expected to sit idle while the new challenge to supremacy in Arabia developed and took shape.

Certain features made Madinah particularly suited to host the new state which was just about to emerge. Its natural fortification was unique. On both eastern and western sides of the city, there were two extended areas with volcanic stones which could not be traversed by man, horse or camel. It was practically impossible for an attacking army to go through these areas. Only its northern front offered access to an army because on all other sides there were thick plantations and a countless number of date trees. It should perhaps be mentioned here that it was in the north of the city that the Prophet and his companions dug the moat to fortify the city further when, five years later, a great concentration of tribes marched to Madinah with the declared aim of eradicating Islam altogether.

From the military point of view, then, Madinah was easily defensible. A small number of guard units was enough to intercept a large army and to stop its march. From another point of view, the Arabs of Madinah, Aws and Khazraj tribes, were known for their pride, integrity, bravery and high standard of military excellence.

They were never subjugated by an attacking enemy, nor did they have to pay any tax or tribute to an occupying force. Any individual or small tribe who enjoyed the protection of the two Arab tribes of Madinah felt very secure.

The two tribes were considered, according to Arabian traditions of the time, as maternal uncles of the Prophet. His grandfather, ʿAbd al-Muṭṭalib, was born to a woman from the clan of al-Najjār of Madinah, known as Salmā bint ʿAmr. ʿAbd al-Muṭṭalib was born in Madinah and lived there until he almost reached adolescence.

The two Arab tribes in Madinah belonged to Qaḥṭān, while the Muslims of Makkah belonged to ʿAdnān, the two main groupings in Arabia. Indeed, every Arabian tribe belonged to either one of these two divisions. When the Prophet settled in Madinah, his supporters belonged to both groupings. However, any possible quarrel between them was prevented by the fact that they were now Muslims.

The Prophet was definitely aware of all this when Muṣʿab reported to him on his mission in Madinah. One can feel his awareness in his careful planning of his future steps over the next year or so. The immediate decision, however, was taken to the effect that Madinah offered a suitable place for the establishment of the new base of Islam. The first step was to meet the new followers. A meeting was fixed for the last night of pilgrimage at ʿAqabah. This was probably the most important meeting in the 13 years of Islam in Makkah. Seventy-three men and two women from Madinah attended in the middle of the night. When everyone was fast asleep, those believers came out of their tents quietly in ones and twos to keep their appointment. The Prophet was the only Muslim from Makkah to attend. He apparently had to confide his plans to someone very close to him. This was his uncle, al-ʿAbbās, who was not yet a Muslim. Al-ʿAbbās was the only non-Muslim to attend the meeting. He wanted to be sure that his nephew was on a safe course.

A Pledge of Unwavering Support

Al-ʿAbbās's presence and his speech, which opened the proceedings of the meeting, must be seen in the light of the future development of relations between the state yet to be born and the Quraysh. What was about to take place was a radical realignment of loyalties. In the tribal society of Arabia, that was very serious indeed. Al-ʿAbbās began by stressing that the Prophet's clan had so far fulfilled its obligations according to the prevailing social values:

> You know how highly we rate Muhammad. We have protected him against our own people, with whom we share the same opinion of his call. He is indeed well protected within his own people and in his own city. Nevertheless, he is determined to join you. If you feel that you will indeed fulfil your pledges to him and will indeed protect him from his enemies, you are welcome to do as you please. Should you, however, feel that you may let him down, after having taken him away to your city, it would be better for everyone if you decide here and now to leave him alone, for he is well looked after in his home town.

They answered him: "We have truly understood what you have said." They then turned to the Prophet and invited him to lay down his conditions.

The Prophet began his short speech by reading a passage from the Qur'ān. He then explained the message of Islam and its profound influence on the lives of its followers. He concluded with this very brief statement of the conditions of the pledge he wanted from them: "You pledge to me that you will protect me as you protect your own womenfolk and your own children."

Al-Barā' ibn Maʿrūr, a leading figure among those present, said: "By Him who has given you the message of the truth, we will defend you as we defend our women. Take up our pledges, for we are the children of war and the best people with arms."

The distinguished figure of Abū al-Haitham ibn al-Tayyihān intervened here: "We have relations with the Jews which are now bound to be severed. If we live up to our pledges and God grants you victory, would you, Messenger of God, leave us then to return to your people?"

Smiling, the Prophet assured him that he would not do that. He said: "I belong to you as you belong to me. I fight your enemy and make peace with your friend."

As they queued to make their personal pledges, a man called al-ʿAbbās ibn ʿUbādah stopped them, saying:

> Do you know what you are pledging to this man? You are committing yourselves to go to war against the whole world. If there is any doubt in your minds or if you feel that if your wealth is looted and your honoured leaders are killed you will give him up, it is more honourable for you to leave him alone now. Giving him up in such an eventuality will dishonour you in both this life and the life to come. If, on the other hand, you feel you will honour your commitments come what may, then go ahead, because this will increase your honour in both this world and the next.

They all said, without hesitation: "We are committed, come what may." The question they were naturally keen to put to the Prophet was: "What will our reward be if we honour our commitments?" The Prophet's answer came in a single word: "Paradise."

Then they all shook hands with the Prophet in a gesture concluding the deal. They asserted that they would never seek release from their commitments, nor would they accept any cancellation.[14]

A few points should be made here in connection with this meeting. Firstly, the fact that al-ʿAbbās, the Prophet's uncle who was still at that time following pagan beliefs, was present may suggest to some people that Muslims may take non-Muslims into their confidence, even in the most serious matters which affect their community. The Qur'ān indeed warns against this and advises us to be on guard. We must remember that al-ʿAbbās was the Prophet's own uncle and the Prophet knew for certain that he wished him and his followers well. Furthermore, al-ʿAbbās was an interested party. As a leading figure of the Hāshimite clan, which was responsible for the protection of Muhammad, he needed to be sure that the Madinah people were serious in taking over this responsibility.

Secondly, it was clear at the meeting that the two parties knew very well what was involved in making that covenant. The Prophet spelled out what sort of protection he required. The speakers from the other side made it absolutely clear to their fellow delegates that they were effectively taking on the whole world. When they made their commitment, therefore, they made it with their eyes open.

Thirdly, the reward the Madinah Muslims were promised for their fulfilment of their part of the deal had nothing to do with this world. They were not told that they would be given so many ministries in the government of the state or that the Prophet's successor would be one of them. Indeed, they were promised what every Muslim who serves his faith with tireless dedication and devotion is promised: admittance to heaven.

This promise helps always to keep those who work for Islam on the right track. Their motives remain pure and their goal is always the same: to earn the pleasure of God. They do not seek any worldly reward and they do not have any personal ambitions, not even that the victory of Islam should come about through their own efforts. They leave such matters to God. He alone determines when and through whose efforts His call achieves victory. The advocates of Islam know that their task is to work for that victory, but what happens to them is immaterial, for their dedication and tireless efforts are sure to bring them their most precious reward: the pleasure of God and Paradise.

When everyone at the meeting had given his personal pledge, the Prophet asked them to select from among them 12 representatives who would be in charge of the Muslims in Madinah. The selected 12 were: Asʿad ibn Zurārah, Saʿd ibn al-Rabīʿ, ʿAbdullāh ibn Rawāḥah, Rāfiʿ ibn Mālik, al-Barā' ibn Maʿrūr, ʿAbdullāh ibn ʿAmr, ʿUbādah ibn al-Ṣāmit, Saʿd ibn ʿUbādah and al-Mundhir ibn ʿAmr ibn Khunais, all of whom belonged to the tribe of Khazraj. The remaining three, Usaid ibn Ḥuḍair, Saʿd ibn Khaithamah and Rifāʿah ibn al-Mundhir, were of the Aws tribe.

The Quraysh Learns of the Meeting

It was unlikely that a meeting of this size, in an open place like ʿAqabah, would remain secret. Before it was over, a loud voice was heard shouting: "There is Muhammad meeting with those who have deserted their religion."[15]

The Prophet told his new allies, whom we shall now call by their Islamic name, al-Anṣār (meaning, 'the supporters'), to go back to their tents. Under cover of darkness they dispersed quietly, thanking God for enabling them to conclude their business with the Prophet. None of them was missed by his people during his absence at the meeting. The shouting, however, was enough to betray the secret. When morning broke, the Quraysh learnt enough about the meeting to prompt immediate action.

They undertook intensive enquiries about what had happened. Their investigation led them in the right direction. A group of their leaders, therefore, went to the camp of the Madinah pilgrims and said: "We have learnt that you have been in contact with our man and that you have requested him to join you in your city and pledged to fight us alongside him. Now we want to assure you that you are the last people with whom we want to have a fight."

The non-believers among the Madinah group – and there were quite a few of them – were quick to deny the whole story. They assured the Makkans that they had no knowledge of any contact or meeting between their people and Muhammad. Their denials were, of course, true. They were kept in ignorance of the whole affair – a fact which suggests that the Prophet and the Muslims viewed their developing relationship and its prospects very seriously and realized that they must tread very carefully if they were to turn a new page in the history of Islam.

The Muslims from Madinah simply kept quiet as this conversation between non-believers from Makkah and Madinah went on. One man of high standing in Madinah, ʿAbdullāh ibn Ubayy, who was to have an unhappy relationship with Islam, reassured the Qurayshi delegation: "This is indeed a very serious matter. My people would not keep me in ignorance of it, should the whole thing be in their minds. I simply have no knowledge that such a thing has taken place, so I must assume that it has not."

Reassured, the Makkans went back home. But a couple of days later, when the pilgrims set off on their return journey, the suspicions of the Quraysh were confirmed. They sent some squads to chase the Madinah people. They could do no more than seize two men: al-Mundhir ibn ʿAmr and Saʿd ibn ʿUbādah, who were among the 12 leaders of the Muslim group. Al-Mundhir managed to escape but Saʿd was taken prisoner. His hands were tied to his neck and he was dragged back to Makkah. They kept beating him and pulling his thick hair. As the torture continued, one man who felt sorry for Saʿd whispered in his ear: "Have you ever had any covenant or dealing with anyone from the Quraysh?"

Saʿd replied: "Yes, indeed. I have always protected the trade caravans of Jubayr ibn Muṭʿim and al-Ḥārith ibn Ḥarb, ensuring that they came to no harm in our parts." The man said: "Then shout their names aloud and mention your friendship with them."

This man, Abū al-Bakhtarī ibn Hishām, went quickly looking for Jubayr and al-Ḥarith. He found them in the mosque and told them: "I have just come from al-Abṭaḥ where I saw a man from al-Khazraj being badly beaten. He kept shouting both your names and saying that you have an agreement of mutual protection with him." When they realized that it was Saʿd who was being tortured, they quickly went and saved him from his tormentors.[16]

That, however, was all that the Quraysh could do about the new covenant between the Muslims from Madinah and the Prophet. The agreement was concluded and sealed, marking the beginning of a new stage in the history of Islam which was to be totally different from the stage that was coming to its close. Shortly afterwards, the Prophet advised his followers in Makkah to emigrate to Madinah. He said: "God has provided you with a new home and new brethren." They started to leave in small groups secretly, so that they would not be stopped by the Makkans. The Prophet himself stayed on in Makkah waiting for God's permission to leave. Within a few weeks, the majority of the Makkan Muslims had settled in Madinah. Only those who were physically prevented from making the trip were left behind, along with the Prophet, Abū Bakr and ʿAlī. Abū Bakr indeed sought the Prophet's permission to go but the Prophet asked him to delay his departure, giving him a significant hint: "God may provide you with a companion."[17]

Notes

1. Ibn Hishām, *al-Sīrah al-Nabawiyyah*, Dār al-Qalam, Beirut, Vol. 1, pp. 64-65. Also, Ibn Sayyid al-Nās, *ʿUyūn al-Athar*, Dār al-Turāth, Madinah, 1996, p. 257.
2. Ibn Hishām, op.cit., pp. 65-66.
3. Ibid., p. 65.
4. Ibid., pp. 68-69. Also, Ibn Sayyid al-Nās, op.cit., p. 260.
5. Ibn Hishām, op.cit., pp. 69-70. Also, Ibn Sayyid al-Nās, op.cit., p. 261.
6. Ibn Hishām, op.cit., pp. 21-24.
7. Ibn Hishām, op.cit., pp. 70-73. Also, Ibn Sayyid al-Nās, op.cit., pp. 262-263.
8. Ibn Hishām, op.cit., pp. 73-77.
9. Ibid., p. 76. Also, Ibn Sayyid al-Nās, op.cit., p. 265.
10. Ibn Hishām, op.cit., p. 76.
11. Ibid., pp. 77-80.
12. Ibid., pp. 95-96.
13. Ibid., p. 81. Also, Ibn Sayyid al-Nās, op.cit., p. 271.
14. Ibn Hishām, op.cit., pp. 81-85. Also, Ibn Sayyid al-Nās, op.cit., pp. 271-273.
15. Ibn Hishām, op.cit., pp. 85-90. Also, Ibn Sayyid al-Nās, op.cit., pp. 273-276.
16. Ibn Hishām, op.cit., pp. 90-94.
17. Ibid., p. 111. Also, al-Ṭabarī, *Tārīkh al-Rusul wa al-Mulūk*, Dār al-Maʿārif, 4th edition, Vol. 2, p. 369.

14

The Journey to Madinah

THE MUSLIMS OF Makkah started to leave for Madinah when the Prophet told them that they were welcome there. They left, mostly in small groups, in the middle of the night, abandoning their homes and belongings. It was clear to everyone that this time the break was final. It had been apparent for some time that rigidity and stubbornness had taken over the people of Makkah. None of its leaders were prepared to look at the real issues with objectivity. Their immediate and narrow interests blinded them; they could see nothing else.

In such circumstances, the exodus of the Muslims acquires an added significance. It was, as everybody realized, a physical separation of the two camps which would make the breakout of hostilities between them much easier. For this to happen in a tribal society such as Arabia was very significant. The exodus was indeed a declaration by the Muslims of Makkah that a new system of loyalties had been established, which placed the bond of faith over all else. This new system was fully endorsed and implemented in practice by the Muslims of Madinah, who welcomed their immigrant brethren with open arms and shared with them their homes and their income. Every Muslim who arrived in Madinah was immediately settled in a welcoming brotherly home. The new arrivals helped to spread an air of delightful expectation among the Muslims in Madinah who by now formed a considerable section of its population.

Chasing Individual Emigrants

The departure of Muslims from Makkah was soon obvious to the Quraysh leaders, despite the fact that, in the majority of cases, departures were made late at night when the whole city was fast asleep. Such an exodus, however, could not be concealed. Houses became uninhabited and familiar faces disappeared. The danger attendant upon such an exodus was soon apparent to the leaders of Makkah. They tried hard to prevent the Muslims from emigrating. Some of these Muslims were locked up by their own tribes; others were chased into the desert. In one case at least, Abū Jahl chased ʿAyyāsh ibn Rabīʿah, his half-brother, right to Madinah and, by a series of lies, tricked him into going back with him to see his mother. As they approached Makkah, Abū Jahl and his brother al-Ḥārith managed to deceive their half-brother, tie him up and drag him back to Makkah, where he was forced to stay.[1]

An example which illustrates the attitudes of both camps is that of Ṣuhayb. He was a former slave who proved his value in running his master's business, bought his freedom and stayed on in Makkah as an ally of his former master's tribe. He soon became very rich. When he left Makkah on his own, he was chased by a group led by Abū Jahl. When they were about to catch up with him, he stopped to speak to them. He made it clear that he was prepared to fight them to the bitter end. On the other hand, he was willing to buy himself off by letting them have all his wealth. They accepted and he told them where they could find his money, so they left him alone. When Ṣuhayb arrived in Madinah and the Prophet learned of the deal he made with his pursuers, he commented: "Ṣuhayb has made a profitable deal." Needless to say, the Prophet was referring to the reward Ṣuhayb would receive from God for sacrificing his wealth in order to join the Prophet and be among his followers.[2]

ʿUmar was the only one to announce his intention to emigrate. He challenged the Quraysh to stop him, telling them: "I am emigrating. He who wants to leave behind him a bereaved mother, a widow or orphan children can meet me beyond this valley." No one did, as they knew ʿUmar to be a fighter of exceptional qualities. Moreover they did not want any trouble with the ʿAdiy clan, to which he belonged.[3]

It did not take long for the Muslims in Makkah to leave. In a short spell of time everybody was gone except those who were locked up by the Quraysh. The Prophet himself awaited God's instructions as to the timing of his departure. He realized that his passage would not be made easy by the Quraysh. He asked his most intimate friend and follower, Abū Bakr, and his young cousin ʿAlī to stay behind.

The Quraysh were aware that if Muhammad could establish a new base for his faith, their tribe stood to lose its dominant position in Arabia. Action had to be taken without wasting any more time. Therefore, a conference was called to discuss the matter urgently. The venue was Dār al-Nadwah, a house where the Quraysh leaders met to discuss grave matters. The participants were leading Quraysh personalities, most prominent among whom was Abū Jahl, representing the hard-line, extremist view.

Stop Muhammad at All Cost

The meeting opened with a review of the situation in the light of the new development. It was clear to everyone that the situation was very serious and there was a danger that Muhammad might be able to mount an attack on Makkah with his new followers. His imminent departure to Madinah was viewed as a step which heralded a threat to the Quraysh's supremacy in Arabia or, to use modern political terminology, a threat to its national security. It had to be stopped, whatever the price.

The more moderate propositions surfaced first. Someone suggested that Muhammad should be kept in solitary confinement until he died. This was rejected out of hand as someone explained that Muhammad's imprisonment might spur his followers to try to save him by force.

Rabīʿah ibn ʿAmir said: "Let us send him into exile. Once he is far away, he will cause us no more trouble. We, on the other hand, will be able to repair the damage he has caused in our ranks and restore our national unity."

In reply someone pointed out that Muhammad was an excellent speaker with sound logic and convincing argument. His appeal to people's hearts was so strong that if he was received well by any Arab tribe he might be able to win them to his cause. If he was able to do that, the danger to Makkah and the Quraysh would be very serious indeed.

Abū Jahl, who had so far kept quiet, felt the moment was ripe to put his point of view. He explained that 'the problem' called for a radical solution which would cause minimum repercussions. Thus, every clan should provide a strong, brave young man of noble birth. Each would be given a good, well-sharpened sword. They would all go to Muhammad and strike him simultaneously, so that all clans would have shared in his murder. The ʿAbd Manāf clan (which is a degree higher than the Hāshimites) would be faced with the choice of either going to war against the rest of the Quraysh – and they would be no match for them – or accepting a financial indemnity, which "we will be glad to pay".

Abū Jahl's proposal was met with unanimous approval. Everybody also agreed that the plan should be carried out immediately. Indeed it was decided that the assassination of Muhammad should take place that same night. The leaders of Makkah left the meeting-place to select their representatives in the 'collective murder'.[4]

Taking All Precautions

But Muhammad was God's Messenger. God had guaranteed his protection until he had completed his mission. So, the Angel Gabriel came to him and told him not to sleep in his bed that night. He was to start his journey to Madinah. The Prophet moved with maximum urgency and extra care. His counter-plan was to take all precautionary measures and set out on his way to Madinah with extreme caution, trusting that God would look after him.

Shortly before midday, he went to Abū Bakr and spoke to him alone, telling him that he had permission to leave Makkah. Abū Bakr had bought two fast camels in the hope that he would be the Prophet's companion on this journey. It was agreed that the Prophet would come at midnight to Abū Bakr's house and the two would immediately set out on their way.

The only other person to know of the Prophet's departure was his cousin ʿAlī, who was one of the very first people to accept Islam, when he was a boy of ten or twelve. Now a young man of 23, ʿAlī was to sleep in the Prophet's bed so that the assassins would imagine that the Prophet was in bed. ʿAlī's role involved a considerable measure of risk. The Prophet, however, assured him that he would come to no harm.

As the would-be assassins took their positions, sleep overpowered them all. The Prophet came out and put some dust over all their heads. He then went straight to Abū Bakr, who had prepared the two camels for their journey. The Prophet insisted that he should pay for his camel. Abū Bakr tried to persuade him to consider it a gift from him. "This journey", the Prophet said, "is taken for the sake of God, and I like to spend my own money to cover my expenses, so that I may reap the reward for what I spend."

Although Madinah is to the north of Makkah, the Prophet and his companion took a southerly direction. They headed towards a cave in one of the numerous mountains surrounding Makkah. There, in the cave of Mount Thawr, they stayed for three days. The Prophet realized that the people of the Quraysh would be chasing him, so in a bid to out-manoeuvre them, he went south.

Pursuit in the Desert

Back at the Prophet's house, the would-be assassins were fast asleep when someone came to check on what they were supposed to do. Amazed at what he saw, he woke them up and said that the dust on their heads was a sign that Muhammad had managed to escape. They were incredulous. Looking through the door, they said: "Here is Muhammad in his bed." They then forced the door open and went in, only to receive the shock of their lives, as they realized that the man lying in bed was ʿAlī. They did not want to add to their problems by killing ʿAlī, so the cry was raised that Muhammad had escaped. Hurried meetings were held. Everyone concerned was alarmed. Abū Jahl took command of the situation. Several groups of horsemen were dispatched to chase Muhammad and his companion. A prize of one hundred camels was set for anyone who could bring Muhammad back, dead or alive. The pursuers went in all directions. One group even went south and they came very close to the cave.

The Prophet and Abū Bakr settled safely in the cave of Mount Thawr. Abū Bakr had insisted that he should go in first, to make sure there was no wild animal or snake there and that it was safe for the Prophet to go in. In the desert of Arabia, squads of pursuers were frantically searching for them. The Prophet's plan was an elaborate one: as soon as he arrived at the cave, he gave the two camels to ʿAbdullāh ibn Arqat, a guide they had hired, and told him to take them to Madinah using an unfamiliar route. Thus the camels were not a burden to them in their three days of hiding in the cave. ʿĀmir ibn Fuhayrah, Abū Bakr's servant and his shepherd, took his sheep for grazing during the day. As the sun declined he went to the cave to give the Prophet and Abū Bakr their supply of milk and meat.

Abū Bakr's own son, ʿAbdullāh, was given an important task to fulfil. He was their intelligence man, moving around in Makkah during the day, listening at meeting-places before going to the cave as the evening approached, to keep his father and the Prophet informed of what was going on in Makkah. ʿAbdullāh then returned home followed by the shepherd and his flock, so that no trace of his footsteps would remain.

ʿAlī, the Prophet's cousin, was also given the task of returning people's deposits which were given to the Prophet for safekeeping. Despite all the hostility of the people of Makkah to Muhammad and his message, they had no doubt whatsoever of his integrity and honesty. Anyone who had something precious would entrust it to Muhammad, certain that he would find it safe whenever he wanted it. What is amazing in this situation is that they did not realize that a person of such honesty and integrity would not lie to God. ʿAlī, then, was asked to return people's deposits.

After three days in the cave, the Prophet and Abū Bakr were ready to resume their journey. Their guide, ʿAbdullāh ibn Arqat, brought them their camels and Asmā', Abū Bakr's daughter, brought them their supply of food. As she went to tie it to the saddle of her father's mount, she realized that she had forgotten to bring a string or a small piece of rope for the purpose. She therefore took off her belt and divided it in two, using one half to tie the food with. This action earned her the title Dhāt al-niṭāqayn, or 'the lady with two belts'.

When everything was ready, the Prophet and his companion set off on their risky trip, in the full knowledge that a very large prize – one hundred camels – was set on their heads.[5]

We should note that although the Prophet was assured of God's help and protection, he took all the precautions necessary to evade his pursuers. He moved first in the direction opposite to that of his destination and spent the first three days, when the chase would be at its height, in hiding. He ensured a regular supply of food and a daily intelligence report. His selection of a guide was based on the guide's skill, experience and honesty. ʿAbdullāh ibn Arqat was not a Muslim then. Full secrecy about his movements was maintained throughout. Only those who needed to know anything about his trip, because they had certain duties to do in connection with it, were given enough information to help them fulfil their duties. Beyond that, nobody knew anything about the timing of the trip or the route the Prophet was taking. Having done everything that was humanly possible to ensure his safety, the Prophet then relied on God to do the rest. He has thus taught us the true meaning of reliance on God.

It has already been mentioned that the pursuers went very close to the cave. As the two men sat quietly inside, Abū Bakr whispered to the Prophet: "If any one of them looks down, he is sure to see us." The Prophet's reassuring answer was: "Don't worry: God is with us."

Certain reports of the Prophet's journey speak of a pair of pigeons nesting outside the cave, and a spider spinning its threads over its opening. It is said that when the pursuers saw the nesting birds and the spider's web, they felt certain that no one was in the cave.

Obviously, God could easily have made the birds come and nest at the cave entrance and the spider weave its web there.[6] One should not, however, exaggerate any such visible manifestations of His work. Such a report has primarily a sentimental value. For the pigeons and the spider to do as the report says they did does not in any way increase our belief that God is able to accomplish His will. He could just as easily divert the non-believers' attention away from the cave, having brought them so close to it, in order to show them that they simply could not challenge Him.

Back on the March

After three days hiding in the cave of Mount Thawr, the Prophet and his companion resumed their journey. ʿAbdullāh ibn Arqat came at the appointed time with the two camels and they started their journey to Madinah, taking a totally unfamiliar route. The Quraysh's frantic chase had somewhat subsided, but it did not totally stop. The journey was around 500 kilometres and there were many caravans moving across the desert. Besides, people went about their business and any group of travellers in the desert, however small, might be a source of grave danger. The temptation of the high reward set on their heads would incite anyone to try to stop them. The Prophet then had to travel the whole distance, virtually unnoticed by anyone. This was very difficult indeed – hence the need for a guide with a great deal of experience and knowledge of all desert routes.

As they moved on their way towards Madinah, they realized that almost everybody in Arabia was fully aware of their flight and the reward offered for handing them over to the Quraysh. The Quraysh made sure that all the tribes whose quarters lay on the route to Madinah, and all familiar resting places, were informed of their wishes.[7]

Trying for the Prize

When the Prophet and his companion passed close by the quarters of the Mudlij tribe, they were spotted by a man who went straight to his people's meeting-place to report the fact. A man called Surāqah ibn Mālik was the first to realize the opportunity of winning the reward. To make sure that no one else joined him in chasing the Prophet and share in the reward, he said: "I have seen those people myself; they belong to such and such tribe and they are only chasing a camel which has gone astray."

Shortly afterwards, Surāqah left the meeting-place and went into his home, where he ordered his servant to get his horse ready and meet him a short distance away from the tribe's encampment. He took his spear and his sword and rode fast. In no time he spotted the travellers and was catching up with them. This is Surāqah's own story of events:

> As I was riding fast chasing them, my horse tumbled and I fell down. I wondered how this could happen to me. Still I persisted and rode on. When they reappeared fully in my view my horse tumbled and I fell down for the second time. I was not deterred, and I rode on. As I approached them, my horse's front legs sank into the sand and I fell down. As the horse pulled his sinking legs out, I saw that they were followed by a column of smoke. I realized that there was no way I could overpower Muhammad. I, therefore, shouted to them and asked them to stop. I assured them that I simply wanted to speak to them and I would not do them any harm. They stopped. I asked the Prophet to write me a note which would serve as a token he would recognize at a later date. He asked Abū Bakr to write me the note, which I used at the time of the conquest of Makkah to gain access to the Prophet and declare my acceptance of Islam.
>
> Having taken the note, I set off to return home. The Prophet called me and said: "What would you say, Surāqah, if you were to wear the bracelets of the Emperor of Persia?" I said: "Khosaru ibn Hormuz?" He said: "Yes." I did not answer. I went back and met several people chasing in that direction. I told everyone I met that I was sure Muhammad did not go that way.

It is worth noting here that when the Muslim armies overran the Persian Empire, a few years after the death of the Prophet, ʿUmar, the second Caliph, called in Surāqah and gave him Khosaru's bracelets to wear, in fulfilment of the Prophet's promise.[8] Needless to say, the promise was given in the most unlikely circumstances. A man chased by his own people, with a huge reward on his head, was promising complete and total victory over a great empire. At that moment, anyone else in his position would have been fully preoccupied with his own safety. This man of faith, however, has given us by this promise a feeling of what it means to be absolutely certain of the truthfulness of one's faith and its eventual victory.

Escaping Real Danger

The episode of Surāqah ibn Mālik was the nearest the non-believers could get to the Prophet during his historic journey to Madinah. Nothing else which could be described as serious happened on the way, which in itself says much for the careful planning of the journey. Yet on three occasions the Prophet could have been in a position of grave danger. Every time he was saved by something over which he had no control whatsoever. Firstly, when his house was encircled by the would-be assassins and sleep overpowered them all. Secondly, when his pursuers stood at the entrance to the cave in which he was hiding, and left without looking into it. Finally when Surāqah, spurred by the temptation of the high reward, was at a striking distance from the Prophet and his repeated falls from his horse turned him into a friend. On each of these three occasions, it may be said, the Prophet was saved by direct intervention of Providence.

One may wonder whether such intervention was a special act of kindness to the Prophet because of his unique position. Can we also expect similar acts from Providence when we ourselves are also in danger? Muslims believe that nothing can happen in the universe against the will of God; He supervises everything. This does not mean that He Himself does everything or causes it to happen. It simply means that the laws of the universe operate according to His will. He has made them and set them in motion. Only He has the power over them and can cause them to stop as He wills.

He can also cause any law of the universe to operate where it normally does not. This results in what may be termed 'miracles', which may appear to be supernatural. To God they are simply part of His creation. They are just as easy for Him to accomplish as the natural phenomena which we tend to accept as 'easy' and 'natural' because of our familiarity with them.

Indeed, God does this all the time. He operates His laws of the universe as He wills. He acts in every situation in the way which serves His purpose. As He is an active participant in the camp of the believers, He may intervene in any situation in order to accomplish what He pleases. This may seem miraculous or lucky, according to our interpretation of it. Muslims, however, believe that nothing in the universe could come about as a result of blind coincidence. Such a term has no entry in the Muslim lexicon. Hence, the Prophet came out of each of those three situations of grave danger as a result of a deliberate act of intervention by God. The same could happen to anyone in a whole variety of situations.

This does not mean that Muslims stop working and wait for God's intervention. One cannot expect a miraculous escape every time danger approaches. Such a fatalistic attitude has no Islamic sanction. One is, indeed, required to take, in every situation, all the measures which are necessary for the accomplishment of one's purpose. Once that has been done, one may add to it reliance on God and prayers to Him to make one's efforts fruitful.

In his planning of his risky trip, the Prophet left nothing to chance. He planned it with meticulous care. He did all that was humanly possible to ensure his safety. When he had done all that he moved with complete reliance on God and confidence that He would bless his efforts. This is the true Islamic attitude which has brought Muslims unparalleled success throughout history.

Completing the Journey

The Prophet continued his journey, stopping for a little while with Umm Maʿbad, a Bedouin woman who camped somewhere on his way. She had no milk or food to offer. Her husband had taken their sheep to graze, leaving only one sheep which was too weak to join the rest. Obviously, she did not have any milk. Times were very hard in that desert area. There were very few parts where animals could graze. Hence, few sheep produced any milk. Umm Maʿbad expressed her deep regret that she had practically nothing to offer her guests.

Having sought and received his hostess's consent, the Prophet wiped the dry breasts of the sheep and mentioned God's name. Milk came gushing out in abundance. Everyone drank his fill and Umm Maʿbad was left with a large quantity of milk before the travellers continued their journey.[9]

When the Prophet arrived at Qubā', a village only a few miles from Madinah, he was received well there and stopped for a few days. A mosque was built there which was the first ever to be built in the Islamic era. To this day it is visited by many pilgrims.[10]

At Madinah, the believers were anxiously awaiting the arrival of the Prophet and his companion. Although he had not informed them of his departure, or his expected date of arrival, they were aware that he was on his way. Indeed, all Arabia was aware of that, as may be deduced from various reports of varying degrees of authenticity.

As they realized that the Prophet was soon to arrive in Madinah, the believers started going out daily to the outskirts of the city, waiting for his arrival. They went out early, with the first breath of morning, and waited until midday, when they could no longer have any shelter from the burning sun.

Warm Reception at Madinah

One day, when they were on their way home after waiting the whole morning, a Jew, having climbed a tree in his orchard, noticed two people and a guide approaching. He shouted to the dispersing crowd, addressing them by a name the Jews used to refer to the people of Madinah: "Children of Qaylah, here comes your fortune."

Everybody rushed back to welcome the Prophet. They chanted a song of welcome which is still chanted today by Muslims who wish to express their love of the Prophet. The believers, both from the Muhājirīn (Makkan Muslims who emigrated to Madinah) and the

Anṣār (Madinan Muslims) escorted the Prophet and his companion as they proceeded into the city on their camels. Many of the Anṣār had not seen the Prophet before. They were able to recognize him by the respect Abū Bakr showed him. The Prophet's arrival at Madinah was on the twelfth of the lunar month of Rabīʿ al-Awwāl, in the year which was to become the first in the Islamic calendar. This date has been calculated to correspond to 24 September 622 AD.

As the procession went into Madinah, every clan invited the Prophet to be their guest. It was difficult to please them all. At the same time the Prophet did not want to offend any group of the Anṣār. He therefore told every group, as they held the rein of his camel, to let her proceed. "She has her orders," he said. She continued to walk in the streets and alleys of Madinah until she finally stopped near the home of Abū Ayyūb who immediately took the Prophet's luggage into his home, delighted that the Prophet had honoured him by being his guest.

There was nothing special about the place where the Prophet would lodge in his first few weeks in Madinah. One home was as good as another. But how could the Prophet make a choice which would keep everyone happy? One must remember that the Arabs of Madinah were still divided on tribal lines. Islam was the unifying force, and it had just begun to work for their unity. If the Prophet were to lodge with any clan, at their own invitation, they would take his action as a source of pride and honour, of which they would remind the other clans for a long time to come. To avoid this, the Prophet let loose the rein of his camel and left her to stop where she liked. God made her stop at Abū Ayyūb's home because, delighted as Abū Ayyūb was to be the Prophet's host, his understanding of Islam was so good that he kept this honour to himself and did not use it as a source of petty vanity and conceit.

Abū Ayyūb's home was a small two-storey house. The Prophet chose to lodge downstairs. Abū Ayyūb felt embarrassed to stay with his wife upstairs and talked about this to the Prophet, but the Prophet said it was more convenient for him and his visitors to stay downstairs.[11]

Thus the Prophet's risky trip was over, and he was to start immediately laying the foundations of the new state.

Notes

1. Ibn Hishām, *al-Sīrah al-Nabawiyyah*, Dār al-Qalam, Beirut, Vol. 1, pp. 118-120.
2. Ibid., p. 121.
3. Amīn Duwaydār, *Ṣuwar Min Ḥayāt al-Rasūl*, Dār al-Maʿārif, 4th edition, Cairo, p. 237.
4. Ibn Hishām, op.cit., pp. 124-126. Also, al-Ṭabarī, *Tārīkh al-Rusul wa al-Mulūk* , Dār al-Maʿārif, 4th edition, Vol. 2, pp. 370-372; and Ibn Kathīr, *al-Bidāyah wal-Nihāyah*, Maktabat al-Maʿārif, Beirut, Vol. 1, pp. 175-176.
5. Ibn Hishām, op.cit., pp. 127-131. Also, al-Ṭabarī, op.cit., pp. 373-379.
6. Ibn Kathīr, op.cit., Vol. 3, pp. 181-188.
7. Ibn Hishām, op.cit., pp. 133-135. Also, Ibn Sayyid al-Nās, *ʿUyūn al-Athar*, Dār al-Turāth, Madinah, 1996, pp. 301-302.
8. A. al-Suhaylī, *al-Rawḍ al-Unuf*, Dār al-Kutub al-ʿIlmiyyah, Beirut, Vol. 2. p. 323. Also, Mahdī Rizqullāh Aḥmad, *al-Sīrah al-Nabawiyyah fī Ḍaw'i al-Maṣādir al-Aṣliyyah*, Markaz al-Malik Fayṣal, Riyadh, 1996, p. 280; and Ibn Ḥajar al-ʿAsqalānī, *al-Iṣābah fī maʿrifat al-Ṣaḥābah*, Dār al-Mu'assasah, Beirut, Vol. 2, pp. 115-120.
9. Ibn Hishām, op.cit., p. 132.
10. Ibid., p. 137. Also, A. al-Suhaylī, op.cit., pp. 330-333.
11. Ibn Hishām, op.cit., pp. 139-141. Also, Ibn Kathīr, op.cit., pp. 198-199.

15

Madinah

IN HIS BOOK on the life of the Prophet, Shaykh Abū al-Ḥasan ʿAlī al-Ḥasanī Nadwī devotes a full chapter to a detailed picture of the social order which existed in Madinah at the time when the Prophet and his companions from Makkah settled there with their brethren who belonged to that city. Such a study is very useful in the understanding of the events that took place in the following years, which witnessed the rise of the first Islamic state in history. He points out that in Madinah, different faiths, cultures and communities lived side by side to give the city a particularly rich and colourful social life. In this it was markedly different from Makkah, which had a single faith and a single community. Here follows a summary of Shaykh Nadwī's account.

It is thought that the Jews arrived in Arabia, particularly in Madinah, in the first century AD. Dr Israel Wilfonson mentions that after the Jews suffered a heavy defeat at the hands of the Byzantines in AD 70 they sought shelter all over the world. Large Jewish groups headed for Arabia. There were three main Jewish tribes in Madinah, whose adult males numbered more than 2000. These tribes were the Qaynuqāʿ, al-Naḍīr and Qurayẓah. It is estimated that the Qaynuqāʿ tribe had around 700 men under arms, and al-Naḍīr had a similar fighting force, while adult males in Qurayẓah might have been 900 in number. Relations between all these tribes were not all that peaceful. They might go to war against each other. Perhaps the other Jewish communities in Madinah were hostile to the Qaynuqāʿ tribe because of the latter's alliance with the Arab tribe of Khazraj. In the battle known as Buʿāth, the other two tribes, the al-Naḍīr and Qurayẓah, fought hard against the Qaynuqāʿ and killed a large number of their men. At the same time, they paid ransom money for all Jewish soldiers who were captured by them. These hostilities continued after the Battle of Buʿāth. When the Anṣār prepared to fight the Jews of the Qaynuqāʿ, none of the other Jewish communities was ready to join them against the Anṣār.

The Jews lived in their own quarters and villages. The Qaynuqāʿ tribe had their special quarters inside the city of Madinah, after they had been expelled by the al-Naḍīr and the Qurayẓah from their forts outside it. The al-Naḍīr had their quarters about two or three miles to the north of Madinah, in a fertile valley called Bādhān. The Qurayẓah quarters were situated at a district called Mahzūr, a few miles to the south of Madinah. All Jewish tribes had their forts and districts where they lived independently, but they could not form a central authority dominated by the Jews to govern the city. On the contrary, they had their autonomy under the protection of the chiefs of the Arab tribes, to whom they paid annual tributes so that they could be secure from aggression. Every Jewish leader had an Arab ally from among the chiefs of Arab tribes.

They used to boast of their knowledge of religions and laws and they had their own schools where they studied their faith, legal code and history. They had special places for worship and they had their legal schools where they discussed all their affairs. Some of their laws and regulations were taken from their scriptures, while others were enacted for them by their rabbis. They had their special festivals and their days of fasting, such as the tenth of Muḥarram, when their fasting commemorated the saviour of Moses.[1]

Most of their financial and commercial dealings with others were according to a system based on taking pledges and usury. Since the economy of Madinah had an agricultural base, it was easy for the Jews to operate their usurious system because farmers often needed to borrow money until harvest time. In their pawn shops, the Jews did not only accept valuable articles as pledges, but would also take women and children as security against the repayment of loans. Such deals involving pledging one's wife or child inevitably generated a feeling of hatred between lenders and borrowers, particularly with the Arabs, who were famous for their keen sense of honour, which was overpowering in matters related to wives and children. This system, however, secured a strong financial position for the Jews, which enabled them to manipulate the market and exploit it to their own advantage. Hence, the whole population hated them for their selfishness, usury and for the means they adopted to get rich.

Their relations with the two Arab tribes in Madinah, the Aws and the Khazraj, were governed by their own interests. They would do anything which ensured any material gain. Hence, they tried to cause war to flare up between the two tribes, whenever they judged that such a war would be to their own advantage. Indeed, it was the Jews who caused all the civil wars which considerably weakened both the Aws and Khazraj tribes. Their unwavering aim was to gain full control of the city finances. When they talked about the imminent advent of a new Prophet, the Arabs of Madinah had all the encouragement they needed to embrace Islam.

The language the Jews spoke in their daily life was Arabic, with a distinct Hebrew accent, since they did not abandon Hebrew altogether, but continued to use it particularly in their prayers and scholarly work.

Had they wished, the Jews would have been able to exercise a strong religious influence among the Arabs, to give Judaism firmer roots in Arabia. Students of Jewish history, however, know that the Jews were never keen to persuade people to follow their own religion. Indeed, to try to propagate Judaism is not allowed in certain cases. There is no doubt that a number of Arabs from the Aws and Khazraj tribes, as well as others, embraced Judaism willingly, or owing to their marriage with Jews, or simply because of their upbringing among Jews. One prominent Jew, Kaʿb ibn al-Ashraf, a merchant and a poet, belonged to the Arab tribe of Ṭayy, but his father married a Jewish woman of al-Naḍīr, and Kaʿb was brought up as a Jew. Moreover, if an Arab lost two or three children in infancy, he might vow that if he had a surviving son, he would make him a Jew. Hence, some Arabs followed Judaism in this manner.

The two major Arab tribes in Madinah, the Aws and the Khazraj, branched out of Yemeni and Azd tribes as a result of repeated waves of emigration at different times. There were several reasons for such emigration, including the conquest of Yemen by Abyssinians and the major economic setback following the collapse of the Ma'rib dam. This suggests that the Jews were already settled in Madinah when the Aws and the Khazraj arrived. The Aws clans occupied the southern and eastern areas of Madinah, which were known as the Upper Part, while the Khazraj inhabited the Lower Part in the central and northern areas. There were four clans branching out from the Khazraj, all of whom belonged to Banū al-Najjār, who lived in the central area around the mosque which was later to be built by the Prophet. The Aws had their quarters in the very fertile areas, living side by side with the major Jewish communities, while the Khazraj lived in a less fertile area, neighbouring the Jewish tribe of the Qaynuqāʿ.

It is extremely difficult to estimate the Arab population in Madinah, but one can make a good estimate of their fighting force in the battles which they fought after the Prophet's settlement in Madinah. Their regiment in the Muslim army on the day when Makkah fell to Islam was 4,000 strong.

At the time of the Prophet's emigration to Madinah, the Arabs had the upper hand there. The Jews could not unite in opposition to the Arabs. Indeed, some of the Jewish clans formed an alliance with the Aws, while others were allied to the Khazraj. When they fought each other, they were fiercer in their mutual hostility than the Arabs. The enmity between the Qaynuqāʿ tribe on the one hand and the al-Naḍīr and the Qurayẓah on the other was so fierce that it compelled the Qaynuqāʿ tribesmen to abandon their farms and become manual workers.

Similarly, the Aws and the Khazraj fought several battles against each other, the first of which was known as the Battle of Samīr and the last as that of Buʿāth, which took place five years before the Prophet's emigration to Madinah. The Jews played a major part in perpetuating the hostility between the Aws and the Khazraj in order to keep them preoccupied with it. This earned the Jews the title 'Foxes', as they were called by the Arabs.

The geographical situation of Madinah left it divided into several quarters, each of which belonged to an Arab or Jewish clan. Each quarter included an agricultural part with its dwellings, and had another part in the form of a fort or several forts. There were 59 Jewish forts in Madinah. They were of particular importance because they provided shelter, particularly for women, children and the elderly in times of war. The forts were also used as barns for storing grains and agricultural produce; arms were kept there as well. In addition, some forts provided a resting-place for trade caravans. Moreover, the forts incorporated temples and schools with their own libraries. It is the combination of these quarters that made up the city of Madinah, which meant that the city was a combination of a group of villages which expanded to become one city.

The religious and social order was practically determined by the Quraysh. All Arabs recognized the authority of the Quraysh in matters of religion, because the Quraysh were the custodians of the Sacred House in Makkah. Hence, Arabs followed the Quraysh in their religious practices. This led to the spread of pagan beliefs. All Arabs worshipped the idols which the Quraysh worshipped, although they might have revered particular idols more than others. The idol named Manāt was known as the goddess of Madinah. It was the most ancient of all idols, and both tribes of al-Aws and al-Khazraj paid great homage to it. Its place was next to Qa'dīd Mount, near the sea on the road from Makkah to Madinah. Al-Lāt was the idol of the people of Ṭā'if, while al-ʿUzzā was the idol of the people of Makkah. Any inhabitant of Madinah who wanted to have his own idol of wood or any other substance would call it Manāt, after their main goddess. The Arabs in Madinah did not seem to have a particular idol within the city which earned any great prestige – such as al-Lāt, Manāt, al-ʿUzzā or Hubal – and which other people would have revered. It seems that idols were not as common in Madinah as they were in Makkah, where every household had its own idol. This meant that the people of Madinah were simply followers of what the people in Makkah invented.

The Quraysh recognized the high position of the Aws and the Khazraj, since they belonged to the major Arabian branch of the Qaḥṭān. Intermarriages between them and the Quraysh were quite common. Hāshim ibn ʿAbd Manāf, the Prophet's great-grandfather and the master of the Quraysh, married Salmā bint ʿAmr of the clan of al-Najjār, which belonged to the Khazraj. But the Quraysh continued to give itself the most prominent position of all. Moreover, the Quraysh looked down on agriculture as a means of livelihood. The people of Madinah, on the other hand, relied on agriculture for their living, in view of the fertility of their land.

The economic situation was generally comfortable. Madinah and its surrounding area was very famous for its dates and grapes. The staple diet of the local population was dates, particularly during periods of drought. Indeed, dates were used as currency with which it was possible to buy other articles. The date tree was also used in building and industry and as fuel and animal food. The farmland of Madinah yielded a large variety of dates and its people were highly experienced in maximizing their produce.

However, this did not prevent the people of Madinah from being active in commerce, albeit to a lesser extent than used to be the case in Makkah, which relied heavily on brisk import and export activity. A number of industries flourished in Madinah, but it was the Jews who excelled in these. It is said that the Qaynuqāʿ Jews were experienced jewellers, which meant that they were very rich compared to other Jews and Arabs.

The major crops which the land of Madinah produced were barley and wheat, in addition to vegetables and different types of beans. They had several practices with respect to renting agricultural land and selling agricultural produce. But Islam forbade some of these, permitting only what involved no injustice to either party. What helped agriculture flourish in addition to the fertile volcanic soil was the abundance of water sources. There were numerous streams and wells which ensured that water remained available throughout the year.

Makkah and Madinah had the same currency, either the Byzantine currency or the Persian one, but both were made of silver. In trade, the people of Madinah used volume more than weight. They had several recognized measures of volume.

It is important to mention that despite the fertility of its land, Madinah could not produce enough food to meet its needs. Hence it was necessary to import certain types of food from abroad. They used to import, for example, flour, fat and honey from Syria. Moreover, they had a wealth of cattle: camels, cows and sheep. Camels were used in irrigation. They also had their own grazing grounds where many people gathered wood for burning and took their horses and cattle for grazing. The people of Madinah used horses in their wars, but the number of horses they had was relatively smaller than those in Makkah. The Sulaym clan, however, were famous horsemen and imported their horses from various places.

There were several bazaars and markets in Madinah: the most important of all were the jewellery market of the Qaynuqāʿ Jews and a textile market where silk, cotton and other fabrics were sold, as well as the perfumery bazaars. Methods of trade were various, but Islam banned a number of practices. A small number of Arab businessmen from the Aws and Khazraj tribes based their dealing on usury, but they were very few compared to the Jews.

Generally speaking, life in Madinah before the advent of Islam was a comfortable one. A number of houses had more than one storey, and some had their own gardens. Some people might have fetched their water supply from a distant place because they wanted the best available drinking water. They had their tools, fine objects of furniture, decorative articles and jewellery. Women worked in weaving, sewing and dying. Sculpture and brick-making were among the skills known in Madinah.

In short, life in Madinah was much more complex than in Makkah, because of the presence of several religions, cultures and communities. Hence, the Prophet was bound to face a variety of problems. To mould the population of Madinah into a united community could be achieved only through the penetrating force of faith. Thus, Prophet Muhammad, who enjoyed God's support, was the only one able to achieve that unity at that particular time.[2] (This ends Shaykh Nadwī's summary.)

It was into this set-up that the Prophet arrived to build a coherent community and a new state. As already mentioned, his host was Abū Ayyūb al-Anṣārī, who was extremely happy to have the Prophet as his guest. Abū Ayyūb was not a very rich person but he was very hospitable, aware that to have the Prophet as a guest was a blessing for which he had to thank God all the time. Hence, both he and his wife tried their best to make the Prophet comfortable as long as he stayed in their home. One day, a jug in which they used to keep their water was broken and the water was spilled. They were worried lest any drop should filter through the floor and fall onto the Prophet. They rushed to dry the water, using a thick piece of velvet material which they used to cover themselves when they slept. They had no other blanket. To use it to dry the spilled water meant that their blanket was wet and they could not use it that night. Nevertheless, they would have preferred to stay up all night rather than disturb the Prophet by allowing water to leak through the floor.

Umm Ayyūb used to prepare dinner for the Prophet. Neither she nor her husband would eat anything before the Prophet finished his meal. If he returned the plate with some food in it, both of them would begin eating at the spot where the Prophet ate, hoping for God's blessings. With such people, the Prophet was made more than welcome for as long as he wished to stay. However, he did not wish to stay any longer than was necessary. He was soon to have his rooms built close to the mosque where he was to settle with his wife, Sawdah. She was soon to be joined by ʿĀ'ishah, another wife of the Prophet.[3]

Shortly after the Prophet's arrival in Madinah, he sent his companion, Zayd ibn Ḥārithah, together with Abū Rāfiʿ, to Makkah and gave them two camels and 500 dirhams. They brought back with them the Prophet's two daughters, Fāṭimah and Umm Kulthūm, together with his wife, Sawdah. Ruqayyah, another daughter of the Prophet, had already emigrated to Madinah with her husband ʿUthmān ibn ʿAffān. The Prophet's eldest daughter, Zaynab, remained in Makkah with her husband Abū al-ʿĀṣ ibn al-Rabīʿ, who was not yet a Muslim. Zayd ibn Ḥārithah also brought with him his own wife, Umm Ayman, who was the Prophet's wet nurse in his childhood. She had a son, Usāmah, whom the Prophet loved very much. They were also joined by ʿAbdullāh ibn Abī Bakr, with the members of Abū Bakr's family, including ʿĀ'ishah. When they arrived in Madinah, the Prophet settled them in the home of Ḥārithah ibn al-Nuʿmān.[4]

As the Muslims who emigrated from Makkah settled into their new homes in Madinah, they realized that it would be a long time before they would be able to see Makkah again. It was natural, therefore, that they would feel homesick. What made things worse for them was the fact that there was a malaria epidemic in Madinah at the time. Abū Bakr and Bilāl were among those who contracted the disease. Hence, the Prophet had to reassure his companions and quieten their uneasiness. He prayed to God to make Madinah as appealing to his companions as Makkah was, and to bless it and to end its epidemic.[5]

The Prophet realized that he had very important tasks to which he needed to attend in order to establish his new state. The first thing he did was to build a mosque. Opposite Abū Ayyūb's home there was an open area used to dry dates. The Prophet enquired about its owner and was told that it belonged to two young boys whose parents had died. Muʿādh ibn ʿAfrā' said he would compensate them handsomely for it and that the Prophet was free to use it as a mosque.

The Prophet called upon his companions to work together in the building of the mosque. He himself worked as hard as any of them. As they saw him working hard, they put in a great effort so that they could finish it in the shortest possible time. They cut down a number of date trees in the area; they levelled those parts which were uneven; then they laid the foundation, which was about two metres deep. The walls were made of unburnt brick. It was a square building, about 65 metres long each way. The *Qiblah* [i.e. the direction one faces while praying] was made towards Jerusalem, as Muslims were still facing it in their prayers. The ceiling was made of stalks of the branches of palm date trees which did not prevent rain leaking through. No special flooring or carpeting was used. A few mats were laid down which did not cover the whole area. Many worshippers prayed on the bare sandy floor.

Next to the mosque two rooms were built for the Prophet to use as a home. Similar material was used to build them and the roofing was also of palm date branches. When they were ready, the Prophet moved in.[6]

Building the mosque was the first major step the Prophet took as he settled in Madinah. He also built a mosque at Qubāʿ, where he had stopped for a few days before completing his journey to Madinah. One wonders, therefore, why he attached such a great importance to mosque-building.

The mosque is not simply a place for worship. Had it been so, it would have been given a secondary priority by the Prophet. Muslims can pray and offer their worship anywhere. Indeed, the mosque is a symbol of Islam as a complete and comprehensive way of life. The Prophet's mosque in Madinah was a spiritual centre for worship, the political and military headquarters of the new state where internal and external affairs were conducted, an institute of learning where discussions and seminars were held, and a social institution where Muslims learnt and practised discipline, equality, unity and brotherhood.

Thus the mosque was a place where many functions were performed. It was indeed the basic cell in the structure of the new community. From this mosque all the great men of that era of Islamic history graduated. It was a simple place, giving magnificent results. But when mosques lost their basic role in the life of the Muslim community, they became huge, magnificent edifices which could give only meagre results.

The Prophet wasted no time in tackling the major problems of building the first Islamic state. One major issue to which he immediately addressed himself was the consolidation of permanent ties between the various elements which constituted the Islamic community.

One must remember that the Anṣār [Madinah Muslims] belonged to two tribes which had been, until very recently, at each other's throats. Both camps were full of hope that with their adoption of Islam, they substituted a permanent, unwavering tie of brotherhood for their old hostility. There was also in Madinah a community of immigrants [the Muhājirīn] who belonged to several distinct and independent branches of the Quraysh. Although the Muhājirīn were well received in Madinah, they were not used to the type of life which prevailed in that city. They were mostly merchants, like the rest of the Quraysh, while the Anṣār were mostly farmers. A great deal of adjustment had to be made in order to reduce potential friction to a minimum.

The Prophet, therefore, called upon all his followers to establish a special bond of brotherhood. Each one of the Muhājirīn had to be the brother of one of the Anṣār.[7]

This new bond of brotherhood was different from the common fraternal ties which formed the basis of social relations within Islamic society. Those common ties of brotherhood are central in any community which adopts Islam as a faith and a code of living. The bond of brotherhood the Prophet established among the Muhājirīn and the Anṣār was special for the Madinah Islamic society. It meant much more than a spiritual bond. It translated itself in reality into something much stronger than any tribal or family relationship. It was so real to the people concerned that a Muhājirīn brother would inherit from his Anṣārī brother when he died and vice versa.

To illustrate how real the new bond was to its parties, one may quote the example of ʿAbd al-Raḥmān ibn ʿAwf of the Muhājirīn whose Anṣārī brother was Saʿd ibn al-Rabīʿ. Saʿd realized that he had to make his brother feel at home in Madinah. He therefore said to him: "Thanks to God, I am quite well-off, and I have decided to share my wealth with you in equal halves. I also have two wives; let me know which one of them you prefer and I will divorce her so that you may marry her."

ʿAbd al-Raḥmān was deeply touched by this very generous offer. However, he declined to take anything from his brother. He simply asked him to show him the marketplace, where he quickly began a small buying and selling business.

A few days later, ʿAbd al-Raḥmān went to the Prophet, who noticed that he must have had a celebration of some sort. ʿAbd al-Raḥmān explained that he had just got married to an Anṣārī lady. The dowry he gave her, as he told the Prophet, was a piece of gold equal in weight to a date stone.[8]

This little incident is indicative of the sort of feelings which existed among the two main groups of Muslims in Madinah: an unparalleled generosity from one side and a high standard of integrity from the other. Such feelings helped mould the two groups into a single cohesive community which continued to be an example for future Muslim generations to follow.

Expressing their feelings at the sort of welcome they had in Madinah, the Muhājirīn said to the Prophet: "We have never heard of any people who are as kind as our hosts: they are the best comforters when their means are limited, and they are the most generous when they are well off. They have spared us all effort and shared with us their luxuries. We fear they will get all the reward from God, while we are left with very little." The Prophet answered: "This will not be the case, if you are truly thankful to them and pray to God for them."[9]

Thus, the Prophet fostered firm and close relations among the Muslim community. He also had to look into his community's relations with others in Madinah.

Notes

1. It is authentically reported that when the Prophet settled in Madinah, he noted that the Jews fasted on the tenth of the lunar month, Muḥarram. He asked them the reason for their fasting and they answered: "It is a day on which God saved Moses." The Prophet said: "I have a stronger claim to Moses than theirs." He started to fast on that day and recommended his followers to do the same. The report does not mention the nature of the danger from which Moses was saved.
2. A. Nadwī, *Muhammad Rasulallāh* (English Translation by Muhiuddin Ahmad), Academy of Islamic Research and Publications, Lucknow, India, 1979, pp. 157-177.
3. Ibn Hishām, *al-Sīrah al-Nabawiyyah*, Dār al-Qalam, Beirut, Vol. 1, pp. 143-144. Also, Ibn Kathīr, *al-Bidāyah wal-Nihāyah*, Maktabat al-Maʿārif, Beirut, Vol. 1, pp. 201-202; and A. al-Suhaylī, *al-Rawḍ al-Unuf*, Dār al-Kutub al-ʿIlmiyyah, Beirut, pp. 340-341.
4. Ibn Kathīr, op.cit., p. 202.
5. Ibid., pp. 221-222.
6. Ibn Hishām, op.cit., pp. 140-141.
7. Ibid., p. 150.
8. Ibn Kathīr, op.cit., p. 228. Also, Ibn Sayyid al-Nās, *ʿUyūn al-Athar*, Dār al-Turāth, Madinah, 1996, p. 326.
9. Ibn Kathīr, op.cit., p. 228.

16

Peace and Confrontation

SEVERAL REFERENCES HAVE been made to two groups of Muslims in Madinah: those who came from Makkah, or the Muhājirīn, and the ethnic people of the Anṣār. It should be emphasized, however, that the distinction was of no lasting consequence. Both groups formed a single cohesive unit based on equality and brotherhood. It is perhaps impossible to exaggerate the strength of the ties between members of that first Islamic community. Internally, the structure of the Muslim nation was very sound. The Prophet, then, had to attend to the nation's 'external' relations.

There were two levels of these relations: firstly, with the Quraysh, who felt very hostile to the new state. It was inevitable that the Quraysh would pose a serious threat, though perhaps not immediately. The rest of Arabia adopted an attitude of wait and see, preferring not to commit themselves to Islam until the conflict with the Quraysh had been resolved. Secondly, there were the other communities in Madinah itself. Islam had been accused over the years of being intolerant to other religions. Nothing can be further from the truth. The example of Madinah gives an insight into the true nature of this religion.

There were two additional main communities in Madinah besides the Muslim nation. The Jews had their own independent community. They could easily separate themselves from the rest of the population of Madinah. There were also the Arabs who had not yet accepted Islam. These belonged to the same tribes as the Anṣār. No open hostility between them and the Anṣār was noticed. On the contrary, amicable relations were expected to continue between the two sides. Indeed, it was expected that more and more of those Arabs would come to realize the truth of Islam and adopt it.

The Prophet, however, proceeded to put relations with the two communities on a clear and firm footing. He also regularized relations and commitments within the Muslim community. A covenant was drawn up defining the responsibilities of every group within the Muslim community and outlining the nature of its relations with the Jews. Here is a translation of this constitutional document, which defined obligations, responsibilities and loyalties within the new state and towards other groups and communities:

> In the name of God, the Merciful, the Beneficent.
>
> This is a document drawn up by Muhammad, the Prophet (peace be upon him) for the believers and the Muslims from the Quraysh and Yathrib, and whoever joins them and takes part in their struggle for their cause: they are one nation, distinguished from all other people. The Muhājirīn of the Quraysh remain the same, bearing responsibility for the blood money they incur.[1] They pay for the release of those taken prisoner from among them, according to what is reasonable and fair among believers. The ʿAuf clan remain the same, bearing responsibility for the blood money they incur. Every group pays for the release of its prisoners, in accordance with what is reasonable and fair among believers.

The document repeats these terms with each of the Anṣār clans: Ṣāʿidah, Al-Ḥārith, Jusham, Al-Najjār, ʿAmr ibn ʿAwf, Al-Nabīt and Al-Aws. It then goes on:

> The believers shall not leave any one of them bearing heavy debts without reasonably helping him in the payment of blood money or ransom. No believer shall contract an alliance with the slave of another believer in preference to himself.

The God-fearing believers stand against any one among their number who transgresses or is guilty of oppression or indulges in an act of sin or aggression or corruption among the believers. They shall stand together against him even though he may be the son of any one of them.

No believer shall kill another believer in retaliation for the killing of a non-believer, nor shall he support a non-believer against a believer. Pledges of protection given under an oath apply to all. The least distinguished among the believers may offer a pledge of protection which is binding on all of them. Believers are one another's allies against all people. Anyone from among the Jews who joins us shall have our support and equal rights with us, suffering no oppression and fearing no alliance against them. Believers shall have a single pledge of peace. No believer shall make a peace agreement to the exclusion of another believer concerning any fighting for God's cause unless this agreement applies to all of them equally and fairly. Every group which joins us in an expedition of *jihād* shall carry its own numbers. The believers are equal with regard to sacrificing their lives for God's cause. The God-fearing believers are committed to the best and straightest guidance.

No non-believer shall extend protection to any property or any person belonging to the Quraysh, nor shall he stand between them and any believer. Anyone who kills a believer and is proven guilty shall be taken in retaliation, unless the victim's next of kin forgoes his right. All the believers shall unite against the killer and it shall not be lawful for them to do anything other than bring him to justice.

No believer who accepts this treaty and believes in God and the Last Day may give support or shelter to any criminal. Anyone who gives such support or shelter to a criminal incurs God's curse and His anger on the Day of Judgement. No compensation shall be accepted from him. On whatever you may differ, the final verdict rests with God and with Muhammad (peace be upon him).

The Jews shall share expenses with the believers as long as they are at war [with others]. The Jewish allies of the ʿAuf clan shall support the believers. The Jews have their own religion and the Muslims have their own. This applies to them and their allies. Anyone who is guilty of oppression or commits a sin only brings himself and his household to ruin. The Jewish allies of the clans of Al-Najjār, Al-Ḥārith, Sāʿidah, Jusham, Al-Aws and Thaʿlabah enjoy the same rights as the Jewish allies of ʿAuf. Anyone who commits injustice or a sin only brings himself and his household to ruin. Jafnah is a branch of Thaʿlabah, who enjoy the same rights. The Shuṭaybah clan have the same rights as the Jewish allies of ʿAuf. Honouring and fulfilling these conditions should be a barrier which prevents their violation. Whatever applies to the clan of Thaʿlabah also applies to their allies. The families and households of the Jews are in the same position as themselves. No one of them shall leave without the permission of Muhammad [peace be upon him]. Nothing shall be allowed to prevent retaliation for an injury. Whoever kills actually kills himself and brings his household to ruin, with the exception of one who is a victim of injustice. God certainly approves these terms.

The Jews shall bear their expenses and the Muslims shall bear theirs. They are required to render support against anyone who fights any party to this agreement. They owe it to each other to give sincere counsel. Fulfilment of the terms of this agreement should prevent its violation. No one shall be held responsible for a sinful action perpetrated by his ally. Support shall be given to the oppressed. The Jews are required to share the expenses with believers as long as the latter are engaged in a war. The centre of the city of Madinah is forbidden to the parties of this agreement. It shall be the same for oneself as a neighbour: he shall not be allowed to suffer any harm and commit a sin. No sanctity shall be protected without the consent of its people. Anything that takes place between the parties to this agreement, or any dispute that may develop between them,

> is to be referred for arbitration to God, the Almighty, and to Muhammad, His messenger [peace be upon him]. God approves the best and most pious elements that this agreement contains. Nothing that belongs to the Quraysh or to those who support it shall be protected. The parties to this agreement shall support each other against anyone who attacks Yathrib. If they are called upon to enter into any peace agreement, then they will do so. If they are invited to something like that, then the believers are required to support it, except with those who fight to suppress the faith. Every group shall bear its share of responsibility in the part closest to them. The Jewish allies of Al-Aws, their own people and their allies, have the same rights and obligations as the parties to this agreement, and this shall be sincerely honoured by the parties to this agreement. Fulfilment of the terms and conditions of this agreement shall prevent their cancellation. Everyone shall bear the responsibility for whatever action he perpetrates. God approves the best and most truthful of what this agreement contains. This agreement does not give immunity from punishment to anyone guilty of oppression or sin. He who leaves Madinah shall be safe and he who stays shall be safe unless he is guilty of injustice or sin. God is the protector of those who fulfil their pledges and are God-fearing, and so is Muhammad, God's messenger [peace be upon him].[2]

This agreement was the first of its kind in Arabia. It defines the sort of relationship that should exist within the Muslim community, and it defines the position of the Jews and their relationship with the Muslim state. The agreement considers the Jews as citizens within the Muslim state. They enjoyed their religious freedom and state protection. They were required to support the Muslim state against any enemy that attacked it. The Jews were also required to give sincere counsel to the Muslim state and never to conspire against it or to withhold information which was important to the security of the Muslim state. On the other hand, they were not allowed to leave Madinah without permission from the Muslim state, which enjoyed all sovereignty and would arbitrate in any dispute that might arise between the Jews and the Muslims.

The arrival of the Prophet (peace be upon him) in Madinah heralded the establishment of the first Islamic state in history. That the foundations of this state needed continuous consolidation was very clear to the Prophet, right from the beginning. His initial major actions as he took charge in Madinah reflect his keen awareness of that need. He built the mosque, which was a place of worship, a people's assembly and the palace of government, all in one. He established a new and strong bond of brotherhood between his followers to consolidate the inner structure of his community. He also signed a treaty with the Jews to ensure peace in Madinah and to free himself to face outside threats, which were only to be expected.

The Quraysh could not remain idle while the new state in Madinah acquired increasing strength. The Quraysh was bound to conclude that the Islamic state in Madinah was going to challenge for supremacy in Arabia. It was expected that the Quraysh might before long try to launch an all-out campaign to eliminate such a challenge before it had a chance to gather strength. A show of force by the Muslims in Madinah was therefore important, in order to make the Quraysh think twice before embarking on any such hazardous course of action.

One may note here that up to the last few months of the Prophet's active work for Islam in Makkah, Muslims were commanded by God not to resort to arms in any confrontation with non-believers. Several reasons may be advanced for such a policy. Firstly, the Makkan period was one of education of a certain people in a new tradition. The Muslim Arabs had to be trained not to retaliate for personal injury, but to look beyond their own persons and interests and to think first of their new community. Secondly, the use of force in the Makkan period might have led to increased stubbornness on the part of the Quraysh and, consequently, to a never-ending series of killing for vengeance. The blame for such an event would undoubtedly have been laid at the door of Islam. Thirdly, the use of force might have led to numerous little family wars, as the believers still lived with their own families and clans. Since the Muslims were still small in number, they might have been totally exterminated. Fourthly, the

Muslims would have lost all the support of their clans. We have seen how the support of the Hāshimites guaranteed for the Prophet all the protection he needed to continue his efforts in fulfilment of his mission.

As the Makkan period drew to an end, permission to fight the non-believers was given to the Prophet and his followers. This came in a Qur'ānic verse which was revealed shortly before the Anṣār made their second covenant with the Prophet. No fighting, however, took place before the Prophet's emigration. There was every indication that it would come soon. Hence preparations for such an eventuality were called for.

The Muhājirīn and the Anṣār were good fighters. Almost every one of them had fought with his tribe. As already related, the two tribes to whom the Anṣār belonged were involved in a fierce battle shortly before they came to know about Islam. But all this experience was not quite enough for the Prophet's purposes. The Muslim community would never fight a tribal war. A new army had to be built on a basis totally different from anything known in Arabia: the basis of faith. Thus, the purpose of war would be different. The soldiers' attitude to death in battle would be based on the Islamic view that a martyr is certain to be admitted to heaven. His attitude to his fellow soldiers would also be completely different. The Prophet wasted no time in building such an army.

The Prophet had moved without a moment's delay to consolidate the foundations of his new state. Internally, the fabric of the social structure of the new society was of the highest quality. Relations with other communities in Madinah were put on a sound basis. A well-trained army, which was soon to prove its calibre, was built up.

The establishment of the new state was indeed a great achievement which crowned the Prophet's hard work over the past 14 years. Since Madinah was not an isolated city, its relations with its neighbours were highly important. All around Madinah there were Bedouin tribes which did not have much of an idea about Islam. Independent though these tribes were, their natural sympathies were with the Quraysh. Like the Quraysh, they were pagans for whom religious values did not count for much. More importantly, the Quraysh was still the recognized superpower in Arabia. Something had to be done to persuade those Arab tribes that things had changed.

Moreover, the Prophet's mission was universal. That is, he was commanded by God to make his message known to all mankind and to call upon them to believe in it. At no time did the Prophet envisage the establishment of the new state as his final objective. It was simply the base from which he would move to explain his message to the rest of Arabia, and thence to the world at large.

To achieve both objectives, the Prophet started to send out armed groups of his companions in what historians have called Sarāyā, which may be roughly translated as 'expeditions'. Practically speaking, these were manoeuvres through which the Muslims learnt a great deal about their enemies: their capabilities, their strong influence on other tribes and the depth of their feelings against the new state. At the same time, these manoeuvres enhanced the Muslims' fighting ability and enriched their knowledge of the surrounding area.

The first expedition set out barely six months after the Prophet's arrival in Madinah. Thirty men from the Muhājirīn, commanded by Ḥamzah, the Prophet's uncle, went towards the coast to stop a Quraysh trading caravan. The leader of the caravan was none other than Abū Jahl, who had 300 men with him. No clash took place, as a tribal chief called Majdī ibn ʿAmr of Juhaynah intervened to prevent it. This expedition took place in Ramaḍān of the first year of the Islamic calendar.[3]

The following month (Shawwāl), the Prophet's companion, ʿUbaydah ibn al-Ḥārith, commanded a 60-man-strong expedition with the Prophet's instructions to go deep into the district of Rābigh, which was closer to Makkah than Madinah. There, at a spring called Aḥyā', they met Abū Sufyān leading a Quraysh force of 200 men. The two sides shot their arrows at each other but no direct fighting took place.[4]

A few weeks later in Dhul-Qaʿdah, Saʿd ibn Abū Waqqāṣ was the commander of a 20-man-strong expedition which went on foot, travelling by night and hiding during the day. On the fifth day they arrived at a place called al-Kharrār which was, according to their instructions, the furthest point they could reach. Having learnt that the Quraysh caravan they were supposed to intercept had been a whole day ahead of them, they had to go back.[5]

Nearly three months later, in Ṣafar of the following year, the Prophet himself led a group of his companions and set out until he reached a place called Waddān. There he concluded a peace agreement with a tribe called Ḍamrah. He met no enemy and went back. Having rested in Madinah for a short while, he set out again, leaving Abū Salamah to deputize for him in Madinah. He went as far as al-ʿAshīrah, close to Yanbuʿ, where he stayed for a few days and made another peace agreement with the allied tribes of Mudlij and Ḍamrah. He then went back to Madinah.[6]

Shortly afterwards, Kurz ibn Jābir of the Fihr tribe raided the grazing grounds on the outskirts of Madinah. The Prophet himself chased him with a group of his companions up to the valley of Ṣafwān, close to Badr. Kurz escaped. Historians call this chase the first Badr expedition.[7]

As time passed, expeditions increased in frequency and significance. A particular one deserves to be mentioned here because of its eventual outcome. A very small group of people went on this expedition, having had clear instructions. As the company was ready to depart, the Prophet gave ʿAbdullāh ibn Jaḥsh, its commander, his written instructions. He told him not to read them until he had been on his way for two days. There he would learn more about his mission. He was specifically told not to force any of his men to go along with him. Should any of them want to go back, he was free to do so.

When the company had been travelling for two days, ʿAbdullāh opened his sheet of instructions and read: "When you have read this, proceed until you reach the valley of Nakhlah, midway between Makkah and Ṭā'if. Try to get whatever information you can about the Quraysh." ʿAbdullāh said: "I shall, most willingly." He then turned to his companions and said: "God's messenger has commanded me to go as far as Nakhlah on a spying mission, to learn some news of the Quraysh. He has bid me not to force any of you to come along with me. Those of you who aspire to martyrdom are welcome; those who have other ideas may go back. As for myself, I am going to do as

I have been bid by the Prophet." All his companions went along with him; none went back.

Every pair of the group had one camel, which they rode in turn. At one point, one camel went astray. Its two riders, Sa'd ibn Abū Waqqāṣ and 'Utbah ibn Ghazwān, went chasing him, while the rest of the company proceeded with their mission until they reached the Nakhlah valley, their appointed place. Presently a small Quraysh caravan encamped close by them. When the Qurayshīs noticed the presence of the company, they panicked. 'Ukkāshah ibn Muḥsin of the Muslim group made himself visible to the Qurayshīs. He had shaved his head, which was a ritual most pilgrims and visitors to the Ka'bah perform. The Qurayshīs were thus led to believe that the other group, whom they did not recognize as Muslims, were ordinary pilgrims. A feeling of reassurance replaced their fear.

Meanwhile, the Muslim company were debating among themselves what to do about the caravan. There was a complication. The date was the last day of Rajab, one of the four lunar months in which fighting was strictly forbidden. This applied to both the Quraysh and the Muslims. The problem for the Muslim company was that if they waited a day, the caravan would have reached the sanctuary of Makkah, where it could not be intercepted. If they attacked, they would violate the injunction of the four sacred months. Eventually, however, they decided to attack.

'Amr ibn al-Ḥaḍramī was killed by an arrow shot at him by Wāqid ibn 'Abdullāh. Two more non-believers, 'Uthmān ibn 'Abdullāh and al-Ḥakam ibn Kaysān, surrendered to the Muslims. The fourth person from the Quraysh, Nawfal ibn 'Abdullāh, managed to escape. The Muslim company was thus able to confiscate the caravan and head back to Madinah.

When they arrived, the Prophet refused to take the two prisoners or the caravan, saying to the company: "I have not asked you to fight in the sacred month." The company felt very distressed. Their Muslim brethren reproached them for their action. They did not know what to do and felt truly lost.

This incident led to a fresh propaganda campaign by the Quraysh, who tried to smear the Prophet and his companions in the eyes of the other Arabs. They harped on the theme of their violation of the sacred month. The whole thing was a matter of affliction for the Muslims until God allayed their worries with fresh revelations of the Qur'ān which declared that to turn the Muslims out of Makkah was a much graver sin than the killing of a non-believer in the sacred month:

> They ask you about fighting in the sacred month. Say: "Fighting in it is a grave offence; but to turn people away from the path of God, to disbelieve in Him and in the Sacred Mosque and to expel its people from it – all this is a much graver offence in God's view. Indeed, religious persecution is worse than killing." They [that is, your enemies] will not cease to fight against you until they force you to renounce your faith, if they can. But he who renounces his faith and dies a non-believer, his works shall come to nothing in this world and in the world to come. It is such people who are destined for the Fire, therein to abide for ever. (2: 217)[8]

When the Prophet received that revelation he took custody of the two prisoners and divided the caravan among his companions. The Quraysh sent for the release of the two prisoners in return for ransom. The Prophet told them nothing could be done before the return of the other two of his companions, Saʿd and ʿUtbah, who were delayed chasing their camel. "If you kill them," he said, "we will kill your two men." Saʿd and ʿUtbah arrived shortly afterwards. The Prophet accepted the ransom for the two prisoners. One of them, al-Ḥakam ibn Kaysān, however, declared his acceptance of Islam and stayed in Madinah. The other went back to Makkah, where he later died.

The smear campaign launched by the Quraysh against the Prophet and his companions, making use of the fighting that took place in one of the four sacred months, soon died down after the Qur'ān had put the whole issue in the right perspective. The Quraysh was guilty of much graver violations of divine laws and, therefore, had no right to claim any virtue for themselves or to shame the Muslims for their action, serious though it might have been.

It is noteworthy here that despite the fact that the Quraysh and the rest of the Arabs did not believe in Islam and did not accept Muhammad as a Prophet, they could not refute the argument of the Qur'ān, whose words enjoyed much weight with the majority of Arabs.

The expedition related above, led by ʿAbdullāh ibn Jaḥsh, was in a sense the turning point which transformed the early military manoeuvres into well-organized military activity, including a number of major battles. That expedition was, perhaps, an early short peak which was a prelude to a climb of very high mountains. It was an expedition of eight men penetrating deep into enemy territory to demonstrate the vulnerability of the southern trade route from Makkah to Yemen. The clash took place over 500 kilometres away from Madinah in a valley midway between two centres of population which were very hostile to the Muslims: Makkah and Ṭā'if. It was therefore a demonstration of the Muslims' dedication to their cause and their willingness to take great risks, to secure a strong, well-protected base for their faith.

The early expeditions achieved considerable results for the Muslims. They enabled them to form a good idea of the geography and topography of the area surrounding Madinah. They identified the routes followed by trade caravans travelling between Makkah and Syria. They also established contacts with several tribes in the area and entered into alliances with some of them. The Muslims also proved that they were powerful enough to defend themselves and their faith against any external or internal threat. They were aware that threats could potentially come from either direction. Internally, the Jews and the Arabs who had not accepted Islam could pose a threat, while externally the Quraysh and her allies were on the lookout for a chance to crush the new Muslim state.

The Prophet also introduced certain new tactics which he employed in these expeditions. Most important among these was secrecy, which helped in taking the enemy by surprise.

As a result of these expeditions, the Quraysh recognized that its trade route to Syria was no longer secure. As Makkah relied on trade, such insecurity and the threat of an economic siege were restraining factors against the Quraysh making any rash move against the Muslims in Madinah.

The Prophet also established the necessary government machinery in Madinah which could function smoothly in his absence. He utilized these expeditions to put the economic and trade relations between Madinah and the surrounding areas on a sound basis. Madinah was a city in the centre of a largely Bedouin area. Bedouin raids on population centres are commonplace in all areas and ages. To avoid them, a city must take the necessary steps in two directions: peaceful, through alliances made with at least a significant section of the Bedouin tribes; militant, by demonstrating the ability to inflict painful, measured punishment when the need arises.

The Prophet utilized his expeditions for this ultimate goal, in both these two directions, with remarkable success. Yet the struggle against paganism could not be won merely by sending out small expeditions to demonstrate Islamic force. A long, hard struggle was yet to come.

An important event which took place some 16 or 17 months after the Prophet had settled in Madinah was the change of direction Muslims face when they offer their prayers. While the Prophet was still in Makkah, he was ordered to turn towards Jerusalem when he prayed. Muslims complied with this divine instruction and continued to do so after they had emigrated to Madinah, where they came in close contact with the Jews. The Jews used the fact that Muslims adopted their own holy city as their *qiblah* to claim that Judaism was the religion of truth and that Muhammad and his companions should adopt Judaism, instead of calling on the Jews to accept Islam.

Now, nearly 18 months after the establishment of the Islamic state in Madinah, new Qur'ānic revelations instructed the Prophet and the Muslims to turn towards the Ka'bah in Makkah when they prayed. The Prophet himself was very pleased with this change, which he keenly desired but dared not request.

The Jews in Madinah countered with a sustained campaign of criticism, as they felt that the change deprived them of their argument for refusing to accept Islam. Their new campaign sought to create doubts in the minds of Muslims as to the basis of their own religion.

If it was right, the Jews argued, that the Muslims should formerly face Jerusalem in their prayers, then the new direction is wrong. They also told the Muslims: "Your prayers from now on would then be of no value. If, on the other hand, the new direction is right and the Kaʿbah is the true *qiblah*, then your prayers in the past were in vain." The Jews also argued that God, the Lord Who knows all, does not change His instructions in that manner. The change clearly showed, the Jews went on, that Muhammad did not really receive any revelation from God.[9]

Reading the verses which speak of this subject and the argument that ensued in Madinah shows that the Jewish campaign was not without results. Reassurance was needed and was, indeed, provided in a long passage in the Qur'ān, which runs from verse 106 to verse 150 in the *sūrah* entitled The Cow. A word of explanation here may be useful.

Arabs revered the Kaʿbah before the advent of Islam. To them it was the symbol of their national glory. It was also one of the factors which held the Arab tribes together. Islam, however, requires of its followers total, undivided loyalty. Muslims must dedicate themselves wholly to God and the cause of Islam. The Prophet's companions must, therefore, abandon all their former loyalties, tribal, racial or national. Hence the need to separate their worship from their traditional reverence of the Kaʿbah. To accomplish this they were ordered to turn towards Jerusalem when they prayed.

After a period of time, when the Muslims had accepted the new situation – moving away, in the process, from the rest of the Arabs – they were taught to regard the Kaʿbah in a different light. They were told to face it in their prayers because it was built by the two Prophets, Abraham and Ishmael, as a place wholly devoted to the worship of God alone. Thus it becomes part of the heritage of the Islamic nation, which has come into existence by way of answering Abraham's prayers to raise among his seed a Prophet who would teach them the true religion.

Thus, having achieved the objective of making the Muslims turn to Jerusalem in their prayers for a while, it was now time to give them their own distinctive *qiblah* – the Kaʿbah, the first house of worship ever built. This process made the Muslims keenly aware that they were the true heirs of Abraham and his religion, based on total submission to God.

To be distinct from others is very important when one speaks of faith and worship, for worship is the visible expression of the beliefs which take root in the soul. If worship is visibly distinct from that of other religions, then it strengthens the perception that the religion itself is unique. The purpose of giving the Muslims their own *qiblah* must be seen in this light.

Notes

1. This condition ensures the collective responsibility of a family, clan or tribe to pay blood money to the family of any person accidentally killed by any one of them. The phrase 'remain the same' approves these commitments as they existed immediately before Islam.
2. Ibn Hishām, *al-Sīrah al-Nabawiyyah*, Dār al-Qalam, Beirut, Vol. 1, pp. 147-150. Also, Ibn Kathīr, *al-Bidāyah wal-Nihāyah*, Maktabat al-Ma'ārif, Beirut, Vol. 1, pp. 224-226.
3. Al-Wāqidī, *Kitāb al-Maghāzī*, Oxford University Press, 1966, Vol. 1, pp. 9-10. Also, Ibn Hishām, op.cit., pp. 245-248; and Ibn Kathīr, op.cit., pp. 144-146.
4. Al-Wāqidī, op.cit., pp. 10-11. Also, Ibn Hishām, op.cit., pp. 241-245.
5. Al-Wāqidī, op.cit., p. 11. Also, Ibn Hishām, op.cit., p. 251.
6. Ibn Hishām, op.cit., p. 248. Also, al-Wāqidī, op.cit., pp. 11-12.
7. Al-Wāqidī, op.cit., p. 12.
8. Ibid., pp. 13-19. Also, Ibn Kathīr, op.cit., pp. 248-252.
9. Ibn Hishām, op.cit., p. 257. Also, Ibn Kathīr, op.cit., pp. 252-254; and Ibn Sayyid al-Nās, *'Uyūn al-Athar*, Dār al-Turāth, Madinah, 1996, pp. 363-372.

17

Badr: The First Major Battle

THIS ACCOUNT HAS now reached the second year of the Prophet's settlement in Yathrib, which has come to be permanently associated with Islam. No decree or order of any sort was issued to change its name, but from now on it has become *Madīnat al-Rasūl*, or 'the city of God's Messenger', Madinah or The City, for short. Events have been moving fast there. The clash which took place between the expedition led by ʿAbdullāh ibn Jaḥsh and a Quraysh trade caravan was at the end of Rajab (the seventh month of the lunar calendar) of that year. The change of direction in prayer took place two or three weeks later, in the month of Shaʿbān. The following month, which was Ramaḍān, was to witness a great event which marked a turning point in the history of Islam.[1]

Intelligence was brought to the Prophet (peace be upon him) that a large trade caravan, in which almost every household in the Quraysh had a share, was returning to Makkah after completing a successful business trip to Syria. The caravan was led by Abū Sufyān, a prominent figure in Makkah and the chief of the Umayyah clan.

It should be remembered that when the Makkan Muslims emigrated to Madinah they left almost all their belongings behind, and the Quraysh lost no time in confiscating their property. The caravan, therefore, seemed to offer a good opportunity of getting some compensation for the Muslims' losses. The Prophet suggested to his companions: "Here is a caravan of the Quraysh, with much of their wealth. If you intercept it, God may reward you with it."[2]

It is clear that the Prophet did not issue an order to the Muslims to mobilize for the mission at hand, otherwise everyone would have taken part. In the event, a force of 313 men marched with the Prophet. Besides, they were not fully equipped for a major clash with the enemy.

The Prophet had in mind another aim in addition to the compensation of former losses. He wanted to demonstrate the inability of the Quraysh to protect its own trade routes. This would shake the Quraysh and weaken their reputation as the master tribe in Arabia.

Abū Sufyān, the leader of the caravan, was a shrewd man. He was aware of the danger posed by the Muslims in Madinah. He, therefore, sought intelligence of the Prophet's movements. Learning that a Muslim force had marched to intercept his caravan, he took two steps at the same time. He hired a messenger called Ḍamḍam ibn ʿAmr of Ghifār to go with a message to Makkah asking the Quraysh to provide him with protection. He also took extreme care to evade the Prophet and his intercepting force. When he was at Badr, he realized that the Muslims were very close to him. He moved fast and changed his route, taking the coastal way, in the hope of avoiding the Muslims.

A Dream Warning of Immediate Danger

Three days before the arrival of Ḍamḍam in Makkah, ʿĀtikah bint ʿAbd al-Muṭṭalib, the Prophet's paternal aunt who still lived in Makkah, had a significant dream. She sent for her brother al-ʿAbbās and told him that in her dream she saw a man riding a camel coming to a place in Makkah called al-Abṭaḥ, where he stood and shouted: "Rise, you people, and move to your deaths in three days' time." People gathered round him and followed him as he moved towards the mosque, where he repeated his warning. He then moved hastily towards a nearby mountain called Abū Qubays, where he repeated his warning for the third time. He then picked up a large stone and threw it down. As it reached the bottom of the mountain, it split up into small pieces, each going into one of the houses in Makkah, leaving no house without a piece of the stone in it.

Al-ʿAbbās told his sister that her dream was certainly significant but he advised her to keep it to herself. However, he related it to his friend al-Walīd ibn ʿUtbah who in turn narrated it to his father. In no time everybody knew the story.

The following day al-ʿAbbās went to the Kaʿbah to do his *ṭawāf* and he was seen by Abū Jahl, who asked him to come over and have a word when he had finished. Upon joining Abū Jahl and his group, al-ʿAbbās was asked by Abū Jahl: "When did this female prophet appear among you?" Al-ʿAbbās said: "What are you talking about?" Abū Jahl indicated that he was referring to ʿĀtikah's dream, but al-ʿAbbās pretended that he had no knowledge of the matter.

Abū Jahl then said: "You, the ʿAbd al-Muṭṭalib clan, are not satisfied to claim a man prophet. You are now claiming a woman prophet. ʿĀtikah alleges that the man in her dream said, 'Rise in three days'. Well, we will wait these three days, and if nothing happens to confirm her dream, we will write a formal assertion that you are the biggest liars in the whole of Arabia."

Al-ʿAbbās did not say much to him apart from denying that ʿĀtikah dreamt anything. In the evening, all the women of the ʿAbd al-Muṭṭalib clan came to al-ʿAbbās and remonstrated with him for not answering Abū Jahl firmly. Al-ʿAbbās apologized and promised to rectify his omission.

On the third day, al-ʿAbbās went to the House (the Kaʿbah) hoping to provoke Abū Jahl so that he may have a chance to answer him back. However, he saw him moving towards the door as he heard Ḍamḍam shouting. Ḍamḍam stood on his camel, having cut the camel's nose and torn his own shirt to indicate the gravity of the message he was delivering. He shouted as loudly as he could: "A tragedy! A disaster! Your property with Abū Sufyān is being intercepted by Muhammad and his companions. I doubt whether you can save the caravan. Help! Help!"

A general feeling of anger spread among the people of the Quraysh when they heard Ḍamḍam delivering Abū Sufyān's message in this dramatic manner. It was soon overtaken by a determination to put an end to the threat posed to their trade caravans by the Muslims in Madinah. Everyone was saying: "Does Muhammad think that this caravan is an easy prey, like the caravan of Ibn al-Ḥaḍramī? He will be proved wrong."

The Quraysh, therefore, mobilized a large army, 1,000 men strong. It was raised in a very short period of time. All men of distinction joined in. Those who could not go with the army in person sent other men in their place. The example of Umayyah ibn Khalaf of the Jumaḥ clan gives a clear idea of the pressures and motives for everyone who enjoyed any degree of honour among the Quraysh to join the army. He was on friendly terms with Saʿd ibn Muʿādh of the Anṣār. Saʿd had visited Makkah some time before all these events took place, where he was the guest of Umayyah. He informed Umayyah that the Prophet mentioned that the latter could be killed soon. Now when the Quraysh mobilized, remembering that conversation, Umayyah decided to stay behind. Learning of his intention, a friend of his called ʿUqbah ibn Abū Muʿayt came to him carrying a small pan with burning incense. He said to Umayyah: "You had better smell this, because you are a woman."

Umayyah replied: "Confound you and what you have done!" He then got ready and joined the army. Abū Lahab, the Prophet's uncle who strongly opposed him, decided to stay behind. He sent al-ʿĀṣ ibn Hishām in his place. The latter had gone bankrupt, owing Abū Lahab 4000 dirhams. Abū Lahab asked him to deputize for him in the army, then he would write off his debt.

A Demonstration of Power

When the Quraysh army had fully mobilized and started to move, they received a new message from Abū Sufyān to the effect that he had succeeded in evading his pursuers and the caravan was now safe. They might spare themselves the trouble of marching out to challenge the Muslims. This news was greeted with evident relief. Many of the Makkans wanted to demobilize. Abū Jahl, however, had the final say: "We will not go back, but we shall march on to Badr [a venue for an annual celebration for the Arabs], where we shall stay for three days to celebrate. We shall slaughter camels for food, feed whoever cares to come to us, drink wine in abundance and be entertained by singers and dancers. The whole of Arabia shall hear about us and hold us in awe for the rest of time."

Thus Abū Jahl wanted to demonstrate the Quraysh's power and the fact that they were able to defend themselves and protect their caravans. Obviously Abū Jahl was keenly aware of the morale-boosting successes the Muslims were able to score against the Quraysh, both militarily and psychologically. He therefore felt the need to stem the tide, counterbalance those successes and preserve the Quraysh's reputation as the main tribe of Arabia.[3]

Meanwhile, the Prophet marched at the head of his 313-man strong expedition. They had only 70 camels and two horses to ride. They therefore had to take turns in riding their camels. The Prophet, ʿAlī and Marthad al-Ghanawī shared one camel. When the Prophet's turn was over, his two companions would try to persuade him to continue on the camel's back and they would walk on. He insisted that he also should walk, and said: "You are not any more able to walk than I, and I am not any less in need of the extra reward from God than you." Abū Bakr, ʿUmar and ʿAbd al-Raḥmān ibn ʿAwf took turns in riding one camel; so did Ḥamzah ibn ʿAbd al-Muṭṭalib, Zayd ibn Ḥārithah and the two servants of the Prophet: Abū Kabshah and Anasah.

The Prophet's march brought him and his companions nearer to Badr, which was on the caravan route to Makkah. When the Prophet left Madinah, he organized his men so that they would be ready to meet any eventuality and to face any surprise attack. After all, they were marching in enemy territory. He assigned an advance group under the command of al-Zubayr ibn al-ʿAwwām and a rear group commanded by Qays ibn Abī Ṣaʿṣaʿah. He had one main, white flag carried by Muṣʿab ibn ʿUmayr and two black ones carried by ʿAlī and a man from the Anṣār. They did not march in close ranks or in groups since they were traversing open ground. Their formation was an open one so that they could move fast, guarding against any surprise. Thinking that Abū Sufyān's caravan should still be in the area, the Prophet sent two of his companions to gather intelligence. The expedition followed the two men at a distance. As the sun set, the Prophet and his companions encamped very close to Badr. He sent out a group of his companions including three who were highly prominent, ʿAlī, al-Zubayr and Saʿd ibn Abū Waqqāṣ. He asked them to try to ascertain the position of the caravan and to gather whatever information they could. They came back with two boys who were looking for water for the Quraysh army. The Prophet's companions mistakenly thought that they belonged to Abū Sufyān and his caravan.

When the Prophet interrogated the boys, it became clear that they belonged to the Quraysh army. From the information they gave him the Prophet realized that the army was at least three times stronger than his own force. He was also certain that they were far better equipped. The Muslims did not set out from Madinah in order to engage in a major clash, as the Quraysh did. They simply hoped to intercept a trade caravan. Furthermore, he learnt that a large number of the Makkan leaders were in the army. He turned to his companions and said: "Makkah has sent you its dearest children."

To Fight or Not to Fight

The Prophet felt that the caravan he set out from Madinah to intercept had eluded him. A large army, three times stronger than his force and much better equipped, had set out on a mission of power demonstration. A totally new situation had thus developed and had to be faced. The Prophet (peace be upon him) felt he needed to consult his men before taking any decision. He, therefore, put the matter to them, explaining that a confrontation was inevitable, if the Quraysh were to be prevented from scoring a moral victory. The Prophet wanted to gauge his companions' readiness for war.

Abū Bakr was the first to speak. He assured the Prophet that they were solidly behind him. ʿUmar then said something to the same effect. Al-Miqdād ibn ʿAmr, the next man to speak, said:

> Messenger of God! Go ahead and do whatever you feel best. We will never say to you as the Israelites had said to Moses: "Go with your Lord and fight the enemy while we stay behind!"

> What we will say is: "Go with your Lord and fight the enemy and we will fight alongside you." By Him Who has sent you with the message of truth, if you ask us to march with you to Bark al-Ghimād [a place in Yemen] we will fight with you anyone who stands in your way until you have got there.

The Prophet thanked him and prayed for him, yet he still asked his men to come forward with their opinions.

The point here was that the three who spoke belonged to the Muhājirīn (that is, the Muslims who emigrated from Makkah with the Prophet). Their willingness and determination to defend the cause of Islam was never in doubt, no matter what they were asked to do. Yet they formed a small part of the Prophet's army. The majority of the troops were from the Anṣār (that is, the Muslims of Madinah). None of them had yet spoken when the Prophet repeated his request to hear other people's points of view.

There was another point of which the Prophet was keenly aware. When the Anṣār made their covenant with him at ʿAqabah that they would support and protect him against his enemies, they made it clear, at the time, that they would not be responsible for him until he had reached their city. "When you have arrived at our quarters," they said at the time, "you will be in our charge and we will protect you as we protect our women and children." The Prophet therefore thought that the Anṣār might feel that their pledge of support applied only to cases when the enemy attacked him in Madinah itself. In other words, the pledge of protection did not include marching out to engage the enemy in battle away from home. The Prophet, therefore, needed to be sure of his companions' feelings.

Saʿd ibn Muʿādh, a prominent figure among the Anṣār, was the first to realize what the Prophet meant by his repeated request for further opinions. He said: "You seem to want to know our opinion, Messenger of God?" Having received an affirmative answer, Saʿd continued:

> We have declared our faith in you and accepted your message as the message of truth. We have made firm pledges to you that we will always do as you tell us. Go ahead, therefore, Messenger

> of God, and do whatever you wish, and we will go with you. By Him who has sent you with the message of truth, if you take us right to the sea, we will ride with you. None of us shall stay behind. We have no qualms about encountering our enemy tomorrow. We fight hard and with strong determination when war breaks out. We pray God to enable us to show you what would please you. You march, then, with God's blessings.

The Prophet was very pleased with what Saʿd had said. He said to his companions: "I can give you the happy tidings that God has promised me that one of the two enemy hosts [the caravan or the army] would fall to us. I can discern now their leaders being killed when we clash."[4]

Here again one notes the Prophet's masterly tact in carrying his followers with him when he faced a serious situation. Of course he could have issued an order and all his companions would have had to comply. By allowing them to make their free choice, however, he achieved a much better result. Besides, he wanted to make sure of their own understanding of their pledges. Had they told him they did not covenant with him to march out for a military clash away from Madinah, he would not have asked them to do more than they had pledged. He never breached a promise or solicited such a breach by others. All this helps to show the nature of the relationship between the Prophet and his companions.

Having made sure through consultation with his companions that they were solidly behind him should a battle with the Quraysh prove inevitable, the Prophet (peace be upon him) marched forward until he reached Badr. There were plenty of wells and the Prophet decided to encamp by the first well he reached. One of the Anṣār, al-Ḥubāb ibn al-Mundhir, asked him: "Are we encamping here because God has told you to do so and we are not to move forward or backward from here? Or is it your own judgement that this is the right place to gain advantage against the enemy?"

When the Prophet answered that it was the latter, al-Ḥubāb said: "Then this is not the right place at which to encamp. We would be better advised to move forward, right to the nearest well to the enemy, where we can encamp and make a basin full of water. We would then close the rest of the wells so that we may have our supply of water and they can have none." The Prophet unhesitatingly endorsed this opinion and ordered that it be carried out.[5]

Here, one notes again that the Prophet was always ready to listen to advice and put it into effect. The fact that he himself might have had different ideas was never an obstacle to the implementation of sound advice. Incidents like this one tended to emphasize that he was a human being whose views on matters not related to the faith or to his task of conveying God's message to mankind could be subject to review and amendment. Such incidents were also practical lessons to all future Muslim rulers that no man could always be right.

Saʿd ibn Muʿādh suggested that a shed should be erected for the Prophet as his headquarters. He said: "You will have your horse ready. If we win, then that is what we want. If it is the other eventuality, then you will ride your horse to join the rest of our people. Those who have been left behind love you as much as we do. Had they thought you were going into war, they would not have stayed behind. They will protect you, give you good counsel and fight your enemies alongside you."

The Prophet thanked Saʿd and prayed for him. A shed was built in accordance with Saʿd's proposal. Soon afterwards there was a light drizzle which helped make the ground a little firmer to enable the Muslims to move swiftly.[6]

In the Enemy Camp

As for the Quraysh, they were still marching on. When the Prophet saw them coming into the valley, he made this supplication: "My Lord, this is the Quraysh demonstrating all its conceit to contend against You and call Your Messenger a liar. My Lord, grant me the victory You have promised me. My Lord, destroy them today."

When the Quraysh encamped, a group of them came up to the basin the Muslims had built. The Prophet told his companions not to oppose them. Every one of them who had a drink was killed in the battle, with the exception of Ḥakīm ibn Ḥizām, who was later to convert to Islam.

Both sides sent spies to learn about the conditions in the other camp. ʿAmmār and ʿAbdullāh ibn Masūd, the Prophet's emissaries, came back with this report: "There is an air of fear in their camp, so much so that if a horse wants to snort, they hit him in the face. It is also raining heavily over there."

ʿUmayr ibn Wahb of Jumaḥ was asked to make a good guess at the number of Muslim troops. He went far into the valley to make sure there were no forces held in reserve. His report was as follows: "They are three hundred, give or take a few. But I can see a catastrophe and much killing. They simply have no protection apart from their swords. I think that we will not kill any one of them without him killing one of us first. Should they be able to kill their number from our side, life would not be worth living. You make your own decision."[7]

His report caused a stir among the Quraysh. One must remember that not all of the Qurayshī leaders were keen on a confrontation with the Prophet. Many would have preferred not to go out at all after the caravan managed to escape its pursuers. But it was a situation where the hard-liners held sway.

They managed to carry the rest of the Quraysh with them when they defined the purpose of their expedition as a demonstration of power which would enable the Quraysh to protect its position as the leading tribe in Arabia. Now that war was looming large, some people felt it was totally unnecessary. To start with, the two clans of ʿAdiy and Zuhrah decided to withdraw. Al-Akhnas ibn Sharīq said to the Zuhrah soldiers: "God has saved your property and spared your tribesman Makhramah ibn Nawfal. You have mobilized to save him and his property. Put the blame on me if you are accused of cowardice, and let us go back. There is no need for you to go on a fighting course for nothing. Do not listen to what this man [meaning Abū Jahl] says." They accepted his advice and went back home. The rest of the Quraysh clans succumbed to the pressure which was brought to bear on them by Abū Jahl and his clique of hard-liners. Some of them still felt that they were on the wrong course.[8]

The Prophet realized that the Quraysh were not all united in wanting a military confrontation with him. He himself felt uneasy about going to war against his own people. Although he never shrugged off his responsibilities and never hesitated to go to war when war was inevitable, still he would have preferred that the Quraysh did not force him into battle. For force him they did, by the mere fact that they were marching through Arabia demonstrating their strength and trying to impose their supremacy over all tribes.

In an attempt to avoid a clash, the Prophet sent his companion ʿUmar ibn al-Khaṭṭāb to tell the Quraysh to go back, for he would rather meet some other people in battle.[9] This message, coupled with what ʿUmayr ibn Wahb said about the number of the Muslim troops and their determination and high morale, caused a considerable stir among the Quraysh. After all, they had nothing much to avenge against the Prophet and his companions. When he was in Makkah they were the aggressors. After his departure the only real grievance they held against him was the killing of one man, ʿAmr ibn al-Ḥaḍramī, and the looting of his trade caravan.

Rejecting Wise Counsel

It was Ḥakīm ibn Ḥizām who tried to do something to avoid a confrontation. When he heard the Prophet's message from ʿUmar, he said to his fellow Qurayshīs: "You have been offered a fair deal. You would do well to accept it." He then went to ʿUtbah ibn Rabīʿah and said to him: "You are the honourable man of the Quraysh and its obeyed master. Shall I tell you something which would bring you high praise for the rest of time?" When ʿUtbah showed his interest, Ḥakīm said: "Tell the Quraysh to go back and you will pay the indemnity for the death of Ibn al-Ḥaḍramī, for he was your ally. You also bear the loss of his looted caravan."

Recognizing the great advantages of this course of action ʿUtbah immediately accepted and asked Ḥakīm to act as his witness. He also asked him to go to Abū Jahl to try to persuade him not to oppose ʿUtbah's proposal.

ʿUtbah himself then stood up and addressed the Quraysh:

> Take it from me and do not fight this man [meaning the Prophet] and his companions. I will shoulder all the responsibility. You may put all the blame on me for this cowardice. Among these people many are our kinsfolk. Should we win, many a man among us will look around and see the killer of his father or brother. This will lead to much enmity and hostility in our ranks. You cannot kill them all before they have killed an equivalent number of you. But then the tide may turn against you. What do you seek to avenge, apart from one killed person and the caravan they have looted? I shall bear all that myself. Fellow men, if Muhammad is a liar, the wolves among the Arabs will rid you of him. If he is a king, you will benefit from the kingdom of your nephew. If, on the other hand, he is truly a Prophet you will be the happiest of all people for having him. My fellow men, do not reject my counsel or belittle my view.

Little is reported about the effect of ʿUtbah's speech among the Quraysh soldiers. When Ḥakīm ibn Ḥizām went to Abū Jahl with the same message, it did not cut much ice with him. He said: "ʿUtbah's cowardice has surfaced now that he has seen Muhammad and his companions. We shall not go back until God has judged between our two parties. ʿUtbah does not believe what he says. It is simply that having seen that they are few in number and that his son is among them, he fears that his son may be killed."

Despite the contradiction in Abū Jahl's argument, he harped a great deal on this theme. He also sent to ʿAmr ibn al-Ḥaḍramī, the brother of the man killed by a Muslim expedition, and incited him to appeal to the Quraysh to avenge his brother's death. This appeal drowned ʿUtbah's peaceful counsel, and most Qurayshīs were now determined to fight. The Prophet's companions at Badr were a little worried when they realized that the enemy forces were at least three times as big as their own, let alone that they had far superior equipment. But God was on their side. Suddenly they were overtaken momentarily by sleep. When they woke up, their worry had gone altogether. It was replaced by a feeling of reassurance. Their sleep served to transform their morale completely. Their confidence was sky high after they woke up. This is recorded in the Qur'ān: "He made slumber fall upon you as a reassurance from Him." (8: 11) The Muslims were now eagerly awaiting the start of the battle.

Back in the unbelievers' camp, ʿUtbah's attempt to persuade the Quraysh to go back met with complete failure. Abū Jahl was a master in arousing passions and spreading an atmosphere of high tension. His sustained efforts to ensure that the Quraysh's resolve to have a military showdown did not weaken have already been referred to. He further caused word to go round that ʿUtbah had adopted that conciliatory attitude towards the Muslims because he feared for the life of his son, Abū Ḥudhayfah, who was in the Muslim army. He further accused him of being cowardly. ʿUtbah felt deeply hurt by all these malicious accusations to which he was subjected by Abū Jahl, and wanted to show how untrue they were. He therefore came out of the rank of the Quraysh army accompanied by his brother Shaybah and his son al-Walīd and challenged the Muslims to a six-man duel.[10]

The Quraysh army had already started to move when ʿUtbah, his brother and his son made their personal move. As the army moved, one of its number, al-Aswad ibn ʿAbd al-Asad of the Makhzūm clan, sprang out of the ranks, saying: "I pledge to God to drink from their reservoir, or I will pull it down, or I will die in my attempt." Ḥamzah ibn ʿAbd al-Muṭṭalib, the Prophet's uncle, struck him with his sword, chopping off his leg. Al-Aswad, however, continued to crawl towards the reservoir and Ḥamzah followed him until he killed him at the reservoir. Thus al-Aswad was the first casualty of that battle.[11]

The Muslim army was very well organized. The Prophet himself had supervised its deployment. He addressed his companions, stressing the importance of putting up a determined fight. He then said to them: "Do not move forward until I have given you the order. When they approach, try to repel them with your arrows. Do not draw out your swords until they have reached you." He then went into the shed which had been built for him. Saʿd ibn Muʿādh and a group of the Anṣār stood by the shed, swords in hand, to guard the Prophet against any attack by the unbelievers.

ʿUtbah, his brother and his son made their challenge, saying: "Muhammad, let our equals come out for a duel." The Prophet sent out three of his own relatives: Ḥamzah, his uncle, and his two cousins ʿAlī ibn Abī Ṭālib and ʿUbaydah ibn al-Ḥārith. The three duels were: ʿUbaydah against ʿUtbah, Ḥamzah against Shaybah and ʿAlī against al-Walīd. In no time, Ḥamzah and ʿAlī succeeded in killing their two opponents, while ʿUtbah and ʿUbaydah struck each other at the same time. Both fell to the ground. ʿAlī and Ḥamzah then made sure that ʿUtbah was killed, both striking him with their swords, and carried ʿUbaydah with them to the Prophet, who laid his head on his leg. ʿUbaydah's main injury was to his leg, which was cut off. The marrow of his bone was spilling out. The Prophet gave him the happy tidings that he was about to be the first martyr of Badr.[12]

The end of these duels served as a signal for starting the battle in earnest. The Quraysh army moved into attack immediately. The Prophet had marshalled his troops very well. Now he ordered them to wait until the attackers were very close. As already mentioned, they were allowed to try to repel them with arrows.

The Prophet took a handful of dust and said: "Let these faces be hung down." He then blew the dust at the Quraysh.

As the two armies drew closer, Abū Jahl said: "Lord! Let the side which severs relations of kinship, and invents falsehood, be destroyed today." His was a prayer to ensure his own ruin.[13]

The Prophet made the prize very clear to his companions as he told them: "By Him Who holds Muhammad's soul in His hand, anyone who is killed fighting these people, dedicating his life for the cause of God, moving forward not backward, shall be admitted by God into heaven." As the enemy troops closed on the Muslims, the Prophet gave them his command to go into battle.

It was a hard fight between two unequal forces. The Muslims, however, were motivated by their faith. They hoped for ample reward from God and many of them wished dearly for martyrdom, knowing that a martyr is certain to be rewarded by admission into Paradise. Therefore, they counter-attacked with courage and determination. No enemy leader was too far for them, no company of soldiers was too strong.

Their attitude is epitomized by that of ʿUmayr ibn al-Ḥamām, who was eating a few dates when he heard the Prophet's words about those killed in battle. He said: "Well, Well! All that separates me from heaven is that these people should kill me!" He then threw away his dates and said: "If I live until I have eaten these dates, I have lived too long." He then fought very hard until he was killed.[14]

The fact that they were outnumbered three to one was a great inspiration to the Muslims, who were soon to overpower their enemy. The Quraysh troops were overwhelmed by their determined onslaught.

The Prophet went into his shed, overlooking the raging battle. He then came down and took part in the fighting. He kept going up into the shed and down into the battlefield, encouraging his companions and raising their already high morale. When he was in his shed he prayed to God: "My Lord, I appeal for the fulfilment of Your promise to me. Should this company of believers be overrun, You will not be worshipped again on earth. Grant me the victory You have promised me. My Lord, strike fear in their hearts. Let them be shaken." He kept praying earnestly and seeking God's help, with his hands raised to the sky. His garment fell off his shoulder. Abū Bakr, his only companion to go into the shed with him, held the Prophet's garment and put it back on his shoulder. He said soothingly: "Messenger of God! Not so hard with your appeal to Your Lord. He will surely grant you what He has promised you." The Prophet, however, went on with his appeal and prayers, but he was soon momentarily overtaken by sleep. When he woke up he was markedly more cheerful. He said to his companion: "Rejoice, Abū Bakr. Victory is certainly coming from God. This is the Angel Gabriel holding the rein of his horse on top of the battle dust." The Prophet then went down to give his companions the happy tidings that they would be victorious.[15]

A word should be added here about the role of the angels. In all the campaigns the Muslims fought with the Prophet against the unbelievers, God sent angel troops to support them. The angels would normally stand in support, without taking part in the actual fighting. Only in Badr did they fight. The reports about their joining the battle are too numerous to be contradicted.

As the battle was about to start, the Prophet said to his companions: "I have come to know that a few men from the Hāshim clan and others have been made to join the army against their will. They have no quarrel with us. Any one of you who meets any Hāshimite should not kill him. If you come across Abū al-Bakhtarī ibn Hishām, do not kill him. If you meet al-ʿAbbās ibn ʿAbd al-Muṭṭalib, do not kill him. He came out against his will."

Abū al-Bakhtarī, who was not a Hāshimite, was singled out by the Prophet because he was, perhaps, the most moderate among the Quraysh in his attitude towards the Prophet. He was indeed one of the five men who successfully mounted the campaign to end the three-year boycott of the Prophet's clan by the rest of the Quraysh.

Abū al-Bakhtarī, however, was met in battle by an Anṣārī man called al-Mujaddhar ibn Ziyād, who told him of the Prophet's specific instruction in his case. Pointing to a friend who was walking alongside him, Abū al-Bakhtarī said: "What about my colleague?" Al-Mujaddhar said: "We will not let him off. The Prophet's instruction applies only to you." Abū al-Bakhtarī said: "Then both of us will die together. No woman in Makkah shall say that I have abandoned my friend in order to save my own life." He then fought al-Mujaddhar, who killed him. Al-Mujaddhar then went to the Prophet to apologize and explain that Abū al-Bakhtarī refused to be taken captive and was determined to fight.[16]

The Battle of Badr was the first major clash between the young Islamic state in Madinah and the Quraysh, the predominant Arab tribe which had opposed Islam ever since its very first day. As such, its importance cannot be exaggerated. A win for the Quraysh might have tempted them to march on to Madinah to put an end to Islam altogether. A victory for the Muslims, on the other hand, would establish them as a major force in Arabia on a parallel level with the Quraysh. This explains the Prophet's earnest prayers for a complete victory.

The Muslims were aware that nothing less than a clear victory could serve their purpose. Hence they went into battle, eager to prove that numerical and material strength could not withstand the power of faith. Having seen two of the most distinguished figures in the Quraysh, ʿUtbah and Shaybah, fall in the initial duels, they went for other leading figures.

Umayyah ibn Khalaf was the chief of the Jumaḥ clan. In the early days of Islam, he assumed a leading role in torturing the new Muslims in an attempt to force them to renounce their new religion. His main victim was Bilāl, who endured a great deal of hardship from Umayyah until he was finally bought by Abū Bakr, who set him free.

As related earlier, Umayyah did not want to join the Quraysh army but he was shamed into joining it by one of the Qurayshī hard-liners. As the battle broke out, Umayyah was keen to save his own life. He was therefore pleased to come across ʿAbd al-Raḥmān ibn ʿAwf, one of those who adopted Islam in its very early days. ʿAbd al-Raḥmān, who was an old friend of Umayyah, was carrying a few armour plates. Umayyah asked him: "Would you like to take me instead of your armour plates? This would be a much better deal for you."

ʿAbd al-Raḥmān agreed, threw away the armour plates he was carrying, and moved to lead Umayyah and his son ʿAlī away from the battlefield to a place where they could be safe as captives. As they walked together, Umayyah remarked that the most notable thing about the battle was that the Muslims were not keen to take prisoners, who could bring them a great deal of money in ransom.

At that moment Bilāl saw Umayyah being led away. He shouted: "Umayyah, head of idolatry, may I perish if he survives!" He then drew near to them. ʿAbd al-Raḥmān made it clear to Bilāl that the two men were his prisoners and should not be harmed. Bilāl repeated his determination to avenge himself on Umayyah. When ʿAbd al-Raḥmān implied that he would defend his captives, Bilāl appealed to the Anṣār: "Supporters of God's cause! Here is Umayyah, head of idolatry! May I perish if he survives."

A group of the Anṣār surrounded them. ʿAbd al-Raḥmān tried to protect them but one of the Anṣār struck ʿAlī, Umayyah's son, on the leg. He fell down. His father uttered a loud cry, and both he and his son were killed instantly.

Abū Jahl himself was among those killed in Badr. A man from the Anṣār called Muʿādh ibn ʿAmr reported that during the battle he noticed that several men from the Quraysh stood in a circle round Abū Jahl and said to one another: "Abū al-Ḥakam [that was his name among the Quraysh] shall not be reached." Muʿādh said:

> When I heard them saying that, I resolved to get to him. I made a determined attack towards him and when he was within my reach I struck him with my sword once, which was enough to send half his leg high into the air, as a date stone flies from underneath the date-stone crusher. His son, ʿIkrimah, struck back at me and cut off my arm, which remained attached to my body by a thin piece of my skin. I was prevented by the raging battle from coming back on him. I, however, kept on fighting for the rest of the day, pulling my arm behind me. When it became too troublesome I bent down and put my hand under my foot and stood up to cut off my arm.

Muʿādh lived more than thirty years after that day.[17]

Later during the battle, another Anṣārī, Muʿawwadh ibn al-Ḥārith, passed Abū Jahl and hit him hard until he could not get up. He then left him, not quite dead.[18]

When the battle was over, the Prophet asked some of the Muslims to look for Abū Jahl among the dead. The man who found him was ʿAbdullāh ibn Masʿūd, a little man who used to be a shepherd in Makkah and was once at the receiving end of Abū Jahl's aggression against the Muslims. ʿAbdullāh put his foot on his neck and said: "You enemy of God, haven't you been humiliated?" Abū Jahl replied: "How? I am only a man killed by his people. Tell me, who has secured victory in battle?" ʿAbdullāh told him that victory belonged to 'God and His Messenger'. He then chopped his head off and took it to the Prophet. That was the end of the arch-enemy of Islam.[19]

Many leading Quraysh personalities met their death in Badr. Both moderates and hard-liners suffered, for both were in the same camp. Those mentioned, like ʿUtbah, Shaybah, Umayyah, Abū Jahl, Abū al-Bakhtarī, were only a few from the leading class who were killed. Others, like Zamʿah ibn al-Aswad and the two brothers Nabīh and Munbbih, sons of al-Ḥajjāj, met the same fate. The Muslims simply launched a fierce attack which no Quraysh army could have hoped to repel. It is not surprising, therefore, that at the end of the day the Quraysh losses amounted to 70 dead and 70 taken prisoner. Fourteen Muslims fell as martyrs in the battle.[20]

These figures can be taken as evidence of the ferocity of the battle and the sort of effort the Muslims put into achieving their resounding victory. After all, they were outnumbered three to one, yet they managed to claim nearly half their own number either killed or taken captive. Such a remarkable victory was certainly achieved with the help of God. A number of factors combined to make it possible.

Firstly, the Muslims were fighting under one command. The Prophet himself was their commander-in-chief. His sense of timing was superb. The relationship between commander and soldier was exemplary. Discipline among the Muslim forces was of the type any army commander would love to have. All these aspects made the Muslim army highly efficient; this compensated for its numerical weakness.

While the Prophet consulted his companions before every step he took, the unbelievers lacked unity of purpose. A large number of notables were in the army, but the most distinguished among them were ʿUtbah and Abū Jahl. The views of these two men were widely different. Suffice it to say that one of them, ʿUtbah, felt compelled to start the battle because the other, Abū Jahl, tried hard to make him appear cowardly.

Secondly, the Prophet marched from Madinah to Badr using a strategy similar to the one adopted today in desert warfare. He also sent out patrols to gather information.

Thirdly, the goals of the two camps were worlds apart. The Muslims wanted to ensure freedom of thought, worship and expression for everyone. The message of Islam had suffered much repression by the Quraysh for a decade and a half. Now it was time for the Quraysh to be taught a lesson in respecting man's basic rights. The Quraysh's goals were simply those outlined by Abū Jahl. When many in the

Quraysh army wanted to go back home after having learnt that Abū Sufyān's caravan was safe, Abū Jahl said: "We will march on to Badr and stay there for three days. We will slaughter camels for food, organize a big feast and make it open to everyone to come and eat. We will drink much wine and will be entertained by singers and dancers. When this is known, all Arabian tribes will hold us in awe for the rest of time." These cannot be the goals of a serious army; this is a short-sighted objective of people driven by conceit.

Lastly, morale among the Muslims was sky-high, even among those who had their first taste of battle at Badr. Good equipment and numerical strength cannot win a battle if morale is low. This is true of all wars, both ancient and modern.

When the battle was over and the Quraysh army withdrew, having suffered a crushing defeat, the Prophet ordered the burial of the dead. The 14 Muslim martyrs were buried in graves dug for them by their brethren. A disused well which had dried up was used to bury the enemy soldiers. When all 70 of them were buried, the Prophet stood at their grave and said, "People of the well! Have you seen how God's promises always come true? God's promise to me has certainly been fulfilled." Some of the Prophet's companions wondered how he could speak to the dead. He said: "They now know that what God has promised is fulfilled."[21]

The Prophet then sent ʿAbdullāh ibn Rawāḥah and Zayd ibn Ḥārithah to convey the good news to the people of Madinah. Usāmah ibn Zaid mentions that his father arrived to give the news of victory shortly after the burial of Ruqayyah, the Prophet's daughter who was married to ʿUthmān ibn ʿAffān. She was ill when the Prophet set out from Madinah. He asked her husband, ʿUthmān, not to join the expedition. Instead, he was to stay and look after her. ʿUthmān later married the Prophet's third daughter, Umm Kulthūm.[22]

Notes

1. The events in this chapter are reported in every work on the Prophet's life. However, the basic and earliest sources are: Ibn Hishām, *al-Sirah al-Nabawiyyah*, Dār al-Qalam, Beirut, Vol. 2, pp. 257-297, and al-Wāqidī, *Kitāb al-Maghāzī*, Oxford University Press, 1966, Vol. 1, pp. 19-101.

2. Ibn Hishām, op.cit., pp. 257-258. Also, Ibn Kathīr, *al-Bidāyah wal-Nihāyah*, Maktabat al-Ma'ārif, Beirut, Vol. 3, p. 256.
3. Ibn Hishām, op.cit., pp. 258-263.
4. Ibid., pp. 263-267. Also, Ibn Kathīr, op.cit., pp. 260-268.
5. Ibn Hishām, op.cit., p. 272.
6. Ibid., pp. 272-273.
7. Al-Wāqidī, op.cit., Vol. 1, p. 62.
8. Ibn Hishām, op.cit., pp. 270-271.
9. Al-Wāqidī, op.cit., p. 61.
10. Ibn Hishām, op.cit., pp. 274-276.
11. Ibid., pp. 276-277. Also, al-Wāqidī, op.cit., p. 68.
12. Ibn Hishām, op.cit., pp. 277-278.
13. Ibid., p. 280.
14. Ibid., p. 279.
15. Ibid.
16. Ibid., pp. 283-285.
17. Ibid., pp. 287-288. Also, al-Wāqidī, op.cit., p. 87.
18. Ibn Hishām, op.cit., p. 288.
19. Ibid., pp. 288-289. Also, al-Wāqidī, op.cit., pp. 89-90.
20. Ibn Kathīr, op.cit., Vol. 3, pp. 300-301 and 303-304.
21. Ibid., pp. 292-293. Also, Ibn Hishām, op.cit., p. 292, and al-Wāqidī, op.cit., pp. 102 and 112.
22. Ibn Hishām, op.cit., pp. 296-297.

18

In Madinah After Badr

AS THE DUST of the battle settled and the dead were buried, the Muslim soldiers looked at the booty they had gained in the war. It was plentiful but there was a problem with it. Those who collected the booty claimed it on the grounds of their action. On the other hand, those who fought the Quraysh army and, as it began to withdraw, chased it in order to ensure that it did not regroup to launch a new attack, also put a claim to it. Their argument was that their efforts enabled their brethren to collect the booty. A third group who kept guard at the Prophet's shed also staked their claim. They argued that they could have joined in its collection or in chasing the enemy. However, they feared that if they did either, they would leave the Prophet vulnerable to any counter-attack or raid.[1]

Observing this dispute among his companions, the Prophet did not try to adjudicate between them. Instead, he told them to pool the booty until God had revealed His judgement. When they had done so, the *sūrah* entitled The Spoils of War or *al-Anfāl,* was revealed. It opens with this verse: "They will ask you about the spoils of war. Say: 'All the spoils of war belong to God and the Messenger. Remain, therefore, conscious of God and set aright your relationship with one another. Obey God and His Messenger if you are true believers'." (8: 1)

This dispute may seem highly uncharacteristic of the Prophet's companions. After all, those who fought the Battle of Badr belonged either to the Muhājirīn or the Anṣār. The first group had left all their property and possessions in Makkah in order to emigrate and help build the new Islamic state in Madinah. As for the Anṣār, God describes them in the Qur'ān as people "who love those who have emigrated to their city..., and give them preference over themselves, even though they may be very poor indeed". (59: 9)

Several reasons may be advanced for that momentary aberration on the part of the Prophet's companions, who normally set an example in almost all aspects of life. Firstly, it was normal in Arabia that one's contribution in battle was measured by the booty one secured. Everyone, therefore, was keen to have the best practical testimonial to his part in this, the very first major clash with the enemies of Islam. Everyone would have loved to show his guests and his children and grandchildren the sword or the body armour he gained in Badr. Secondly, it was normal in the Arabian society to cherish what one gained in battle. Thirdly, one must not forget that Muslims generally lived in dire poverty. It was normal, therefore, that the question of personal shares in the booty should be paramount, once the enemy had been defeated and the booty had been collected. After all, the Prophet's companions were human beings, and all human considerations had their effects on them. The heights of nobility and self sacrifice they reached did not take away from them their human feelings or cares and considerations. When they slipped, however, they were expected to correct their errors once they had been reminded of them. This is the reason the Qur'ān appeals to their sense of faith whenever they need fresh instruction in the qualities of the faithful. This is evident in the verse quoted above, which gives the answer to their questions about the spoils of war.

Fair Distribution of the Booty

The Prophet and his army spent that night in Badr. Early in the morning they set out for Madinah, taking with them their prisoners and their booty. Later that morning the Prophet stopped to distribute the booty. He divided it equally among all those who were in the army, assigning one share for the man fighting on foot and two shares for the horseman (the additional share was for the horse). He also included those like Ṭalḥah and Saʿīd ibn Zayd whom he had sent on special missions and those like ʿUthmān whom he had asked to stay behind in Madinah for specific reasons. The shares of those who died in battle were given to their heirs.

Some of the Prophet's companions queried this method of equal distribution. Saʿd said to him: "Do you, Messenger of God, give the horseman who causes havoc among the enemy the same as you give to a weak person?" The Prophet answered: "Do you think that you are given victory except for the sake of the weak among you?"[2] The Prophet's answer indicates that might on its own is not a guarantee of victory. Cooperation, unity and the exertion of maximum collective effort are also essential for the achievement of victory. After all, the weak fighter gives the best he can, in the same way as the strong one. That is all Islam requires from anyone. The reward, therefore, should be shared equally.

The Prophet did not distribute the booty on the battlefield in order not to make it a tradition. If the Muslim army remained in position and preoccupied itself with the spoils of war, the enemies might regroup and attack again. For this reason, division of the booty was delayed, as it was considered a matter of secondary importance.

When the Prophet reached a place called al-Rawḥā', he was met by the Muslims from Madinah who offered their congratulations on his victory. They also apologized for not joining the battle. Usayd ibn Ḥuḍayr was speaking for them all when he said to the Prophet: "God be praised for having given you the victory which brings you happiness. Had I thought that you would be going to war I would not have stayed behind. I thought it was only a caravan you were intercepting, not an enemy you were fighting." The Prophet accepted their congratulations and excuses, saying to Usayd: "You are certainly stating the truth."[3]

As congratulations were offered, Salamah ibn Salāmah said: "What are you congratulating us for? We have only met bald old men who looked like tied-up camels and we slaughtered them." The Prophet smiled and said: "Nephew! Those were the men of honour." What he meant was that no one should underrate their position or fighting ability.

As has already been mentioned, when the battle was over the Muslim army found itself with no fewer than 70 prisoners. Many enemy men preferred to surrender rather than get killed in the battle. In his shed the Prophet was watching the battle and a group of Muslim soldiers was guarding him lest a band of enemy troops should launch an attempt on his life. A notable personality amongst these was Saʿd ibn Muʿādh, who did not look very pleased with what he saw. The Prophet asked him and he confirmed his displeasure: "This is the first defeat God has caused the idolaters to suffer, and I would have preferred that we spare none of their men."[4]

Saʿd's view, however, was not shared by most Muslim fighters, who hoped that the prisoners of war would bring in some badly needed income as the Quraysh would be keen to pay their ransom.

Singled Out Prisoners

When the Prophet marched from Badr with his troops, they took the prisoners with them. They stopped at a place called al-Uthayl, where the Prophet looked at all the prisoners. When he saw among them al-Naḍr ibn al-Ḥārith, his look struck fear into al-Naḍr's heart. The latter said to the man next to him: "By God, Muhammad will surely kill me. He looked at me with an eye full of death." The man said: "He would not kill you; you are only scared."

Al-Naḍr, however, had good reasons for his fears. He therefore started to look around for someone who might put in a good word for him. He tried with Muṣʿab ibn ʿUmayr, who was a relative of his: "Plead for me with your crony so that he may apply to me the same treatment as the rest of the Quraysh prisoners. He will certainly kill me unless you do."

Muṣʿab said: "You used to speak ill of God's book and His Messenger, claiming that the Qur'ān was 'legends of the ancients' and that the Prophet was a liar. You also used to inflict torture on Muslims." Nevertheless, al-Naḍr continued to plead with Muṣʿab: "Had you fallen prisoner to the Quraysh, they would never have killed you while I was alive." Muṣʿab answered: "I do not believe you. But then, I am not like you. I am a Muslim. My adoption of Islam means that all my other ties have been severed."[5]

Indeed, al-Naḍr was not the sort of enemy anyone would wish to spare. He literally did all he could to turn people away from Islam, inflicting great torture on anyone upon whom he could lay his hands. He started a propaganda campaign against Islam. Whenever the Prophet addressed a group of people and read a passage from the Qur'ān to them, he would come and sit in the Prophet's place and say: "Do not listen to Muhammad. What he claims to be Divine revelations is nothing but some legends of the ancients. I have a book better than his!" He would go on and tell them of the histories of ancient empires. His campaign of smear and defamation was effective with some people. His allegations about the Qur'ān are referred to no fewer than eight times in the Divine Book.

For all this the Prophet gave his command that al-Naḍr be beheaded. That was done on the spot. The man who had taken al-Naḍr prisoner, al-Miqdād, wished that he should be spared so that he would get his ransom, but the Prophet prayed to God to give al-Miqdād of His bounty and he was satisfied.

Another prisoner, ʿUqbah ibn Abū Muʿayṭ, was also killed on the Prophet's order when he reached a place called ʿIrq al-Ẓabyah. As he was taken to be killed, he shouted: "Whom are you leaving to look after my boys, Muhammad?" The Prophet's answer was: "The Fire". ʿUqbah asked: "Do you single me out from all your prisoners?" The Prophet replied in the affirmative, pointing out to his companions some of the crimes the man had perpetrated. He said: "As I prostrated in my prayers once in the Mosque, he put his foot over my neck and pressed hard. He did not release me until I felt my eyes would come out of my face. On another occasion he threw over my head the stomach of a dead sheep while I was praying. Fāṭimah came to wash it off my head."[6]

Kind Treatment of Prisoners of War

When the Prophet arrived in Madinah, he assigned the prisoners to various groups of his companions and asked them to look after them well. That meant, in effect, that the prisoners received the sort of treatment no prisoners of war could have expected or even dreamt of. Abū ʿAzīz ibn ʿUmayr who was among them, reported: "I was assigned to a group of the Anṣār. When they laid out their lunch or dinner, they would give me the bread while they themselves ate dates without bread. [Dates were the most common food in Madinah, while bread was not always available. Bread is also filling; thus someone who ate bread would not feel the pangs of hunger like someone who ate only dates.] This was because of the Prophet's instructions to them. Every time any one of them had a piece of bread he would give it to me. Sometimes I felt embarrassed by their hospitality and I gave the bread to any one of them who was around. He would return it without taking a single bite."[7]

This was the sort of treatment Muhammad's prisoners received. The only reason for this noble treatment was that the Muslims did not go into war in the first place for any material or military gain. Their objective in war was the same as their objective in peace: to make their message known to other people and to remove all obstacles that prevented people from accepting it. The Quraysh's military might was one such obstacle.[8] When the Quraysh came out in a demonstration of strength which, if successful, would have prevented many people from even listening to the message of Islam with open minds, then that exercise had to be challenged and smashed, even if that meant killing people who were very close relatives. But when that immediate objective had been achieved and the Quraysh army retreated in defeat, those who were taken prisoner would receive kind treatment because they could not, in their position, cause the Muslims any harm. Indeed, the Muslims looked on them as people who could become believers, if they were to know what Islam was all about.

One very important characteristic of the religion of Islam is that it teaches its followers to evaluate every situation within its own perspective. During the battle and when the Muslims started to take prisoners from among the unbelievers, the same man who reported the type of treatment he and the rest of the prisoners received, Abū ʿAzīz ibn ʿUmayr, was seen by his brother, Muṣʿab, a companion of the Prophet, when a man from the Anṣār was taking him captive. Muṣʿab drew near and said to the Anṣārī man: "Hold him fast. His mother is wealthy. She may pay you a generous ransom." In this case, Muṣʿab was pointing out something in the interest of the Muslim community. His kinship with his brother was then of little importance. When the battle was over, the course of action which served the interests of Islam was to treat the prisoners well so that their hostility to Islam would be at least reduced, if not totally removed.

The immediate problem which had to be resolved when the Prophet (peace be upon him) arrived in Madinah after his victory in Badr was that of the prisoners of war. Apart from the two who were killed because of their active hostility to Islam and the Prophet, all the prisoners of war were treated well. The Quraysh were expected to send for their release and a decision had to be taken on what to do with them.

Back in Makkah, the Quraysh leaders tried to put on a brave face. They instructed everyone not to cry in public over their relatives killed at Badr. They also decided not to rush to the Prophet with offers of ransom to obtain the release of their men who had been taken prisoner in order not to be asked to pay hefty sums of money. But sooner or later someone would have had to make a move to get their prisoners released. Al-Muṭṭalib ibn Abī Wadāʿah was the first to go to Madinah to buy the release of his father.[9]

Consultation Concerning the Prisoners

Meanwhile, the Prophet consulted his companions on what to do with the prisoners of war. Abū Bakr said: "They are, Messenger of God, your own people and tribesmen. If you spare them and accept ransom from them, the ransom will be useful to us and they may, in time, realize that Islam is the truth and accept it."

When the Prophet asked ʿUmar his opinion, he received a totally different suggestion. ʿUmar said: "I suggest that you give me my relative to kill, and you allow ʿAlī [the Prophet's cousin] to kill his brother ʿAqīl, and you let Ḥamzah [the Prophet's uncle] kill his brother, so that we all demonstrate in front of God that we have no love or loyalty whatsoever to the unbelievers. These prisoners are their leaders."

ʿAbdullāh ibn Rawāḥah of the Anṣār suggested that they should be thrown in a huge fire, specially made for the purpose.

The Prophet went into his rooms for a while. When he came out he said: "God makes some hearts so soft that they are softer than milk, and He makes others even harder than stones." He then likened Abū Bakr's attitude to that of Abraham and Jesus, who had taken a soft line towards their peoples. He also likened ʿUmar's attitude to that of Noah and Moses, who invoked hard punishment for those who belied their messages. In conclusion he gave his ruling: "You are poor indeed. No prisoner of war may, therefore, be released without a ransom, otherwise he shall be beheaded." Thus the process of releasing the prisoners was started.

Some time later, when the prisoners were already released, the Prophet received new Qur'ānic revelations taking the Muslims to task for accepting ransom from their prisoners. The Qur'ān made it clear that, in the circumstances, putting the prisoners to death was the right course to follow. The relevant verses may be rendered in English as follows:

> It does not behove a Prophet to keep captives without shedding blood in the land. You may desire the fleeting gains of this world, but God desires [for you the good of] the life to come: God is Almighty, Wise. Had it not been for a decree from God that had already gone forth, a tremendous chastisement would indeed have befallen you, on account of what you took. Now enjoy what you have gained as lawful and good, and keep your duty to God. God is Forgiving, Merciful. (8: 67-69)[10]

The message of these verses is very clear indeed. In the circumstances of the Muslims at that time, the prisoners should have been put to death. It is not difficult to discern the reasons which called for that line of action.

For one thing, Badr was the first major battle between the Muslims and the unbelievers. The Muslims were still a small minority in Arabia, while the non-believers heavily outnumbered them. Hence, to kill those captives who were physically strong and able to fight would weaken the unbelievers and contribute to their humiliation. That would have made them think twice before making another attempt to settle their scores with the Muslims by resorting to war. Thus it would have been a step towards ensuring the security of the Muslim community in Madinah. No ransom obtained for the release of those prisoners could have given the Muslims comparable results.

Another reason was that to which ʿUmar had referred when he suggested that the captives should be put to death and that those among the Muslims who had relations among them should be the ones to carry out the death sentence on their relatives. His argument was "that we all demonstrate in front of God that we have no love or loyalty whatsoever to the unbelievers." Such an attitude would have made the issues abundantly clear between the two camps.

It is for these two reasons that the Muslims were rebuked for preferring to take ransom from the captives in their first major battle: "You may desire the fleeting gains of this world, but God desires [for you the good of] the life to come: God is almighty, wise."

But then it had been God's earlier decree that He would forgive the fighters of Badr all their errors. Hence no punishment was to be exacted from them. Instead, God, out of His grace, decided also to make the ransom they had taken, as well as the booty they gained, lawful for them. Such booty was forbidden to earlier nations which followed other prophets: 'Now enjoy what you have gained as lawful and good.'

ʿUmar reported that he met the Prophet and Abū Bakr with tears in their eyes. He asked why they were crying and said: "If I find that you are crying for a good reason, I will join you; if not, I will feign crying in sympathy." The Prophet said: "We are crying for what your fellows have persuaded me to do: take ransom from the captives. I was made to see your approaching punishment closer than this tree."[11]

One cannot but see the overriding reasons which called for a much tougher attitude over the prisoners of war, yet the fact that the Muslims made this error of judgement was not without benefit to them. They were spared killing more of their kinsmen and thus aggravating the feelings of hatred between them and their fellow tribesmen. Moreover, at least sixteen of the prisoners were later to become Muslims and that, in itself, was a tremendous gain.

It must be pointed out also that there were several relatives of the Prophet among the prisoners, such as his uncle al-ʿAbbās, his cousin ʿAqīl ibn Abū Ṭālib and his son-in-law Abū al-ʿĀṣ ibn al-Rabīʿ. The Muslims would have hesitated to kill the Prophet's own relatives. One cannot but sense that it was God's will to spare the Prophet the pain of having to kill his own relatives and to spare the Muslims the embarrassment of killing them, as well as the pain of killing their own people.

Ransom Waived

Not all the prisoners had to pay ransom in order to be freed. ʿUmar ibn ʿAbdullāh of the Jumaḥ clan was one of the poor among them. He had several daughters. He appealed to the Prophet in these words: "Messenger of God, you know that I have not got any money to speak of. I am indeed one of the needy and I have a large family to support. I, therefore, appeal to your generosity to set me free." The Prophet granted his appeal and set him free after taking from him a firm pledge never to join any force which aimed to fight the Prophet. Indeed, ʿUmar ibn ʿAbdullāh was one of quite a few prisoners whom the Prophet released for no ransom because they were poor.[12]

A shrewd decision was made by the Prophet when he stipulated that any prisoner who could read and write would be set free for no ransom, if he taught ten Muslim children to read and write. Most of the Arabs at the time were illiterate. The Prophet himself received no education when he was young and could not read and write. His decision, therefore, shows that his grasp of all matters was so good that he realized that to provide basic education for ten Muslim children equalled the large amount of money (1,000-4,000 dirhams) many of the prisoners had to pay in order to buy their freedom.

As the declaration that the prisoners might buy their freedom went around, the first to be released was Abū Wadaʿāh ibn Ḍubayrah of the Sahm clan. His son, al-Muṭṭalib, left Makkah quietly one night, when the Quraysh were still playing it cool with regard to negotiating the prisoners' release, hoping to get easier terms. Al-Muṭṭalib went straight to Madinah, where he bought his father's freedom for 4,000 dirhams.[13]

There were several cases worthy of special mention with regard to the release of the prisoners. An important personality among those prisoners was Suhayl ibn ʿAmr, a fine public speaker. He used his talent to speak ill of the Prophet and Islam. Mikraz ibn Ḥafs was sent to Madinah to negotiate his release. When terms were agreed, the Anṣārī who held him asked Mikraz to pay the agreed ransom. However, he did not have the money. He offered to stand in for Suhayl, who would be released to fetch the money and get Mikraz released. This was indeed the way Suhayl was set free. Before that, however, ʿUmar ibn al-Khaṭṭāb suggested to the Prophet that he be allowed to pull out all Suhayl's front teeth so that his speech would be impaired and he would never have the chance to speak in public against the Prophet. It was, in effect, a suggestion which aimed at depriving Suhayl, and the Quraysh generally, of a powerful weapon which they used in spreading false propaganda against the Prophet and against Islam. The Prophet, however, would have nothing of the sort. He taught us in this incident a very important principle of maintaining our moral standards even with our enemies, in times of peace or war. He said to ʿUmar: "I would not mutilate him, lest God should mutilate me, even though I am a Prophet." Thus, the mutilation of any person, dead or alive, is strictly forbidden in Islam, in all circumstances, even if he is our worst enemy. It is also reported that the Prophet said to ʿUmar that Suhayl might in future 'take a stand of which you will not disapprove'.[14]

The Prophet's Relatives

Among the prisoners was the Prophet's son-in-law, Abū al-ʿĀṣ ibn al-Rabīʿ, who was married to his eldest daughter, Zaynab. She continued to live with him in Makkah after the Prophet's emigration to Madinah, despite the fact that she was a Muslim and he was not. At the time, the rulings concerning such marriages were not yet revealed. Abū al-ʿĀṣ was the nephew of the Prophet's first wife Khadījah. At her request, the Prophet approved his marriage with

Zaynab before he received his first revelations. Zaynab was very happy with her husband, who was a man of great honesty and integrity.

When relations between the Prophet and the Quraysh reached a low ebb at the time when he was still in Makkah, preaching his message and speaking against idolatrous worship, some of the Quraysh leaders thought of causing the Prophet personal problems by getting his daughters divorced. They, therefore, went to Abū al-ʿĀṣ and asked him to divorce Zaynab, promising him that he could instead marry any woman of his choice. He turned down their request, saying that he would not divorce Zaynab for any other woman. ʿUtbah ibn Abī Lahab, who was engaged to one of the Prophet's other daughters, accepted the offer. He left her and chose in her place the daughter of Saʿīd ibn al-ʿĀṣ.

Now that Abū al-ʿĀṣ was a prisoner of war in Madinah, Zaynab sent money for his release. She included in her offer of ransom a necklace which was her mother's gift to her on her wedding night. When the Prophet saw the necklace he was deeply touched. He said to his companions: "If you feel it proper to release her prisoner for her and refund her her money, you may do so." They said: "Of course" and released Abū al-ʿĀṣ, taking no ransom from him.[15]

Among the prisoners of Badr was also the Prophet's own uncle al-ʿAbbās. He was the one the Prophet ordered not to be killed in the battle. Now the Muslims wanted him to pay his ransom. Obviously the matter was left to the Prophet, because no one dared demand a ransom from the Prophet's own uncle. Al-ʿAbbās, however, pleaded that he was a Muslim, though he did not declare the fact to the Quraysh. The Prophet answered: "God knows whether you were truly a Muslim. If so, He will certainly reward you. To all appearances, however, you were against us. You have, then, to pay the ransom for yourself, your two nephews Nawfal ibn al-Ḥārith and ʿAqīl ibn Abī Ṭālib, and also for your ally ʿUtbah ibn ʿAmr." Al-ʿAbbās replied that he did not have the money to pay all that. The Prophet asked him: "What about the treasure you and your wife Umm al-Faḍl buried in the ground? You said to her that if you were killed, the money should be divided among your three children, al-Faḍl, ʿAbdullāh and Qutham."

Al-ʿAbbās said: "I certainly know that you are God's Messenger. This was known to nobody apart from myself and my wife." He then asked the Prophet to count towards the ransom demanded 20 ounces of silver the Muslims gained from him during the battle. The Prophet refused, saying that was of the spoils of war which belonged, by right, to the Muslims. Al-ʿAbbās, therefore, had no choice but to pay the ransom in full for himself, his two nephews and his ally.[16]

This shows very clearly how the Prophet maintained a high standard of fairness. He did not allow his uncle to get off lightly. He made him pay for his release and for that of his relatives who did not have the means to buy their own freedom. In the case of his son-in-law the Prophet merely suggested to the Muslims that they might forego the ransom. When they did so, they were not under any pressure to comply. It was a matter of free choice. Had any of them refused – and everyone was entitled to refuse – Abū al-ʿĀṣ would have had to pay the ransom like his fellow prisoners.

Abū Sufyān's Son

This discussion of the prisoners of war taken in the Battle of Badr cannot be complete without mentioning two more incidents. The first relates to Abū Sufyān ibn Ḥarb, the leader of the caravan which the Muslims tried to intercept. That was the incident which led to the outbreak of hostilities. As learnt earlier, Abū Sufyān succeeded in evading the Muslim troops and led his caravan to safety until he reached Makkah. Two of his children, however, were in the Quraysh army. One of Abū Sufyān's sons, Ḥanẓalah, was killed in the battle, while the other, ʿAmr, was taken prisoner. When most of the prisoners were released after the payment of ransom, some people in Makkah were surprised that Abū Sufyān did not try to get his son released. They spoke to him about the payment of ransom for him. His argument for leaving his son prisoner, without trying to get him released, was that he did not want to suffer a financial loss in addition to the loss of his other son. He said he was prepared to leave ʿAmr prisoner for as long as the Muslims cared to keep him. Eventually, he said, they will have to let him go.

A short while later, an elderly man from the Muslims of Madinah went out with his wife to Makkah for *ʿUmrah* (mini-pilgrimage). It did not occur to the old man, Saʿd ibn al-Nuʿmān, that he would be in any danger because it was a long-established tradition in Arabia that the Quraysh would not harm anyone who visited Makkah for pilgrimage, no matter how good or bad their relations with his tribe were. This time, however, Abū Sufyān and his men caught Saʿd and kept him prisoner. Nobody in the Quraysh objected to Abū Sufyān's action, which was a blatant violation of their time-honoured traditions. Obviously everyone in the Quraysh was feeling the agony and humiliation of the defeat and felt that, in the circumstances, Abū Sufyān's action was not without justification.

Back in Madinah, the Anṣār who belonged to the same clan as Saʿd were disturbed when they heard that he was captured. They went to the Prophet and asked him to approve an exchange deal whereby they would give Abū Sufyān his son and get their man released. The Prophet approved and the exchange deal was effected. This was just another incident where the time-honoured values and traditions of Arabia were violated for the sake of limited gain. Indeed, the Quraysh stopped at nothing in their hostility to Islam and the Prophet. All values and moral standards went out of the window once a petty gain was looming for the Quraysh.[17]

The Prophet's Daughter

The other incident relates to Zaynab, the Prophet's eldest daughter, whose husband Abū al-ʿĀṣ ibn al-Rabīʿ was released for no ransom. Obviously, Zaynab was a Muslim while her husband was not, although he was a man of great integrity. When Abū al-ʿĀṣ was about to leave Madinah for Makkah, the Prophet took him aside and said something to him before he left. Nobody knew exactly what the Prophet said to his son-in-law, but it is generally assumed that it was either a condition of Abū al-ʿĀṣ's release or that he simply promised the Prophet that as soon as he arrived in Makkah after his release, he would let his wife join her father. Shortly afterwards, the Prophet asked two of his companions, Zayd ibn

Ḥārithah and a man from the Anṣār, to go to a place called Ya'jaj, about eight miles from Makkah, and wait there until Zaynab arrived and then to escort her to Madinah.

When Abū al-ʿĀṣ arrived in Makkah, about a month after the Battle of Badr, he told his wife that she should get ready to travel to Madinah where she would join her father. It is interesting to relate here that Hind bint ʿUtbah, Abū Sufyān's wife, met Zaynab once by chance and asked her whether she was getting ready to go to Madinah. Zaynab denied that for fear that Hind would do something to stop her from going. After all, Hind's father, brother and uncle were all killed in the Battle of Badr. Hind, however, persisted and offered to help Zaynab get ready for her journey, which would take a few days. She said to her: "If you need anything that I have which would make your journey easier, do not hesitate to ask it of me, because we women have our own relationship, which is different from that of men." Zaynab later said that she believed Hind was sincere in her offer; nevertheless she feared to make her true intention known to her and continued to get ready without anyone's help.

When Zaynab was ready for her journey, her brother-in-law Kinānah brought her a camel to ride and, having armed himself with his bow and a bag full of arrows, he went out with her, leading her camel, in broad daylight. There was some whispering among the Quraysh about Zaynab's travelling to Madinah and a group of men from the Quraysh chased her until they caught up with her in a place called Dhū Ṭuwā. The first to catch up with her was called Habbār ibn al-Aswad; he threw his spear at her in her howdah. It is said that at the time Zaynab was in the early stages of pregnancy and that the shock caused a miscarriage. It is also said that Habbār frightened the camel and Zaynab fell on a rock and that her miscarriage was caused by that fall. She continued to bleed intermittently until she died some years later in Madinah.

When her escort Kinānah realized that the men were intent on forcing Zaynab to go back, he put his arrows in front of him and held his bow ready to strike. They retreated a little when he said: "By God, anyone who draws near shall have one of these arrows in his body."

Abū Sufyān, now the most important personality in the Quraysh, also came over with a few of the Quraysh notables. He said to Kinānah: "Hold back your arrows, man, until we have spoken to you." Kinānah did so and Abū Sufyān came over to him and said quietly:

> You have certainly been unwise in taking the lady out in broad daylight, while you are fully aware of the catastrophe that has befallen us at the hands of Muhammad and his followers. Should you take his daughter to him from among us in such an open way, people would say that we are so humiliated that we were unable to stop her. Many tribes would think that we are very weak and cowardly. We certainly have no desire to prevent her joining her father. We do not see that we could get any revenge on him by stopping her. I would counsel you to go back with her now and stay back in Makkah until the incident is forgotten. Once it is known that we have caused her to return, you may, if you wish, take her out quietly and resume your journey.

Kinānah felt that that was sound advice, so he went back with Zaynab and she came to no harm. A few days later, when the storm over the incident had subsided, Kinānah took Zaynab out quietly, under cover of darkness. Nobody intercepted them before they reached Ya'jaj, where they met Zayd ibn Ḥārithah and his companion, who escorted Zaynab the rest of the way to Madinah.

It is said that when the people who frightened and attacked Zaynab went back to Makkah, they were met by Hind who rebuked them for their thankless task: "In time of peace you show all your ruthlessness and boldness, while in war you are just like women weakened by their periods."[18]

The fact that the Prophet asked for his daughter to join him in Madinah was simply in compliance with Islamic teachings that a Muslim woman could not remain married to an unbeliever. Now that the Muslims had their state in Madinah and were masters of their own affairs, a situation like that of Zaynab – being a Muslim while her husband was not – could not have been allowed to continue. God's ruling on this is very clear. Zaynab remained in Madinah but did not marry anyone until her husband, Abū al-ʿĀṣ, became a Muslim several years later and the two were re-united in Madinah. This will be discussed in Chapter 27.

Abū Lahab's Humiliation

The Battle of Badr had profound effects both on the unbelievers in Makkah and on the Muslims in Madinah, as well as on people throughout Arabia. In Makkah, the Quraysh were never happy at the fact that the Prophet had managed to establish a state in Madinah which competed with it for supremacy in Arabia. The Quraysh's leaders – or at least the hard-liners among them – nurtured the hope that they would be able to put a quick end to the challenge presented by the Muslims in Madinah. In Badr, however, they saw their dreams come to a sudden end. The challenge presented by the Muslims was now seen to be greater than ever. Many of the unbelievers had obviously thought that nothing could stand up to the might of the Quraysh. To be soundly beaten by a force which was just one-third their number and far inferior in equipment was a humiliation that they neither expected nor could tolerate for long. Every one of them was cherishing a hope, which seemed far too remote, that something could just happen to restore, at least partially, their shattered pride.

One man, Abū Lahab, was an uncle of the Prophet but opposed him violently throughout his life. As has been seen, he did not join the Quraysh army but sent a man in his place. However, he was very badly shaken and shattered by the defeat when he first heard the news. One day he went to Zamzam, the well very close to the Kaʿbah, where his sister-in-law Umm al-Faḍl, wife of al-ʿAbbās, was watching one of her servants doing his work. The servant was a Muslim like his master and mistress, although al-ʿAbbās decided not to break his ties with his people and preferred to keep the fact that he was a Muslim a secret.

Shortly after Abū Lahab had sat down, a nephew of his called al-Mughīrah ibn al-Ḥārith arrived, one of the very first Quraysh soldiers to reach Makkah. Abū Lahab shouted to him to come over. As he did so, a few people also came over to learn how things went in the battle. Abū Lahab asked him to explain how the Quraysh could suffer such a defeat.

Al-Mughīrah replied: "As soon as we clashed, we allowed them to hold to our shoulders and lead us wherever they wished, and take us prisoners at will. Nevertheless, I do not blame anyone. We certainly saw white men riding white and black horses walking over the horizon, wiping out all in front of them, simply no one was able to resist them."

The servant called Abū Rāfiʿ turned and said: "Those are certainly the angels." Abū Lahab was furious and hit him in the face. Abū Rāfiʿ tried to hit back but he was a small man. Abū Lahab lifted him, threw him to the floor and sat on him, hitting him very hard.

Umm al-Faḍl, however, took a post and hit Abū Lahab, cutting his head very badly. She said to him: "You think you can hit him as you wish because his master is away!" Abū Lahab rose and left, feeling the humiliation of being hit in public by a woman, on top of the general humiliation of the Quraysh. Apparently the humiliation was too much for Abū Lahab and he lived for only seven days afterwards.[19]

Abū Lahab's was a case of a man overpowered by his sense of humiliation, his realization that all his opposition to Muhammad was in vain, that the cause he was fighting for was a lost cause and that the tide of Islam would sweep through everything that stood in its way. For Abū Lahab, there was nothing more to live for.

Seeking Quick Revenge

Other Quraysh notables were thinking hard about how to achieve a quick revenge. One man, Ṣafwān, was extremely depressed by the fact that his father, Umayyah ibn Khalaf, and his brother, ʿAlī, were both killed at Badr. Shortly after the battle he was talking to a friend of his called ʿUmayr ibn Wahb about the defeat of the Quraysh at the hands of the Muslims. ʿUmayr was a man of courage and intelligence. He was the one who accurately guessed the number of the Muslims for the Quraysh just before the start of the battle. Before the Prophet's emigration to Madinah, ʿUmayr used to cause the

Prophet and his followers much harm. Although he escaped death and captivity in Badr, his son Wahb was taken prisoner. Ṣafwān and ʿUmayr sat next to the Kaʿbah and the topic of discussion was, inevitably, the Battle of Badr.

Speaking of the Qurayshīs who were killed, Ṣafwān said: "Now that they have gone, life is not worth living." ʿUmayr rejoined: "That is very true. Had it not been for the fact that I am encumbered by debt which I cannot repay and that my children are so young that, if something should happen to me, they would suffer much hardship, I would have gone to Muhammad and killed him. After all, I have a very good pretext for going there: they hold my son prisoner and I can pretend that I have come to get him free for a ransom."

Ṣafwān realized that a great opportunity was opening up for him. He said to ʿUmayr: "Do not worry about your debt; I will pay it all. Be reassured about your children; I will look after them for you. They will not be in need of anything I can provide."

ʿUmayr was indeed serious in his intention and did not make the proposition in order to hold back from implementing it. He promised his friend that he would depart as soon as possible and he made Ṣafwān promise that he would not say a word about their agreement to anyone. Secrecy was extremely important for the success of their venture.

ʿUmayr ordered that his sword should be sharpened for him and poisoned. He then set off secretly, not telling anyone of his purpose.

In Madinah, ʿUmar ibn al-Khaṭṭāb was sitting with a group of Muslims, talking about their victory at Badr. They praised God for the great help He had given them, enabling them to overpower their enemies. Everyone realized that without the grace and help of God, they would never have been able to achieve such a great victory. This sort of discussion is, by its very nature, very pleasing to the participants. Suddenly ʿUmayr appeared. ʿUmar was the first one to notice him as he dismounted at the doorstep of the Prophet's mosque. He immediately noticed that ʿUmayr had his sword with him. ʿUmar said to his fellow Muslims: "This dog, ʿUmayr ibn Wahb, is an enemy of God and he could only have come here for an evil purpose. He was the one to stir up trouble and to guess our number to our enemies on Badr day."

Straightaway ʿUmar went to the Prophet and said: "Prophet, ʿUmayr ibn Wahb, God's enemy, has just arrived carrying his sword." The Prophet asked ʿUmar to let ʿUmayr in. ʿUmar went to him and took the belt on which he hung his sword, put it round his neck and let him through. He also said to the Anṣār who were sitting with him: "Come in and sit with the Prophet. Be on your guard against this evil man; he is sly and cunning." Then ʿUmar let ʿUmayr go in to see the Prophet.

When the Prophet saw ʿUmar pulling ʿUmayr with the belt of his sword around his neck, he told him to release ʿUmayr and told ʿUmayr to come nearer. To break the tension, ʿUmayr greeted everybody with the greeting used by the unbelievers: "Happy be your morning." The Prophet said to him: "God has blessed us with a greeting better than yours, ʿUmayr. That is the greeting of peace, the greeting of the people in heaven." ʿUmayr replied, "By God, Muhammad, I have heard that only very recently."

The Prophet then asked him about the reason for his journey to Madinah. ʿUmayr used his pretext and said: "I have come for the prisoner you are holding. I would like to request you to be kind to him."

The Prophet then asked him why he was carrying his sword on him. ʿUmayr answered: "Confound these swords! They are indeed useless." The Prophet repeated his question about the purpose of his journey and emphasized that he wanted to know the truth. ʿUmayr again said that he simply came for his prisoner and there was nothing more to his being in Madinah at that moment.

"There is indeed," the Prophet said, "a different purpose. You sat with Ṣafwān ibn Umayyah at al-Ḥijr and spoke about the losses of the Quraysh in Badr, then you said to him: 'Had it not been for my debts and my children, I would have gone to kill Muhammad.' Ṣafwān then said he would pay your debts and look after your children in return for your killing me. But God will see to it that your purpose is foiled."

Astonished, ʿUmayr said: "I declare that you are the Messenger of God. We used to say that you were lying when you spoke to us about faith and about the revelations you received. Now this is something that nobody witnessed except Ṣafwān and myself. By God, I know that no one could have told you about it except Him. Praise be to Him that He has guided me to adopt Islam, and has shown me the right path. I declare that there is no deity but God, and that you are His Messenger."

The Prophet turned to his companions and said: "Educate your brother in His faith and teach him the Qur'ān, and release his prisoner for him." These orders, naturally, were carried out.

Enemy Turned Brother

It is interesting to note here that the Prophet (peace be upon him) referred to ʿUmayr as the brother of his companions once ʿUmayr had declared his acceptance of Islam. This declaration is, indeed, the only thing that is required of any person to join the brotherhood of the Muslims. Throughout the ages, this bond of brotherhood has been very real and very strong among the Muslims. It is a bond which supersedes all other ties and relationships. Once ʿUmayr had made his declaration that he believed in God's oneness and in the message of the Prophet, he became the brother of all Muslims who had been, until a moment earlier, his enemies.

Some days later ʿUmayr came to the Prophet and said: "Messenger of God, I have worked very hard to put out God's light, and caused much harm to those who were following God's faith. I am now seeking your permission to go to Makkah and call its people to believe in God and His Messenger, and to accept Islam. I hope they will listen to me and that God will guide them aright. If they do not, I will inflict harm on them in the same way as I used to inflict harm on your people." The Prophet granted him his request and ʿUmayr set out on his return journey.

Back in Makkah, Ṣafwān could not hide his excitement about ʿUmayr's mission. He said to some of his friends: "In a few days you will receive a piece of news which will make you forget the Battle of Badr." If anyone arrived in Makkah coming from the direction of Madinah, Ṣafwān went to him and asked him about ʿUmayr. He soon learned that ʿUmayr had adopted Islam. Ṣafwān was greatly distressed and felt that he was badly let down. He made an oath that he would never speak a word to ʿUmayr and would never do him a good turn.

When ʿUmayr arrived in Makkah, he started to call its people to adopt Islam. As mentioned earlier, he was a man of great courage. He was very harsh to those who did not respond to his call. Indeed, a number of people responded favourably and adopted Islam. The Battle of Badr had a tremendous effect on those who were in Makkah thinking about Islam and feeling a little reluctant to take the big step of adopting it. Many who kept the fact that they were Muslims secret were now more open about having followed the Prophet. Quite a number of people joined the ranks of the Muslims and went to Madinah. ʿUmayr's efforts would have produced totally different results, had it not been for the great victory God had granted the Muslims.[20]

Notes

1. Ibn Hishām, *al-Sīrah al-Nabawiyyah*, Dār al-Qalam, Beirut, Vol. 1, p. 295. Also, Ibn Kathīr, *al-Bidāyah wal-Nihāyah*, Maktabat al-Maʿārif, Beirut, Vol. 1, pp. 301-302.
2. Amīn Duwaydār, *Ṣuwar Min Ḥayāt al-Rasūl*, Dār al-Maʿārif, 4th edition, Cairo, p. 318.
3. Ibn Kathīr, op.cit., p. 305.
4. Ibid., p. 284. Also, Ibn Hishām, op.cit., pp. 280-281.
5. Ibn Hishām, op.cit., p. 298. Also, Amīn Duwaydār, op.cit., p. 319.
6. Ibn Hishām, op.cit., p. 298. Also, Ibn Kathīr, op.cit., pp. 303-304.
7. Ibn Hishām, op.cit., pp. 299-300.
8. Ibid., pp. 299-300.
9. Ibid., p. 303. Also, Ibn Kathīr, op.cit., p. 310; and al-Wāqidī, *Kitāb al-Maghāzī*, Oxford University Press, 1996, Vol. 1, p. 129.
10. Ibn Kathīr, op.cit., pp. 297-298.
11. Ibid., p. 297.
12. Ibn Hishām, op.cit., p. 315. Also, Amīn Duwaydār, op.cit., p. 322.
13. Ibn Hishām, op.cit., p. 303.
14. Ibid., pp. 303-304. Also, Ibn Kathīr, op.cit., p. 310.
15. Ibn Hishām, op.cit., pp. 307-308. Also, Ibn Kathīr, op.cit., p. 311.
16. Ibn Kathīr, op.cit., p. 299.
17. Ibid., p. 311. Also, Ibn Hishām, op.cit., pp. 305-306.
18. Ibn Hishām, op.cit., pp. 308-312.
19. Ibid., pp. 301-302.
20. Ibid., pp. 316-318.

19

New Trends of Hostility

THE VICTORY ACHIEVED by the Muslims at the Battle of Badr sent a shiver into the hearts of all those who did not wish Islam well. It is wrong to assume that the Quraysh in Makkah were the only enemy of Islam. The Prophet had his state in Madinah, where an alliance and a bond of brotherhood was established between its Muslim inhabitants and the few hundreds who emigrated with the Prophet from Makkah. Newcomers to Islam were joining every day. Nevertheless, a large section of the population of Madinah simply preferred to stick to idolatrous beliefs. It is extremely difficult to ascertain the relative strength of the Muslims and the non-believers in Madinah. It is certain, however, that the Muslims had the upper hand and were the masters in the city. Several factors contributed to this state of affairs, the most important of which was that the Muslims were united under the leadership of the Prophet whose care and compassion were never in short supply. Moreover, his undoubted wisdom was greatly enhanced by the guidance he received from God. The opposition, on the other hand, lacked any sort of wise leadership and was certainly far from united.

Realizing that the victory in Badr could only add to the strength of the Muslims and enhance their reputation throughout Arabia, many of those Arabs in Madinah who chose not to become Muslims felt that they could protect their interests only if they joined the new camp. This realization, however, was not based on any appreciation on their part of the truth of Islam; it was simply motivated by their instinct for self preservation. They feared that the Prophet and his companions would follow the victory achieved at Badr with more resounding victories which would make them undisputed masters in the whole of Arabia. If that eventuality would come to pass while they themselves remained non-believers, they would miss out, they thought, on their opportunity to be part of this mastery. Joining the ranks of the believers seemed to them a very attractive proposition, because it would spare them any hostility on the part of the Muslims. If they continued to stay aside, leaving the tide of Islam to go its way while they kept to their old practices, they feared they might be reduced to total insignificance.

But how could they be assimilated into the new set-up when they did not believe in Islam and could not accept Muhammad as God's Messenger? To them that was a difficult question. From another point of view, who could tell that the victory achieved in Badr was not the result of the Muslims being able on that day to rise to the big occasion? Who could be sure that the same would happen again and again? What would happen when the Quraysh had recovered from their setback and marshalled forces to attack Muhammad and his companions? If the Quraysh were able to inflict a crushing defeat on the Muslims in the next battle, would that not signify the end of Islam? If that came to pass, these people thought, they would have gained nothing from joining the Muslims now. Instead they would have gained the hostility of their Jewish neighbours and the hostility of their co-religionists, the unbelievers in Makkah and elsewhere.

Jumping on the Bandwagon

This was the dilemma facing many a non-believer in Madinah. They did not take long to discover their way out. They decided to take a hypocritical stand. They simply pretended to be Muslims, while deep in their hearts there was no shred of faith in Islam. God has described their attitude in the Qur'ān: "When they meet the believers, they claim: 'We, also, are believers.' But when they are alone with their devils, they declare to them: 'We are truly on your side: we are simply mocking'." (2: 14) Their decision was to hold the stick in the middle. To all appearances they became Muslims. They would pray and fast and speak as if they belonged to the Muslim community. Deep at heart, however, they remained non-believers. They simply had nothing in common with the Muslims. Their hearts were full of hatred towards the Prophet and his companions and they longed for something to happen that would put an end to Islam altogether. What was worse was that these people were able to know many a secret of the Muslims and to pass these secrets on to other enemies of Islam. They would spare no effort in their attempts to cause the Muslims harm.

The Muslims were at a loss to know how to deal with this group of people. They did not state their rejection of Islam openly so that they could be treated as enemies; neither were they true believers with whom the Muslims could share all their cares and concerns. They were simply in between, neither here nor there. For this reason God decries their behaviour in the Qur'ān, condemns them in numerous verses and threatens them with the most painful punishment in the hereafter: "Surely, the hypocrites shall be in the lowest depth of the Fire, and you will find none who could support them." (4: 145) He has made it clear that He alone will decide their punishment, because He alone knows their true motives and their deceptive appearances; He knows what they say to each other in private and He knows the lies behind which they hide their true nature. Indeed, they managed to put on such a highly deceptive appearance that the Prophet himself did not know much of the truth about them. Even this fact is stated in the Qur'ān: "Among the Bedouin who dwell around you, there are hypocrites; and among the people of Madinah there are such as have grown insolent in their hypocrisy. You do not always know them, but We do know them. We shall cause them to suffer doubly in this world and then they will be given over to awesome suffering in the life to come." (9: 101)

These hypocrites were certainly the worst and most dangerous enemies of Islam. Their objective – which was always present in their minds, and for the achievement of which they worked very hard – was the elimination of Islam altogether and the Muslims generally. They seized every opportunity to cause the Muslims all the damage they could. They adopted several means and tactics for the achievement of their goal. They tried hard to demoralize the Muslims when they went to war and worked hard to bring about a split in their ranks; they belittled Muhammad's message so that Muslims would look at it with less respect; and they maintained secret contacts with other enemies of Islam inside and outside Madinah, in order to forge an alliance which would group all these forces in an all-out effort to exterminate Islam.

The Prophet, however, was ordered by God to accept from them what they professed and leave them to God to judge them as He knew their reality. The Prophet, however, felt very sorry for them because they were aware of the teachings of Islam and could realize that it was a message from God. Nevertheless, they decided to reject it and continue with their erring ways and false beliefs. On several occasions he would hint to them that he was aware of their hypocrisy. He did not take any measure to harm them, except for the fact that he described them, as a group, as insignificant cowards. But he did not publicly attach such a description to any one of them personally.

Different Jewish Attitudes

The hypocrites certainly played a significant role in the events that took place in Madinah and elsewhere at the time of the Prophet. This will be discussed together with their schemes and tactics in the war against Islam later in this book. Another trend of hostility, which was to come into the open soon after the Battle of Badr, came from the Jews. It was mentioned earlier that there was a large concentration of Jews in and around Madinah. According to their own statements, the Jews came to live in Madinah because they knew it was the place to which the last of the Prophets would emigrate and establish his state. They hoped that the last of the Prophets would be one of them. They gathered in Madinah in the hope that they would follow him and establish with him a new kingdom, similar to that of David and Solomon.

The Prophet might have hoped that the Jews would follow him because theirs was a Divine religion which emanated from the same source as Islam. Little did he think at the beginning that blind hatred of anything that did not emanate with the Israelites would determine the Jews' attitude towards Islam. In the early days of the Prophet's settlement in Madinah, there were a few encouraging signs about the Jewish attitude, but the indications of a forthcoming hard struggle were much more numerous. A few examples of both types of indicator will give us a clear idea of Jewish attitudes to Islam in those early days.

The first report concerns an old Jewish man who travelled from Syria to settle in Madinah a few years before its people heard of Islam. This man, called Ibn al-Hayyabān, soon acquired a high reputation for his devotion and scholarship. His behaviour was testimony to his keen sense of devotion. He gained great respect among Jews and Arabs alike. If rain was scarce, people asked him to pray for rain. He would refuse unless they were willing to make a sizeable donation to the poor. He would then go outside the city with the people to pray God for rain. He would hardly have finished when clouds would appear and rain would be pouring down. He did this several times.

He was soon taken ill, and it appeared that his illness was terminal. When he was certain of that, he spoke to his people, putting to them this question: "My Jewish people, what do you think was the reason for me to leave the land of fertility and fine produce in order to settle in this land of poverty and hunger?" They told him that he must have had a good reason. He said: "I have come here only to await the appearance of a prophet who is due to appear any time now. It is to this city that he will emigrate. I had hoped that I would see him and follow him. As I say, it is time for him to appear. Let no one beat you to follow him, my Jewish people. He will be given permission to shed blood and to enslave the women and children of his opponents. Let that not be a barrier which prevents you from following him." Ibn al-Hayyabān died soon afterwards.

Several years later, when the Prophet had settled in Madinah and when he besieged the Jewish tribe of Qurayẓah for their treachery, several young men of that Jewish tribe spoke out reminding their people of Ibn al-Hayyabān's prophecy and asserting that Muhammad was the Prophet he had mentioned. The elders of the tribe denied that he was the promised Prophet. Those young men were certain of their ground and told their people that all descriptions of this prophet were met by Muhammad. Therefore, they came out of the forts of Qurayẓah and declared their acceptance of Islam. By so doing, they protected their property and their families.[1]

Another encouraging sign was provided by Mukhayrīq, a Jewish rabbi of high renown and a man of vast wealth, which was mostly in date palms. He recognized the Prophet according to his description in the Jewish scriptures. However, he found it hard to abandon Judaism and follow Islam. He continued to hesitate for more than two years. When the Quraysh tried to attack Madinah in the third year of the Prophet's settlement there, and the attempt led to the Battle of Uḥud (which shall be described in detail in the next chapter), Mukhayrīq said to his people: "My Jewish people, you certainly know that supporting Muhammad is your bounden duty." They said that it was the Sabbath and they could do nothing. He told them that they had no Sabbath. He picked up his armour and went to see the Prophet at Uḥud. Before leaving, he made a will that should he die on that day, all his property should go to the Prophet Muhammad to do with it whatever he liked. When the battle broke out, he fought hard until he was killed. The Prophet received Mukhayrīq's wealth and it was from this money that the Prophet made most of his *ṣadaqah* or charitable donations.[2]

A Test of Honesty

An even more telling report is the one which concerns ʿAbdullāh ibn Sallām, a highly prominent Jewish rabbi. This is his story:

> When I heard about God's Messenger (peace be upon him) I recognized his description, name, and the time in which we were awaiting his appearance. I did not disclose any of this information, but kept it to myself until God's Messenger arrived in Madinah. When he arrived at Qubā' and stayed with the clan of ʿAmr ibn ʿAwf, a man came to tell us of his arrival.

I was at the top of a date tree doing some work, while my paternal aunt, Khālidah bint al-Ḥārith, was sitting underneath. When I heard the news of the arrival of God's Messenger (peace be upon him) I glorified God. When my aunt heard me, she said: "Confound you! By God, had you heard of Moses himself coming, you could not say anything more." I told her: "Aunt, he is, by God, the brother of Moses and he follows Moses' faith and he has been sent with the same message as that of Moses." She said: "Nephew, is he the Prophet whom we have been told would be sent with the approach of the Hour? [The term 'the Hour' refers to the end of life and the arrival of the Day of Judgement.] I told her that he was. She said: "That is it, then." I then went to meet God's Messenger (peace be upon him) and adopted Islam. I have turned to my family and told them to do likewise, and they also adopted Islam.

At first, I kept my adoption of Islam a secret. I then went to the Prophet (peace be upon him) and said to him: "Messenger of God, the Jews are always ready to follow falsehood. I would like you to put me in one of your rooms and ask them about me when they are unaware of my presence, so that they can tell you what position I have among them, before they come to know of my adoption of Islam. Should they know it initially, they would abuse me and speak ill of me." The Prophet allowed me to go into one of his rooms. They came to him and spoke to him, putting some questions. He then asked them: "How do you view al-Ḥuṣayn ibn Sallām? [the man's real name]." They answered: "He is our master and his father was also our master. He is a rabbi of great scholarship." When they had said that, I came out and said to them: "My Jewish people, fear God and accept what Muhammad tells you. By God, you certainly know that he is God's Messenger who is mentioned by name and qualities in your Torah. I, for my part, bear witness that he is God's Messenger and I believe in him and know him to be a Prophet." They said: "You are telling lies," and started to abuse me. I turned to the Prophet and said: "Messenger of God, have I not told you that they follow

> falsehood, and they are treacherous people who do not hesitate to lie. I declare that I and my household follow the religion of Islam." My paternal aunt, Khālidah bint al-Ḥārith, also adopted Islam and became a good Muslim.[3]

A Confrontational Attitude

This last report is of a rabbi who was honest with himself. When he ascertained that Muhammad was the Prophet God had promised to send to mankind, he could not oppose him. He had to act on the basis of his knowledge and he accepted Islam. However, the majority of the Jews were not ready to do likewise. They preferred to oppose the Prophet, knowing that by so doing they would incur God's wrath. There are similar incidents which confirm this hostile attitude. The first is reported by Ṣafiyyah bint Ḥuyayy, who was later to be married to the Prophet. Her father was a highly prominent Jewish rabbi, well versed in the Jewish scriptures. She reports:

> I was my father's favourite child, and I was also the favourite of my uncle, Abū Yāsir. They would never see me with a child of either of them without picking me up in preference to the other child. When God's Messenger arrived in Madinah and stayed at Qubā', my father, Ḥuyayy ibn Akhṭab and my uncle, Abū Yāsir, went to see him before sunrise. They did not return home until sunset. They were so tired when they came back that they could have dropped as they walked. My face was beaming with a smile as I went towards them. Neither, however, took any notice of me, because they were obviously very depressed. I heard my uncle, Abū Yāsir, say to my father, Ḥuyayy: "Is it truly he?" My father answered: "Yes, indeed. By God, it is he." My uncle said: "Do you recognize him perfectly?" My father answered in the affirmative. Then my uncle asked: "What are you going to do?" My father answered: "By God, I will be his enemy as long as I live."[4]

Indeed, these last two examples illustrate a conscious decision by the Jews to oppose the Prophet, knowing that he was God's Messenger and the last Prophet who would be sent to mankind. This is indeed the worst type of opposition because it is adopted in spite of a clear recognition that such opposition flies in the face of the truth. Hence, its proponents will always be hardened by this knowledge, knowing that any weakening in their opposition would expose their falsehood and would show them to be untrue to their own faith. Indeed Ḥuyayy ibn Akhṭab was to give credence to his statement and later spared no effort in trying to suppress the voice of Islam. Nevertheless, the Prophet did not despair of calling on the Jews to be honest to themselves and to accept Islam. For example, he wrote a letter addressed to the Jews of Khaybar, in the north of Arabia, reminding them of God's grace and confirming that it was their duty to follow him:

> In the name of God, the Merciful, the Beneficent.
>
> From Muhammad, God's Messenger, Moses's colleague and brother, who confirms the message conveyed by Moses. God has said to you, people of the Torah, what you surely find in your scriptures: "Muhammad is God's Messenger; and those who are with him are firm and unyielding towards all disbelievers, yet full of mercy towards one another. You see them bowing down, prostrating themselves in prayer, seeking favour with God and His goodly acceptance. Their marks are on their faces, traced by prostration. This is the example given of them in the Torah as well as in the Gospel: [They are] like a seed that brings forth its shoot and then He strengthens it, so that it grows stout, and in the end stands firm upon its stem, delighting the sowers, so that through them He might confound the unbelievers. God has promised those of them who attain to faith and do righteous deeds His forgiveness and supreme reward.
>
> I appeal to you by God and by what has been revealed to you and by what God has fed your predecessors of Manna and Quails, and I appeal to you by Him who parted the sea for your predecessors to save them from Pharaoh and his might, to tell me: Do you find it in your scriptures which have been revealed to you that you must believe in Muhammad? If you

> do not find this in your scriptures, then let it be so. The right way has now become distinct from the way of error. I, therefore, call on you to believe in God and His Messenger.[5]

No such appeal could be of much avail with people who had determined to fight the truth of Islam tooth and nail. Indeed, they stopped at nothing to undermine the new faith. They would have done anything to bring back hostility between the tribes of the Aws and the Khazraj.

Stirring Up Old Hostility

Shās ibn Qays was an old Jew with unparalleled hatred for Islam. One day he passed a group of the Prophet's companions including members of both tribes. He was appalled to see them with one another. He recognized that this friendship was brought about only by Islam. He thought that with such unity the position of the Jews in Madinah was threatened. He called the young Jewish man who was sitting with them and told him that when he went to rejoin them, he should remind them of the Battle of Buʿāth and other battles that took place between the two tribes and that he should recite some of the poetry composed on those occasions in which each tribe extolled its fighters and abused its opponents. The young man did as Shās said. That was sufficient to make some of the Prophet's companions speak highly of those days and this led to ill-feeling being stirred up again between them. This went on for some time and anger replaced their friendliness. Some suggested that they could resume fighting that very day to prove who was superior.

In no time, the Prophet learnt of this. He came to them as fast as he could, accompanied by some of the Muhājirīn. He appealed to their sense of faith: "Muslims, fear God. Are you to resume the enmity of ignorance when I am still among you, after God has guided you to believe in Islam and submit to Him? Do you forget God's blessing as He has saved you from ignorance and disbelief and planted love and friendliness in your hearts instead of hostility?"

They immediately recognized that they had allowed themselves to be deluded by their enemies. They were in tears and hugged one another. They went with the Prophet, praying God to forgive them.[6]

All this goes to show that the Jews in Madinah were fierce enemies of Islam, waiting for every chance to deal a devastating blow to Muslims.

Despite the fact that the Prophet made a treaty with the Jews when he first came to Madinah which stipulated that the Jews would support the Muslims in any fight against any enemy who threatened the Muslims in Madinah, it was soon to become clear that the Jews had no intention of putting that provision into effect. Indeed, their hatred of Islam, which had no cause except the fact that the Prophet himself was not Jewish, became self-evident – so much so that when they realized that the Muslims had achieved a resounding victory at Badr, they felt very sorry for the unbelievers and felt insecure in Madinah. One of their leaders, Kaʿb ibn al-Ashraf, commented on the Prophet's victory over the nobility of Arabia: "Those are the most noble among the Arabs, the true kings. If Muhammad has dealt them such a heavy blow, death is certainly preferable to life."[7] Hence the Jews gave every indication that they considered their peace treaty with the Prophet broken. Their poets started to ridicule the Muslims and belittle their victory. Unashamedly they also spoke ill of the Prophet and started a barrage of ridicule against him.

Trying for a Showdown

There were several Jewish tribes in and around Madinah. The tribe of Qaynuqāʿ was renowned for its bravery amongst all Jews. They were also closest to the Arabs in their quarters. It was perhaps this proximity that led the Jewish tribe of Qaynuqāʿ to show more hostility to the Muslims than the rest of the Jews. The atmosphere between the Muslims and the Jews became very tense. Any provocation would surely be enough to start a war between the two parties. Such a provocation was soon to come.

A Muslim woman went to the Qaynuqāʿ market and sat in front of a jeweller's shop. In order to have a laugh at her, a Jew came from behind her and took the lower edge of her dress and stuck it to her shoulders, but she was totally unaware and felt nothing of what was being done to her. When she stood up, the lower half of her body was visible and all the Jews around her laughed. She cried for help and a Muslim man nearby attacked the Jew who perpetrated this and killed him. Several men then attacked the Muslim and killed him. There was much chaos and confusion. Both Jews and Muslims were calling for help and people started gathering. The situation would surely have led to a massacre. The Prophet, however, was informed and he quickly came over and tried to calm everybody down.[8]

The Prophet called the notables in the Qaynuqāʿ tribe and spoke to them, warning them against any breach of their treaty: "You had better guard against a calamity, like that which befell the Quraysh. You will be well advised to adopt Islam, because you know that I am a messenger from God. You find this in your own Book, and it is contained in God's promise to you."

Their hatred, however, had become very strong and they would not listen. Their answer was far from conciliatory: "Muhammad, do you think that we are an easy prey? Do not let euphoria overtake you. You simply met some people who had no knowledge of war and its tactics, which enabled you to score an easy victory. If we were to fight you, you would certainly know that we are the true fighters."[9]

Thus the situation had undergone a total change. The Jewish tribe of Qaynuqāʿ moved over to the enemy camp, after they had been friends with the Muslims. Their hostility was not passive. They themselves were calling for a fight with everything they did or said. The Muslims then had to face the situation with appropriate means and with the firmness it called for.

There was certainly no chance that the Muslims would feel easy about probable treachery by the Qaynuqāʿ Jews when the state of war still existed between the Muslims and the Quraysh. The Prophet received the following instruction from God: "If you have reason to fear treachery from people with whom you have made a covenant, cast it back at them in an equitable manner. For, indeed, God does not love the treacherous." (8: 58)

It was clear that the Qaynuqāʿ Jews had embarked on treachery, broken their pledges and promises and started a provocation campaign which might lead to full-scale war.

Overcoming the New Threat

One must remember here that their district in Madinah was very close to the Muslim areas, which meant that there was constant contact between the two. The Jews certainly knew a great deal about the Muslims and were aware of many of their secrets. All this called for decisive action on the part of the Prophet in order to put an end to this threat. This is exactly what the Prophet did. He declared to them that the treaty between the two parties no longer had any value. He also warned them that he considered himself at war with them. They, on their part, went into their fortifications while the Muslims put them under siege. The siege continued for 15 days, during which the Qaynuqāʿ Jews received no help whatsoever from any quarter.[10]

It is interesting to note that the two other main Jewish tribes, namely al-Naḍīr and Qurayẓah, who both lived on the outskirts of Madinah, did not attempt to help the Qaynuqāʿ Jews in their confrontation with the Prophet. This, in itself, could be taken as evidence of the treachery of the Qaynuqāʿ Jews. The other Jews were no less hostile to Islam than the Qaynuqāʿ tribe, although they did not show it at the time. If the case of treachery was not clear cut, the other Jews would at least have mediated between the Prophet and their cousins. The fact that these tribes remained neutral suggests that the Qaynuqāʿ Jews would have lost their case even if it had been put to a Jewish jury.

It was mentioned earlier that there were alliances between the Jews and the Arabs in Madinah. Every Jewish tribe had alliances with several clans of the Arab tribes. This was natural in a tribal society like that of Arabia, and a multi-national community like that of Madinah. Obviously the Qaynuqāʿ Jews hoped that their former allies would come to their aid. The two leaders who had firm alliances with the Qaynuqāʿ Jews were ʿUbādah ibn al-Ṣāmit and ʿAbdullāh ibn Ubayy. ʿUbādah was now a good Muslim. He went to the Prophet, having realized that his allies were guilty of treachery, and said to him: "Messenger of God, my only loyalty is to God, His Messenger and the believers. I renounce the alliance with these unbelievers and I will give them no support whatsoever."

ʿAbdullāh's case was totally different. He simply professed to be a Muslim while his actions did not give credence to his claim. Over the following years he would emerge as the leader of the hypocrites. On this occasion he felt that if the Qaynuqāʿ Jews, his allies, were to suffer a heavy defeat, his strength in Madinah would be completely eroded. He therefore went to the Prophet and said to him: "Be good to my allies."

The Prophet made no reply and ʿAbdullāh harshly repeated what he had said. The Prophet simply turned away from him. ʿAbdullāh then put his hand inside the Prophet's armour and the Prophet asked him to let him go. ʿAbdullāh did not listen. The Prophet became angry and said: "Let me go!" ʿAbdullāh then said: "I will not let you go until you are good to my allies. They are 700 fighters who protected me against all my enemies and you come to finish them off in one day. I am a man who fears the turns of fortune." The Prophet then said to him: "They are yours."

When the Qaynuqāʿ Jews felt that the siege was biting and that they would receive no support from the other Jews or from their allies, they realized that their case was hopeless. They were overtaken by fear and decided to ask the Prophet to let them leave Madinah. He accepted their offer to leave and let them go with their women and children, provided they left behind their property and their arms. He appointed their former ally, ʿUbādah ibn al-Ṣāmit, to supervise their departure, which was a very good gesture from the Prophet because ʿUbādah was sure to be kind to them. Thus the first Jewish tribe left Madinah.[11]

A Truly Moderate Attitude

To all appearances, the Prophet took a relatively mild attitude towards the hypocrites and the Jews. Although ʿAbdullāh ibn Ubayy behaved so insolently and made the Prophet angry, the Prophet did not let his anger dictate his actions. He allowed ʿAbdullāh to keep his alliance with the Qaynuqāʿ Jews and allowed them to leave Madinah in peace with their women and children.

This moderate attitude made little impression on ʿAbdullāh, who remained hostile to Islam despite his declaration that he was a Muslim. On several occasions he adopted attitudes which were highly detrimental to the cause of Islam. Some historians may suggest that had the Prophet adopted a strong attitude towards him right from the beginning, he was bound to think twice before he took another hostile position. This argument does not take into consideration the fact that ʿAbdullāh had a large following in Madinah amongst the Arabs who viewed Islam with suspicion and hatred. ʿAbdullāh was indeed a man of strong influence. Before the Prophet's emigration to Madinah, preparations were under way to crown him as king of Madinah. It was only owing to the rise of Islam in Madinah that he was deprived of that position. He, however, continued to wield great influence among all those who did not readily accept Islam. Had the Prophet taken him to task on this first occasion of insolence, many of the Arabs who considered him as leader would have been quick to defend him. There might have been a situation of polarization which could have led to a confrontation between the Muslim Arabs and the non-Muslim Arabs in Madinah. That would have meant civil war. Only the Jews and the Quraysh would have benefited from that situation. The Qaynuqāʿ Jews would have felt much stronger and, together with ʿAbdullāh ibn Ubayy and his followers, would have tried to deal a crushing blow to the Prophet and his companions.

Yet the fact that the Prophet decided to take a conciliatory attitude towards ʿAbdullāh did not mean that he felt himself to be weak. Indeed, it is the strong who can afford to take such an attitude. The Prophet was sure to win any confrontation with the hypocrites in Madinah, or with their Jewish allies. He had an army composed of fighters who cared nothing for life when it came to rendering sacrifice for the cause of Islam. Death in battle meant martyrdom, which ensured the highest position in heaven in the life to come. Such an army was more than a match for any force the enemies of Islam could muster. But it is more important sometimes to win the peace than to win the war. The Prophet's attitude to ʿAbdullāh was one which could win hearts and peace.

Moreover, the Prophet's prime objective was to widen the base of Islam and to propagate it far and wide. He considered that if he let a confrontation develop between his followers and the Arabs of Madinah, this would adversely affect the cause of Islam outside the city. Other Arabian tribes would have seen it as a purely internal feud between two groups of Muslims. They had no way of knowing that ʿAbdullāh and whoever chose to follow him were not truly Muslims. To all appearances they were. Reports would go far and wide that Muhammad was killing some of his own followers. That was bound to make other tribes and other nations take an extremely mistaken view of Islam and its message. Surely the harm that such an attitude could cause would outweigh the benefit that might have accrued from adopting a strong attitude towards the hypocrites.

The confrontation with the Jews, on the other hand, was inevitable. Things had not gone smoothly between them and the Muslims over the 18 months that had passed since the Prophet's emigration to Madinah. It was clear that the Jews encouraged the hypocrites to oppose Islam and tried to sow the seeds of discord between the two main groups of Muslims, the Muhājirīn (who emigrated from Makkah) and the Anṣār (who originally lived in Madinah). They even tried to persuade the Prophet to leave Madinah and go to Jerusalem. They also tried to embarrass him with questions concerning all aspects of faith and religion, hoping that such questions would make some of his followers reconsider their attitude towards Islam. The Prophet, however, stood firm against all these attempts. As the Qur'ān was in the process of revelation, it dealt with all their queries and gave the Muslims the final word about all the aspects of faith and religion, leaving no room for suspicion as to which of the two religions was the one acceptable to God.

A Fundamental Challenge

All this, however, led to an escalation of the tension between the two camps. The Qaynuqāʿ Jews, living in the midst of the Muslims, were the first of the Jewish tribes to attempt to confront them. It is difficult to see what made the Qaynuqāʿ Jews feel that they could stand up to the might of the Muslims, especially when the Muslims had just scored a resounding victory against the Quraysh. Their morale was bound to be sky-high. They were sure of God's help and that He alone had granted them victory at Badr. They realized that if they were true in their submission to God, He would not let them down in any confrontation.

The Qaynuqāʿ Jews had probably thought that unless the Muslims were made to suffer a blow or a defeat, they would only get stronger and would soon become unstoppable. They might have argued that an encounter with the Muslims at that particular moment was their best chance to achieve victory.

Some non-Muslim historians believe that it was possible for the Prophet to achieve a *modus vivendi* with the Jews in Madinah. After all, they argue, Islam and Judaism are two monotheistic religions. They have a great deal in common. A little flexibility from both sides would have been enough to ensure that a state of cooperation existed between them which would have enabled them to face the pagan Arabs and put an end to idolatry. These historians forget that the Prophet had made a sincere attempt to achieve such a state of peaceful coexistence and cooperation with the Jews. The treaty he signed with them could have ensured peaceful coexistence between the two sides for a long time to come, provided that good-will existed on both sides. The Qaynuqāʿ Jews, however, showed no sign of good-will. As already mentioned, they were very sorry when they learnt that the idolaters of the Quraysh had suffered a heavy defeat at the hands of the Muslims. One Jewish leader, Kaʿb ibn al-Ashraf, went to Makkah to offer his condolences to the Quraysh leaders and wept for their dead.

There was indeed one significant factor which made peace between the Jews and the Muslims very difficult to achieve. This factor had its roots in the very nature of the two religions. Islam adopts a universal outlook. It opens its arms to every human being to adopt it. All Muslims, regardless of their ethnic origin, colour, race or nation, are absolutely equal. All people are invited to adopt

Islam, and all are treated absolutely equally once they become Muslims. It was a great achievement of Islam in the tribal society of Arabia, based on class and race, that a man like ʿUmar who, before the advent of Islam, was considered among the nobility and became after Islam the second most important follower of the Prophet, should refer to Bilāl, a former slave, as 'our master'. In the early days of Islam in Makkah, Bilāl, as discussed earlier, was subjected to severe torture by his master who tried to force him to renounce Islam. To save Bilāl, Abū Bakr, the Prophet's companion, bought him and set him free. Referring to this incident ʿUmar said: "Abū Bakr was our master and he set our master free."

It is this attitude of open arms to welcome all men or women, humble or noble, free or slave, white or black, to the fold of Islam, considering them all as equals, which distinguishes this great religion. Islam is indeed a religion of all mankind. It is this openness and this universality which make it so different from Judaism. The Jews consider themselves God's 'chosen people'. As such, they believe themselves to be above the rest of mankind. Their sense of the superiority of their race was the prime cause of their hostility to Islam. They knew that a Prophet was bound to come. Indeed, their choice of Madinah as a place for their settlement was motivated by the fact that they knew from their scriptures that Madinah was the place to which the last of the Prophets would emigrate. They went there in order to receive him and follow him. But when they realized that the last of the Prophets was not an Israelite but an Arab, an Ishmaelite, their narrow sense of racism blinded them into harbouring unwavering hatred towards Islam and cut for them a course of unnecessary resistance.

This was the true reason why the Qaynuqāʿ Jews wanted to deal a quick blow to Islam and put an end to it. They sensed that, brave and strong as they were, they could achieve their purpose at that particular time. Perhaps they banked on support from the hypocrites on the one hand and their fellow Jews on the other. That would have meant that they would have the numerical strength which was bound to bring them victory. However, they reckoned without the power and the wisdom of God, Who was guiding His Prophet to victory over all His enemies.

The Case of a Prominent Jew

A prominent personality of the Jewish tribe of al-Naḍīr, Kaʿb ibn al-Ashraf, was so distressed at the defeat of the Quraysh at Badr that he felt and said that death was preferable to life since the Quraysh leaders were killed. Shortly after the Muslims' victory at Badr, Kaʿb went to Makkah to offer his condolences to the pagan Arabs there and to encourage them to look forward to another encounter when they could avenge themselves on Muhammad and his companions. While in Makkah he wrote poems condemning the Muslims and the Prophet in particular, and openly declaring his sympathy with the idolaters of the Quraysh. After a long stay in Makkah, during which he did his utmost to persuade the Quraysh to prepare for an assault on the Muslims, he came back to Madinah where he started to hit the Muslims below the belt, as it were. He wrote obscene love poems mentioning Muslim women. This was extremely offensive to the Muslims, who valued their honour very highly. It was also meant to cause domestic problems in the homes of some of the Muslims. Thus the man was openly an enemy who did not disguise his hostility to the Prophet and to the Muslims in general.

Reviewing the case of Kaʿb ibn al-Ashraf, the Prophet felt that he must be stopped. He therefore said to some of his companions: "Who will rid us of Ibn al-Ashraf, for he has declared his hostility to us openly?" A man from the Anṣār called Muhammad ibn Maslamah said: "I volunteer for that. I will kill him." This man requested and was granted permission from the Prophet to pretend to Kaʿb that he and his friends were against the Prophet and against Islam. It is important to note here that the Prophet did not hesitate to grant them such a permission because he realized that if they succeeded in deluding Kaʿb into thinking them hostile to the Prophet, they would be able to accomplish their mission much more easily and without loss.

A group of the Anṣār – including Muhammad ibn Maslamah and Silkān ibn Salāmah – went to Kaʿb. Silkān was Kaʿb's brother by virtue of their both being breastfed by the same woman. There was therefore an element of trust between them. For this reason Silkān was the first to go to Kaʿb. They chatted together for a while and

Silkān and Kaʿb read some of their poetry to each other in a happy social evening. After a while Silkān said that he had come for a certain purpose but he wanted Kaʿb first to promise that he would keep his secret. When Kaʿb gave him that promise, Silkān said: "The arrival of this man [the Prophet] and his stay among us has been a real disaster for us. All the Arabs are now against us and they have joined forces in their hostility to us. We are now virtually besieged; our children are suffering; we are all enduring real hardship and we cannot really provide well for our children."

Kaʿb answered: "I am Ibn al-Ashraf! I did tell you repeatedly that you would be facing this situation." Silkān then said: "I have come to you to buy food from you, and we will pledge with you something which could secure our debt."

Kaʿb asked whether they were prepared to pledge their women with him. Silkān pointed out that he was the playboy of Madinah and it was impossible for them to trust him with their women. He then proposed that they should give him their children as a pledge. Silkān said: "You want to shame us among the Arabs. I am telling you I have friends who share my opinion. I would like you to meet them and sell them what they need. We will all be making a good deal. We will give you enough of our armour to secure for you the price of the food you would be selling us." Silkān's aim was that Ibn al-Ashraf would not be surprised or suspicious at their bringing their armour with them. Kaʿb said: "Your armour would be good security."

Silkān went back to his companions and told them to get ready. They all met at the Prophet's place. Then they set out and the Prophet walked with them part of the way. Before they left him, he blessed their mission and prayed God to help them.

When they arrived at Kaʿb's fort Silkān shouted for him to come down. Apparently Kaʿb was newly married but he jumped out of bed and answered. His wife, standing aside, said to him: "You are a man at war, and people at war do not go out of their forts at this time of night." Kaʿb said: "This is Silkān, Abū Nā'ilah. Had he found me asleep, he would not have woken me up." She rejoined: "I can hear treachery in his voice." Kaʿb said: "The man [meaning himself] would answer even if he is called in order to be stabbed."

He went down to them and they chatted for a while before they proposed that he should join them for a walk down to Shiʿb al-ʿAjūz, a place at the outskirts of Madinah, where they would spend a few hours together. He agreed and they walked together.

The Killing of Kaʿb ibn al-Ashraf

A little while later, Silkān put his hand in Kaʿb's hair and then smelt his hand and said: "I have never smelt such a nice perfume." Walking on for a little longer, he repeated the gesture, and then once again, so that Kaʿb would not suspect anything. When they had walked for quite a while, Silkān suddenly held Kaʿb by his head and shouted to his friends: "Kill the enemy of God." They hit him with their swords, but he apparently had his armour on and their swords did not harm him.

Kaʿb sent up such a loud cry that all the Jewish forts and castles around them were lit up and there was no more time to waste. Muhammad ibn Maslamah, however, had a knife. He stabbed Kaʿb in the lower part of his abdomen and pulled the knife down. Kaʿb fell. When they had made sure that Kaʿb could not live, they started to run. But they realized that one of them, al-Ḥārith ibn Aws, was wounded and could not move as quickly as they did. They waited for him when they reached a safe area and when he arrived they carried him and went straight to meet the Prophet. It was late into the night when they arrived and the Prophet was at his prayer. When he finished, he went out to see them and they told him of the success of their mission. He wiped al-Ḥārith's wound with his saliva and it cleared up. They then went to their homes and stayed till the morning. The incident struck fear into the hearts of the Jews, who realized that the Muslims would tolerate hostility from no one.[12]

Many Orientalists have denounced the killing of Kaʿb ibn al-Ashraf as 'political assassination'. Those among them who are hostile to Islam find in it material for denouncing Islam and the Prophet himself. The moderates, however, say that it left a stigma in the otherwise bright history of the Prophet. The incident, however, must be viewed in its proper perspective. All historical reports agree that when the Prophet arrived in Madinah he entered into a treaty with the Jews that they and the Muslims would live together in peace, with neither party interfering in the affairs or religion of the other. The treaty also stipulated that the Jews would never give any support to any enemy who attacked Yathrib or fought its people. The treaty also contained the following provisions:

> He who wrongs another brings retribution only on himself and his household. The parties to this agreement will support one another against any third party who wages a war against its signatories. They will give each other mutual advice and approve only good deeds, to the exclusion of bad ones. Support shall be given to the oppressed. No protection shall be given by any party to the Quraysh or to any of its supporters. They shall come to each other's support against whoever attacks Yathrib. This treaty shall not give any immunity to any transgressor or any perpetrator of wrongs. He who leaves Madinah is secure, and he who stays is secure except for those who transgress.[13]

It is clear that the treaty could have provided for peaceful coexistence between the Muslims and the Jews. Its provisions were very clear and far-reaching. If each party had fulfilled its obligations under this treaty, the Muslims and the Jews could have lived peacefully, without any small incident to disturb that peace. One should note here that the treaty provided for mutual support against all enemies, but it mentioned the Quraysh in particular, because the Quraysh were the immediate enemy of the Muslims. It also declared that any individual who transgressed would bear the responsibility for his transgression.

It is difficult to see any reason for Kaʿb ibn al-Ashraf's support for the Quraysh and the feelings of hostility which he showed towards the Muslims when he realized that they had scored a resounding victory against the unbelievers. Indeed he should have been delighted at the victory of the Muslims, for it was a victory of his neighbours and allies who followed a monotheistic religion like his own.

One could ask and wonder: why did Kaʿb ibn al-Ashraf go to the Quraysh, the most hardened enemy of Islam, to weep for its dead and to encourage its leaders to launch a fresh campaign to avenge themselves against the Muslims? Authentic reports suggest that he stayed in Makkah until he was certain that an irreversible decision to attack the Muslims had been taken. Some reports even say that he entered into an alliance with the Quraysh to fight the Muslims alongside them. Besides, why did he write those obscene poems about Muslim women, when he knew that nothing could be more offensive to the Muslims?[14]

All Kaʿb ibn al-Ashraf's actions had engaged him in a war against the Muslims. It was he who decided to take that attitude. Even his wife tried to persuade him not to answer the call, pleading what she knew to be a fact: that he was an enemy in active warfare against the Muslims. As an enemy he deserved to be killed. The fact that the Muslims adopted a method to achieve that end which did not cause any bloodshed between the Muslims and the Jews, apart from killing Kaʿb, was a credit to them. It they had made false pretences to him, these were made for a good purpose: to cause as little bloodshed as possible.

A Jewish delegation came to the Prophet to protest against the killing of Kaʿb ibn al-Ashraf. The Prophet explained that Kaʿb, unlike them, was involved in active hostility against the Muslims. He said: "Had he stayed here in peace, like others who shared his opinion, he would not have been assassinated."[15] The delegation accepted that Kaʿb had chosen to be an active enemy and to support the camp hostile to Islam, and as such had made himself liable to be killed.

An Attempt at Revenge

It is not in the nature of things that a major power in any region will accept a serious setback easily, without doing something to restore its pride. The pressures, both internal and external, in such cases are enormous. Everybody clamours for some sort of revenge, especially if the enemy which has inflicted the setback is, by normal standards, weaker than the side suffering it.

This is exactly the situation that prevailed in Arabia after the defeat of the Quraysh at Badr. Although the Arabian tribes enjoyed full independence, with each of them conducting its own affairs, making its own alliances and fighting its own wars, the Quraysh was without question, the major tribe to which all other tribes deferred for leadership and guidance. The idea of revenge was therefore present in everybody's mind in Makkah where the Quraysh resided, although nothing definite was proposed or considered. The nature of Arabian society at the time made the idea of revenge not merely desirable but dearly cherished. It was a society where tribal wars broke out every other day and revenge for a defeat – or indeed, for one person's death – came very high on any tribe's list of priorities. Hence, everyone in Arabia felt that the Quraysh must do something to wipe out its humiliating defeat at Badr.

But the Quraysh were in a state of shock. They were stunned by the defeat. After the death of many elders, there was no one to fill the vacuum of leadership. The Quraysh wept for their dead for a whole month. They then stopped, not because the wounds had healed or the sorrows were any less felt, but because someone suggested that the Prophet and his companions would be glad to see them weep. Other appearances of mourning were, however, kept. Everybody in the Quraysh wore mourning dress. Women cut their hair very short and left their husbands' beds while men, despondent and unkempt, went about their business wearing an expression of gloom. Something had to happen to bring the Quraysh back to life.

The tragedy was felt most strongly by Abū Sufyān and his wife, Hind bint ʿUtbah ibn Rabīʿāh. At Badr, Hind lost her father, her brother and her uncle, while another brother was in the Muslims' camp. Abū Sufyān was the leader of the caravan which the Prophet and the Muslims attempted to intercept. That attempt was the immediate cause of the Battle of Badr. He now sought the position of leader of the Quraysh. He saw that the time was ripe for him after the death of so many of the Quraysh's leaders. Hind was the first woman in the Quraysh to banish herself from her husband's bed. She vowed that she would wear no perfume until she had taken revenge. Her husband, on the other hand, vowed that he would not have a bath until he had exacted some revenge to restore the Quraysh's pride. Nearly two and a half months after the Battle of Badr, Abū Sufyān mobilized a force of 200 horsemen and went towards Madinah. They went first to the quarters of the Jewish tribe of al-Naḍīr. They called on Ḥuyayy ibn Akhṭab to get some information about the Prophet and his companions, but Ḥuyayy refused to receive them. Their second choice was Sallām ibn Mishkam, who received them well, entertained them and told them everything he knew about the Prophet and the Muslims. Before dawn of the following day, Abū Sufyān and his men went to a place called ʿUrayḍ, nearly three miles out of Madinah, where they killed two men of the Anṣār and burnt down several houses. Abū Sufyān felt that that was enough to honour his vows, so he left quickly with his men.

When the Prophet heard of this incident, he called on his companions to pursue the raiders. He went out at the head of a force of 200 men of the Muhājirīn and the Anṣār in pursuit of Abū Sufyān and his men. When the latter realized that they were being followed they started to drop their supplies of food to give themselves a better chance of escape. Most of the provisions they carried with them were of a foodstuff called *sawīq,* which was made of cereals and could keep for a long time. The raiders were a long way ahead of their Muslim pursuers and they managed to escape. The Muslims, however, were happy to take the provisions thrown away by the Qurayshīs, which were, indeed, plentiful. This is the reason why this pursuit in the desert was called 'the *sawīq* expedition'.[16]

Efficient Economic Siege

Nothing much was achieved by this raid from the Quraysh's point of view. Preparations were therefore started for a major clash, although no definite plans were yet made. However, the need to restore the pride of the Quraysh was coupled with its need to secure its trade routes to Syria, which had come under constant threat from the Muslims in Madinah. Their alternatives were indeed very limited, as indicated by Ṣafwān ibn Umayyah, who said: "Muhammad and his companions have ruined our trade, while we do not know what measures to take against them. They are constantly threatening the coastal area, while its inhabitants are either at peace or in alliance with them. Where shall we live and where shall we stay? If we stay here, in our home town, we will be forced to eat from our capital which will soon be consumed. We depend for our lives on trade with Syria in the summer and with Yemen and Abyssinia in winter."

Al-Aswad ibn al-Muṭṭalib advised him to avoid the coastal route and to take the route leading to Iraq, through Najd, for that was an area not frequented by Muhammad's followers. He also advised Ṣafwān to employ Furāt ibn Ḥayyān as a guide.

Thus a caravan was equipped with all the normal exports of the Quraysh and Ṣafwān went at its head towards Iraq. The Prophet, however, had his informers looking in all directions. He soon learnt of the caravan and its route. He sent a force of 100 men of the Muhājirīn and the Anṣār, led by Zayd ibn Ḥārithah, to intercept the caravan. They came into contact with it at a spring called Qaradah in Najd. When Zayd and his men suddenly surrounded the caravan, all its men fled with the exception of the guide, who was taken prisoner and was soon to embrace Islam. The Muslims took possession of the caravan, which was worth 100,000 dirhams, a considerable amount by the standards of the time. The Prophet distributed the booty among his companions.[17]

Thus the economic siege imposed by the Prophet and his companions on the Quraysh was now biting hard. There was no chance that the Quraysh could tolerate that for long. It was no longer just a matter of wounded pride. As far as the Quraysh were concerned, the situation was a matter of life and death. If it was to submit to the ascendancy of the Muslims, it was bound to lose all its prestige and forfeit its cause altogether. Hence preparations for a new encounter were given a boost. A decision was unanimously taken by the Quraysh that the caravan led by Abū Sufyān, which had escaped interception by the Muslims, would be utilized in full for the preparations for the new battle. Yet it was several months before the Quraysh could raise a well-equipped army to attack the Muslims. In the meantime, several clashes took place between the Muslims and some of the Arab tribes who lived near Madinah. The Prophet adopted the tactic of surprise. Every time he learnt that a tribe or a group of tribes were preparing to attack the Muslims, he would take them by surprise with a pre-emptive strike against them.

Historians give different reasons for these skirmishes. Some suggest that these tribes were in alliance with the Quraysh, while others suggest that they depended for a large portion of their revenue on the Quraysh's usage of the trade route from Makkah to Syria, passing through their areas. When the economic siege imposed by the Muslims on the Quraysh put a virtual end to the Quraysh's usage of that route, the siege hit those tribes as well. Whatever the reason, those clashes were only minor ones and could not affect the Muslims in any major way. Nor could these skirmishes divert the Muslims from concentrating on being ready for any attack which might be launched by their main enemy, the Quraysh.[18]

Notes

1. Ibn Hishām, *al-Sīrah al-Nabawiyyah*, Dār al-Qalam, Beirut, Vol. 1, pp. 227-228.
2. Ibid., Vol. 2, pp. 164-165 and Vol. 3, p. 94. Also, A. al-Suhaylī, *al-Rawḍ al-Unuf*, Dār al-Kutub al-ʿIlmiyyah, Beirut, pp. 375-376; and Ibn Kathīr, *al-Bidāyah wal-Nihāyah*, Maktabat al-Maʿārif, Beirut, Vol. 1, p. 237.
3. Ibn Hishām, op.cit., Vol.2, pp. 163-164.
4. Ibid., pp. 165-166.
5. Ibid., p. 193.
6. Ibid., pp. 204-205.
7. Ibid., Vol. 3, p. 55.
8. Ibid., p. 51.
9. Ibid., p. 50.
10. Ibid., pp. 51-52. Also, Ibn Sayyid al-Nās, *ʿUyūn al-Athar*, Dār al-Turāth, Madinah, 1996, pp. 443-445.
11. Ibn Kathīr, op.cit., Vol. 4, pp. 3-4. Also, A. al-Suhaylī, op.cit., Vol. 3, pp. 225-226; and Ibn Sayyid al-Nās, op.cit., p. 445.
12. Ibn Hishām, op.cit., Vol. 3, pp. 54-60.
13. A. al-Suhaylī, op.cit., Vol.2, pp. 346-350.
14. Amīn Duwaydār, *Ṣuwar Min Ḥayāt al-Rasūl*, Dār al-Maʿārif, 4th edition, Cairo, p. 343.
15. Ibid., p. 343. Also, al-Wāqidī, *Kitāb al-Maghāzī*, Oxford University Press, 1996, Vol. 1, p. 192.
16. Ibn Hishām, op.cit., pp. 47-48.
17. Ibid., pp. 53-54. Also, Ibn Kathīr, op.cit., Vol. 4, pp. 4-5.
18. Amīn Duwaydār, op.cit., p. 350.

20

A Bitter Defeat

NO ONE IN Arabia expected the Quraysh to accept defeat at Badr without making a determined effort to avenge themselves. The skirmishes that took place in the following months between the Muslims and certain pockets of resistance to the Islamic cause could inflict no harm on the Muslims. Indeed the Prophet and his followers made use of these skirmishes to consolidate their reputation as a major force in Arabia. When the Quraysh also felt that the economic siege imposed by the Muslim state on them was biting hard and that it had become a major danger threatening its well-being, it realized that it could regain its prestige and break the economic siege only through scoring a military victory over the Muslims.

The Quraysh allocated for the new war effort every penny it had made in its trading with Syria by means of the caravan led by Abū Sufyān who managed to escape his Muslim pursuers just before the Battle of Badr. Delegations were sent to several Arab tribes to seek their support in the campaign to be launched. Arms were sought and bought everywhere they could be found. These preparations continued for a whole year, after which the Quraysh felt that they were strong enough to make a strike and exact revenge.

In the month of Shawwāl of the third year of the Prophet's emigration, that is, a little over a year after the Battle of Badr, the

Quraysh army, now 3,000-men strong, set out on its way towards Madinah. A large number of 'volunteers' and supporters from Tihāmah and Kinānah, Abyssinians living in Arabia, and others were also in the army. Fourteen women, most prominent among whom was Hind bint ʿUtbah, Abū Sufyān's wife, went out as well in order to provide encouragement and to deter any would-be defectors. Also in the army was Abū ʿĀmir, a man from the Aws, one of the two main tribes of the Anṣār. Abū ʿĀmir was a man of knowledge who had learnt about the appearance of the last Prophet. He used to tell his people about the qualities and description of that Prophet, making it clear that the time was due for his appearance. When the Prophet Muhammad emigrated to Madinah, however, and the Anṣār followed him, Abū ʿĀmir, a prominent figure, occupying in the tribe of the Aws a similar position to that of ʿAbdullāh ibn Ubayy in the tribe of the Khazraj, rejected his message. Both men felt envious of the Prophet because he had gathered such a large following, but they adopted different attitudes. ʿAbdullāh ibn Ubayy professed to be a Muslim although his actions gave no credence to what he professed. Abū ʿĀmir, on the other hand, rejected Islam and went out to Makkah along with 50 men and youths of his tribe, giving support to the Quraysh and now joining its army to fight the Prophet and his own people. Abū ʿĀmir also told the Qurayshīs that he would make his tribesmen desert the army of the Prophet and that the Quraysh had nothing to fear from the Aws. Obviously, he made these promises on the basis of his former standing with his people. Little did he think that Islam had superseded all tribal loyalties. He was soon to be bitterly disappointed.

The Element of Surprise

The Quraysh's army moved forward. Abū Sufyān was its overall commander; Ṭalḥah ibn Abī Ṭalḥah was the flagman; Khālid ibn al-Walīd and ʿIkrimah ibn Abī Jahl were commanders of the right and left flanks respectively; Ṣafwān commanded the infantry. The army included 200 horsemen and 700 soldiers wearing body armour. A large number of camels were utilized to carry the soldiers and to be slaughtered for food. There were plenty of slaves and servants to carry out the menial jobs.

The Quraysh had apparently set a plan for the achievement of well-defined objectives. They wanted to surprise the Muslims in their own city and take them unawares. If that initial aim was thwarted and the Muslims were aware of the impending attack, the Quraysh's plan was to attempt to cause division among the Muslims when the clash became imminent. Should that also fail, the immediate aim when war broke out was to kill the Prophet himself and the leaders of the Muslims, especially the prominent figures among the Muhājirīn, in the same way as the Muslims did in Badr when they killed many prominent figures of the Quraysh.

The Quraysh's army moved in total secrecy. No demonstration of strength was attempted this time, as was Abū Jahl's aim in Badr. Whatever the goal, it was to be accomplished with speed. Hence the army moved very fast until it reached the valley of Uḥud, only eight kilometres from Madinah, where it encamped. Perhaps the Quraysh would have taken the Muslims by surprise, had it not been for the fact that al-ʿAbbās, the Prophet's uncle, who still lived in Madinah and had not yet declared his adoption of the Islamic faith, sent the Prophet a letter informing him of the Quraysh's march and giving him all the details of the army and its equipment.

Al-ʿAbbās's emissary travelled day and night until he reached Madinah, where he learnt that the Prophet was in Qubā', a short distance away. He went to him there and gave him the letter. As is well known, the Prophet could not read or write. He therefore gave the letter to Ubayy ibn Kaʿb, who read it for him. The Prophet asked Ubayy not to circulate the news. He then informed Saʿd ibn al-Rabīʿ of the Anṣār of what he had learnt. Saʿd said: "I pray to God to give us the benefit of all this."

Back in the Quraysh encampment, Abū Sufyān said as he woke up in the morning: "I swear that they have informed Muhammad of our march and he has now learnt all the information he needs about us. I should not be surprised if his followers are staying in their forts and we will see none of them face to face."

Ṣafwān said: "If they do not come out to meet us we will cut down the date palms which belong to the Aws and the Khazraj. They will be left without any produce. If they come out and meet us, we outnumber them and we are better equipped. We have more horses than they have and we are here for revenge, while they seek no revenge with us."

The Prophet's informers came back with the news that the Quraysh army was encamped at Uḥud. They gave him their estimates of their number and their equipment. They also told him that the unbelievers let their camels and horses loose in the farms of Madinah and they were causing havoc. Thus the danger was abundantly clear and the Muslims realized that they could not afford to waste any time. That night, guards were keeping an all-night vigil at the approaches of Madinah. Many of the Muslims stayed the night in the mosque, with their arms ready. The Prophet's rooms were adjacent to the mosque and the Muslims were worried lest the Quraysh should mount an attack on the mosque with the aim of killing him.

The next day was a Friday. After the dawn prayer, the Prophet consulted his companions in order to achieve a consensus of opinion for an effective plan of action. He told them that he had a dream the previous night. Long before he became a Prophet, every dream Muhammad had came true in every single detail. This was one of the early signs of his prophethood. It goes without saying that after he became Prophet, his dreams continued to be indicative of forthcoming events. Now he said that he saw in his dream a few cows which belonged to him being slaughtered, and a little notch in the edge of his sword, and that he had put his hand in a strong shield of armour. He said that he felt optimistic about his dream and he interpreted that the cows indicated that a few of his companions would be killed, while the notch indicated that a member of his household would be killed. The shield of armour, he felt, was a reference to Madinah itself. He then suggested that they should stay put in Madinah and leave the Makkans where they had encamped. "If they stay there, they will find that their position is an unenviable one. If they attempt to force their way into Madinah, we will fight them in its streets and alleys, which we know far better than they, and they will be attacked with arrows and all sorts of missiles from rooftops."

Consultation Over a Plan

ʿAbdullāh ibn Ubayy, a leading personality of the Khazraj, who at one time spoke very harshly to the Prophet when he feared for his Jewish allies of the Qaynuqāʿ tribe, supported the Prophet's view on this occasion. He said:

> Messenger of God, before the advent of Islam we used to fight in Madinah. We would keep our women and children in our fortified homes, giving them plenty of stones. We would also build shelters and fortifications to close the gaps between the outer buildings so that the whole city would be like a big fort. Women and children would throw stones and other missiles from rooftops while we fought in the streets and alleys. Our city is indeed a virgin. No enemy has ever tried to enter it without being defeated, and we have never gone out to meet an enemy without regretting it. Let them, Messenger of God, stay where they are. They are in an uncomfortable abode, and if they go back they will have achieved nothing. Their objectives will have been foiled. Take my word on this, because it is the opinion supported by history.

Several young men advanced a different view. They felt that they had missed much by not turning out at Badr and they were keen to meet the enemy this time. They asked the Prophet to lead them to meet the enemy outside Madinah.

A number of mature men, known to have the best interests of Islam at heart, said: "We fear that the enemy may think, if we do not go out to meet them, that we feel weak and cowardly. This may tempt them to launch a bold attack on us. In Badr you had only 300 people and you achieved a great victory. Today we can provide a much larger number of soldiers. We have been hoping for such an encounter and praying God to make our hopes come true. Now we have the enemy at our doorstep, so let us meet them where they are."

Mālik ibn Sinān said to the Prophet: "We can have one of the two best alternatives: either we shall achieve victory with the help of God – and that is decidedly our aim – or we shall die as martyrs. As far as I am concerned, I do not care which will come to pass. Both are very good."

Ḥamzah ibn ʿAbd al-Muṭṭalib, the Prophet's uncle, who was in his early fifties, said: "By Him who has sent down His Book to you, I shall taste nothing today until I have fought them with my sword outside Madinah."

Al-Nuʿmān ibn Mālik said: "Messenger of God, why do you keep us from heaven? By God Who is the only deity, I will get into it." The Prophet (peace be upon him) asked him: "On what grounds?" He answered: "Because I am a man who loves God and the Prophet and does not flee from battle."

Iyās ibn Aws said: "It worries me that the Quraysh should be able to return and say: 'We have besieged Muhammad and his companions in the fortifications and hills of Yathrib [Madinah].' They will then feel that they can have a go at us at any time. Moreover, they have grazed on our farms, and unless we defend our farms they will not be fit to be planted again."

Khaythamah – whose son Saʿd was killed at Badr – said:

> I missed the Battle of Badr when I was keen to take part in it. I was so keen then that I tossed with my son for which of us would have the privilege of joining you there. He won the toss and became a martyr. I was so eager that martyrdom would be mine. Last night I saw my son in my dream, looking his best, enjoying the fruits of Paradise. He said to me: "Come and join us here in heaven, for I have found that God fulfils His promises." I swear, Messenger of God, that I am longing to join him in heaven. I am very old and I would love to meet my Lord. Pray God to grant me martyrdom soon, so that I can join my son in heaven.[1]

ʿAbdullāh ibn Jaḥsh said: "My Lord, I pray you to enable me to meet the enemy tomorrow, and that they kill me and open my stomach and cut my nose and ear. When you ask me why they have done that to me, I will answer: Because I believe in you!"[2]

It has been frequently said that only the young Muslims in Madinah were keen to go out and meet the enemy outside, while the more mature people supported the view of the Prophet. These quotations provide a more accurate picture. Indeed, those who preferred to go out and meet the enemy where they had encamped were not only in a majority, they also represented a broad section of the Muslim community. Had he wished, the Prophet was able, indeed, to impose his opinion, and no one would have questioned him. He, however, wanted to teach his companions a lesson in leadership. He wished to drive home to them the fact that he who has the authority must not impose his own will. He must consult his companions because through consultation the right course of action will emerge. He also wanted them to face up to their responsibilities. The decision was that of the majority and they all shared in the responsibility for taking such a decision.

The Prophet then accepted the will of the majority. At noon, when it was time for Friday prayer, he emphasized in his sermon the need for consolidated action in fighting and told them that they would achieve victory if they fought hard and endured whatever hardship they might face. Most people were happy with the Prophet's decision, but some of them felt that they had forced him to take action against his better judgement. Many Muslims went to their homes to get ready for battle and came back to the mosque. The Prophet led them in the mid-afternoon prayers, *ʿAṣr*, and instructed them to keep their women and children in their fortified homes, before he went into his rooms to get ready.

Second Thoughts

Discussion was still going on among the Muslims in the mosque on the advisability of going out to meet the enemy or staying in Madinah. Right from the beginning, quite a few shared the Prophet's opinion that it was better to stay. Many others had second thoughts, not because they were reluctant to meet the enemy but because they felt that it was wrong for them to make the Prophet do something against his own wishes. Two of the leading figures of the Anṣār, Saʿd ibn Muʿādh and Usayd ibn Ḥuḍayr, said to them: "You have forced the Prophet to decide to go out and meet the enemy, when you know that he receives revelations from on high. You would be better advised to leave the matter to him. Whatever he commands you, you should do, and when you see that he is inclined to something or to a certain point of view, you had better follow his inclination."

While they were having this discussion the Prophet came out of his rooms wearing his armour. Those who had pressed for meeting the enemy outside Madinah said to him: "Messenger of God, it is not for us to disobey you. Do as you please and we will follow you." He answered: "I have asked you to stay and you refused. It is not for a Prophet who has worn his armour to lay it down until God has judged between him and his enemies. Obey my orders and remain steadfast and you will achieve victory."[3]

The Prophet realized that it was important that he should not seem to vacillate between two different points of view. Once a decision is made, it should be carried out. Hesitation, especially at a time when the enemy is on the doorstep, is exceedingly dangerous. This lesson in consultative government which he taught his companions was of paramount importance. They realized, as all Muslim generations would come to realize, that a ruler may have to take an attitude contrary to his own opinion if it meets the wishes of a broad section of the Muslim community. This is an essential characteristic of Islamic government. But once a decision is made, everybody, including the ruler – or the Prophet in this case – should help to see it implemented.

When the Muslims completed the mobilization of their forces, their army was about 1,000-men strong. The Prophet split them into three divisions, with a flag for each division. Usayd ibn Ḥuḍayr was given the flag of one of the two Anṣārī tribes, the Aws, while al-Ḥubāb ibn al-Mundhir was given the flag of the Khazraj. The third flag was that of the Muhājirīn, which was carried by Muṣʿab ibn ʿUmayr. Only a hundred of the Prophet's companions had body armour. Ibn Umm Maktūm,[4] a blind man from the Muhājirīn, deputized for the Prophet in conducting the affairs of Madinah and led the prayers in the mosque.

When the Prophet reached a place called al-Shaykhayn, he stopped to inspect his army. He found that there were several young boys in the ranks and ordered them to go back. Among these boys were Rāfiʿ ibn Khadīj and Samurah ibn Jundub. The Prophet was told that Rāfiʿ was a good marksman with bow and arrows, so he let him stay with the army. On hearing that Rāfiʿ was allowed to stay, Samurah wept and said: "The Prophet has allowed Rāfiʿ and refused me, while I am stronger than him and can beat him." When the Prophet learnt of this, he asked the two boys to wrestle. As Samurah came out the winner, the Prophet allowed him also to stay.

A Split in the Ranks

Before long, it was night and the army spent the night at al-Shaykhayn. Muhammad ibn Maslamah was put in charge of the guards who kept watch over the army and Dhakwān ibn Qays was in charge of the Prophet's own bodyguard. Before dawn, the Muslim army started to move until it reached an orchard between Madinah and Uḥud called al-Shawṭ. At that point, ʿAbdullāh ibn Ubayy – who, as we have noted, had opposed the idea of the Muslims meeting the enemy outside Madinah – deserted the army and went back with no fewer than 300 soldiers. The reason he gave for his desertion was that the Prophet "had obeyed the young boys in preference to me. Why should we, then, kill ourselves at this place?"

ʿAbdullāh ibn ʿAmr ibn Ḥarām went after the deserters, trying to persuade them to return. He appealed to them not to split the ranks of the Muslims and not to let down their people and the Messenger of God when the enemy was on the doorstep. His entreaties, however, were in vain. They simply were not prepared to listen. They said in a tone of sarcasm: "We do not believe that there will be any fighting. If we knew that fighting would take place, we would join you." When he realized that his words were falling on deaf ears, ʿAbdullāh ibn ʿAmr gave them a piece of his mind and left them.[5]

This was certainly no small matter. The breach in the ranks of the Muslims was very serious indeed. One-third of the army had left. Now the Muslims were outnumbered four to one. But the desertion was not without its advantages. It was clear that those people who left with ʿAbdullāh ibn Ubayy did not have the interests of Islam at heart. As such, they could not be expected to fight for it, risking their own lives. Their presence would then have been of no great use. The cause of Islam can be served only by those who are dedicated to it and are prepared to risk their lives for it. Hence the desertion by the hypocrites meant that only such people remained as could be counted upon to fight hard and remain steadfast regardless of the consequences.

The Qur'ān says that two groups of the believers were so badly affected by the desertion of the hypocrites that they were on the point of losing heart. These were the soldiers from the two clans of Ḥārithah and Salamah. Only God's grace helped them regain their confidence and put their trust in God: "Two of your groups were about to lose heart, but God was their protector. In God shall the believers trust." (3: 122) Here God is telling the believers about their own thoughts. What took place in the minds of those two groups was known only to themselves, but God knows every single thought that flashes into anybody's mind. He is here reminding the Muslims that only through His grace are they protected against any evil thought that occurs to them.

Seeking Help from Non-Muslims

Perhaps because of the departure of ʿAbdullāh ibn Ubayy with his 300 supporters, and the consequent feeling of weakness that spread among the Muslims, some of the Anṣār put to the Prophet the proposition that they should ask their Jewish allies to fight alongside them. The Prophet, however, rejected this proposition out of hand, saying: "We do not need them."[6]

It should be pointed out here that the Prophet was not against seeking help from non-Muslims in principle. On several occasions he sought, and received, help from people who did not, at the time, accept his message or that he was God's Messenger. Several years before the

Battle of Uḥud, the Prophet sought the support of al-Muṭʿim ibn ʿAdiy to enter Makkah safely after the failure of his mission in Ṭā'if. When he left Makkah to emigrate to Madinah, he employed ʿAbdullāh ibn Arqat as a guide to take him through unfamiliar routes. Later, when he was making preparations to fight the Battle of Ḥunayn, the Prophet borrowed 100 shields of body armour and a large quantity of weapons from Ṣafwān ibn Umayyah. He also asked Maʿbad ibn Abī Maʿbad of the tribe of Khuzāʿah to try to discourage the Quraysh from attacking the Muslims at Ḥamrā' al-Asad. None of these people was a Muslim at the time when the Prophet sought his help. One of them at least – al-Muṭʿim ibn ʿAdiy – died without ever embracing Islam. Thus the idea of seeking outside help – or more specifically, seeking help from non-Muslims – is not unacceptable to Islam or to the Prophet. Yet he rejected the proposition made by the Anṣār to seek the help of their Jewish allies. This case then needs to be considered in order to determine the cause of the Prophet's attitude.

If one reviews these cases where the Prophet sought outside help, one finds that in none of them was there any question of compromise being asked or given with respect to any principle of Islam. Thus the Prophet teaches that if this condition is fulfilled, seeking help from outsiders for the benefit of the Muslim community is both acceptable and sound. The sort of help offered in these incidents was either technical expertise or armament or protection in case of defencelessness against an overpowering enemy. At no time did the Prophet seek advice (apart from that based on technical expertise) or military support from non-believers.

It is not difficult to determine the reasoning behind this attitude. With regard to advice in order to formulate an opinion and adopt an attitude, the reason for limiting it to Muslims only is that there can never be complete trust that a non-Muslim will give absolutely objective advice to help a religion in which he does not believe. Military support is also ruled out, because the admission of non-Muslims into an Islamic army constitutes an ever-present danger of their causing a split by withdrawing their support at any time, just as ʿAbdullāh ibn Ubayy did when he persuaded one-third of the Muslim army to desert, even before the Muslims reached the battlefield.

From another point of view, if the help of non-Muslims is sought in the actual fighting of a war fought for the cause of God, there could be only two situations. Firstly, there are enough of them to make their presence in the army felt by every soldier. In such a case, they themselves constitute an apparent danger should they ever contemplate moving against the Muslims in any way, such as joining forces with the enemy, or merely by withdrawing their support when Muslims are in the thick of battle. If, on the other hand, they represent no danger because there are so few of them, then their presence cannot significantly affect the outcome of the battle. It is better, therefore, not to seek their help at all to guard against any possibility that any one of them should act as a spy for the enemy. This, then, is the lesson the Prophet taught the Muslims when he said to those who proposed that they should seek help from their Jewish allies: "I do not seek help from a non-Muslim."

One should distinguish here between 'seeking help' from non-believers and 'cooperation' with a non-believer. Seeking help places Muslims in a weak position *vis-à-vis* the non-believers. The Muslims are thus the beneficiaries of such help while the non-believers stand to gain nothing from helping. Cooperation, on the other hand, signifies a situation where both cooperating parties benefit. The fact that the other party stands to benefit from such cooperation serves as a guarantee of its good intentions. Islam approves of such cooperation, provided that it is limited to the field where cooperation is needed and that the benefit accruing to the Muslims should be greater than that accruing to the non-Muslims.

At Uḥud Before the Battle

The Prophet and his 700 companions who remained with him marched on until they reached Uḥud. Their determination to defend the cause of Islam with their lives was unshakeable. Every one of them was more than ready to give his life for the sake of Islam. The fact that they were heavily outnumbered did not cause them to be down-hearted. They realized that they were on God's side. As Muslims, they believed that victory can be achieved only with God's help. He alone can grant victory to any particular group of people. They, therefore, prayed God to grant them His help so that they might achieve victory. Every time the Muslims faced an enemy, they always felt that they would come out with one of two very welcome results: either victory or martyrdom.

Uḥud is a mountain with numerous well-defined passages and routes, intersected by a number of valleys, stretching out into a wide semi-circle opposite the narrow plain where the Quraysh had encamped. There are numerous pockets in its slopes where soldiers may hide if a defensive strategy is adopted. The Prophet encamped by the side of the mountain, close to a hill called Mount ʿAynayn which overlooked the plain. The Prophet marshalled his troops, taking advantage of the position of the hill so that they would face their enemy with the hill at their back providing protection against any possible pincer attack. He deployed 50 marksmen, who were good with arrows, on top of Mount ʿAynayn, giving their command to ʿAbdullāh ibn Jubayr. The Prophet's strict orders to these marksmen were that they should protect the Muslims from behind and not allow the enemy to overrun their positions at any cost. He also ordered them not to leave their positions whatever the outcome of the battle. This last order the Prophet stressed so strongly that he told them that they were not to move, even if they saw with their own eyes their fellow Muslims being killed left, right and centre. If the Quraysh's horsemen were to try to climb the hill in order to attack the Muslims from behind, they were to repel them with their arrows. When the Prophet had deployed his troops, he spoke to them, encouraging them to fight and exert their maximum efforts. He also told them not to start fighting until he gave the battle order.[7]

At that moment the enemy troops appeared in the plain below and the two armies were now face to face. The women from the Quraysh were singing and playing music to encourage their troops and boost their morale. When the two armies stood facing each other, Abū Sufyān, now the undisputed leader of the Quraysh, started implementing the strategy he had devised. He addressed the Anṣār in the vain hope of splitting the Muslim ranks. He said to the Aws and the Khazraj that the Quraysh had no quarrel with them and did not wish to fight them. If the Aws and the Khazraj would leave the Quraysh to settle their score with their kinsmen – that is, the Muhājirīn – then they had nothing to fear from the Quraysh. No one replied, and no one was interested in what Abū Sufyān said.

Next spoke Abū ʿĀmir, the man who used to foretell that the Prophet was soon to appear, but when the Prophet emigrated to Madinah, Abū ʿĀmir left his people, the Aws, and joined the Quraysh with 50 of his kinsfolk. He now made his speech, hoping to persuade his tribesmen to leave the Muslim ranks. He called to the Aws to respond to him. A response was made, but it was the opposite of what he used to assert to the Quraysh. He always claimed that he was the undisputed leader of the Aws and that they would not do anything which displeased him. Their response, however, was to curse and stone him. Humiliated, he ran back to the Quraysh, saying: "Some unknown evil overtook my people after I left them." Thus the Quraysh failed in their two initial aims: to take the Muslims by surprise and to cause a split in their ranks. The only option left to them was to fight.

The Battle Starts in Earnest

The Quraysh started the battle with an attempt to encircle the Muslims with a pincer movement. The left flank of the Quraysh army, commanded by ʿIkrimah ibn Abī Jahl, tried to turn the Muslims round but was unable to accomplish its purpose. The right flank, commanded by Khālid ibn al-Walīd, then made a similar attempt to achieve the same purpose. It was repelled, however, by a heavy bombardment with the arrows from the unit on top of Mount ʿAynayn. The two armies were back to their starting positions.

A man came out from the ranks of the non-believers calling for a duel. Al-Zubayr ibn al-ʿAwwām accepted his challenge, fought and killed him, to the delight of the Muslims who shouted their ever inspiring slogan: 'God is Supreme'. The battle now began in earnest and the Muslims were ready to repeat their splendid victory at Badr. The fact that they were fighting an enemy four times their size did not discourage them. Indeed, to most of them victory was a certainty which was soon to come to pass, because they had long realized that victory is granted by God. Since they were fighting for God's cause, victory was assured.

An incident which epitomizes the attitude of the Muslims at the Battle of Uḥud was that of Abū Dujānah Simāk ibn Kharashah. The Prophet held out a sword in his hand and asked his companions as he was marshalling them: "Who takes this sword for its proper value?" Several men showed interest but the Prophet did not give it to any of them. Abū Dujānah, however, stood out and asked: "What is its proper value, Messenger of God?" The Prophet answered: "That you strike the enemy with it until it is bent." Abū Dujānah said: "I take it for its proper value." He was known to be a brave fighter and in time of war he would walk in a certain way which showed pride. He took out a red band and tied it to his forehead, a gesture that signified that he was ready to fight. When the Prophet saw him doing that, he said: "This type of walk is hateful to God, except in time of war."

As the battle raged on, Abū Dujānah fought hard and killed every one of the enemy army who tried to stop him. While Abū Dujānah advanced in this fashion, there was an enemy soldier who made it his duty to seek any one of the Muslims who was wounded and kill him. Soon he found himself face to face with Abū Dujānah and each of them levelled a strike at the other. Abū Dujānah managed to make his opponent's strike hit only his shield and he then killed him. He moved on to meet another soldier wearing a mask. As he was about to strike him, the soldier cried out and Abū Dujānah realized that he was facing a woman. He let her go because, as he said later, he felt it was improper to strike a woman with the Prophet's sword. That woman was Hind bint ʿUtbah, Abū Sufyān's wife.

Keeping Up the Quraysh Flag

With the battle raging fiercely, it was clear to everyone that it surpassed all previous encounters between the two sides in its ferocity. The Muslims concentrated their attack on the unit which held the flag of the Quraysh. Traditionally, the clan of ʿAbd al-Dār had the honour of holding the flag of the Quraysh in any battle. Since their showing at Badr had not been very impressive, Abū Sufyān spoke to them before the outbreak of war, saying that it might be better to give the flag to some other unit if the ʿAbd al-Dār fighters were to give a similar performance to that of Badr. His real intention was to provoke them so that they would be determined to put up a good fight. They told him that no one would be able to criticize their performance this time.

Their performance was indeed impressive by any standard. As the Muslims concentrated their attack on them, the ʿAbd al-Dār fighters fought back with courage and determination. But they were no match for their attackers. Ṭalḥah ibn Abū Ṭalḥah, the Quraysh flag-holder, was soon killed by Alī. The flag was then held by his brother, ʿUthmān, who was killed in turn by Ḥamzah and the pattern was repeated. No fewer than seven brothers carried the Quraysh flag, and they were all killed. Three more of their relatives were also killed as they held the flag. The flag was then on the ground and the Quraysh army was in chaos.

It was the smaller army which was putting in the more determined fight. Although the Quraysh came to avenge its previous defeat, the Muslims had higher hopes and stronger inspiration to do well in battle. After all, they were defending their faith. It was not surprising, therefore, that they fought hard, and in no time they were gaining ground on their enemy. Ḥamzah ibn ʿAbd al-Muṭṭalib, the Prophet's uncle who had been the scourge of the Quraysh at the Battle of Badr, repeated his exceptional performance. He killed at least two of the flag-holders as well as some other Quraysh soldiers. But he had an enemy whom he could not see.

A Great Martyr Falls

Waḥshī, an Abyssinian slave, was an excellent marksman with the spear. His master, Jubayr ibn Muṭʿim, had promised to set him free if he killed Ḥamzah to avenge the killing of Jubayr's own uncle, Ṭuʿaymah ibn ʿAdiy, who was killed at Badr. Also Hind bint ʿUtbah promised Waḥshī a good reward if he killed Ḥamzah in revenge for her father, brother and other relatives. Waḥshī was with the Quraysh army, but he did not take part in the actual fighting. He looked only for Ḥamzah and found him fighting with exceptional courage. As Ḥamzah was closing in on a man from the Quraysh called Sabba' ibn 'Abd al-'Uzzā, he came within the range of Waḥshī's spear. Ḥamzah missed Sabbā''s head with his sword when Waḥshī aimed his spear at him, hitting him in his lower abdomen. The spear went through his body and appeared between his legs. He tried to move towards Waḥshī but could not and fell down. Waḥshī waited until Ḥamzah died and went to pull his spear out. As Waḥshī did not have any more interest in the fighting he left, having ensured his freedom.[8]

Hind bint 'Utbah, who for a full year had nursed her grudge against Ḥamzah, now started to disfigure him. She opened his stomach and took out his liver and tried to eat it. She could not cut it with her teeth, so she threw it out.[9]

The death of Ḥamzah, however, did not much affect the way the battle was going. It was soon very clear that the Muslims were gaining the upper hand. Confusion spread in the Quraysh army. Many of its soldiers started to run away. The Muslims, on the other hand, started to collect their booty.[10]

Disobedience by Believers

All that, however, was round one, which went clearly in favour of the Muslims. They overwhelmed their enemy despite the fact that they gave away a great deal in numerical strength. They were simply fighting for a cause. Nothing can motivate people more than faith and that the Muslims had in abundance. But even the most ardent of the faithful have their moments of weakness. One such moment came when, to all appearances, the Muslims had all but won the battle.

That unit which the Prophet placed on Mount 'Aynayn and entrusted with the task of repelling any attempt by the Quraysh army to launch a pincer attack on the Muslims had a very important role in achieving the initial victory. One should recall that that unit was under strict orders from the Prophet not to leave its position in any eventuality. They were the rearguard of the Muslim army. The Prophet could not have impressed on them more strongly the importance of their keeping their position: "Even if you see us being killed left, right and centre."

Despite such strong emphasis, when the Mount ʿAynayn unit of archers – which may be compared in modern warfare terms to artillery units which give cover to the advancing infantry – saw their Muslim brethren start to collect the booty, they felt that the battle was over and that they were free to leave their positions. Their commander, ʿAbdullāh ibn Jubayr, was under no illusion that their action went clearly against the express wishes of the Prophet. He reminded them of their instructions. He told them that they were taking the risk that the Prophet would be displeased with them. However, they did not listen. They sought to interpret the Prophet's instructions as valid only until victory was achieved. Since victory was achieved – or so they thought – there was no reason for them to stay in their positions, leaving all the booty to their fellow fighters. Therefore, they descended into the battlefield to join in the collection of the booty. Only ʿAbdullāh ibn Jubayr remained on top of the hill with a handful of his fellow soldiers, in strict obedience to the Prophet's instructions.

It is difficult to explain the behaviour of those companions of the Prophet and their keenness to collect the booty themselves. Not long before the Muslims had fought the Battle of Badr and the dispute over the booty had arisen between different groups of soldiers. The matter was then resolved by clear instructions from God which gave all those who fought equal shares in the spoils gained by the Muslims. The action could be explained only by assuming that memories of the recent past came into play. Just before the advent of Islam, the Arabs were always fighting each other over petty gains. Their battles were never well organized. They were more like two unruly mobs fighting each other. To stick to certain positions when everything appeared to be over was not exactly comprehensible to their way of thinking.

Attack from Behind

Khālid ibn al-Walīd, the commander of the right flank of the Quraysh army, was a brilliant fighter. His qualities of military leadership were proven in the numerous battles which he subsequently fought for the cause of Islam. In the Battle of Uḥud, however, he was fighting against Islam. He realized that the only hope the Quraysh had of turning the scales against the Muslims was in the possibility that a chance might offer itself to mount an attack against the Muslims from behind. While the Quraysh fighters were beating a retreat, his eyes were fixed on what was taking place on Mount ʿAynayn. He was assessing the situation and considering the possibility of repeating his earlier unsuccessful attempt to climb the hill from behind. Suddenly he saw the Muslim unit – or rather, most of it – leaving its position in order to join their fellow fighters in the battlefield. Without the slightest hesitation, Khālid ibn al-Walīd drove his troops wide, away from the main area of fighting, in a semi-circular movement, until he reached the back of Mount ʿAynayn, where he and his soldiers fought the now very thin unit remaining with ʿAbdullāh ibn Jubayr. Khālid was followed closely by ʿIkrimah ibn Abū Jahl, the commander of the left flank of the Quraysh army, and the two made a quick job of finishing off whatever brave resistance those who remained on top of the hill, as the Prophet had bid them, could put up.

Khālid and ʿIkrimah then launched a determined attack on the Muslims from behind. They penetrated their ranks, hailing their main idols like al-ʿUzzā and Hubal. This caused some initial hesitation among the Muslims and a pleasant surprise for the retreating units of the Quraysh army. Those units were now able to counter-attack, benefiting from the hesitation of the Muslims. A woman called ʿAmrah bint ʿAlqamah of the Ḥārithī clan picked up the Quraysh flag, which was trampled upon on the ground, and lifted it up so that it was a gathering point for the returning Quraysh soldiers. The speed with which all this happened caught the Muslims by surprise and left them confused. They did not know how the army which a short while ago had been withdrawing in defeat, could attack them from both the front and the rear. Quite a number of Muslim soldiers were killed, but the state of confusion that spread among them was more disastrous than the number of casualties they suffered.

At that moment, someone shouted very loudly: "Muhammad has been killed!" The outcry was repeated and it caused much disturbance to the Muslims. Most of them were truly shaken and many felt that defeat was inevitable.[11]

To Flee or to Fight

The Muslims did not know what was really happening to them. Some of them went right up into the mountain, trying to reach a position of safety. Others simply fled the battlefield. Some were fighting on, defending themselves as strongly as they could. They felt that if they fought until they were killed, that would be the best they could achieve. Others were so surprised and confused that they laid down their swords and arms and stopped fighting. Some of them started to question themselves and their brethren: "If Muhammad is dead why do we fight on? Is it not better for us to go back to Madinah where our people could work for an accommodation with the Quraysh?" Others felt that it was the moment of decision between Islam and Ignorance, and that they would inevitably be killed.

The Prophet, however, was not dead. He was not a man to be shaken by defeat, or to give up when death looked him in the face. He was the example for all believers in all generations. His courage was never in doubt. He stood firm, shouting to his companions: "Come to me, you who worship God; come back to me; I am God's Messenger."[12] He even shouted to certain people, calling them by name. Most of his companions, however, did not even hear him as he shouted to them. A handful of them, not more than ten according to the highest estimates, remained steadfast with him and gave him their pledges to fight with him until they died. They moved to a position which afforded them a little protection and fought most determinedly.

Aiming to Kill the Prophet

It was mentioned earlier that the Quraysh aimed, if war broke out, to try to kill as many of the leading Muslim figures as possible.

Now it went for the highest prize of all: Muhammad himself. A determined attack was launched with the single aim of killing the Prophet. The Quraysh realized that the Muslims would not be able to survive if they were to be deprived of the guidance the Prophet provided. Their sense of nationhood was not yet strong enough to weather such a storm as the killing of the Prophet would bring about. Thus, by attacking the Prophet personally, the Quraysh indeed went for the one aim which would be the realization of all it had been hoping for.

The Prophet himself stood firm, with a handful of his companions exerting every effort to defend him and ready to die in order to protect God's Messenger. The best show in this defence was put up by one of the Muhājirīn called Ṭalḥah ibn ʿUbaydellāh. He was only 15 or 16 when he adopted Islam in the very first week of the Prophet receiving God's revelation. Now a man of 30, he was continuing his unblemished record of devoted service to the cause of Islam. At Uḥud, he surpassed himself. He fought as hard and as determinedly as anyone could imagine. He carried his sword and dashed here and there in front of the Prophet or behind him or to his left or to his right, beating off whatever danger was approaching. He walked round the Prophet, making his own body a shield, protecting the Prophet from the swords and spears of his attackers. He continued to do so until the Quraysh attack was beaten off. Indeed, no one was as effective as Ṭalḥah in protecting the Prophet that day. For this reason the Prophet praised him and said: "Ṭalḥah has made it a must."[13] What the Prophet meant was that Ṭalḥah had made it inevitable that God would admit him to heaven because of his determined defence of the Prophet. The Muslims recognized the role played by Ṭalḥah in Uḥud and that he alone did the work of a whole unit. Abū Bakr himself, the Prophet's closest companion and one of those who stood firm when the Muslims were badly shaken, used to say of the Battle of Uḥud: "That day belonged totally to Ṭalḥah."[14]

Shammās ibn ʿUthmān of the Makhzūm clan of the Quraysh was another man who defended the Prophet well. Every time the Prophet looked right or left, he found Shammās fighting in that direction. Apparently the attackers came very close to the Prophet, so that a few of his defenders had to shield him with their own bodies. One of those was Shammās who dug his feet into the ground as he shielded the Prophet until he was killed. The Prophet said: "I have never seen the like of Shammās except in heaven."[15]

Abū Dujānah, who was seen earlier taking the Prophet's sword "for its proper value", which was "to fight the enemy with it until it was bent", was one of those who shielded the Prophet with their own bodies. This action is credited to only three of the Prophet's companions: Ṭalḥah, Shammās and Abū Dujānah. The last of the three received numerous hits with arrows on his back as he bent his body over the Prophet to protect him.[16]

Other companions of the Prophet tried to repel the attack by fighting extremely hard. Two of them were among the best marksmen with arrows. One of them, Abū Ṭalḥah, a man from the Anṣār, put down all his arrows in front of the Prophet and used them one by one. When the Prophet saw any of his companions with a bag of arrows, he would ask him to give it to Abū Ṭalḥah. The Prophet followed every arrow Abū Ṭalḥah threw to see whom it hit. Abū Ṭalḥah used to say to him: "Prophet, may my father and mother be sacrificed for you. Do not look lest one of their arrows hit you. I would rather receive the arrow aimed at you in my own neck or face." Saʿd ibn Abū Waqqāṣ was perhaps the best marksman among the Muhājirīn. He also remained steadfast with the Prophet, trying to repel the attackers with his arrows. The Prophet himself handed him the arrows and every time he did so he said to him: "Throw it, Saʿd, let my father and mother be your ransom." He would even give him an arrow without a head and Saʿd would use it.[17]

This expression of sacrificing one's parents for another person was a common expression used by the Arabs. It was not meant literally but it signified a great degree of love and devotion. The Prophet did not use that expression with anyone except Saʿd ibn Abū Waqqāṣ, who was related to the Prophet's own mother. Indeed, the Prophet used to take pride in Saʿd and say: "This is my uncle, let everyone show me his uncle." It should be mentioned that Saʿd was more than 20 years younger than the Prophet.[18]

In Defence of the Prophet

One cannot truly appreciate the strength of the attack mounted by the Quraysh against the Prophet himself unless one realizes what sort of fight his companions had to put up in his defence. A woman, Nasībah bint Kaʿb of the Anṣār, went out with the Muslim army carrying water to give the soldiers a drink. When she realized that the Prophet was being attacked so determinedly and that most of the Muslims were in a state of total confusion, she put down her water and took up a sword. Tying her dress up round her waist, she fought harder than any man and received at least 13 wounds. One of them, in her shoulder, was so deep that it would never heal. It was inflicted by a man called Ibn Qami'ah who tried hard to be the one who killed the Prophet. The Prophet said of her: "I saw her defending me every time I looked right or left."[19]

Al-Ḥubāb ibn al-Mundhir stood like a rock as he fought off a full unit of the unbelievers. Eventually, they overwhelmed him and those who witnessed this felt that he could never come out alive. However, he managed to fight his way out before taking the role of the attacker. Those fighting him were soon fleeing.[20]

Muṣʿab ibn ʿUmayr, one of the Prophet's defenders, put himself in the way when ʿAmr Ibn Qami'ah levelled a blow at the Prophet. Muṣʿab was killed and Ibn Qami'ah thought he had achieved his goal of killing the Prophet. He went back to the unbelievers to tell them so. This was how the news of the Prophet being killed was spread around.[21] A few men from the Anṣār also fought hard in the defence of the Prophet until they were killed one by one. The last of the group was Zaid ibn al-Sakan, who was fatally wounded. The Prophet laid him down and put his head on his foot until he died.[22]

More Muslims came to the defence of the Prophet. Every one of them came and spoke to him: "I give my life to save you, I leave you in peace without saying farewell."[23] Perhaps as many as 30 people were killed as they defended the Prophet.

Four men of the Quraysh were more determined than ever to kill the Prophet. They pledged to one another that they would not be deterred from killing him. This was well known in Makkah, where everyone of the Quraysh expected them to be true to their word.

When the assault on the Prophet was at its height, the four of them were in the thick of it. ʿAbdullāh ibn Shihāb managed, indeed, to hit the Prophet, causing a cut in his forehead; his beard was red with blood. ʿUtbah ibn Abī Waqqāṣ, the brother of Saʿd who was defending the Prophet so bravely, managed to hit the Prophet in his lower lip and break one of his lower front teeth. ʿAmr ibn Qami'ah succeeded in hitting him on his cheek; two links of the Prophet's iron mask penetrated into his flesh. ʿAmr then hit the Prophet on the shoulder with his sword and the Prophet fell in a hole in the ground and was unable to rise again. ʿAlī ibn Abī Ṭālib held the Prophet's hand while Ṭalḥah ibn ʿUbaydellāh lifted him. This injury to the Prophet caused him pain for a whole month.[24]

Ubayy ibn Khalaf aimed his spear at the Prophet and said: "You liar, where will you flee from me?" The Prophet hit him in his shoulder with a spear and he went back, snorting like a bull. When the Quraysh army was on its way back, Ubayy had given up all hope of survival. His fellow soldiers said to him: "There is hardly any injury in your shoulder. Why are you behaving like a dying man?" He said: "Have you not heard what Muhammad said? He said he would kill me. By God, had he spat on me, he would kill me." Ubayy died before reaching Makkah.[25]

Some Muslims began to realize that the Prophet was not dead and they rejoined the battle. As they rallied, the first to recognize the Prophet was Kaʿb ibn Mālik, who said: "I recognized him with his eyes beaming through his head mask. I shouted this piece of happy news to the Muslims but the Prophet motioned me to keep quiet."[26]

More support was coming to the Prophet and a group of his companions moved him to a well protected area at the foot of the mountain, where he was kept safe by a number of his followers. He wanted to climb a rock in the mountain but he was unable to do so because he had lost so much blood. Ṭalḥah ibn ʿUbaydellāh, however, sat underneath him and lifted him to help him climb the rock until he was over it. The Prophet was touched by Ṭalḥah's gesture and gave him the title 'Ṭalḥah al-Khayr', meaning that he was the symbol of goodness.[27]

Thus the determined assault made by the Quraysh to kill the Prophet failed in its objective. The role of Ṭalḥah ibn ʿUbaydellāh as the most effective of his defenders was acknowledged even by those who remained steadfast with the Prophet. One of them, Saʿd ibn Abū Waqqāṣ, said later that Ṭalḥah was the hero of the day. "He remained close to the Prophet while the rest of us made some leaps forward and came back to him." Ṭalḥah was badly injured: he received an arrow in his hand which paralyzed the lower part of it. He was also hit with a stone on his head and lost consciousness. The Prophet asked Abū Bakr to attend to him, and Abū Bakr washed his head. As Ṭalḥah regained consciousness, he asked Abū Bakr about the Prophet. When Abū Bakr told him that he was all right, Ṭalḥah praised God and said: "Any catastrophe that may befall us now is but a small matter."[28]

One of the Anṣār to show great courage in the battle was Anas ibn al-Naḍr, the uncle of Anas ibn Mālik. He was sorry that he missed the Battle of Badr and pledged that if he were to take part in a battle for the cause of Islam, God would see his heroism. He was indeed true to his word. When the Muslims were in confusion, he said: "My Lord, I apologize to You for what these people [meaning his fellow Muslims] have done, and I disown what these others [the unbelievers] are after." He then fought heroically until he was killed. No one could recognize his body until his sister recognized him by a mark on his finger. About 80 wounds were found on his body.[29]

More and more of the Prophet's companions were coming to their senses and joining the party which remained steadfast throughout. They were still confused. Some of them fought without knowing whom they were fighting. In this confusion one of the Muslims, al-Yamān, an elderly man who was the father of a great Muslim commander named Ḥudhayfah, was killed by mistake at the hands of the Muslims. Ḥudhayfah saw his father being attacked by his Muslim brothers and tried in vain to warn them. After the battle he relinquished any claim against his father's killers.[30]

Sweet Slumber

Something extraordinary then happened to the Muslims. As they were rallying over to the Prophet, they were overcome by sleep. They were moving towards the Prophet in the thick of the battle, yet many of them felt sleep overtaking them. Everyone so overtaken dropped his sword but as he did so he awoke, fresh, strong and reassured. Such momentary sleep happens to many people as they experience great hardship. When they wake up, they feel that they have shed a very heavy burden. That it happened to the Muslims in their hour of difficulty, when defeat was staring them in the face, was a blessing from God. The Qur'ān records this fact as it relates the events of the Battle of Uḥud. "Then, after the sorrow, He sent down peace of mind upon you in the shape of a slumber that overcame a party of you."[31] (3: 154)

Now the fighting was less one-sided. The Muslims who had rallied were prepared to go on. They were putting up a determined fight. Both parties, however, were extremely exhausted. The commanders of the Quraysh felt that they had achieved a victory which would wipe away the memories of their earlier defeat at Badr. As the situation stood, there was no way the Quraysh could bring the Muslims to the sort of crushing defeat it had hoped for. Soon the fighting died down and each party gradually disengaged from the battle.

Abū Sufyān, the Quraysh leader, walked around the battlefield looking at those who had been killed. He was hoping to find the body of the Prophet. When he could not find it, he grew suspicious and went back to his camp. They were preparing to leave the battlefield. Just before they left, Abū Sufyān stood on a high place and shouted: "Great are our deeds. The score is even. A day for us which compares with Badr. Glory to Hubal." (Hubal was the main idol the pagan Arabs worshipped.)

The Prophet asked ʿUmar to answer him and ʿUmar answered with the Prophet's words: "God is more glorified, supreme. We are not even. Our martyrs are in heaven and your dead are in hell."

Abū Sufyān asked ʿUmar to draw nearer to him and the Prophet gave permission to ʿUmar to go and see what he wanted. Abū Sufyān said: "I ask you by God, ʿUmar, have we killed Muhammad?" ʿUmar replied: "By God, you have not. He is hearing you as you speak now." Abū Sufyān said: "In my view, you are more truthful than Ibn Qami'ah." Ibn Qami'ah was the man who claimed that he had killed the Prophet.

Abū Sufyān then shouted: "There was some disfigurement of your men who were killed. I swear by God I was neither pleased nor displeased. I neither sanctioned this nor forbade it." Abū Sufyān was referring to what some men and women from the Quraysh, including his own wife, Hind bint ʿUtbah, did with the bodies of those Muslims who were killed. They cut the noses and ears of the Muslim martyrs and made bracelets and necklaces with them; Hind's treatment of Ḥamzah has already been described.

Before he left, Abū Sufyān also said: "Let us meet again in Badr next year." The Prophet instructed ʿUmar to accept the challenge.[32]

Now that the Quraysh army was preparing to leave, the Prophet was worried that they might launch an attack on Madinah itself. He dispatched his cousin, ʿAlī ibn Abī Ṭālib, and said: "Follow them and look what they do and what they intend. If they ride their camels in preference to their horses, then their direction is Makkah. If, on the other hand, they ride their horses and let their camels follow them, then their aim is Madinah." After ʿAlī had gone, the Prophet said: "By Him who holds my soul in His hand, if they want to attack Madinah I will march to them there and will fight them tooth and nail in Madinah." ʿAlī soon came back with the news that the Quraysh army were going back home.[33]

Tending the Wounded

The Prophet's companions were tending to him and trying to treat his wounds. Abū ʿUbaydah ʿĀmir ibn al-Jarrāḥ pulled out the two links of the Prophet's head mask which were stuck in his cheek. The best way Abū ʿUbaydah could do that and cause the Prophet the least pain was to pull them out with his own teeth. As he pulled out each one he lost one of his teeth. But he was so happy to do that that he refused to let anyone but himself pull out the second link when they saw that he had lost a tooth.[34]

The Muslims began to check whether any of the fallen fighters were still alive. The Prophet asked some of them to look for one of his companions, Saʿd ibn al-Rabīʿ. A man found him badly wounded and told him: "The Prophet has asked me to find out whether you are dead or alive." Saʿd said: "I am one of the dead. Convey my greeting to God's Messenger and tell him on my behalf that Saʿd ibn al-Rabīʿ prays God to reward him as best He rewards a Prophet of His. Convey also my greetings to our people and tell them that Saʿd ibn al-Rabīʿ says to them that they can have no excuse before God, if they let the Prophet be killed while one of them is still alive."[35]

The Prophet himself went round the battlefield to check on the dead. When he stood over the body of his uncle Ḥamzah and saw how badly disfigured he was, he felt deeply anguished and distressed. He said: "I have never seen a more distressing and agonizing sight."[36] He then looked at Muṣʿab ibn ʿUmayr of the Muhājirīn who was also killed, wearing a short simple dress and said: "I saw you in Makkah when no one was better dressed and more handsome than you. Now here you are with dust over your head, wearing nothing but this simple dress." He then looked at all those who were killed in the battle and said: "I am a witness for these. Anyone who receives a wound while fighting for God's cause shall be resurrected with his wound bleeding, the colour is that of blood and the smell is that of musk."[37]

The Prophet then ordered that the victims be buried where they were killed. He asked his companions to wrap them as they were, without washing their wounds. Every two or three were placed in one grave. In each grave the one who had more knowledge of the Qur'ān was put ahead of his companions. The Prophet realized that his own companions were extremely tired and he did not wish to exhaust their energies with digging a grave for every single person. The Muslims lost 70 martyrs at the Battle of Uḥud. Four of them were from the Muhājirīn, the rest were from the Anṣār. The Quraysh, on the other hand, lost 24 men.[38]

When the burial of the 70 Muslims was completed, the Prophet and his companions rode back to Madinah. Many of them, including the Prophet himself, were wounded. Some of them, like Ṭalḥah and ʿAbd al-Raḥmān ibn ʿAwf, received something like 20 wounds each. All of them were blaming themselves for their error and disobedience of the Prophet's orders. They prayed God to forgive them.

Back in Madinah

As they arrived at the entrance to the city, they were received by a group of women weeping for their dead. As they saw the Prophet, the women stopped crying and hurried to him to reassure themselves that he was all right. Two women of the ʿAbd al-Ashhal clan spoke to him. Umm ʿĀmir said: "With you safe, any catastrophe is trivial." Saʿd ibn Muʿādh's mother rushed to him and, having made sure that his condition did not call for alarm, said: "Now that I see you are safe, the magnitude of our disaster grows less and less."

The Prophet offered her his condolences for the death of her son ʿAmr and said to her: "Umm Saʿd, be happy and give the families of the martyrs the happy news that their dead are all friends in heaven." She answered: "We are happy with the Messenger of God among us. Who would cry for them now? Please pray for those whom they have left behind, Messenger of God." The Prophet prayed for them: "My Lord, let their sorrow be momentary, ease their disaster and give those who are left behind good reward."[39]

The Prophet then asked the wounded among his companions to stay in their homes and tend their wounds. He himself went home but could not dismount without assistance. He leaned on his two companions, Saʿd ibn ʿUbādah and Saʿd ibn Muʿādh, until he was inside his home. When Bilāl called for the *Maghrib* prayer, he came out into the mosque in a similar manner. When the prayer was finished, he went back home. A number of leading personalities of the two Anṣār tribes, the Aws and the Khazraj, spent the night in the mosque guarding the Prophet, for they feared that the Quraysh might decide to mount a raid on his home during the night.

The Prophet gave permission to weep for the dead. He realized that tears eased people's sorrow. However, he forbade any other manifestation of grief, such as pulling one's hair, scratching one's face, tearing off one's clothes or wailing. These were common practices in the pre-Islamic era. The prohibition remains in force.[40]

Reflecting on what had happened, the Prophet realized that the forces hostile to Islam in Madinah itself and in its surrounding area would find in the Muslims' defeat a motivation to try to cause them further harm. He was keenly aware that the Muslims were still the weaker party in Madinah itself. Although their resounding victory at Badr had given them added security in the sense that all their enemies held them in awe, their military defeat now would replace that with a feeling that the Muslims were vulnerable. If the Quraysh were to decide to renew their attack, or if the Jews and the pagan Arabs of Madinah were to join forces in a military action against Muhammad and his companions, the Muslims would find themselves in a highly perilous position. Some sort of action was therefore needed to restore to the Muslims their self-confidence and make their enemies think twice before contemplating attacking them.

Pursuit in the Desert

The following day, Sunday 16 Shawwāl, callers went out into the streets of Madinah, calling on people to get ready for an immediate military operation. At the Prophet's instructions they made it clear that "only those who took part in yesterday's battle are to join the army."

The Prophet's companions were quick to respond to the new call. All of those who took part in the battle came along, including those who were wounded. None of them thought that his injury excused him from attending the new operation. Two brothers, ʿAbdullāh and Rāfiʿ, sons of Sahm, had received several wounds at Uḥud. They did not hesitate to respond to the new call. As Rāfiʿs injuries were far greater than those of his brother, he could not walk the whole distance to the mosque. ʿAbdullāh therefore carried him on his back part of the way, then put him down to walk a little further. The Prophet was touched when he saw them in this condition, and prayed for them.

Several people who did not attend the Battle of Uḥud sought permission to join the troops now, but the Prophet declined their offer. Indeed, ʿAbdullāh ibn Ubayy, the man who deserted with one-third of the army just before reaching the battlefield, came to the Prophet and asked him to let him join the army. His request was declined. The Prophet did not wish to give immediate rehabilitation to the deserters or to those who were reluctant to go out in the first place. If some of them had repented, their repentance would be recognized in their future behaviour. The Prophet preferred to wait until God had pardoned them.

The only exception was Jābir ibn ʿAbdullāh. He was a young man and the Prophet knew that he was one of his most faithful companions. He came to the Prophet and said: "Messenger of God, it was my father who ordered me to stay behind in order to look after my seven sisters. He told me: 'Son, the two of us cannot leave these women without a man to look after them. I am not the man to favour you with joining the struggle with the Prophet in preference to myself. So, you have to stay behind and look after your sisters.' This was my reason for not joining you in the first place." The Prophet recognized the validity of Jābir's reason for staying behind. His father was among those who were killed in the battle. He therefore allowed Jābir to join him.

When the troops had gathered, the Prophet led them in a short prayer in the mosque before mounting his horse, fully dressed for battle. He gave the flag to ʿAlī ibn Abī Ṭālib (although some reports say that he gave it to Abū Bakr) and asked his blind companion ʿAmr ibn Umm Maktūm to deputize for him in Madinah. They marched to a place called Ḥamrā' al-Asad, 14 kilometres from Madinah where they spent Monday, Tuesday and Wednesday.

Battle of Wits

During the day, the Prophet ordered his companions to collect as much wood as they could manage; as night fell, he ordered them to light as many fires as possible. Thus the fires could be seen from a very great distance, giving an impression that the Muslim army was much larger than its actual strength. Reports travelled far and wide that the Muslims had mobilized all their forces and were ready for action.

Not long after the Prophet and his companions had encamped at Ḥamrā' al-Asad, a man called Maʿbad from the tribe of Khuzāʿah, which was on friendly terms with the Prophet, came to him and offered his commiserations. Maʿbad said to the Prophet: "We are very sorry indeed for what has befallen you and your companions.

We wish that God had given you the victory we were looking for, and that the disaster had befallen your enemies." Ma'bad then asked the Prophet whether he could do anything to help. The Prophet instructed him to make haste and follow the Quraysh army and try to dissuade Abū Sufyān from any attempt to launch a second attack on the Muslims.

Ma'bad travelled fast and caught up with the Quraysh army at a place called al-Rawḥā', about 60 kilometres from Madinah on the route to Makkah. The Quraysh leaders were having a discussion among themselves, reflecting on what they had achieved. Most of them were disappointed. They blamed themselves for withdrawing so quickly after victory was assured. They realized that the defeat of the Muslims was not a crushing one. Their leading figures, who were able to mobilize their forces, were still alive. The Prophet himself survived, despite his wounds. Many in the Quraysh army were pressing for a return attack.

When Ma'bad caught up with them, Abū Sufyān welcomed him, hoping to gather some intelligence about the situation of the Muslims. Abū Sufyān asked what news Ma'bad had, to which question he replied: "Muhammad has mobilized such a large force as I have never seen in my life. They are all boiling with rage. All those of his followers who did not take part in the encounter between your two sides are with him now, having felt sorry for letting him down in the first place. They are in a state of anger so great that it is very rarely seen."

Shocked and alarmed, Abū Sufyān tried to make sure that Ma'bad was certain of what he was saying. Ma'bad played his part astutely. He said: "If you were to order your troops to march now, I would imagine that by the time you have started to move, you will be seeing their horses." Abū Sufyān told him that they had made up their minds to re-attack the Muslims in an effort to wipe them out. Ma'bad said: "I would counsel you not to do anything of the sort."

This shows that the Prophet's move was a very shrewd one. He felt that it would not be long before the Quraysh would realize that the victory they had achieved was far from decisive. Their logical move would be to try to hit the Muslims at their moment of weakness. Had the Quraysh come back to attack the Muslims again in Madinah, there would be no shortage of people who would advise making peace with them on terms which would be far from satisfactory to the Muslims. Many would be reluctant to fight. Many others, those who were injured at Uḥud, would be unable to fight. The situation would be very difficult indeed for the Muslims. They would lose a great deal of what they had built in the three years since the Prophet's emigration to Madinah. By going out to Ḥamrā' al-Asad, encamping there, having such great fires in a demonstration of strength, and waiting in anticipation – by these tactics, along with the psychological trick played by Maʿbad on Abū Sufyān, the Muslims secured a breathing space after which they would be able to enter any new battle in a far better shape.

Abū Sufyān marched quickly with his army towards Makkah. He was a shrewd politician and an excellent army commander. On his way to Makkah, he met someone heading towards Madinah. He asked: "Would you give a message to Muhammad, and I will give you a camel load of raisins when you are next in Makkah?" When the man indicated his willingness to do as requested, Abū Sufyān said to him: "Tell Muhammad that we are coming back to wipe him and his companions out."

When the message was conveyed to the Muslims, they said, as the Qur'ān relates: "God is sufficient for us; He is the best guardian." (3: 173) Thus Abū Sufyān was trying the same tactic the Prophet used, in order to dissuade the Muslims from going on the attack. The Muslims remained in their camp at Hamrā' al-Asad for three days, by the end of which they realized that the Quraysh were simply bluffing and they were sure, according to the intelligence they had received, that the Quraysh army had gone back to Makkah.[41]

Notes

1. All the above quotes are mentioned in more or less all works on the Prophet's life. Reference may be made to: Ibn Hishām, *al-Sīrah al-Nabawiyyah*, Dār al-Qalam, Beirut, Vol. 3, pp. 64-67; al-Wāqidī, *Kitāb al-Maghāzī*, Oxford University Press, 1996, Vol. 1, pp. 199-213; A. al-Suhaylī, *al-Rawḍ al-Unuf*, Dār al-Kutub al-ʿIlmiyyah, Beirut, Vol. 3, pp. 240-243; Ibn Sayyid al-Nās, *ʿUyūn al-Athar*, Dār al-Turāth, Madinah, 1996, Vol. 2, pp. 5-8; and Ibn Kathīr, *al-Bidāyah wal-Nihāyah*, Maktabat al-Maʿārif, Beirut, Vol. 4, pp. 9-13.
2. A. al-Suhaylī, op.cit., pp. 284-285.

3. Ibn Hishām, op.cit., p. 68. Also, al-Wāqidī, op.cit., pp. 213-214.
4. Ibn Umm Maktūm's blindness meant that he could not join the army, so he often deputized for the Prophet when he travelled. His name was ʿAmr, although some reports refer to him as ʿAbdullāh.
5. Al-Wāqidī, op.cit., pp. 215-219.
6. Ibn Hishām, op.cit., p. 68. Also, Ibn Kathīr, op.cit., p. 14.
7. Ibn Hishām, op.cit., pp. 69-70. Also, Ibn Kathīr, op.cit., pp. 14-15; and Ibn Sayyid al-Nās, op.cit., pp. 10-11.
8. Ibn Hishām, op.cit., pp. 72-74. Also, Ibn Kathīr, op.cit., pp. 15-16.
9. Ibn Hishām, op.cit., pp. 96-97.
10. Ibn Kathīr, op.cit., p. 25. Also, al-Wāqidī, op.cit., pp. 231-232.
11. Al-Wāqidī, op.cit., pp. 231-235.
12. Ibid., pp. 236-237.
13. Ibid., pp. 246-247. Also, Ibn Hishām, op.cit., pp. 91-92; and Ibn Kathīr, op.cit., pp. 29-30.
14. Ibn Kathīr, op.cit., p. 29.
15. Al-Wāqidī, op.cit., p. 287.
16. Ibid., pp. 251-256. Also, Ibn Hishām, op.cit., pp. 71-72.
17. Al-Wāqidī, op.cit., pp. 241-244.
18. Ibn Kathīr, op.cit., p. 27.
19. Al-Wāqidī, op.cit., pp. 268-269.
20. Ibid., pp. 256-257.
21. Ibn Hishām, op.cit., p. 77. Also, al-Wāqidī, op.cit., pp. 245-246.
22. Ibn Hishām, op.cit., p. 86.
23. Al-Wāqidī, op.cit., p. 240.
24. Ibid., pp. 243-244.
25. Ibid., pp. 251-252. Also, Ibn Hishām, op.cit., p. 89; and Ibn Kathīr, op.cit., p. 23.
26. Ibn Hishām, op.cit., p. 88.
27. Ibid., pp. 91-92.
28. Ibn Kathīr, op.cit., pp. 26-27; Also, al-Wāqidī, op.cit., p. 255.
29. Ibn Hishām, op.cit., p. 88.
30. Ibid., pp. 92-93. Also, al-Wāqidī, op.cit., pp. 233-234.
31. Ibn Kathīr, op.cit., pp. 27-28. Also, al-Wāqidī, op.cit., pp. 295-296.
32. Ibn Hishām, op.cit., pp. 99-100. Also, al-Wāqidī, op.cit., p. 297.
33. Ibn Hishām, op.cit., p. 100.
34. Amīn Duwaydār, *Ṣuwar Min Ḥayāt al-Rasūl*, Dār al-Maʿārif, 4th edition, Cairo, p. 365.
35. Ibn Hishām, op.cit., pp. 100-101.
36. Ibid., pp. 101-102.
37. Ibid., p. 104. Also, Amīn Duwaydār, op.cit., p. 366; al-Wāqidī, op.cit., p. 309; and Ibn Kathīr, op.cit., p. 42.
38. Ibn Hishām, op.cit., pp. 129-135. Also, Ibn Kathīr, op.cit., pp. 41-46.
39. Ibn Hishām, op.cit., pp. 104-106. Also, Ibn Kathīr, op.cit., pp. 46-47; and Amīn Duwaydār, op.cit., p. 367.
40. Amīn Duwaydār, op.cit., p. 367.
41. Ibn Hishām, op.cit., pp. 107-110. Also, al-Wāqidī, op.cit., pp. 334-340; and Ibn Kathīr, op.cit., pp. 48-51.

21

The Lessons of Uḥud

DEFEAT AT THE Battle of Uḥud came as a great shock to the Muslims who fought that battle. They could not understand how they could achieve a resounding victory at Badr, when they were heavily outnumbered and shabbily equipped, and then suffer a defeat at the hands of an army which they had already forced on the retreat. The dramatic turn of events in the battle just finished, which turned an assured victory into a disastrous defeat, was more than baffling to them.

Their defeat, however, made it clear to the early Muslims that victory was not theirs by right and that they could not expect to win every battle they fought under any conditions and in whatever circumstances, without having taken the necessary actions and preparations which made victory a certainty. God wanted His servants, the believers, to know that victory could not be assured unless they first set themselves on the road to victory. This meant that their attitude must be the right attitude in battle: they must be willing to fight and be totally obedient to God and the Prophet. They must show determined perseverance in situations of hardship and they must overcome their own desires and whatever temptations they faced. God has assured the believers of victory against any enemy, as long as they serve Him with sincerity of action and purpose. Whenever they give priority to their own narrow interests, He leaves them to their own priorities.

Perhaps the first sign of weakness to appear in the Muslim camp was when ʿAbdullāh ibn Ubayy deserted with about one-third of the army. His pretext was that his opinion was overlooked in favour of that of the more enthusiastic Muslims who wanted to engage the enemy straight away. He overlooked the fact that the Prophet himself was initially in agreement with him. The Prophet had to accept the other view when he realized that it was held by the broad majority of the Muslims. The Prophet did not see anything wrong with discarding his own view in favour of that of the majority. But ʿAbdullāh ibn Ubayy considered that humiliating. His desertion did not only weaken the army but was about to cause a further split when the soldiers from the Salamah and Ḥārithah clans of the Anṣār were about to desert as well.

But all this did not cause much harm at the beginning of the battle, when the Muslims overran their enemies and were able to achieve a clear advantage. The Muslims' determined attack was achieving the desired results and all seemed to be sweetness and light. At this point, however, a costly mistake was made when the rearguard of the Muslim army, the unit placed on Mount ʿAynayn, left their position to share in the collection of the booty.

Every military commander maintains that strict obedience by all his troops is absolutely necessary for the success of his plan, whether offensive or defensive. Obedience by all soldiers in war is taken for granted. Without it, no army can achieve victory even against a weaker enemy. In this instance, the Muslims suffered from disobedience.

It is extremely difficult to explain why soldiers in that unit went against the express orders of the Prophet, the commander-in-chief of the Muslim army, as well as the clear orders and advice of their own commander, ʿAbdullāh ibn Jubayr. There is no doubt that their desertion of their position, in order to get their share of the booty, was the act which caused the disaster. Yet the Muslims have always been obedient to the Prophet. All authentic reports confirm that ʿAbdullāh ibn Jubayr did advise his soldiers against leaving their positions and reminded them of the Prophet's instructions and warnings. All reports also indicate that they did not leave their positions until they were certain that the battle was over and the Quraysh army was defeated. They saw their brethren collecting the booty. Several reports indicate that there was no deliberate attempt on the part of those soldiers to disobey the Prophet. They simply felt that his orders were valid as long as the battle was going on. Once it was over, and they might have sincerely felt that it was over, then they were free to do as they liked. Whatever the explanation, there is no doubt that the action was one of disobedience, as it is described in the Qur'ān. It was a moment of weakness which overcame those believers to divert them from the noble goal they were fighting for and to distract them by petty gain. They had to learn, therefore, that God's unfailing rule was that He supported the believers as long as they supported Him and His cause with all their hearts. They witnessed with their own eyes the quick victory they achieved when they were fighting for the sake of God. But when their purpose differed, the result was different.

Weakness and Confusion

Another sign of weakness exposed at the Battle of Uḥud was the fact that when the Quraysh army launched its counterattack, the Muslims did not fight a determined battle. They were scattered everywhere instead of closing ranks together. Some of the Muslim soldiers were preoccupied with saving their own souls. They did not respond to the Prophet as he called them to join him. In fact, most of them left him to face the determined attack which the Quraysh launched with the aim of killing him personally. In those very difficult moments, he had only a handful of his companions to defend him. In a situation like that which developed when the rearguard unit left its positions, the proper thing for the rest of the army to do was to gather round their commander, who was in that particular case the Prophet, and to fight tooth and nail. But many of the Muslim soldiers were confused, stunned, distracted and perhaps did not realize what they were doing as they climbed high up in the mountain to protect themselves. It is not strange, therefore, that those who stayed with the Prophet and defended him bravely, like Ṭalḥah ibn ʿUbaydellāh, Abū Dujānah and several men of the Anṣār, should receive the highest praise from him.

In a situation of weakness and confusion, it is difficult to achieve clarity of thinking and to hit on the right course of action. For this reason, when the rumour spread that the Prophet had been killed some of the believers stopped fighting and conceded defeat. Some of them thought: "What about sending a messenger to ʿAbdullāh ibn Ubayy to arrange for a truce with Abū Sufyān. If Muhammad is killed, our best course is to return to our people before the Quraysh come to kill us." This attitude betrayed a reluctance which was highly uncharacteristic of the believers. It gave the impression that they did not come to fight for their faith, prepared to give the sacrifice required, but rather came because they had to come. They either felt they could not disobey the Prophet when he asked them to go out to fight or they might have felt that they had no option but to honour their pledges to him to support him against any enemy who attacked him in Madinah. Now that the Prophet was dead, there was no reason to continue fighting.

It was necessary for the Muslims to realize their mistake. They were not simply defending and protecting the person of the Prophet. They were not fighting for the man, God's Messenger. Their only aim must be to support the cause of God and to help it triumph. They were fighting for their faith and defending it against the forces which wanted to smother and suppress it. Hence, it is not appropriate for a people who believe in God and submit themselves to Him to stop fighting if the Prophet is killed. God addresses them in the Qur'ān: "Muhammad is but a messenger before whom other messengers have passed away. If, then, he dies or is slain, will you turn about on your heels? He who turns about on his heels will not harm God in any way. God will reward those who are grateful [to Him]." (3: 144)

Thus the Qur'ān puts the case in its proper perspective. The Muslims must always be advocates of the cause. They live for it and die for it. Their own persons, no matter what high ranks they enjoy, are of no importance. The Prophet himself could die or be killed, but the cause of Islam remains alive and must be served. Moreover, the fortunes that may befall the advocates of Islam need not be taken as a criterion by which to judge how sound Islam is. Islam remains the faith of the truth. Its followers will achieve the right results for their own efforts. God does not give the Muslims victory in order to prove to them that Islam is the truth. They first have to believe in the truthfulness of their faith and to confirm their belief by their actions in order to achieve victory. God is in no need of anyone. Muslim worship does not benefit Him. He is, therefore, under no obligation to the followers of His Messenger. Indeed, they are obliged to Him. Hence, one cannot judge Islam by the degree of success against the enemy. Success is a reflection of one's condition and a proof of whether one is a good Muslim or not. Besides, one has to make the right preparations. In the same way as people may die in war as well as in peace, whenever the appointed time for each one of them arrives, victory is granted only to those who deserve it through their preparations and purity of purpose.

Bright Elements

So much for the negative aspects of the performance of the Muslim army at the Battle of Uḥud. No objective study of any event is complete unless it makes a full list of both the positive and negative points. One must not let the fact that the Muslims lost their second major encounter with the unbelievers overshadow the fact that that encounter revealed a number of positive points in the general situation of the Muslims.

No one can take away from the Muslims the fact that their early efforts in the battle forced the Quraysh army to retreat. Victory was surely within the grasp of the Muslims. They fought a hard, determined battle, which was well planned and sure to bring about a decisive result. Despite the fact that they were heavily outnumbered, their tactics, which centred on creating chaos in the ranks of their opponents, coupled with ensuring protection for their own rear, were very sound. Many of their fighters displayed a standard of heroism which can hardly be paralleled. Yet the heroism was not only at the beginning of the fighting, when the Muslims were winning. There was much heroism as well when the small group of fighters who surrounded the Prophet managed to withstand the determined assault launched by the bulk of the Quraysh army with the aim of killing him. Heroism was also displayed when more and more people were rallying to the Prophet at the end of the day, preventing the Quraysh from levelling a final crushing blow at the Muslims. It was this heroism which was displayed throughout the battle, albeit by varying numbers of the Muslim fighters, that enabled the Prophet and his commanders to save the bulk of their army. In a battle which turned against the Muslims, forces outnumbering them by four to one did not manage to inflict on the Muslims the type of heavy losses which could have made them much weaker, for a long period. In the event, 90 per cent of the Muslim army was safe and sound, despite injuries, and was able to go on a demonstration of strength the following day.

When one speaks of heroism at Uḥud, there are numerous examples. Enough have been mentioned and repetition is hardly necessary. One need say only that Muslim fighters generally, throughout the ages, have displayed such heroism every time they went to battle with the issues clear in their minds. There is something in the faith of Islam which brings out in the followers of this religion a high standard of courage and the will to sacrifice one's soul for one's faith. This is something planted by Prophet Muhammad himself, as he carefully reared the first generation of Muslims to make them an example for all Muslim generations.

Rare Heroic Examples

The greatest example of heroism, however, was displayed by the Prophet himself (peace be upon him). One must remember that he was against going out of Madinah to meet the enemy. He would have preferred the Muslims to stay in their city and defend it against the attacking force. But he accepted the other view when he realized that it was shared by a broad section of the community. When his companions felt that they might have to go back to his opinion, he would have nothing of it. This is a lesson in sound leadership. The leader may consult with his advisers and review all options. When the implementation of the decision made after such consultation is under way, there is no more room for hesitation because hesitation can only lead to confusion and weakness. Yet when things did not go the way the Muslims desired, it was the Prophet who remained steadfast, when most people around him were interested only in their own safety. Despite the extremely difficult situation in which he found himself, he stood out, calling his companions, pointing out to them the right course to follow, caring nothing for his own safety as the enemy soldiers were rushing towards him, motivated by unalloyed hatred.

The soldiers who were turning away from battle, trying to find a secure place in the mountain, were not cowardly. They were only overtaken by confusion. The Prophet's stand was not one of a commander who, when things went wrong, wanted to show that he knew better and that they should have listened to him in the first place. He only demonstrated what true conviction and true courage meant. Indeed, he did not rebuke any of his men after the event. He graciously forgave them their errors. He consoled them and encouraged them, saying: "They shall never have a similar advantage over us until we enter the Ka'bah." God has praised the Prophet's generous attitude in the Qur'ān: "It was by God's grace that you (Prophet) dealt gently with your followers: for if you had been harsh and hard of heart, they would indeed have broken away from you. Pardon them, then, and pray that they be forgiven. Take counsel with them in matters of public concern; then, when you have decided upon a course of action, place your trust in God; God loves those who place their trust in Him." (3: 159)

The Battle of Uḥud was of great significance to the Muslims. That first generation of Muhammad's followers was able to draw on its lessons for the rest of their lives. Some 60 verses of the third *sūrah* of the Qur'ān, 'The House of 'Imrān', which is one of the longest *sūrahs*, comment on this battle. One should note that they contain only a mild reproach to the Muslims for their failures. The reproach, however, is mixed with advice which sets the Muslims on the right course for better results in the future. Perhaps the most important lesson was that the Muslims must not be complacent. The fact that they believe in God does not ensure victory in battle unless they are well prepared and willing to make the necessary sacrifice.

The Prophet's Position in Muslim Society

A point of reproach concerned their attitude when the rumour was spread around that the Prophet had been killed. When the Prophet started to convey his message and called people to Islam, he made his position absolutely clear: "I am God's servant and messenger." This meant that his task was to deliver his message in order to enlighten the hearts and minds of his followers. Once a person is thus enlightened, having received God's message, he should have enough wisdom to prevent him sinking back into the darkness in which he formerly lingered. Those who have followed Muhammad as God's servant and messenger have seen in him a leader guiding them along the path of truth and establishing that link with God. If God's servant dies in any circumstances, that link which he has established for them with God must not just disappear; it must stay and increase in strength.

The Qur'ān further tells the Muslims that the setback they suffered was not without advantages. The Battle of Badr gave the Muslims a great moral advantage over their enemies. The Battle of Uḥud distinguished the true believers from the hypocrites. It thus helped purge the Muslim ranks of any weak links. Those who were true believers in God and followed His Messenger with sincerity and conviction were able to pass the test. From among them God selected a number of martyrs. The martyr, in the Islamic view, has an important role in the advancement of the Islamic call.

A martyr is selected by God to give a testimony to the truth of the faith of Islam. The Arabic term *shahīd*, which signifies martyr, is derived from the same root as the term *shahīd*, which signifies a witness. As the martyr sacrifices his life for the cause of Islam, he takes the stand as a witness testifying for the cause in which he believes. The cause in this instance is that of God: His being the overall Lord of all the universe, the Creator and Sustainer of all, and the only deity to be worshipped. The cause of God's oneness is the cause of truth absolute. He who stands witness to this truth, sacrificing his life in the process, deserves to be rewarded as only God can reward. Such witnesses, or martyrs, are called on to testify only at times of hardship. At Uḥud, the Muslims experienced such a time and 70 of them were called to the witness box.

According to Islam, martyrs who sacrifice their lives for the cause of God are not dead. They remain alive in heaven. The Prophet said to his companions:

> When your brothers were killed at Uḥud, God placed their souls in the chests of green birds which were admitted into heaven. They drink of its rivers, eat of its fruits and have their abode in gold lanterns underneath God's throne. As they enjoyed their food, drink and abode they said: "Would that our brothers knew what God has given us as a reward, so that they may not weaken in *jihād* or hesitate in war." God said to them: "I shall convey this to them on your behalf." He then revealed the following verses: "Do not think of those that have been slain in God's cause as dead. Nay, they are alive. With their Lord they have their sustenance, exulting in that which God has bestowed upon them out of His bounty. They rejoice in the happy news given to those of their brethren who have been left behind and have not yet joined them, that no fear need they have and neither shall they grieve: they rejoice in the happy news of God's blessings and bounty, and that God will not fail to reward the believers." (3: 169-71)

22

Vulnerability and Treachery

ALTHOUGH THE DEMONSTRATION of strength the Prophet organized at Ḥamrā' al-Asad was effective – where he encamped with his army for three days, lighting fires throughout the night and causing it to be known that they were ready and prepared to meet the Quraysh in a second encounter if such was its intention – it could not completely erase the fact that at Uḥud the Muslims suffered a military defeat. The Jews and the hypocrites in Madinah did not conceal their pleasure at what had befallen the Muslims. They started a campaign of ridicule with the Prophet himself as their main target. The Jews in particular started to raise doubts as to whether Muhammad was indeed a Prophet.

The Muslims' defeat was the favourite topic of conversation for the Jews and the hypocrites. Wherever they were, and whoever they talked to, the question was asked: "How can a Messenger of God be defeated by pagan, idol-worshippers?" Their emphatic statement which they used to repeat every time and everywhere was: "Had Muhammad been a true Prophet, he would not have suffered that defeat. He is no more than an ambitious adventurer who seeks a kingdom. As such, he sometimes wins and sometimes loses." The hypocrites, on the other hand, tried hard to turn people away from the Muslim camp. They tried to portray the defeat at Uḥud as an unmitigated disaster. They took pride in the fact that they deserted the army before the battle. The Muslims, they argued, would have been better advised to follow suit.[1]

That, however, was the least of the Muslims' worries. After all, nothing else could have been expected from the Jews, who had already taken a hostile attitude to the Prophet and the Muslims generally. The hypocrites also found that the Muslims' defeat provided them with a chance to have a go at them. Those Muslims who were firm in their faith would not be shaken or diverted from their course by the taunts of the Jews and the ridicule of the hypocrites. The Prophet worked hard at reassuring the Muslims and consolidating their faith. The overwhelming majority of them responded positively. The Muslim community in Madinah closed ranks and started to repair the damage.

Attending to External Danger

The external danger, however, was becoming more serious. Many a tribe considered that they had not much to fear from the Muslims and adopted a hostile attitude towards them. The Bedouin tribes in the area close to Madinah felt that they could launch looting raids on the city without fearing any great punishment. The Asad tribe was the first to contemplate such a looting raid. They started to get ready, mobilizing their forces. The Prophet, however, had already established a wide intelligence network so that he might always be informed of any development that would affect the security of Madinah and its Muslim population. When he received intelligence of the intentions of the Asad clan, he raised a force of 150 men from the Muhājirīn and the Anṣār under the leadership of Abū Salamah, his companion.

The Muslims moved fast and were able to attack the Asad tribe in their own place, taking them by surprise. The attacking Muslim force was able to disperse the enemy and drive their cattle with them as they went back to Madinah, having achieved a total victory without suffering any casualties. Abū Salamah, who was wounded at Uḥud, suffered a recurrence of the same injury. Medical attention was of no avail and he died a few days later.[2]

Then the Prophet received information that Khālid ibn Sufyān of the Hudhayl tribe was raising a large force in order to attack Madinah. The Prophet called his companion ʿAbdullāh ibn Anīs and told him of the information he had received. He asked him to go to Khālid ibn Sufyān, who was at ʿUrāna, and kill him. ʿAbdullāh ibn Anīs asked the Prophet to describe him so that he would know the man. The Prophet said: "When you see him, he will remind you of Satan. The sign which will confirm to you that he is your man is that when you look at him, you will feel as if he is trembling."

ʿAbdullāh ibn Anīs reported what he did:

> I saw him with his women; he was trying to locate a place for them to encamp. It was time for the *ʿAṣr* prayer. When I saw him I recognized the sign the Prophet told me of his trembling. I walked towards him, but then I feared that there might be some engagement between the two of us which would not enable me to offer my prayers. I therefore offered my prayers while walking towards him, making signs with my head instead of the normal movements of the prayers. When I reached him, he asked me who I was. I said: "I am an Arab and I have heard that you are mobilizing a force to attack that man and have decided to join you." He said: "I am doing that indeed." I walked with him a little until I could take him unawares. Then, at the right moment, I hit him with my sword and killed him. I left the place, with his women crying over his body. When I arrived in Madinah the Prophet saw me and said: "Successful is the mission." I said: "I have killed him, Messenger of God." He said: "That is right."[3]

Playing a Dirty Trick

The Hudhayl were enraged at the assassination of their leader. They realized that they could not avenge themselves against the Muslims, if they were to attack them in Madinah. Realizing that deceit was the only way to revenge, they sent a delegation to the Prophet from two tribes named ʿAḍal and al-Qārah. As the delegation spoke to the Prophet, they claimed that their tribesmen had a desire to learn about Islam and possibly embrace it. They requested the Prophet to send a few of his companions to explain Islam to them and to teach them how to read the Qur'ān. The Prophet sent six of his companions with them and appointed Marthad ibn Abū Marthad as their leader. The other five were Khālid ibn al-Bukayr, ʿĀṣim ibn Thābit, Khubayb ibn ʿAdiy, Zaid ibn al-Dathinnah and ʿAbdullāh ibn Ṭāriq. The two groups travelled together until they reached a spring called al-Rajīʿ which belonged to the Hudhayl, where they encamped. Secretly, the delegation sent to the Hudhayl to come over and arrest the Muslim group.

Taken by surprise, the six Muslims found themselves surrounded by over 100 people from the Hudhayl. They managed to find shelter in a nearby hill and showed that they were prepared to fight. The men from ʿAḍal and al-Qārah told them: "We do not wish to kill you. All that we are after is to hand you over to the people of Makkah in return for some money. We swear to you by God and give you our solemn pledges that we will not kill you."

The first three, Marthad, Khālid and ʿĀṣim, told them that they would never accept a pledge from, or enter into any agreement with, anyone who associates partners with God. They fought along with their companions against their treacherous attackers and all three of them were killed. The other three were inclined to accept the offer of the attacking force. They laid down their arms and were taken prisoner. As soon as they came down from their place on the hill, ʿAbdullāh ibn Ṭāriq realized that his captors were bent on treachery. He managed to release his hands, which had been tied, took up his sword and moved back. The people, however, bombarded him with arrows, stones and other missiles until he was killed. The other two Muslims were kept under guard.

Honouring a Dead Man's Pledge

ʿĀṣim ibn Thābit represented a special prize for the traitors. At the Battle of Uḥud he killed two of the non-believers who were brothers.

Their mother Sulāfah bint Saʿd was among the Quraysh women who joined the army at the Battle of Uḥud. She knew that ʿĀṣim was the man who killed her two sons. She made a vow that if she ever got hold of ʿĀṣim, she would use his skull as a glass with which she would drink wine. Now his killers wanted to cut off his head in order to sell it to Sulāfah. They felt they could ask a high price for it.

ʿĀṣim had pledged to God that he would never touch an unbeliever or let an unbeliever touch him. Although this is not required of a Muslim, ʿĀṣim made this pledge, feeling that the unbelievers were impure and as such he should have no physical contact with them at all. When he fell dead, he was obviously at the mercy of his killers who were unbelievers. When they approached him to cut off his head, they found great numbers of hornets, wasps and bees almost covering him. They felt the wasps and hornets would turn against them if they were to carry on with their intentions. Someone suggested that they should wait until night had fallen, when these insects would go back to their nests. As the sun started to decline, however, floods came and carried the body of ʿĀṣim ibn Thābit to an unknown destination. When he learnt that ʿĀṣim was protected by hornets and wasps, ʿUmar ibn al-Khaṭṭāb said: "God will always protect His faithful servants. ʿĀṣim made a pledge that he would never touch an unbeliever as long as he lived, and God kept his pledge for him after he died."

The remaining two prisoners, Khubayb ibn ʿAdiy and Zaid ibn al-Dathinnah, were taken to Makkah where they were sold to the Quraysh. ʿUqbah ibn al-Ḥārith bought Khubayb in order to kill him in retaliation for the killing of his own father, al-Ḥārith ibn ʿĀmir, and Ṣafwān ibn Umayyah bought Zaid in order to avenge the death of his own father, Umayyah ibn Khalaf, who was killed at the Battle of Badr.

Since the two men were captured during the month in which all killing and fighting was traditionally prohibited in Arabia, they were kept prisoner until that period was over. Shortly afterwards, the two men were taken to a place called al-Tanʿīm, about 6 kilometres to the north of Makkah, to be killed. A large number of men, women and children went out there to witness the killing of the two defenceless prisoners. Ṣafwān ibn Umayyah ordered one of his slaves, called Naṣṭaṣ, to kill Zaid. As he was placed to be killed, Abū Sufyān spoke to Zaid: "I ask you in the name of God, Zaid, would you prefer that Muhammad was in your place, being killed now by us, and you were safe with your family?" Zaid answered: "I don't wish to be with my family now and Muhammad is troubled by a thorn in his body, wherever he is now." Abū Sufyān commented: "I have never seen anyone have so much love for another as the followers of Muhammad love him."

When Khubayb was brought up to be killed he made a request to his killers: "I should be grateful if you would let me have a short prayer." They granted him his request and he offered two *rak'ahs* as calmly as anyone absorbed in his devotion. When he had finished he said to them: "I would have prayed more but for the fear that you may think that I am afraid of death." His action has become a *sunnah* (a religious Islamic term meaning 'a recommended practice'). If a believer is taken prisoner by the enemies of Islam, and if they want to kill him, it serves him well to pray two *rak'ahs* if he is allowed to do so, just as Khubayb did before he was killed.

The non-believers put Khubayb on a cross of wood, tied him up and then put up the cross. He raised his eyes to the sky and said: "My Lord, we have conveyed the message of Your Messenger. Inform him of what has been done to us." He then looked at his killers and said: "My Lord, count them all and kill them all and let none of them escape."

When they realized that he was making his prayer they fell on their sides, as it was their tradition. They believed that if they did so, they would evade the curse invoked against them. One report says that they gathered the children of those people whom he killed at the Battle of Badr and gave them spears with which they stabbed him repeatedly, but only lightly, so that they could prolong his torment.[4]

This was the end of an episode which caused the Muslims in Madinah great agony, especially because of the element of treachery involved in the killing.

Further Treachery on the Way

About the same time as the treacherous killing of Muslims at al-Rajīʿ, another group of the Anṣār fell victim to an even more ghastly and treacherous crime. The event started when a man from Najd named ʿĀmir ibn Mālik – or, more respectfully, Abū Barā', in the Arabian tradition of calling a man as the father of his eldest son – came to Madinah and met the Prophet. The Prophet explained the message of Islam to him and called on him to believe in God's oneness and the message He vouchsafed to Muhammad. Abū Barā', a highly respected chief among his people, neither accepted Islam nor rejected it outright. However, he suggested to the Prophet that he should send a group of his followers to Najd, where they could speak to its clans and tribes and call on them to believe in Islam. He told the Prophet that he had high hopes that the response of the Arab tribes of Najd would not be unfavourable. The Prophet expressed his fears that the people of Najd, well known for their bravery and ferocity, would try to kill them. Abū Barā' said that he would extend his protection to them.

In the traditions of Arabia at that time, any man could extend his protection to any other person by publicizing the fact that he had done so. This meant that the tribe of the protector was under an obligation to defend the protected person against anyone who tried to cause him any harm. It was the normal practice that Arabian tribes observed the protection given to anyone by members of any tribe with whom they did not want any friction. All tribes considered that the breach of their protection by any person or tribe an act of aggression which could not be repelled by any measure short of war, or at least the killing of the persons who perpetrated such a breach, or a similar number of people of that particular tribe.

The Prophet sent out a mission which included at least 40 (though some reports put the number as high as 70) of his companions, all from the Anṣār, with the exception of ʿĀmir ibn Fuhayrah, Abū Bakr's servant, who played an important role in the arrangements of the Prophet's emigration to Madinah. When the delegation arrived at a place called B'ir Maʿūnah, midway between the area inhabited by the tribe of ʿĀmir and the area of the Sulaym tribe, they sent one of their number, Ḥarām ibn Milḥān, to the chief of the ʿĀmir tribe, a man called ʿĀmir ibn al-Ṭufayl, with the Prophet's letter addressed to him. ʿĀmir ibn al-Ṭufayl, however, did not even look at the letter. Instead, he killed Ḥarām ibn Milḥān on the spot. It must be emphasized here that the ʿĀmir tribe were aware that Abū Barā', one of their chiefs, had extended his protection to this mission. He travelled from Madinah ahead of them and communicated to all tribes the fact that the Prophet's companions were under his protection. Hence, ʿĀmir ibn al-Ṭufayl's action in killing Ḥarām constituted a violation of historically observed values and traditions on two counts: he killed a messenger when it was normal practice to grant messengers safe conduct, and he was in breach of a pledge of protection given by a chief of his own tribe.

ʿĀmir ibn al-Ṭufayl then called on the people of his tribe to attack the Muslim mission. They would not have anything to do with it. They told him quite clearly that they were not prepared to violate Abū Barā's pledge of protection. He then called on the people of Sulaym to come to his aid. From them, he received the response he was hoping for. They marched in force, with him as their commander. Soon they encircled the Muslim mission whose members, concerned over the long absence of their messenger, had started to move towards the place of the ʿĀmir tribe.

The Muslims found themselves besieged by a force much bigger than theirs. The odds were heavily against them. There were no negotiations or exchanges of any sort. The attackers had one objective in mind and they immediately set about achieving it. The Muslims naturally defended themselves and bravely fought a very hard battle. They were, however, heavily outnumbered. As the Arabic saying goes: "Numbers beat courage." The Muslims were no match for their attackers. All the Muslim men in that mission were killed with the exception of Kaʿb ibn Zaid, who was wounded and looked all but dead. He lived, however, and was able to fight another battle with the Prophet which took place about a year later when he achieved martyrdom.

The Survivors

Two men from among the Muslims had been sent earlier with their cattle to graze. They went quite a long way and did not witness the horrible events of the day. They suspected that something serious had happened when they saw a large number of birds concentrating on the spot where they had left their people. They realized that something must have happened to attract the birds. They hurried back to find out. The sight they encountered was a ghastly one. All their brethren were dead; their blood was everywhere. Their attackers' horses were still on the spot: they had not left yet. One of the two men, ʿAmr ibn Umayyah of the Muhājirīn, expressed his view to his Anṣārī brother, al-Mundhir ibn Muḥammad, that the best thing they could do was to go back home and tell the Prophet what had happened. The Anṣārī man said: "I would not spare myself a battle in which al-Mundhir ibn ʿAmr [a friend of his] has been killed. I certainly would not like to be told by others how he met his death." He then attacked the aggressors and fought them single-handedly, killing two of their men before he was killed. ʿAmr ibn Umayyah was left alone and, realizing that it was futile for him to try to fight such a large force on his own, he allowed himself to be taken prisoner. When he told ʿĀmir ibn al-Ṭufayl that he belonged to the Muḍar tribe, he was set free. ʿĀmir told him, after shaving his head as a sign of humiliation, that he was setting him free on behalf of his mother, who had to free a prisoner or a slave.

ʿAmr ibn Umayyah headed towards Madinah. When he arrived at a place called Qarqarah he stopped to rest. Two men from the ʿĀmir tribe came and joined him in the shady place where he was resting. These two men had been to see the Prophet and were carrying a pass from him. In other words, the Prophet had extended his protection to them. Unaware of this fact, ʿAmr decided to kill the two men when he learnt of their tribal affiliation. He waited until they fell asleep, whereupon he carried out his intention. He felt that killing them was the first instalment of the revenge to be exacted from their tribe.

When ʿAmr arrived in Madinah he told the Prophet what had happened to his followers. The Prophet was sad, outraged and hurt at what had happened. He said: "This is the result of Abū Barā's advice. I was unwilling to send them and I feared the consequences." Perhaps the Prophet never felt as much sorrow as he felt for his companions who were killed in this incident. This is perhaps because it was nothing less than murder in cold blood, coupled with treachery. In his sorrow, the Prophet prayed God to punish the clans which took part in the killing of his companions. He did so every day for 15 days during his *Fajr* prayers. He mentioned each clan by name. He also prayed to God to help certain individuals who were detained in Makkah by the Quraysh.[5]

The two episodes of al-Rajīʿ and B'ir Maʿūnah occurred at roughly the same time. Some reports suggest that the Prophet received information about the killing of both groups of his followers on the same day. While he, as a Prophet entrusted with a message and an advocate of a cause, could not adopt an over-cautious attitude when people came to him and asked for teachers to instruct their people about Islam, he actually took reasonable precautions to ensure the safety of his followers. This is why he was unwilling to send his companions to Najd until Abū Barā' extended his protection to them. The fact that this protection was not of much use to them was a risk the Prophet could not have done much about. After all, he was in the business of conveying the message to the largest possible number of people. When a reasonable opportunity arose to extend the area of Islam, that opportunity must be seized without hesitation. While the safety of soldiers and companions is a paramount consideration, precautions must be kept to a reasonable limit. An over-cautious approach could not win too many followers for Islam.

The events also showed that the enemies of Islam were not in a compromising mood. After all, the Quraysh's victory at Uḥud encouraged them and gave their morale a boost. They were determined to level one blow after another at the Muslims of Madinah, hoping that with every blow the Muslims would weaken and their end would be brought in sight.

The Muslims, on the other hand, went through a difficult period. The difficulty, however, did not weaken their faith. They realized that they were surrounded by enemies. Even in Madinah itself they had the hypocrites and the Jews to contend with. Hence, they had to tread carefully. The Prophet was always watchful. He made sure he received good and timely intelligence. He was like a captain of a ship, steering it carefully in rocky waters and rough seas.

Trusting or Vulnerable?

The two tragic incidents of al-Rajīʿ and B'ir Maʿūnah served to indicate the vulnerability of the situation of the Muslim community in Madinah. Following closely on the heels of the Battle of Uḥud, the two incidents suggested that many of the forces hostile to Islam were strongly tempted to test the Muslims' resistance. The Muslims were never short of enemies. At the time of the Prophet there were three main danger areas. In Makkah, the Quraysh still represented a major force. With its honour restored and morale boosted as a result of its victory at Uḥud, the Quraysh did not need much persuasion to go on the offensive again in order to smother the call of Islam. Closer to Madinah, and in the desert area surrounding the Muslim state, there were several Bedouin tribes who had no love for the Muslims. Inside Madinah there were the Jews and the hypocrites who represented the internal enemy. All these groups had one thing in common: hatred of Islam and the desire to get rid of Muhammad and his companions. Needless to say, in such circumstances, the closer threat is far greater than the distant enemy, the internal danger far more serious than the external one. Conspirators are in their element in such a situation.

The two events of al-Rajīʿ and B'ir Maʿūnah gave the impression that the Muslims could easily be taken in by false pretences. The internal enemy in Madinah took their cue from these two events and felt that a well-planned attack on the person of the Prophet might achieve for them the one success which would cap all others. With this in mind, the internal enemy was awaiting a suitable chance.

It may be asked here whether it would not have been easier for the Muslims had God chosen to unveil to the Prophet the identity of each of the hypocrites so that the Muslims could at least be on their guard against them. That was certainly easy for God to do, if He so wished, but He chose not to. One must not forget that the hypocrites pretended to be Muslims. Were the Prophet to take any positive action against them, he would appear, in the eyes of others, to be punishing a section of his followers for no apparent crime. This might have frightened away from Islam many people who would otherwise have decided to accept the faith. The Prophet would have also appeared to be a tyrant who passed arbitrary judgement on some of his followers. Moreover, he was setting an example for the following generations of Muslims. Since no other Muslim ruler would receive revelations from God, the identity of the hypocrites in succeeding Muslim generations could not be ascertained. These generations needed guidance on how to deal with the problem of hypocrisy. Such guidance could be provided only by the Prophet. He was therefore instructed by God to accept people as they professed to be, leaving judgement on their true intentions and their true motives to God alone. Thus the hypocrites represented a danger of an unknown quantity. The Muslims were to keep on their guard, but they were not to strike the first blow.

In the case of the Jews, they had a treaty of coexistence with the Prophet. Neither party was to interfere in the religious affairs of the other. The Jews had pledged not to give support to any enemy of the Prophet or the Muslims. Past experience, however, showed that the Jews could violate the provisions of their treaty if they felt that such violation would serve their interests. Besides, they showed indications of treachery on several occasions. A year or so earlier the Jewish tribe of Qaynuqāʿ had taken a position of open hostility to the Prophet. Certain individuals among them tried to plot against the Muslims. All this took place shortly after the resounding victory achieved by the Muslims at the Battle of Badr. The Muslims were then in a position of great strength, but that did not deter the Jews from plotting against them. Now that the Muslims had been shaken by the defeat at Uḥud and the treacherous events of al-Rajīʿ and Bi'r Maʿūnah, the temptation for the Jews to do something against the Muslims was too great to ignore. Hence, the Prophet had to be constantly watchful for any sign of treachery which might come from either side or both. The Prophet also felt that he should seize any opportunity that might arise to test the loyalty of the Jews.

Testing Jewish Loyalty

Such an opportunity presented itself when ʿAmr ibn Umayyah, the one companion of the Prophet who was not killed at B'ir Maʿūnah, came back and told the Prophet of what happened to his companions and what he himself had done on the way back. The Prophet had to pay blood money to the relatives of the men ʿAmr had killed on his way back. Since the Muslim state in Madinah was still a very poor one – especially because the Muhājirīn had to be supported by their brethren, the Anṣār, who received them well and were very generous to them – outside help was needed in this particular instance.

The Prophet, therefore, went to the Jewish tribe of al-Naḍīr, who were allies with the ʿĀmir tribe. He asked their chiefs to contribute to the blood money he had to pay. When he made his purpose clear to them they showed their willingness to meet his request. They were careful to show respect to him and addressed him by his title of Abū al-Qāsim, meaning the father of his eldest son, al-Qāsim, who, incidentally, had died in infancy. They said to him: "We will certainly help you in this matter."

The Prophet had a few of his companions with him. Among them were Abū Bakr, ʿUmar and ʿAlī. He sat down with his companions close to a house which belonged to the Jews. The chiefs of the al-Naḍīr tribe left them there pretending that they were about to raise some money to contribute to the ransom the Prophet had to pay. When they were alone, some of the Jews said: "You will never find the man as easy prey as he is now. Let a strong person go onto the roof of the house next to which Muhammad is sitting and drop a large stone or rock over his head and rid us of him." One of them, ʿAmr ibn Jiḥāsh ibn Kaʿb, volunteered to commit this treacherous crime. However, the Prophet was informed by God of the design of the al-Naḍīr tribe, so he left his companions in their place, giving the impression that he was coming back soon, and went straight to Madinah.

When the Prophet's companions who were with him felt that he had been absent for too long, they started to worry and went looking for him. Soon they met a man coming from Madinah who told them that he had seen him entering the city. They went back immediately until they reached Madinah, where they met the Prophet, who told them of the treacherous design of the Jews.

When the Prophet left his place and escaped this assassination attempt there was no reason for the al-Naḍīr tribe to continue with their plot. They realized that they had missed their chance of their greatest prize and hoped that the Prophet's escape was merely a coincidence. Little did they realize that he was made aware of what they had plotted. They were soon to learn that treachery could not go unpunished. After all, there was no reason whatsoever for the Jews of al-Naḍīr to plot against the life of the Prophet, with whom they had a treaty of peaceful coexistence and cooperation. Their only motive for such action was their uncompromising hatred of the Prophet and Islam. Their hatred was absolutely inexplicable in the sense that the Jews in Arabia were a small minority who followed a monotheistic religion amidst a pagan nation which worshipped idols represented by statues of stone, gold and wood. The rise of a powerful monotheistic religion in that society should have given them pleasure. Instead, they viewed it with hatred because it did not subscribe to their feeling of supremacy over all other nations and religions.

An Ultimatum to Evacuate

The Prophet sent the Jews of al-Naḍīr one of his companions, Muhammad ibn Maslamah, to convey to them the following message: "Betake yourselves out of my city. You are no longer allowed to share it with me now that you have plotted your treacherous action against me. I give you ten days' notice to carry out this ultimatum. Any of you seen after this period in Madinah shall be executed."

This message was absolutely clear and left no room for compromise. In the circumstances of Madinah – where in the same city three different communities, the pagan Arabs, the Jews and the Muslims lived side by side – an act of blatant treachery like the one perpetrated by the al-Naḍīr Jews could not easily have been tolerated. Trouble from within Madinah had to be stamped out immediately, with all the vigour and determination necessary to make everybody understand that severe punishment awaited any traitor.

Raising Prospects of Support

The Jews of al-Naḍīr started to get ready for their evacuation. The terms of the ultimatum allowed them to carry with them all their belongings and to appoint agents to look after their farms and orchards. These terms can thus be seen to be highly humanitarian. They were not to be dispossessed of any property they had. Since they were no match on their own for the Muslims from the military point of view, it was only common sense that they should leave without further trouble. A new development, however, caused them to revise their position. They received a message from ʿAbdullāh ibn Ubayy, the most prominent of the hypocrites, who split the Muslim army before the Battle of Uḥud and deserted with 300 of his followers. He asked them to reject the Prophet's ultimatum and to refuse to evacuate Madinah. He promised them support, saying that he had 2,000 men who were ready to fight with them. They were prepared to go into their forts to fight alongside them and the Jewish tribe of Qurayẓah. The Arab tribe of Ghaṭafān, who were allies with the al-Naḍīr tribe, could also come to their support. ʿAbdullāh ibn Ubayy also pledged that his own people would give them full backing to the extent that if the worst came to the worst and the al-Naḍīr tribe were made to evacuate Madinah, they would leave with them.

Ḥuyayy ibn Akhṭab, the chief of the al-Naḍīr tribe, was very excited by ʿAbdullāh ibn Ubayy's offer. He felt that there was an excellent chance of defeating the Muslims. After all, the Muslims' morale, he imagined, was very low after their defeat at Uḥud and the massacres of their companions at al-Rajīʿ and B'ir Maʿūnah. He therefore sent a message to the Prophet: "We are not prepared to evacuate our homes. We will resist any attempt to evacuate us. You can do as you please." When the Prophet received this message he and his followers glorified God and said: "The Jews have decided to fight." The Muslims mobilized and the Prophet marched at the head of a considerable force, with ʿAlī carrying the flag. He asked his companion, Ibn Umm Maktūm, to deputize for him in Madinah. They encircled the Jewish quarters of the al-Naḍīr, who retreated inside their forts awaiting support from ʿAbdullāh ibn Ubayy and their co-religionists of the tribe of Qurayẓah. They armed themselves with arrows and other types of missiles in preparation for the forthcoming battle. All these events are recorded in the Qur'ān in *Sūrah* 59, entitled The Exile or *al-Ḥashr*. On the promise of the hypocrites, the *sūrah* states:

> Have you not seen the hypocrites? They say to their brethren who disbelieve among the people of the Scriptures: "If you are driven out we will go with you. We will never obey anyone who seeks to harm you. If you are attacked we will certainly come to your support." God bears witness that they are liars. For indeed, if they are driven out, they will not go out with them, nor, if they are attacked, would they come to their support. Indeed, if they did help them they will turn their backs in flight and leave them to their fate. (59: 11-12)

This was surely true. The al-Naḍīr tribe waited for support, but support was long in coming. Neither their allies of Ghaṭafān nor their co-religionists of the Qurayẓah nor their supporters, the hypocrites, came to their aid. They continued to be under siege and the situation was becoming more and more difficult. The Prophet ordered that some of their date palms should be burnt. When his command was carried out, the Jews sent him a message asking why he was doing this when he had always criticized those who did any similar action. The Qur'ān makes it clear that this was sanctioned by God. The siege continued for 26 days. The besieged Jews grew restless and scared. They sent word to the Prophet that they were willing to evacuate under the original terms.

The Prophet answered their message, stating that they could not have the same terms he originally offered them. Had they evacuated in peace, they would have spared themselves any trouble. But the fact that they were willing to join forces with others against the Prophet and the Muslims meant that they would do the same whenever a new opportunity presented itself.

The Prophet, however, was keenly aware that any internal trouble or dispute had better be resolved with speed and minimum bloodshed. Muslims are never keen to fight and shed blood anyway.

Since the Jews were prepared to leave, the Prophet was ready to let them go under new terms of evacuation. The new terms were that they would have safe conduct to leave Madinah with their women and children. Each of them could have a camel load of his belongings but no arms were allowed. Their farms and lands were to be given up. Thus they carried whatever they could on their camels and took their women and children and left for Khaybar, a city of Jewish concentration in Arabia. Some of them went to Syria. Those of them who had immovable property destroyed their homes before leaving so that the Muslims would not benefit from them. God states in the Qur'ān: "Their dwellings were destroyed by their own hands as well as by the believers." (59: 2)

Thus the encounter with the second Jewish tribe came to its conclusion. The Muslims did not have to fight and no blood was shed. The position of the Muslims in Madinah was much stronger now that another Jewish tribe was evacuated; the hypocrites were seen to be very weak indeed. The Muslim state was considerably richer now with the lands and property that the Muslims had gained from the Jews.

What Caused al-Naḍīr's Downfall

This second encounter between the Muslims in Madinah and their Jewish neighbours was the direct result of an attempt by those Jews to take advantage of the setbacks that befell the Muslims in quick succession. Within a period of four months the Muslims suffered a major defeat at Uḥud and the two treacherous attacks of al-Rajīʿ and B'ir Maʿūnah which altogether claimed the lives of at least 120 of their fighters. The figure could be as high as 154, which was a large proportion of their total number, considering that Islam was largely confined to the city of Madinah at that time. It was these setbacks which induced the Jews of al-Naḍīr to violate the treaty they had with the Muslims and to plot against the life of the Prophet. Little did they consider that Muslims never tolerate serious pledges and treaties being deliberately broken. It is not in the nature of the religion of Islam to allow its followers to be easy targets for their enemies who wish to take advantage of any setback that may befall them. Islam inspires its followers with a feeling of dignity and pride in their religion, the main pivot of which is the belief in the oneness of God, the Creator of the universe. This explains why, kind and tolerant as the Muslims are, they never allow anyone to take advantage of their weakness, if they can help it. Hence, when the al-Naḍīr Jews tried to do something of this sort they had to be taught a lesson. The lesson was, for anyone who cared to see, that a treaty or a covenant violated by the other party was no longer binding on Muslims once the violation had taken place.

The Qur'ān comments on this encounter and makes it absolutely clear that whatever the Muslims did, mobilizing their forces and besieging the Jews in their strongholds, was only a secondary element in the whole affair. It was God who directly conducted this encounter and brought about its conclusion. *Sūrah* 59 of the Qur'ān, entitled The Exile or *al-Ḥashr*, was revealed shortly after this encounter and commented on several aspects of it, laying down general principles for the Muslims to implement in their dealings with other people. It first reminds the Muslims that they were not called upon to fight the Jews in order to accomplish their evacuation:

> It was He that drove the unbelievers among the people of earlier revelations out of their homes into the first exile. You did not think that they would go; and they, for their part, fancied that their forts would protect them from God. But God reached them whence they did not expect, and cast terror in their hearts so that their homes were destroyed with their own hands and the hands of the believers. Learn from their examples, you that have eyes. (59: 2)

Here is an absolutely clear statement that the Muslims themselves did not expect the Jews of al-Naḍīr to be evacuated. This is because of the strength and forces that the Jews possessed. One can imagine then what task the Muslims would have had on their hands, had the hypocrites fulfilled their promise and raised a force of 2,000 men to support the Jews of al-Naḍīr and had the other Jews of Qurayẓah come also to their support. God, however, prevented such gathering of forces which might have caused the morale of the Muslims to sink, considering that memories of their setbacks were still fresh in their minds.

The Qur'ān also states that the only factor which caused the Jews of al-Naḍīr to succumb to the rule of the Prophet was the fact that God cast terror into their hearts. After all, no fighting took place and the Jewish forts constituted an impregnable stronghold. They themselves thought that no force could penetrate their stronghold but they did not reckon with the force of God and that He accomplishes whatever He wills. Hence they did not take any precaution against what might have come from within themselves. They could not guard against fear possessing them so suddenly that they could do nothing but surrender.

This is the way God accomplishes His purpose. Since He knows everything and is able to do whatever He wants, and since He has the means and the tools for accomplishing His purpose, and since both cause and effect are of His own making, and the means and the end of His own creation, nothing can stop Him and nothing can be too difficult for Him. He is indeed the Almighty, the Wise. When the Jews of al-Naḍīr retreated into their forts and thought that those forts would protect them against their enemies, defeat came to them from within themselves when God cast fear into their hearts, which resulted in the destruction of their own homes with their own hands.

It was mentioned earlier that the Prophet ordered his companions to cut down and burn some of the date palms which belonged to the Jews of al-Naḍīr. They were shocked at his action and sent him a message reminding him that he used to deplore such actions by other leaders. The Prophet did not bother with their representation. His companions felt uneasy about this. It was totally uncharacteristic of the Muslims to cut down trees and ruin farms as conquering armies did and still do to the present day. God tells them in the Qur'ān that He Himself has sanctioned their action: "Whatever palm trees you cut down or left standing on their roots, it was by God's leave, so that He might humiliate the evil-doers." (59: 5)

Indeed the Muslims were never allowed to indulge in such action of burning and destruction except in this instance. Hence this verse reassures them that it was God who wanted them to do it. After all, He had taken charge of this encounter and conducted it in the way He wished, in order to achieve His own purpose. Everything that took place was with His express permission. The purpose of cutting down some palm trees and leaving some others standing was simply to cause humiliation to the evil-doers. Their hearts were indeed broken to see their palm trees cut down and burnt. They were even more heartbroken when they had to evacuate Madinah and to leave their farms and orchards behind, including all their remaining palm trees, and let the Muslims enjoy them as they wished. Therefore, it was to cause them all this humiliation and sorrow that the trees were cut down and burnt and the orchards and farms confiscated.

After the Evacuation

The Prophet divided the land and property left by the Jews after their surrender only among the Muhājirīn. Only two people from the Anṣār, Sahl ibn Ḥanīf and Abū Dujānah, were included. This was a departure from the established rule of sharing the spoils of war, and therefore needs an explanation.

In Badr the spoils of war were the result of a major clash between the Muslims and the unbelievers which involved the Muslims in very hard fighting. The encounter with the al-Naḍīr Jews, on the other hand, did not require the Muslims to do any fighting. No one raised a sword and no fighting took place. Hence the property gained by the Muslims as a result of the al-Naḍīr encounter is of a different category altogether and cannot have the same treatment as the spoils of war. This type of gain is known in Islamic terminology as *fay'*. The established principle is that *fay'* belongs to the Muslim state. The way it is shared out is explained in the Qur'ān:

> That which God gives as spoil to His Messenger from the people of the townships, is for God and His Messenger and for the near of kin and the orphans and the needy and the wayfarer, so

> that it [that is, wealth] does not become the property of only the rich among you. Whatever the Messenger bids you, take it, and whatever he forbids you, abstain from it. (59: 7)

This verse makes it clear that *fay'* belongs in total to the Muslim state. It is for the Muslim ruler to share it out among those who have a claim to it, on the basis of this verse, according to his discretion. The term 'the near of kin' refers to the relatives of the Prophet. They do not have a share in *zakāt* and cannot inherit from the Prophet. Hence they are compensated by their share of *fay'*.

The Qur'ānic verse also establishes a far-reaching rule of the Islamic economic and social system: the rule which makes it absolutely clear that wealth must not be confined only to the rich. Islam allows private ownership as legitimate but qualifies it with this rule, which makes it clear that the poor have a claim to a share in the wealth of the community. Hence, any situation or system that results in money being monopolized by the rich only, or any class of society, is not in line with the Islamic economic theory and system. Financial dealings and relations within Islamic society must be so organized as not to create such a situation, or allow it to continue if it happens to exist.

Indeed, the whole economic system of Islam is based on this principle. The *zakāt* system and the inheritance system are two important factors which contribute to the division and distribution of wealth in Islamic society which, generally speaking, militates against the rise of a small, aristocratic class which monopolizes the greatest part of the wealth of the community. The rule concerning the distribution of *fay'* helps to remedy any situation which creates an imbalance among different sectors of Islamic society.

The way the Prophet divided the *fay'* which was gained from the Jews of the al-Naḍīr must be seen in the light of this general rule. The Muhājirīn, who emigrated from Makkah leaving all their property behind, were still a burden to their Anṣārī brothers. Some of them managed to find work and become independent but the majority were still sharing with their Anṣārī brethren whatever they had. Now the Prophet had a chance to rectify this situation. He called the Anṣār and spoke to them, praising their kindness and generosity and the way they treated their Muhājirīn brothers. He then said: "I will divide this *fay'* God has bestowed on me from the al-Naḍīr tribe among you and the Muhājirīn alike, if you so desire. In this case they will continue to live with you in your own houses and have a share in your money. Alternatively, I will divide the *fay'* among them only and they will leave your homes, if you so prefer."

Saʿd ibn ʿUbādah and Saʿd ibn Muʿādh, the two leaders of the Anṣār, said: "You divide it among them and we are happy to have them continue living in our houses as they are now." The rest of the Anṣār endorsed their leaders' decision and the Prophet prayed for them and for their children.

The two men of the Anṣār who were also given a share of the *fay'* – Sahl ibn Ḥanīf and Abū Dujānah – were poor. Apparently, they were the only two poor people among the Anṣār and in consideration of their poverty they had a share of the *fay'*. It is clear, then, that the Prophet wanted to correct an imbalance which existed in the Muslim community. The Muhājirīn did not deserve to be favoured with the *fay'* on any grounds other than their poverty. It is up to any Muslim ruler to identify the poor in his community and to distribute among them whatever *fay'* he may have.

The encounter with the Jews of al-Naḍīr, coming as it did soon after the setbacks of Uḥud, al-Rajīʿ and Bir' Maʿūnah, boosted the Muslims' morale to a new high. They achieved a total victory which they themselves had not expected. The internal enemy suffered a crushing blow. Indeed, the victory of the Muslims was a thorn in the flesh of all their other enemies. Although the Quraysh was not directly involved, the Muslims' victory meant that they were in a much better shape now for any new clash between the two sides. The remaining Jews in Madinah felt much weaker with the evacuation of their co-religionists, which was achieved without shedding a drop of blood. The Arab hypocrites in Madinah, who demonstrated their total inability to take part in any armed conflict against the Muslims, were greatly weakened by the evacuation of their Jewish allies. They realized that they could no longer hope to regain any control in Madinah unless the Quraysh and the other Arab allies could win a decisive victory against the Muslims, which did not seem at all likely in the circumstances. Thus within six months of the Battle of Uḥud, no traces of weakness could be detected in the Muslim community. Indeed, all hostile forces realized that they underrated the strength of the Muslim state at their own peril. It was a major force to be reckoned with in Arabia.[6]

Notes

1. Ibn Kathīr, *al-Bidāyah wal-Nihāyah*, Maktabat al-Ma'ārif, Beirut, Vol. 1, p. 48.
2. Ibn Sayyid al-Nās, *'Uyūn al-Athar*, Dār al-Turāth, Madinah, 1996, p. 59.
3. Ibid., pp. 59-61.
4. Ibn Hishām, *al-Sīrah al-Nabawiyyah*, Dār al-Qalam, Beirut, Vol. 1, pp. 178-182. Also, Ibn Sayyid al-Nās, op.cit., pp. 63-66.
5. Ibn Hishām, op.cit., pp. 193-196. Also, Ibn Sayyid al-Nās, op.cit., pp. 67-72.
6. Ibn Hishām, op.cit., pp. 199-202. Also, Ibn Sayyid al-Nās, op.cit., pp. 73-78.

23

Consolidation

BARELY TWO MONTHS after the encounter with the al-Naḍīr Jews, the Prophet learned that the two Arabian tribes of Muḥārib and Thaʿlabah were mobilizing to attack Madinah. Working on the basis that attack is the best defence, the Prophet assembled a force of 700 of his followers and appointed ʿUthmān ibn ʿAffān to deputize for him in Madinah. The Muslim force marched a very long way until they reached a place called Nakhl in the area which belonged to the tribes of Ghaṭafān in the Najd province, right in the heart of the Arabian Peninsula. There the Muslims came face to face with a very large concentration of enemy forces. The two sides drew very close to each other. The Muslims were worried because they realized that they were heavily outnumbered. Despite their numerical strength, their enemies felt very fearful as well. Neither party was keen to attack and both hoped that a clash could somehow be averted.

This was a very hard campaign for the Muslims. They had covered a great distance from Madinah and they had to travel over very hard terrain. The expedition is known in Muslim history books as 'The expedition of cloth pieces', or Dhāt al-Riqāʿ. The name is taken from the fact that the Muslims had to wrap their feet in pieces of cloth to relieve the pain as they walked over rocky areas. When the two forces stood face to face, the feeling of fear was common to both of them. It was indeed on this expedition that the Prophet used in his prayers with the Muslims the method known as 'Prayers in the case of fear'. This method means that the army is divided into two halves and they take turns as they pray with the Prophet. He himself would pray the whole prayer while one half of his men joined him for the first part of the prayers, then they would finish their prayers individually. When they had finished, the other half would join the Prophet for the rest of his prayers. Thus everyone in the army would have joined the same prayers while one half would always be free, watching the enemy and making sure that they did not exploit the time of prayers in order to attack the Muslims. This method of prayer is outlined in verse 102 of *Sūrah* 4, entitled Women. For a more detailed discription refer to Chapter 26, p. 502.

No clash, however, took place between the two sides. The Prophet managed to withdraw with his forces intact without engaging the enemy.[1]

A great part of the history of Islam at the time of the Prophet is devoted to the military activity of the Muslims. This is natural because those ten years during which the Prophet established the first Islamic state were full of military operations, owing to the fact that several forces were keen to fight the Muslims and suppress Islam altogether. When relating history, great events overshadow small or ordinary ones. One should not, however, overlook those small events which give a good impression of the type of life the Muslims lived in Madinah. From them one can understand a great deal about how the Muslims treated one another, what sort of relations they had with the Prophet and how far they were devoted to their cause. In this connection, some events which took place during this expedition are worth mentioning.

A Friendly Conversation

One such incident is related by Jābir ibn ʿAbdullāh, a young companion of the Prophet who went on this expedition. He was riding a weak camel, which meant that he kept falling behind. When the Prophet noticed him and learnt that the camel was not a strong one, he asked Jābir to sit him down. When he did, the Prophet said to him: "Give me the stick in your hand, or cut a stick for me from a tree." The Prophet pricked the side of the camel with the stick several times and asked Jābir to mount the camel. Jābir says: "By Him who sent the Prophet with the message of truth, the camel was then as fast as any."

The Prophet was then chatting to Jābir and asked him: "Would you sell me this camel of yours, Jābir?" Jābir replied: "It is yours as a gift." The Prophet said: "No, but sell it to me." Jābir said: "Make me an offer then." The Prophet said: "I will give you one dirham [the silver currency at the time] for it." Jābir declined the offer and said: "Then you would give me an unfair price." The Prophet said: "What do you say to two dirhams?" Jābir declined again. The Prophet kept increasing the price and Jābir kept declining, until the Prophet offered him an ounce of silver. Jābir then said: "Would you be happy to pay this price, Messenger of God?" The Prophet answered in the affirmative and Jābir accepted the price.

The Prophet asked Jābir whether he was married and Jābir answered that he was. The Prophet then asked him about his wife and whether she was a virgin getting married for the first time or a woman who had been married before. Jābir's wife was of the latter type. The Prophet said: "Would it not have been better if you had married a young virgin with whom you can play and have fun?" Jābir who was perhaps less than 20 years of age at that time said: "Messenger of God, my father was killed at Uḥud, leaving me my seven sisters to look after. I therefore married a woman who could look after them and keep the family together."

The Prophet replied, "Then you have done the right thing, God willing. When we arrive at Ṣirār, we will have some camels slaughtered and we will celebrate. Your wife will then hear that we have celebrated her marriage and she will put her cushions." (Putting up cushions was apparently a sign of celebrating a happy occasion.) Jābir said: "But we have no cushions, Messenger of God." The Prophet said, "But you will have. When you arrive at Madinah you should arrange a good feast."

When the Muslim army arrived at Ṣirār, which was only about five kilometres from Madinah, the Prophet had a number of camels slaughtered and cooked. The whole army shared in the celebration of the recent wedding of one of its soldiers. When the sun went down, the Prophet and his companions went into Madinah. Jābir told his wife what the Prophet said and she advised him to do as the Prophet told him.

The following morning Jābir took his camel and sat him down outside the Prophet's mosque. Then Jābir went into the mosque. When the Prophet came out, he asked about the camel and was told that Jābir had brought it. He asked for Jābir to be called and when he arrived the Prophet said: "Take your camel, my nephew; it is yours." He then called Bilāl (who acted as treasurer) and told him to go with Jābir and to give him an ounce of silver. Bilāl did as the Prophet bade him and gave Jābir a fraction more. Jābir said that the camel stayed with him a very long time.[2]

This incident shows the degree of care the Prophet used to show to his companions. There are numerous stories about the Prophet doing certain things of a similar nature. These were taken by his companions as signs which consolidated their belief in him as a Messenger of God. It is not that they had any doubts, but miraculous acts like his treatment of the camel's weakness tended to confirm for them what they already knew to be true. The fact that the Prophet asked a young companion of his about his family affairs in such a way, as happens between intimate friends, serves to show that the Prophet really cared about every individual among his companions. He was not like a leader who viewed his troops as people whom he could utilize to achieve his personal glory. The Prophet was after no glory for himself but he wanted to be informed about the affairs of his companions so that they would feel much closer to him. When he realized that Jābir was newly married, he was keen to make the whole community share in the celebration.

It is also obvious that the Prophet did not need to buy the camel but he realized that Jābir was poor and he knew that he was supporting a family. Buying the camel and giving it as a gift to its previous owner was highly characteristic of the Prophet. He was indeed the best example of generosity. When he asked to buy the camel, he intended all the time to give it back to Jābir as a gift, but he wanted Jābir to name his price so that he felt that the matter was serious. According to one report, the terms of the deal stipulated that Jābir could utilize the camel until they had arrived in Madinah. Throughout the journey, then, Jābir was convinced that he had sold the camel. But what better wedding gift could he have hoped for than having his camel as well as its price.

An Assassination Attempt

Two more little incidents that took place during the expedition of Dhāt al-Riqāʿ are worth mentioning because they shed considerable light on the depth of faith of the Prophet and his companions in their religion. They show how seriously that first generation of Muslims viewed their faith and how literally they took the word of the Qur'ān.

A man called Ghawrath from the tribe of Muḥārib, one of the two tribes who were mobilizing to attack Madinah, said to his people: "Shall I kill Muhammad for you?" They replied: "Yes, but how will you do it?" Ghawrath said: "I will take him unawares and kill him." He then went to the Prophet and found him sitting alone. He said to him: "Muhammad, may I have a look at your sword?" The sword was decorated with silver. The Prophet let him have it and the man drew it out of its scabbard. He shook the sword repeatedly and tried to hit the Prophet, but every time he did so he found himself restrained. He then addressed the Prophet: "Muhammad, do you fear me?" The Prophet answered, "No. Why should I fear you?" The man said: "How can you not fear me when I have the sword in my hand?" The Prophet said: "But I do not fear you. God will protect me from you." The sword dropped to the ground and the Prophet picked it up, and said to Ghawrath, "Who will protect you from me?" Ghawrath replied: "You can, if you wish, be the best man to overpower an opponent." Ghawrath apparently realized that he could save himself only by appealing to the Prophet's generosity. The Prophet then asked him to declare that he believed in God as the only deity and that Muhammad was His Messenger. He said: "I give you my solemn pledge that I will never fight you and I will never join any people who want to fight you." The Prophet then let him go and Ghawrath went to his people and said: "I have been with the best man on earth."

This small incident shows how the Prophet's trust in God was total. God had promised him that he would not come to any harm while he conveyed His message. The Prophet showed on numerous occasions that his confidence in God's promise was both complete and unshakeable. Here we see him alone with a man holding a sword in his hand, a man who had come to him for the sole purpose of killing him. Yet he allows him to look at his own sword and when the man speaks about killing him, the Prophet is in no way perturbed.[3]

Uninterrupted Prayer

The second incident concerns two of the Prophet's companions, ʿAmmār ibn Yāsir of the Muhājirīn and ʿAbbād ibn Bishr of the Anṣār. The Prophet had encamped close to a mountain trail and he asked for volunteers to keep a night watch. The two men came forward to volunteer for the task and the Prophet asked them to stay close to the opening of the trail. When they went there ʿAbbād asked his companion whether he preferred to have a nap straight away or stay awake and have his nap later in the night. ʿAmmār preferred to sleep early. When he lay down, his Anṣārī brother stood up to pray.

Apparently an unbeliever was following the Muslim army. When he drew near, he noticed the figure of the Anṣārī man saying his prayers. He realized that the man was keeping watch. He aimed an arrow at him and hit him. ʿAbbād did not move but took the arrow off and continued praying. The man hit him with a second arrow and ʿAbbād did the same. A third arrow hit him as he was praying, so he took it off and continued with his prayer, bowing down and then prostrating himself. He then woke his companion and told him that he was wounded. ʿAmmār stood up and when the man saw the two of them together, he fled. Realizing that ʿAbbād was badly wounded, ʿAmmār said to him: "Why did you not wake me up when he hit you the first time?" The Anṣārī man replied: "I was reading a *sūrah* and I did not like to cut it short. I hoped to be able to finish it before I did anything. When he hit me three times I bent down and woke you up. I swear that had it not been for the fact that I feared that I would not carry out the Prophet's order to keep watch in the way I should, I would not have cut the *sūrah* short even if he had slit my throat."[4]

As it is well known, there is nothing wrong with reading only a portion of the *sūrah* in prayers, be it a short or a long portion. Prayers are valid even if one reads only one verse of a very long *sūrah*. Yet the man realized that every *sūrah* of the Qur'ān is a complete unit. Keeping that in mind, he was keen to read the whole *sūrah* in one session, whether he was praying or not. Since God made the division of the Qur'ān into *sūrah*s, the Anṣārī man wanted to keep strictly to that division. When he found that in that particular instance, reading the whole *sūrah* might have put the Muslims in danger, he cut his prayers short and did his duty. This is just one example of the devotion of the Prophet's companions to their cause.

This expedition was highly beneficial to the Muslims, despite the fact that no encounter with the unbelievers took place. The mere fact that the Muslims were ready to march a considerable distance in order to meet their enemies before they could attack them in Madinah was an indication of unshaken self-confidence. The fact that the unbelievers did not manage to engage the Muslims in a battle, despite the fact that theirs was a much larger force, showed that the Muslims were truly feared by their enemies. Coming so soon after the second encounter with the Jews, which resulted in the evacuation of a strong Jewish tribe from Madinah without shedding a drop of blood, this expedition gave a new boost to the Muslims' morale, which went a long way to wipe out the effects of their defeat at Uḥud. It meant that the external enemy was unsure of its strength, worried that the Muslims could not be overcome.

Turning Up for a New Clash

The Prophet stayed in Madinah for about three months after this expedition and then called on the Muslims to get ready for their appointment with the Quraysh. At the end of the Battle of Uḥud,

Abū Sufyān had suggested that the two sides meet again in one year's time at Badr. That eventful year was now coming to its conclusion and the appointed time was drawing near. The Muslims were therefore getting ready, cherishing the hope that this time they would inflict on the Quraysh a heavy defeat which would destroy their reputation as the major tribe in Arabia.

In Makkah, Abū Sufyān did not look forward to the approaching appointment. He would have preferred to continue to capitalize on the victory he achieved at Uḥud in order to preserve the Quraysh's reputation. He realized that a new battle might change the whole situation. Besides, that year brought a prolonged drought in Makkah which adversely affected its resources. If one adds to this the fact that the Muslims in Madinah continued to impose a trade boycott on the Quraysh, not allowing their caravans to go through towards Syria, one can realize that the Quraysh suffered an economic crisis that year. Abū Sufyān, however, could not just miss out on the appointment. That would have been an unmistakable sign of weakness which he was unwilling to give. He therefore resorted to trickery, hoping that he would be able to frighten the Muslims off going out to meet the Quraysh. He hired a man called Nuʿaym ibn Masʿūd and asked him to spread rumours in Madinah that the Quraysh had raised a very large force to fight the Muslims and that the Muslims were no match for that force. Nuʿaym did as he was instructed and spread that rumour as far as he could. The Prophet, however, was determined to keep the appointment. He said: "By Him who holds my soul in His hand, I am going out to meet them even if no one joins me."

The Muslims, however, were very keen to join the Prophet and he marched at the head of 1,500 of his followers. He appointed as his deputy in Madinah ʿAbdullāh ibn ʿAbdullāh ibn Ubayy, the son of the hypocrites' leader. Unlike his father, ʿAbdullāh was a man of sincere and strong faith.

When they arrived at Badr, which was about 160 kilometres from Madinah, they found no trace of the enemy. What happened was that an army from the Quraysh marched from Makkah towards Badr. Abū Sufyān was very uneasy about meeting the Muslims. He was convinced that the time was not suitable for the Quraysh. He addressed his soldiers pointing out the difficulties they had experienced that year and said that they could not hope to win a war in such a year of drought. They had to wait for a good season when there would be an abundance of crops and dairy products. He advised the army to return and they took his advice.

Although Abū Sufyān's action might have been prudent in the circumstances, it did not help the Quraysh's cause in any way. In fact, it helped the cause of the Muslims. Even the people of Makkah itself accused the army of cowardice. The fact that they went back after they had started to march was unjustifiable to many of the Arabs who started to doubt the significance of the Quraysh's victory at Uḥud.[5]

Badr was a seasonal market of Arabia. People from all tribes assembled there during the month of Shaʿbān and exchanged goods and commodities. The trading fair lasted for eight days. The Prophet and his companions benefited a great deal from being at Badr at that time. Their financial gains from the market were considerable. Their more important gain was the recovery of their reputation as a strong fighting force, equal to any in Arabia. These events and expeditions of al-Naḍīr, Dhāt al-Riqāʿ and the final expedition to Badr, close on each other's heels, were of great psychological significance to the Muslims. They made the defeat at Uḥud seem to be an event in the ancient past, despite the fact that it had taken place only a year earlier. When the market was over, the Muslims returned to Madinah having demonstrated that they feared no one in Arabia.

A New Marriage

Shortly after their return to Madinah, the Prophet married Umm Salamah, whose name was Hind. The title of Umm Salamah was given to her according to the traditions of Arabia which are still valid in many Arab countries. The word 'Umm' means 'mother' and Salamah was the name of her eldest son. To call any person, man or woman, by the fact of their parenthood of their eldest son is a sign of respect. Umm Salamah was so much better known by her title that few books record her original name.

Apparently, Umm Salamah was middle aged. This is evident from the fact that her own son, Salamah, acted for her when the marriage contract was made. However, she was good looking and belonged to a distinguished family. Her husband, Abū Salamah, was one of the first companions of the Prophet to emigrate with his wife first to Abyssinia and then to Madinah. He was certainly a good soldier of Islam and a good military commander. He received a wound at the Battle of Uḥud when he remained steadfast with the Prophet while many others of his companions were overtaken by confusion. Although his wound healed and he was well enough to be the commander of another expedition (where he fought against the tribe of Asad), he suffered a recurrence of his injury which led to his death.

When the Prophet sent someone over a year later to propose to her on his behalf, Umm Salamah was overjoyed. To be married to the Prophet was an honour no Muslim woman would hesitate to accept. Yet she was worried lest she should not be able to fulfil her duties as the wife of God's Messenger. After all, she was no longer young; she had children, some of whom were still young; and the Prophet had other wives. She, therefore, sent a kind apology: "I cannot help my jealousy, I am old and burdened with young dependents."

The Prophet, however, answered: "If you are old, I am older than you. God will relieve you of your jealousy. You may commend your dependents to God and His Messenger."[6]

Umm Salamah was either the third or fourth wife of the Prophet in Madinah. He was already married to Sawdah, who was an elderly woman; 'Ā'ishah, who was in the prime of youth; and possibly Ḥafṣah, who was of mature age.

Another Expedition

The fact that the Quraysh did not wish to engage the Muslims in a new battle meant that the initiative was now completely in the Muslims' hands. The Prophet was eager that the Muslim state in Madinah should not be considered an easy target by any prospective enemy. His informers brought him intelligence that the Arab tribes in the area of Dūmat al-Jandal in the north of Arabia, close to Palestine and Syria, had been attacking trade caravans and threatening all travellers. Their exploits had convinced them that they were too powerful for anyone – so much so that they contemplated attacking Madinah. Moreover, he was told that a large force had been raised to launch such an attack.

The Prophet therefore raised a force of 1,000 men of his companions and marched northwards with them. They marched at night and encamped during the day so that they could take their enemy by surprise. It was a long journey, taking 15 nights to cover the distance. An expert guide was employed to show them the way. The Muslims were indeed able to take their enemies by surprise and swept through their encampments. Thus the forces which were raised to attack Madinah were left with no choice but to flee. They went in every direction, abandoning their cattle which the Muslims gained.

The Muslims encamped there for several days, during which the Prophet sent a number of pursuing squads to make sure that the enemy was not regrouping. No one, however, was willing to fight the Muslims who went back to Madinah after they had established their authority in the northern area as well. This expedition took place in the third month of the fifth year of the Prophet's emigration to Madinah.[7]

The expedition to Dūmat al-Jandal was significant in more ways than one. First of all, it complemented the earlier military activity which the Muslims had undertaken when they sent their forces eastwards to Najd, in the heart of Arabia, before going south to meet the Quraysh at Badr, a meeting which did not take place because the other party did not turn up. Now, this expedition northwards confirmed the Muslims' authority in all areas surrounding Madinah. No one would now entertain the idea that a quick raid on Madinah would meet with any success. After all, everyone realized that the Muslims' internal position in Madinah was much stronger after the evacuation of the Jewish tribe of al-Naḍīr. Hence the principal enemies of the Muslims, the Quraysh and the Jews who evacuated from Madinah, realized that unless an alliance which brought together all forces hostile to Islam could be forged, they had no hope of causing even a dent in the solid structure of the Muslim state.

Another factor which made this expedition necessary was the fact that the Prophet realized that another source of danger – although perhaps not in the very short term – was the Byzantine Empire. All areas to the north of Arabia, from Palestine and beyond, belonged to the Byzantine Empire, which ruled over Syria and as far east as the borders of present-day Iraq. The Arabian tribes in the north of the Arabian Peninsula feared no authority more than they feared the Byzantines. The Byzantine Emperor, on the other hand, did not even think it possible that anything could happen in Arabia which might cause him any worry. It was necessary, therefore, to plant the fear of the Muslim state in the hearts of the Arabian tribes which lived in the north, so that they would realize that their best hope was to be at peace with the Muslim state. This would help in the longer term, when the Muslims would have to engage the Byzantines in battle, because it would restrain these Arabian tribes from attacking the Muslim army from behind. They would also hesitate before giving any aid to the Byzantines against the Muslims.

The expedition to Dūmat al-Jandal was also important in that it gave the Muslims a foretaste of what they might expect if they had to face the Byzantines in battle. It gave them the necessary experience in going through the long desert route from Madinah to northern Arabia and prepared them for making this journey again if that were to prove necessary.

The Muslims were thus involved in four major events without actually having to fight. In each of these events a bloody encounter might have taken place. In none of them was blood shed. Yet they all tended to enhance the Muslims' reputation, boost their morale and cause their enemies to be even more fearful of them. There can be only one explanation for all this: God was watching over this young Muslim community and helping it through its difficulties when the Muslims demonstrated that they valued nothing more than the triumph of Islam.

Yet these events – significant as they were and enhancing the reputation of the Muslims as a fighting force – did not mean that the battle for Islam was anywhere near resolution. The Muslim state in Madinah was still in its early days, when its numerous enemies were taking the initiative to raise forces and attack the Muslims. The Prophet's tactics of attacking any would-be aggressors before they had time to mobilize fully was highly successful in saving the Muslim state from several situations where it could have suffered a great deal of harm. Indeed, throughout this stage, the Muslim state was on the defensive. All the attacks the Muslims launched were, in essence, counterattacks. The power of their enemies however, was gradually being eroded and a major rethink and reconsideration of tactics was soon to be conducted by the enemies of Islam, who were always on the watch for an opening which might give them a breakthrough in their fight against Islam.

Notes

1. Ibn Hishām, *al-Sīrah al-Nabawiyyah*, Dār al-Qalam, Beirut, Vol. 1, pp. 214-215. Also, Ibn Sayyid al-Nās, *'Uyūn al-Athar*, Dār al-Turāth, Madinah, 1996, p. 79.
2. Ibn Hishām, op.cit., pp. 216-218. Also, Ibn Kathīr, *al-Bidāyah wal-Nihāyah*, Maktabat al-Ma'ārif, Beirut, Vol. 1, pp. 86-87.
3. Ibn Hishām, op.cit., p. 216. Also, Ibn Sayyid al-Nās, op.cit., pp. 79-80.
4. Ibn Hishām, op.cit., pp. 218-219.
5. Ibid., p. 220. Also, Ibn Sayyid al-Nās, op.cit., p. 82; Ibn Kathīr, op.cit., pp. 87-89.
6. Ibn Kathīr, op.cit., p. 90.
7. Ibid., p. 92. Also, Ibn Hishām, op.cit., p. 224; al-Wāqidī, *Kitāb al-Maghāzī*, Oxford University Press, 1996, Vol. 1, p. 402-404; and Ibn Sayyid al-Nās, op.cit., p. 83.

24

How to Mar a Splendid Victory

THE SETBACKS SUFFERED by the Muslims at Uḥud, al-Rajīʿ and B'ir Maʿūnah were perhaps erased from the memories of both the Muslims and their enemies by the successful campaigns launched by the Muslims against both their internal and external enemies. Following one another in quick succession, these campaigns re-established the Muslims' reputation as a fighting force which did not cower in the face of any challenge. Hence the enemies of Islam had to take stock of these recent events and reconsider their strategy. Until that time their hostility to Islam was open and direct. Now some of them at least recognized the need to change their tactics.

Some of the Arab inhabitants of Madinah resorted to hypocrisy right from the early days of the establishment of the Muslim state. They recognized at the time that they could not go against the wishes of a large portion of their community who accepted the new religion. They therefore pretended to be Muslims, hoping to share in the gains of Islam when it met with success. Deep inside, however, they did not believe in God or His Messenger. They were ready to join forces with any enemy of Islam seeking to crush it. Yet they were always on shifting ground. They could not afford to throw in their lot completely with the enemies of Islam. They did not have the necessary strength and courage to make their feelings clear and to join the other enemies of Islam in an open campaign.

Over the previous few years, the hypocrites in Madinah had been playing a dirty game against the Muslims. Their wickedness and their hatred of Islam surfaced whenever the Muslims suffered a setback. On the other hand, they were quick to suppress their true feelings and claim to be loyal to Islam and to the Prophet whenever the Muslims achieved a significant victory. This, however, did not prevent the hypocrites from resorting to taunts and ridicule and spreading false rumours against the Muslims whenever they had an opportunity to do so. Indeed, the hypocrites' hatred of Islam increased in proportion as the Muslims' authority became more firmly established. We have seen how they tried to persuade the Jews to fight the Muslims, pledging them their own support. However, they did not fulfil their promises when they realized that the Muslims' victory was inevitable.

The hypocrites continued to try to make others fight Islam. As for their own efforts in the attempt to defeat Islam, they preferred to work from within. Perhaps the best example of their tactics and treachery is provided by the events of the Prophet's expedition against the tribe of al-Muṣṭalaq.

A Pre-Emptive Attack

The Prophet received information that this tribe, under the leadership of its chief, al-Ḥārith ibn Abī Ḍirār, was preparing to launch an attack on Madinah. In keeping with his successful strategy of surprising his enemies before they had time to launch their attack, the Prophet marched at the head of a large force of Muslims, towards his enemies. It was the Prophet's custom when he went on an expedition of any kind, to have at least one of his wives with him. He would have a toss between them to decide which of them was to join him. This time, he took ʿĀ'ishah with him.

This expedition was marked by the large number of hypocrites who joined the Muslim army. They normally did not join any army raised by the Prophet. Remember how, at the Battle of Uḥud, their leader, ʿAbdullāh ibn Ubayy, deserted the army before the battle with 300 of his followers. Since then, the hypocrites had not participated in any expedition until the Prophet moved against the tribe of al-Muṣṭalaq.

There were two obvious reasons for the hypocrites' change of tactics. Recent encounters between the Muslims and their enemies had all been successful. Moreover, the Muslims had won with little or no bloodshed. There was no reason why the same should not happen again this time. The coming clash was with a single Arab tribe who was, perhaps, no match for the Muslims. Success coupled with a large booty were to be expected. The hypocrites felt they had little to lose by joining the Muslim army. Indeed, there was the opportunity of sharing the booty if they went.

The other reason was perhaps in the minds of the hypocrites' leaders who were always looking out for an opportunity to undermine the Muslims. Such an opportunity might well arise in an expedition of this sort. Moreover, by joining the Muslim army, the hypocrites would reduce their alienation from the Muslim community. Many of them who were not known to be hypocrites felt that they would allay any suspicion about their sincerity by joining the army. This would help them even more in their plotting against Islam.

The Muslim army marched until they reached a spring called al-Maraysīʿ where al-Ḥārith and his men had gathered. There are two different reports of the events that took place. The first account, which is perhaps less authentic, speaks of the Prophet asking his companion ʿUmar ibn al-Khaṭṭāb to call on the people of al-Muṣṭalaq to accept Islam. He stood out and shouted to them asking them to declare that they believed in God as the only deity; then they would be safe, and their property would be untouched. They declined the offer and both sides started to aim their arrows against each other. After a while the Prophet ordered his companions to go on the attack. In no time they overwhelmed their enemies, who surrendered *en masse* after ten of their number had been killed. Only one Muslim soldier was killed by mistake. Thus the whole tribe, with all its belongings, was taken over by the Muslims.

The other account – which, on balance, seems to be more accurate – suggests that the Muslims took their enemies by surprise when they were camping close to the spring. The two armies moved towards each other but little or no fighting took place. Victory was soon assured to the Muslims. Whichever account was true there was no doubt about the results of the expedition: the whole tribe had fallen prisoner to the Muslims.[1]

We need to explain here that although the Prophet often used the element of surprise in his battles with the unbelievers, never did he launch a surprise attack, moving with a full military force against people who were unprepared for war. This sort of surprise known in old and modern warfare was never part of his tactics. What he did was to move swiftly and face his enemies before they have completed their preparations. His presence, with his fighting force, would be sudden so as to bring the fear factor into the confrontation. His enemies would be hesitant, unsure whether to fight or to lay down their arms. We will see his tactics in their clearest example at the time when he moved to take over Makkah [Chapter 34]. The people of Makkah found the Muslim army at their doorstep when they were least prepared for a battle, although they had violated their peace agreement with the Prophet and were guilty of blatant aggression. However, when the Prophet was very close and darkness had fallen, he ordered that every soldier in the army should light up a fire. Upon noting the large number of fires, and believing the Muslim force to be even larger than it really was, the Quraysh leaders were convinced that they were no match for the Muslim force. They were willing to accept the Prophet's terms. Thus, we see that the Prophet used the surprise factor in order to reduce the possibility of war and bloodshed.

According to the traditions which prevailed at that time both in Arabia and outside, prisoners of war became slaves. This applied both to men and women. Two hundred families of al-Muṣṭalaq faced slavery as a result of their ill-considered plan to attack the Muslims. It should be emphasized here that such a prospect was not as terrible as one may think today. Slaves in the Muslim state enjoyed all their human rights as fellow human beings to their masters. This was true only in the land of Islam. Islam treats every individual as a human being who is susceptible to be a good servant of God. Hence no one is despised or looked down upon simply because he lacks in fortune or is in bad circumstances.

Freeing a Whole Tribe

The Prophet, however, did not like this prospect for his vanquished enemies. His primary thoughts did not follow the tendencies of kings and emperors. First and foremost, he was a Messenger of God whose task was to save mankind from subjugation to false gods. He did not view the material wealth of the Muslim community as his top priority. He realized that an act of kindness might win over the hearts of yesterday's enemy.

Yet the Prophet could not enact special legislation for the tribe of al-Muṣṭalaq. As long as slavery was an international practice, the Muslims could not abolish it unilaterally. If any Muslims were ever taken prisoners in a battle, they would have been enslaved by their enemies. Hence enemy prisoners had to be treated likewise. Yet the situation called for immediate action to help al-Muṣṭalaq people before it was too late.

The Prophet played a master stroke which brought about the desired result without any adverse repercussions. Among the women taken prisoner was Barrah, daughter of al-Ḥārith, chief of al-Muṣṭalaq. The Prophet took her for himself, granted her freedom from slavery and proposed to her. When she accepted, he married her and renamed her Juwayriyyah. When the Muslims realized what the Prophet had done, they felt that they could not keep the people of al-Muṣṭalaq as their slaves. The whole tribe were considered relatives of the Prophet now that he had married one of their women. This is in keeping with the tribal traditions of Arabia. So all the Muslims who had slaves from al-Muṣṭalaq voluntarily set them free. The Muslims loved the Prophet more than they loved themselves, therefore it was natural that they did not like to have his relatives as their slaves. Thus Juwayriyyah was celebrated by her tribe as a woman of unparalleled blessing. She was the cause of their change of fortunes from slavery to freedom. Shortly afterwards, many of them embraced Islam.[2]

It is tempting to explain most of the Prophet's marriages in terms of the political, social or religious aims which attended each one of them. One must be wary, however, of oversimplifying matters, seeking justification for things which one should accept without too much worry. The Prophet was allowed by God to marry as many women as he wished. If he therefore availed himself of this permission for no reason other than that for which people normally get married, this should be an absolutely satisfactory explanation. The fact that he made use of this concession in order to achieve beneficial results for Islam and for the Muslim community increases one's love and respect for him. One need not unduly bother with what he did in this connection. Sufficient is the fact that this permission was given to him by God and that he, God's Messenger, could judge best when to use this concession.

It was indeed a splendid victory that the Muslims achieved in the expedition of al-Muṣṭalaq. They had every reason to be satisfied with their achievement. Not only did they score a total victory, they also made considerable financial gains in addition to the most important gain of all: that a large number of their former enemies became their friends and brethren in faith. Yet it was only natural that the large number of hypocrites who joined the Muslim army in this instance should do everything possible to mar that victory and spoil the Muslims' achievements. Two incidents which took place after the Muslims had scored their success were exploited by the hypocrites to the detriment of the Muslims.

Stirring Up Trouble

The first incident took place when the Muslims were still encamping at the spring which provided the stage for their battle. Servants were taking horses to the water to drink. Among them was Jahjāh, 'Umar ibn al-Khaṭṭāb's servant. Apparently, there was some scrambling at the water among the servants. Jahjāh clashed with an 'ally' of the Khazraj, named Sinān ibn Wabr. Neither man seemed to be endowed with much wisdom: punches were exchanged and each appealed to his 'group' for help. Jahjāh called on the Muhājirīn to defend him, while Sinān called on the Anṣār.[3] Perhaps one should emphasize here that these two noble groups of Muslims did not feel themselves to be two separate communities. Indeed, they were on the best of terms. Their mutual kindness and care for each other were exemplary. One must not forget, however, that Islam in Madinah was still in its early days. These events we are relating here took place in the fifth year of the Prophet's emigration to Madinah. It is well known that old loyalties die hard. Despite the great and highly successful efforts the Prophet had made to make all Muslims feel themselves to be a single community, regardless of their tribal or national allegiances, it was not to be expected that age-long values and traditions could be forgotten overnight. Tribal values meant that any member of a tribe who found himself in a position of difficulty was defended by the whole tribe before anyone could determine whether he was at fault or not. Their maxim was: "Support your brother, whether he is right or wrong." Hence it was not surprising that some individuals hastened to the combatants' rescue.

The Prophet was informed of what was happening. He felt very angry that the Muslims should stand against one another. He went out quickly to the spring where the event was taking place. Speaking strongly to the Muslims, he enquired: "How come you are invoking the loyalties of ignorance." He calmed the two sides and told them plainly that the loyalties they were invoking – tribal and national loyalties – were unworthy of them. They must abandon such ties because they were alien to Islamic values. He described such loyalties as 'stinking' and ordered the Muslims to abandon them altogether.

It is indeed worth noting that the Prophet moved quickly to stamp out any tribal or communal division among the Muslims. Indeed, he feared nothing more than internal division in his newly formed community. This should serve as a reminder to all Muslims that their differences should at no time cause a split into separate camps which are hostile to each other, when the bond of Islam exists between them all. Muslims may have different points of view, but such differences must not be allowed to alienate any group of them from the other. They must always feel that any Muslim remains a brother with whom they have the strongest of ties. The Muslim community must always remain a single, united community, with mutual love and compassion prevailing among all its members.

The incident at the spring provided the hypocrites with a golden opportunity to fish in troubled waters. ʿAbdullāh ibn Ubayy, their leader, tried hard to stir up the trouble which subsided after the Prophet's intervention. Since he still enjoyed a position of honour among most of his people who were not aware that the man was a hypocrite, he tried to play on their emotions. To his own circle he said: "I have never known such humiliation as has befallen us today. They [the Muhājirīn] are now standing up to us in our own home town. They are ungrateful to us for our favours. Our case with the refugees of the Quraysh is an apt example of the proverb: 'Fatten your dog and he will eat you.' When we go back to Madinah the honourable among the two of us will certainly chase the humble out of it." He then reproached his people for their hospitality which they had shown to the Muhājirīn:

> You have only yourselves to blame for all this. You have taken them into your own homes and given them your own money until they have become rich. I swear that if you stop helping them with what you have, they will leave you and go elsewhere. Yet you are not satisfied with all the hospitality you have given. You have exposed yourselves to danger, and you have had your men fight and die in their defence. You have made your children orphans. You have decreased your numbers while they are on the increase. I counsel you not to spend any more money to help them until you see them depart.

While making his remarks, ʿAbdullāh ibn Ubayy took little notice of the presence of a boy of about 14. This boy, Zaid ibn Arqam, went straight to the Prophet, who was attended by a number of his companions from both the Muhājirīn and the Anṣār. Zaid recounted to the Prophet all that he had heard from ʿAbdullāh ibn Ubayy. The Prophet felt hurt and his face changed colour. However, he did not want to act on the report of a boy before he made certain that the report was true. He said to Zaid: "Do you have any reason to be angry with him?" Zaid said: "I swear that I have heard that from him." The Prophet asked him again: "Maybe you did not hear properly?" Zaid answered that there was no chance of that. The Prophet again asked: "Maybe you thought you had heard him saying that?" Zaid answered again: "I swear by God that I have heard all that from him, Messenger of God."

Dealing with Strife

It was then clear to the Prophet, and to those of his companions who were present, that ʿAbdullāh ibn Ubayy was correctly quoted. ʿUmar ibn al-Khaṭṭāb suggested that the Prophet should command ʿAbbād ibn Bishr to kill ʿAbdullāh ibn Ubayy. The Prophet said: "How would you like it, ʿUmar, if people started to say that Muhammad is killing his companions? Indeed, I shall not do that. However, give orders to depart now."

ʿAbdullāh ibn Ubayy learnt that the Prophet had been told what he had said. He therefore hastened to him and denied any knowledge of what had been attributed to him. He swore by God that he did not say anything of the sort. Those of the Prophet's companions who were present tried to pacify matters. They were still keen that ʿAbdullāh ibn Ubayy should be given his chance to accept Islam. After all, he had been well respected among his people before the advent of Islam. They suggested to the Prophet that Zaid ibn Arqam might have misquoted or misheard ʿAbdullāh. The Prophet said nothing.

When the orders were given to march, Usayd ibn Ḥuḍayr, a prominent figure among the Anṣār, came to the Prophet, greeted him with the respect due to him as Messenger of God and said: "Prophet, I see that you are marching at a time of day when you used not to march." The Prophet said to him: "Have you not heard what your friend said?" When Usayd asked for details, the Prophet told him that ʿAbdullāh ibn Ubayy had said that "the honourable among the two of us will chase the humble out of Madinah." Usayd said: "Yes indeed, Messenger of God. You can turn him out of Madinah if you like. You are the honourable and he is the humble." Usayd then pleaded clemency and told the Prophet: "God has sent you to us when his people were preparing to crown him king. He may think that you have robbed him of his kingdom."

The Prophet marched at the head of the Muslims for the rest of the day and throughout the night, and continued marching until mid-morning, when it was burning hot. He then allowed his companions to stop. Hardly had they sat down when they all fell asleep. This the Prophet did in order that people would not be preoccupied with what ʿAbdullāh ibn Ubayy had said.[4]

The Prophet realized that those evil comments might cause strife within the ranks of the Muslims. He felt that if he tired the Muslims out by marching most of the time and taking as little rest as possible, the whole episode might be forgotten before the army had reached Madinah. Hence, haste and speed were the marks of the Muslims' return from their successful expedition against the tribe of al-Muṣṭalaq.

Shortly afterwards, the *sūrah* entitled *al-Munāfiqūn*, or The Hypocrites, was revealed. It describes the hypocrites and their feelings towards the Muslims and it also states the very words said by ʿAbdullāh ibn Ubayy and conveyed to the Prophet by Zaid ibn Arqam. There was no longer any doubt as to the accuracy of Zaid's report. The Prophet held Zaid's ear in his hand and said: "This is the one who made good use of his ear for the sake of God."[5]

A Son's Agony

ʿAbdullāh ibn Ubayy had a son whose name was also ʿAbdullāh. Unlike his father, ʿAbdullāh was a good believer who entertained no doubt about the truthfulness of Muhammad's message. Indeed, the Prophet was so certain of ʿAbdullāh's strong faith that he appointed him to deputize for him in his absence when the Prophet headed the Muslim army on their final expedition to Badr. Moreover, ʿAbdullāh was a dutiful son to his father. It was a cause of distress to him that his father acted against the Prophet. He would have done anything to bring his father within the Muslim fold. When he heard that his father had uttered those wicked comments against the Prophet and the Muhājirīn he realized that this crime was a capital one. He also learnt that some of the companions of the Prophet had counselled him to get rid of ʿAbdullāh ibn Ubayy. ʿAbdullāh, the son, went to the Prophet and spoke to him:

> Messenger of God, I have heard that you intend to kill ʿAbdullāh ibn Ubayy for what was reported to you as his words. If you must kill him, then you have only to command me and I will bring you his head. The tribe of al-Khazraj [his own tribe] is fully aware that I am its most dutiful son to his father. However, I fear that if you order someone else to kill him, I may not be able to look at my father's killer walking in the street. I may be moved to kill him. If I do so, I would be killing a believer in revenge for an unbeliever. Hell would then be my doom.

The Prophet smiled and calmed him down. He said to ʿAbdullāh: "We will be kind to him and treat him well as long as he is with us."[6]

This event and the following one, in which ʿAbdullāh ibn Ubayy took the leading part, were enough to make every Muslim aware of his true position towards Islam. ʿAbdullāh remained in Madinah and he never lost an opportunity to speak ill of Islam and the Prophet. His credibility, however, was eroded. Whenever he said or did something, his own people were the first to take issue with him and remonstrate with him, trying to make him see his error. When this was apparent, the Prophet said to ʿUmar ibn al-Khaṭṭāb, the first to suggest that ʿAbdullāh ibn Ubayy should be killed: "Now do you see, ʿUmar? Had I killed him when you suggested that to me, some people would have been very angry, while they themselves would be prepared to kill him now if I would only order them to do so." ʿUmar replied: "I certainly know that God's Messenger knows better than I do and his actions are more blessed than mine."[7]

The Wicked Designs of Hypocrisy

A brief reference has already been made to another incident which the hypocrites tried to exploit to the detriment of the Muslims, during the expedition of al-Muṣṭalaq. Perhaps it was the Muslims' hurried return which gave rise to this incident. It has already been mentioned that the Prophet used to have one of his wives with him whenever he travelled. The choice was decided by toss between them. It was ʿĀ'ishah who joined the Prophet on al-Muṣṭalaq expedition. The second incident involved the spread of rumours accusing ʿĀ'ishah of adultery. It shall be seen in the course of this narrative that this accusation cannot stand even the most casual examination. It is in the nature of hypocrisy, however, to utilize any incident, or any circumstantial evidence, for ulterior motives. One has seen how ʿAbdullāh ibn Ubayy came to the Prophet and swore by God that he did not say what he actually did. There exists not only the testimony of Zayd ibn Arqam to prove that ʿAbdullāh ibn Ubayy uttered his evil comments: "When we go back to Madinah the honourable among the two of us will certainly chase the humble out of it", and "I counsel you not to spend any more money to help them until you see them depart." God Himself tells us that the hypocrite did say these very words. Yet had ʿAbdullāh ibn Ubayy recognized his error, and had he repented saying those words and sought forgiveness, he would have been received by the Prophet with open arms. God would have forgiven him if he was sincere. But the man was not to be won over by kindness. The Prophet's policy was to show him all the kindness he could, yet ʿAbdullāh ibn Ubayy could only sink to a new low in his wicked attempts to undermine Islam. He was so different as an enemy of Islam from a man like Abū Jahl, the arch enemy of the Muslims in Makkah. Abū Jahl's hostility was open: he held his sword in his hand and fought as hard as he could; he carried his tribe with him from one determined attempt to crush Islam to another, until he was killed at Badr. ʿAbdullāh ibn Ubayy, on the other hand, was like a snake creeping stealthily to bite and inject his poison while maintaining a smooth appearance, pretending that he was a Muslim.

Yet ʿAbdullāh was too clever to be caught. After all, how can you catch a man of honour lying when he can easily deny under oath what he had said a moment earlier?

Nevertheless, a man like ʿAbdullāh ibn Ubayy could not have let the opportunity which presented itself go without utilizing it fully for his wicked ends. He sought to undermine the Prophet's own family life. From his own point of view, thinking in terms of this world and having all sorts of doubt about the truthfulness of the Prophet, he saw that the ultimate prize was within his reach. Abū Bakr, ʿĀ'ishah's father, was the Prophet's closest friend and companion. Their friendship dated back to their childhood. If ʿAbdullāh ibn Ubayy could make the accusation of adultery against ʿĀ'ishah stick – and he saw no reason why it should not – that firm friendship between the Prophet and Abū Bakr, which was a source of strength to the Muslim community ever since the Prophet had received God's message, would collapse. Moreover, the Muslim community would sink into confusion and distress.

Before reporting the details of this singular event, it would be useful to remember that every event in the life of the Prophet must be studied carefully in order to learn how to respond should one find oneself in similar circumstances. That the Prophet's own wife should stand accused of one of the gravest sins should provide a clear lesson on what to expect from the hypocrites. While reading the details of this remarkable event one should bear in mind that any Muslim might face any type of false accusation. Before rushing to condemn him or her, one should reflect upon what would have happened if the Prophet's wife had been hastily condemned by those who heard the hypocrites' accusations against her.

The False Story

"The Story of Falsehood" is the name given by God in the Qur'ān to the accusation made by the hypocrites against ʿĀ'ishah. Perhaps the most comprehensive view of this story can be gained through ʿĀ'ishah's own account of it:

> Every time the Prophet went abroad he made a toss among his wives to decide which of them should accompany him. At the time of al-Muṣṭalaq expedition, the toss favoured me and I travelled with him. At the time, women did not eat much, which meant that they were slim and light. When my transport was prepared for me, I would sit in my howdah which would

then be lifted onto the camel's back. When they had secured it, the camel driver would march with it.

When the Prophet had done his business on that expedition and was on his way back, he encamped one night at a spot not very far from Madinah. He stayed there only part of the night before the call to march was again made. People started to get ready and in the meantime I went out to relieve myself. I was wearing a necklace, and I did not feel it drop off me before I returned. Back in the camp I felt for my necklace and, realizing that it was gone, I looked for it there, but could not find it. People were just about to move. I therefore went quickly back to that particular spot and searched for my necklace until I found it.

In the meantime, the people who prepared my camel finished their task and took up the howdah, thinking that I was inside, and lifted it onto the camel's back and secured it. It did not occur to them that I was not inside. They therefore led the camel away. When I came back to where we had encamped, there was no one to be seen. The army had marched. I, therefore, tied my dress round my body and lay down. I realized that when I was missed, someone would come back for me. I soon fell asleep.

Ṣafwān ibn al-Muʿaṭṭal of the tribe of Sulaym was travelling behind the army. He was apparently delayed by some business and did not spend that night in the camp. When he noticed someone lying down, he came towards me. He recognized me since he used to see me before we were ordered to wear veils. He said: *Innā lillāhi wa innā ilayhi rājiʿūn*, "We all belong to God and to Him we shall return." I woke up when I heard him. I did not answer him when he asked me why I had been left behind. However, he made his camel sit down and asked me to ride it, which I did. He led the camel seeking to catch up with the army. Nobody missed me before they had stopped to rest. When everybody had sat down to relax, Ṣafwān appeared, leading his camel, on which I was riding. This prompted those people to invent the story of falsehood. The whole army was troubled with it, but I heard nothing.[8]

It is worth noting here that when ʿAbdullāh ibn Ubayy saw ʿĀ'ishah approaching, he enquired who she was. When he was told that she was ʿĀ'ishah, he said: "Your Prophet's wife has spent the whole night with a man, and now she turns up with him leading her camel!" This statement gave rise to the falsehood that was spread about ʿĀ'ishah. ʿĀ'ishah's narrative continues:

> Shortly after our arrival in Madinah, I felt very ill. Nobody told me anything about what was going on. The Prophet and my parents heard the story, but they did not mention anything to me. However, I felt that the Prophet was not as kind to me during this illness of mine as he used to be. When he came in, he would ask my mother who was nursing me: "How is that woman of yours?" He said nothing else. I was distressed and requested his permission to be nursed in my parents' home. He agreed. I went there and heard nothing. I was ill for 20-odd nights before I began to get better.
>
> Unlike other people, we, the Arabs, did not have toilets in our homes. To us, they were disgusting. What we used to do was to go out at night, somewhere outside Madinah where we would relieve ourselves. Women went only at night. One night I went out with Umm Misṭaḥ [Abū Bakr's cousin]. While we were walking, she was tripped by her own dress and fell down. As she did so, she said: "Confound Misṭaḥ' to her own son.
>
> I said: "Improper indeed is what you have said about a man of the Muhājirīn who fought at Badr." She asked me: "Have you not heard the story then?"
>
> When I asked her what story, she recounted to me what the people of falsehood said about me. I swear I could not relieve myself that night. I went back and cried bitterly until I felt that crying would break me down. I said to my mother: "May God forgive you. People said what they said about me, and you mentioned nothing to me."
>
> My mother said: "Calm down, child. Any pretty woman married to a man who loves her will always be envied, especially if she shares him with other wives."

I said: "Glory be to God. That people should repeat this sort of thing!" I cried bitterly throughout that night till morning, without a moment's sleep.

The Prophet called ʿAlī ibn Abū Ṭālib and Usāmah ibn Zaid to consult them about divorcing me. Usāmah, who felt that I was innocent, said: "Messenger of God, she is your wife and you have experienced nothing bad from her. This story is a blatant lie."

ʿAlī said: "Messenger of God, God imposed no restriction on you in matrimonial matters. There are many women besides her. If you would see fit to ask her maid, she would tell you the truth." The Prophet called in my maid, Barīrah, and asked her whether she had seen anything suspicious. Barīrah said: "By Him who sent you with the message of truth, there is nothing I take against her other than, being so young, she would doze off and let the hens eat the dough I had made to bake."

The Prophet addressed the Muslims in the mosque when I was still unaware of the whole matter. He said: "I have seen nothing evil from my wife. Those people are also involving a man from whom I have seen no evil. He never entered my wives' rooms except in my presence.

Saʿd ibn Muʿādh, the Aws leader, said: "Messenger of God, if these men belong to the Aws, our tribe, we will spare you their trouble. If, on the other hand, they belong to our brethren the Khazraj, you have only to give us your command."

Saʿd ibn ʿUbādah, the leader of the Khazraj, who enjoyed a good reputation, allowed his tribal feelings to get the better of him this time and said to Saʿd ibn Muʿādh: "By God, you shall not kill them. You are saying this only because you know that they are of the Khazraj."

Usayd ibn Ḥuḍayr, a cousin of Saʿd ibn Muʿādh, said to Saʿd ibn ʿUbādah: "You are no more than a hypocrite defending other hypocrites." People who belonged to both tribes were very angry and were about to fight. The Prophet was still on the pulpit and he tried hard to cool them down, until finally he succeeded.

I continued to cry for the rest of the day. I could not sleep. Next morning both my parents were with me – I had spent two nights and a day crying hard. My tears never stopped. Both of them felt that my crying would break my heart. While we were in that condition, a woman from the Anṣār came to me and started to cry with me.

Shortly afterwards the Prophet came and sat down. He had not sat in my room ever since the rumour started. For a whole month he received no revelations concerning me. When he sat down, he praised and glorified God before going on to say: ʿĀ'ishah. People have been talking as you are now well aware. If you are innocent, God will make your innocence known. If, however, you have committed a sin, then you should seek God's forgiveness and repent. If a servant of God admits her sin and repents, God will forgive her."

When the Prophet finished, my tears dried up completely and I turned to my father and said: "Answer the Prophet." He said: "By God, I do not know what to say to God's Messenger, peace be on him."

I then said to my mother: "Answer the Prophet." She said: "I do not know what to say to God's Messenger, peace be upon him."

I was still a young girl, and I did not read much of the Qur'ān. However, I said: "I know that you all have heard this story repeated again and again until you now believe it. If I tell you that I am innocent, and God knows that I am, you will not believe me. If, on the other hand, I admit something when God knows that I am innocent of it, you will believe me. I know no comparable situation to yours except that of Joseph's father (I tried to remember Jacob's name but I could not) when he said: 'I will be calmly patient and I will seek God's help against your claims.'" I then turned round and lay on my bed. I knew that I was innocent and that God would make my innocence known. It did not occur to me for a moment, however, that God would reveal a passage of the Qur'ān concerning me. I felt myself too humble for God to include my case in His revelations. All I hoped for was that the Prophet should see something in his dream to prove my innocence. Before the Prophet left us, however, and before anyone left the house, God's revelations started. The Prophet was covered with his own robe, and a pillow was placed under his head. When I saw that, I felt no worry or fear. I was certain of my innocence, and I knew that God, limitless as He is in His glory, would not be unjust to me. As for my parents – well, by Him Who holds ʿĀ'ishah's soul in His hand, while they waited for the Prophet to come back to himself, they could have died for fear that Divine revelations might confirm what people said. Then it was all over. The Prophet sat up, with his sweat looking like pearls on a wet day. As he wiped his forehead, he said: "ʿĀ'ishah, I have good news for you. God has declared your innocence." I said: "Praise be to God."

The Prophet then went out and spoke to people, and recited to them the Qur'ānic revelations he had received concerning the matter.[9]

First Impressions

There is no doubt that the story of falsehood had far-reaching effects on the life of the Muslim community generally and, for a certain period of time, on the Prophet's own family life. Honour was of paramount importance to all Arabs, even before the advent of Islam. Islam places very high importance on chastity for both men and women. Fornication and adultery are grave crimes which merit very severe punishments. Adultery, in particular, is punishable by death when proven by a clear testimony of four witnesses or free confession. For the Prophet's own family to be subjected to such rumours was therefore very disturbing to him personally and to all those who believed in him as God's Messenger. It was incomprehensible to them that God would allow the Prophet's own honour, and that of his beloved wife, to be the subject of wanton conversations by hypocrites and other enemies of Islam.

The Prophet, however, conducted himself with the sort of dignity which only a Prophet could show. He did not hold his wife guilty of anything while he had no proof of her guilt or innocence. He continued to care for her and to enquire after her when she was ill. Not a word did he say to her which suggested that he believed anything he heard. Nor did he speak to Ṣafwān, the man who was accused of being her lover, in any way which suggested that he held him responsible for anything in the absence of any clear evidence. When the Prophet spoke to the people in order to make his feelings clear, he said: "I have seen nothing evil from my wife. Those people are also involving a man from whom I have seen no evil. He never entered my wives' rooms except in my presence." The Prophet, then, did not have any intention of judging anyone except on the basis of clear evidence. Lacking that, he was prepared to wait until God had given him guidance on what to do, leaving those people, in the meantime, to say what they wanted to say. To him, libel of this sort was something he had to bear as part of his sacrifice for the fulfilment of his mission.

When one considers this story, it takes no time to come to the conclusion that a small incident was blown up out of all proportion. ʿĀ'ishah's delay was caused by her search for her necklace. It is only natural that her jewellery should be very important for any young wife, especially when her husband, the Prophet, has other wives and she is his favourite among them. Again, it was only natural that she would be found by one of the men who were given the task of picking up anything that was left by the army where they had encamped. When Ṣafwān found her, he did his duty by letting her ride the camel and leading her until they caught up with the army. There was nothing else he could or should have done. This was all that happened. It should have raised no doubt in anybody's mind. After all, ʿĀ'ishah was not the first woman to miss her travelling company. This happens every day, throughout the world, as long as people travel in groups. Moreover, there was nothing so peculiar about a woman on the back of a camel, being led by a man. A few years earlier, Umm Salamah, whom the Prophet was later to marry, left Makkah alone with her young child to emigrate to Madinah in response to the Prophet's invitation to the Muslims of Makkah. On her way, she was met by a man who was an unbeliever. This man, ʿUthmān ibn Ṭalḥah, felt that he could not leave a woman to travel such a long distance (500 kilometres) in the desert on her own. He escorted her for the rest of her journey. She said later that his behaviour was exemplary.[10] No one at the time ever raised any doubt as to the conduct of either ʿUthmān or Umm Salamah, despite the fact that he was not a Muslim. Indeed, he was still an enemy of Islam. Everybody understood that ʿUthmān's noble attitude was motivated by Arabian traditions which required a man to protect a woman travelling on her own in the desert.

Comparing these two incidents, one finds great similarity between them. That one of them should raise such false rumours while the other did not seems surprising. After all, the second incident – that is, the one involving ʿĀ'ishah – should have given no reason for raising any doubts or spreading any rumours. The man involved, Ṣafwān, was a very good Muslim, famed for his honesty and integrity. Islam is a religion of very serious morality, and all Muslims observe the Islamic standards. Besides, no one, however negligent of his moral duties, could have thought of the Prophet's own wife as someone to respond to promiscuous overtures. ʿĀ'ishah was of a family which enjoyed an unblemished reputation, even before the advent of Islam. The family had enjoyed even greater respect since. Married to the Prophet, she could not have entertained the slightest thought of infidelity.

Self-Evident Falsehood

Moreover, the accusation levelled at ʿĀ'ishah and Ṣafwān is self-refuting. Had there been any truth in it (God forbid), ʿĀ'ishah and Ṣafwān would have tried to hide their guilt. They would have not come in the open to join the army, as soon as they could, in broad daylight. It is in women's nature that even those who are promiscuous try to maintain an appearance of decency in public. ʿĀ'ishah was the only woman travelling with the army. Had she entertained any thought of guilt, she would not have appeared with her companion as she did. She would have at least tried to slip into her howdah unnoticed. But neither she nor her companion thought of that, because they had nothing to hide. Besides, even if she did not care for appearances, she would have been deterred by the severity of punishment which awaited her, if her guilt was proven. As already stated, in Islam, adultery is punishable by death. Moreover, the Prophet's wives enjoyed a special status. They were doubly rewarded for their good actions while their grave sins, if any, incurred double punishment (*Sūrah* 33, verses 30-31).

One should not be surprised that ʿĀ'ishah missed the returning army. The Prophet marched at high speed, allowing his companions little rest in order to divert their attention from the incident which had taken place earlier. He deliberately tired them out on their way home so that they had no chance to discuss that unfortunate incident, which the Prophet viewed with the utmost seriousness.

All this makes it absolutely clear that the accusation was false. It was a lie which no person of common sense could believe. It should have been rejected out of hand, even if it was supported by any further evidence. A leading contemporary writer, ʿAbbās al-ʿAqqād, says:

> The accusation is supported by no evidence, circumstantial or otherwise, apart from that ʿĀ'ishah was delayed for a few minutes, when the army moved suddenly, in a journey which was full of surprises with regard to the timings of stops and departures. Such a delay is not enough to raise any suspicion about any woman among the Muslims who were on a campaign of *jihād* with the Prophet. If every woman who was delayed on a journey were suspected of immorality, raising doubts and suspicions about the honour of women would have been the simplest matter.

That, however, is alien to Islamic morality.

The truth is that ʿAbdullāh ibn Ubayy, the hypocrites' leader, was dismayed that his earlier remarks, which he had made in the presence of people whom he thought shared his hypocrisy, were reported to the Prophet by Zaid ibn Arqam. He realized that his position among his people would be jeopardized as a result of those remarks which put him on a course of confrontation with the Prophet, since he classified himself as the honourable of the two of them threatening to oust the Prophet from Madinah, and describing him as 'humble'. This is something no Muslim could tolerate, not even those who still hoped that ʿAbdullāh ibn Ubayy would rid himself of his personal grudges and accept Islam wholeheartedly. When it came to the crunch, Muslims placed much higher importance on their love for the Prophet and their obedience to him. ʿAbdullāh ibn Ubayy realized that although some Muslims who belonged to the Khazraj, his own tribe, still cared for him, there was no doubt that they were prepared to drop all their loyalty to him when that clashed with their loyalty to their new faith. His position, therefore, was much more shaky than before. Having missed his chance to create strife between the Muhājirīn and the Anṣār over the first incident, which was caused by some argument over water, he felt that he now had a chance to raise doubts in the Muslims' minds about the honour of the Prophet and his own standing with God. Failing that, he thought he could create a rift between his own tribe and the rest of the Muslims, if he could play on the tribal loyalties of his own people. These were the motives behind his dirty game. But God would not allow this to happen. He revealed a passage of the Qur'ān, declaring ʿĀ'ishah's innocence and providing guidance to Muslims on how to behave in similar circumstances.

It is therefore abundantly clear that the story of adultery was false from start to finish. It should have been rejected out of hand by all Muslims, even before God declared ʿĀ'ishah's innocence in His revelations in the Qur'ān. Indeed, some Muslims did just that and dismissed the accusation as absolutely false. Khālid ibn Zayd, better known as Abū Ayyūb of the Anṣār, was one such person. His wife spoke to him about the rumours and asked whether he had heard them too. He said: "Yes, indeed. That is a blatant lie. Would you, Umm Ayyūb, have done such a thing?" She replied: "No, by God, I would not do it." He said: "By God, ʿĀ'ishah is better than you." This is indeed the attitude which is praised in the Qur'ān, but more of this later.[11]

Delaying the Declaration of Innocence

The rumours continued to spread for about a month without any counter action by the Prophet or by anyone else. During most of this time, ʿĀ'ishah was very ill: this meant that she could not be told of what people were saying about her. The Prophet was worried by the whole episode and, in the absence of any clear evidence either way, he could not take any action. It is appropriate to reflect here what would have been the attitude of any king, president or head of state in similar circumstances. It is easy to imagine that any king or president at that time would have executed those who spread the rumours and would perhaps have arranged for the disappearance of Ṣafwān. He would undoubtedly have issued a decree forbidding, under penalty of death, any reference to those rumours or to the episode as a whole, whether explicit or otherwise. He would have declared that his wife was above suspicion if he loved her, or might have arranged for her disposal if he did not.

The Prophet, however, was neither king nor president. He was, above all, God's Messenger and he awaited His guidance. This was not given to him for a whole month, during which the Prophet must have felt the agony of any man whose beloved wife stands accused of adultery while he is unable to prove her innocence. The fact that revelations on this matter were not vouchsafed to him for a whole month served more than one purpose. The Prophet trusted in God's wisdom and that He would do to him only what was right and good. He conducted himself with perfect dignity and forbearance until God saw fit to reveal ʿĀ'ishah's innocence. Indeed, the delay added to the strength of her defence. It is also evidence of the truthfulness of Muhammad's message. Had he been a false prophet who invented the Qur'ān, as the unbelievers alleged, he would probably have hastened to fabricate some sort of statement which gave judgement on this matter. Far was it from Prophet Muhammad to do any such thing. What should be emphasized here is that human nature could not, of its own accord, have seen the wisdom for such a delay. When people were speaking ill of the honour of the Prophet, human nature dictated that all those rumours should be stamped out immediately. The Prophet, however, realized that the decision was not his to make.

He waited for guidance. This fits well with the fact that the Prophet did not have any control on matters which affected the Muslim community as a whole, or his own affairs as a human being.

When ʿĀ'ishah's innocence was declared, it was done in the strongest possible way. God revealed a passage of the Qur'ān making her innocence absolutely clear and reproaching the Muslims for entertaining any doubts about her. This passage is contained in *Sūrah* 24, entitled *al-Nūr* or Light (verses 11-20). The *sūrah* opens with an abundantly clear prohibition of all adultery and fornication, followed by an equally firm prohibition of accusing any woman of committing a crime of adultery without producing four witnesses to prove the accusation. Since these rules had been made clear to the Muslims beforehand, they should have required the same evidence when ʿĀ'ishah was accused. The passage which concerns ʿĀ'ishah's innocence opens with a clear-cut statement, describing the rumours as absolutely false, and the whole story as the story of falsehood. It makes it clear that the story was fabricated by a group who wanted to cause the Muslims considerable damage, but God wants to turn it to their benefit. The fabricators would receive their due punishment, especially the arch-villain, who would receive 'grave suffering'.

The Qur'ān then teaches the Muslims a lesson and educates them in how to behave in similar circumstances. It is proper for the Muslims to think well of their brothers and sisters. They must not believe anyone who whispers in their ears with such rumours unless he supports them with clear evidence which leaves no room for doubt. If Muslims fail to do that, then they participate in spreading a blatant falsehood, the aim of which is to cause damage to the whole Muslim community. The Qur'ān warns the Muslims against ever making the same mistake. In no circumstances are they allowed to take an attitude which helps spread promiscuity in their society. It reminds them of God's grace when He has guided them to adopt the right faith. Indeed, their action of not having rejected those rumours out of hand made them liable to God's punishment, if it was not for His grace and mercy and forgiveness.

A religion like Islam, which is characterized by its serious attitude to morality, could allow no room for making the honour of innocent women the subject of idle talk. To accuse any woman of adultery without providing clear evidence of her guilt is in itself a serious crime which merits severe punishment. The Qur'ān states that those who spread such rumours without producing four witnesses to testify that they have seen the crime of adultery being committed with their own eyes, are to be punished by flogging (80 lashes) and that they are not to be accepted as witnesses in a court of law, unless they repent and prove their good conduct in future. Accusation of adultery is viewed so seriously by Islam, because it is easy to indulge in such idle talk. Unless deterred by faith, people find such gossip interesting. Hence, the Qur'ānic warnings against it are plain, firm and decisive.

The End of the Story

When God's ruling was made clear, the Prophet ordered the punishment for falsely accusing a Muslim woman of adultery to be inflicted on three people: Misṭaḥ ibn Athāthah, Hassān ibn Thābit and Ḥamnah bint Jaḥsh. Those three repeated the accusations in plain terms. Others who did not speak so plainly were forgiven. ʿAbdullāh ibn Ubayy managed to escape unscathed: he was too clever to allow himself to be taken in such a manner. His role, however, was known to everyone and he lost all his people's respect.

It is worth pointing out that Ḥamnah's participation in these rumours was motivated by jealousy. Her sister, Zaynab bint Jaḥsh, was married to the Prophet. Zaynab and ʿĀ'ishah competed for the Prophet's love ahead of the rest of his wives. When the Prophet asked Zaynab whether she had seen or heard anything suspicious of ʿĀ'ishah, she said: "Messenger of God, I would rather protect my eyes and ears. I have seen nothing but good from ʿĀ'ishah."[12] Her sister, Ḥamnah, went too far in pleading Zaynab's case for the Prophet's favours, and this led her to slip. Misṭaḥ, a relative of Abū Bakr, ʿĀ'ishah's father, depended on Abū Bakr's charity to meet his own expenses. This, however, did not deter him from repeating the rumours like a parrot. Yet the man was of good character and he had fought at Badr. Abū Bakr was annoyed with Misṭaḥ and decided not to support him any longer. In the following verses of the same *sūrah*, however, God directs the believers not to let their own personal feelings get the better of them. It is better for them to continue to support their brethren, even if those brethren are sometimes rash in their behaviour. God asks of these believers: "Do you not love that God should forgive you?" (24: 22) Abū Bakr said when he heard this verse: "I indeed love that God forgives me." And he continued to support Misṭaḥ.[13]

The fact that such companions of the Prophet took part in these rumours proves that even Muslims of good conduct may slip and make mistakes. If they do, they are supposed to repent and ask God's forgiveness. If their mistakes are punishable by a specified punishment and that punishment is inflicted on them, it atones for their mistakes. If they are not punished, the matter is left to God, Who may either forgive them or punish them in the hereafter for their mistakes.

Notes

1. Ibn Hishām, *al-Sīrah al-Nabawiyyah*, Dār al-Qalam, Beirut, Vol. 1, p. 302. Also, Ibn Sayyid al-Nās, *'Uyūn al-Athar*, Dār al-Turāth, Madinah, 1996, pp. 134-135; and Ibn Kathīr, *al-Bidāyah wal-Nihāyah*, Maktabat al-Ma'ārif, Beirut, Vol. 1, p. 156.
2. Ibn Hishām, op.cit., pp. 307-308. Also, Ibn Sayyid al-Nās, op.cit., p. 138.
3. Ibn Hishām, op.cit., p. 303. Also, Ibn Sayyid al-Nās, op.cit., p. 136; and Ibn Kathīr, op.cit., p. 157.
4. Ibn Hishām, op.cit., pp. 303-304. Also, Ibn Sayyid al-Nās, op.cit., pp. 136-138.
5. Ibn Hishām, op.cit., p. 305.
6. Ibid. Also, Ibn Sayyid al-Nās, op.cit., p. 137.
7. Ibn Hishām, op.cit., p. 305.
8. Ibid., pp. 310-311. Also, Ibn Sayyid al-Nās, op.cit., pp. 139-140.
9. Ibn Hishām, op.cit., pp. 311-315. Also, Ibn Kathīr, op.cit., pp. 161-162; and Ibn Sayyid al-Nās, op.cit., pp. 140-143.
10. Ibn Hishām, op.cit., Vol. 2., p. 113.
11. Ibn Hishām, op.cit., p. 315.
12. Ibid., pp. 312-313.
13. Ibid., p. 316.

25

A Fresh Storm Gathers

THERE WAS NO mistaking the fact that the Muslim state in Madinah had considerably consolidated its position in Arabia. Under the Prophet's leadership, the Muslims were able to score several successes which put them in an even stronger position than they had been in after their remarkable victory at Badr. If the defeat at Uḥud tempted some tribes to mount raids on groups of Muslims or try to trap them in a hopeless position, no one could any longer think of anything similar to al-Rajīʿ or B'ir Maʿūnah. Indeed, neither the Quraysh nor the Jews felt that they could score a victory in an open battle against the Muslims, similar to the Quraysh's victory at Uḥud, if they were to fight on their own. Both the Quraysh and the Jews, however, could only grow more bitter as they realized that Islam was getting stronger every day.

There were certain circumstances which indicated that a new major encounter between the Muslims and their enemies was bound to come soon. One such factor was that the Quraysh had to justify itself for not turning up for its appointment with the Muslims by planning a new attack on them. The Jews of al-Naḍīr, however, were the first to realize that the only chance of suppressing Islam was for its enemies to join forces in a consolidated attack which would wipe out the

Muslims altogether. A group of the leaders of al-Naḍīr tribe, including Sallām ibn Mishkam ibn Abī al-Ḥuqayq, his cousin Kinānah ibn al-Rabīʿ ibn Abī al-Ḥuqayq and Ḥuyayy ibn Akhṭab, as well as Hawthah ibn Qays and Abū ʿAmmār of the Jewish tribe of Wā'il, went out of Khaybar where the al-Naḍīr had settled, to try to forge an alliance with the Quraysh and other enemies of Islam.

The group went first to the Quraysh and proposed an alliance which would have the sole purpose of annihilating the Muslims. They told them: "We will fight alongside you until we exterminate Muhammad and his men." The Quraysh needed little persuasion to agree to such an alliance; they could lose nothing by it. Besides, they could only increase their own firepower when it came to actual fighting.[1]

Here is a singular incident which cannot be easily justified. Some of the Quraysh leaders were a little hesitant about the whole affair. It may be that when they reviewed their earlier encounters with the Prophet, they realized that they were always the aggressors. Muhammad and his companions were always fighting in defence of their lives and their new religion. They did not try to force their religion on anyone. They simply wanted to be free to convey God's message to people and let them choose whether to accept it or not. Perhaps some of them were having doubts about their own religion of idolatrous worship when they compared it to Islam, which is based on the belief in God's oneness. Hence, the Quraysh leaders addressed the Jewish chiefs, some of whom were Rabbis: "You, the Jewish people, are the people of ancient scriptures. You know our quarrel with Muhammad. We now want to ask you: which is better of the two religions – ours or his?" Unhesitatingly, the Jewish chiefs said to those who worshipped idols: "Your religion is certainly better than his and you are nearer to the truth than he."[2]

How can one explain such a testimony? Obviously, the grudge, bitterness and hostility those Jews felt towards the Prophet and Islam had blinded them totally so as to testify that pagan beliefs and the worship of statues and idols were better than believing in God, the Lord of the Universe, the Creator of all. In so doing, those Jews contravened the very basis of their monotheistic religion, which shared with Islam the belief in God's oneness. The Qur'ān denounces their attitude in strong terms, in verses 51 and 52 of *Sūrah* 4, entitled Women: "Have you not seen those who were given a portion of the Scriptures, and yet they believe in sorcery and digression, and assure the unbelievers that they are better guided than the believers. It is those indeed whom God has rejected. Whomever God has rejected shall have help from no one."

The Quraysh, however, were very happy to receive such a statement from the Jewish leaders and the alliance was thus firmly established.[3]

The Jewish delegation then sought to expand the alliance in order to ensure that in their coming battle the balance would be heavily tilted against the Muslims. They went to the tribe of Ghaṭafān, a major Arab tribe with several clans. They tried to persuade Ghaṭafān to join the alliance and were finally successful when they promised Ghaṭafān their entire date harvest for a whole year after they had achieved their victory against Muhammad. They were also able to enlist the support of other Arab tribes such as Sulaym, Asad, Ashjaʿ and Fazārah. When all these tribes mobilized their forces, they raised a strong army of 10,000 men which marched towards Madinah under the command of Abū Sufyān in the month of Shawwāl in the fifth year of the Prophet's settlement in Madinah (February AD 627).

Defence Plan

When the Prophet received intelligence of the new threat which the Muslims were about to face, he consulted his companions on the best way to defend Madinah against the attackers. Realizing that his companions were no match for the large army of their enemies, the Prophet felt that he had no choice but to adopt a defensive plan. Most reports suggest that it was Salmān, the Persian companion of the Prophet, who suggested digging a moat around Madinah, so that the attackers would be physically prevented from engaging the Muslims in an open fight. The idea was a novel one, as far as fighting between Arab tribes was concerned. Arabs were used only to fighting in open space. In no previous military engagement did they ever have to build a bridgehead over a river or a similar natural barrier. This time, however, they had to face such an obstacle. The geography of Madinah was perfectly suited to the execution of this idea. Only the northern parts of the city were vulnerable to attack. Other parts were naturally fortified. To the east, an old volcanic area called Wāqim stretched a considerable distance, and a similar old volcanic area called Wabarah stretched to the west. In the south, orchards thick with palm trees stretched over a considerable area and formed a natural barrier to any attack. Behind these fields the Jewish tribe of Qurayẓah lived in fortified homes, and they were bound by their peace treaty with the Muslims.

To complete the fortifications and defences of Madinah the moat had to be only wide enough to prevent any possible crossing and deep enough to make driving across it impossible.

The Prophet and his companions found the idea of digging the moat attractive and he called on his companions to start working on it without delay. The Prophet divided his 3,000 companions, who constituted the fighting force of the Muslim state, into groups of ten, and assigned to each group a distance of 40 yards to dig. As they worked hard, the companions of the Prophet chanted suitable rhymes indicating their determination to defend their faith. By the time the allied forces of evil arrived, the Muslims' defensive plan was fully operational. The moat stood as an impregnable barrier between the two parties. It should be pointed out that the Muslims must have found the task of digging the moat rather difficult because they were not used to such manual activity. The Arabs generally worked in trade, leaving menial jobs to their slaves and servants. The Muslim community in Madinah, however, was a poor community with few slaves. They, therefore, had to take part themselves in that remarkable project.

The Prophet himself shared in the digging of the moat. His position was unlike that of present-day heads of state who initiate large national projects in a spectacular ceremony designed to make use of the mass media in order to gain political advantage. The Prophet shared in the work like any individual of the Muslim community. He worked with the axe and the shovel and he carried the soil away like every single member of his community. Once he was so tired that he sat down to rest and leaned against a rock. As he did so, he fell asleep. His two companions, Abū Bakr and ʿUmar, stood nearby, motioning others to move away so that they did not disturb the Prophet in his sleep. When he suddenly woke up, he said to them: "Why did you let me sleep? You should have woken me up."

The Prophet's action motivated the Muslims to work as hard as they could in order to complete digging the moat in a spectacular period of six days. Some reports suggest that it took them 17 days, while others put the number as high as 24. Perhaps the smaller figure is more accurate considering the urgency of the matter, with the hostile forces already on the march when the digging started.

Working together in digging the moat, the Muslims felt their communal ties to be stronger than ever. Nothing cements the ties of brotherhood more than joining such a grand effort in the service of the common cause. This was markedly visible among the Muslims as they continued digging the moat.

As mentioned earlier, there were in Madinah a group of hypocrites who pretended to be Muslims. These people resented having to do such a menial job as digging a moat. They were always bent on seeking some excuse to absent themselves from the site. Many of them would come for a short while, then sneak away. When their conduct was noticed by the rest of the Muslims, they were determined not to leave the site without first obtaining permission from the Prophet. Any believer who wanted to go away for any reason, even the most pressing, preferred to tell the Prophet first and ask his permission. Thus, every short absence was reported in advance. This discipline was voluntary, not imposed. God, therefore, praises the Muslims for their conduct and denounces the behaviour of the hypocrites in the last three verses of *Sūrah* 24, entitled *al-Nūr* or Light.[4]

A Meal for an Army

There were several incidents during the digging of the moat which confirmed that Muhammad was truly a Prophet. As has already been pointed out, the Prophet worked in the digging of the moat as an individual among the community. As they dug, the Muslims chanted in chorus and the Prophet joined in. The Muslims were very poor. At the time, most of them suffered from hunger. With their hard work, hunger was especially biting. Many of them used the device of putting a stone against their stomach and wrapping it tight to overcome the pangs of hunger. The Prophet had two stones on his stomach. As he was working, one of his companions noticed that he must have been extremely hungry. This man, Jābir ibn ʿAbdullāh, was deeply affected by the sight and sought permission for a temporary absence. He went straight home and said to his wife: "I have seen the Prophet in a condition which I cannot tolerate. Have you got any food?" She told him that she had a small quantity of barley and a small goat. He immediately slaughtered the goat and prepared it for cooking. His wife ground the barley and started to cook the goat in a large saucepan.

When the cooking and baking were nearly finished, Jābir went to the Prophet and said: "Messenger of God, I have some food at home. Would you like to be my guest with one or two of your companions?" The Prophet asked him how much food he had, and when he heard Jābir's reply he said: "This is good and plenty. Tell your wife not to take her saucepan off the fire, or her bread out of the oven until I come." Then he addressed his companions and invited them to Jābir's dinner. All those digging the moat, from among the Muhājirīn and the Anṣār, went with him.

In Jābir's own account of the story, he says that he was exceedingly embarrassed because his little goat and small amount of bread were very inadequate for that large number of people. He preceded everybody, went straight to his wife and said: "The Prophet has come and brought with him all the Muhājirīn and the Anṣār." She said: "Has he asked you what food we have?" When he answered in the affirmative, she said: "God and His Messenger know better." Her answer was enough to relieve Jābir of his embarrassment.

When he arrived at Jābir's house, the Prophet said to his companions: "Come inside, but do not push one another." The Prophet himself started to cut the bread, put it in dishes and put meat on top of it. Meanwhile, he kept the pot simmering and covered it as well as the oven, after taking some bread from it. He served dish after dish to his companions until they had all eaten a full meal. Both the saucepan and the oven were still full of bread and meat when everyone had finished eating. The Prophet then said to Jābir's wife: "Eat of that and send presents to other people, for we have suffered something approaching a famine." She did so, and sent large quantities of bread and meat during the rest of that day.

There are several reports which relate this story. Some of them put the figure of those who shared in Jābir's dinner at 800. If everyone who was working on digging the moat accepted the Prophet's invitation to Jābir's house, the number would be much higher. This is not surprising, not because a little goat – or a large one, for that matter – was enough to feed such a large number of people, but because God blessed that repast and gave the Prophet such a privilege at that particular time.[5]

A similar incident took place during the digging of the moat, which confirms that the Muslims in Madinah were very short of food at the time when the Quraysh resolved to attack them along with other Arab tribes and the Jewish tribe of al-Naḍīr. A young daughter of Bashīr ibn Saʿd reported that her mother, ʿAmrah bint Rawāḥah, gave her a small quantity of dates and told her to take them to her father and her uncle, ʿAbdullāh ibn Rawāḥah, for their lunch. On her way, she passed the Prophet who asked her what she was carrying. She replied: "Some dates my mother has sent to my father, Bashīr ibn Saʿd, and my uncle, ʿAbdullāh ibn Rawāḥah, for their lunch."

The Prophet said: "Give them to me." She put them in the Prophet's hands and noted that he could have held more. The Prophet ordered a cloth to be spread and then put the dates all over it. He asked someone nearby to invite all the people to lunch. They all came and started eating. The dates increased and increased until everybody had eaten, with the cloth still full of dates.[6]

Indicative Signs

Although such incidents are signs which testify to the truth of Muhammad's message and the fact that he was a Prophet and a Messenger of God, they are not the basis of belief in Islam. They simply confirm an accepted truth. The best evidence of that truth is the Qur'ān itself, God's message which provides guidance for mankind, and creates, whenever implemented, a perfect human society which is run by human beings and ensures a happy human life for everyone. That is the main proof of Muhammad's message. Incidents of a miraculous nature such as have been related are of secondary importance, despite the fact that they confirmed, especially for the companions of the Prophet who witnessed them, what they had already taken for granted.

Another incident which took place at that time was that a unit of the Prophet's companions complained that they had in their portion of the moat a large piece of rock which was too hard for their shovels and axes. They could do nothing about it. The Prophet said: "I am coming." He picked up an axe, hit the rock, and it turned into a heap of dust which was very easy to tackle.[7]

When the Prophet and his companions finished digging the moat, they felt much more secure in their position. The moat was too wide and too deep for any horseman to jump over. The rubble and sand left over from digging the moat were piled in a parapet which formed an additional barrier between the Muslims and their enemies. Women and children were guarded in fortified buildings. The Prophet and his fighting forces encamped at the foot of Mount Silʿ with their backs to the mountain.[8]

The Quraysh and the confederate Arab tribes which joined the army of unbelievers which marched towards Madinah had a clear motive and a definite aim. They wanted to finish Muhammad and his companions, leaving no trace of Islam whatsoever. Ḥuyayy ibn Akhṭab and the other leaders of the Jewish tribe of al-Naḍīr, who were the initiators of this alliance and worked very hard to have it forged and to see the large army of the confederate tribes raised, made it clear to the leaders of the Quraysh and the Ghaṭafān that this time they must never lose sight of their ultimate aim of exterminating the Prophet and his companions. The pledges made by all the parties involved were clear indicators that all understood the objective and agreed to it. Thus, when this large army moved towards Madinah, its commanders were thinking of a total sweep of the city, leaving to the Muslims there no chance to put up any kind of resistance which would enable Islam to survive, even with a considerably reduced following. In short, the effort they had undertaken was nothing less than a war of extermination.

The picture on the other side was totally different. The Muslims were a community motivated by faith. Their newly established bonds of brotherhood, superseding all previous bonds of tribal loyalties, had given them a sense of unity which they had not experienced in the past. They trusted in the leadership of the Prophet, knowing that he was guided by God who, alone, could give victory to whomsoever He willed. When the Prophet called on his companions to dig the moat, in order to complete the fortification of Madinah, their collective effort, hard and tiresome as it was and undertaken at a time of famine, helped to enhance their unity and their feeling of strength. They realized that they would probably be no match for their enemy in an open fight if they were to rely solely on their own power. That, however, did not weaken them, because they trusted in God and in the leadership of the Prophet. When they settled on their defensive plan, they realized that perseverance and steadfastness were of the highest importance if they were to win this encounter. They knew that they had to exhaust the patience of their enemies in order to draw them into making costly mistakes. In other words, their effort was largely a war of nerves.

The Unexpected Barrier

When the Quraysh and its allies arrived and realized what the Muslims had done to defend themselves and their city, they were shocked and baffled. This plan was something they had never encountered before. They did not know how to build a bridgehead over the moat. Even if they did, their effort would be very costly in lives. They therefore encamped near to the moat, waiting for something to happen. Units of horsemen paraded day and night near the moat. They tried to find a weak point where a crossing could be effected. They watched for a chance to take the Muslims unawares and cross over to them. The Muslims, on the other hand, were fully aware what a breach of their defences would mean to them. They encamped very close to the moat and every time a unit, large or small, approached, a shower of arrows from the Muslim side forced them to retreat.

The Muslims guarded their defensive lines day and night. They were alert, watchful and determined. Muhammad ibn Maslamah, a companion of the Prophet, said: "Our night was turned into day. The leaders of the unbelievers took turns to demonstrate their power on the other side of the moat. We saw Abū Sufyān leading some units of his troops beyond the moat, then other commanders took turns each following day – Khālid ibn al-Walīd, ʿAmr ibn al-ʿĀṣ, Hubayrah ibn Ubayy, ʿIkrimah ibn Abī Jahl and Ḍirār ibn al-Khaṭṭāb."[9]

While this exhibition suggested that the unbelievers had great forces at their command, it also showed that there was no recognized supreme leader of the confederates, to whom they all deferred. Perhaps this was the main factor of weakness in the ranks of the unbelievers. The defenders of Madinah, however, did not show any indication to that effect. They could, therefore, be excused their worry over the outcome of this long and drawn-out encounter.

When several days had passed and the situation did not alter, a group of the Quraysh's renowned heroes tried to cross the moat. Indeed, a few of them managed to get their horses to jump over at the narrowest point. A group of Muslim fighters, led by ʿAlī ibn Abī Ṭālib, rushed to stop this breach and face the attackers. Those who crossed were either forced to retreat or killed. One of them, ʿAmr ibn ʿAbd Wadd, was highly renowned for his bravery and fighting ability. ʿAlī said to him: "ʿAmr, you have pledged that if you were ever invited by a man from the Quraysh to accept one of two alternatives you would certainly do so." ʿAmr confirmed his pledge. ʿAlī then said to him: "Then I call on you to believe in God and His Messenger and to accept Islam." ʿAmr answered: "I have no time for that." ʿAlī then said: "Then I challenge you to a duel." ʿAmr said in a condescending tone: "And why do you do that, my nephew? By God, I do not want to kill you." ʿAlī said: "But I do want to kill you." Enraged, ʿAmr dismounted and faced ʿAlī. The two were locked in a bitter fight which ended with ʿAlī, the young man, killing the hero of the unbelievers, whose bravery was no match for the courage and confidence of ʿAlī, the trusted companion of the Prophet.[10]

All indications suggested that the siege would be prolonged. Any far-sighted person would have realized that unless the Muslim lines were breached at some point or another, the defenders would be able to survive for a long time. They were in their city and their farms were behind them. Thus, their supply lines could not be disrupted. Their position was by no means a comfortable one, but it was not desperate either. Their enemies were in a worse position. Their supply lines were virtually non-existent. They had to rely on what they had with them. Soon, that would be exhausted. They could not maintain their siege for very long. The first to realize that something dramatic must be done to break the stalemate was Ḥuyayy ibn Akhṭab, the rabbi of the Jewish tribe of al-Naḍīr.

Of all the leading enemies of the Muslims, Ḥuyayy ibn Akhṭab was perhaps the most determined to bring the whole enterprise to a successful conclusion. The whole idea of joining together all the forces hostile to Islam was his brainchild. He realized that a failure this time could be total. The deadlock had to be broken and no one else could be trusted to come up with a suitable idea to break it.

Treason by Temptation

Right at the back of Madinah and beyond its fields lived the Qurayẓah, the largest of the Jewish tribes who had settled in Madinah a long time ago, in anticipation of the emergence of the last of the prophets. Like the rest of the Jewish tribes, the Qurayẓah were bound by a peace treaty which the Prophet signed with them shortly after his settlement in Madinah. So far, the Qurayẓah had kept to their obligations under the agreement. The other two tribes of the Qaynuqāʿ and the al-Naḍīr were evacuated from Madinah after having violated the treaty. Hence, the Qurayẓah Jews feared nothing from the Muslims. Trusting that there was no danger to guard against from the Qurayẓah's side, the Muslims took no precautions against them.

Now, Ḥuyayy ibn Akhṭab realized that the only chance to achieve his goal of bringing about the collapse of Islam and the annihilation of Muhammad and his companions was to persuade the Qurayẓah to join forces with the Arab unbelievers and their Jewish allies to launch a pincer attack against the defending Muslim army. He, therefore, found his way to the fortified house of Ka'b ibn Asad, the Qurayẓah leader.

The Jews in Madinah lived in houses like forts. In the days before the advent of Islam, they stirred up trouble between the two main Arab tribes in Madinah, the Aws and the Khazraj, making alliances with both sides and joining them in their battles. Each house of theirs was fortified. In such troubled times as Madinah was going through, the Jews took every precaution and locked up their fortified houses. When Ḥuyayy ibn Akhṭab knocked at Ka'b ibn Asad's door, the latter refused to open up. Ḥuyayy called out to him and asked him to open, but he refused, saying: "Ḥuyayy, you are a man of ill fortune. I have a treaty with Muhammad which I intend to observe. I have seen nothing from him except honesty and faithful observance of his obligations."

Ḥuyayy would not take no for an answer and his entreaties to Ka'b to open the door grew more and more passionate. But Ka'b would not open his door. Eventually, Ḥuyayy deliberately insulted Ka'b to provoke him into admitting him into his home. He said: "You have bolted your door only because you do not want me to share your dinner."[11] The trick was successful and Ka'b admitted his unwelcome friend.

When he sat down, Ḥuyayy ibn Akhṭab said: "Ka'b, can you not see that I have come to bring you the glory of all time. I am giving you a sea of goodness." Ka'b enquired: "What is that?" Ḥuyayy answered: "I have brought you the Quraysh, with all its chiefs and leaders, right to their encamping place at Mujtama' al-Asyāl, where all streams converge. I have also brought the Ghaṭafān, with all their chiefs and leaders, right to where they are encamping, close to the mount of Uḥud. Both have given me their most solemn pledges that they will not depart until we have annihilated Muhammad and all his followers."

Ka'b answered: "You have indeed come to me with an everlasting shame. You bring me nothing but a cloud which has already shed its rain. It may produce lightning and thunder, but it has nothing good to offer. Leave me alone, Ḥuyayy, for I have seen nothing from Muhammad but honesty and faithful observance of our treaty."

A man from the Qurayẓah called ʿAmr ibn Saʿd put in a few good words. He reminded his people of the treaty they had with the Prophet and that they were required, under that treaty, to support Muhammad against his enemies. He then said: "If you do not want to fight with Muhammad, then leave him alone to face his enemies."

Ḥuyayy ibn Akhṭab was not deterred by this negative answer. His power of persuasion was indeed great. He kept pressurizing and persuading Kaʿb ibn Asad until the latter yielded to the temptation of joining the allied forces hostile to the Prophet. In return, Ḥuyayy pledged to him by God that if the Quraysh and the Ghaṭafān were to leave before they could inflict a defeat on Muhammad, he and the Jews under his command would join Kaʿb ibn Asad and the Qurayẓah in their fortified houses and share with them their fate, whatever that fate might be. When that was done, the Qurayẓah followed their leader Kaʿb ibn Asad in his unilateral abrogation of their treaty with the Muslims.[12]

The Prophet soon heard of the treachery of the Qurayẓah. He was aware that if the news became known to the Muslim army, it was bound to have adverse effects on their morale. He therefore wanted to be absolutely sure of the new situation. He sent four of his companions – Saʿd ibn Muʿādh, the chief of the Aws tribe, Saʿd ibn ʿUbādah, the chief of the Khazraj tribe, ʿAbdullāh ibn Rawāḥah and Khawāt ibn Jubayr – to the Qurayẓah to ascertain their position: "If you find out that the intelligence we have received is true, give me a hint which I will understand. Try to avoid affecting the Muslims' morale. If, on the other hand, you find that the Qurayẓah remain faithful to their treaty with us, make the news known to everyone."

The delegation went to the Qurayẓah and met the people there, calling on them to maintain their peaceful relations and to confirm their alliance with the Prophet. The Qurayẓah, however, took a defiant attitude. They said: "You want us to confirm the alliance now, when we have been weakened by the evacuation of al-Naḍīr. Who is God's Messenger? We do not know him."

Saʿd ibn ʿUbādah abused them and they returned the abuse. Saʿd ibn Muʿādh told him: "We have not come here for this. The matter is much more serious than entering into a slanging match with them." Then he said to them: "Qurayẓah, you know our past relations. I fear for you a destiny similar to that which befell al-Naḍīr, or even worse." At this point they abused him, in some of the most vulgar and obscene terms. He said: "You would have been well advised to use different language."

The Muslim delegation then left the Qurayẓah and went back to the Prophet with the bad news that the Jews no longer recognized the peace treaty which they had with him. On arrival Saʿd ibn Muʿādh and Saʿd ibn ʿUbādah found the Prophet with a group of his companions. Following his advice that they should give him a hint of the Qurayẓah's treachery rather than give the fact full publicity, they mentioned in their report the names of the two Arab tribes, ʿAḍal and al-Qārah, in reference to the treachery they had perpetrated at al-Rajīʿ. The Prophet was not perturbed. On the contrary, he said: "God is supreme. Rejoice, you Muslims, for the end will be a happy one."[13]

An Attitude of Unshaken Faith

It is important to consider the attitude of the Prophet when he received the unhappy news of the Qurayẓah's treachery. At no time during his life did the Prophet show that he was given to fanciful ideas or carried away into the high flights of imagination. Indeed, the reverse is true. He was a very practical and realistic man. He was fully aware of what the treachery of the Qurayẓah meant. The Muslims were, in effect, besieged by two enemies who were determined to attack them on two fronts in an all-out effort to exterminate them. Yet, at the very moment when he received the news of the imminent danger, he advised his companions to rejoice for the end would be a happy one.

This reflects his total trust in God and his realization that despite the great forces of their enemies, the Muslims would be victorious if they were truly on God's side. After all, victory is given by God to those who fight for His cause with sincerity of purpose and intention.

The Prophet's attitude in this case can be contrasted to his attitude when friction and conflict were about to erupt within the ranks of the Muslims after their victory in the expedition of al-Muṣṭalaq. At that time, the hypocrites were successful in stirring up hostility. Then the Prophet was very worried, and hastened to settle the differences between the Muslims. His wise, quick measures enabled him to overcome the trouble created by the hypocrites. He was genuinely worried by that incident. That shows that the Prophet considered the internal trouble much more serious than having to face the might of all forces hostile to Islam in open battle. He considered that it was enough for the Muslims to be united in their determination to fight the enemies of God and Islam and to do their utmost in that direction to be sure of God's help against their enemies. If, on the other hand, strife erupts between the Muslims themselves, then God will leave them to their own devices and will not help one group of them against the other.

The Muslims soon realized that the Jews of the Qurayẓah had gone back on their promises and joined the campaign to wipe them out. Everyone was extremely worried and feared the outcome. Their greatest worry was that the Qurayẓah had easy access to Madinah. They would be able to let in units of the Quraysh and their allies to join them in an attack on the civilian population of the city. Obviously all strong and able-bodied Muslim men were with the army and only women, children and old people were left in Madinah. They could no longer be left on their own without protection. If the Muslims were to split their forces in order to fight on both fronts, their lines would be very thin and they could not resist a determined attack from either side, let alone a concerted one from both for a long period. Hence, the worry and the fear were great indeed.

The Prophet tried hard to comfort the Muslims, telling them to relax and trust in God. He told them: "By Him who holds my soul in His hand, God will provide you with a way out of this hardship. I indeed hope to go around the Kaʿbah feeling absolutely safe, and that God will enable me to hold the keys of the Kaʿbah in my hand. God will surely destroy the Persian and Byzantine Emperors, and their treasures will be spent to further the cause of God."[14]

In this critical period, the hypocrites revealed their true feelings and the fact that they had little faith in God and the Prophet. What they wanted most was to spare themselves. Some of them came to the Prophet and asked permission to go back to their homes, which were vulnerable to attack. Some of them remarked that the Prophet was promising them the treasures of the great empires of Persia and Byzantium "when none of us feels safe even to go to the toilet." Others said that the Prophet's promises were false and tried to persuade some of the Muslims to go back home.[15]

God describes their attitude in clear terms in the account given in the Qur'ān of this encounter between the Muslims and their enemies. This account occurs in *Sūrah* 33, entitled *al-Aḥzāb* or The Confederates. Only the hard core of the true believers remained steadfast and accepted the Prophet's assurances of victory.

A War of Nerves

Meanwhile, Ḥuyayy ibn Akhṭab went back to the command of the Quraysh with the news that the Qurayẓah were joining their campaign. This gave them such a boost that they were lighting great fires every night to intimidate the Muslims and weaken their morale. The Qurayẓah asked to be given ten days to get ready before they could fight. One of their conditions was that, in the meantime, the Quraysh and their allies would increase the pressure against the Muslims, so that they could not attempt to settle with the Qurayẓah first. As a result, skirmishes intensified and there were repeated attacks from across the moat which only served to emphasize that the Muslims were the weaker party.[16]

The Prophet thought hard about a way to cause a split in the enemy ranks. He thought of persuading the Ghaṭafān to withdraw from the alliance with the Quraysh and the Jews. He sent a messenger to ʿUyaynah ibn Ḥiṣn of Fazārah and al-Ḥārith ibn ʿAwf of Murrah, the two main leaders of the Ghaṭafān, with an offer by which they would get one-third of the crops of Madinah if they were to withdraw their forces from the campaign. They accepted the offer and the text of the agreement was written. Before having the agreement signed and witnessed, the Prophet called in the two leaders of the Anṣār, Sa'd ibn Mu'ādh and Sa'd ibn 'Ubādah. He wanted to consult them about the agreement because the Anṣār were the ones most affected by its provisions. When he had told them what he had proposed to the Ghaṭafān, Sa'd ibn Mu'ādh asked him: "Is this something you would like us to do? In this case, we will accept it for your sake. Or is it something God has ordered and we shall have to accept it? Or is it something you are doing for our sake?"

The Prophet answered that he was doing it for them, because of their extremely difficult situation, now that all the Arabs and their allies had joined forces against them. He added that all he wanted was to break up the unity of their enemies for the present.

Sa'd ibn Mu'ādh said:

> Messenger of God, when we were, like these people, idolaters, unaware of any religion other than the worship of idols, they did not hope to get a single fruit from Madinah except as a present from us or if we sold it to them. Now that God has honoured us with Islam and guided us to it and has given us the honour and strength of having you in our midst, would we willingly give them our goods? We have no need for this agreement. We will give them nothing but the sword until God makes His judgement between us.

The Prophet replied: "The matter is entirely up to you." Then Sa'd took the sheet on which the agreement was written and erased the writing. He said: "Let them do their worst. We are ready to meet them." Thus no peace was made with any party and the siege continued as hard as ever.

The attempt to reach an accommodation with the Ghaṭafān came to nothing. There was, however, an indirect result: the Prophet was now absolutely certain of the Anṣār's determination to fight to the end. There was no weakening in the Muslims' ranks. The fact that they were facing the greatest danger they had ever faced did not shake their faith. Their trust in God was as strong as ever.

Nevertheless, the Muslims were facing a very difficult situation indeed. The army of the pagan Arabs of the Quraysh and the Ghaṭafān intensified their pressure, keeping the Muslims engaged all the time in order to give the Qurayẓah a chance to get ready for fighting and to prevent any attempt by the Muslims to launch a lightning attack against the Qurayẓah in order to restore the situation that prevailed before the Qurayẓah's treachery.

The Quraysh and their allies were so pleased with the feat accomplished by Ḥuyayy ibn Akhṭab in persuading the Qurayẓah to change sides that they were now absolutely certain of achieving the victory they were seeking. Skirmishes on the Quraysh front were now much more frequent. Parades of forces taken in turn by the Quraysh commanders were a daily occurrence. One has to remember here that each time a division of the enemy forces went on parade, the Muslims went on full alert. Their position was a defensive one. They, therefore, had to guard against any action their enemies might take. Every movement was watched and every eventuality was prepared for.

While these parades attracted the Muslims' attention for a time, skirmishes of an ever-increasing intensity presented an imminent danger. One such engagement took place when a battalion of the Quraysh army launched an attack on the position where the Prophet himself stood. He and his companions fought hard to repel it. The fighting continued all day and well into the night. The fighting was so fierce that neither the Prophet nor any of his companions was able to offer any of the obligatory prayers on that day. All of them missed the three prayers of *ẓuhr, ʿaṣr* and *maghrib*. Some reports suggest that the engagement was of a shorter duration and that the Prophet and his companions missed only the *ʿaṣr* prayer and offered it together with *maghrib*. All reports, however, agree that prayers were missed and could be offered only after sunset. When the Prophet and his companions were ready to offer their prayers, Bilāl made one call, *adhān*, for them all and one *iqāmah* for each one.[17]

Pressure at Its Highest

The Qurayẓah themselves took part in the systematic intensification of the pressure on the Muslims. It seems that they were creating impressions that they were ready to launch an attack on the Muslims at any moment in order to divert their attentions and make it easy for the Quraysh to cross the moat and put their plan into operation. The situation was so critical as far as the Muslims were concerned that the Prophet did not allow any of his companions to go back to Madinah for any reason without carrying his full armour. This was a precaution against any trap the Qurayẓah might have set for the Muslim soldiers.

One evening, it was reported to the Prophet that the Qurayẓah were about to launch a night attack on Madinah and its civilian population. This was not just idle talk. The Prophet had to treat the report seriously. He sent two units of his companions to guard Madinah that night. The first unit of 200 men was commanded by Salamah ibn Aslam and assigned the task of guarding one side of the city. The other unit was even larger: Zayd ibn Ḥārithah commanded 300 men and was given the task of providing a guard for the rest of Madinah.[18] Some of the Prophet's companions described the difficulty of their situation in those days by saying that they were much more worried about their women and children being attacked by the Qurayẓah than about facing the much larger force of the Quraysh and the Ghaṭafān. It was apparently a time when every moment brought something to worry about. The Jews of the Qurayẓah had easy access to Madinah and apparently they sent some of their men to frighten the Muslim women and children. One of them was killed by Ṣafiyyah bint ʿAbd al-Muṭṭalib, the Prophet's aunt, when she saw the man moving suspiciously very close to the quarters of the Muslim women.[19]

All Courage and Caution

It is useful to relate the following example in order to have a feeling of the thoughts and feelings of the Muslims in that period. Saʿd ibn Muʿādh, the leader of the Aws tribe of the Anṣār, was apparently attending to some business in his home, obviously with the Prophet's permission. When he was ready to go back, he waited a little for a friend of his called Ḥamal ibn Saʿdānah. He was chanting a few words which described that particular situation: "Tarry a while and Ḥamal will take part in the fighting. Death is welcome if one's end is due." His mother was urging him not to wait.

ʿĀ'ishah, the Prophet's wife who related this incident, was with his mother. In her account, she remarked that the body armour Saʿd was wearing was not as good as it should have been. It left him with one arm totally unshielded. She said to his mother: "I wish that Saʿd had a better shield." She feared that he might be hit on the arm.

When Saʿd joined the army that day, he took part in one of the engagements that had become very frequent. He was hit on the arm by an arrow. Apparently, his wound was very deep. Saʿd, so keen to see Islam well established in Arabia after the defeat of its enemies, prayed to God in these words: "My Lord, if we are to fight the Quraysh again, spare me now for that fight. There are no people I like to fight for Your cause, more than those who have opposed Your Messenger, rejected him and forced him out of his home town. If You have willed that this encounter between us would be the last, I pray You, my Lord, to make this wound of mine my way to martyrdom, but spare me until I see our affair with the Qurayẓah have a happy ending for Islam."[20]

Saʿd's earnest prayer describes fully the Muslims' feelings in their very difficult situation. However, they had done everything in their power to defend the cause of Islam. They neither weakened nor allowed their worry and fear to dictate their behaviour. They continued to do as the Prophet bade them, trusting that the outcome would be in their favour as long as they were ready to continue to give their utmost. They had learnt from the Prophet that that was all that God asked anyone to give. When any group of people have given that and have done all they can for the sake of God, God takes over and gives them victory in the way He pleases.

In the Islamic view, victory in war is given only by God. When two armies meet in battle, the decisive factor which determines the outcome of that battle is God's help, which He gives only to those who serve His cause. If both armies turn their backs on the cause of God and do not recognize it, He abandons them both to their own devices and lets the laws of nature, which He has set and determined, produce the result on the basis of their interaction. One may indeed say that the interaction of the laws of nature determines the outcome of any battle between any two armies provided that we include among these laws of nature the one which determines that those who believe in God, live their faith and practise it in their daily lives, are entitled to be helped by God. This help is their right, which He Himself has given them. He has committed Himself to helping His servants whenever they fight His and their enemy, setting for themselves the only objective of serving His cause. With this law, which supersedes all others, victory is always assured to the believers.

Islam requires its adherents to exert every effort and to do their utmost for the achievement of victory for Islam. They must not set their aim as the achievement of victory for themselves. Their personalities do not matter. What matters is the victory of the cause, regardless of who achieves it. After all, that cause is God's not theirs. Their role is to serve it as best as they can and let God do with it, and for it, what He wills. That unique generation of Muslims, the Prophet's companions, understood this principle very well and acted on it. Every time they met their enemies, they prayed God to give them "either one of the two great prizes: victory or martyrdom."

It must be emphasized that fatalism is alien to the Islamic concept of life. Muslims do not go to war thinking that victory is guaranteed them by the fact that they are Muslims. They must do their own duty, exerting their best efforts to achieve victory before they can earn God's help.

As the Muslims with the Prophet continued their defence of Madinah, in this encounter known in the history books as The Expedition of the Moat or The Encounter with the Confederates, they were able to demonstrate most convincingly that their aims were absolutely free of any gain they might have sought for themselves. For 27 nights they remained under siege, with hostile forces close to them, threatening to attack them on two fronts, hoping to put an end to Islam altogether. Worrying about their faith, their families and the Prophet, those Muslims did not think about their own lives. All they were thinking about was what they could do to ensure that the call of Islam would continue to spread. When they were attacked, they fought hard. None of them thought about his own safety. Indeed, their women and children were always urging them on, encouraging them to do that little bit more.

War Is But a Trick

In such a situation, God's help is always assured. Those Muslims were required to continue to exert their best efforts, and victory was theirs. One can detect that victory was achieved only with the help of God, when one realizes that those circumstances which helped achieve that victory could not have happened at that time, in that place, and in that particular way, all by coincidence. It was all the work of God. When He willed that those Muslims should reap the fruits of their efforts, He caused a man from the Ghaṭafān tribe to come to the Prophet. This man, Nuʿaym ibn Masʿūd, was apparently a highly intelligent and resourceful person who had formed many friendships and acquaintances with all sorts of people. He said to the Prophet: "Messenger of God, I am now a Muslim and my people are not aware of the fact. You may give me whatever orders you wish."

Keenly aware that the thing which the Muslims needed most was for their enemy to split ranks, the Prophet said to Nuʿaym: "If you join us, you increase our number by one. But try, if you can, to dissuade the people from attacking us. War is but a successful trick."

Nuʿaym was the right person to bring about a split in the ranks of the enemies of Islam. He had many friends among the Jews of the Qurayẓah, who were getting ready to attack the Muslims from behind. He went to them and said: "You know that I love you truly and that I am a good friend of yours." They replied: "Indeed your friendship to us is undoubted." He said:

> The Quraysh and the Ghaṭafān are not in the same position as you. This city is your own home city, where you live with your own women and children and have all your assets and property. The Quraysh and the Ghaṭafān have come to attack Muhammad and his companions, and you have now joined them. But their women and children and their money and property are somewhere else. This places them in a position different from

> yours. If they have an opportunity to seize, they will not fail to seize it. But if things turn sour for them, they will certainly depart and leave you alone to face Muhammad in your own home town. If you are to face him alone, you are certainly no match for him. My advice to you is to guard against that eventuality. You must not fight alongside the Quraysh and the Ghaṭafān unless you take some hostages from among their leaders so that you may be absolutely sure that they will fight with you until Muhammad is defeated.

The Qurayẓah recognized the validity of Nuʿaym's argument and thanked him for his advice.

Leaving the Qurayẓah, Nuʿaym went straight to the Quraysh encampments, where he met the overall leader, Abū Sufyān ibn Ḥarb, and the other chiefs. He said to them: "You know me to be your friend and that I am no follower of Muhammad. I have come to know something which I feel I must convey to you as a piece of advice, but please do not tell anyone that I am your source of information." Having obtained Abū Sufyān's promise, Nuʿaym continued:

> I would like you to know that the Jews have repented their breach of their treaty with Muhammad. They sent him messengers to communicate to him their regret for what they had done. In order to show him their goodwill, they asked whether he would be satisfied if they were to give him a number of men from among the nobility of the Quraysh and the Ghaṭafān to kill. They also promised that they were ready to fight with him against you until you have been exterminated. He answered that their offer was satisfactory. Now, if the Jews ask you to send them some of your people to stay with them as a guarantee that you will not abandon them, do not send them a single person.

Nuʿaym then went straight to the Ghaṭafān and said to their leaders: "You are my own people, whom I love most dearly. I believe I am not a man you suspect of any ill will towards you." When they assured him of his good standing among them, he told them the same thing he told the Quraysh and warned them against sending anyone to the Qurayẓah.

In this way, Nuʿaym was successful in planting suspicion among the three major groupings of the forces hostile to Islam. Each side wanted to make absolutely sure of the intentions of the other. Abū Sufyān and the chiefs of the Ghaṭafān sent a delegation to the Qurayẓah led by ʿIkrimah ibn Abī Jahl with representatives from both tribes. It so happened that the delegation went on the Sabbath night. It had totally escaped Abū Sufyān's notice that the Jews of the Qurayẓah were very strict in observing their Sabbath. The delegation said to the Qurayẓah: "This siege has caused us so much trouble. We cannot maintain it much longer. We are getting exhausted, so we have to make a move. Get ready and let us attack Muhammad and finish him off with his Companions."

The Qurayẓah answered:

> You are surely aware that today is our Sabbath day, when we do nothing. Some of us, in former times, violated the sanctity of this day and were subjected to God's punishment, of which you are aware. This point apart, we cannot fight Muhammad alongside you unless you give us some of your own people to stay with us so that we are absolutely sure that you are as determined as we are to fight Muhammad to the bitter end. We fear that if you find the going hard, and if the fighting goes against you, you will depart and go home, leaving us to face the man in our home town while we are no match for him on our own.

When the delegation went back with this message, both the Quraysh and the Ghaṭafān concluded: "Nuʿaym ibn Masʿūd's report is certainly true." They sent the Qurayẓah a message that they were not prepared to send them a single person: "If you want to fight, then come out and fight." Receiving this message, the Qurayẓah concluded that Nuʿaym's advice was right and valid. Messages were exchanged between the two sides, but neither of them was willing to accept the other's condition.[21]

Thus Nuʿaym ibn Masʿūd was the means by which God caused this split in the ranks of the enemy forces. There was no longer any chance of a double-fronted attack on the Muslims. The army besieging Madinah was in a worse position than that with which it started. The 27-day siege did not weaken the Muslims. Besides, the great hopes which the enemy came to cherish when the Qurayẓah pledged its active support and participation in battle were now shattered. The besieging forces had to rely on their own strength.

Perhaps it is worth repeating that the circumstances which combined to produce the split in the ranks of the enemies of Islam could not have occurred by chance. They were the work of God, Who decided to help the Muslims after they had proved that their faith was unshakable and that they were ready to fight for the cause of Islam, no matter what sacrifice they were called upon to make. The split in the enemy ranks was the first part of the help God gave to the Muslims at that point in time. It was also through His help that the siege of Madinah was ended.

The Campaign is Aborted

Hudhayfah ibn al-Yamān, a companion of the Prophet who belonged to the Anṣār, was with a group of people in the city of Kūfah in Iraq many years later when he was asked by someone from that city: "Did your people really see God's Messenger, and were you truly in his company?" When Hudhayfah answered in the affirmative, the man asked: "How did you serve him?" Hudhayfah said: "We used to try our best." The man said: "Had it been our fortune to be his companion we would not have let him walk. We would have carried him on our shoulders." Hudhayfah wanted to give the man an idea of what it really meant to be a companion of the Prophet. He related the following incident which took place on the night when the Quraysh and the Ghaṭafān realized that their mission was destined for total failure:

> It was a night when very strong winds blew over the forces hostile to Islam. The night was extremely dark and very cold. The unbelievers could not light a fire, because of the wind

> and rain. They were unable to cook, because their pots and pans were being turned upside down by the wind. Their tents began to collapse, and they were worried that the Muslims might attack them that very night. In this atmosphere, thoughts of departure started to creep into their minds.
>
> Back in the Muslim camp, the Prophet stood up praying for a part of the night. He then turned to his companions and asked: "Who is willing to go and find out what our enemies are doing and come back. [To come back was a condition the Prophet attached to that particular mission.] I shall pray God to make any volunteer for this mission my companion in Heaven."

Although nothing is more tempting to a Muslim than being admitted to Heaven in companionship with the Prophet, the conditions which prevailed that night were far from encouraging. Hudhayfah continued:

> No one volunteered because of our great fear and hunger in that very cold night. When no one answered, the Prophet called me to come forward. I then had no choice but to go. He said to me: "Hudhayfah, go inside the camp of those people and find out what they are doing. Do not do anything on your own initiative until you come back." I went into their quarters to see the wind and God's other soldiers playing havoc in that camp. No pot or pan stood upright, no fire could be maintained and no structure stood up. Abū Sufyān then addressed his people: "People of the Quraysh, let everyone make sure of the person sitting next to him."
>
> I took the man next to me by the hand and asked him who he was. He answered me, mentioning his name and his father's name. Abū Sufyān then said: "People of the Quraysh, you realize that we cannot stay much longer. We have endured great hardship and the Jews of the Qurayẓah have not fulfilled their promises to us. Indeed, we have received highly disturbing reports about their attitude. You see what these strong winds are doing to us. We cannot stay much longer in these conditions,

> and my advice to you is to go back home where I am going." He then mounted his camel, which was tied to a peg. He hit the camel, which jumped to its feet, and released itself as it stood up.
>
> Had it not been for the Prophet's clear instructions to me that I must not do anything serious before I went back, I could have killed Abū Sufyān with my arrow.

Hudhayfah then went back to the Prophet with his report. He found the Prophet praying, and sat very close to him. Continuing his prayers, the Prophet drew Hudhayfah closer to him until he was sitting between his legs and he covered him with his robe. When he finished his prayers, he listened to Hudhayfah's report.[22]

The Ghaṭafān, the other tribe of the pagan Arabs who mounted the siege of Madinah, decided to follow suit when they learned that the Quraysh were leaving.

In the morning, the Muslims looked around them and found that their enemies had gone. All their forces had disappeared. To the believers, this was decisive evidence that they were supported and protected by God Himself. Their faith in the truthfulness of His message was now much greater. It was clear to them that they had only to carry out their part of the deal they had made with God – that is, do their best in the service of Islam – and He would surely fulfil to them His promise to always give them the upper hand over their enemies.

This encounter with the enemies of Islam was not a battle in the straightforward sense. It was, however, a war of nerves and a great test. For this reason, the believers passed the test comfortably while the hypocrites failed. The worry, fear and weakness of the hypocrites were more than matched by the perseverance, endurance and courage of the believers, who were certain that God would soon ease their difficulty. When they passed the test so remarkably well, they found God, by His grace, helping them out of their difficulty and causing their enemy to flee. The whole episode is recorded in the Qur'ān, in God's own words, in the *Sūrah* entitled *al-Aḥzāb*, or The Confederates. Verses 9-27 of the *sūrah* refer to the various stages of this encounter between the Muslims and their enemies and draw lessons for all Muslims in successive generations in order that they can follow in the footsteps of their forefathers in any period of great difficulty. Here is a translation of the verse which speaks of the conclusion of the encounter: "Believers, call to mind the blessings which God bestowed on you at the time when enemy hosts came down upon you, whereupon We let loose against them a storm wind and other forces which you could not see." (33: 9)

When the Prophet looked at the now deserted place where the enemies of Islam had encamped, he felt that it was only through God's grace that the Muslims were saved. His companions recognized in his looks a feeling of great hope and great confidence in God. He looked at them and said: "Now we will no longer be on the defensive; they will not attack us again."[23] In complete humbleness before God, the Prophet repeated the following words which Muslims always repeat, especially on their happy occasions: "There is no deity other than God, who has fulfilled His promise, given victory to His servant, and dignity to His soldiers, and Who has defeated the confederates single-handed. No one was before Him and no one remains after Him."[24]

Notes

1. Ibn Hishām, *al-Sīrah al-Nabawiyyah*, Dār al-Qalam, Beirut, Vol. 1, p. 225. Also, Ibn Sayyid al-Nās, *ʿUyūn al-Athar*, Dār al-Turāth, Madinah, 1996, p. 84; and Ibn Kathīr, *al-Bidāyah wal-Nihāyah*, Maktabat al-Maʿārif, Beirut, Vol. 1, p. 94.
2. Ibn Hishām, op.cit., p. 225. Also, Ibn Kathīr, op.cit., p. 94; and Ibn Sayyid al-Nās, op.cit., p. 84.
3. Ibn Hishām, op.cit., p. 226. Also, Ibn Sayyid al-Nās, op.cit., p. 84.
4. Ibn Hishām, op.cit., pp. 226-227. Also, Ibn Sayyid al-Nās, op.cit., pp. 85-87.
5. Ibn Hishām, op.cit., p. 229. Also, Ibn Sayyid al-Nās, op.cit., pp. 87-88.
6. Ibn Hishām, op.cit., pp. 228-229. Also, Ibn Sayyid al-Nās, op.cit., p. 87.
7. Ibn Hishām, op.cit., p. 230. Also, Ibn Sayyid al-Nās, op.cit., p. 88.
8. Ibn Hishām, op.cit., pp. 230-231. Also, Ibn Sayyid al-Nās, op.cit., pp. 88-89.
9. Ibn Sayyid al-Nās, op.cit., p. 89.
10. Ibn Hishām, op.cit., pp. 235-236.
11. Ḥuyayy's statement was a thinly veiled threat that he would embark on a campaign of defamation against Kaʿb, describing him as miserly. In Arabia, any passer-by could knock on a door and be sure of a hospitable welcome. A traveller would be an honoured guest before he is even asked where he was heading.

12. Ibn Hishām, op.cit., pp. 231-232.
13. Ibid., pp. 232-233. Also, Ibn Sayyid al-Nās, op.cit., pp. 90-91.
14. Ibn Kathīr, op.cit., p. 109.
15. Ibn Hishām, op.cit., p. 233.
16. Ibn Sayyid al-Nās, op.cit., pp. 91-92. Also, Ibn Kathīr, op.cit., pp. 104-105.
17. Ibn Kathīr, op.cit., pp. 109-111. Also, Ibn Sayyid al-Nās, op.cit., pp. 95-96. It should be pointed out here that these are three of the five obligatory prayers Muslims must offer every day. Each has a time range when it must be offered and each takes only a few minutes. The first of these three, *ẓuhr*, begins at midday and its time lapses after about three hours. The time range of the second, *ʿaṣr*, lasts until sunset, while *maghrib* may be offered any time until about 90 minutes after sunset. Each prayer is called by an *adhān*, which is normally announced from a minaret. The *iqāmah* is a shorter version of the *adhān* and it is called immediately before starting the prayer.
18. Ibn Sayyid al-Nās, op.cit., p. 89.
19. Ibid.
20. Ibn Hishām, op.cit., pp. 237-238.
21. Ibid., pp. 240-242.
22. Ibid., pp. 242-244.
23. Ibn Sayyid al-Nās, op.cit., p. 99.
24. Ibn Kathīr, op.cit., p. 111.

26

An Account to Settle

THERE IS NO doubt that the Muslims were saved by Divine Providence when, to all appearances, they had no chance whatsoever of survival, let alone victory. Had the enemies of Islam carried their designs to their natural conclusion, they would have accomplished their aim of exterminating all the Muslims in Madinah. It was God, however, who willed it otherwise. All sides were aware that the Muslims were no match for their enemies. This was in the mind of the Prophet himself as he appealed to God for help and said: "My Lord, You may not be worshipped on earth if You so desire." Had God abandoned the Muslims and left them alone to face their enemies, the victory of the Quraysh and their allies would not have been in doubt. The small Muslim community would certainly have been exterminated. But the Muslims passed their test and proved themselves as sincere and faithful followers of Islam. When they were called upon to sacrifice their all for their cause, they did so without hesitation. Hence, God's help was certain to be forthcoming.

There can be little doubt that it was the treachery of the Jews of the Qurayẓah which put the Muslims in that perilous situation. Without that treachery, the pagan Arabs could not have penetrated the Muslim defences. Long did they encamp and parade in front of the moat which the Muslims had dug. Much did they try to find a weak point in the Muslim defences. All their efforts were in vain.

The Muslims were totally determined to defend their faith and to sacrifice their all to achieve victory for their cause. At no time did they show any weakness of any sort. Had the Qurayẓah been faithful to their peace treaty with the Muslims, the unbelievers would have been faced with a situation which offered only two alternatives: either to try to cross the moat and suffer very heavy casualties and eventual defeat at the hands of the heroes of Islam, or to accept that their aims had been foiled and to retreat with ignominy. The treachery of the Qurayẓah, however, gave a boost to their morale and a fresh assurance that their ultimate objective was in sight. Furthermore, the treachery of the Qurayẓah worried the Muslims greatly. As mentioned earlier, they worried about their women and children being attacked by the Qurayẓah more than they worried about any attack the unbelievers might have possibly launched. The Qur'ān describes their situation in the following terms: "Their eyes were dazzled, their hearts reached their throats, and suspicions carried them everywhere." (33: 10) Such was the situation of the Muslims up to that blessed morning when they awoke to find that their Arab enemies had gone. They realized that this was accomplished through no effort of their own, except their demonstration that they were prepared to give any sacrifice they were called on to give. As said earlier, it was accomplished by Divine Providence.

The departure of the Quraysh and the Ghaṭafān did not settle matters completely. Another score had to be settled: with the Qurayẓah.

That morning the Prophet and all the Muslims went back to Madinah and put down their arms for the first time in nearly a month. They tried to relax and refresh themselves. At noon, however, the Angel Gabriel came to the Prophet to tell him: "God commands you, Muhammad, to march to the Qurayẓah. I am now going there to shaken their hearts."

Where to Offer a Certain Prayer

The Prophet ordered a call to be made all over Madinah: "He who obeys God must not pray *ʿaṣr* except at the Qurayẓah."

The Prophet himself asked Ibn Umm Maktūm to deputize for him in Madinah before he set out. No sooner did the companions of the Prophet hear the call than they set about joining the new expedition. Their response provided a great example for Muslims everywhere. One might have expected them to opt for a few days' rest before settling their account with the Qurayẓah, had they been given a choice. But no choice was offered. After 27 days of enduring a harsh siege and great worry, they were ordered to start a new campaign. No other community would have shown such a response. There was absolutely no dissent. Indeed, the Muslims hurried to join the new campaign. The time for *ʿaṣr* prayers fell when they were on their way towards the Qurayẓah. How were they expected to behave? Should they interrupt their journey to pray *ʿaṣr*, as they would have done in any other circumstances? Or should they delay offering this obligatory prayer until they had reached the Qurayẓah, since the Prophet had enjoined them not to pray *ʿaṣr* elsewhere?

There were two different opinions among the Prophet's companions. Some of them argued that the Prophet only wanted to emphasize the need for speed. He did not want them to omit an obligatory prayer or to delay it until its time had lapsed. They, therefore, stopped to pray before continuing their journey. Others, however, argued that they were only doing the Prophet's bidding. Hence, they could not be at fault if they delayed offering *ʿaṣr* prayer until they had reached the Qurayẓah. Thus, some of the Muslims prayed on their journey and others did not pray until they reached the place. The Prophet did not criticize either party. This is evidence of the fact that Islam respects all opinions arrived at in good faith.

Which group of Muslims were correct? Some people take religious statements, either in the Qur'ān or the *sunnah*, at their face value. They simply do as they are told, believing that God and the Prophet make their purpose absolutely clear, without any need to dig deep for a hidden meaning in order to understand that purpose. Others try to determine the aim beyond any particular statement and act according to their understanding, even if this differs from the immediate meaning of the statement. Both parties are rewarded for their actions even if their understanding is wrong, since they arrive at it in good faith. Some scholars, such as al-Bukhārī, believe that the timings of the prayers can be overlooked during fighting. This is a matter of ordering our priorities. Muslims can understand their faith properly only if they set their priorities right. As Muhammad al-Ghazālī, a contemporary scholar, says in his book on the life of the Prophet: "We must be aware that God does not accept a recommended act of worship unless the obligatory act has been completed. A person who offers many a voluntary act of worship while omitting some obligatory ones does wrong."

If a teacher abandons his class or a trader neglects his trade or an employee disregards his work in order to indulge in voluntary prayers, he neglects an important duty in order to do something which is not required of him, while it is, at the same time, much less important.

In that particular case of speeding towards the Qurayẓah, the Prophet felt that taking the Qurayẓah by surprise, and before they had fortified their positions and prepared themselves to meet the Muslims, was the most pressing task. Hence nothing, not even obligatory prayers, should be allowed to interfere with it. On balance, it seems that those companions of the Prophet who delayed prayers until they had arrived at the Qurayẓah, after sunset, understood the Prophet's purpose correctly.

As the first groups of Muslims began to arrive at the fortified quarters of the Qurayẓah, they found them in a defiant mood. Perhaps the Qurayẓah did not expect the Muslims to arrive in force so soon after the departure of the pagan Arabs. It might be that the Qurayẓah did not realize that the Quraysh and the Ghaṭafān had already departed and perhaps they thought that only a small force of Muslims were given the task of engaging the Qurayẓah in a diversionary encounter, to prevent them from helping the Arabs on the other front. ʿAlī ibn Abī Ṭālib, the Prophet's cousin who was renowned for his fearless bravery in war, was the Muslim standard-bearer. As he began to deploy his forces, the Qurayẓah Jews made a deliberate attempt to provoke the Muslims by insults. They poured abuse on the Prophet and his wives in such an offensive manner that, when the Prophet arrived, ʿAlī rushed to him and asked him not to come too close to the Jewish quarters. The Prophet realized what was happening and told ʿAlī that he need not worry over this: "When they see me, they will stop abusing me."

The Muslims imposed a siege on the Qurayẓah Jews. Thus, those who were besieged by their enemies were now meting out the same treatment to a section of those enemies. The difference was that those who were besieged now had no hope whatsoever against the Muslims, who had already got rid of the largest section of their enemies.

The Jews withstood the siege patiently at first. But as the days passed with no sign of a let up, they were weary and realized that their only hope was to try to come to a compromise with the Muslims.

An Offer of Surrender

They sent a message to the Prophet requesting treatment similar to that which their fellow Jews of al-Naḍīr tribe had received. Al-Naḍīr were allowed to leave Madinah with their women and children, and each one of them was allowed a camel load of his property. Now the Qurayẓah offered to leave on the same terms. However, there was no chance that the Prophet would accept this. The crimes perpetrated by both tribes were vastly dissimilar. Both violated their treaties with the Muslims, but al-Naḍīr tried to kill the Prophet. The Qurayẓah, on the other hand, entered into an alliance with the pagan Arabs with the aim of exterminating the Muslims altogether, when the terms of their treaty dictated that they should give them support against those very Arabs. Their guilt was more open and far more serious. Hence, to give them the same treatment as their fellow Jews would have been totally unjust.

Still they tried to come to a peaceful arrangement. When they were told that the Prophet was not prepared to accept their offer, they sent another message asking him to allow them to evacuate Madinah with their women and children, taking nothing with them and carrying no arms. Again, the Prophet refused. They were told that their only choice was to submit to the judgement of the Prophet, whatever that might be – that is, an unconditional surrender.

The Qurayẓah Jews were at a loss. They recognized that their crime was enormous. They also realized that they were no match for the Muslims, whose morale was boosted by the departure of the pagan Arabs and whose power remained intact since they were not called upon to fight against such a large force as the Quraysh and the Ghaṭafān mustered between them. When the siege was biting hard and they were demoralized, they sent to the Prophet requesting him to send them one of his companions to consult him regarding their best course of action. Their choice was Abū Lubābah Rifāʿah ibn al-Mundhir, of the Aws tribe of the Anṣār. The Aws had been allies with the Qurayẓah in the days before the advent of Islam. There were still strong ties between many Muslims of that tribe and the Qurayẓah. Abū Lubābah in particular was a very close friend of theirs. His home was in their quarters and his business was also in their area. They trusted that from him they would receive sound advice. The man was, however, a sincere Muslim and he realized that his place was with the Muslim army. He, therefore, refused to go to them unless the Prophet gave him permission to do so.

As soon as he arrived, having obtained the Prophet's permission, their men went to receive him and their women and children cried loudly to soften his heart. He felt for them and wished that they did not put themselves in that position. They surrounded him and asked his advice: "What do you think, Abū Lubābah? Muhammad has refused every offer we have made and would accept nothing from us except our submission to his judgement." Abū Lubābah said: "You have no choice, then, but to submit." As he said this he pointed to his throat in a gesture which meant that the Prophet's judgement would be to have their throats cut.

Repenting a Treasonable Act

As soon as Abū Lubābah made this gesture, he realized that his action was treasonable. He felt that he had betrayed God and the Prophet. With such a feeling, he could not face the Prophet. He left the Qurayẓah and went away, not returning to the Prophet but going straight to the mosque. He tied himself to a post in the mosque and swore that he would not leave that spot unless God forgave him his error. He also pledged to God that he would never step into the

Qurayẓah quarters again and that he would never be seen in the place which witnessed his treachery.

When the Prophet felt that Abū Lubābah had been gone a long time, he wondered: "Has Abū Lubābah not finished his consultations with his allies?" He was informed of Abū Lubābah's action and decision. The Prophet said: "Had he come back to me, I would have prayed God to forgive him. Now that he has done this, I am not the one to release him until God has pardoned him."

For six days Abū Lubābah remained tied to the post in the mosque, eating and drinking nothing. At every prayer time, his wife came to release him so that he could join the prayers, then she tied him up again after the prayers had finished. His pardon was given when God revealed the following verse to the Prophet: "There are others who have acknowledged their sins after having mingled righteous deeds with evil ones. It may well be that God will accept their repentance. God is indeed Much-Forgiving, Merciful." (9: 102) This verse was revealed at night, just before the dawn prayers. Umm Salamah, the Prophet's wife, noticed him smiling. When she asked him the reason for his smile, he mentioned to her that God has forgiven Abū Lubābah his error. She asked his permission to give Abū Lubābah the happy news and, upon receiving his permission, she went out to him and told him. People rushed to congratulate him and tried to release him, but he insisted: "I swear that no one but the Prophet himself will release me." Shortly after that, the Prophet went out to offer the dawn prayer in the mosque and he released Abū Lubābah.

Three Choices to Avoid Surrender

The Qurayẓah Jews were now left to contemplate their position. After 25 days of the siege, they were totally demoralized and they recognized that they could not hold out much longer. Their leader, Kaʿb ibn Asad, outlined to them the options they had, as he saw them: "You are aware of the difficult position in which we find ourselves. I am offering you three possibilities to choose from. The first one is to believe in this man, Muhammad, and to follow him.

By God, we are now certain that he is a Prophet and a Messenger sent by God. He is indeed the one described in our own Book. If you do so, you spare your own lives and protect your children and families." They objected to this solution and said: "We will never abandon the Old Testament and substitute anything else for it."

Ka'b then said: "Since you refuse me this possibility, I suggest to you that we kill all our women and children and go out to fight Muhammad and his followers. If we do so, we can fight much harder, since we have no responsibility behind us. We can fight him until God rules between us. If we are exterminated, then we will face death without any worry about our offspring. If, on the other hand, we achieve victory, we will soon find new women and have new children." They said: "What would be the purpose of our lives when we have killed our poor women and children?"

He went on: "Since you refuse this also, the only thing I can suggest to you is that since tonight is the Sabbath night, it may well be that Muhammad and his companions may relax their watch, thinking that we would not do anything serious on the Sabbath night. Let us then take them by surprise and fight them to the bitter end." To this suggestion, they answered: "Do you want us to spoil our Sabbath and violate it in a way that has never been done before, except by those whom you know and who received the punishment you know?" One of them, Nabbāsh ibn Qays, said: "How do you expect us to take them by surprise when you can see that they are getting stronger every day? In the early days of the siege they were in their positions during the day, and retreated at night. Now we see them maintaining the siege day and night. The surprise element is not in our hands." Ka'b then said: "None of you has ever made a firm decision since he was born."

The following morning the Qurayẓah Jews surrendered and accepted the judgement of the Prophet. Their surrender was the final outcome of a conflict which brought Islam face to face with the united forces of its enemies of pagan Arabs and Jews. The determination and steadfastness which the Muslims had shown over a period of great difficulty lasting over three months were now yielding their fruits. The Arabs had departed in humiliation, then the Jews followed by submitting to the judgement of the Prophet.

On the same night when the Qurayẓah surrendered, three Jews of the clan of Hodal came down from the Qurayẓah forts and requested to be taken to the Prophet. The three men, Thaʿlabah ibn Saʿyah, his brother Usayd and Asʿad ibn ʿUbayd, declared their acceptance of Islam. Another man, ʿAmr ibn Suʿdā, who had refused to share in the treachery of his people and counselled them against it, also came down. He passed by Muhammad ibn Maslamah, the Muslim chief guard, who recognized his special position. He said: "My Lord! Let me not be unkind to people of honour." He let him go. Nobody knows where ʿAmr went. The Prophet said later that God saved ʿAmr ibn Suʿdā for being faithful to his pledge.

A brief reminder may not come amiss here. The Muslims of Madinah who are generally called the Anṣār belonged to two main tribes, the Aws and the Khazraj. Before Islam, the two tribes were often at war with each other. In their intermittent clashes they sought alliances and it was natural that they should have looked to the Jewish groupings in Madinah for such alliances. The Khazraj were allies with the Jewish tribe of Qaynuqāʿ, while the Qurayẓah were the allies of the Aws. The Qaynuqāʿ Jews were the first of the Jewish tribes to be in conflict with the Prophet, shortly after the Battle of Badr. That conflict has been related in detail (Chapter 19). Its outcome was the evacuation of the Jews of Qaynuqāʿ after their chief ally of the Khazraj, ʿAbdullāh ibn Ubayy, had interceded with the Prophet on their behalf. They were given safe conduct out of Madinah with their women and children, and every one of them was allowed a camel load of personal belongings.

End of the Qurayẓah

Now that the Qurayẓah had surrendered, the Prophet ordered that their men be handcuffed and put to one side and their women and children put to the other side. The Muslims of the Aws tribe felt that they should try to plead for mercy with the Prophet for their former allies. It was clear that the old ties which existed between the Aws and the Qurayẓah were very strong; that the Aws people were more inclined to reprieve their former allies, despite their treachery. When the Aws people pressed their request for clemency to the Prophet, he said to them: "Would you accept if I refer the matter between me and your former allies to one of you?" The Aws were very pleased with this offer and accepted it readily. The Prophet then told them to ask the Qurayẓah to choose any person from the Aws to be their arbiter. Their choice was the chief of the Aws tribe, Sa'd ibn Mu'ādh.

Some reports suggest that it was the Prophet who chose Sa'd ibn Mu'ādh to judge the case of the Qurayẓah. Whether the choice was made by the Prophet or by the Qurayẓah, Sa'd was the right man to judge in this case. The Aws would have certainly been more satisfied with the judgement if it was made by their own chief. Besides, nothing would have been fairer to the Qurayẓah than appointing their own ally to judge them.

It was mentioned earlier that Sa'd ibn Mu'ādh was wounded in the clashes that took place during the siege imposed by the Quraysh and the Ghaṭafān on the Muslims. He was being treated for his wound in a tent clinic established by a woman called Rufaydah bint al-Ḥārith, the first clinic of its type in the Islamic period. Indeed, it was the Prophet who had asked the Aws to have Sa'd treated in Rufaydah's clinic, so that he could visit him during the siege of the Qurayẓah. When he was appointed arbiter of the Qurayẓah, some of his people came to take him to the Prophet. They brought him a donkey to ride and tried to persuade him to be lenient. They said to him: "Be kind to your allies, Abū 'Amr. The Prophet has chosen you to judge them in order that you be kind to them. You know that 'Abdullāh ibn Ubayy was kind to his allies."

Sa'd chose to be silent at first. When he was tired of their insistence, he said: "It is time for Sa'd to disregard all criticism when it comes to something through which he hopes to please God." It is said that his words indicated to his people that he was not going to let his and their sympathies interfere with his judgement. Hence, some of them went back to their people and announced to them that the Qurayẓah faced a terrible judgement, even before Sa'd reached the Prophet's tent.

When Sa'd arrived, the Prophet said to his companions: "Stand up to greet your master." They stood up in two ranks and each one of them greeted Saʿd. The Prophet then told him that he had been chosen to pass judgement on the Qurayẓah.

Saʿd said: "It is God and His Messenger who are entitled to pass judgement." The Prophet told him that it was God's command that he should give his verdict. Saʿd then turned to the Muslims and asked them: "Do you give me your most solemn oath by God that my verdict is acceptable and final?" When they answered in the affirmative, he lowered his head in deference to the Prophet, pointed his hand in the direction where the Prophet was sitting, and said: "Does this apply also to those who are on this side?" The Prophet answered, "Yes."

Saʿd then asked the Qurayẓah whether they would accept his verdict, whatever it was. They said his verdict was acceptable. He asked them to give him their most solemn pledges and oaths that they would accept whatever judgement he made. When they did, he pronounced his verdict in these words: "I hereby rule that all the men of the Qurayẓah are to be killed, their properties to be divided and their women and children be enslaved." The Prophet endorsed the ruling and said it was God's.

The judgement was then implemented. At the Prophet's orders, all the people of the Qurayẓah were taken to Madinah, where the men were detained in the house of Usāmah ibn Zayd while the women and children were detained in the house of a woman called Kayysah bint al-Ḥārith. Their armaments and movable properties were also taken to Madinah and their cattle were left in their fields. They were given dates to eat. Moats were dug in the marketplace of Madinah for the execution of the Qurayẓah men, who were taken in groups to be beheaded.

Some reports suggest that the number of men killed was 400. Others put it at 600 and others put it even higher at 800 or 900. Perhaps it is more accurate to say that the number was 600-700 people, including Ḥuyayy ibn Akhṭab, who honoured his pledge and shared the fate of the Qurayẓah. When he was taken to be killed, the Prophet said to him: "Has not God handed you over to me, you enemy of God?" Ḥuyayy replied: "Indeed, God has chosen to give you power over me. I have never blamed myself for taking a hostile attitude towards you. But he who is not given support by God is left to suffer humiliation." He turned to those around him and said: "We cannot object to God's judgement. It is a fate we have to suffer because God has imposed it on the Israelites." He was then executed.

The Prophet ordered that the prisoners be treated well and given food and drink before they were killed. The execution was left until late in the afternoon, so that the condemned were not made to suffer the burning heat of a midsummer day in addition to their execution. One man, Rifāʿah ibn Samuel, sought the protection of a woman from the Anṣār called Umm al-Mundhir. She went to the Prophet and asked him to pardon Rifāʿah, and the Prophet granted her request. Later, Rifāʿah embraced Islam. An old man from the Qurayẓah called Zubayr ibn Bāṭā had done a good turn to a man from the Anṣār called Thābit ibn Qays. Now Thābit wanted to return his favour, so he went to the Prophet and requested a pardon for him. The Prophet pardoned Zubayr and allowed him to save his family and property. Zubayr, however, told Thābit when he brought him the news that he would prefer to join his beloved friends who were killed.

ʿĀ'ishah said that one woman from the Qurayẓah was sitting with her chatting and laughing while their men were being killed. Someone called out her name and she responded. When ʿĀ'ishah asked her why she was being called, she answered: "I am taken to be executed for something I had done." ʿĀ'ishah said: "I still wonder at her relaxed manner and her chatting and laughing when she knew that she was to be killed." This was the only woman from the Qurayẓah to be killed, and her crime was that she threw a large piece of stone at a Muslim man called Khallād ibn Suwayd and killed him.[1]

The Prophet then ordered that the properties of the Qurayẓah and their women and children be divided among the Muslims. He chose for himself one of their women called Rayḥānah bint ʿAmr. He offered to marry her if she would accept Islam, but she refused and said that she would rather remain a bondswoman. He left her for a while. He was not happy that she refused Islam. Some time later, Rayḥānah voluntarily accepted Islam and the Prophet was very pleased.

How Fair Was the Judgement

This was the end of the Qurayẓah. The judgement which Saʿd passed on the Qurayẓah and their execution merit some explanation. The first point to be made is that the precautions Saʿd took before declaring his judgement, in order to ensure that his verdict would be binding on all parties and acceptable to them, suggest that he had carefully considered his verdict before he passed it. His character and his history in the service of Islam make it clear that Saʿd was a well balanced, mature and broadminded person who was devoted to Islam, ready to give any sacrifice asked of him and endowed with the rare quality of looking at every situation in its proper and broad perspective. Nevertheless he was only 35 at that time. Those rare qualities of his were the ones which secured for him the leadership of his great tribe the Aws.

Saʿd's judgement condemned all the Qurayẓah men to death and the women and children to slavery. There are some people who criticize his judgement as too severe. Since Islam is a religion of mercy, could it be said that the judgement passed on the Qurayẓah was the just one?

A universally accepted principle makes it clear that: "The punishment must fit the crime." Having stated this principle, one should perhaps remind oneself of the full extent of the Qurayẓah's crime before commenting on the severity or otherwise of their punishment. The Qurayẓah were the last of the Jewish tribes still living in Madinah. They had a peace treaty with the Prophet requiring them to defend the city alongside the Muslims against any outside enemy which attacked it. Ḥuyayy ibn Akhṭab came to Kaʿb ibn Asad, chief of the Qurayẓah, and persuaded him to break that treaty and join forces with the enemies of the Prophet and the Muslims in their attack, which was mounted with the declared aim of exterminating the Muslims altogether. Kaʿb ibn Asad allowed himself to be persuaded of this treachery, despite the fact that he realized that Ḥuyayy was, in Kaʿb's own words, "a man of ill fortune". When Ḥuyayy first stated the purpose of his visit to Kaʿb, the latter's response was: "By God, you have come to me with an everlasting shame and with a cloud that has shed its rain." He also declared: "I have seen nothing from Muhammad but honesty and faithful observance of our treaty." Despite all that, Kaʿb ibn Asad led the Qurayẓah to perpetrate a wicked act of treachery which could have left thousands of Muslims dead in the streets of Madinah and a fatal doom befalling their women and children. The Quraysh, the Ghaṭafān and the Jews of al-Naḍīr had set as their objective the extermination of all the Muslims. The Qurayẓah joined them and started preparing for a battle which would have ensured the fulfilment of that objective, had it not been for God's intervention on the side of the Muslims.

The punishment meted out to the Qurayẓah, then, was nothing more than turning the scales against them and giving them the treatment they themselves had prepared for the Muslims, who had done them no wrong. It was the Qurayẓah's own crime that they switched alliances and chose to follow the course of treachery. They were indeed criminals of war who could not be treated with mercy.

Some people may suggest that the Prophet had shown mercy to other Jewish tribes earlier; why could he not have shown the same kind of mercy to the Qurayẓah? After all, the same peace treaty held true between the Muslims and all the Jewish tribes of Madinah. When the Jews of Qaynuqāʿ and al-Naḍīr broke their treaty, they were allowed to leave Madinah carrying with them a specified portion of their belongings together with their families. The question to be asked here is whether the treachery of all these tribes was of the same magnitude.

Comparing Acts of Treason

The Jewish tribe of Qaynuqāʿ were evacuated from Madinah after they had abused a Muslim woman who was shopping at their jewellery market which, in turn, led to the killing of the jeweller by a Muslim man who happened to be at the market and the revenge killing of the Muslim man by the Jews. The whole incident took place in a period of mounting tension between the Qaynuqāʿ Jews and the Muslims, shortly after the Muslims had achieved their resounding victory at Badr.

Al-Naḍīr, on the other hand, tried to kill the Prophet when he went to them shortly after the Battle of Uḥud, requesting them to honour their treaty obligations by contributing to the blood money which the Prophet proposed to pay for the accidental killing of two Bedouin Arabs by one of his companions. Al-Naḍīr chiefs tried to win the Prophet's confidence by pretending that they were meeting his request while they were in fact engaged in carrying out an assassination plot, the victim of which would have been the Prophet himself.

In both cases, the Prophet allowed the Jewish tribe concerned to leave Madinah and go anywhere they liked in or beyond Arabia, giving them safe conduct from Madinah with their women and children. One should realize here that in both cases the crime perpetrated by the Jews was an individual one. The victim would have been one person: an ordinary Muslim woman in the first case and the Prophet himself in the second. There was also some abuse of the Prophet and other Muslims, especially in the case of the Qaynuqāʿ. Neither crime can be treated on the same footing as that of the Qurayẓah, who set their target as nothing less than the extermination of the whole Muslim community. Moreover, the Qurayẓah had actually started putting their plans into effect: they were getting ready for war and prepared to launch a rearguard attack against both the civilian quarters of the Muslims and their besieged army.

When one compares the three cases and considers carefully the relative crime of each of the three Jewish tribes, one is bound to conclude that the Prophet treated the first two graciously and leniently. In the third case, of the Qurayẓah, he was duty bound to abide by the rules of justice, as he actually did. We use the term "duty bound" advisedly, since the Prophet, as a head of state, could not disregard the feelings and interests of the whole Muslim community, which would have been the victims of the Qurayẓah's treachery. One must also consider what would have been the likely results of any kindness shown to the Qurayẓah.

The Jews, who were shown kindness and mercy by the Prophet on previous occasions, were indeed the promoters of the alliance which threatened the whole Muslim community. Ḥuyayy ibn Akhṭab in particular was the most instrumental in forging the alliance which attacked Madinah. Yet al-Naḍīr were less hostile to the Muslims than the Qurayẓah, since their treachery was confined to an assassination attempt against the Prophet. The Qurayẓah were much more hardened in their attitude against Islam by their very preparation to annihilate the Muslims. Had they been allowed to settle somewhere else in Arabia, they were certain to try to have another go at the Muslims by raising new forces and forging new alliances. No wise government would have allowed its enemy such a chance. Islam adopts a very serious and down-to-earth attitude in developing relations between the Muslim community and other communities. It leaves no room for naïvety or complacency. When the hostility of any group of people towards Islam prompts them into taking any measures against the Muslim community, such a group must be treated with justice when the Muslims overcome them and foil their hostile designs. This applies to the Qurayẓah as much as it does to anyone else. The Qurayẓah were treated with justice, as their own sacred books outline it.

If one must apportion blame in the tragedy of the Qurayẓah, one is bound to conclude that the greater part of it belongs to Ḥuyayy ibn Akhṭab. It was his obstinate hostility to the Prophet, and Islam generally, from the first day of his realization that Muhammad was indeed the man God had chosen to carry His last message to mankind and to conclude the line of Prophethood which, for generations, had rested with the Israelites. Every time the Muslims, under the Prophet's leadership, scored a new victory, Ḥuyayy's bitter grudge against Islam intensified. Every time the Muslims suffered a setback, as they did at Uḥud, he was overjoyed. He allowed his grudge to be his overall motive. Once he and his tribe were evacuated from Madinah, he set out on his evil mission, working hard to forge that ungodly alliance, making his target the extermination of the whole Muslim community. This view is shared by another leader of the Jewish tribe of al-Naḍīr, Sallām ibn Mishkam, who said on hearing of what happened to the Qurayẓah: "This is all Ḥuyayy ibn Akhṭab's doing. Judaism will never have a base in Hijaz in future."

When the Qurayẓah affair was finally settled, the Muslims' position in Madinah was far stronger. The hypocrites among its residents lost their Jewish allies and so felt themselves to be in a much weaker position. The Muslims also benefited economically from the wealth left by the Qurayẓah. Indeed, the confrontation with the confederate Arab tribes first and with the Qurayẓah later marked an important turning point in the history of Islam. Never again were the Muslims to be attacked in their own city. It was now time for them to consolidate their own position and to spread Islam across Arabia.

So the Muslims emerged much stronger from those three months which were perhaps the most difficult period in their history. However, they suffered a few casualties, the most important of whom was Saʿd ibn Muʿādh, the man who sat in judgement in the case of the Qurayẓah.

A Noble Soul Gathered

It has already been related that Saʿd was hit on the arm by an arrow and received a serious wound during the siege of Madinah. At the time, with the fortunes of Islam weighing heavily on his mind, he prayed to God: "My Lord, if we are to fight the Quraysh again, spare me now for that fight. There are no people I like to fight for Your cause, more than those who have opposed Your Messenger, rejected him and forced him out of his home town. If You have willed that this encounter between us would be the last, I pray You, my Lord, to make this wound of mine my way to martyrdom, but spare me until I see our affair with the Qurayẓah have a happy ending for Islam." The events that followed indicated clearly that God answered Saʿd's prayers. His wound healed temporarily while the siege of the Qurayẓah went on. When it was over, he was chosen to arbitrate in their case. When his verdict was carried out Saʿd was taken back to the mosque where he was being nursed.

During the night, his wound opened up and he bled heavily. There are several reports which, taken together, confirm that the Angel Gabriel came to the Prophet that night and asked: "Muhammad, who is this dead man for whom the gates of the heavens have opened up and for whom God's throne has stirred?" The Prophet hurried from his rooms to the tent where Saʿd was being nursed to find that he was dead. The Prophet was heartily grieved to lose that great servant of Islam, but he was also pleased for him because he had earned his martyrdom, with its great reward.[2]

With the execution of the Qurayẓah's men, there was no longer any great concentration of Jews in Madinah. There were obviously some who had not taken part in any act of treachery and they, as individuals, were allowed to stay on in Madinah as long as they did not participate in any hostile action against Islam or the Muslims. They were allowed to work and practise their religion freely, without any pressures. Indeed, when the Prophet died a few years later, his own body armour was pledged with a Jewish pawnbroker. Those who were active against Islam were not allowed to carry on their hostile activities.

Liquidating a Hardened Opponent

One of those was Sallām ibn Abī al-Ḥuqayq, whom the Prophet wanted punished. Sallām was one of the chiefs of the Jewish tribe of al-Naḍīr. Along with Ḥuyayy ibn Akhṭab, he was instrumental in forging the alliance of the Arab tribes which attacked Madinah. Ḥuyayy was killed with the Qurayẓah. Sallām, however, took refuge in Khaybar, a city in the middle of Arabia which housed the greatest concentration of Jews in the land. The Prophet did not merely want him punished for revenge; he knew that the man would continue with his efforts to undermine the Muslim state. He was therefore an enemy with whom no accommodation could be made.

The two tribes of the Anṣār, the Aws and the Khazraj, were determined to show the Prophet that they were equally devoted to the cause of Islam. If either tribe was successful in accomplishing a good deed for Islam, the other tried hard to get on the same level with them. When the Prophet wanted to get rid of Kaʿb ibn al-Ashraf, the Jewish chief from the tribe of the Qaynuqāʿ who abused Muslim women and sided with the Quraysh after their defeat at Badr, it was some men from the Aws who carried out the task of liquidating him. The Khazraj were on the lookout for something of equal significance to get back on the same footing with the Aws. This competition for honours, however, must not be blown up out of proportion. There were no jealousies between the two tribes; it was more of a sporting competition, after they had been united by their faith in Islam.

The Khazraj people felt that Sallām ibn Abū al-Ḥuqayq offered them the right choice for matching the Aws's deed. A group of them sought and received the Prophet's permission to plot his assassination. Five of them, led by ʿAbdullāh ibn Anīs, went to Khaybar to have him liquidated. Just before they left, the Prophet issued them his instruction that they must not kill a child or a woman under any circumstances.

One evening, they forced their way into Sallām's home. ʿAbdullāh ibn Anīs spoke the language of the Jews and it was he who locked all the doors and told Sallām's wife when she asked his name that he came with a present for Sallām. The woman opened the door and tried to shout for help when she realized that the men were armed. They threatened her with their swords, but without hitting her, because they were eager to obey the Prophet's instructions. When they went inside, they hit Sallām with their swords. However, he had his body armour on and was only slightly wounded. One of them, nevertheless, forced his sword into his stomach and leant on the sword with all his weight until he realized that Sallām was dead.

When they had accomplished their task, they withdrew hurriedly. Sallām's wife shouted for help. As the five men were on their way out, ʿAbdullāh ibn Anīs, who was short-sighted, fell down the stairs and hurt his leg badly. His Muslim brothers carried him and sought refuge in a safe place. They were chased everywhere by groups of Jews from Khaybar but they managed to evade their pursuers. They remained in their refuge for two days before they could continue their journey, helping their injured brother the whole way.

When they arrived at Madinah, they gave the Prophet the news of Sallām's death. Every one of them, however, claimed that he had killed Sallām. The Prophet asked them to show him their swords and when he had seen them he determined that it was ʿAbdullāh ibn Anīs who had killed Sallām. The Prophet said that traces of Sallām's food were visible on the sword. Thus, a hardened enemy of Islam was liquidated.[3]

Their great victories in the two encounters of the moat and the Qurayẓah gave the Muslims great prestige in Arabia. They became truly feared by all Arabian tribes. Their state was recognized as immune to attack. The Prophet had discerned the future turn of events when he saw the Arabian armies of the Quraysh and the Ghaṭafān which withdrew from battle without engaging the Muslims in a full-scale war. He remarked then: "Now we will no longer be on the defensive; they will not attack us again."

Consolidating the New Position

The Prophet also realized that he had to consolidate the new position of the Muslims by demonstrating that the balance of power in Arabia continued to move in their favour. At the beginning of the third month of the sixth year of his emigration to Madinah (July AD 627), the Prophet set out from Madinah at the head of a force of two hundred of his companions to attack a tribe called Liḥyān who lived at Fazzān Valley in Hijaz, not far from Makkah. He had a score to settle with that tribe. As related earlier, the tribe of Liḥyān perpetrated an act of ghastly treachery when they persuaded the Prophet to send a few of his companions to teach them the Qur'ān and explain to them how to live as Muslims. He had sent six of his companions. When they arrived in their neighbourhood, the Liḥyān attacked them and killed four of them and sold the other two to the Quraysh in Makkah where they were executed. That act of treachery is known in history books as the Day of al-Rajī'.

Attacking the tribe of Liḥyān meant going very close to Makkah, where the Quraysh would dearly have loved to meet such a small force of Muslims in open battle. Should the Quraysh learn of the Prophet's intention, they would be able to raise a large army very quickly, come to the aid of the Liḥyān and try to settle their score with the Muslims. They would be able to call on other tribes to support them. The prize would have been too great for them to miss, especially with the Prophet himself leading the Muslim expedition.

The Prophet, however, was a shrewd military commander. He knew that the Liḥyān watched his movements carefully, realizing that one day he might decide to punish them for their treachery. He therefore moved northwards in the direction of Syria. He went quite a long distance in that direction until he felt that no one would suspect that his real objective was southward. He then turned south on the route to Makkah and moved at a very high speed towards Fazzān. He hoped that in this way he could take the Liḥyān unawares. They, however, were greatly afraid that their turn would inevitably come. They watched the Prophet's movements very, very carefully. When he arrived at the place where the act of treachery was actually committed, the Liḥyān tribesmen realized that the Prophet aimed to attack them. They fled and sought refuge in the nearby mountains. When the Prophet arrived at the Liḥyān quarters he found nobody there. He encamped there for a couple of days and sent several detachments of his forces in all directions, looking out for the Liḥyān, but they discovered nothing. Trying to make the most of his expedition, the Prophet suggested to his companions: "If we can go as far as ʿAsafān and encamp there, the Quraysh would realize that we have reached Makkah itself." He led his companions then until they arrived at ʿAsafān. Having encamped there, the Prophet then sent a number of his companions, under the leadership of Abū Bakr, towards Makkah. They arrived at Kurāʿ al-Ghamīm on the outskirts and came back.[4]

When the Quraysh realized that the Prophet was at ʿAsafān, they hurriedly raised a large force under the leadership of Khālid ibn al-Walīd. When the two forces were facing each other, it was time for *ẓuhr* prayers. The Prophet and his companions offered that prayer while the Quraysh force was watching them. When their prayers were over, the Quraysh started to blame themselves for not attacking the Muslims while they were praying. They felt that they had missed a chance to strike when the Muslims could not hit back. Someone from the Quraysh army then reminded his fellow soldiers that the Muslims would be praying again before long. Referring to *ʿaṣr* prayers, the Quraysh fighters thought: "Before long, the Muslims will be engaged in a prayer which is dearer to them than their own children, and even their own lives."

Prayer When Fearing Attack

At this point, the Prophet received revelations explaining how he should offer his prayers with his companions in such a situation when they are afraid that their enemies may attack them. This is fully explained in the Qur'ān (4: 102) and is known in religious books as 'Prayers in the case of fear'. It has already been described briefly at the beginning of Chapter 23 but here is a more detailed account.

When it was time for *ʿaṣr* prayer, the Quraysh soldiers were watching and hoping to attack the Muslims when they prostrated themselves, putting their heads on the ground. The Prophet's companions, however, lined up in two rows behind him as he led the prayers. When he finished his recitation of the Qur'ān he bowed and all of his companions bowed with him. All of them then stood up in the normal way. The Prophet then knelt and prostrated himself, and the first row of his companions did likewise. The second line remained in a standing position to guard their brethren as they prostrated themselves. When the first line finished their two prostrations and stood up, the second line did their two prostrations and joined them in the standing position. The two lines then changed places and the Prophet continued with his second *rakʿah*, which was conducted in the same way as the first. The second line (which was in front in the first *rakʿah*) took up the guard duty as their brethren prostrated themselves with the Prophet. When they had finished their prostrations, the first line guarded them as they did theirs. The whole community of Muslims then joined the Prophet in the final part of the prayers, which was conducted with all of them sitting down. They all finished their prayers together.[5]

This is how prayers are offered in a situation where the Muslims fear that they may be attacked while they are praying. Since Muslims prostrate themselves and put their heads on the ground when they pray, that moment gives their enemies a chance to hit them hard and cause considerable casualties in their ranks. Islam, however, is a practical religion and faces every situation squarely and directly. Prayers must be offered by Muslims regardless of the situation in which they find themselves, but prayers may be offered in a modified manner to meet a certain emergency. In this instance, half the Muslim community remained on guard while their brethren continued with their prayers. Hence, their enemies could not take them unawares. The changeover, which is carried out after the first *rak'ah*, is done so that every one of the Muslim army shares equally in all duties of fighting, guarding and praying. This is in line with the Islamic view of fighting and prayers.

Islam views all human activities as acts of worship when they are done for God's sake and to earn His pleasure. When a Muslim prays he demonstrates his continued willingness to submit himself to God. When he goes to fight the enemy, he makes it clear that he is ready to sacrifice his life for the cause of God. When he follows a command given him by the Prophet or by anyone who is assigned a position of responsibility in the Islamic state, he makes his contribution to the overall work of the state for the sole purpose of pleasing God. Within this framework, a Muslim expects to be rewarded by God for everything he does. This, however, is conditional upon his intention and the aim behind his action. Any action a Muslim does in order to please God or to contribute to the welfare of the Muslim state is an act of worship which is sure to be rewarded by God. On the other hand, a pure act of worship, such as prayer, is rejected by God and earns no reward from Him if it is done for any motive other than to please God. Thus, if a person prays in order for it to be known that he is regular in his prayers, all the reward he receives for his prayers is the reputation he gains among his fellow human beings. God, Who is well aware of people's intentions, will reward him accordingly.

Notes

1. All this account of how the Prophet dealt with the tribe of Qurayẓah after their treachery is based on the account given in Ibn Hishām, *al-Sīrah al-Nabawiyyah*, Dār al-Qalam, Beirut, Vol. 1, pp. 244-256. Similar accounts are given in all other books cited here.
2. Ibn Hishām, op.cit., p. 262.
3. Ibid., pp. 286-288.
4. Ibid., pp. 292-293. Also, Ibn Sayyid al-Nās, *'Uyūn al-Athar*, Dār al-Turāth, Madinah, 1996, p. 124; and Ibn Kathīr, *al-Bidāyah wal-Nihāyah*, Maktabat al-Ma'ārif, Beirut, Vol. 1, p. 149 and pp. 81-83.
5. Ibn Kathīr, op.cit., p. 81.

27

Family Matters

SHORTLY AFTER THE Prophet started to receive God's message, Zaynab, the eldest daughter of the Prophet, along with the rest of the household, embraced Islam. Her husband Abū al-ʿĀṣ ibn al-Rabīʿ, however, did not. No ruling was given at that time about the validity of marriages where one partner remained a non-Muslim. Zaynab therefore continued to live with her husband for a number of years and their marriage was a happy one. When the Prophet emigrated to Madinah, Zaynab stayed behind in Makkah with her husband. As has already been related, at the Battle of Badr Abū al-ʿĀṣ took part in the battle as a soldier of the Quraysh, against the Muslims. He was taken prisoner and he received the same treatment as the rest of the Quraysh prisoners who were invited to buy their release. Zaynab sent the due ransom and included in it a necklace which her late mother, Khadījah, had given her to wear on her wedding night. When he saw the necklace, the Prophet was deeply touched and said to his companions: "If you feel it proper to release her husband for her and refund her money, you may do so." Thus Abū al-ʿĀṣ was released for no ransom.

Shortly after his return to Makkah, Abū al-ʿĀṣ sent his wife to Madinah to join her father, the Prophet. This he did in fulfilment of the promise he gave the Prophet just before he left Madinah. The events of Zaynab's journey and the Quraysh's attempt to prevent her from leaving Makkah were related in detail earlier. Zaynab continued to live in Madinah with the Prophet, while her husband remained in Makkah. This is because she was a Muslim and he still followed idolatrous beliefs that associate partners with God. Their separation continued for about four years before the following events took place.

A Caravan is Intercepted

In the month of Jumādā al-ʿŪlā of the sixth year after the Prophet's emigration to Madinah (September AD 627) the Prophet sent an expedition of 170 men under the leadership of Zayd ibn Ḥārithah to intercept a Quraysh trade caravan on its way back from Syria. Zayd's mission was highly successful. He managed to intercept the caravan and gain all its cargo. Some of the men who were travelling with the caravan were taken prisoner. Abū al-ʿĀṣ was in charge of that caravan, but he managed to escape when the attack took place. When he was certain that he had evaded his pursuers, he sat down for a moment to reflect on his position and realized that he was in difficulties. The fact that he was so closely related to the Prophet would have made him open to the charge that he did not exercise due diligence in safeguarding his trust. He might have been accused of complacency or complicity in what had happened. He felt that he could not just return to Makkah and inform the Quraysh that his caravan was intercepted, despite the fact that his was by no means the first trade caravan to be intercepted by the Muslims in Madinah.

Abū al-ʿĀṣ therefore went to Madinah. He had to approach it very carefully, lest he should be taken prisoner. As he drew nearer, he moved only during the night. When almost everybody in Madinah was asleep, he moved stealthily until he gained access to Zaynab's home, just next to the mosque. He sought to be her guest and under her protection. She granted him that, since there was nothing in the teachings of Islam which prevented any Muslim from doing so. Indeed, there is every encouragement to extend protection to those who fear for their lives.

Soon, it was time for dawn prayers and the believers were assembled in the mosque where the Prophet led them in prayers. When the congregational prayer began and all the Muslims were engaged in their prayers, Zaynab came out of the women's quarters and spoke loudly: "Let everybody know that I have extended protection to Abū al-ʿĀṣ ibn al-Rabīʿ."

When the prayers were over, the Prophet turned towards the congregation and asked them whether they had heard what he did. When they replied in the affirmative, he said: "By Him who holds my soul in His hand, I knew nothing of this until I heard what you heard. The believers are a single unit. The most humble among them may speak for them all and extend protection on their behalf. We will honour her pledge." When people left the mosque, the Prophet went to his daughter and told her to be hospitable to Abū al-ʿĀṣ. He made it clear to her that she was not to treat him as her husband despite the fact that they were not divorced. Since Abū al-ʿĀṣ was not a Muslim, his wife was separated from him because of his faith. He could not, therefore, expect a husband's treatment in Zaynab's home: they could not have a sexual relationship. That did not preclude kind treatment and hospitality.

Zaynab then pleaded with the Prophet to return to Abū al-ʿĀṣ everything that had been taken from him. It was a case of Zaynab feeling that such a treatment might produce a better result. The Prophet was the kindest of people to his children and to the Muslim community generally. There are numerous examples of requests made by ordinary Muslims in all sorts of circumstances and one can easily conclude that the Prophet would always grant any such request provided it did not involve a contradiction of something that God had decreed. In this instance, the matter was not wholly up to him. He said to his companions: "You know the sort of relationship that binds us to this man. You have taken some money and property from him. If you are kind enough to give him back what you have taken from him, we will appreciate that. If you refuse, you are totally within your right to do so. What you have gained is something that God has given you." Needless to say, there was no pressure from the Prophet on the Muslims to give back to Abū al-ʿĀṣ what had been taken from him. The Prophet made it plain that to keep the booty was to act within everyone's rights. Those Muslims who were the companions of the Prophet refused him nothing. Once they realized that he would be pleased if they behaved in a certain way, they were keen to do what pleased him. In this instance, they brought back even the smallest of items which had been taken from Abū al-ʿĀṣ and his caravan. He commented that it was all given back intact, as if it had never been taken.

Abū al-ʿĀṣ then went to Makkah. He paid back the property of everyone who had a share in the caravan. No one suffered any loss. Indeed, they received all the profit Abū al-ʿĀṣ made in this business venture. When he had done that and everybody was happy with what they got, Abū al-ʿĀṣ asked them: "Do I owe anyone anything still?" When they answered in the negative, he said: "Have I fulfilled my trust and discharged my mission to your satisfaction?" All of them said: "Yes indeed. We have found you, as we have always known you, a man of honesty and integrity."

He said: "I would like you to know, then, that I declare that there is no deity except God, and that Muhammad is His Messenger. I want further to say that nothing stopped me from declaring my belief in Islam when I was in Madinah except my fear that you might think that I wanted to keep your money. Now that God has given you back your money and I have fulfilled my charge, I feel free of any obligation towards you and I declare my belief in Islam." Abū al-ʿĀṣ then went back to Madinah, where he was reunited with his wife. No new marriage contract was necessary for this reunion.[1]

This is a case where the Prophet and his family shared fully and without hesitation in whatever their faith required of them. A separation which lasted for about four years was effected between the Prophet's own daughter and her husband because he was not quick enough to adopt Islam. This should provide some comfort to those women who convert to Islam without their husbands. They should trust in God and hope for a happy outcome.

A Marriage at Long Distance

The Prophet's own married life shows a remarkable change after his emigration to Madinah. When he was in Makkah, the Prophet had one wife, Khadījah, with whom he lived for 25 years until her death three years before his emigration. There is no report whatsoever of the Prophet entertaining any thoughts of another marriage while Khadījah was alive, despite the fact that polygamy was a common practice and a recognized institution in the social life of Arabia. There was no limit to the number of wives a man could have. Under Islam, polygamy was restricted to a maximum of four wives for a man at any time. Hence there was nothing, socially or religiously, to prevent the Prophet from having another wife during that long period of his life. It was the Prophet's own choice to have a single wife with whom he led a very happy life.

In Madinah, the Prophet married several wives in a period of ten years. Indeed, when he died he left nine widows. God exempted the Prophet from the restriction applicable to all Muslims with regard to the number of wives they could have. A careful consideration of the Prophet's marriages is certain to reveal important reasons for each marriage which cannot be overlooked. These reasons relate mostly to the establishment of strong ties between the Prophet and important figures among the Muslims, with unmistakable effects on the future of the Islamic state the Prophet established in Madinah. Some of his marriages were highly beneficial to the tribes to which the wives concerned belonged.

One has already seen what it meant to the al-Muṣṭalaq tribe that the Prophet married Juwayriyyah, the daughter of al-Ḥārith ibn Abū Ḍirār, their chief. His marriage to her ensured the freedom of all her people from bondage, after they were taken prisoner. The Muslims felt that they could not enslave people who were related by marriage to the Prophet. Some of his marriages had legislative reasons; some had definite purposes.

One marriage of the latter group was that which united the Prophet with Umm Ḥabībah Ramlah bint Abū Sufyān. Ramlah – or Umm Ḥabībah as she is better known – was the daughter of none other than Abū Sufyān, the Quraysh's leader who commanded its armies in several battles against the Prophet and the Muslims.

Umm Ḥabībah was one of the early Muslims. She was married to a man called ʿUbaydullāh ibn Jaḥsh, who also adopted Islam. Some 12 or 13 years before her marriage to the Prophet, Umm Ḥabībah emigrated with her husband to Abyssinia when the Prophet advised his companions to go there in order to escape the Quraysh's persecution and to establish a new base for Islam in a country where there was no religious persecution. It so happened that her husband, ʿUbaydullāh ibn Jaḥsh, converted to Christianity during his stay in Abyssinia. He continued to live there with Umm Ḥabībah but he was always taunting the Muslims who stayed there, saying that he was the only one who saw the clear light of Christianity. He used to say to them: "I am the only one with clear vision, while you have only a dim view of the truth."[2] This was heartbreaking for Umm Ḥabībah, who continued to live with him because the legislation which separated Muslim women from their non-Muslim husbands was not yet revealed.

Shortly after the expeditions of the moat and the Qurayẓah, the Prophet learnt of the death of ʿUbaydullāh ibn Jaḥsh. He realized that Umm Ḥabībah was in a very difficult position in Abyssinia, living on her own with her daughter, while her father, Abū Sufyān, was engaged in a long struggle against Islam. There was no question of her returning to her parents, while staying on her own in Abyssinia did not offer any great prospects for her.

From another point of view, the situation between the Muslim state in Madinah and the Quraysh was now very different. After the failure of the grand design which brought together all the hostile forces in a determined attempt to crush Islam and annihilate the Muslims, the initiative was now in the Muslims' hands. There was no question that the balance continued to move in their favour. The Prophet was not an ordinary ruler who wanted to build an empire or to extend the area of his rule. He wanted all people to recognize the validity of Islam and the benefits they were bound to get from becoming Muslims. He wanted his enemies to see the light of Islam and to appreciate the great change in their lives which would be produced by adopting it. Hence, he was thinking of the future relations between the Muslims and the Quraysh when he sent his emissary, ʿAmr ibn Umayyah al-Ḍamrī to Negus, King of Abyssinia, who was so hospitable to the Muslims and became a Muslim himself. The Prophet wanted arrangements to be made for his marriage to Umm Ḥabībah.

Umm Ḥabībah reports:

> During the time when I was in Abyssinia, I had an unexpected visit from a maid of Negus called Abrahah, who attended to his dress and toilet. She asked permission to see me and I let her in. She came straight to the point and said to me: "The King would like you to know that the Messenger of God (Peace be upon him) has sent to him a letter with his proposal to you and asked him to supervise your marriage to him." I said to her: "May God give you great and happy news." She went on to say that the King would like me to appoint a man to act for me in making the marriage contract. I sent for Khālid ibn Saʿīd ibn al-ʿĀṣ and appointed him as my representative. I gave Abrahah two silver bracelets and two foot bracelets and a number of silver rings which I wore on each of my toes. This I did because I was overwhelmed with joy at the news she had just given me.
>
> Towards the evening Negus sent for Jaʿfar ibn Abī Ṭālib and the rest of the Muslims to attend him. When they had gathered in his court, he made the following speech: "Praise be to God, King of the Universe, the most praiseworthy, the Almighty. I declare that there is no deity other than God and that Muhammad is His servant and Messenger and that he is the one of whose mission Jesus, son of Mary, had spoken. The Messenger of God has asked me to marry him to Umm Ḥabībah bint Abū Sufyān and I am attending to his request. He has given her a dowry of 400 dinars." He then put the money in front of those who attended him.
>
> Khālid ibn Saʿīd spoke next: "Praise be to God. I praise Him and pray Him for forgiveness. I declare that there is no deity but God and that Muhammad is His servant and Messenger. He has sent him with right guidance and with the religion of truth so that it may supersede all other religions in spite of the unbelievers. I accept the proposal of God's Messenger and I marry him to Umm Ḥabībab bint Abū Sufyān. May God bless this marriage and give His Messenger all His blessings."
>
> Negus then paid Khālid ibn Saʿīd the dowry and the Muslims indicated their desire to leave. Negus told them to sit

> down because it was a tradition of all the Prophets that a table would be laid for people to eat when any Prophet got married. He ordered a table to be laid and all of them shared in the repast before they left.

Shortly afterwards, Negus ordered all the arrangements to be made for Umm Ḥabībah's departure for Madinah. Her escort was Zayd ibn Ḥārithah, a companion of the Prophet. Negus also paid all the expenses of the marriage. It should be noted here that Umm Ḥabībah received the highest dowry of all the Prophet's wives. Their dowries were normally 400-500 dirhams, while hers was 400 dinars, equivalent to 4,000 dirhams. (The dirham was the silver currency of the day. Ten dirhams equalled one dinar, the gold currency.)

When Abū Sufyān heard of his daughter's marriage to the Prophet, he said: "Muhammad is a person of high calibre against whom no one can say anything bad." He recognized that it was an honour for anyone to be related to the Prophet by marriage.[3]

A Marriage Contrary to Norms

Another of the Prophet's marriages took place at this time. This was the one which united God's Messenger with Zaynab bint Jaḥsh.[4] The enemies of Islam have always sought to use this marriage as a vehicle for their false propaganda against Islam and the Prophet. There will always be some people who try hard to twist plain facts in order to achieve their personal ends. This marriage of the Prophet is an example of the type of incident which should raise no curiosity and stir no controversy if taken in its proper perspective. It is also the type of event which can be given a totally different colour through the distortion of some details leading to, or resulting from, it.

When Muhammad was only a young man of 25 – that is, some 15 years before he received his message – he married Khadījah bint Khuwaylid, who gave him a slave boy named Zayd ibn Ḥārithah to serve him. Even at that early stage in his life, Muhammad felt that slavery was extremely repugnant. He did not wish to own a slave. He therefore set Zayd free and allowed him to stay in his service as a free man. When Zayd realized what sort of man Muhammad was, and what a fine character he had, he became so fond of him that he did not wish to change his situation in relation to him.

Zayd had originally belonged to an Arabian tribe and was taken prisoner when another tribe raided the quarters of his own people. He was then sold in Makkah and came into Khadījah's possession as mentioned earlier. Zayd's father and uncle tried to buy his freedom, but Muhammad told them that Zayd was free to go with them if he wished. "If he, on the other hand, chooses to stay with me, I would not part with him for anything you offer." Zayd unhesitatingly chose to stay with Muhammad, saying to his incredulous father and uncle that he had known Muhammad for several years and he would not part company with him for anything in the world. As a result, Muhammad declared in front of everybody in Makkah his decision to adopt Zayd as his own son.

All these events took place long before Islam. When the Prophet received his first revelations, Zayd was the first man to embrace Islam. He knew Muhammad too well to entertain any doubt about the truthfulness of his message. He served Islam as one of its best followers and soldiers. The Prophet assigned to him the command of several expeditions. Perhaps the Prophet did not love any man better than he loved Zayd, with the possible exception of Zayd's own son Usāmah.

When the Prophet had settled in Madinah, he wanted to marry Zayd to one of his own relatives, Zaynab bint Jaḥsh, whose mother was Umaymah bint ʿAbd al-Muṭṭalib, the Prophet's own parental aunt. She was not keen on the marriage. Her brother was even less agreeable. After all, Zaynab belonged to the same family as the Prophet, which was the noblest family in the whole of Arabia. In comparison to such a great lineage, who was Zayd? Was he not a mere slave to whom the Prophet had shown great kindness? He was being called Zayd ibn Muhammad, it is true; but that appellation did not change the facts.

Zaynab, however, did not have much choice. She was a good Muslim and as such she could not refuse a wish expressed by the Prophet. The Prophet's purpose behind marrying his own cousin to a former slave was to destroy for ever all class distinction. Zaynab and her brother consented to the marriage, with reluctance, to ob the Prophet. They realized that it was not up to them to dissen especially when God revealed in the Qur'ān that an order by the Prophet was final, even when it involved the personal life of any believer. "No believer, man or woman, may have a choice in their own personal affairs when God and His Messenger have determined something (respecting such affairs.) He who disobeys God and His Messenger goes demonstrably astray." (33: 36)

Zayd's marriage with Zaynab was not a happy one. She had no love for him and could not rid herself of her class feelings. She always made him conscious that she thought herself far above him socially.

Zayd, who never accepted that he was a slave and never had a slave's mentality, could not tolerate Zaynab's attitude. He complained to the Prophet on several occasions. The Prophet was always ready to help. He counselled Zaynab to restrain her pride and to accept God's decision with regard to her marriage. But the situation in Zayd's home continued to flare up every now and then.

The Prophet was then instructed by God to let Zayd divorce his wife, since he expressed his desire to do so frequently, although he did not do so in deference to the Prophet's wishes. The Prophet was further instructed to marry Zaynab when her divorce process was completed.

The Prophet was greatly perturbed when he received these instructions. He was apprehensive about what such a marriage might bring. He kept the matter to himself and spoke of it to nobody. He realized that if he married Zaynab, people would start talking and accuse him of marrying his daughter-in-law. God's purpose, however, was to put an end to such false pretensions. No one may claim to be the father of anyone other than his own children. The system of adoption, with all that it entails, was to be stopped forever.

The Prophet, however, did not proceed promptly to implement God's instructions on this particular occasion. Perhaps he hoped that God might relieve him of this unwelcome duty which caused him so much worry. He went even further. When Zayd came again complaining of his wife and expressing a renewed desire to divorce her, the Prophet said to him: "Hold on to your wife and have fear of God."

At this point, Qur'ānic revelations were received by the Prophet which criticized his attitude and encouraged him to allow Zayd to divorce Zaynab. He was again commanded to marry Zaynab when she was fully divorced. That certain people might say that Muhammad was marrying his daughter-in-law should not be a reason to stop the Prophet from fulfilling God's instructions. Adoption is, after all, a form of forgery. Since the system of adoption was well entrenched in Arabian society, only a practical example by the Prophet himself would be sufficient to put an end to it.

The source of information on these events is nothing less authoritative than the Qur'ān itself. God addresses the Prophet in the Qur'ān, making clear that He was fully aware of the Prophet's feelings:

> You say to the man whom God has favoured with His grace and you have favoured with your bounty: hold on to your wife and fear God. You keep to yourself what God wants to make public. You fear people when God is the one whom you should fear. When Zayd has finished his business with her, We married her to you so that the believers would have no reluctance to marry the former wives of those whom they used to claim as their own children, when they have finished their business with them. (33: 37)[5]

Here is the clearest of statements. The Prophet was counselling Zayd not to divorce his wife, keeping to himself something that God wanted to be known. Furthermore, here is a statement that the marriage of the Prophet and Zaynab was made in fulfilment of God's own instructions: "We have married her to you." The whole purpose is also made absolutely clear: it is to put an end to this system of adoption and all that it entails.

Despite these clear statements by God, the enemies of Islam continued to spread rumours and make false accusations. One of the most stupid of their accusations is the one which claims that the Prophet was in love with Zaynab and tried to hide his love. When it was known, it is so claimed, he felt he should marry her. Those who maintain such an indefensible view also claim that the Qur'ānic verse quoted above criticizes the Prophet for suppressing his feelings towards Zaynab.

Such claims are self-contradictory, to say the least. Who could have prevented the Prophet from marrying Zaynab, his own cousin who was a devout Muslim? It was he who asked her to marry Zayd against her own wishes. He also tried repeatedly to comfort her so that she would be satisfied with her marriage. Moreover, the claim that the Prophet is criticized for not making his love to Zaynab known to people cannot stand any analysis. Suppose that a man falls in love with another man's wife – is he morally bound to speak of that love in public? Would God criticize a man who could not help his feelings if he suppressed such a love and kept it to himself? Would he be better rewarded if he were to write some love poems expressing his feelings? It is this kind of ludicrous interpretation that is advanced as the meaning of the Qur'ānic verse. The Qur'ānic statement admits only the incidents just related. The Prophet is being told by God that he also cannot delay the implementation of God's orders. He need not feel any worry about breaking former social traditions when he has received God's instructions to do so, for God's will must be done. Hence, the Prophet had no option but to proceed with this marriage.

When Zayd divorced his wife and she had completed her waiting period, the Prophet asked Zayd to go over to Zaynab and propose to her on his behalf. He went to her home, where she was making the dough to bake her bread. Zayd reported: "When I saw her, I felt uneasy. I could not even look at her because God's Messenger (peace be upon him) was her suitor. I, therefore, turned my back to her and said: 'Zaynab, I bring you a happy piece of news. God's Messenger has sent me to tell you that he wishes to marry you.' She said: 'I am not prepared to do anything until I have sought guidance from my Lord'." She immediately went to pray. Then the Qur'ānic verse which speaks of this marriage was revealed and the Prophet came to Zaynab's home and entered without waiting for permission.

The Prophet's action in entering Zaynab's house without waiting for permission is, in itself, an indication that the matter was no longer in his or Zaynab's hands. This is a marriage which was ordered by God for, among other things, legislative purposes.

Zaynab was a woman of fine character, devout and kind. Few women could equal her in her kindness to the poor. She was indeed an example for Muslim women in her strength of faith and voluntary devotion. She used to fast frequently and spent part of the night in voluntary devotion. Nothing, however, could take away from her the feeling that her marriage to the Prophet gave her a highly unique position. She used to say to the Prophet: "I am proud of three things, none of which can be possessed by any of your other wives: you and I have the same grandfather [this refers to the fact that Abd al-Muṭṭalib was the father of ʿAbdullāh, the Prophet's father, and Umaymah, Zaynab's mother]. And I was married to you by God, glorified be He, with an order sent down from heaven, and the emissary in our marriage was the Angel Gabriel (peace be upon him)."[6]

A Lesson of Good Manners

It is a tradition of the Prophet that marriage should be celebrated with a banquet to which people should be invited. This is in order to publicize the marriage. A banquet is not merely a very good method of publicity, in any society, regardless of that society's state of development; it is also a means of making the occasion of marriage a happy one for the community as a whole. When the Prophet married Zaynab, a woman called Umm Salīm prepared some food and gave it to Anas ibn Mālik and told him: "Take this to God's Messenger (peace be upon him) and tell him that this is a humble present from us to him." Anas, the reporter of this event, observes that it was a time when most commodities were scarce. He took the food to the Prophet and conveyed Umm Salīm's message. He says:

> The Prophet looked at it and told me to put it aside, and to go and invite some people to come and eat. He named a large number of people and then added, "and every Muslim you meet". I went around and invited the people he named as well as everyone I met on my way. When I came back, the house and the area outside in the mosque were full of people. The Prophet told me to come over to him and I brought him the food. He put his hand over it and prayed to God and said: "Whatever God wills is done." He then asked the people to make small groups of ten men each and to mention God's

name before they started eating. He also instructed them that everyone should eat what was nearest to him. They did as he told them and started eating. Every one of them ate his fill. When they had all finished, the Prophet asked me to take the food away. I looked at the pan and I am not sure whether it was fuller when I put it down, before anybody ate anything, or when I lifted it after they had finished eating.

Most people left after they had eaten their meal, but some men stayed behind, inside the Prophet's house. The Prophet's bride was also there. She turned her face to the wall, because she was shy. The men, however, continued to talk for a long while, and the Prophet felt embarrassed. He was extremely shy. Had they known that their behaviour embarrassed the Prophet, they would have been very sorry. The Prophet went out to see his other wives. He went first to ʿĀ'ishah. As he entered her room he said: "Members of this household, peace be to you along with God's mercy and blessings." She returned his greeting with a similar one and asked him, "How have you found your new wife, may God give His blessings to you?" He called on every one of his other wives, and each one of them said the same thing as ʿĀ'ishah. When he had finished, he came back towards Zaynab's room to find that three men still remained. Feeling very shy and embarrassed, he turned back to go to ʿĀ'ishah's room again. The men realized that they should leave and went out hurriedly. I am not sure whether it was me who told him or that he was informed by God that the men had left. He came again to Zaynab's room and as soon as he put his first foot in, the curtain was drawn between us.[7]

It is indeed on this occasion that the special teachings about the Prophet's wives and their appearance in public was revealed. These instructions make it absolutely clear that although the Prophet's wives enjoyed a special status by virtue of the fact that every one of them is considered 'the mother of the believers', they could not speak to men except from behind a screen of some sort – a door or a curtain for example. The teachings also make it absolutely clear that the

Prophet's wives could not marry anyone after his death. These instructions are included in the following verse:

> Believers, do not enter the houses of the Prophet unless you are given leave [to come in] to eat food for which you do not wait until it is ready. But enter when you are invited, and when you have eaten, disperse. Do not linger on for conversation. This was a cause of embarrassment for the Prophet, and yet he felt shy of [asking] you [to leave]. Of what is right, however, God is not shy. When you ask anything of them [the Prophet's wives], ask for it from behind a screen: this will heighten the purity of your hearts and theirs. It is not for you to give offence to the Messenger of God, nor should you ever marry his wives after him. That, indeed, would be an enormity in God's sight. (33: 53)

This is the story of Zaynab's marriage. A postscript for this story is provided by two statements by ʿĀ'ishah. In the first, she says: "I have never seen a woman more devout than Zaynab. She was exemplary in her fear of God, truthfulness, kindness to relatives, sincerity and generosity." ʿĀ'ishah also says: "We, the Prophet's wives, asked him who would be the first among us to follow him after his death. He said: 'The one with the longest arm among you.' We used to measure our arms to find out which of us had the longest arm. When Zaynab was the first among us to die after the Prophet had died, we realized that he meant by that description the most generous among us. Zaynab used to work with her own hands and give her earnings for charity."[8]

Notes

1. Ibn Hishām, *al-Sīrah al-Nabawiyyah*, Dār al-Qalam, Beirut, Vol. 2, pp. 312-313.
2. Ibid., Vol. 4, p. 6.
3. Ibn Kathīr, *al-Bidāyah wal-Nihāyah*, Maktabat al-Maʿārif, Beirut, Vol. 1, pp. 143-145.
4. Ibid., pp. 145-147.
5. Ibid.
6. Ibid., p. 144.
7. Ibid., pp. 147-148.
8. Ibid., pp. 148-149.

28

Peace in the Making

THE SIXTH YEAR of the Prophet's settlement in Madinah, and the establishment of the first Muslim state there, was indeed a remarkable year. Its early months witnessed the splendid victory achieved by the Muslims over the confederate Arab tribes and their Jewish allies in what came to be known as 'The Expedition of the Moat'. This was followed soon afterwards by the punishment of the Jewish tribe of the Qurayẓah, the last major Jewish tribe in Madinah. Both events gave the Muslims a great morale boost and enhanced their standing in Arabia. The hypocrites in Madinah were in a state of overwhelming depression. They used to think that the combined forces of the Jews and the Quraysh and the other Arab tribes were enough to overwhelm the Muslims and destroy them completely. They did not reckon with the power of God, Who can bring about any result He desires with whatever means He chooses. This was manifest in the way the 'Expedition of the Moat' ended when a ferocious storm overwhelmed the Arabian armies surrounding Madinah and forced them to depart. After what happened to the Arabian armies and to the Jewish tribe of the Qurayẓah, the hypocrites in Madinah felt themselves powerless and could cause no harm to the Muslim state.

Moreover, the Arabian tribes in the area surrounding Madinah, which were mainly Bedouin tribes who seized every chance to launch looting raids on their neighbours, felt totally subdued. They realized that they could not challenge the power of the Muslim state. Hence, most of them tried to avoid coming into conflict with the Muslims, especially after the Prophet had sent several expeditions to subdue any tribe which contemplated attacking Madinah.

So the Muslims were in a very favourable position, enjoying a period of relative peace and tranquillity which they had not experienced ever since the establishment of their state. The situation, however, was not without potential dangers. The Jews who were evacuated from Madinah settled in Khaybar, in the north-east of Arabia, which was already a place of Jewish concentration. A revival of the alliance between the Quraysh in Makkah and the Jews of Khaybar to launch a new attack on the Muslims was always on the cards. The Prophet realized that to forestall any attempt at reviving such an alliance was far better than trying to break it after it was made. Hence, some sort of demonstration was needed to remind everybody that the Muslims in Madinah were too strong and alert to allow the emergence of any such alliance.

The Prophet was also keenly aware that the Muslims needed to demonstrate to the outside world that to them war was no more than a necessary evil and that they preferred to live in peace with everyone. The wars of the last few years might have persuaded some people to look on the Muslims as a nation which enjoyed war and fighting. Nothing could be farther from the truth. The Muslims were the trustees of God's message and they realized that their most important duty was to convey that message to mankind. To fulfil that duty properly, they needed peace more than anything else. Therefore, a demonstration which fulfilled both purposes was needed.

A Very Pleasant Dream

One night, the Prophet saw in his dream that he went to the Ka'bah with his companions to offer their worship, and that some of them shaved their heads there while others cut their hair. Shaving one's head or cutting one's hair is part of the rituals of pilgrimage and *'Umrah* (mini-pilgrimage). They were able to do that, as the Prophet saw in his dream, without fear of any enemy and meeting no obstacles in their way. He felt very happy about his dream, which he reported to his companions. They were overjoyed because they realized that Prophets do not have idle dreams. When a Prophet has a dream, his dream is an indication of what is about to happen to him or to his community. Hence, the Muslims in Madinah viewed what the Prophet had told them about his dream as a happy piece of news, fulfilling something which they dearly loved to do. Every Muslim wanted to go to the Kaʿbah but they had been forcibly prevented from doing so for the last six years.

Shortly afterwards, the Prophet announced to his companions and to the Arabian tribes around Madinah that he intended to visit Makkah to honour the Kaʿbah and to worship there. He invited them all to join him. Most of the Arabian tribes which had not yet accepted Islam were highly reluctant to join this peaceful expedition because they feared that the Quraysh were bound to resist the Muslims and prevent them from entering Makkah. If the Quraysh were determined to stop the Muslims, an armed conflict might erupt. Hence, those Arabian tribes wanted to stay out of it. The Muslims, however, were very glad to join the Prophet, who marched at the head of some 1,400 of his followers.

The Prophet's journey created a very tricky situation indeed. The Kaʿbah was in Makkah, the home town of the Quraysh which, so far, had taken a very hostile attitude towards Islam and the Muslims. The Quraysh were still the most important and most powerful tribe in Arabia. On the other hand, they were the custodians of the Kaʿbah. The unique position which they enjoyed among the Arabs was due in part to the fulfilment of this role, which demanded that no one who wished to visit the Kaʿbah for pilgrimage or devotion was to be prevented from doing so for any reason. Over the last few years the Muslims had not been allowed in Makkah because of the state of war which prevailed between them and the Quraysh. Now that the Prophet and his companions were coming on a peaceful mission, to honour the Kaʿbah and demonstrate their respect for it, what would the Quraysh's attitude be? Would they be justified, in the eyes of other Arabs, if they were to turn the Muslims back? Would such an action not cast a stigma on the Quraysh's honour as custodians of God's house?

The Prophet wanted to give the Quraysh no excuse whatsoever to adopt a hostile attitude, so he took every possible step to demonstrate to the Quraysh and to all the Arabs that his mission was a peaceful one and that he intended to do nothing other than to honour the Kaʿbah. Hence, in the month of Thul-Qaʿdah (February AD 628) the Prophet marched at the head of his companions, carrying no arms except swords in their sheaths. No traveller in Arabia at that time could go about without his sword. The Prophet mounted his she-camel, al-Qaswā', driving with him 70 camels. He intended to slaughter them after completing his *ʿUmrah* and to distribute their meat to the poor in the Ḥaram area in Makkah. Sacrifice is part of the rituals of pilgrimage and is recommended after *ʿUmrah*. The pilgrim partakes of the sacrificial meat but distributes most of it to the poor in the Ḥaram, the area surrounding Makkah. The Prophet asked his blind companion, Ibn Umm Maktūm, to deputize for him in Madinah and took Umm Salamah, one of his wives, with him on this journey. When he arrived at a place called Dhul-Ḥulayfah, some nine kilometres from Madinah, he stopped to pray *ẓuhr*. He then marked the camels, according to Arabian practice, so that they would be known as camels intended for slaughter after the completion of devotional rituals. His companions followed suit with whatever animals they had with them for slaughter. The Prophet and his companions then went into the state of consecration, that is, *iḥrām*, wearing their *iḥrām* garments. They marched on, repeating the phrases which stressed that they were going out in response to God's call to mankind to honour the Kaʿbah and glorify Him there. No one who saw the Muslims in their procession would have doubted that they were on a peaceful mission. Everyone would have realized that their purpose was simply one of worship.

Taking Resistance Measures

The Prophet asked his companion, ʿAbbād ibn Bishr, to take a company of 20 men and march ahead of the rest of the procession in order to make sure that there was no danger *en route*. He also sent Bishr ibn Sufyān to spy on the Quraysh and find out what they intended to do. This was typical of the Prophet, who attended to every detail. He made sure that the Muslims would never be taken unawares. Hence, it was important on this first peaceful mission for the Muslims to be well informed of the intentions of their traditional enemies. The Quraysh were highly agitated when they heard of the Prophet's intentions, and his march at the head of some 1,400 of his followers. Their immediate reaction was that Muhammad would never be allowed to enter Makkah under any circumstances. This meant that force would be used if necessary to prevent the Muslims from entering Makkah to worship at the Kaʿbah. Preparations for war were immediately started. Two renowned commanders, Khālid ibn al-Walīd and ʿIkrimah ibn Abī Jahl, were sent at the head of a force of 200 men to intercept the Muslims at Kurāʿ al-Ghamīm, which was well outside Makkah. The force was also joined by volunteers from two other tribes and was able to establish a system of communication to convey messages about the Prophet's movements to their headquarters.

The Prophet, however, marched on until he arrived at a place called Ghadīr al-Ashṭāṭ where Bishr ibn Sufyān gave him his report that the Quraysh were mobilizing and seeking the help of others to fight him and prevent him from entering Makkah. The Prophet consulted his companions and asked them whether they felt that it would be better to attack their living quarters, because they were preventing people from worshipping. Abū Bakr, his closest companion, said to him: "Messenger of God, you have set out in order to pay a visit to this Sacred House. You have no intention of fighting or killing anyone. Proceed, therefore, towards the House. If any people try to prevent us from reaching it, then they are the ones whom we shall fight." The Prophet was pleased with this answer and commanded his companions to proceed.

The events of that day suggest that the Prophet had no intention of carrying out any attack or starting any war. It seems that when he voiced that suggestion he only wanted to make sure of the feelings of his companions. He himself was very eager to make his expedition a perfectly peaceful one. He had no desire to fight or to score a victory. He felt that peaceful success would serve the interests of his message in a far better way. That was the Prophet's main objective. However, he always adopted a positive attitude which meant that he considered every situation on its merits before determining his reaction. Reflecting on the new situation after he had learnt that the Quraysh were preparing for armed conflict, the Prophet decided to try to avoid such an eventuality. Hence, he asked whether anyone in his camp was able to lead them through a route which took them away from the Quraysh, so that they could avoid an armed conflict with their advance force. A man from the tribe of Aslam came forward and led them through a very rough route which was very hard for the Muslims. Eventually, they found themselves in an open area which was easy to cross. The Prophet commanded them to take the right-hand route until they finally arrived at the plain of al-Ḥudaybiyah, to the south of Makkah, which was only a day's walk from the Holy City.

A Declaration of Peace

Suddenly, the Prophet's she-camel sat down. People shouted at her to make her rise again, but she would not move. Some people suggested that she refused to go forward. The Prophet told them that such a refusal was not in her nature. He said: "She is held back for the same reason which held back the elephant." This was a reference to an incident which took place nearly 60 years earlier when Abrahah, the ruler of the Yemen, was riding an elephant at the head of a large force, whose aim was to destroy the Ka'bah. Shortly before arriving in Makkah, the elephant sat still and would not move forward; it was ready to go back. Shortly afterwards, Abrahah's army was attacked by birds which dropped stones on the army and destroyed it. The story is mentioned in a short *sūrah* of the Qur'ān entitled The Elephant, and which may be translated as follows: "In the name of God, the Merciful, the Beneficent. Have you not seen how your Lord dealt with the people of the Elephant? Did He not cause their treacherous plan to be futile, and send against them flights of birds, which pelted them with stones of sand and clay? Thus He made them like devoured dry leaves." (105: 1-5)

The Prophet then declared: "By Him Who holds my soul in His hand, I shall respond favourably to any proposal the Quraysh puts to me today which helps establish good relations and guarantees respect to God's sanctuaries." He then ordered his companions to encamp.

The place was almost dry, with only one well with very little water. The companions of the Prophet economized on water as much as they could, but the well soon dried up. When they were very thirsty, they complained to the Prophet. He came to the well, sat next to it and asked for a pail to be brought to him with whatever quantity of water they could find. He took some water in his hand, rinsed his mouth and prayed to God. He then asked his companions to pour the water back into the well and told them to leave the well for a while. Some reports also suggest that the Prophet took an arrow from his bag and asked his companions to throw it into the well. Soon the well was full of water and provided all the water the Muslims needed to drink, perform ablutions and give to their camels and other animals. They suffered no shortage of water until they departed.

Successive Emissaries

When the Quraysh realized that the Prophet had managed to evade their advance forces and that he was encamped at al-Ḥudaybiyah, they decided to send a messenger to him. They were also aware that should they succeed in stopping Muhammad from entering Makkah when he had come with no purpose other than to visit the Sacred Mosque, their action would not go unquestioned by the other Arabs. Their prestige was derived from the fact that they were custodians of the Sacred House and that they prevented no one from worshipping there. The first emissary they sent was Budayl ibn Warqā' of the tribe of the Khuzāʿah, who went with a group of his fellow tribesmen. The tribe of the Khuzāʿah was always sympathetic to the Prophet. Some of its men had embraced Islam, but even those who had not were far from hostile to the message of Islam. Budayl spoke to the Prophet and told him that the Quraysh were determined to prevent him from entering Makkah. The Prophet assured him that he had no intention of fighting anyone. He wanted only to visit the Kaʿbah and to demonstrate the Muslims' recognition of its sanctity. The Prophet's comment on the Quraysh's attitude was given in these words: "The Quraysh are now in such a state that they can think only of war. I am prepared to agree a truce with them, if they so desire. I ask them only to leave me alone to speak to people. If I am successful and other people follow me, then the choice is theirs to do likewise. If they refuse, they will have preserved their strength. If they are determined to stop me, I swear by God that I will fight them over this cause of mine until I die, and even then they cannot prevent what God wills."

Budayl went back to the Quraysh and said to them: "We have come to you after seeing this man and hearing what he says. Would you like to hear what he told us?" Some of them shouted: "We do not wish to hear anything he says." Some wiser people requested him to report what he had heard. When he finished his report, he pleaded with them, saying that they were rash in their attitude because Muhammad did not intend to fight them. He wanted only to visit the Kaʿbah.

The Quraysh leaders were not persuaded to moderate their attitude. They said: "Even if he does not want to fight, he will never be allowed to enter Makkah against our will. No one shall say that we allowed that to happen."

The Quraysh then sent Mikraz ibn Ḥafs to speak to the Prophet, and he came back with the same message as Budayl. The third envoy the Quraysh sent was al-Ḥulays ibn ʿAlqamah, the leader of the Ḥabshī tribe. When the Prophet saw him coming from a distance, he said to his companions: "This is a man who belongs to a religious community. Drive the sacrificial animals towards him so that he may see them." When al-Ḥulays saw the sacrificial animals, he returned to the Quraysh without speaking to the Prophet, because he realized that there should have been no cause for contention. He advised the Quraysh to leave Muhammad alone and allow him to worship at the Kaʿbah. They spoke harshly to him and told him to leave them alone. Al-Ḥulays was angered by the Quraysh's attitude, but they were not to be persuaded by any argument.

The Fourth Envoy

Having rejected the advice of all three envoys to allow Muhammad to enter Makkah and worship at the Kaʿbah, the Quraysh decided to send a fourth emissary. None of the existing reports throws any light on the reasons which made the Quraysh feel that sending another envoy to speak to the Prophet would bring about any change in the situation. It is not known what the Quraysh hoped to achieve by sending these envoys when it was not prepared to listen to their advice. Perhaps it was all a mark of the Quraysh's confusion. On the other hand, it may have been an exercise in self-justification. The Quraysh might have wanted to be able to say that they tried all they could to reach an accommodation with Muhammad. Be that as it may, the man the Quraysh chose this time was ʿUrwah ibn Masʿūd, a leader of the tribe of Thaqīf, which lived in the town of Ṭā'if. ʿUrwah, however, wanted first to make sure that on his return he would not receive the same harsh treatment as the other envoys the Quraysh sent, should he come back with advice which the Quraysh might not like. He, therefore, addressed the people of the Quraysh: "I have noted what sort of abuse you have poured on the heads of those you have sent to Muhammad. You know that to me you are parents and that I am your son. When I heard of your trouble, I gathered those of my people who obeyed my orders and have come to give you support." The Quraysh answered: "This is certainly true, and we have no doubts about you." When he sat down to speak to the Prophet, he said:

> Muhammad, I have left your people mobilizing their forces. They are swearing that they will never let you reach the Sacred House until you have overwhelmed them. Should there be a fight between you and them, you are faced with one of two eventualities: either you conquer your own people – and we have never heard of any man who has conquered his own people – or your soldiers will let you down. Have you gathered this mob to smash your own people? It is the Quraysh you are fighting, and the Quraysh have mobilized even their women and children, and are now in a very determined mood, pledging

> to God that you will never enter their city. My feeling is that you will be in a very difficult situation tomorrow, when this mob let you down. I certainly recognize no one among them and cannot see that any one of them comes from a respectable background.

At this moment Abū Bakr interrupted him and told him to be more respectful.

As he talked to the Prophet, ʿUrwah kept trying to hold the Prophet's beard, following the Arabian habit which indicated a sincere desire to maintain good relations. Al-Mughīrah ibn Shuʿbah, a Muslim nephew of ʿUrwah, was standing behind the Prophet, holding his sword in his hand and wearing his shield. Every time ʿUrwah raised his hand to touch the Prophet's beard, al-Mughīrah hit him with the bottom of his sword on his hand and said: "Keep your hand off the Prophet's face before it is chopped off." ʿUrwah did not recognize him, but when he persisted, ʿUrwah said: "Confound you – how ill-mannered you are." The Prophet smiled at this demonstration of his companion's love and respect for him.

ʿUrwah tried his best to weaken the Prophet's determination to enter Makkah, raising before him the prospect of defeat and counselling him against causing a military conflict. The Prophet assured him that he wanted nothing more than to pay a visit to the Kaʿbah in the same way as anyone else could visit it to worship, and was not prevented from doing so. After all, the Kaʿbah did not belong to the Quraysh; they were only its custodians and as such they had no right to prevent anyone from worshipping there.

ʿUrwah did not fail to notice the Muslims' respect for the Prophet. When he went back to the Quraysh he advised them:

> People of the Quraysh, I have seen Khusru, the Persian Emperor, and Caesar of the Byzantine Empire and Negus of Abyssinia, in their respective kingdoms. I swear that I have never seen a king enjoying among his people a similar position to that of Muhammad among his companions. They do not fix their eyes when they look at him; they do not raise their voices when they speak to him. He does not need to give more than a signal to any one of them for that man to do what he is bid.

> I have looked at those people and I have seen that they do not care what may happen to them if they are able to protect their master. Make up your minds. He has made a proposal to you and I counsel you to conclude a peace agreement with him, and to accept his offer. I am giving you my sincere advice and I certainly fear that you will not be able to overcome him.

The Quraysh, however did not like ʿUrwah's opinion and were not willing to consider the idea of peace. ʿUrwah, therefore, left them with his people and returned to Ṭā'if.

Thus, every envoy the Quraysh sent returned and counselled them to moderate their attitude and allow the Muslims to offer their worship at the Kaʿbah. None, however, was able to persuade the Quraysh that its hard line did not serve its own interest. Motivated by pride and anger, the Quraysh was determined not to give in, whatever the cost.

The Muslims, on the other hand, did not wish to overrun Makkah. That course would result in more bloodshed and a fight against their own people. They stayed calm, hoping that some solution to the problem could still be found.

One report suggests that the Quraysh sent a small force of 40 or 50 men, giving them orders to go around the Muslims' camp and try to take one of the Prophet's companions prisoner. As it turned out, they were taken prisoner themselves and were brought before the Prophet. He, however, pardoned them and set them free. God mentions in the Qur'ān that He has bestowed calmness on His Messenger and the believers and caused them to abide by the rules of faith and piety. That is the attitude which best becomes them. (The events that took place at al-Ḥudaybiyah are commented on in *Sūrah* 48, entitled *al-Fatḥ* or The Conquest.)

The Prophet's Envoy

Considering the situation and the fact that he had received four emissaries from the Quraysh without any sign that the Quraysh were mellowing their opposition to the Muslims' entry to Makkah, the

Prophet thought it might be useful to bring some pressure to bear on the Quraysh. He therefore decided to send them an envoy to assure them that his objective was only to worship at the Ka'bah, not to pick a fight with anyone. His envoy was Kharrāsh ibn Umayyah of the tribe of Khuza'ah. As soon as Kharrāsh arrived in Makkah, however, his camel was wounded by the Quraysh people, who also wanted to kill him. He was saved by the Ḥabshi tribe, whose master al-Ḥulays was one of the Quraysh's envoys to the Prophet. The treatment Kharrāsh received was against the age-honoured traditions of diplomacy which gave immunity to messengers and envoys. The Prophet, however, did not wish to allow this incident to be an obstacle in his attempt to reach a peaceful solution to the problem. He therefore overlooked the matter and concentrated on maintaining contact with the Quraysh. He thought that sending a more prominent figure from among his companions might be more useful.

The Prophet first thought of 'Umar ibn al-Khaṭṭāb as a suitable messenger. 'Umar, however, pointed out that his own clan, Banī 'Adiy, no longer had any influence in Makkah. No one would protect him should he come to any harm. He suggested that 'Uthmān ibn 'Affān of the Umayyad branch of the Quraysh was better placed to act as the Prophet's ambassador.

Despite the fact that 'Uthmān's clan was very influential in Makkah, he had to go under the protection of his own cousin, Abān ibn Sa'īd ibn al-'Āṣ. Enjoying that protection, he was able to deliver his message, speak to the Quraysh elders and explain to them that the Muslims had come for the purpose of worship only and had no other intention. It was better for the Quraysh, 'Uthmān argued, that they should be seen by the Arabs as faithful to their charge as custodians of the Sacred House. The Quraysh, however, were adamant in their hard line attitude. The only concession 'Uthmān could get from the Quraysh was that they allowed him to do the *ṭawāf* should he so desire. He made it clear to them that under the circumstances, he would not do so until the Prophet had done his own *ṭawāf.*

'Uthmān's discussions with the Quraysh leaders were prolonged and he was in Makkah for three days. Moreover, he was apparently able to contact some people from among the Quraysh who had adopted Islam and remained in Makkah, keeping the fact of their conversion to Islam a secret. Apparently there were quite a few of these people, who yearned for the day when they would be able to declare their stand and enjoy freedom of faith. ʿUthmān carried a message from the Prophet to them telling them that victory would be coming soon. They were greatly encouraged by that message and requested ʿUthmān to give the Prophet their respects and to tell him on their behalf that they believed that God, Who had enabled him to encamp at al-Ḥudaybiyah, was able to open the gates of Makkah for him.

Some reports suggest that ʿUthmān was arrested by the Quraysh when they discovered that he had made these contacts with the Qurayshi Muslims. Soon a rumour began to spread that ʿUthmān had been killed. It did not take long before this rumour was heard in the Muslim camp. ʿUthmān's prolonged absence could only lend credence to that rumour. Receiving no indication to the contrary, the Prophet concluded that the report of ʿUthmān's death was correct. The treatment which was meted out to his first envoy, Kharrāsh ibn Umayyah, served as supporting evidence. He felt that the situation had reached a stage where tolerance could only be counter-productive.

A Pledge to Fight and Die

Deeply hurt and very sad, the Prophet felt that by killing ʿUthmān, his companion and envoy, the Quraysh had closed the door on all efforts which aimed at reaching a peaceful settlement. The other alternative was the one which he had tried hard to avoid: namely, war. He called on his companions to give him a pledge to fight the Quraysh to the bitter end. He was standing underneath a tree when he requested that pledge, and his companions rushed to give him what he asked of them. Every one of them pledged that he would fight and never flee from battle even if that meant his own death. The Prophet was pleased with his companions' responses. He also made a pledge on behalf of ʿUthmān: "ʿUthmān is on a mission given him by God and His Messenger. I, therefore, make a pledge on his behalf." He clasped his hands together and said, "This is for ʿUthmān." In a comment on this pledge, the Qur'ān says: "Indeed, well pleased was God with the believers when they pledged their allegiance to you under that tree, for He knew what was in their hearts; and so He bestowed inner peace upon them from on high, and rewarded them with a victory soon to come and many war gains which they would achieve. God is indeed almighty, wise." (48: 18-19)

That pledge is known in Islamic history books as Bayʿat al-Riḍwān, or 'the pledge earning God's pleasure', in view of the clear statement that God was pleased with those who took part in it. Indeed, the pledge warmed the Prophet's heart, since it was yet another demonstration that his companions were always prepared to render whatever sacrifice they were called upon to make in defence of the cause of Islam. Those companions of the Prophet realized that numerically the Quraysh were far superior to them. Besides, when they started their journey, they did not bring their war equipment with them. War was completely absent from their minds. None of them wore body armour or carried it with him. They carried only the minimum armament which was absolutely necessary for travelling in the desert of Arabia: their swords in their sheaths. Their pledge meant, in effect, that they were determined to face the far superior strength of the Quraysh, on the Quraysh's own ground with swords only, leaving no room for withdrawal or escape. They were fully aware of what they had pledged to do. When they were subsequently asked about the terms of their pledge and what it entailed, their answer was: 'Death'. Such a pledge, readily given and sincerely meant, would definitely earn God's pleasure, as those people had definitely earned it. Jābir ibn ʿAbdullāh, a companion of the Prophet who took part in that pledge, said: "The Prophet (peace be upon him) told us on the day of al-Ḥudaybiyah: You are the best people on earth."

We should stress here a small but significant point about that tree beneath which the pledge was given. The tree was subsequently cut down and the place where it used to stand was forgotten. This is certainly good for Islam. Had it survived, people who are quick to give exaggerated significance to places and to things associated with historical events might have raised a monument in its place or built a mosque or some other building on that site and made it a shrine to visit. Islam does not recognize the sanctity of any such place or object. Had it been allowed to survive, the tree might have acquired, with the passage of time, more significance than the event which took place beneath it. The tree, however, is immaterial, while the pledge itself remains a lesson for every Muslim.

Shortly after the pledge was made, ʿUthmān arrived to give the Prophet an account of his mission. His arrival took the heat out of the situation. The Prophet was very pleased to see him alive but was not happy to learn of the Quraysh's adamant attitude. He reflected on the situation, trying to assess the choices open to him.

The Quraysh, on the other hand, heard of the pledge given by the Muslims to the Prophet. Their chiefs were engaged in high-level consultations. They realized that the Muslims' pledge meant that their determination to achieve their purpose was not in doubt. Past experience suggested that should the two sides be engaged in a military conflict, the outcome might very well be a victory for the Muslims, despite their relatively small numbers and poor equipment. That the Muslims could always be relied upon to fight hard and well and not to weaken in the face of adversity was something not to be doubted. Now that they had given the Prophet such a clear commitment to fight to the bitter end, the Muslims would not just go away. Moreover, the Quraysh might not have been fully convinced that they acted within their rights when they tried to prevent the Muslims from worshipping at the Kaʿbah. Their motives for their attitude were nothing more than pride of position and conceit. Hence, the Quraysh realized that they must think seriously of the consequences, especially if the military conflict went against them.

A Delegation for Peace

Some wiser men among the Quraysh must have suggested that achieving a peaceful settlement might preserve the Quraysh's dignity better than war, even if the war ended in its favour. The views of its earlier envoys – particularly those of al-Ḥulays of the Ḥabshī tribe and ʿUrwah ibn Masʿūd of the Thaqīf – began to appear highly valid. Moreover, should the Quraysh push matters to the point of a flare-up, their action might mean a fight near the Sacred House and in the sacred month. This would, in effect, be setting a precedent which was certain to do more harm than good to the Quraysh. Hence the arguments for moderation suddenly began to appear much weightier. A delegation headed by Suhayl ibn ʿAmr was, therefore, dispatched to negotiate the terms of a peace settlement with the Prophet.

The Prophet received Suhayl ibn ʿAmr and his delegation well. He instructed his companions to show their sacrificial animals and to raise their voices with phrases expressing the fact that they had come only in response to God's call to honour the Sacred House.

The talks between the two sides were not easy. Despite the fact that the Prophet was keen to achieve a peace settlement, the negotiations had to deal with several issues of substance. The topics included: the Prophet's visit to the Sacred House; the Quraysh's determination not to seem to have given in to force; the possibility of agreeing a long truce between the two sides, putting an end to their frequent military clashes; the sort of relations which should exist between the two sides; and the freedom of each side to make any political moves on the wider horizon of the whole of Arabia.

There was, however, no reason to prolong these discussions. The Prophet accepted all the Quraysh's conditions readily. It was Suhayl ibn ʿAmr who took a long time in his presentation of each of those conditions and what each of them entailed. Indeed, the Quraysh side were surprised that all their conditions were accepted by the Prophet without too much trouble. It was necessary, however, to write the agreement down and to have it signed by representatives of both sides.

Unease in the Muslim Camp

The Prophet's attitude caused a stir in the Muslim camp. They were not used to seeing the Prophet taking such a very soft attitude. It was also surprising for the Quraysh negotiators themselves. Not only did the Prophet accept all the terms the Quraysh stipulated, he did not consult his companions in the matter, contrary to his normal practice. Moreover, the terms of the peace agreement were extremely surprising to the Muslims, because they tended to cast the Muslim side as much weaker than the Quraysh. To the Muslims, accepting such terms was neither useful nor necessary. Some of them could not hide their dissatisfaction. This is epitomized by the attitude of ʿUmar ibn al-Khaṭṭāb. When the terms of the peace agreement were finalized and were about to be written down, ʿUmar came to Abū Bakr and said: "Abū Bakr, is he not God's Messenger?" Abū Bakr answered in the affirmative. ʿUmar again asked: "Are we not the Muslims?" When Abū Bakr gave the same answer, ʿUmar went on: "Are they not the idolaters?" Abū Bakr again answered: "Yes." ʿUmar then asked him: "Why then should we accept humiliation in matters of our faith?" Abū Bakr answered with a piece of advice, saying to his questioner: "Follow him whatever he does, ʿUmar. I believe that he is God's Messenger." But ʿUmar was still perturbed and said: "And I too believe that he is God's Messenger."

ʿUmar's argument was that since what separated the two sides was really a single issue – right against wrong, faith against lack of faith – those who were on the side of right and truth must not give in to those who championed the cause of wrong and falsehood. The believers must never accept any sort of humiliation when it came to matters relating to their faith. Indeed, they should always show pride in their religion. Hence, ʿUmar was not to be deterred. He went to the Prophet and put to him the same questions: "Are you not God's Messenger? Are we not the Muslims? Are they not the idolaters?" To all these questions, the Prophet answered in the affirmative. The final question ʿUmar put was again the same: "Why then should we accept humiliation in matters of our faith?"

The Prophet's answer provided the clue to his attitude: "I am God's servant and Messenger. I shall not disobey Him and He will never abandon me." The Prophet was indeed following Divine orders which he must have received at that time.

The Prophet then called in ʿAlī ibn Abī Ṭālib to write down the peace agreement so that it might be signed by both sides. Again,

Suhayl ibn ʿAmr showed maximum rigidity, while the Prophet showed complete flexibility.

The Prophet told ʿAlī to write: "In the name of God, the Merciful, the Beneficent." Suhayl interrupted: "I do not know this. Write down: 'In your name, Our Lord'." The Prophet told ʿAlī to write the phrase Suhayl proposed. He continued with his dictation: "These are the terms of the peace agreement negotiated between Muhammad, God's Messenger, and Suhayl ibn ʿAmr." Again, Suhayl interrupted: "Had I accepted that you are God's messenger, I would not have fought you. You have to write down your name and your father's name." The Prophet accepted Suhayl's point and revised his dictation, telling ʿAlī to write:

> These are the terms of the peace agreed by Muhammad ibn ʿAbdullāh and Suhayl ibn ʿAmr.
>
> - Both have agreed to a complete truce for a period of ten years, during which all people will enjoy peace and security and will not attack one another.
> - Moreover, if anyone from the Quraysh joins Muhammad without permission from his guardian or chief, he shall be returned to the Quraysh.
> - If anyone from those in the camp of Muhammad joins the Quraysh, they are not required to return him.
> - Both sides agree that they harbour good intentions towards each other.
> - No theft or treachery shall be condoned.
> - Whoever wishes to enter into an alliance with Muhammad may do so, and whoever wants to enter into an alliance with the Quraysh may do so.
> - It is further agreed that you, Muhammad, shall return home this year without entering Makkah. At the end of one year, we shall evacuate Makkah for you so that you may enter it with your followers to stay for three days only. You shall carry only the armament necessary for a traveller – namely, your swords in their sheaths. You shall not carry any other arms.

A Hard Test of Muslim Intentions

These were the terms of the peace agreement. When they were written down, witnesses from both sides were asked to sign the document. At that moment, something happened to test the patience of the believers and to give them another opportunity to prove the strength of their faith. A man from Makkah arrived in handcuffs and with his legs in chains. He was being kept prisoner there because he was a Muslim. This man was none other than Suhayl's own son, Abū Jandal. It was his father who imprisoned him and fastened his shackles. Nevertheless, he was able to escape and to take an unfamiliar route through the mountains surrounding Makkah until he arrived at al-Ḥudaybiyah. When the Muslims saw him, they were very glad that he had been able to escape and gave him a fine reception.

While the peace agreement was being written down, Suhayl was too busy to notice anything. When it was finished, Suhayl looked up and saw his son among the Muslims. He went up to him, hit him in the face and took him by the collar. Abū Jandal cried aloud: "My fellow Muslims, am I to be returned to the unbelievers to try to turn me away from my faith?" Those words were very painful to the Muslims, some of whom started to cry.

Suhayl ibn ʿAmr, however, was unmoved. He said to God's Messenger: "This is the first person whose case I take up. You must return him to me." The Prophet referred to the fact that Abū Jandal arrived before the agreement was completed: "We have not finished drawing up the document yet." Suhayl said: "Then I have not agreed any terms with you whatsoever." The Prophet pleaded: "Then allow me him."

Suhayl said that he would not. Mikraz, another member of the Quraysh delegation, said that they should allow Muhammad to have Abū Jandal. The father was adamant and refused all appeals to let his son join the Muslims. He went even further and began to hit his son with a thorny branch of a tree. The Prophet again pleaded with him to let his son go, or at least not to torture him. But Suhayl would accept nothing. Some of Suhayl's friends, however, extended their protection to Abū Jandal and his father stopped hitting him. The

Prophet explained to Abū Jandal his inability to help him, speaking to him in a loud voice so that he could hear: "Abū Jandal, be patient and endure your situation for God's sake. He will certainly provide for you and those who are suffering with you a way out of your hardship. We have made a peace agreement with those people, giving them a pledge by God that we will be faithful to the terms of our agreement. We shall not violate our pledges.

Kill Your Father

ʿUmar ibn al-Khaṭṭāb was again outraged by the situation. He could not understand why the Muslims should accept such humiliating terms or stand idle when a brother of theirs was subjected to harsh treatment for no reason other than the fact that he believed in God and His Messenger. As Abū Jandal was being led away, ʿUmar went up to him and walked by his side. He spoke to him: "Be patient, Abū Jandal. These people are unbelievers. They are worthless. The blood of anyone of them is no more precious than the blood of a dog."

As he was walking by Abū Jandal's side and talking to him, he continued to move the handle of his sword towards Abū Jandal, hoping that Abū Jandal would take ʿUmar's sword and kill his father. Abū Jandal either did not wish to kill his father or did not understand or notice ʿUmar's gesture. He submitted to his fate until God would help him get his release. He was led away in his shackles and chains. As the Muslims looked at him, their hearts were full of agony because they were unable to help him.

When the document detailing the peace terms was written down, the Prophet asked a number of his companions to witness the agreement, in addition to witnesses from the Quraysh side. The Muslim witnesses were Abū Bakr, ʿUmar ibn al-Khaṭṭāb, ʿAlī ibn Abī Ṭālib, ʿAbd al-Raḥmān ibn ʿAwf, Saʿd ibn Abū Waqqāṣ, Maḥmūd ibn Maslamah and ʿAbdullāh ibn Suhayl, another son of the chief Quraysh negotiator himself. Mikraz ibn Ḥafṣ and Ḥuwayṭib ibn ʿAbd al-ʿUzzā were the Quraysh witnesses. When the witnessing was finally done, the Quraysh delegation went home.

This peace was supposed to last for ten years. Very few Muslims were able to bring themselves to accept it without experiencing a feeling of unease. What added to their bitterness was the fact that the terms of the agreement meant that they had to go back home without being able to fulfil their purpose of worshipping at the Kaʿbah. It should be remembered that the Prophet and his companions were in *iḥrām*, the state of consecration, having left Madinah in order to perform the *ʿUmrah*. They were first prevented from entering Makkah by the declared intention of the Quraysh to use force to stop them. Now they were prevented by the terms of the agreement which they signed with the Quraysh. They were, in effect, in the position of a *muḥṣar*, a person who sets out from home to do his pilgrimage or *ʿUmrah* but is unable to reach his destination owing to some reason beyond his control. God declares in the Qur'ān that such a person can release himself from *iḥrām* by slaughtering a sheep or some other sacrificial animal at the point where he cannot continue his journey.

Cancellation of Intended Worship

The Prophet said to his companions: "Slaughter your animals and shave and release yourselves from *iḥrām*." No one showed any sign of willingness to comply with this order. The Prophet repeated his command three times and still no one was willing to do as he was told. The Prophet was very angry indeed. He went into his tent where Umm Salamah, his wife who accompanied him on this expedition, was waiting. She immediately noticed how angry he was. She asked him the reason and he answered: "The Muslims are ruining themselves. I have given them a command and they have not obeyed." He explained to her how his companions received his orders with indifference and how not one of them was willing to obey. She tried to pacify him: "Messenger of God, do not blame them. They have been under great pressure because of all the trouble you have taken to achieve this peace settlement and because they now realize that they have to take the long way home without achieving their purpose." She then gave him a very sound piece of advice: she told him to go out and slaughter his own sacrificial animals and shave, without speaking to any one of them. The Prophet acted on his wife's advice and went out and slaughtered his camels. He then called someone to shave his head. When his companions witnessed what he did, they rushed to do likewise. Some of them helped others to shave and they were extremely unhappy with themselves for not responding to the Prophet's orders in the first place.

Not all of the Muslims at al-Ḥudaybiyah shaved their heads: some of them just cut their hair. The Prophet said: "May God have mercy on those who have shaved." Some of his companions said: "Messenger of God, what about those who have cut their hair?" He answered by repeating the same prayer: "May God have mercy on those who have shaved." The same question about those who had cut their hair was put to him, but he answered by repeating the same prayer a third time. Once more, he was asked about the other group and the Prophet included them in his prayers, saying: "And those who have cut their hair." When he was asked the reason for repeating his prayers for mercy to the shavers three times before he included the other group, he answered: "They have entertained no doubt." This is always a very important point. If people start to doubt, then they soon find that their doubts dictate their actions. Sound faith means accepting such matters as may appear to be against the immediate interests of the believer, once he is certain that they are required by Islam. At al-Ḥudaybiyah, the Muslims were absolutely certain of that because they were receiving direct orders from the Prophet himself.

When the Prophet's companions finished slaughtering their sacrificial animals and released themselves from *iḥrām*, they started their journey back home. They had stayed at al-Ḥudaybiyah a little over two weeks; some reports suggest that their stay lasted 20 days. However, they were still perturbed about this peace agreement in which they had no say. It was something totally different from what the Prophet had told them before they started their journey. He had given them the happy news of worshipping at the Kaʿbah. However, they were unable to reach the Sacred Mosque. Hence they started to put questions to him. It was ʿUmar first and then some other companions of the Prophet who asked him: "Have you not told us that we would go to the Kaʿbah and do our *ṭawāf* there?" The Prophet answered by asking them: "Have I told you that you will go there this year?" When they answered in the negative, he said: "You will certainly go and do your *ṭawāf* there, God willing."

The other point which the Muslims found very difficult to accept was the one which stipulated that they should return any person from the Quraysh who came to them declaring that he was a Muslim, while the Quraysh was allowed to accept anyone who turned away from Islam and joined its ranks. They asked the Prophet how he could accept such unequal treatment. He answered: "He who leaves us to join them, let him never return to us. If we return to them someone who is a Muslim, God will certainly provide him with a way out of his troubles."

A Grand Victory

On the way back to Madinah, the Prophet received new revelations – the *Sūrah* entitled *al-Fatḥ* or The Conquest. He asked ʿUmar ibn al-Khaṭṭāb to come forward and said to him: "A *sūrah* has been revealed to me tonight, and it is much dearer to me than all that the sun overlooks put together." He then recited the new revelation, which spoke of what happened at al-Ḥudaybiyah in terms of its being a grand victory. ʿUmar asked him: "Is it a conquest, Messenger of God?" He replied: "Yes indeed. By Him Who holds my soul in His hand, it is a grand victory."

A man from among the Muslims said: "This is not a victory. We have been prevented from entering the Sacred Mosque, and our sacrificial animals were not allowed to reach their appointed destination. The Prophet also had to return to the unbelievers some Muslims who have tried to join us."

When these words were reported to the Prophet, he said:

> What bad words. It is, indeed, the greatest victory. The unbelievers were willing to use only peaceful means to prevent you from going into their homeland; they were also willing to come to you to negotiate a peace agreement and a pact of mutual security. Your good, overall condition has worried them.

> God has given you the upper hand over them. He has enabled you to go back safely, having earned His reward. All this makes it indeed the greatest victory. Have you forgotten the day of Uḥud, when you were running as fast as you could in the mountain, fleeing before them, caring for nothing, and I was calling you to stop and fight for your Hereafter? Have you forgotten the day when they allied their forces against you and tried to organize a pincer assault on you, attacking you from front and behind? Have you forgotten how you were utterly distressed, you could not fix your eyes on anything, your hearts almost reached your throats and all sorts of doubts and suspicions were prominent in your minds?

These words were very soothing to the Muslims. When they considered them carefully, they realized that what they had achieved at al-Ḥudaybiyah was no trifling success. They said to the Prophet: "God and His Messenger tell the truth indeed. It is certainly the greatest victory. Prophet, we have not thought on these lines which you have pointed out. You certainly know better than us what God wants for us. We are very happy and satisfied."

The Muslims' doubts were gradually replaced by reassurances. They were now satisfied that this peace agreement would bring them only something good. They trusted in God and the Prophet and this trust meant that as long as they obeyed their orders, nothing harmful or evil would come to them. Little did they realize, however, what sort of benefits would result from this peace agreement. Not one of them was able to look towards what would happen a few months or a year hence. They were not to be blamed for that. The sort of history they were writing had never been written before. There was no way of knowing how events would develop. The Prophet, however, told them that it was the greatest victory of all. God has entitled the *sūrah* He revealed on this occasion The Conquest. A great victory it indeed was.

If any leader adopts an attitude similar to that of the Prophet when the terms of the peace agreement have been negotiated, accepting all the terms the other side proposes without seeking to extract a concession for every concession given and without consulting any of his advisers, he cannot escape accusations of dictatorship and selling out to the enemy. Hence, the irritation of the Muslims as they saw the Prophet adopting such an attitude was quite understandable. The Prophet, however, was neither a traitor to the cause nor a dictator – far from it. As already said, the clue to his attitude and policy in that period lies in his answer to ʿUmar's questions: "I am God's servant and Messenger. I shall not disobey Him and He will never abandon me." He was simply carrying out the orders he was receiving from God. His mission was to establish God's message on earth. Therefore, to disobey God was to go against the most essential element in his message: namely, submission to God. He fully realized that God wanted only what was good for the Muslim community. So, if He had given an order which seemed to be against the immediate interests of the Muslim community, there must be something good behind it which would become apparent in due course, and would far outweigh the harm it seemed initially to produce. Keeping this in mind, the Prophet followed the line indicated for him, paying no attention to the unwise opposition from his companions or to the Quraysh's provocations.

The Early Fruits

The Muslims did not have long to wait for the benefits of this peace agreement to materialize. To start with, for the first time in their history the Muslims enjoyed a period of calm when they did not have to worry about the Quraysh. Indeed, the Quraysh had represented the greatest obstacle in the path of Islam, ever since the Prophet started his mission. Its determined opposition to Islam had prompted most of the Arabian tribes to follow its example and adopt a hostile attitude to the Prophet. The Jews also found in the Quraysh a great source of strength to help their scheming against the Prophet and Islam. In effect, the Quraysh was the catalyst which produced enmity to Islam all over Arabia. When the peace agreement was made, the catalyst became idle and hostility towards Islam abated.[1]

When the Prophet explained to his companions, on their way back to Madinah, why the peace he made at al-Ḥudaybiyah was 'the greatest victory of all', one of his reasons was: "The unbelievers were willing to use only peaceful means to prevent you from going into their homeland; they were also willing to come to you to negotiate a peace agreement and a pact of mutual security." In order to appreciate the import of these words one must remember that the Quraysh had stopped at nothing in their hostility towards the Prophet and Islam, ever since he started conveying his message. They accused him of different things at different times, calling him a sorcerer, a fortune-teller, a madman and a liar. They warned every visitor to Makkah of his 'evil sorcery'. They boycotted him and his people in their quarters in Makkah until they almost starved to death. They inflicted all sorts of torture on his companions to drive them away from their homes and their property. They plotted against his life when he was in Makkah and raised one army after another to attack him in his new place, plotted with the Jews to assassinate him and helped forge an alliance of forces against him.[2]

Now the Quraysh had to climb down. It was the Quraysh who sought peace, recognizing the legitimacy of the Muslim state and dealing with it on an equal footing. It was even prepared to send a delegation to the Prophet to negotiate the terms of the peace agreement. That was indeed a moral victory for Islam which should not be taken lightly. The Prophet realized that this moral victory opened up great new horizons for the cause of Islam.

In order to appreciate fully the prospects that the peace of al-Ḥudaybiyah opened up for Islam, one should remember that the Muslims had remained on the defensive in Madinah ever since they established their state there. They could not have any meaningful relations with any Arabian tribes, because theirs was a state surrounded by enemies on all sides. No one could be sure of its chances of survival in that ocean of hostility. Now that peace was made with the Quraysh, the Muslims were able to establish contacts with other tribes and to explain to them the principles of Islam and the true nature of its message. The other tribes were thus able to understand Islam without fearing the Quraysh and to recognize its valid principles and noble objectives. When they associated these with what they had known of the Muslims' high moral standards and their implementation of the principles of their faith in their practical life, and added that to what they had already known of the character of the Prophet and his fine nature, they responded to the Islamic call without fear or hesitation. Thus, Islam was able to make inroads into many tribes, and to win new followers all over Arabia, including the Quraysh's own stronghold, Makkah. The number of Muslims multiplied rapidly – so much so that the Prophet was able to raise an army of 10,000 only two years later, while his army on the day of al-Ḥudaybiyah was no more than 1,400. It is for this reason that most historians regard the peace of al-Ḥudaybiyah as a great victory. Al-Zuhrī, an early Muslim historian, says:

> No preceding victory in the history of Islam was greater than al-Ḥudaybiyah. Those were victories achieved after fighting. When the truce was made and peace was achieved, people feared no danger from one another. They met and made contacts and talked with one another. No one with any degree of sound reason who was approached about accepting Islam could reject it. Indeed, in the two years following the peace of al-Ḥudaybiyah, the Muslims more than doubled in number.[3]

A Chance to Choose Freely

From the Islamic point of view, being able to talk freely to people and to call them to Islam is much more important than winning battles. It has never been the aim of Islam to conquer countries or subjugate people. Its aim is to win followers through conviction. Indeed, compulsion as a method of conversion has never been used by Islam or Muslims. Ever since the Prophet started to convey his message, the advocates of Islam have never asked for anything more than to be able to address people freely and explain the principles and the nature of Islam to them. At al-Ḥudaybiyah, the Prophet saw a chance for Islam to achieve that and he was determined not to lose it. In the event, it worked wonders. It will always work wonders provided that the advocates of Islam go about their task of conveying its message with sincerity and vigour.

After the peace agreement the Prophet was also able to open new avenues to spread Islam outside Arabia. He wrote to the kings and rulers of all the states surrounding Arabia, or ruling in the far corners of the Arabian Peninsula, informing them about Islam and calling on them to believe in it. He entrusted the delivery of his messages to some of his companions who were known to have two important qualities: courage and wisdom. Most of these kings and rulers did not adopt Islam. Some of them were indeed extremely hostile. The Persian Emperor was particularly insulting in his attitude. He also ill-treated the messenger the Prophet sent. Nevertheless, sending these messengers made Islam known in those countries and stressed the universal character of Islam. It did not mean to confine its interest to Arabia only. It was a religion for all mankind. History shows that within 30 years all those countries to which the Prophet sent his messengers were to become predominantly Muslim.

The peace agreement also gave the Prophet a chance to concentrate on his other enemies. As already seen, the Jews were just as hostile as the Quraysh towards Islam. They were prepared to stop at nothing to destroy the Muslim state and to exterminate the Muslims totally. On their own, the Jews were not powerful enough to achieve their objectives. This was what prompted them to try to work together with the Quraysh in the first instance, and with other tribes afterwards. Now that peace had been made between the Muslims and the Quraysh, and many Arabian tribes were willing to listen to Islam, the Jews faced the prospect of total isolation. The peace agreement indeed provided the Muslims with a chance to eliminate any potential danger from the Jews. They had to put an end to all Jewish treachery. Hence the battles of Khaybar, Fadak and Taymā', which were to take place in the following year, greatly enhanced the standing of the Muslims in Arabia and brought the Muslim state additional strength.

Moreover, the Muslims did not have to grant too many concessions. The fact that they agreed to return to Madinah without visiting the Sacred Mosque was made on the understanding that they would be able to do so the following year, so the purpose of their journey was not totally thwarted. It was only put back a year – which, in practical terms, did not constitute such a great concession as the Muslims felt at the time, when passions were running high. The alternative would have been war which was sure to bring about much worse results. That prospect was totally averted, and this was indeed a great achievement.

One reason for not allowing events to develop into a military conflict was that there were a number of Muslims in Makkah who had adopted Islam but did not publicize the fact of their conversion. They did not wish to sever their ties with their families and hoped that there would soon come a time when the Quraysh would relent in their attitude towards Islam. Some of them, on the other hand, would not have been able to emigrate to Madinah if they had tried, because their circumstances did not allow them freedom of action. Some of them were kept in Makkah by force, as seen in the case of Abū Jandal ibn Suhayl, the son of the Quraysh's chief negotiator at al-Ḥudaybiyah. Neither the Prophet nor the Muslims knew precisely how many Muslims there were in Makkah. God says in *Sūrah* 48 of the Qur'ān that had there been a clash at al-Ḥudaybiyah, the Muslims would have been victorious and the unbelievers would have turned their backs and run away. In such an eventuality, the Muslims might have probably killed a number of those Muslims in ignorance of the fact that they were their brethren. That would have led to considerable embarrassment for the Muslims and would have meant that they had to pay blood money to their relatives for killing them accidentally. Moreover, it would have constituted a real blemish in the history of Islam. For these reasons – and because God was aware that most, if not all the people of Makkah would soon change their hostile attitude to Islam and become Muslims – God instructed His Messenger to make peace his overriding objective. Military victory is not a paramount consideration in the Islamic view. The most important consideration is to win people over to Islam through conviction, not compulsion. Peace, not military conflict, is more conducive to that. Hence, peace was to be given priority.

Counterproductive Rigidity

Events subsequent to the peace agreement of al-Ḥudaybiyah proved, as often in history, that the side which adopted a rigid and inflexible attitude, trying to dictate very harsh terms, would eventually come to regret them. The condition which the Quraysh thought to be its most important face-saver with anyone who might seek to criticize its change of attitude from confrontation to negotiation was the one which required the Muslims in Madinah to return to the Quraysh anyone from among its members who went to the Prophet declaring that he had adopted Islam. This condition was not to be reciprocated in the case of any Muslim joining the Quraysh. The Muslims themselves bitterly resented this condition and felt that it was humiliating to their young state, and unwarranted. The Prophet, however, was acting on God's instructions in concluding the peace agreement. He, therefore, did not bother to weigh up probabilities and compare eventualities. He trusted that God would take care of the Muslims and would turn everything to their benefit.

It was not long before the Quraysh started to realize that that very condition through which they sought to save face was the one that would cause the most trouble. A man from the Thaqīf called ʿUtbah ibn Usayd, but better known by his title Abū Buṣayr (following the Arabian tradition of addressing a man as the father of his eldest son), came to the Prophet declaring that he was a Muslim. Shortly after he had made his escape, Azhar ibn ʿAbd ʿAwf and al-Akhnas ibn Sharīq of his own tribe, wrote to the Prophet requesting that he should honour his pledges by returning him. They sent their message with a man from the tribe of ʿĀmir who travelled with a servant of his. When they gave the Prophet the letter addressed to him, he spoke to Abū Buṣayr and explained that the Muslims did not violate their pledges or go back on their promises. He, therefore, had no option but to send him back with those two people. He also told him: "God will certainly provide for you, and those subjugated people like you, a way out of your trouble." When Abū Buṣayr protested that he was being returned to those people who would certainly try to turn him away from his faith, the Prophet could do no more than repeat his words.

Abū Buṣayr went with those two people on the long journey from Madinah to Makkah, a distance of more than 500 kilometres. Apparently, Abū Buṣayr tried to win the confidence of his captors as they travelled on that journey which took several days to complete, giving them no hint whatsoever of what was in his mind. When they sat down to rest at some stage, the man from the tribe of ʿĀmir was playing with his sword and boasting: "I shall work this sword of mine hard in the Muslim tribes of the Aws and the Khazraj one day."

To this statement, Abū Buṣayr rejoined: "Your sword must be a very sharp one, then." The man said: "Yes, indeed. Would you like to have a look at it?" Abū Buṣayr accepted the sword from him thankfully. No sooner had he taken it in his hand than he started to hit the man hard with it until he had killed him. When the servant saw this, he was absolutely terrified. He ran away towards Madinah and continued to run until he reached the city.

When the Prophet saw him from a distance coming in that state, he said: "This lad must have seen something horrifying." When the servant had caught his breath, he told them what had happened. Shortly afterwards, Abū Buṣayr arrived. He greeted the Prophet and said: "You have honoured your pledge. God has fulfilled your promises. You have given me up to those people, but I have managed to escape persecution."

The Prophet told him to go wherever he wished. He explained that he could not allow him to stay in Madinah because that would constitute a breach of the peace agreement. When Abū Buṣayr left, the Prophet commented on his action: "This man would surely cause a war if he had some men to support him."

A Guerrilla Campaign

As he left Madinah, Abū Buṣayr realized that he had to cause the Quraysh some trouble in order to survive. He, therefore, sought a place on the coastal route of the Quraysh's caravans where he stayed in hiding. Whenever a Quraysh trade caravan passed he would attack it, looting as much as he could of its goods. As these attacks were reported in Makkah, they provided encouragement to the Muslims there. Abū Jandal and his fellow Muslims in Makkah carefully planned their escape, and as many as 70 of them were able to join Abū Buṣayr in his hiding place. Thus, the first force of freedom fighters in the history of Islam came into existence. Together, those

Muslims mounted guerrilla attacks on the Quraysh, making the trade caravans their primary target. Soon afterwards, they were joined by a number of people from various tribes such as the Ghifār, Aslam and Juhaynah, who were not bound by the peace agreement between the Prophet and the Quraysh. The guerrilla force was now 300 strong. They were able to cause the Quraysh a great deal of trouble. Moreover, the Quraysh could not do much about them. No matter how many people the Quraysh sent with their caravans to provide protection for them, those Muslim fighters were able to mount a successful raid on every caravan, taking its goods and killing its guards.[4]

History in all its ages, including today's, shows that there is no simple answer to the problem of determined guerrilla fighters. Despite the great advances in modern weaponry and the large resources states are able to mobilize against freedom fighters, a guerrilla war is the hardest to win for any regular army. Moreover, no victory can be achieved against guerrilla fighters without great losses for which no logical justification may reasonably be found. It is therefore not surprising that the Quraysh was soon very tired of the new situation created by Abū Buṣayr, Abū Jandal and their men. They started appealing to the Prophet to take those guerrilla fighters into his fold and spare the Quraysh the trouble they created. According to this request, the Prophet summoned Abū Buṣayr and Abū Jandal to join him in Madinah together with their men who had nowhere else to go. The Prophet also ordered those who had joined Abū Buṣayr from other tribes to go back to their people, where they were safe and could carry on with their efforts to propagate the cause of Islam.

Abū Buṣayr had apparently received a serious wound in one of his latest raids. The wound proved fatal and when the Prophet's letter to him arrived, he was on the point of death. He learnt that his efforts had achieved the results for which he had been working and he died peacefully. Abū Jandal and his companions buried him in the place where he launched his campaign against the Quraysh and joined the Muslims in Madinah.[5] Thus the unfair and rigid condition which the Quraysh imposed on the Muslims in the peace treaty was abrogated by the Quraysh itself.

A Believer's Psychology

As explained, there were several developments which made the Muslims restless during the events of al-Ḥudaybiyah from the moment of the Prophet's departure with his companions from Madinah to the point of their return without being able to offer their worship at the Kaʿbah. To them, a visit to the Sacred Mosque would have fulfilled a long-cherished hope. The fact that the Prophet saw in his dream that they would be visiting the mosque and worshipping there was, to them, a firm promise. Prophets' dreams always come true. Yet this time it was not so – or so it seemed to the believers at the time.

Restlessness among the believers also manifested itself in their reaction to the inflexibility of the unbelievers during the negotiations of the terms of the peace agreement. It is reported that when the chief negotiator of the Quraysh, Suhayl ibn ʿAmr, objected to the title 'Messenger of God' being attached to the Prophet's name in the peace agreement, the Prophet asked ʿAlī, his companion who was writing the agreement, to erase that title. ʿAlī did not do so because he could not bring himself to erase something in which he firmly believed. The Prophet then erased it himself after the words were pointed out to him.

Again, that restlessness showed itself in various acts and attitudes shown by different companions of the Prophet. It also manifested itself much more clearly when the Muslims did not comply straightaway with the Prophet's order that they should slaughter their sacrificial animals and release themselves from the state of consecration.

Despite all this restlessness, the Qur'ān comments that God has "sent down tranquillity into the hearts of the believers so that their faith might grow stronger." (48: 4) How can one fit this description of tranquillity with that restlessness?

The believers' restlessness was the result of actions by the Quraysh which could only be described as unwarranted provocations. At that stage in the life of the Muslim community, the believers had grown much stronger in their faith and in their willingness to make whatever sacrifice they were called on to make. To them, that was elementary to their role as the vanguard of the new faith. They were the followers of the truth and their enemies were only defending falsehood. Hence the forces of truth must on no account yield before the forces of falsehood without putting up a determined fight. At al-Ḥudaybiyah, they were called on to forgo their rights in return for nothing – or so it seemed to them. Moreover, they felt that they were more than a match for the Quraysh forces, despite being heavily outnumbered. No army which found itself in a position similar to that of the believers in al-Ḥudaybiyah would have waited long before launching a surprise attack to force its way into Makkah. The temptation to do so was indeed great. Yet the Prophet declared that he would accept any peace proposal the Quraysh put to him. Moreover, he acted on his word despite the seemingly unfair conditions the Quraysh imposed. Although that was the first time the Muslims felt that a promise by the Prophet did not immediately come true, and in spite of all the humiliation they felt at being dictated to by the Quraysh and also in spite of all their restlessness and anger, they did not entertain any idea of doing anything against the Prophet's wishes. If they did not immediately comply with his orders to release themselves from consecration, that was due to the frustration of their high hopes that they would be worshipping at the Sacred Mosque. It was always present in their minds that theirs was a position of obedience to God and the Prophet. Any army in similar circumstances to those of al-Ḥudaybiyah might have organized a mutiny to replace its commander with someone who was more of a hard-liner. Such an action was totally absent from the thoughts of the Muslims at al-Ḥudaybiyah. As has been seen, when the Prophet provided the practical example by releasing himself from *iḥrām*, his companions rushed to do likewise.

In *Sūrah* 48, entitled The Conquest, there is a verse which may be rendered in translation as follows: "God was well pleased with the believers when they pledged their allegiance to you underneath the tree. He knew what was in their hearts, and He sent down reassurance on them, and has rewarded them with a victory coming soon." (48: 18) This refers to the pledge the believers made to the Prophet when he received news that his envoy ʿUthmān had been killed. He felt that the murder of his envoy had set the two sides on a collision course. He called on his companions to pledge that they were prepared to fight to the bitter end. Not one of them hesitated. In the event, there was no need to fight since it soon became clear that ʿUthmān was not dead. That, however, did not detract from the fact that the Prophet was very happy with his companions' response. In this verse, they received the happy news that God Himself was well pleased with them.

As a believer, one cannot emphasize the importance of this statement too strongly. Sayyid Quṭb, the highly renowned contemporary scholar, says in his famous work *In the Shade of the Qur'ān*:

> Any one of us who reads or hears God's statement: 'God is the patron of the believers' must feel happy. His thoughts would be: 'I do indeed hope that I am included among the believers God patronizes.' When he reads or hears the other Qur'ānic statement: 'God is on the side of those who persevere', he is reassured. He thinks: 'I surely hope that I will be one of those who show perseverance. Hence, I sincerely hope that God is on my side.' But those companions of the Prophet are told individually that God means them in person. He communicates His message to every single one of them that He is well pleased with him. He knows what is in everyone's heart and He accepts it and is well pleased with it. This is indeed great, far greater than words can describe.[6]

This is an honour which God has bestowed on those companions of the Prophet. Their happiness with it cannot be described. They are told that they are the people who have earned God's pleasure. The Qur'ānic statement mentions the very place they have been in and the very action they have done. God's pleasure is communicated to them by the Prophet, whom they know to be always truthful. In their experience, he never said a word which was not absolutely true.

History books do not tell how this Qur'ānic statement was received by the believers. It is known that the Prophet himself said about the *sūrah*: "A *sūrah* has been revealed to me tonight, and it is much dearer to me than all that the sun overlooks put together."[7] He said this because the *sūrah* opens with a couple of verses which are addressed directly to him: "We have given you a manifest victory, that God may forgive you your sins, past and future, and may perfect His favour to you, and may guide you on a right path. God may also grant you a strong victory." (48: 1-3) This was addressed to the Prophet, who had already been forgiven his sins. Nevertheless, he was so pleased with this *sūrah* that he said it was dearer to him than the whole world. His companions – who, like all other believers, were not sure of God's forgiveness, although they hoped for it – must have been overwhelmed with joy at the happy news that God was well pleased with them. That piece of news must have made the rest of their lives joyful and must have increased their determination to serve Islam as much as they could for the rest of their lives.

Notes

1. Detailed accounts of the events leading to the signing of the peace agreement are given in all major sources on the Prophet's life. See for example: Ibn Hishām, *al-Sīrah al-Nabawiyyah*, Dār al-Qalam, Beirut, Vol. 1, pp. 321-336; al-Wāqidī, *Kitāb al-Maghāzī*, Oxford University Press, 1996, Vol. 2, pp. 572-617; Ibn Kathīr, *al-Bidāyah wal-Nihāyah*, Maktabat al-Maʿārif, Beirut, Vol. 1, pp. 164-177; and Ibn Sayyid al-Nās, *ʿUyūn al-Athar*, Dār al-Turāth, Madinah, 1996, pp. 160-172.
2. Ibn Sayyid al-Nās, op.cit., p. 172.
3. Ibn Hishām, op.cit., pp. 336-337.
4. Ibid., pp. 337-338. Also, al-Wāqidī, op.cit., pp. 624-627; and Ibn Sayyid al-Nās, op.cit., pp. 179.
5. Ibn Hishām, op.cit., p. 338. Also, Ibn Sayyid al-Nās, op.cit., pp. 179-180; and al-Wāqidī, op.cit., p. 629.
6. Sayyid Quṭb, *Fī Ẓilal al-Qur'ān*, Dār al-Shurūq, Beirut, 1974, Vol. 6, p. 3326.
7. Ibn Kathīr, op.cit., p. 177.

29

Back on the Move

WHEN THE MUSLIMS arrived in Madinah after the conclusion of their peace agreement with the Quraysh, the Prophet let them rest for only a few weeks before he called on them to be ready again for a major encounter with the enemies of Islam. One should remember here that the Quraysh represented only one of the three major sections of people hostile to Islam. The other two were the Bedouin Arabs, scattered all over Arabia and always on the lookout for a chance to attack Muslims and cause them some harm, and the Jews. As has been seen, three major encounters took place between the Muslims in Madinah and the three leading Jewish tribes in that city. Now the main centre of Jewish concentration in Arabia was Khaybar, which was in the northern part of the Arabian Peninsula, quite a long way from Madinah.

In Khaybar, the Jews were wavering between their burning desire to launch a successful attack on the Muslims and their fear that their renewed efforts might have the same result as earlier ones. Their wish to resume the fight against Islam was almost as strong as their keenness not to do something which would threaten their very existence. They realized that their enemy was neither weak nor cowardly. Indeed, they knew that the Muslims could not be easily overcome, regardless of the size of the forces allied against them. Yet the Jews wanted to put an end to Islam, so they could not bring themselves to accept the idea of coexistence with the new faith. Their leaders, one after the other, followed the same hostile line, conspiring against the Prophet and joining every effort and every campaign launched against Islam.

It was from Khaybar that Jewish leaders like Sallām ibn Abū al-Ḥuqayq and Ḥuyayy ibn Akhṭab started their conspiracies against Islam. The latter Jewish leader was the architect of the campaign known as 'The Expedition of the Moat' launched by the allied Arab forces to destroy Madinah (Chapter 25). Furthermore, the idea of persuading the Qurayẓah to join that effort was his own brainchild. When those two Jewish leaders were removed from the scene, the leadership of the Jews in Khaybar fell to a man called Usayr ibn Rizām. Usayr followed the same policies and tactics of his predecessors. He started by renewing the pact which the Jews of Khaybar had with the Arab tribe of the Ghaṭafān against the 'common enemy' – the Muslims. Among Arab tribes, the Ghaṭafān was known for hard fighting. Their quarters were not very far from Khaybar. They were the tribe which joined the Quraysh in marching on Madinah a year earlier, in response to the Jewish efforts, with the declared objective of annihilating the Muslims.

Treachery Always at Hand

Since alliances were usually short-lived in Arabia at that time, Usayr felt that a renewal of alliances was necessary as a sound precaution in case a new confrontation with the Muslims took place. Never did Usayr ibn Rizām think that the course which had been followed by the Jews ever since the advent of Islam was the cause of their defeat at the hands of the Muslims, or that common sense required him to move in a totally different direction. When the Prophet heard of Usayr's activities, he sought to neutralize that source of danger. He sent 30 of his companions from the Anṣār, headed by ʿAbdullāh ibn Rawāḥah, with instructions to try to persuade Usayr ibn Rizām to follow a more sensible approach to the relationship between the Jews and the Muslims. When ʿAbdullāh ibn Rawāḥah and his men arrived at Khaybar they had a meeting with Usayr. Both sides agreed to exchange pledges of security and safety until they had finalized the business in hand. ʿAbdullāh ibn Rawāḥah explained that the Muslims did not want any military conflict with the Jews or anyone else. They would much rather have peaceful relations with all parties. He assured Usayr that the Jews need not fear any threat or danger from the Muslims if they were willing to live in peace with them. He proposed that Usayr should go to Madinah where he could conclude a peace agreement with the Prophet. Usayr agreed to this and went with them, accompanied by a number of his fellow Jews, with that aim in mind. They had not been travelling long, however, when Usayr started to have second thoughts. These prompted him to try to assassinate ʿAbdullāh ibn Rawāḥah. The latter, however, was quick to see what Usayr was trying to do and he managed to kill him on the spot.[1] Yet another Islamic effort at peaceful coexistence with the Jews was thus nipped in the bud. As usual, the bitter fruits were reaped by the treacherous.

Usayr ibn Rizām was succeeded by Sallām ibn Mishkam as leader of the Jews in Khaybar. Singular as it might seem, Sallām could not benefit from past lessons. He followed the same course as his predecessors and went about confirming past alliances and concluding pacts of hatred against Islam.

Eye for an Easy Gain

After the pact of al-Ḥudaybiyah, the Prophet felt that the Muslims were now in a position to neutralize the threat posed by the Jews in Khaybar. He therefore called on his companions to mobilize again and start the march towards Khaybar. He made it clear that only those who went with him for the *ʿUmrah* at al-Ḥudaybiyah were allowed to join him this time. As already seen, many people did not wish to join him then because they feared that the Quraysh were in a position to stop the Muslims by force and inflict a heavy defeat on them. These same people, however, realized that the Muslims were now set on a winning course. In the *sūrah* which comments on the events of al-Ḥudaybiyah, there is a definite promise by God to the Muslims that they would have more chances to gain spoils of war. The very people who had grave misgivings about the prospects of the Muslims when they marched towards Makkah were now absolutely certain that there was great booty to grab. Deep inside them, they realized that Qur'ānic promises always came true. It was natural, then, that they should try to join the Muslim army on this expedition, which promised great immediate benefits. The Prophet, however, told them that they were allowed to join the army only if they were keen to serve the cause of God. If they were after the booty which would result from an Islamic victory, their services were not required.

Thus, only those who went with the Prophet on the mission of al-Ḥudaybiyah were allowed to go with him this time – in addition, perhaps, to a few others who were known to be good Muslims. The Muslim army was only 1,400 men strong, with only 200 horsemen, and the task confronting it was formidable indeed. Khaybar was a well fortified city and the Jews could raise very large forces. Moreover, the Prophet always tried to take his enemies by surprise. This time, however, the Jews of Khaybar received intelligence of his intention. It is reported that ʿAbdullāh ibn Ubayy, the man usually described as the chief of the hypocrites, sent them a warning the moment he realized that the Prophet was planning to attack Khaybar. As soon as they received this information, the Jews started to make their preparations. They put their city on a war footing, keeping their women and children well protected in their forts and holding military exercises and training every day outside their city.

Khaybar was about 160 kilometres to the north of Madinah, a distance which took five days of travelling by camel. Appointing his companion Sibāʿ ibn ʿArfaṭah to deputize for him in Madinah, the Prophet set out in the month of al-Muḥarram of the seventh year of his emigration to Madinah (August AD 628), realizing that speed was an essential factor in taking the Khaybar Jews by surprise. He covered the whole distance in only three tiring stages, each taking one day, and arrived in the vicinity of Khaybar at dawn of the fourth day. The Muslims encamped in an open valley called al-Rajīʿ, on the route between the Ghaṭafān and Khaybar. They wanted to block the route so that the Ghaṭafān could not come to the aid of their Jewish allies.

Some reports suggest that the Ghaṭafān decided to send some of their forces to help the Jews. Shortly after setting out, they heard noises in their own quarters. They thought that the Muslims were planning to attack their quarters after they had left. They, therefore, went back and stayed in their own town, to defend it against the Muslims, should the latter attack it. What had probably taken place was that the Prophet had actually sent a detachment of his forces when he realized that the Ghaṭafān were planning to support the Jews, in order to frighten the Ghaṭafān away from supporting their allies. Other reports suggest that the Prophet actually asked the Ghaṭafān not to support the Jews of Khaybar, and he promised to give the Ghaṭafān a portion of what the Muslims stood to win when they achieved victory. Whichever report was true, the practical result was that the Ghaṭafān did not actually help the Jews, and left them to face the Muslims on their own.

It is necessary to explain here that Khaybar was not a city in the traditional sense of the word. It was a large oasis, very fertile, with farms and orchards stretching over a very large area indeed. Its people were not concentrated in a single built-up area forming the city; they were scattered over the neighbouring hills and valleys. Their homes were fortified in the middle of their farms and orchards. The terrain was very difficult for any attacking army because it would have had to fight in the farms, in the valleys and over several hills.

From the military point of view, Khaybar was divided into three sections, al-Naṭāh, al-Shaqq and al-Katībah. Each section included several forts. Al-Naṭāh, for example, incorporated the forts of Nāʿim, al-Ṣaʿb and al-Zubayr. The most prominent forts al-Shaqq included were Ubayy and al-Barī'. The al-Katībah section also comprised numerous forts which included al-Waṭīḥ, Sulālem and Nizār. All these forts were built on high land; some of them were on top of hills.

The population of Khaybar were, generally speaking, experienced fighters. Indeed, the Jewish concentration in Khaybar was the strongest, richest and best armed in Arabia, so it was very difficult for the Muslims to attack such a city. But the Jews generally were not the sort of people who fought in open battlefields. They preferred to fight in front of their forts and castles. Should the battle go against them, they were then able to retreat into their castles and forts and try to withstand a long siege. Obviously, they hoped that their attackers would grow weary of the long siege and go away. This was the reason which prompted the Prophet to march to Khaybar. Had he not done so, the Jews of Khaybar would have continued to urge others to attack the Muslims. The pattern of raising Arab tribes against the Muslims would be repeated again and again. There was no other way of stopping the Jewish aggression except by attacking the Jews in their own castles.

When the Muslim army arrived in the vicinity of Khaybar, the Prophet wanted to encamp near al-Naṭāh section and its forts. One of his companions, al-Ḥubāb ibn al-Mundhir, said to him:

> The people of al-Naṭāh are highly renowned for their marksmanship. They can cast arrows a greater distance than most people, and they are better than most at hitting their targets. Moreover, they are well above us in their forts. This gives them an added advantage, with their arrows gathering more speed as they travel down towards us. If we encamp here we cannot guard ourselves fully against a night attack which they may plan and in which they would take advantage of their palm trees, which would give them added cover. It would be wiser to encamp at some other place.

The Prophet said to him: "Your advice is certainly sound." He ordered his army to move backwards so that they were well away from the forts and would not be hit by sniper arrows. This attitude of the Prophet is reminiscent of his attitude at Badr, when al-Ḥubāb ibn al-Mundhir also objected to the place in which the army was planning to encamp. There also the Prophet acted on the advice of al-Ḥubāb who apparently had a keen strategic eye. Indeed, the Prophet was always willing to act on any sound advice put to him in matters of strategy or policy. Such areas were left for him to decide as a human being. Hence, he acted at his own discretion, without imposing his will on his companions. No matter how grave or trivial the business in hand was, the Prophet was always willing to accept sound advice. By so doing, he has given an example for Muslim rulers in following generations. He has shown the true meaning of the fact that Islam is a system based on consultative government.

Taken by Surprise

The people of Khaybar were fast asleep when these events took place. They did not notice anything until their farm workers went out of the forts, carrying their tools, to go about their farm work. When they saw the Prophet and his companions, they were panic-stricken. They shouted: "Muhammad and his army! Muhammad and his army!" They ran away to their forts warning their people against the impending calamity. The Prophet wanted to add to their panic and shouted: "God is supreme. Khaybar is destroyed. When we arrive in the enemy's land, those who have been forewarned will have a very bad morning."

The people of Khaybar awoke to this very unpleasant surprise. They realized that the initiative was totally with the Prophet. The options open to them were either to surrender or to fight to the last man. As the Prophet and his companions encamped at such a close distance, it was impossible for the Jews of Khaybar to launch an offensive. They had to go on the defensive. This gave the Muslims a great psychological advantage. But the Jews also realized that in their previous encounters with the Muslims, their forts and castles were of no great use to them. Eventually, the Muslims were able to score total victory. Some of the Jews in Khaybar were evacuees from Madinah. To them, seeing the Muslims besieging their forts again did not bode any good omen. They felt fear creeping into their hearts. That in itself was half the battle.

Fighting began at the fort of Nāʿim, in which the Jews had amassed a large force. Their leader in that fort was Sallām ibn Mishkam, the overall chief of the Jews of Khaybar. Here, the Jews were prepared for a long and fierce battle. The Prophet, however, tried to score a psychological victory which he hoped would avert the need for actual fighting. Knowing that the Jews considered their money to be as dear to them as their own lives, he wanted to demonstrate to them that they might be better off if they surrendered. If they insisted on fighting, he wanted them to understand that their loss would be financial as well as military. He, therefore, ordered his companions to cut down the palm trees which belonged to the Jews. Nearly 400 trees were felled on his instructions, but he realized that there was no sign of the Jews surrendering. He then ordered a halt to the tree-felling and prepared to launch his attack.

Shrewd Military Strategy

The Prophet realized that in order to achieve a total victory over the Jews in such an unusual city as Khaybar, he had to smash their power in every one of these forts and castles. His strategic plan was to assign to small detachments of his forces the task of engaging the Jews in several forts while concentrating the larger part of his forces against one fort, putting it under siege until it surrendered. He would then move on to the next fort. He divided his forces into small sections according to their clans and tribes. He also appointed a commander for every unit, so that there would be a great deal of competition between the different units. This also helped in alternating several units between the tasks of engaging enemy forces and of mounting a siege. In this way, no unit was overtired through sustained pressure. All the Muslim units shared in the military effort, with none of them bearing the larger share of the burden on its own. Here the Prophet was clearly a great military commander, putting a different plan for each encounter with the enemy according to the nature of the encounter, taking all factors into consideration: the terrain, the size of his forces in relation to enemy forces, the psychological advantage. In Khaybar, the Prophet's plan did not differ from the most advanced military plans for urban and forest fighting.

The first battle was fierce and the Jews showed solid resistance to the Muslims every inch of the way. The Muslims, however, were more than a match for the defenders. Every time the Jews tried to come out of their fort to repel their attackers, the Muslims forced them to retreat inside. The siege continued day after day, as the fierce fighting could not tilt the balance decisively either way. The battle of the fort of Nāʿim continued for seven days, with the Prophet assigning the Muslims' banner to a different one of his companions on each successive day. None, however, was able to force the doors of the fort open. Finally, on the seventh day, the Prophet assigned the banner to ʿAlī ibn Abī Ṭālib, who was able to break the power of the defenders and force the fort wide open. It is said that ʿAlī was suffering from a severe eye inflammation so he could hardly see his way. When the Prophet assigned the banner to him, ʿAlī drew the Prophet's attention to his complaint and the Prophet wiped ʿAlī's eyes with his saliva and prayed for his recovery. ʿAlī's complaint was immediately relieved and he never again experienced a recurrence of his eye inflammation.

At one point in the battle of the fort of Nāʿim, one of the bravest and best renowned Jewish fighters, Marḥab, challenged the Muslims to a duel. ʿAlī himself fought him and was able to kill him. A Muslim soldier, Maḥmūd ibn Maslamah, was sitting at one point next to the wall of the fort, and someone from inside the fort threw a large stone which fell on his head and killed him. His brother, Muhammad ibn Maslamah, was able to take revenge for his dead brother. The Jewish commander, Sallām ibn Mishkam, died during the siege and was succeeded by al-Ḥārith ibn Abī Zaynab.

When the fort of Nāʿim fell to the Muslims, the Jews who were there withdrew to the fort next to it, al-Ṣaʿb. When the Muslims put them under siege, the Jews made a determined fight and attacked with large forces. The Muslims were forced to retreat some distance, but the unit commanded by al-Ḥubāb ibn al-Mundhir was able to stand firm. The Prophet encouraged the Muslims to double their efforts in their *jihād* and al-Ḥubāb was able to check the Jews' advance and then force them on the retreat. They went back into their fort and closed its gates. In their counterattack, the Muslims were able to force the gates of the fort open and started to kill anyone who resisted them, or to take him prisoner. The fort of al-Ṣaʿb then surrendered to the Muslims.

In al-Ṣaʿb fort, the Muslims found large amounts of provisions – barley, dates, butter, cooking oil, honey and several other items. Before that, they were without any provisions of their own; they were more or less in a famine. The Prophet was worried that the Muslims might be preoccupied with carrying away these provisions and he asked one of his companions to convey his orders that they were allowed to eat and to give their horses and camels what they needed, but not to carry with them any amount of those provisions.

In that fort, the Muslims found buried under the ground a large quantity of mangonel, shields, swords and other weapons. They used them for the rest of the battle and thus they were far better equipped than they were when they had started. The discovery was made through a Jew who had fallen prisoner during the siege of the fort of Nāʿim. This man was in fear for his life and he came to the Prophet and volunteered this information in return for an assurance from the Prophet that neither he nor anyone of his family would be killed.

A Battle at Every Fort

The next fort where the Jews were planning to fight was that of al-Zubayr. The Muslims mounted a three-day siege, but the Jews would not come out. Then the Prophet discovered that a stream of water ran into that fort from the back. He ordered the stream to be diverted so that the besieged would not have their supply of water. The trick worked and the Jews were forced to come out and fight. The battle was ferocious, with casualties on both sides. The Muslims, however, were able to gain the upper hand and al-Zubayr, the last fort in al-Naṭāh section, fell to them. The Jews were now in the next section, al-Shaqq, defending the nearest of its forts which had the name of Ubayy.

This fort was on a hill known as Mount Shamran, where the Jews fought a determined battle. There were several duels between the best known fighters of both sides. These went in favour of the Muslims. The Muslim commander in the battle of the fort of Ubayy was Abū Dujānah, whom we have seen in early battles, especially Uḥud, demonstrating his fearless courage and exceptional determination. This time he was able to force his way into the fort and its defenders lost no time in escaping to the next one, al-Barī'.

When the Prophet and his companions moved to that fort, the Jews had made up their minds to do all they could to halt the Muslim advance. The defenders of the fort of al-Barī' were perhaps the best marksmen with arrows among all the Jews of Khaybar. In this encounter, they justified their reputation by pouring on the Muslims a shower of arrows and stones. Indeed, some arrows hit the Prophet's own clothes. At this point, the Prophet ordered his companions to bring out the mangonel and start using it. The Jewish defendants of the fort were terrified and fled to the next section. Thus the al-Shaqq section of Khaybar and its forts had fallen completely to the Muslims.

Retreating into the last section of al-Katībah, the Jews put up their defences first at the fort of al-Qamous where the chiefs were the family of al-Ḥuqayq, to which belonged several of the Jewish leaders who shared in the earlier conspiracies against the Muslims. The Muslims besieged this fort for 20 days until it surrendered to the Muslim commander, ʿAlī ibn Abī Ṭālib. A large number of women were taken prisoner from this fort. Following the universal traditions of the time, these women prisoners were enslaved. The Prophet chose from among them a woman called Ṣafiyyah bint Ḥuyayy, the daughter of Ḥuyayy ibn Akhṭab, who was the Jewish leader perhaps most hostile to Islam. The Prophet set Ṣafiyyah free before marrying her. So she became a mother of the believers.

After the Surrender

With all these forts falling to the Muslims, the Jews were forced to retreat to their two final forts, al-Waṭīḥ and Sulālem. These were besieged for over two weeks, before the Jews realized that they had no hope of turning the scales against the Muslims. Hence, they offered to surrender in return for their safety. Their leader, Kinānah ibn al-Rabīʿ ibn Abī al-Ḥuqayq, came down to sign a document of surrender with the Prophet. The surrender agreement stipulated that none of their fighters would be put to death. They would be allowed to leave Khaybar and its vicinity, taking with them their women and children. They would abandon all their claims over their land, money, horses and arms. To these conditions, which were voluntarily offered by the Jews, the Prophet added: "But all guarantees given you would be abrogated if you withhold anything from me." Thus all Khaybar fell to the Muslims, who were now in possession of all its wealth and land.[2]

When the peace agreement was made, the people of Khaybar started to have second thoughts about leaving their land. Hence, they came to the Prophet, requesting him to allow them to stay and work in the farms and orchards. They said to them: "We are better at this sort of job than you, and the land would yield much better crops if we work on it." They offered to give the Muslims half the yield of all the land in Khaybar in return. The Prophet accepted these offers and amended the peace agreement accordingly, but added the proviso that the Muslims would evacuate the Jews from Khaybar whenever they chose.[3]

Remaining Jewish Centres

There were other centres of Jewish population in Arabia. One of these was at Fadak. When the Jews there heard of the peace agreement reached between the Prophet and the people of Khaybar, they decided not to go to war against the Muslims. They sent a delegation to meet the Prophet and a similar peace agreement to that with the people of Khaybar was reached. Thus the Muslims won Khaybar by force of arms, while Fadak was gained without any need to fight. Hence, Fadak became the property of the Prophet as the head of the Muslim state, according to Islamic legislation.[4]

The next Jewish concentration was at Wādī al-Qurā, to which the Prophet marched after leaving Khaybar. He besieged the place for several days, upon which its population surrendered and entered a peace agreement with the Muslims on the same terms as those of the agreement with Khaybar. The Jews of Taymā', on the other hand, did not fight. They surrendered voluntarily to the Muslims. Thus, all the Jews in Arabia finally yielded to the authority of the Prophet and relinquished all their own authority. The Muslims in Madinah were now in a much better position with regard to security. They feared no enemy to the north after the surrender of the Jews. Nor was there any enemy to fear to the south now that they had entered into the famous peace agreement with the Quraysh at al-Ḥudaybiyah.[5]

Return of Old Immigrants

When the Muslims had finished the job of conquering Khaybar and all its forts and castles fell to them, they had a pleasant surprise. They were joined there by Jaʿfar ibn Abī Ṭālib, the Prophet's cousin, who had emigrated to Abyssinia about 15 years earlier with a number of the companions of the Prophet. (The events which necessitated that emigration, its effects and consequences on the Muslims and the purposes it served have already been discussed in Chapter 10.) Many who had emigrated with Jaʿfar rejoined the Prophet at Madinah at different times. A group of them, however, continued to live in Abyssinia having been ordered by the Prophet to do so. A short while before the Prophet set out towards Khaybar, he sent his companion, ʿAmr ibn Umayyah al-Ḍamrī, who acted as his ambassador at large, to Negus, the ruler of Abyssinia, asking him to facilitate the return of the Muslims who sought refuge in his country. He himself had adopted Islam. On receiving the Prophet's request, he immediately arranged for two boats to carry the Muslims on their way back home. The immigrants headed to join the Prophet, and that meant that they went straight to Khaybar. There were 16 men and a few women, but there were others with them from Abyssinia and Yemen. The Prophet was very pleased when he saw Jaʿfar and his brethren. He hugged Jaʿfar and kissed him on his forehead between the eyes. He said: "I am not sure which of the two gives me greater pleasure: the conquest of Khaybar or the return of Jaʿfar."[6] The Prophet treated the returning immigrants on an equal footing with those who fought at Khaybar, giving each one of them an equal share of the spoils of war.

Those spoils of war were indeed great. The conquest of Khaybar and the gains the Muslims achieved as a result were part of the fulfilment of the promise God made to the Muslims as a reward for their steadfastness and declared willingness to fight the Quraysh at al-Ḥudaybiyah. That promise is contained in the *Sūrah* 48, entitled The Conquest. The promise was that God would grant the Muslims 'a victory coming soon' and 'a great deal of spoils of war', which they would take for themselves. The Khaybar expedition took place barely two months after al-Ḥudaybiyah.

The Muslims' gains were great, but they were not gold and silver; they were orchards and farms, horses and camels, swords and arrows. It was such a fertile land that its yield of dates alone was estimated for purposes of *zakāt* at 40,000 camel loads. The Prophet set aside one-fifth of all that the Muslims had gained. In effect, this fifth was the land of the military section of al-Katībah. It is reported that that section included at least 40,000 date palms which yielded annually something like 8,000 camel loads. According to Islam, one-fifth of everything the Muslims gain in battle goes to the public treasury. Thus, al-Katībah was the share of the state. The rest was divided into 1,800 shares. These shares were of equal value and were distributed among the soldiers of the Muslim army, each man getting one share. Each horse was given two shares. This confirms that there were 1,400 Muslim men in that army. They had only 200 horses with them.

Some reports suggest that the Prophet divided what the Muslims had gained in Khaybar into two halves. He then divided one half into 1,800 shares, as explained. The other half was given to the Muslim state in order to run its business. If one remembers that the peace agreement which was finally concluded after the battle of Khaybar stipulated that the Jews could work the land for half its yield of all crops, one need only know the yield of each share which the Muslims had in order to have a good idea of the size of their booty. A clue for such a calculation is found in the fact that the Prophet married one of his companions to a young lady. The marriage was consummated without any stipulation of a dowry. The man did not give his wife anything by way of dowry. Since the man was among those who attended al-Ḥudaybiyah, he had a share in Khaybar. When he was about to die, he said to those who attended his deathbed: "The Prophet married me to my wife and I did not give her any dowry. I would like you to bear witness that I give up to her my share in Khaybar as her dowry.' She sold that share for 100,000 dirhams.[7]

When one reads that the Prophet used to store provisions for his family for a whole year in advance, one knows that he was able to do so only after the conquest of Khaybar. It is true to say that the Muslims' fortunes were totally different after Khaybar. Again, this is the result of honest and sincere effort exerted by the Muslims for the cause of God and in anticipation of no return other than winning the pleasure of God. When Muslims do that, they do not only achieve their goal with respect to earning God's pleasure, but they also win material gains which ensure for them a comfortable life in this world.

Compassion

Two incidents which took place in the wake of the Battle of Khaybar give an insight into the widely different attitudes of the Muslims and their enemies. It is reported that Bilāl, a companion of the Prophet, was taking Ṣafiyyah bint Ḥuyayy, whom the Prophet later married, and a cousin of hers from one place to another. Bilāl deliberately planned his route so that they would pass by the place where those Jews who were killed in the battle were about to be buried. When the two girls saw the dead, Ṣafiyyah's cousin cried and lamented loudly. The Prophet disliked what Bilāl had done and reproached him severely: "Are you devoid of mercy? You take a young girl to the place where the killed are."

Bilāl apologized, saying that he did not think that the Prophet would object to what he did. He thought it might be beneficial if the girl was made to see the dead from among her people. But he also promised that he would never do such a thing again.[8]

Here the Prophet reproaches one of his earliest companions for paying little heed to human considerations. To him, the fact that the Jews were hardened enemies of Islam was no reason for treating them unkindly. Indeed, the reverse was true: kind treatment might overcome their hostility and Islam might benefit by the establishment of better relations with them in future.

Revenge

The other incident took place when the Prophet and the Muslims had had some rest after their hard battle. A woman called Zaynab bint al-Ḥārith, the wife of Sallām ibn Mishkam, the chief of Khaybar who died during the siege of the first fort, prepared a lamb for eating. She had enquired beforehand which part of lamb the Prophet liked best. She was told that he liked the shoulder. When the lamb was well cooked, she poisoned it and put an extra dose of poison in the lamb's shoulders. She then took it to the Prophet and gave it to him as a present. The Prophet took one shoulder and had a bite of it, but he did not like the taste and spat it out. He said: "This joint tells me that it is poisoned."

One of his companions, Bishr ibn al-Barā', was with him at the time. Bishr ate a little of the lamb and found it acceptable. The poison soon had its effect and he died quickly. The woman was called in and the Prophet asked her about the lamb. She confessed that she had poisoned it. Under questioning she explained her reason to the Prophet: "You know what you have done to my people. I thought that if you were a king I would get my revenge and we would get rid of you. If you were truly a Prophet, you would be told of the poison." The Prophet pardoned her. Some reports, however, suggest that she was put to death in punishment for killing Bishr ibn al-Barā'.[9] The traditions which suggest that she was pardoned are weightier. Moreover, they are more in line with the attitude of the Prophet. He knew that people were always on the lookout for a chance to get some revenge on their conquerors, especially immediately after their defeat. It was his habit after every success in battle to do something which would help in turning over a new leaf in the relations between the Muslims and those whom they had just defeated.

In the earlier campaign of al-Muṣṭalaq, several hundred people of that tribe were enslaved after being taken prisoner, in the normal tradition of the time. After the battle, the Prophet married Juwayriyyah bint al-Ḥārith, the daughter of the chief of al-Muṣṭalaq. This marriage resulted in the immediate release from slavery of all those who were taken prisoner by the Muslims. The companions of the Prophet would not hear of having his 'in-laws' as their slaves. Hence they gave them their freedom, demonstrating their love and respect for the Prophet.

A New Bride for the Prophet

After Khaybar, the Prophet married the daughter of the man who did more than any other Jew to undermine Islam and to put an end to it. Ḥuyayy ibn Akhṭab, the chief of the Jewish tribe of al-Naḍīr, had determined to fight Islam tooth and nail from the very first day of the Prophet's settlement in Madinah. Ḥuyayy was one of the chiefs of al-Naḍīr who plotted to kill the Prophet when he went to their quarters, seeking their help in accordance with the terms of the covenant which he had concluded with them on his arrival in Madinah. This assassination attempt resulted in the evacuation of the Jews of al-Naḍīr from Madinah. No sooner had they settled in Khaybar than he started to put into effect his plan of uniting all the enemies of Islam in a concerted attack on Madinah, with the aim of exterminating the Muslims altogether. It was Ṣafiyyah, the daughter of Ḥuyayy himself, whom the Prophet decided to marry when the battle of Khaybar was over.

One must not underestimate the significance of such a marriage, especially in the tribal environment of Arabia, where marriage relations between the families of the chiefs of different tribes signified alliances between those tribes. The Prophet wanted his companions and the vanquished Jews to realize that he was opening a new page in his relations with yesterday's enemies. The Prophet would not have married Ṣafiyyah had he intended not to treat her on an equal footing with his other wives. He realized that his marriage would go a long way to reassure the Jews that the door was open for them to have friendly relations with Islam.

Ṣafiyyah was a young woman when the Prophet married her. Some reports suggest that she was only 17, but that may not be very accurate, considering that in Arabia, no group or tribe kept records or dates of events. She might probably have been a few years older, considering that she had been married twice before. Her first husband was Sallām ibn Mishkam, the prominent Jew who took over the overall leadership of the Khaybar Jews a short while before the Battle of Khaybar and died when the Muslims were besieging the fort of Nāʿim. It is not certain how long that marriage lasted, but it seems probable that Sallām divorced his wife sometime before his death. Her second husband was Kinānah ibn al-Rabīʿ ibn Abī al-Ḥuqayq, who belonged to a family which gave the Jews many of their leaders. Kinānah was killed in Khaybar, towards the end of the battle.

In the traditions of the time, Ṣafiyyah would have been a slave girl in the Prophet's household. The Prophet, however, did not keep any slave, man or woman, who was given into his hands in bondage for any length of time. When his companions told him that Ṣafiyyah should not be given to any person other than himself, because of her noble birth – which incidentally was traceable to the Prophet Aaron, Moses' brother (peace be upon them both) – the Prophet gave Ṣafiyyah the freedom of choice. He told her that she could rejoin her family or he would set her free and marry her. She chose to be his wife.

After their marriage the Prophet did all he could to help Ṣafiyyah forget the events of the past, which were naturally a source of grief to her. She is reported to have said later: "God's Messenger (peace be upon him) was very hateful to me because he killed my husband and my father. However, he kept apologizing to me, saying that my father had raised the Arabs against him, and did this and did that, until all my hard feelings disappeared."

One day, the Prophet went into Ṣafiyyah's room to find her crying. When he asked her why, she said that ʿĀ'ishah and Ḥafṣah, who were both his wives, kept talking about her, belittling her position. They said that either of them was far superior to her because they were distant cousins of the Prophet and that he married them for their personalities, not for any other reason. He said to her: "Why did you not reply to them and say: 'how can you be superior to me when Aaron is my father [meaning her lineage ended with him], and Moses is my uncle and my husband is Muhammad?'"

It is reported that when Ṣafiyyah was still a young girl, she saw in her dream that the moon fell into her lap. She mentioned her dream to her father and he hit her hard in the face. He said to her: "You surely wish to be wed to the King of the Arabs." The slap left a visible mark on her face which the Prophet noticed when he married her. He asked her about that mark and she told him its cause.[10]

Winning People's Hearts

It has already been reported that according to their agreement with the Prophet, the Jews at Khaybar would stay and look after the land in return for half its produce. The Prophet accepted that and allowed them to remain on condition that the Muslims could ask them to leave whenever they wished and they would leave without any complaint. This shows how the Prophet did not harbour any hard feelings against his old enemies. He did not wish to take revenge against any one of them, despite their past conspiracies and repeated attempts to cause Islam a great deal of harm. When they had surrendered and it was clear that they could not cause the Muslims any more trouble, no real purpose would have been served by putting their men to death, or sending them into exile. He therefore allowed them to stay.

Moreover, the Prophet emphasized to the Muslims that they should treat the Jews fairly. The Jews complained at one point after they were allowed to stay that some Muslims went into their farms and took away some of the fruits or crops which they found. The Prophet ordered the Muslims to assemble and spoke to them: "The Jews have complained to me that you have been taking things away from their farms and barns. You know that we have reached an agreement with them, giving them security for their lives and possessions in their land. We also agreed that they would work on the land for us. No Muslim is allowed to have anything which belongs to anyone with whom the Muslims have a peace agreement unless he pays him its fair price." All subsequent dealings between the Muslims and the Jews were then conducted on this basis.

When the Muslims had returned to Madinah, the Prophet used to send his companion, ʿAbdullāh ibn Rawāḥah, to Khaybar every year to estimate the amount of the crops, so that it could be shared out equally between the Muslims and the Jews. Sometimes when he had made his estimates and pointed out which share belonged to the Muslims and which belonged to the Jews, they would tell him: "You have been unfair to us." He would answer: "You may have either share." That gave the Jews the best reassurance that they were treated fairly. They told ʿAbdullāh: "On this standard of justice, everything on earth and in heaven can prosper."

Among the things which came into the possession of the Muslims as a result of their victory in Khaybar were a number of sheets and pages from the old Torah. The Jews asked the Prophet to hand back these sheets to them. He did so willingly. To them, those sheets had a special value. To be able to have them back after their defeat filled them with admiration for the Prophet. It is the normal practice in most wars that the victor plays havoc with whatever the defeated regard as holy. When the Byzantines conquered Jerusalem in the year 70 BC they burnt the sacred books which belonged to the Jews. No such practice was followed in any battle the Muslims fought.[11]

The Battle of Khaybar put an end to one source of danger with which the Muslims had had to contend for several years. It smashed the political and economic power of the Jews in Arabia. As the power of Islam continued to increase, the Jewish influence paled into insignificance. What is more, the enemies of Islam had to revise their calculations. In less than three or four months, the Muslims were able to neutralize the Quraysh and to smash the power of the Jews. How different the Arabian scene had become after the Battle of Khaybar!

Back with the Quraysh

When the Muslims, led by the Prophet, marched from Madinah towards Khaybar, their fortunes generated great interest all over Arabia, especially from the Quraysh. As events actually developed, the conquest of Khaybar by the Muslims was a great achievement which few people had expected to come about so relatively quickly and easily. The Quraysh certainly followed the events with great sympathy for the Jews. It was less than 18 months earlier that the Quraysh and the Jews had been partners in an all out attempt to destroy Madinah and exterminate the Muslims. Now the Quraysh was neutralized with the conclusion of the peace treaty of al-Ḥudaybiyah. Sympathies were not expected to undergo a marked change with the mere signing of a peace treaty. Hence, the Quraysh could only wish that the Jews of Khaybar could achieve, on their own, what their combined forces had failed to achieve.

Views differed among the Quraysh people as to the result they expected in the encounter between the Muslims and the Jews. Some of them, who were familiar with the strength and armament of the Jews and with their strong fortifications, and were aware of the alliance which they had with the Ghaṭafān, expected that the battle would end in favour of the Jews. Others who admired the unity of the Muslims, their determination, discipline, mutual cooperation and willingness to sacrifice their all for their faith, did not give the Jews much of a chance. There was much argument between the two sides, and large bets were placed on the outcome of the expected battle. Hence they were very eager for any piece of news which might be carried by a lonely traveller or a caravan. Some of them went to the extent of going out of Makkah to sit on the routes followed by travellers in order to question any passer by.

So much for the situation in Makkah. Back in the Muslim camp at Khaybar, a man who had adopted Islam a short while earlier and taken part in the Battle of Khaybar, came to the Prophet after the battle was over and said: "Messenger of God, I left much of my money with my wife, Umm Shaybah, and a number of businessmen in Makkah owe me large sums of money. I beg leave to go and collect my debts." Having obtained the Prophet's permission to do so, this man, al-Ḥajjāj ibn ʿAllāṭ of the tribe of Sulaym, said to him: "I may have to say things which may not be totally correct." The Prophet allowed him to do so.

Al-Ḥajjāj travelled as fast as he could until he approached Makkah where he found at Thaniyyat al-Bayḍā', on the outskirts, some men from the Quraysh waiting for anyone who would be able to give them any information about the Prophet and the Muslims. Unaware that al-Ḥajjāj had become a Muslim, they said when they saw him coming towards them: "This is al-Ḥajjāj ibn ʿAllāṭ, and he must have the information we are looking for." They rushed towards him and said: "Ḥajjāj, we have heard that the man [meaning the Prophet] has marched towards Khaybar, the Jewish city which is the garden of Hijaz." Al-Ḥajjāj replied: "Yes, I heard of that, and I have very happy news for you." Al-Ḥajjāj reports:

> They quickly gathered round my she-camel and asked me to speak. I said: "Muhammad was soundly beaten, and his companions suffered heavy casualties and Muhammad himself

was taken prisoner. The Jews decided not to kill him but to send him to you here in Makkah so that you could kill him in revenge for those of your leaders who were killed by him."

When they heard this, they rushed to give that news to the people of Makkah and were saying to everyone around that the awaited news had certainly arrived, and that Muhammad was about to be sent to them in shackles and fetters to be killed. As everyone was so elated, I said to them: "Help me collect my money from my debtors, because I want to go to Khaybar and gather as much as I can of what Muhammad's army has left behind, before other traders beat me to it." Many rushed to my aid, and collected my debts for me in a very short time. I then went to my wife and asked her to give me my money which I left with her for safekeeping, giving her the same excuse I gave to the other people of Makkah.

Al-Ḥajjāj's news caused a great stir in Makkah. To the hardened people of the Quraysh, it was an unexpected piece of information which would mark a radical change in the situation in Arabia. With the eclipse of the rising power of the Muslims, the Quraysh was sure to regain its supremacy. On the other hand, there were many people in Makkah who had adopted Islam but kept that fact secret. They were at a loss. If the news was true, they faced a very bleak future. Moreover, the sympathies of the Hāshimites, the Prophet's own clan, were with the Muslims. They did not wish Muhammad to suffer any defeat.

One of their leaders, al-ʿAbbās ibn ʿAbd al-Muṭṭalib, the Prophet's own uncle, was troubled by what he heard but wished to confirm it for himself. He sought to speak to al-Ḥajjāj ibn ʿAllāṭ. Finding him in a tent which served as the shop of a Makkan trader, he came close to him and said: "Ḥajjāj, what is this piece of news you have been spreading?" Al-Ḥajjāj replied: "Can I trust you with the safekeeping of what I wish to deposit with you?"

When al-ʿAbbās answered in the affirmative, al-Ḥajjāj asked him to wait until he had finished collecting his debts, when he would come to see him. When he had done so and was about to leave, al-

Ḥajjāj met al-ʿAbbās and said to him: "Listen carefully and keep what I am going to tell you a secret for three days, because I fear that the Quraysh people would pursue me hard if they know what I am going to tell you. After three days, you are free to say whatever you wish."

Al-ʿAbbās promised to keep his secret for three days. Al-Ḥajjāj then told him: "By God, I have left your nephew having wed their king's daughter [meaning Ṣafiyyah bint Ḥuyayy]. He has certainly conquered Khaybar. The whole city and its surrounding land now belong to him and his companions." He continued: "This is certainly the truth. Keep it a secret please. I am a Muslim and I have come here only to take my money. I feared that if I left it, I would never be paid by my debtors. After three days, you can publicize what I have just told you, because it is certainly the truth." Al-Ḥajjāj then departed, and al-ʿAbbās went back home reassured and happy.

After three days, al-ʿAbbās attended to his appearance so that he looked at his most elegant, put on his best suit and went out towards the Kaʿbah, where he did his *ṭawāf*. Still elated with their happy news, people from the Quraysh remarked as they saw him: "Abū al-Faḍl [this was an appellation of respect for al-ʿAbbās, addressing him as the father of his son, al-Faḍl], you are certainly showing patience in the face of this unexpected calamity."

He retorted: "No, indeed. Muhammad has certainly conquered Khaybar, and married the daughter of the Jewish king, and has taken all Khaybar and its land so that it now belongs to him and his companions." Startled and shocked, the Quraysh people asked: "Who told you this?" Al-ʿAbbās said that he heard it from the man who gave them the news they wished to hear. He also told them that al-Ḥajjāj was a Muslim who came just to take his money and rejoin Muhammad and his companions. Thus, disappointment replaced their earlier elation. They threatened that they would have done 'so-and-so' to al-Ḥajjāj, but they realized that he had escaped them.[12]

This shows what sort of feelings the Quraysh experienced whenever Muhammad and the Muslims were engaged in battle against a third party. When the Quraysh people realized that the

Jewish front had also been neutralized by the Muslims, they could not avoid the conclusion that the Muslims were now the major power in Arabia.

Notes

1. Ibn Sayyid al-Nās, *'Uyūn al-Athar*, Dār al-Turāth, Madinah, 1996, pp. 157-158.
2. Ibn Hishām, *al-Sīrah al-Nabawiyyah*, Dār al-Qalam, Beirut, Vol. 1, pp. 342-352. Also, al-Wāqidī, *Kitāb al-Maghāzī*, Oxford University Press, 1996, Vol. 1, pp. 633-671; and Ibn Sayyid al-Nās, op.cit., pp. 181-187.
3. Ibn Hishām, op.cit., p. 352. Also, Ibn Sayyid al-Nās, op.cit., p. 187.
4. Ibn Hishām, op.cit., p. 352 and p. 368.
5. Ibid., p. 353. Also, Ibn Sayyid al-Nās, op.cit., pp. 197-199.
6. Ibn Hishām, op.cit., Vol. 4, p. 3. Also, al-Wāqidī, op.cit., p. 683; Ibn Kathīr, *al-Bidāyah wal-Nihāyah*, Maktabat al-Ma'ārif, Beirut, Vol. 1, pp. 205-208; and Ibn Sayyid al-Nās, op.cit., p. 192.
7. Amīn Duwaydār, *Ṣuwar Min Ḥayāt al-Rasūl*, Dār al-Ma'ārif, 4th edition, Cairo, pp. 486-488. See also, Ibn Hishām, op.cit., Vol. 3, pp. 363-368; al-Wāqidī, op.cit., pp. 693-699; and Ibn Sayyid al-Nās, op.cit., pp. 191-195.
8. Ibn Hishām, op.cit., Vol. 3, pp. 350-351. Also, Ibn Kathīr, op.cit., p. 197.
9. Ibn Hishām, op.cit., Vol. 3, pp. 252-253. Also, Ibn Kathīr, op.cit., pp. 208-212.
10. Al-Wāqidī, op.cit., pp. 683-685. Also, Ibn Kathīr, op.cit., pp. 196-197; and Ibn Sayyid al-Nās, op.cit., pp. 184-185.
11. Amīn Duwaydār, op.cit., pp. 488-489.
12. Ibn Hishām, op.cit., pp. 359-361.

30

Peace in the Desert

WHEN THE MUSLIMS were settled back in Madinah after their success at Khaybar, they had reason to feel much safer and much stronger. The two enemies which represented the greatest sources of danger to the Muslim community in Madinah, the Quraysh and the Jews, were now neutralized. A third source of danger existed which represented a continuous threat: the Bedouin Arabs. Everywhere in the Arabian Peninsula, there were Bedouin tribes, large and small, which led a life based on aggression and looting. They did not recognize any law apart from that of the desert. Agreements, treaties and alliances counted for little. Whenever a chance of gain presented itself, treaties and friendship were thrown to the dogs and the friends of yesterday became the enemies of today. The victor always treated the vanquished with ruthlessness and contempt. Many Bedouin tribes did not like the rise of the Muslim state in Madinah. They recognized that a totally new order was about to prevail in Arabia if the steady progress and increased strength of the Muslim state were allowed to continue. Hence, they were always planning to launch raids and attacks on Madinah. Their most immediate concern was not to allow the Muslims to settle in peace.

The Prophet's prime objective, however, was that the Muslims should be free to convey the message of Islam all over Arabia, and to the world at large. For this to happen, peace and security must be established. People must feel free to adopt Islam if they were convinced of its truth. The Prophet had long ago adopted a policy based on the principle that attack was the best form of defence. He was not to change that sound policy now when he faced only those terrorist tribes and concentrations of Bedouin Arabs who wanted to preserve lawlessness in Arabia. Therefore successive expeditions were mounted during the next few months against anyone who thought of attacking the Muslims or causing them any trouble.

In the month of Shaʿbān, three such expeditions were mounted. The first was led by ʿUmar ibn al-Khaṭṭāb and included about 30 horsemen. Their aim was one of the clans of Hawāzin. Although ʿUmar moved only by night, those people of Hawāzin received intelligence of his approach and fled. When ʿUmar arrived at their place, he found no one around. He, therefore, started on his journey back home. His guide asked him whether, having missed his target, he wished to attack a group of the Khathʿam who were travelling in the area. ʿUmar told him that the Prophet did not order him to attack anyone other than Hawāzin. Hence, he left them alone. This is only one example of the fact that the Muslims attacked only those Bedouins who intended or plotted to cause them some harm. People who wished to live in peace were given the chance to do so.[1]

The second expedition was led by Abū Bakr, who travelled eastwards to Najd, where his target was the tribe of Fazārah. He was able to take them by surprise, killing a number of their men and taking a number of prisoners. Abū Bakr's own share of the spoils of war included a pretty maid. The Prophet asked him to give him the maid as a present and he did so. The Prophet then sent her to the people of Makkah in return for the release of a number of Muslim prisoners.

The third expedition was led by Bashīr ibn Saʿd from the Anṣār, who marched at the head of 30 men towards the people of Murrah near Fadak, the Jewish township in the north of Arabia, which entered into a peace agreement with the Muslims shortly after the Battle of Khaybar. He managed to take a herd of cattle which belonged to the Murrah people and went back towards Madinah. The people of Murrah, however, pursued them and were able to catch up with them at nightfall. There was a battle of arrows in which the Muslims were not as well armed as their opponents. When their supply of arrows was exhausted and some of them were injured, the others tried to escape because they were heavily outnumbered. Bashīr, the commander, fought very well but the people of Murrah were able to regain their cattle. Bashīr was injured but he was able to walk with difficulty. He managed to reach the Jewish township, where he stayed until his injuries healed. He then returned to Madinah.[2]

Many other expeditions were sent to places all over Arabia, some of them deep into the desert. The purpose was to achieve security so that emissaries from the Prophet to the various tribes could come and go in peace and security to explain the message of Islam to the people. This is the task which the Prophet and the Muslims wanted to accomplish. Any obstacle which prevented them from fulfilling this duty of theirs was to be removed without hesitation. Whatever means were necessary for its removal were to be employed. Hence, these expeditions, which were highly professional and disciplined, were sent out. They abided by the Prophet's instructions as he gave them. They were not looting raids, for the Muslims would not unjustifiably take anybody's property. They did not care for anything other than conveying God's message to people. We have already mentioned that ʿUmar did not wish to interfere with any people other than those who were identified to him by the Prophet as troublemakers.

An example of the discipline which was the mark of these expeditions may be given by relating what happened to a man who was instructed to gather intelligence for his commander, Ghālib ibn ʿAbdullāh, during his expedition to attack the people of the Mulawwaḥ in a place called al-Kadīd. He says that they arrived there before sunset. In order to learn what the people were doing, he climbed a hill which overlooked their dwellings. He lay down at the top of the hill when the sun was just about to set. A man came out of his home and saw him in his position at the top of the hill. He said to his wife: "I see something black on the top of the hill which I did not notice earlier on. Maybe the dogs have pulled some garment or something up there. Look around you and find out if anything is missing." She confirmed that everything was in its place. Then the man asked her to hand him his bow and a couple of arrows. He took the first arrow and shot it and was able to hit the Muslim man at the top of the hill in his side. The man took the arrow out and remained in his place. He then aimed the second arrow and hit the Muslim in the shoulder. Again, the Muslim did not move, apart from pulling the arrow out. The man said to his wife: "Both my arrows have hit that thing. Had it been a man gathering intelligence, he would have moved. We have nothing to worry about. In the morning, go up there and fetch my arrows."

Here is a man who has been hit twice, yet he prefers to suffer the pain rather than alert hostile people to the presence of his companions. With such an attitude, the Muslims could rely on God's help, for God helps only those who demonstrate their willingness to sacrifice whatever is needed for His cause. What took place in that expedition afterwards is sufficient to show how the Muslims were helped by God. The same man reports:

> We waited until all activity in their quarters died down. We then launched our raid, killed a number of their men and took their cattle, and started our journey back home. Soon, they managed to raise help and came after us in hot pursuit. Our pursuers heavily outnumbered us and we were certainly no match for them. We moved as fast as we could, but they were soon catching up with us. When only a short distance in the lower part of the valley separated us, God sent, from wherever He willed, fast floods. We had not seen any rain previously, but the flood water ran so fast that no one dared make an attempt to cross to our side. That gave us a chance to evade our chasers and we managed to reach home with everything we had.[3]

These were only examples of the expeditions which the Prophet sent out to every corner of Arabia where trouble was brewing. The forces sent on these expeditions varied from 30 to 500 men. The size of each force was determined by the task in hand. All of them, however, demonstrated the same degree of discipline and seriousness, so that in a few months all the routes of Arabia were safe for the Muslim preachers to go about and visit the various tribes and towns, calling on them to accept Islam. They were able to explain the message of Islam without fear of being attacked. This was the goal, and it was achieved when the Muslims employed the necessary means for combating tribal terrorism which was the order of the day in Arabia.

The Muslims viewed themselves as trustees of the message of Islam. Their task was to convey it to people. When they had explained its principles and showed that it worked for the benefit of man and for the achievement of human happiness, their task ended there. They were not supposed, nor did they try, to compel people to accept Islam. Conversion by compulsion is alien to the nature of Islam. People, however, are normally not prepared to listen to a new call or a new theory, let alone a new religion, if they live in fear or if they are threatened by different powers. Hence, security was absolutely necessary for the fulfilment of the Prophet's and the Muslims' task of making the message of Islam known to people far and wide. Security was also necessary to ensure that anyone who adopted Islam, in any tribe, was safe from internal persecution. This is another example of the practicality and realism of Islam. It faces every situation with appropriate measures.

But the neutralization of the Quraysh and Jewish fronts gave the Muslims prospects other than spreading the message of Islam in Arabia. One has to remember that Islam is a universal message which God addresses to all mankind. People other than the Arabs had to be informed of it. Hence it was only natural, in those years when the Muslim state was safe from immediate hostilities, that the Muslims should give their advocacy efforts a broader outlook.

Notes

1. Ibn Sayyid al-Nās, *'Uyūn al-Athar*, Dār al-Turāth, Madinah, 1996, p. 199. Also, al-Wāqidī, *Kitāb al-Maghāzī*, Oxford University Press, 1996, Vol. 1, p.722.
2. Ibn Sayyid al-Nās, op.cit., pp. 200-201. Also, al-Wāqidī, op.cit., p. 722.
3. Ibn Hishām, *al-Sīrah al-Nabawiyyah*, Dār al-Qalam, Beirut, Vol. 4, pp. 257-259. Also, Ibn Sayyid al-Nās, op.cit., pp. 205-206; and al-Wāqidī, op.cit., pp. 750-752.

31

Opening Up International Horizons

NO BIOGRAPHER OF the Prophet can fail to note the emphasis he placed, ever since he started to receive his message, on the universal nature of the Islamic faith. He always stated to his people that his message was "to all mankind." At no stage of his life is any special importance given to the Arabs as a nation or a race, despite the fact that the Prophet grew up in a tribal society where narrow pride in one's lineage or tribal ancestry was common to all people. At no time did the Prophet think of himself as an Arab reformer whose task was to put his nation on the right footing. He always emphasized that the message he conveyed to people was meant for everyone and for all ages. If the message of Islam had not until then gone beyond the borders of Arabia, it was because Islam was still fighting to consolidate its base in Madinah and to win supremacy in Arabia. It was not likely that the Prophet should expand his call beyond Arabia, when his position in it was not yet secure.

In the early months of the seventh year of the Prophet's settlement in Madinah, the Arabian scene changed radically. First there was the peace treaty of al-Ḥudaybiyah, which was signed in the last month of the preceding year and which, in effect, neutralized the Quraysh, the major Arabian power opposing Islam. Then

Khaybar fell to the Muslims, thus ending the Jewish threat to the new call of Islam. Shrewd and practical head of state that he was, the Prophet moved quickly to widen the horizon before his followers. He picked a number of his companions who combined charming personality with intelligence and ability to handle difficult situations, and he sent them as envoys who carried his messages to the rulers of neighbouring countries, some of which were the superpowers of the day: Byzantium and Persia. It is important to follow the fortunes of those ambassadors in order to gauge the likely response to Islam worldwide.

To find out whether any of them was successful in his mission also gives us an insight into how Islam moulds the personality of a Muslim. One starts with Diḥyah ibn Khalīfah, of the Kalb tribe, who carried the Prophet's message to Heracules, the Byzantine Emperor. Diḥyah was a charming, handsome man. It is reported that the Angel Gabriel sometimes came to the Prophet in the same shape as Diḥyah. The Prophet asked his companions: "Who is prepared to carry my letter to the Tsar of Byzantium and be guaranteed Heaven?" A man asked: "Even if he rejects it?" The Prophet affirmed that the reward would still be his even if Heracules rejected the message. Diḥyah then took it and travelled to the capital of the Byzantine Empire.

In the Emperor's Presence

Heracules was the man who rescued the Byzantine Empire and gave it a new lease of life after it was about to collapse before the Persian Empire. He was a military commander in Carthage when he was summoned to take up the positions of Emperor and Military Commander of the Empire in AD 610. He was able to bring about a radical transformation in the fortunes of the Byzantine Empire. In a few years, he inflicted a heavy defeat on the Persian Empire which threatened its very existence. This victory took place in AD 625. Four years later, he went to Jerusalem to fulfil his pledge of returning the holy crucifix to it after recovering it from the Persians. He was given a grand reception, with people laying out carpets for him to walk on and saluting him with flowers and cheers. A grand celebration was organized for the return of the holy crucifix to its place. It was during his visit to Jerusalem that Diḥyah, the Prophet's envoy, arrived there to give him the Prophet's message. Heracules read the Prophet's message which ran as follows:

> In the name of God, the Merciful, the Beneficent.
>
> From Muhammad, God's messenger to Heracules, the Byzantine ruler. Peace be to those who follow right guidance. I call on you to believe in Islam. Adopt Islam and you will be safe, and God will give you a double reward. If you decline, you shall bear responsibility for the Arians. (The Arians were the followers of Arius, the Egyptian who believed in the Oneness of God and denied that the father and the son were two manifestations of the Lord.)

Heracules received the Prophet's envoy well, but he wanted to establish for himself the Prophet's true nature. He, therefore, ordered his aides to find any person from Arabia who happened to be in the area, so that he could question him about the Prophet. It so happened that Abū Sufyān, the Quraysh leader, was in Gaza. He was brought to Heracules with a number of his compatriots. Heracules spoke to them through his interpreter, asking them first: "Who is the closest relative among you to this man who claims to be a prophet?" Abū Sufyān told him that he was. Heracules asked him to come forward. He also placed the other Arabs just behind Abū Sufyān and told them that he was about to put some questions to him. He wanted them to point out to him any lie Abū Sufyān might tell. Abū Sufyān, however, did not wish to be known for telling a lie in that company. The conversation went as follows:

The Emperor's Verdict

Heracules:	What sort of family lineage has he among you?
Abū Sufyān:	His ancestry is a distinguished one.
Heracules:	Was any of his forefathers a king?
Abū Sufyān:	No.

Heracules:	Has anyone among you come out with a similar claim before him?
Abū Sufyān:	No.
Heracules:	Do the majority of his followers belong to the aristocracy, or are they poor people?
Abū Sufyān:	They are poor.
Heracules:	Do they increase or decrease?
Abū Sufyān:	They are on the increase.
Heracules:	Does any of them turn away from his religion after having embraced it?
Abū Sufyān:	No.
Heracules:	Have you ever known him to lie before he started to make his claim?
Abū Sufyān:	No.
Heracules:	Is he given to treachery?
Abū Sufyān:	No. We, however, have an armistice agreement with him for the time being, and we do not know what he will do during this period.
Heracules:	Have you ever fought him?
Abū Sufyān:	Yes.
Heracules:	How did your fighting go?
Abū Sufyān:	Sometimes he wins and sometimes we win.
Heracules:	What sort of commandments does he give you?
Abū Sufyān:	He tells us to worship God alone, without ascribing Divinity to anyone else. He tells us not to follow our fathers. He commands us to pray and to be truthful and chaste and kind to our fellow human beings.
Heracules:	You have mentioned that he enjoys distinguished ancestry, and this is the case with all prophets and messengers. Since you say that no one else among you has made similar claims, I cannot say that he is imitating anyone. You also denied that any of his forefathers was a king, which means that he is not a claimant of a kingdom. You also say that he was not known to tell a lie before he came out

> with his message. Well, I know that he would not start by lying to God. You have stated that the poor are his followers, and this is the case with all messengers from God. The fact that his followers are on the increase again confirms a phenomenon which is always associated with true faith, until it is completed. You have also mentioned that no one turns away from his religion after having embraced it. This is a characteristic of faith when its light shines in people's hearts. You also denied that he is treacherous, and no messenger of God was a treacherous person. You also said that he calls on you to believe in the Oneness of God and to pray and to be truthful and chaste. If what you have told me is true, then he will have the supremacy right here where I stand. I knew that his time was due, but I did not think that he would belong to your people. Had it been in my power, I would certainly have taken the trouble to meet him and wash his feet.[1]

This is the most authentic report of Heracules' reaction when he received the message sent him by the Prophet. There are other reports which are less authentic, suggesting that Heracules tried to persuade his bishops and his advisers to embrace Islam, but they were all unanimous (with one exception) in opposing him. One report suggests that the exception was the Archbishop, who was killed on the spot when he declared that he believed in the new Messenger. Whatever the truth about these reports, the fact remains that Heracules did not adopt Islam, and that perhaps this was due to his fear that he would lose his throne as a result.

Heracules also chose to send back a diplomatic reply, pretending that he personally accepted Islam but was prevented from publicizing the fact by the opposition of his Church. He gave Diḥyah, the Prophet's envoy, a sum of money in gold currency and the Prophet distributed it to the poor in the Muslim community.

The Other Emperor

The other superpower of the day was the Persian Empire. Its Emperor was Khusru II, who acceded to the Persian throne in the year AD 590. Shortly afterwards he faced rebellion which ended in his defeat. He was forced to seek refuge at the Court of Maurice, the Byzantine Emperor, who helped him regain his throne. When Maurice was killed by the usurper Phocas, Khusru marched on the Byzantine Empire to avenge the killing of his old friend and patron. He was able to score great victories against 'the old enemy'. It took quite a few years for Heracules to be able to gain power in Byzantium and regain the occupied provinces of the Byzantine Empire. He followed that by a concentrated campaign against the capital city of the Persian Empire. Khusru was thus forced to leave his capital and seek refuge elsewhere. He was later killed in an uprising which took place in the year AD 628.

Historians agree that Khusru II was one of the most powerful emperors of Persia. In his reign, the Persian Empire reached the pinnacle of its affluence. He even claimed that he was a god in the shape of a man.

The Prophet sent his companion ʿAbdullāh ibn Ḥudhāfah with a message to Khusru. The Prophet's letter ran as follows:

> In the name of God, The Merciful, the Beneficent. From Muhammad, God's Messenger, to Khusru, the leader of Persia. Peace be to him who follows right guidance, believes in God and His Messenger, and declares that there is no deity but God, the only God who has no partners, and that Muhammad is His servant and Messenger. I wish to convey to you God's call, for I am God's Messenger to all mankind, sent with the task of warning all those who are alive that doom will befall the unbelievers. If you submit to God you will be safe. If you refuse, you shall bear the responsibility for the Magians.

When Khusru read the Prophet's letter, he tore it to pieces, saying: "How dare he write this sort of letter to me when he is my slave?" Khusru then wrote to Bādhān (or Bādhām), who was governor of Yemen, a Persian province. He ordered him to send two able-bodied soldiers to arrest the Prophet and take him to Persia. Immediately Bādhān sent Abādhaweih, one of his assistants, and a Persian officer called Kharkharah, with a warrant which required the Prophet to surrender himself to them and go with them to Khusru. Bādhān, however, asked his assistant to find out the truth about the Prophet.

Abādhaweih and his companion travelled from Yemen until they arrived in Ṭā'if, which is about 100 kilometres from Makkah. Its people told them that the Prophet was now in Madinah. The Ṭā'if people – who were not Muslims at the time – and the Quraysh were very pleased when they learnt that the Persian Emperor had ordered the arrest of Muhammad. They felt that Muhammad was now facing his most difficult test.

Clean-shaven but with large moustaches, the two officers from Yemen came to the Prophet in Madinah. Abādhaweih said to him: "Khusru, the king of kings, has written to Bādhān, the king of Yemen, commanding him to send us to take you to him. If you comply, Bādhān will write to the king of kings interceding on your behalf. This will spare you a great deal of trouble. If you reject his order, you know how powerful he is. He is sure to destroy you and your people as well as your country."

The Prophet did not like their appearance. He asked them who ordered them to shave their beards and their reply was: "Our Lord", meaning Khusru. The Prophet said: "But my Lord has commanded me to wear a beard and to trim my moustache." He also asked them to wait till the following day when he was to meet them again. In the meantime, the Prophet received information through the Angel Gabriel that God had caused Khusru to be killed by Shirweih, his own son, giving him the exact time of night and the date when Khusru was killed.

The Prophet called in the Persian messengers and told them of the killing of their Emperor. They said to him: "Do you realize what you are saying? Your arrest has been ordered for something much more trivial than this. Do you still wish us to write this down and inform King Bādhān of what you have just said?"

The Prophet replied: "Yes. Tell him also on my behalf that my religion and my kingdom will replace that of Khusru and will sweep all before it. Tell him also that if he accepts Islam, I will give him what he has now under his authority and will make him a ruler in the area he now governs." The Prophet also gave Kharkharah a sack of gold and silver which was sent to him as a present by another king.

The two envoys left and went back to Yemen where they told Bādhān of what the Prophet had said. He told them: "This is not the sort of thing a king would say. To my mind, the man is a prophet, as he claims. If he is, what he has just told you will come to pass. If it is true that Khusru has been killed, the man is a Prophet and a Messenger. If not, we will make up our mind about what to do with him."

Presently Bādhān received a message from Shirweih informing him that he had killed his father after he had adopted despotic measures against the Persian nobility. He also commanded him to ask his commanders to swear allegiance to him as the new emperor. He further asked him not to disturb the Prophet until he had received further instructions.

Bādhān then realized that Muhammad was truly God's Messenger. He called Abādhaweih in and questioned him further about the Prophet. The latter told him that the Prophet did not keep any guard to protect him from his people or from anyone else. "Nevertheless, I have never spoken to a man who has inspired me with awe as much as he does." Bādhān was then certain that Muhammad was truly the Messenger of God and he communicated his conviction to his advisers and counsellors. He declared that he wished to become a Muslim and they all joined him in accepting the message of the Prophet. This was the beginning of the spread of Islam in Yemen. The majority of its population, Christians and Magians alike, started to accept Islam. They conveyed this to the Prophet and he sent them some of his companions to teach them the principles of Islam and instruct them in how to lead an Islamic life.[2]

A Puppet Ruler's Response

An attitude similar to that of Khusru was shown by al-Ḥārith ibn Abī Shammar of the Ghassān Arabs, who was the ruler of Damascus appointed by the Byzantine Emperor. Shujāʿ ibn Wahb, the Prophet's companion, carried his message to al-Ḥārith. When he read the message, al-Ḥārith threw it on the floor and said: "Who can take my kingdom away from me? I will march to him even if he is in the Yemen." He immediately started to mobilize his forces.

One should remember here that al-Ḥārith was no more than a governor whose jurisdiction extended only over his Arabian tribe, which was subjugated by the Byzantine rulers. Nevertheless, he was so boastful that he did not think anyone could take his kingdom away from him. One should note here that his attitude was far more arrogant than that of his master Heracules. However, he wrote to Heracules, making known his intention to march with his forces against the Prophet. Heracules wrote back from Jerusalem ordering him not to proceed with his intention. He also called him to join him in Jerusalem.

Shujāʿ ibn Wahb reported to the Prophet when he arrived back in Madinah that al-Ḥārith had a Byzantine commander of his palace guard named Marrī, a Christian. He questioned Shujāʿ about the Prophet and his message. When Shujāʿ explained that to him, his eyes were full of tears, he said: "I have read plain references to this Prophet in the Bible, but I thought that he would appear in Syria. However, I believe in him as God's Messenger, but I fear that I shall be killed by al-Ḥārith if I were to declare my belief." He asked Shujāʿ to convey his respects to the Prophet and to tell him that he was a believer in him and his message.[3]

Another Message to Negus

ʿAmr ibn Umayyah al-Ḍamrī was the Prophet's fourth envoy, and his mission took him to Abyssinia with a letter from the Prophet to its King, known by his title Negus. Abyssinia is in East Africa, overlooking the south-western end of the Red Sea. It is very difficult to give any correct idea of what sort of borders it had at the time. Most probably, it included what forms present-day Eritrea with other parts of Ethiopia.

Abyssinia was a fully independent country, and its capital was Axum. Its relations with the Byzantine Empire were cordial, since both were Christian countries. In the middle of the third century the Byzantine Emperor, Justinian, appointed a man called Julian as ambassador of Byzantium at the court of Abyssinia.

ʿAmr's trip to Abyssinia was not his first, nor was the letter he carried the Prophet's first letter to the Negus. Already reported are the earlier relations between Islam and the King of Abyssinia, who extended his hospitality and protection to the Muslims who sought refuge in his kingdom and had been living there for about 13 years.

There is some confusion in history books about the identity of the Negus to whom the Prophet sent his letter with ʿAmr ibn Umayyah. Many of them tend to think that he was the same king who ruled throughout this period. This is quite possible, since he was a young man when he succeeded to the throne of Abyssinia, but there is a possibility that the Negus now addressed by the Prophet was a different one. When the Prophet had sent earlier to the Negus requesting him to extend kind treatment to his followers, there is no report to suggest that the Prophet called on him to become a Muslim. Indeed, he did not write to any ruler of any country explaining the message of Islam and calling on him to accept it.

It fits very well in the pattern of events, however, that the Prophet should now send a letter to the Negus in the same terms as he wrote to other kings and emperors. Ibn Kathīr, a prominent historian and biographer of the Prophet, who lived seven centuries ago, says that the Prophet's address to the Negus was at the same time as his "writing to the kings and emperors of the world, with the message of God, prior to the conquest of Makkah."

The Prophet's letter to the Negus ran as follows:

> In the name of God, the Merciful, the Beneficent. From Muhammad, God's messenger, to the Negus, the king of Abyssinia. Peace be with you. I praise God, the only God, the King, the Praised One, the Peace, the One who controls everything. I bear witness that Jesus, son of Mary, was God's spirit and His word given to Mary, the virgin, the chaste. She thus conceived Jesus, whom God created of His own spirit, as He created Adam with His own hand. I call on you to believe in God alone, and to associate no other deity with Him, and

> to continue to obey Him, and to follow me and to believe in what has been revealed to me. I am God's Messenger and I call on you and on your subjects and soldiers to believe in God, the Almighty. I have thus conveyed my message and given good counsel. It is better for you to accept my good counsel. Peace be to those who follow right guidance.

ʿAmr ibn Umayyah also talked to the Negus and he is reported to have said to him:

> You are as kind to us as one of us, and we trust you as if we belong to your people. You have met all our good expectations and we feared nothing from you whatsoever. However, we find in your own words what supports our case. The Bible is our ultimate witness and fair arbiter. There can be no clearer evidence or stronger argument. If you do not submit to its word, then your attitude towards this Prophet is akin to the attitude of the Jews towards Jesus, son of Mary. The Prophet (peace be upon him) has sent his envoys to all people, but he has far greater hopes in you than in them. He has trusted you with what he has not been able to trust them with, for your history of good deeds. Moreover, a fine reward awaits you.

The Negus replied in these words: "I swear by God, he is the Prophet awaited by the people of past revelations. Moses has given news of the impending appearance of the Prophet who rides a donkey in the same way as Jesus has given news of the impending arrival of a Prophet who rides a camel."

Thus, the Negus declared his acceptance of the message of Muhammad and his belief in Islam. He also wrote to the Prophet:

> In the name of God, the Merciful, the Beneficent. To Muhammad, God's Messenger, from Negus. Peace from God be to you, Prophet, along with God's mercy and blessings. I have received your letter, Messenger of God, and noted what you have said about Jesus. By the Lord of the Heavens and the Earth, Jesus, son of Mary, is nothing more than what you have

> stated. I know the truth of what you have said to me, and I have extended hospitality to your cousin and his companions. I bear witness that you are God's Messenger who tells the truth. I pledge my allegiance to you, and I have pledged this allegiance to your cousin and have become a Muslim. I submit myself to God, the Lord of all the Universe.[4]

This was the most favourable response the Prophet received to all his messages and letters to the kings and emperors of other countries. It meant that Islam acquired a solid base on the other side of the Red Sea, stretching well into Africa.

Negus continued in power until his death two years later. When he died, in the ninth year of the Islamic calendar, the Prophet announced his death to the Muslims and offered the prayers for the deceased *in absentia* for his soul.

An Envoy to the Egyptian Ruler

Ḥāṭib ibn Abī Baltaʿah, another companion of the Prophet, carried his letter to the ruler of Egypt in Alexandria, who was a governor-general appointed by the Byzantine Emperor. Most Arab historians refer to the ruler of Egypt at the time by the name al-Muqawqis. There is much disagreement, however, among historians as to his true name, his title and his identity. Some historians – like Abū Ṣāliḥ, who lived in the sixth century of Islamic history (equivalent to the thirteenth century of the Gregorian calendar) – call him Grīg ibn Mīnā al-Muqawqis. The renowned historian Ibn Khaldūn says that he was Coptic, while al-Maqrīzī, another Muslim historian, believes that he was a Byzantine ruler appointed by Heracules, and his name was George. Other historians believe that his appointment took place in the year AD 621. Alfred Butler, the author of a book on the Arab conquest of Egypt, is of the opinion that the Arabs believed that the Governor of Egypt appointed by the Byzantine Emperor, after his victory over Persia, was given the title of al-Muqawqis, and combined the two offices of Governor and Head of the Church. Hence they gave this title to George, who was a deputy for Heracules in Egypt.

He traces this title to Coptic origins. It is perfectly possible that a Coptic bishop took over the government of Egypt in addition to his being Head of the Church when the Persians took over Egypt. The Persian forces withdrew from Egypt in AD 627, but no peace agreement was signed until the following year. It is also perfectly possible that the Prophet's letter to al-Muqawqis was sent during this period when the Egyptian Governor enjoyed a certain degree of autonomy. Hence, the Prophet addressed him as 'The Chief of the Copts'. The Prophet's letter ran as follows:

> In the name of God, the Merciful, the Beneficent. From Muhammad ibn ʿAbdullāh to al-Muqawqis, the Chief of the Copts. Peace be to those who follow right guidance. I wish to convey to you the message of Islam. Accept Islam and you will be safe. Accept it and God will double your reward. Should you turn your back on it, you will bear the responsibility for the Copts. People of earlier revelations, let us all come to a fair agreement among ourselves that we shall not worship anyone but God, and that we will never ascribe divinity to anyone else, and that none of us will give others the status of Lord alongside God. If they refuse, say to them: bear witness that we submit ourselves to God.

Having sealed his letter, the Prophet gave it to his companion, Ḥāṭib ibn Abī Baltaʿah, who travelled straight to Alexandria, where he quickly presented himself to al-Muqawqis. Ḥāṭib opened his address to the Egyptian ruler with these words: "There lived before you a man who claimed to be the overall Lord of the Universe, but God smote him with the punishment of this life and the life to come. He used him to punish others before he himself was punished by God. Take heed, therefore, by what happened to others, before you are made an example to those who come after you." Al-Muqawqis asked Ḥāṭib to elaborate, and Ḥāṭib said:

> We have a religion which we will never forsake unless we find another which is better. Our religion is Islam, with which God compensates all mankind for whatever else they lose.

> This Prophet of ours called people to believe in God. His fiercest opponents were the Quraysh, while the most hostile were the Jews. The Christians were the closest to him. I can assure you that as Moses gave the news that Jesus, son of Mary, would be sent as a messenger later, so did Jesus give the news of the appearance of Muhammad (peace be upon him). Our call on you to believe in the Qur'ān is the same as your call on those who believe in the Torah to accept the Gospel. Any people who happened to be contemporaries of a new Prophet belonged to his nation, so they must follow him. You are certainly a contemporary of this Prophet. We do not forbid you to follow the faith of Jesus; indeed, we ask you to follow it.

Al-Muqawqis replied: "I have examined this matter and considered the message of this Prophet. I have found that he does not order anything which people are better advised to discard, or forbid anything which is not harmful. He is certainly neither a wicked sorcerer nor a lying fortune-teller. I have also found certain indications which confirm his prophethood. I will consider the matter further."

Al-Muqawqis put the Prophet's letter in a box made of ivory and sealed it. He called in someone who could write Arabic from among his people and wrote this reply:

> In the name of God, the Merciful, the Beneficent. To Muhammad ibn ʿAbdullāh from al-Muqawqis, the chief of the Copts. Peace, I have read your letter and understood its contents and what you have called on me to do. I certainly know that one more Prophet is to be sent, but I thought that he would appear in Syria. I have extended my hospitality to your messenger and I am sending you two maids who enjoy great respect among the Copts, and I am presenting you with clothes and a mule for you to ride. Peace be to you.

Al-Muqawqis did not accept Islam, although he described to Ḥāṭib certain features which he knew to be applicable to the remaining

Prophet and which Ḥāṭib confirmed were true of Muhammad. Al-Muqawqis explained that his people would not accept his advice, should he give it, to follow the Prophet Muhammad and become Muslims. He also told him not to tell anybody about his discussion with him because he found it difficult to relinquish his kingdom. Al-Muqawqis also said that Islam was sure to spread into Egypt. He gave some gold clothes to Ḥāṭib as a personal gift.

When Ḥāṭib went back to Madinah and told the Prophet of his interview with al-Muqawqis and the gifts he sent him, the Prophet said the man feared for his authority, which would not last.[5]

Correspondence with the Ruler of Bahrain

Another messenger the Prophet sent was al-ʿAlā' ibn al-Ḥaḍramī, who carried his message to al-Mundhir ibn Sāwā al-ʿAbdī, the ruler of Bahrain.[6] The letter was in the same terms as the Prophet sent to other rulers. Al-Mundhir wrote back: "Messenger of God, I have read your letter to the people of Bahrain. Some of them liked it and they accepted Islam. Others refused. There are Magians and Jews among my population and I await your instructions."

The Prophet wrote back to him:

> In the name of God, the Merciful, the Beneficent. From Muhammad, God's Messenger, to al-Mundhir ibn Sāwā. Peace be to you. I praise to you God who has no partners, and I bear witness that there is no deity but God and that Muhammad is His servant and Messenger. I remind you of God, the Almighty. He who does right, does it only unto himself; and he who obeys my messengers obeys me; and he who gives them sound counsel gives it to me. My messengers have praised you to me, and I accept your intercession on behalf of your people. Allow the Muslims among your people what they have in their hands. I pardon all those who have committed sins, so accept from them their pledges. We will not dismiss you from your office as long as you do well. Those who wish to stay Jews or Magians should pay a tribute as a sign of their loyalty.

Thus, the ruler of Bahrain gave a reply of total acceptance and remained a good Muslim until his death a few years later.[7]

Notes

1. Ibn Sayyid al-Nās, *ʿUyūn al-Athar*, Dār al-Turāth, Madinah, 1996, pp. 344-346. Also, Ibn Kathīr, *al-Bidāyah wal-Nihāyah*, Maktabat al-Maʿārif, Beirut, Vol. 1, pp. 262-264.
2. Ibn Sayyid al-Nās, op.cit., pp. 347-348.
3. Ibid., pp. 356-357.
4. Ibid., pp. 349-350.
5. Ibid., pp. 350-352.
6. The name Bahrain was used at the time for an area in the Eastern parts of present-day Saudi Arabia. It is an inland area, and has nothing to do with the geographical area that bears this name today.
7. Ibn Kathīr, op.cit., pp. 352-353.

32

A Second Trip to Makkah

THE TERMS OF the peace agreement between the Muslims and the Quraysh signed at al-Ḥudaybiyah included the provision that the Prophet would be allowed to visit Makkah with his companions for worship at the Kaʿbah a year later. As already learnt, the Prophet travelled towards Makkah with 1,400 of his companions with the sole intention of offering an *ʿUmrah*, or mini-pilgrimage. The Quraysh did not allow them to proceed and the peace agreement was eventually negotiated because the Prophet did not wish to start a new battle with the Quraysh. As a result, the Muslims in Madinah enjoyed several months of a calm which was not interrupted except by a few limited and confined clashes with certain Arabian tribes who tried to create trouble or to threaten trade routes and travellers. The Prophet also made approaches to several Arab tribes, outlining to them the message of Islam and calling on them to become Muslims. Many people so addressed with the message of Islam did accept it and the Muslims were becoming stronger every day.

When a year was over, and it was again the month of Dhul-Qaʿadah, the Prophet started preparing for his *ʿUmrah* which history books describe as "the compensatory *ʿUmrah*" or "the post-dispute *ʿUmrah*.' He instructed his companions to get ready, and said that no one who was with him at al-Ḥudaybiyah was to stay behind. So the same people who took the first journey, with the exception of those who had died or been killed in battle, joined the Prophet again, along with several hundred others who did not make the first trip. In all, some 2,000 men, in addition to a good number of women and children, went with the Prophet on this *ʿUmrah*. The Prophet asked his companion Abū Dharr al-Ghifārī to deputize for him in Madinah and took with him sixty camels to sacrifice after his *ʿUmrah*. He went into the state of consecration, or *iḥrām*, which is obligatory for all pilgrims, at the doorstep of his mosque in Madinah. As he and his companions moved along, they were repeating phrases asserting their submission to God and the fact that they were undertaking that trip in response to His call.

The terms of the peace agreement stipulated that the Muslims were allowed to carry only their swords in their sheaths, but the Prophet feared that the Quraysh might violate their obligations. Hence he took with him more armaments, including shields, spears and protective headgear. He also took with him 100 horses and instructed Bashīr ibn Saʿd to look after the arms and Muhammad ibn Maslamah to look after the horses. When he had travelled only 11 kilometres from Madinah, he ordered that the horses and the arms should be at the head of his procession.

Muhammad ibn Maslamah went ahead with his horses until he arrived at a place called Marr al-Ẓahrān, which was only about one day's travel, on camel's back, from Makkah. He found there a few men from the Quraysh who questioned him about his mission and why he had so many horses with him. His answer was: "God's Messenger (peace be upon him) will encamp here tomorrow, God willing." They also noticed that Bashīr ibn Saʿd had a large quantity of arms with him. They went quickly to Makkah to tell the Quraysh of what they had seen. A feeling of worry and panic overtook the Quraysh, who started asking: "We have certainly honoured our promises. Why should Muhammad and his companions come to invade us?"

The Quraysh then sent Mikraz ibn Ḥafṣ at the head of a delegation to the Prophet. They said to him: "Muhammad, we have never known you to break a promise ever since you were a young child. Do you wish to enter your home town with all your arms when you have promised that you will come only with the armament of a peaceful traveller: swords in their sheaths?" The Prophet said: "I am not going to carry the arms into the city." Mikraz ibn Ḥafṣ then replied: "This is more like what we have known of your faithfulness." He went back speedily to Makkah to tell its people that Muhammad was honouring his pledges. The Quraysh were then reassured and allowed the Muslims to pass.

The Quraysh's Reception

There are different reports about the attitude of the people of Makkah to the entry of the Prophet and his companions to do their *ʿUmrah.* Some reports suggest that the Quraysh left Makkah and went into the surrounding mountains, because they did not wish to look at the Muslims as they came in to worship. Other reports suggest that the people of the Quraysh moved into close positions on the mountains to have a good view of the Muslims.

Yet other reports suggest that the Quraysh people, or a large number of them, gathered at a place called Dār al-Nadwah, which served as their parliament, to look at the Muslims as they went into the city. There are still more reports which suggest that they sat much closer, within the precincts of the Ḥaram. Again, some reports suggest that only a few of the nobility of Makkah did not wish to look at the Muslims as they came in, because the sight of them infuriated them, since they realized that the very fact that the Muslims were able to come to Makkah enhanced their position in Arabia.

Perhaps all these reports carry some of the truth, and different people in Makkah did indeed do different things. The fact remains that most of the Quraysh people were eager to see the Prophet and his companions coming in, especially because a rumour was spread in the city that Muhammad and his companions were greatly weakened physically by an epidemic which spread in Madinah. Some of them were told that the Muslims could hardly walk because of their illness. That would have been a pleasing sight to the people of

Makkah. Whatever the reason, the Prophet's entry into Makkah, only seven years after he was forced to leave it under the cover of darkness, was a great event which few people would have liked to miss. When they saw it, they started thinking and wondering.

The Prophet Enters Makkah

It was an awe-inspiring scene. The Prophet rode his she-camel, al-Qaṣwā', surrounded by a number of his companions who were watching all directions, lest any one of the unbelievers should try to attack or harm the Prophet. The whole of the procession shouted phrases asserting their submission to God. ʿAbdullāh ibn Rawāḥah, a companion of the Prophet from the Anṣār, held the rein of the Prophet's she-camel and chanted a few lines of poetry which he had composed. When the Prophet was very close to the Ḥaram (the grand mosque at the centre of which is the Kaʿbah), he told ʿAbdullāh ibn Rawāḥah to repeat these phrases: *Lā ilāha illa Allah waḥdah, Ṣadaqa waʿdah, wa naṣara ʿabdah, wa aʿazza jundah, wa hazam al-aḥzāba waḥdah.* This translates as follows: "There is no deity but God alone. He has fulfilled His promise, given victory to His servant, and dignity to His soldiers, and He has alone defeated the confederates." This was a reference to the defeat suffered by the Quraysh and the other tribes and the Jews allied with it when they attempted to invade Madinah in order to annihilate the Muslims. ʿAbdullāh ibn Rawāḥah repeated these phrases and all the Muslims repeated them after him, providing an atmosphere of great strength and enthusiasm.

The Prophet was aware of the rumours which the Quraysh spread about the physical weakness of his companions. He therefore instructed his companions not to show any sign of weakness. Since they were all in their *iḥrām* garments, which consisted of two large pieces of cloth, one wrapped round their waists and covering the lower part of their bodies, the other thrown over their shoulders, he instructed them to bare their right shoulders and to do part of their *ṭawāf* jogging. He went into the mosque and touched the black stone with the piece of stick which he carried. He said to his companions: "May God have mercy on everyone who shows them that he is strong." He started jogging round the Kaʿbah and his companions did likewise for the first three rounds. They continued the rest of their seven rounds walking. The unbelievers were amazed when they saw that the epidemic did not affect the strength of the Muslims. Some of them said to the others: "Are you sure that these people have been weakened by fever? They are jumping and running like deers."

When the Prophet completed his *ṭawāf*, he went to do his *saʿī* which is a walk between the two mounts of al-Ṣafā and al-Marwah. He did the *saʿī* on the back of his she-camel. When he had finished his seven rounds, he stopped and said: "This is the place to slaughter your sacrificial animals, and all Makkah is such a place." He started slaughtering his animals, 60 camels, and everyone who was with him on the first trip and was present at al-Ḥudaybiyah also sacrificed a camel. Camels were not plentiful and the Prophet allowed those who could not buy or get a camel to slaughter a cow. Afterwards, the Prophet and his companions shaved their heads and released themselves from the state of consecration.

Demonstrating Devotion, Power and Equality

The Prophet had left the horses and the arms at a place close to Makkah called Ya'jaj. He left 200 of his companions there as guards. All this he did as a precaution against any possible treacherous attack the Quraysh might contemplate. When he and those of his companions who joined him in his *ʿUmrah* had completed their rituals, he sent 200 of them to Ya'jaj to replace those who stayed there. When they arrived, they relieved their fellow guards, who went straight to Makkah to fulfil the duties of their *ʿUmrah.*

The Prophet remained in the Kaʿbah until it was time for midday prayers, *ẓuhr*, when he ordered his companion, Bilāl, who was in charge of calling for prayers, to go on top of the Kaʿbah to make the call, i.e. *adhān*. Bilāl stood over the top of the Kaʿbah, and with his fine melodious voice he shouted: "God is most supreme. I bear witness that there is no deity but God. I declare that Muhammad is God's Messenger. Come to prayer. Come to a certain success. God is most supreme." These are the words which Muslims have always used to call people to come to prayers, but those words sounded very offensive in the ears of the Quraysh leaders. Many of them expressed their profound dismay. Suhayl ibn ʿAmr and a few of his friends covered their faces when they heard Bilāl calling to prayers as a gesture expressing their anger.

What made Bilāl's action even more offensive to the people of Makkah was the fact that he used to be a slave owned by Umayyah ibn Khalaf, who was later killed at the Battle of Badr. In the Makkan idolatrous society, which was extremely class-conscious, the fact that a former slave could rise on top of the Kaʿbah, where the Quraysh put their idols, was something they could not accept. ʿIkrimah ibn Abī Jahl said: "God has certainly been kind to my father by causing him to die before he could hear this slave saying such words." Ṣafwān ibn Umayyah ibn Khalaf said: "God be praised for taking my father away before he could see this." Khālid ibn Usayd echoed his words and said: "I thank God that my father died before he could see this day, with the son of Bilāl's mother barking on top of the Kaʿbah."

Those people were the young generation of Makkah chiefs, whose fathers were mostly killed in the battles with the Muslims. Bilāl's action, however, was a manifestation of the strength of Islam which emphasizes equality between all people.

The Prophet and his companions stayed three days in Makkah, according to the terms of the peace agreement. They moved about the city without fear. This in itself was a great act of public relations on the part of the Muslims. The people of Makkah were able to see how close-knit the Muslim community was. They realized that the Muslims harboured the most brotherly feelings towards one another. Every one of them loved every other Muslim. Their dedication to the cause of Islam was clearly visible in the way they talked to one another, in their high respect for the Prophet, in the total absence of any division between them. The people of Makkah could not suppress their feeling of admiration and envy as they realized that the Prophet was able to achieve that great degree of unity among the Muslim community despite the fact that his followers belonged to many tribes which had been, until recently, at war with one another.

They also realized that the predominant feelings within the Muslim community were those of mutual sympathy and solidarity. Its objectives were noble and its dedication was complete. Its submission to God was undoubted. The chiefs of Makkah were worried that their own people might start to have second thoughts about Islam, as they realized how profound its effect was on the people of Madinah and on Muslims generally. They therefore sent Suhayl ibn ʿAmr and Ḥuwayṭib ibn ʿAbd al-ʿUzzā, when the three days were over, to tell the Prophet: "Your time is up and you have to leave."

The Prophet was aware that his stay in Makkah was very effective in making its people relent and modify their hostile attitude towards Islam. He tried to soften their hearts further. He said to the two Makkan envoys: "What harm would it cause you if you were to let me have my wedding in your place? We will organize a banquet for you."

Another Marriage

The Prophet was about to marry a woman from Makkah called Maymūnah bint al-Ḥārith. She was a woman of noble descent, and her sister was married to his uncle, al-ʿAbbās ibn ʿAbd al-Muṭṭalib. The Makkan envoys were quick to realize the danger to their religion which this proposal of the Prophet implied. They felt that if Muhammad had a chance to have his wedding in their own grounds and to talk to the people in the friendly atmosphere of a wedding and a banquet, their cause would lose its grip on the hearts of those very Makkan people. They realized that their own religion could not stand up to the logic of Islam. People were bound to be favourably influenced by the strength of the Prophet's personality and his argument. The barriers which they erected to prevent people from going over to him would thus start to collapse. They realized that Muhammad's visit to Makkah was changing the atmosphere which had prevailed between the two camps, but they could not realize that many of the people of Makkah had already softened to the cause of Islam. They nevertheless refused his offer outright. They said: "We have no need for food. You are required to leave. We appeal to you by God, and by the covenant which exists between you and us, to leave our land immediately. Your three days are up."

Their rough attitude angered Saʿd ibn ʿUbādah, the chief of the Anṣār. In his fury, he went up to Suhayl ibn ʿAmr and said: "Liar! This is not your land, nor was it your father's. He will not depart from here unless he wishes to do so of his own free will." The Prophet smiled and said to his companion: "Saʿd, do not be so severe to those people who have visited us in our camp."

Thus a situation which could have been explosive was rendered harmless. The Prophet ordered his companions to prepare to depart, and they moved on to Saref, some 14 kilometres away from Makkah, where they encamped, and the Prophet had his wedding to Maymūnah.[1]

This *ʿUmrah* of the Prophet marked a turning point in the relations between the people of Makkah and Islam. This was soon to be reflected in the attitude of the Quraysh towards the Prophet and Islam generally. The sort of hostility which dictated the attitudes of the Quraysh people was never to return. Moreover, many individuals started to think about adopting Islam. They were drawn from all classes of the Makkan society.

A Family Dispute

As the Muslims were preparing to leave, a daughter of Ḥamzah ibn ʿAbd al-Muṭṭalib, an uncle of the Prophet and a great soldier of Islam who was killed at the Battle of Uḥud, followed the Prophet and called out to him: "Uncle, Uncle." ʿAlī, the Prophet's cousin and son-in-law, took her by the hand and said to his wife, Fāṭimah, the Prophet's daughter: "Take your cousin with you." Three of the Prophet's companions wanted the girl to join them. ʿAlī, his brother Jaʿafar and Zayd ibn Ḥārithah argued with each other over who had the strongest claim to keep her. ʿAlī said: "I took her first, and she is my cousin." Jaʿafar said: "She is also my cousin and I am married to her mother's sister." Zayd said: "Her father was my brother." This was a reference to the fact that the Prophet made Ḥamzah and Zayd brothers when he established the bond of brotherhood among the Muslims, making every couple of them brothers.

The Prophet judged in this dispute and said to the three men: "You Zayd, are the servant of God and of His Messenger. [Zayd, as already mentioned, was a slave given as a present to the Prophet before Islam, but the Prophet granted him his freedom and he had stayed with the Prophet ever since.] And you, Ja'afar, look like me and your manners are similar to mine. And you, 'Alī, belong to me and I belong to you. Ja'afar, however, has the best claim to her because he is married to her aunt. Let me point out that no woman can be married to the husband of her paternal or maternal aunt."

Ja'afar was so pleased that he stood up and hopped round the Prophet on one foot. When the Prophet asked him why he was doing that, he said that he learnt this practice in Abyssinia, where he lived for over 14 years after his emigration there in compliance with the Prophet's orders. If Negus, the ruler of Abyssinia, judged in favour of someone, that person would stand up and hop round the place where the ruler was sitting. The Prophet later married Ḥamzah's daughter to Salamah, the son of one of his wives.[2]

Setting Minds Thinking

By now, over two years had passed since the Expedition of the Moat, with little or no fighting taking place between the Muslims and the Quraysh. Now a formal peace existed between the two sides. The Muslims made use of this new atmosphere by concentrating on their efforts to convey the message of Islam far and wide. As a result, Islam made great inroads in Arabia, winning over the hearts of many people of all tribes. The Quraysh, however, remained hostile. Their enmity to Islam, which extended over a period of 20 years, was not to give way easily to the pressure the Muslims were now exerting. The people of Makkah viewed themselves as the hard core of resistance to the new call of Islam. Even the most intelligent of its leaders were determined not to reconcile themselves to Islam, whatever the circumstances. Nevertheless, this was not easy. Intelligent people cannot always turn a blind eye to the forces of reality. They may try for a while, but eventually they have to give in. The history of two such people of the nobility of the Quraysh is sufficient to appreciate what sort of momentum the cause of Islam was acquiring. It shows how the great structure of idolatry in Arabia was crumbling from within.

ʿAmr's Story

ʿAmr ibn al-ʿĀṣ was a very shrewd person. He had been the Quraysh's envoy to Negus, the ruler of Abyssinia, to demand the extradition of those Muslims from the Quraysh who sought refuge in that country. This was in the fifth year of Islam, some 15 years earlier than the events which are about to be related.

This is ʿAmr's own account of these events:

> I was strongly hostile to Islam. I took part in the Battles of Badr, Uḥud and the Moat, fighting alongside the idolaters, and I was able to survive. Now I started thinking that Muhammad would eventually triumph over the Quraysh. I, therefore, went to my place at al-Ruhṭ where I lived in semi-seclusion. After al-Ḥudaybiyah when the Prophet returned home, having signed his peace agreement with the Quraysh, the Quraysh went back to Makkah. I started thinking on these lines: "Muhammad will enter Makkah with his companions next year. Makkah is certainly not a place to be in. Nor is Ṭā'if. The best thing to do is to go away." I was still very hostile to Islam and I felt that even if every man in the Quraysh would embrace Islam, I would not.
>
> I went to Makkah, where I spoke to a group of my people who valued my opinion and consulted me on every serious matter. When I asked them about their opinion of me, they said: "You are our wise man and spokesman. You have a noble soul and a blessed purpose." I told them that I thought Muhammad was on the crest of a wave. He was bound to overcome whatever resisted him. I then explained that I felt it was wiser to seek refuge in Abyssinia, where we could join Negus. If Muhammad did overcome his enemies, we would

be safe with Negus with whom we would be better placed than if we were to succumb to Muhammad. If the Quraysh turned out to be the winners, they would know that we were on their side. They all agreed with me and we started preparing for our departure. I suggested to them to put together a valuable gift which Negus would like. The gift he liked best from our part of the world was hide. We, therefore, took with us a large quantity of hide and travelled until we reached Abyssinia.

When we were in the court of Negus, ʿAmr ibn Umayyah al-Ḍamrī, the envoy sent by Muhammad, arrived with a message. [Reports vary as to the exact nature of that message. One report suggests that it was the Prophet's proposal to Umm Ḥabībah bint Abū Sufyān, which is probably not accurate because that marriage took place earlier. Another report suggests that the message was a request by the Prophet for the return of his cousin, Jaʿafar, and the rest of the Muslims who emigrated to Abyssinia. It is perhaps more correct to assume that the message was the Prophet's call on the Negus to adopt Islam, which has already been related.]

When I saw ʿAmr ibn Umayyah go in for his audience with Negus and leave soon afterwards, I said to my people: "This is ʿAmr ibn Umayyah. If I can persuade Negus to give him up to me, I will kill him to give the Quraysh infinite pleasure."

When I was admitted into the presence of Negus, I prostrated myself to him as I used to do. He said to me: "Welcome, my friend. Have you brought me any gifts from your part of the world?" I said: "Yes, I have brought you a gift of hide." I presented my gift and he was very pleased with it. He gave some of it to his bishops and patriarchs and ordered that the rest should be kept and recorded. When I saw that he was very pleased with my gift, I said to him: "Your Majesty, I have seen a man coming out of your court. He is the envoy of our enemy, who has killed a number of our chiefs and noblemen. May I request that you give him up to me so that I can kill him?"

He was very angry with me for what I said. He hit me with his hand on my nose and I felt as if my nose was broken. I was bleeding heavily through the nose and tried to wipe the blood with my clothes. I was so humiliated that I wished the earth would open up and swallow me because I was so afraid of him. I then said to him: "Your Majesty, had I known that you would dislike what I said I would not have made that request." He felt a little ashamed and said to me: "ʿAmr, you are asking me to give up to you the envoy of a man who receives the archangel who used to come to Moses and Jesus so that you can kill him?" When I heard his words, I felt a great change overcoming me. I thought that Negus, the Arabs and the non-Arabs, recognized the truth while I was deliberately turning away from it. I said to him: "Do you testify to that, Your Majesty?" He said: "Yes, I bear witness to that in front of God. ʿAmr, do as I say and follow him, for his cause is that of the truth, and he will win over all those who oppose him, in the same way as Moses won against Pharaoh and his soldiers." I said to Negus: "Do you accept on his behalf my pledge to follow Islam?" He answered in the affirmative and put out his hands and I gave him my pledge to be a Muslim.

He then called for a bowl of water to be brought for me to wash. He also gave me new clothes, because my own clothes were full of blood. When I went out, my friends were very pleased to see me wearing new clothes given me by Negus. They asked me whether he had granted my request, and I said that I did not feel the occasion was suitable for such a request, since I was speaking to him for the first time. They agreed with me and I pretended that I was going out for some private purpose and left them there. I went straight to the port area, where I found a ship ready to sail. I went on board and sailed to a place called al-Shuʿbah, where I disembarked. I bought a camel and travelled on towards Madinah. I passed through Marr al-Ẓahrān and went on until I arrived at al-Haddah. I saw two men who had arrived there a short while earlier, trying to find a place to encamp. One of them was inside the tent, while the other was holding the reins of their two camels. Presently, I recognized Khālid ibn al-Walīd. When I asked him where he was going, he answered: "To Muhammad. All people of any significance have become Muslims. If we were to remain non-Muslims, he would catch us by the neck in the same way as the hyena is caught in its cave." I told him that I also was going to Muhammad and wanted to be a Muslim. ʿUthmān ibn Ṭalḥah came out of the tent and welcomed me. We stayed there together that night.

We travelled on together until we arrived at Madinah. I will never forget a man saying as we drew near: "*Yā Rabāḥ*", or 'What a profitable morning!' He repeated that three times. We were very pleased when we heard him saying that. As he looked at us, he said: "Makkah has given up the reign after these two have come to join us." I thought he was referring to me and Khālid ibn al-Walīd. He went quickly towards the mosque. I thought that he went to give the Prophet the news of our arrival. I was proved right.

We stopped for a short while at the old volcanic area outside Madinah, where we put on our best clothes. When the mid-afternoon prayer, *ʿaṣr*, was called for, we went on until we arrived at the mosque to meet the Prophet. His face was beaming with pleasure and all the Muslims were pleased when they learnt that we had adopted Islam. Khālid ibn al-Walīd went first to give his pledge of loyalty to the Prophet. He was followed by ʿUthmān ibn Ṭalḥah. I was third. When I sat down opposite him I could not lift my face up to him because I was feeling very shy. I gave him my pledge of loyalty, provided that God would forgive me all my sins which I had committed in the past. I did not remember to include what I might do in future. The Prophet said to me: "When you embrace Islam, all your past sins are forgiven. When you emigrate for the cause of God, your emigration ensures also the forgiveness of your past sins."

After we embraced Islam, the Prophet placed me and Khālid ibn al-Walīd at the top of his advisers in any serious matter

> confronting him. We enjoyed the same positions with Abū Bakr. I continued to enjoy that position during the reign of ʿUmar, but ʿUmar had perhaps some reservations with respect to Khālid.[3]

This is the account of one of the great servants of Islam who was later to command Muslim armies which liberated both Palestine and Egypt. He also ruled over Egypt for a long time.

Khālid's Story

The other case is that of Khālid ibn al-Walīd, the commander of a division of the Quraysh's army at the Battle of Uḥud. It was he who managed to attack the Muslims from behind and turn their victory into a military defeat. He was a young man of great promise. Indeed, he was to become one of the most distinguished commanders the world had ever known.

Khālid reports in detail how he began to think about Islam and the process of his conversion. He says that at first he started to reflect on his past attitude towards Islam:

> I fought all those battles against Muhammad. Every time I felt that all my efforts were to no avail. I was certain that Muhammad would eventually be the winner. When the Prophet came and encamped at al-Ḥudaybiyah, I commanded a detachment of horsemen from among the idolaters until we met the Prophet and his companions at ʿAsafān. I drew close to him to provoke him. He and his companions prayed *ẓuhr* in front of us. We thought of attacking them, but we refrained. He must have realized what we were thinking of when the next prayer, *ʿaṣr*, was due. He therefore, led his companions in what is known as 'the prayers of fear'. That affected us profoundly and we realized that he was immune from our attack. We therefore drew back.
>
> When the terms of the peace agreement of al-Ḥudaybiyah were eventually negotiated and the Prophet and his companions went home, I started thinking about what might

> come next and what was in store for us. I thought hard: Where should I go? Should I join Negus? But then I remembered that he had already become a follower of Muhammad and that Muhammad's companions were safe under his protection. Should I go and join Heracules? That would have made me a Christian or a Jewish convert. That prospect did not appeal to me. Should I emigrate or should I stay where I was, waiting for something to happen?[4]

This state of confusion was not to be easily resolved for Khālid. He did not wish to emigrate where he would have had to prove his worth. If he stayed in Makkah, on the other hand, he knew for certain that the eventual triumph of Islam was only a matter of time. His confusion, however, clouded his vision and he could not see that the right course of action was to look at Islam objectively. Weeks and months passed and he could not make up his mind. When a year had passed, and Muhammad and his companions came to Makkah for their compensatory *ʿUmrah*, Khālid did not wish to look at the Muslims coming into Makkah. He went into the mountains and stayed until the Prophet and his companions departed.

When he went back home, he found a letter left him by his brother, al-Walīd ibn al-Walīd, who had been a Muslim for some time. Al-Walīd was in the Prophet's company when he came to Makkah for his compensatory *ʿUmrah*. After completing the duties of the *ʿUmrah*, al-Walīd tried to find his brother Khālid. When he could not find him, he realized that Khālid was trying to run away from Islam. Al-Walīd, however, knew that his brother was a man endowed with great intelligence. He felt that a brotherly word might not go amiss. Hence, he wrote him the following letter:

> In the name of God, the Merciful, the Beneficent. I am infinitely amazed at the fact that you continue to turn away from Islam when you are as intelligent as I know you to be. No one can be so blind to the truth of Islam. God's Messenger asked me about you, and said: "Where is Khālid?" I said to him: "God will bring him to us." He said: "A man of his calibre cannot remain ignorant of Islam. If he would use his

intelligence and his experience for the Muslims against the idolaters, he would benefit from it a great deal. We would certainly give him precedence over others." It is high time, brother, for you to make amends for the great benefits you have missed.[5]

Clear Vision

When Khālid read his brother's letter, he felt as if a curtain which had blurred his vision for a long time was removed. He was pleased at the fact that the Prophet himself enquired about him. He felt a strong desire to become a Muslim. That night he dreamt that he was in a narrow strip of land in a barren desert and he was walking on and on until he came into an open, green, limitless field. It did not take him long to make up his mind that the right course for him was to become a Muslim. He decided to join the Prophet at Madinah.

He felt, however, that he needed to have a companion to go with him. He looked for a young man from the nobility of Makkah and the first one he approached was Ṣafwān ibn Umayyah. Ṣafwān's father and brother were killed at the Battle of Badr. His uncle was killed at Uḥud. Ṣafwān belonged to that generation of Quraysh leaders who viewed their conflict with Islam in clear-cut terms. He had resolved not to compromise with Muhammad and he was in no mood to do so when Khālid approached him. Nevertheless, Khālid said to him: "Do you not see that Muhammad is gaining the upper hand against both the Arabs and the non-Arabs? It is certainly expedient for us to join him and share in whatever success he may achieve."

Ṣafwān took a very extreme attitude and said to Khālid: "If all the Arabs followed Muhammad and I was the only one left, I would never join him."

When Khālid heard this reply he thought that Ṣafwān was a man who nursed his grudges and he remembered that his father and brother were killed at Badr. He, therefore, tried to look for someone else. By chance, he met ʿIkrimah ibn Abī Jahl, whose father had always been the most determined enemy of Islam, until he was killed at Badr. ʿIkrimah's reply to Khālid's approach was in terms similar to those of Ṣafwān. Khālid, however, asked him not to mention his approach to anyone and ʿIkrimah promised him that.

Khālid then met ʿUthmān ibn Ṭalḥah, a close friend of his. He thought of probing the matter with him, then he remembered that ʿUthmān's father, uncle and his four brothers were all killed at the Battle of Uḥud. Khālid hesitated, expecting a reply similar to those of Ṣafwān and ʿIkrimah. Eventually, he probed ʿUthmān, speaking first about the fact that the Muslims continued to gain strength. He then said; "I compare our position to that of a fox in a hole. If you pour a bucket of water down into the hole, you can be certain that the fox will come out." Then Khālid proposed to ʿUthmān that they should join the Prophet in Madinah. ʿUthmān responded positively. The two agreed to start their journey after midnight, and each to travel on his own and meet at the break of day at Ya'jaj. They then continued their journey together until they arrived at al-Haddah, where they met ʿAmr ibn al-ʿĀṣ. He said to them: "Welcome. Where are you heading?" Realizing that they all had the same purpose, the three of them travelled together until they arrived on the outskirts of Madinah, where they stopped to change their clothes. Khālid's report is as follows:

> God's Messenger was informed of our arrival, and he was pleased. I put on one of my best suits and went ahead to meet the Prophet. On the way I was met by my brother, who said to me: "Be quick. God's Messenger has been informed of your arrival and he is pleased. He is waiting for you." We then moved faster until we saw him at a distance, smiling. He wore his smile until I reached him and greeted him as God's Prophet and Messenger. He replied to my greeting with a face beaming with pleasure. I said: "I declare that there is no deity but God, and that you are God's Messenger." He said: "Come forward." When I drew nearer, he said to me: "I praise God for guiding you to Islam. I have always been aware that you are endowed with great intelligence and I have always hoped that your intelligence will lead you only to what is right and beneficial." I said to him: "Messenger of God, I am thinking of those battles at which I was fighting against the side of the truth. I request

> you to pray God for me to forgive me." He said: "When you embrace Islam, all your past sins are forgiven." I said: "Messenger of God, is that a condition?" He said: "My Lord, forgive Khālid ibn al-Walīd every effort he exerted to turn people away from Your path." ʿUthmān and ʿAmr then pledged their allegiance to the Prophet. By God, ever since our arrival in the month of Ṣafar in the eighth year of the Prophet's emigration, the Prophet consulted me about every serious matter which cropped up, ahead of all his other companions.

Khālid mentioned his dream to Abū Bakr, the Prophet's first companion. Abū Bakr told him that the narrowness and barrenness of the land in which he saw himself represented the false beliefs he had shared with his people, who were idolatrous. That he came out of it later into an open, fertile land represented the fact that God had guided him to Islam.[6]

Khālid ibn al-Walīd and ʿAmr ibn al-ʿĀṣ were to play great roles in the history of Islam. The Prophet assigned to Khālid the command of one army after another and gave him the title "Sword of Islam". He was to fight numerous battles for the cause of Islam and he achieved a resounding success in almost every battle he fought.[7]

Notes

1. Ibn Hishām, *al-Sīrah al-Nabawiyyah*, Dār al-Qalam, Beirut, Vol. 4, pp. 12-14. Also, Ibn Kathīr, *al-Bidāyah wal-Nihāyah*, Maktabat al-Maʿārif, Beirut, Vol. 1, pp. 226-233.
2. Ibn Kathīr, op.cit., p. 235.
3. Ibn Hishām, op.cit., Vol. 3, pp. 289-291. Also, al-Wāqidī, *Kitāb al-Maghāzī*, Oxford University Press, 1996, Vol. 1, pp. 741-749. Also, Ibn Kathīr, op.cit., pp. 141-142 and 236-238.
4. Al-Wāqidī, op.cit., pp. 745-746. Also, Ibn Kathīr, op.cit., pp. 238-240.
5. Al-Wāqidī, op.cit., pp. 746-747. Also, Ibn Kathīr, op.cit., p. 239.
6. Al-Wāqidī, op.cit., pp. 747-749. Also, Ibn Kathīr, op.cit., pp. 239-240.
7. Amīn Duwaydār, *Ṣuwar Min Ḥayāt al-Rasūl*, Dār al-Maʿārif, 4th edition, Cairo, p. 514.

33

A Foretaste of Fighting the Byzantines

WHEN THE PROPHET sent his envoys to the rulers and emperors of neighbouring countries in order to convey to them the message of Islam and call on them to submit themselves to God, as He requires of all people, he sent his companion al-Ḥārith ibn ʿUmayr to convey a similar message to Shuraḥbīl ibn ʿAmr of the Arab tribe of Ghassān, who was the ruler of Buṣrā in the south of present-day Syria. Buṣrā was a governorate of the Byzantine Empire. It enjoyed a form of political autonomy, since that area was inhabited by immigrant Arabs who belonged to the tribe of Ghassān.

The fact that most of the rulers and emperors received the Prophet's envoys with varying degrees of hospitality is by now apparent. Some of them replied cordially, others sent the Prophet some presents and others, such as Negus of Abyssinia and the ruler of Yemen, were soon to become Muslims. The Emperor of Persia was alone in sending back a rude reply. However, he did not order any maltreatment of the Prophet's envoy. All this was in keeping with the age old tradition that messengers and ambassadors must be treated well, regardless of the nature of the message they carried.

Shuraḥbīl ibn ʿAmr was the exception to all that. His behaviour was in total disregard to all diplomatic standards and values. He was not only rude but also he chose deliberately to be insulting to the Prophet and to Islam generally. He met the Prophet's envoy, al-Ḥārith ibn ʿUmayr, accidentally as the latter was on his way to him. He asked him where he was heading. When he realized that he was an envoy sent by Muhammad, he gave orders for al-Ḥārith to be tied up and then beheaded.

When the Prophet came to know of this, he felt that the treatment of his envoy represented an insult and a challenge which called for a firm reply. Islam was still consolidating its position in Arabia itself. An important factor in the steady progress of the Muslim state was to ensure that it was held in awe by all neighbouring powers. The people in Arabia were convinced that Islam could not be overcome by any other force. The Muslims enjoyed God's support, and that support was enough to defeat all their enemies. This general feeling was responsible for the conversion of a large number of people in Arabia who embraced Islam either because they feared it or because they wanted to be part of its success. If Islam was seen to be weakening in front of larger forces, the position of many of those who were prepared to join the ranks of the Muslims would be violently shaken. The implications would then be very serious indeed. Hence, the Prophet was keen that the position of the new Muslim state should be safeguarded. No one could be allowed to level an insult against Islam or the Muslim state and manage to get away with it. People inside and outside Arabia must feel that Islam was a force to be reckoned with. So, the Prophet decided to send an expedition to teach the aggressor a lesson and to show the world at large that no ambassador of the Muslim state could be killed and forgotten. His killers must be brought to justice and must be made to pay a heavy price for their aggression.

The Three Commanders

The Prophet called on his companions to join the army he was sending to Buṣrā. The response was, as usual, highly favourable. A force of 3,000 soldiers was thus raised. When they were ready to march, the Prophet named three of his companions as commanders who should succeed one another in case any of them was killed. He himself was heavily engaged in Madinah and could not take the command of the army himself.

Thus the army started its march under the leadership of its first commander, Zayd ibn Ḥārithah, who had been the first man ever to become a Muslim.

The Prophet told the army that if Zayd were to be killed, the commander would be Jaʿfar ibn Abū Ṭālib. In case he also was killed, the command would fall to ʿAbdullāh ibn Rawāḥah. If ʿAbdullāh was also killed, then the army could choose its own commander. The Prophet ordered the army to travel until they reached the district where al-Ḥārith ibn ʿUmayr was killed, and to call on the people of that area to accept Islam. If they did, the Muslims were to leave them alone. If they did not, then they should fight them, praying God to help them. He also ordered them not to break any promises they gave and not to kill a child, a woman, an old man or a monk praying in seclusion. They were not to cut down any trees or destroy any buildings. The Prophet went out with the army to the outskirts of Madinah, where he bade the commanders and the soldiers farewell.

The Muslim army tried to conceal its purpose in order to be able to take the enemy by surprise. The news of its march, however, was soon known to its enemies, who started to get ready. Shuraḥbīl ibn ʿAmr mobilized all the Arab tribes under his control. These tribes were able to provide a very large force indeed. Most historians set the figure of their forces in this encounter at 100,000. Moreover, Heracules, the Byzantine Emperor, sent his local governor a further force of 100,000 Byzantine soldiers. Thus, an army of 200,000 was preparing to meet the Muslim army which, although large by the standards of the Muslim state in Madinah, consisted of 3,000 soldiers only. Historians differ as to how Shuraḥbīl ibn ʿAmr was able to mobilize such a large force. Some suggest that the Byzantine force accompanied Heracules for his pilgrimage to Jerusalem, which was intended as a thanksgiving pilgrimage for his victory over the Persian Empire. Whether the historical reports of the exact number of the forces which were preparing to meet the Muslim army were accurate or not, one can be certain that the Muslims were about to confront a force greatly superior to them in numerical strength. This suggests that all people who found themselves in a position of confrontation with the Muslims were aware that they needed a very large force in order to ensure that they could triumph over the Muslims. The victories achieved by the Muslims against the Quraysh and the Jews in Khaybar and in other battles were well known in surrounding areas. Hence, it was not surprising that Shuraḥbīl ibn ʿAmr should resort to raising a very large force to confront the Muslims.

The Muslims, on the other hand, did not fear to meet a larger force. It is reported that Abū Hurayrah, a companion of the Prophet who adopted Islam after the signing of the peace agreement at al-Ḥudaybiyah, was very surprised at the disparity between the forces of the two sides on this occasion. He is reported to have said: "I took part in the battle of Mu'tah. When the unbelievers drew near to us, we saw a great force fully equipped with arms and well dressed. I was dazzled. Thābit ibn Arqam spoke to me and said: 'Abū Hurayrah, you seem to be surprised at their superior forces.' When I answered in the affirmative, he said: 'You were not with us at the Battle of Badr. We do not win on the basis of our numerical strength'."

Nevertheless, the disparity between the two forces was so marked that the Muslims felt that they needed to stop and think about what they were about to face. When they reached Maʿān, in the south of present-day Jordan, they received intelligence of the size of the forces preparing to meet them. They stopped at Maʿān for two nights in consultation on what their next step should be. Some of them suggested that they should write to the Prophet informing him of the situation and of the forces of their enemies, and await his orders. He might either send some support or give them further instructions. ʿAbdullāh ibn Rawāḥah, the third commander named by the Prophet, felt that the matter did not warrant that sort of delay. He encouraged the Muslims not to hesitate before confronting their enemy:

> The cause of your hesitation now is the very prize which you have set out to achieve: namely, martyrdom. We have never fought any enemy on the basis of our numerical strength, or our better equipment, or our superior number of horses. We fight them only with this religion with which God has blessed us. Let us

> march on. I attended the Battle of Badr when we had only two horses. At the Battle of Uḥud, there was only one horseman in our ranks. March on, brothers. We stand to win one of two great prizes: either we will achieve victory – and this is what God and His messenger have promised us, and it is a promise which never fails – or we will achieve martyrdom, in which case we join our brethren who went before us into Heaven.

These words were very touching to the Muslim army. This was no vain discourse. What ʿAbdullāh ibn Rawāḥah said was something in which they all believed. To a Muslim, any fight for the cause of Islam can end either in an honourable victory or in martyrdom. It is a case of either a victory for the community or a victory for the individual. Hence, they marched on. Two more nights and they reached the area to which they were sent. They found out that the enemy forces were encamped in a village called Mashārif. Enemy companies started to draw near them. They, therefore, moved to a village called Mu'tah, where they took their positions.

The Battle of Mu'tah

Although the decision reached by the Muslim army may seem unwise, considering the enormous disparity between their forces and those of their enemies, the Muslims always had their own criteria when they considered any serious matter. That particular army, which included many soldiers who took part in earlier battles the Muslims fought against their enemies, was generally aware that numerical inferiority could be compensated for by superior spiritual strength. The speech of ʿAbdullāh ibn Rawāḥah rekindled the enthusiasm of the Muslim soldiers to the extent that they were eager to face their enemy.

When the Muslim army took its position at the village of Mu'tah, the Byzantine forces marched towards them in great numbers, seeking to overwhelm the Muslims by sheer numerical strength. The Muslims deployed their forces, adopting the tactics of concentrated pressure at the centre while preventing the outside flanks of their enemy from trying to encircle them. The Muslim commander of the right flank was Quṭbah ibn Qatādah; his counterpart on the left flank was ʿUbādah ibn Mālik. These two commanders and their units fought very hard to protect the central units from being overwhelmed. The battle was now being fought in earnest.

Zayd ibn Ḥārithah was the first Muslim commander. He carried the Muslim flag and fought hard. Apparently the Byzantine forces concentrated their efforts on trying to kill the Muslim commander, so they pressed hard where Zayd was fighting and were soon able to kill him. The banner was taken over by Jaʿfar ibn Abū Ṭālib, who again was the target for a concentrated enemy attack. Jaʿfar was a great fighter who struck the enemy soldiers right, left and centre. He could not, however, withstand the continuous pressure against him and he felt that he could fight better if he were to dismount. He continued to fight on foot, still carrying the flag in his right hand. As he fought on, he was hit several times. Then an enemy soldier was able to chop off his right hand, but Jaʿfar automatically carried the flag with his left hand. Again, he was hit hard, and his left hand was chopped off. Nevertheless, he would not drop the flag. He held it tightly with the upper parts of his arms and faced the enemy. His position was no longer tenable and he was soon killed. It is reported that when he was about to be buried, they counted on his body something like ninety wounds.

The flag was taken over by ʿAbdullāh ibn Rawāḥah, who had demonstrated, ever since he joined the army, that he dearly wished to be killed in battle. The fighting was so hard that the Muslim soldiers did not have any food because they were preoccupied with the battle. A cousin of ʿAbdullāh, however, gave him a piece of meat and said: "Eat this and strengthen yourself. You have nearly exhausted your energy today." When he had his first bite ʿAbdullāh heard the noise of fighting from one side and said to himself: "And I am still in this world?" He dropped the piece of meat and fought hard until he was killed.

The Fourth Commander

It was nearly evening when ʿAbdullāh ibn Rawāḥah was killed. According to the Prophet's instructions, the Muslims were to choose their own commander, should all three commanders appointed by him be killed. Thābit ibn Arqam took the banner and shouted to his fellow Muslims: "You now have to elect your own commander." Some of them said to him: "We choose you." He answered: "No, I do not accept." Their choice was Khālid ibn al-Walīd, who had joined the Muslim ranks only a few months earlier.

It was Khālid's first battle with the Muslims. He was a gifted military commander. He realized that total victory could not be achieved by the Muslims in such a greatly ill-balanced confrontation. His immediate thoughts were to engage the enemy for the rest of the day in such a way as to avoid heavy casualties among the Muslims. When darkness fell and the two armies were separated for the night, Khālid still had a great deal to do.

Taking stock of the situation, he realized that the best that the Muslims could achieve in that confrontation was to try to maximize the losses of their enemies while minimizing their own and avoiding an outright defeat. He redeployed his forces completely, moving his right flank to the left and his left flank to the right. He also exchanged the positions of the front and rear forces. This total redeployment was completed during the night. He then ordered a detachment of his forces to raise as much dust as possible behind the army and to cause a great deal of noise.

At daybreak, fighting was resumed. The Byzantine forces were surprised to see new faces all round. They thought that the Muslims must have received fresh help. They were somewhat scared to go into battle in earnest. The Muslims were able to take the initiative and fought hard, killing a large number of enemy soldiers.

Khālid, however, did not intend the battle to go on indefinitely. As his forces were fighting hard, he was, at the same time, drawing back very slowly and skilfully. The Byzantine commanders thought that he was trying to drag them slowly into the desert. They felt that if they were to be dragged that far, they would lay themselves open to greater risks. Hence, they thought it was wiser to resist the temptation. They stood their ground. Khālid, on the other hand, was able to disengage his forces in that way, without incurring any great losses. Historians agree that this withdrawal was a great success. It was indeed, in that particular confrontation, much more difficult than achieving victory, had the forces of the two sides been equally balanced. A lesser commander would not have been able to withdraw safely. Moreover, the Muslims managed to inflict heavy losses on their enemies.

The Muslims lost only 12 martyrs in this battle. Among these were the three commanders of the army named by the Prophet. This was because the Byzantine army concentrated its attack on those commanders because, in those days, killing the commander ensured winning the battle. The discipline of the Muslims, however, brought new factors into the equation and the Muslims lost three commanders without their morale being affected in any way. In order to describe the ferocity of that battle, one need only remember how Jaʿfar ibn Abī Ṭālib fought until he was killed. Khālid ibn al-Walīd said about that battle: "Nine swords were broken in my hand at the Battle of Mu'tah." That was a large number of swords for the Muslim commander to use.

What the Battle Achieved

The great achievement of that battle was that it gave the Byzantines and their Arab agents an idea of what fighting the Muslims meant. At no time afterwards did the Byzantine forces look forward to meeting the Muslim forces. Every time a battle was looming on the horizon, and there were many battles to come between the two sides, the Byzantines approached it with fear in their hearts. Moreover, this battle inspired great respect for the Muslims among the Arabian tribes in the north, such as those of Sulaym, Ashjaʿ, ʿAbs and Dhubyān, who started to join the Muslim ranks.

Back in Madinah, the Prophet informed the Muslims of the events of the battle. He said: "Zayd took the banner until he was killed. It was then taken over by Jaʿfar until he was killed. Then Ibn Rawāḥah carried the flag until he was killed." The Prophet's eyes were tearful as he said this. "It was taken over," he continued, "by a man who is one of God's swords, and he fought until God granted them success." This is a testimony by the Prophet that what Khālid and the Muslims did in that battle was a great success. No other testimony or opinion is needed in addition to this one.

Nevertheless, when the army arrived back in Madinah, children met them with jeers and denunciation. They said to them: "You deserters. You desert a battle being fought for God's cause?" The Prophet, however, set things right when he said to them: "These are no deserters. They will live to fight another day." The children's attitude gives an impression of what sort of society the Prophet built in Madinah, and in Arabia at large.

A few days later, the Prophet was speaking about the commanders who were killed at the Battle of Mu'tah. He said to his companions: "They would not wish to be with us now." This is most certainly the case. No martyr would like to return to his home after enjoying God's blessings which come with his martyrdom.

The Prophet also visited the family of his cousin, Jaʿfar, the second commander. He said to them: "Do not cry for my brother's death any more. Let me see his children." The three boys were brought to him and he called in a barber to cut their hair. He said to them: "Muhammad [son of Jaʿfar] resembles our uncle, Abū Ṭālib. ʿAbdullāh has a likeness to me in shape and manners." He then took ʿAbdullāh by the hand and waved his hand, praying in these words: "My Lord, look after Jaʿfar's family. Bless every transaction ʿAbdullāh makes." He repeated that three times. ʿAbdullāh was to grow up as one of the most generous people that ever lived. Their mother spoke about their being orphans and the Prophet said to her: "Do you fear that they will live in poverty when I am their patron in this world and in the world to come?" This is just an example of the sort of care the Prophet took of his companions, especially those who fought hard for the cause of Islam.[1]

Notes

1. A detailed account of the events related in this chapter is given in all books on the Prophet's life. See for example: al-Wāqidī, *Kitāb al-Maghāzī*, Oxford University Press, 1996, Vol. 1, pp. 755-767; Ibn Sayyid al-Nās, *ʿUyūn al-Athar*, Dār al-Turāth, Madinah, 1996, pp. 208-211; and Ibn Kathīr, *al-Bidāyah wal-Nihāyah*, Maktabat al-Maʿārif, Beirut, Vol. 1, pp. 241-252.

34

A Long Conflict Draws to a Close

GREAT AND LONG, drawn out conflicts are normally resolved when something decisive takes place, tilting the balance of power irrevocably towards one party or the other. This is particularly true when the conflict is not motivated merely by economic or material considerations, but involves ideological factors as well. As seen in this narrative, the conflict between the Muslims in Madinah and the Quraysh in Makkah was essentially an ideological one. The two sides were brought into conflict because they held diametrically opposed ideologies and one of them, namely the Quraysh, wanted to suppress the faith of Islam. Hence, the likelihood of that conflict being resolved by the achievement of a peaceful accommodation was very slim indeed. In any ideological conflict which makes use of the force of arms, once the military activity subsides for any reason, the intellectual debate, in one form or another, takes over until the conflict is brought to a more fundamental resolution.

In the case of the conflict between the Quraysh and the Muslims, the Quraysh had been the aggressor ever since the Prophet declared his message and called on people to believe in the oneness of God and to submit to Him. It has been seen how the Quraysh persecuted those who responded to the call of the Prophet when the Quraysh elders decided to reject it. Over a period of 13 years in Makkah, the intellectual debate was not given any chance. Anyone who decided to embrace Islam realized that he was making that decision at his own peril. The Quraysh was indeed able to impose its authority and contain the new message within its own area, to the extent that in 13 years the Prophet could win over only about 300 followers from among the Quraysh.

Ultimately, the message of Islam was successful in breaking through the imposed siege and a new base was founded for Islam in Madinah. The Quraysh, then, resorted to its superior military force in order to suppress Islam once and for all. But after five years, three major encounters and a large number of localized and sometimes major confrontations involving other Arab tribes as well as the Jews, the Quraysh realized that they were making no headway whatsoever in the confrontation with Islam. Indeed, Islam was growing stronger all the time. Those five years left the initiative decidedly in the hands of the Prophet.

A Peaceful Battle of Ideas

The peace agreement signed by the two sides at al-Ḥudaybiyah was a decisive moral victory for the Muslims. The Qur'ān describes it as "a clear victory". What the Muslims achieved in that peace campaign was that for the first time they were able to address people with their message without having to contend with the fear those people had of the Quraysh. Since the Quraysh were the master tribe of Arabia, all other tribes took their cue from them. Most adopted an attitude of 'wait and see' towards the conflict between the Muslims and the Quraysh. They neither wanted to incur the Quraysh's anger nor wished to involve themselves in a conflict which remained far from clear to most of them. As the peace agreement of al-Ḥudaybiyah stipulated that all tribes were free to join or to be in alliance with either side, Arabian tribes felt that they would incur nobody's anger if they listened to Muhammad and paid thoughtful consideration to his faith. As far as the Prophet and the Muslims were concerned, this was a remarkable achievement. After all, no sound idea required more than objective consideration in order to be accepted. If this applies to human ideas, it is particularly applicable to the true faith based on the oneness of God.

As history shows, the advocates of false beliefs fear nothing more than a situation where they have to come face to face with the true faith under fair rules. Moreover, nothing attracts people to a faith more than seeing with their own eyes that that faith can build a better society than their own. Both factors came into play when the Prophet and his companions offered their compensatory *ʿUmrah*. For three days the Prophet and his companions were in Makkah, talking freely to its inhabitants, who were the relatives of many of the Muslims. Such conversations took place in a relaxed atmosphere. The people of the Quraysh were also seeing the type of society Islam built in Madinah. They realized that the ties of brotherhood, love and mutual compassion Islam made among its followers were very real indeed. As said earlier, this was bound to bring about a change in the attitude of individuals from the Quraysh towards Islam.

The net result of the events of those seven years since the Prophet's emigration from Makkah was that the structure which the Quraysh represented started to crumble from within. After all, its foundation was far from solid, its motives were highly questionable and the ties between its different classes were those of mutual fear and apprehension. In comparison, the Muslim society in Madinah was a shining example of what a human society can and should be, if it is built on a proper foundation.

The Prophet realized that the tide was going against the Quraysh. He was absolutely confident that it was only a matter of time before the Quraysh would give up the fight to suppress Islam. He had no doubt whatsoever in the truth of his message and he was absolutely certain that Islam would continue to spread and move forward.

The chiefs of Makkah also realized that the Muslims had gained a position which was at least equal to their own as far as prestige in Arabia was concerned. They also realized that since the peace agreement of al-Ḥudaybiyah was signed between the two sides, Islam had continued to make fresh gains. While these gains were not at the expense of the Quraysh directly, they had an indirect adverse effect on it. In a two-sided competition within a limited area, any gain one side makes is a loss to the other. Islam was winning the hearts of more and more people and this was the most valuable of gains. Hence, the Quraysh realized that things were not going their way.

At that time, the Quraysh represented the forces of evil. In such an equation as the one portrayed of the relative situations of the Muslims and the Quraysh, it was inevitable that evil would seek some way to reassert its position. If chance offered such a way, scruples could easily be shed. The purpose justified the means. In any such a situation, when matters reached that stage, little wisdom is shown by those who hold sway in the evil camp. As history shows, they are normally groping in the dark for anything which could keep them from falling. What they normally come up with is something stupid and counter-productive. It is generally counter-productive because, ill-considered as it is, it tends to play into the hands of the other side. What happens afterwards is that it accelerates the resolution of the confrontation. All this applied to the Quraysh at the time just before the events about to be related. Those events took place nearly two years after the signing of al-Ḥudaybiyah peace agreement between the Prophet and the Quraysh.

The Violation

What triggered those events was something relatively minor, but nevertheless it represented a blatant violation of the peace agreement. It should be recalled that that peace agreement stipulated that Arabian tribes were free to make alliances with either side. The terms of the peace agreement applied to those allies in the same way as they applied to the main participants. The tribe of Bakr joined the Quraysh camp by way of a formal alliance, while the tribe of Khuzāʿah entered into an alliance with the Muslims.

These two tribes were at loggerheads before the advent of Islam. Although hostilities ceased between them a few years before the signing of al-Ḥudaybiyah peace agreement, they still harboured ill feelings towards each other. A branch of the Bakr known as the clan of Dayl had a score to settle with the Khuzāʿah. Their leader, Nawfal ibn Muʿāwiyah, felt that the truce obtained in Arabia as a result of the peace agreement offered him a chance to settle that score. He, therefore, marched at the head of a large force from his clan and launched a surprise raid against the Khuzāʿah as their men were gathering at a water spring called al-Watīr.

Fighting broke out and the Khuzāʿah were forced to retreat. As the Khuzāʿah lived very close to Makkah their retreat took them inside the consecrated area of the Kaʿbah, where fighting had been strictly prohibited ever since the time of Abraham. All the Arabs recognized the sanctity of that area. Thus, the Bakr's action not only represented a violation of the peace treaty, it was also a violation of the sanctity of Makkah. The Bakr realized that. Some of their men said to their leader: "Nawfal, we have entered the consecrated area. Do not incur the displeasure of your god." Nawfal's desire to take revenge against the Khuzāʿah, however, blinded him to all that. He said: "Today, I have no god. Children of Bakr, take your revenge. I know that you steal in the consecrated area. Would you not take your revenge there?"

That revenge the Bakr did take. They killed a good number of the men of Khuzāʿah. Moreover, the Quraysh gave them a helping hand. They supplied them with arms and some Qurayshi men took part in the actual fighting alongside the Bakr. Hence the peace agreement was violated not only by the Bakr, but also by the Quraysh.

When the fighting was over, the Khuzāʿah sent a messenger to the Prophet to inform him of the events. That messenger was called ʿAmr ibn Sālim. ʿAmr travelled as fast as he could until he arrived in Madinah. He went straight to the mosque, where the Prophet was sitting with a group of his companions. ʿAmr conveyed the news in the most effective fashion of the time – namely, poetry. The Prophet's response was short, clear and decisive. He said to him: "You shall have our support, ʿAmr ibn Sālim."

That messenger was followed by a delegation from the Khuzāʿah headed by Budayl ibn Warqā', who came to meet the Prophet at Madinah. They gave the Prophet a detailed account of what took place. They also informed him that the Quraysh lent active support to the Bakr in their raid against the Khuzaʿah. There was no doubt in the Prophet's mind that the Quraysh had committed a blatant violation of the peace agreement. However, he did not make any promises to the Khuzāʿah apart from his original promise of support. He preferred not to publicize his next move. The delegation went back home satisfied with their meeting with the Prophet.

Staving Off the Consequences

When the Quraysh actively supported their allies, the tribe of Bakr, in their aggression against the Khuzāʿah who were allied to the Prophet, they did not give much thought to the consequences of their treachery. Little did they realize that news travelled fast and that the Prophet would inevitably come to hear of the Quraysh's indefensible action. When the excitement was over, the enormity of what they had done stared them in the face. They realized that for a petty gain they had put themselves in a position where they could incur grave losses. Some of them suggested that it was necessary for them to act quickly in order to avert any possible campaign of revenge which might be launched by the Muslims. They, therefore, sent their leader, Abū Sufyān, to Madinah ostensibly to negotiate a revision of the peace agreement, making it valid for a longer period.

Abū Sufyān in Madinah

The Prophet had expected all that. When he ascertained that the Quraysh had lent active support to the attackers of his allies, he told his companions that he expected Abū Sufyān to come to Madinah with the pretext of improving the terms of the peace agreement. It was only a short time before Abū Sufyān made his appearance in Madinah.[1]

Like any guilty person who plans to hide his guilt by appearing to do something good, Abū Sufyān was worried lest his efforts should come to nothing. He, therefore, thought of enlisting the support of someone in the Prophet's own household. That person was Abū Sufyān's own daughter, Umm Ḥabībah, whom the Prophet had married a couple of years earlier. Abū Sufyān entered her room and, behaving like any father in his daughter's house, proceeded to sit down on the Prophet's mattress. Umm Ḥabībah was faster than him – she folded the mattress and took it away. Surprised, Abū Sufyān asked: "I am not quite sure, child, whether you think that I am above sitting on your mattress or that it is too good for me." She put it to him quite frankly: "It is the mattress of God's Messenger and since you are an idolater you are impure. Hence, I do not like you to sit on the mattress of God's Messenger (peace be upon him)."

That was a totally unexpected blow for Abū Sufyān. He could not have imagined that his own daughter would humiliate him in this way. He said: "I am certain some harm has befallen you since you left me, daughter."

This is an example of how dear the Prophet was to the Muslims: dearer than their own parents or children. Such a relationship was totally incomprehensible to the unbelievers.

Abū Sufyān left his daughter's room nursing that severe blow. He went into the mosque where he met the Prophet. He said to him: "Muhammad, I have come to ask you to confirm our peace agreement and to validate it for a longer period."

The Prophet asked him: "Is this what you have come here for? Have you perpetrated any trouble?" Abū Sufyān hastened to deny any knowledge of any breach of the peace agreement and said: "We are abiding by our peace agreement of al-Ḥudaybiyah. We strictly observe its terms." The Prophet did not say anything further to him and Abū Sufyān's attempt to enter into a dialogue with the Prophet was in vain.

Abū Sufyān then went to meet Abū Bakr, the Prophet's senior companion. He made the same request to him, but Abū Bakr said that he would do only as the Prophet did. He would not speak to the Prophet on behalf of the Quraysh. Abū Sufyān then went to ʿUmar and tried to persuade him to speak to the Prophet on his behalf. ʿUmar said: "You want me to be your advocate? If I could find nothing to fight you with except dust, I would certainly fight you."

Abū Sufyān must have felt very low after this sequence of rebuffs. In different circumstances he would not have continued with his efforts. With every blow he received, however, he realized that the matter was very serious indeed. Failure in his mission was certain to bring about very bad consequences for the Quraysh. He, therefore, persisted in his efforts. He spoke to several of the leading companions of the Prophet, but he received the same reply time after time. Chiefs of both the Muhājirīn and the Anṣār told him: "We only abide by the Prophet's instructions. Whatever promise or pledge he gives, we will honour."

He then went to ʿAlī the Prophet's cousin and son-in-law, and said to him: "ʿAlī, you are my nearest relative among the Muslims and our relations have always been close. I have come for a definite purpose and I do not want to return empty-handed. Will you please intercede with the Prophet on my behalf?" ʿAlī replied: "God's Messenger has made up his mind to do something, and none of us can speak to him about it."

Fāṭimah, the Prophet's daughter, was present and her eldest son, Ḥasan, was playing in the room. Abū Sufyān addressed Fāṭimah: "Muhammad's daughter, would you instruct this young child of yours to declare peace between our two sides and he will be the greatest Arab man for the rest of time." She answered: "My child is too young to declare peace between people. No one can extend protection to anybody against God's Messenger (peace be upon him)."

Abū Sufyān felt that he was running into a blind alley. He said to ʿAlī: "I feel that matters have become too hard for me, and I seek your advice." ʿAlī replied: "By God, I do not know of anything which would be of any use to you. You are, however, the chief of a great tribe of Arabia. Go and declare peace between people, and then go home." Abū Sufyān asked ʿAlī whether he thought that such a step would be of much use. ʿAlī answered in the negative and added: "But I can see no other way for you."

Abū Sufyān went out and said: "Let everybody know that I have declared peace between people, and I do not think that anybody would breach my pledge."

This was a tradition in Arabia. If the chief or chiefs of some tribe made such a declaration, people would normally accept it as a declaration of truce. At that particular time, the situation was greatly different in Madinah. Abū Sufyān wanted to make sure that his pledge would be honoured. He went to the Prophet and said to him: "Muhammad, I have declared peace between people, and I do not expect anyone to breach my pledge or violate my protection." The Prophet answered: "You are the one who is saying that."

It was apparent that the Prophet wanted matters to be very clear to Abū Sufyān. The Muslims gave him nothing whatsoever. His declaration was binding only on him, since they did not approve it.

When Abū Sufyān arrived in Makkah, his people asked him whether he had come back with any document or agreement approved by the Prophet. He reported to them on his failure and told them of ʿAlī's advice and his acting on it. They said: "You have accepted something unilaterally and come back with what is useless for us and you. ʿAlī was only playing games. Your peace and protection have not been accepted and are not binding on them." His own wife was even harsher to him.[2]

Preparations Start

When some time had passed after the departure of Abū Sufyān, the Prophet told his wife ʿĀ'ishah to prepare his fighting equipment. She started to prepare food as well. Her father, Abū Bakr, came in and when he saw what she was doing he asked her why she was preparing that sort of food, but she did not reply. He asked whether the Prophet wanted to mount a fresh expedition, but ʿĀ'ishah remained silent. Abū Bakr went on questioning her and asked whether the Prophet's aim was the Byzantines, or the people of Najd, or, indeed, the Quraysh.

ʿĀ'ishah did not answer any of these questions. At that point, the Prophet came in and Abū Bakr put the same questions to him and the Prophet confirmed that his target was the Quraysh. Abū Bakr mentioned the peace agreement and the Prophet told him that they had breached it. The Prophet had thought deeply about the Quraysh's action. He could not find any excuse for giving them the benefit of the doubt. Theirs was a most flagrant violation of the peace treaty. Hence, they had to pay a heavy price for it. If they were allowed to get away with such a violation, they would soon be thinking of another way to get at the Muslims. Action needed to be taken without delay. The Prophet, however, started his preparations quietly. Even his closest advisers were not initially informed of his purpose.

The Prophet indeed did not inform anyone of his impending expedition, but he ordered his companions to get ready. Moreover, he put ʿUmar ibn al-Khaṭṭāb in charge of security. ʿUmar appointed patrols on all the routes leading out of Madinah or into it, and gave them instructions not to allow anyone whom they suspected to pass through. The Prophet wanted to take the Quraysh by surprise, and employed all means to ensure that they would not receive intelligence of his impending departure. Moreover, as he was the most perfect of believers, he prayed God to help make his precautions effective so that the Muslims could take the Quraysh by surprise.[3]

Treasonable Action

At this point, one member of the Muslim community did something which was totally uncharacteristic of the Muslims. Ḥāṭib ibn Abī Baltaʿah, one of the Muhājirīn who emigrated with the Prophet from Makkah to Madinah, wrote a letter to the Quraysh warning them that the Prophet intended to attack them. He gave it to a woman who concealed it and managed to leave Madinah without being detected by any of the guards appointed by the Prophet on all exits and entrances. The Prophet was informed by God of Ḥāṭib's action. He therefore sent two of his companions, ʿAlī ibn Abī Ṭālib and al-Zubayr ibn al-ʿAwwām, telling them to go as far as a place called Rawḍat Khākh, where they would find a woman who was carrying a letter which they were to retrieve. They went as far as that place, where they found the woman just as the Prophet had told them. They asked her to give them the letter, but she denied all knowledge of any letter. ʿAlī said to her: "I swear by God, the Prophet has not lied. You will either do as we tell you and give us the letter or we will undress you." She realized that he was serious and that she had no option but to comply. She asked them to turn their faces away. As they did so, she undid her hair, in which she had concealed the letter. She gave it to them and they went back straight to Madinah to hand it to the Prophet.

The Prophet called Ḥāṭib in and questioned him about what he had done. Ḥāṭib appealed to the Prophet not to jump to any conclusions. He said:

> I am certainly a believer in God and His Messenger. I have not changed at all. It is not that I have any doubts in matters of faith. I only looked at my situation in Makkah, where I have a family and children. I was only an ally to the Quraysh, not being born among them. Other people among the Muhājirīn who have families or property in Makkah have their relatives and clans to protect them. I only thought that if I did the Quraysh a favour by warning them, they would return it by protecting my children and family. There is nothing more to it than that. I would never revert to unbelief after God has guided me to the right faith.

The Prophet recognized that Ḥāṭib was telling the truth. He said to those around him: "What he has told you is certainly the truth." The case was, however, one of high treason. In any country, a person doing what Ḥāṭib did would be court-martialled. He would be charged with passing top military secrets to the enemy. It was not surprising that ʿUmar ibn al-Khaṭṭāb, one of the leading companions of the Prophet and an outspoken advocate of taking stiff measures against anyone who did something detrimental to Islam, should say to Ḥāṭib: "Confound you. You see God's Messenger placing guards at the exits and entrances of the city, and you still write to the Quraysh?" Then ʿUmar said to the Prophet: "Allow me to behead this hypocrite."

The Prophet felt that he should take a different view of the incident. He surveyed Ḥāṭib's association with Islam and recognized that he was one of those who had fought for Islam in Badr. He became a Muslim when adopting Islam meant exposing oneself to the wrath of the Quraysh and their persecution. He was also the Prophet's envoy to al-Muqawqis, the ruler of Egypt. The Prophet then smiled at ʿUmar and said: "How would you know, ʿUmar, that God has not looked at the soldiers of Badr and said to them: I have forgiven you whatever you will do?" Tears sprang to ʿUmar's eyes as he said: "God and His messenger know better."

It is in connection with this incident that the opening of *Sūrah* 60, The Examined One, was revealed. It orders the believers not to seek as patrons the enemies of God and their own enemies, by doing them a good turn in anticipation of reciprocation.[4] What is absolutely clear in this incident is that Ḥāṭib committed a grievous error by trying to win a position of favour with the unbelievers of the Quraysh when they had adopted a hostile attitude towards the Prophet and Islam and persecuted the Muslims, as Ḥāṭib was well aware. But as mentioned earlier, great men may slip. This was the slip of a great man. He thought that if the approaching big battle becomes too ferocious, the Quraysh might think of taking revenge on the families of those Muslims who had emigrated from Makkah. In this case, the only thing which might secure the safety of his own family and children would be a favour to the Quraysh. He was certainly mistaken. The unbelievers never showed any inclination to recognize past favours or past loyalties in their unrelenting hostility towards Islam. Hence, when the Muslim community stands in opposition to them, it is not for any Muslim to maintain any personal friendly relations with them. How can it be justified that one Muslim individual should do something which was bound to have adverse effects on the Muslim community as a whole?

The Prophet was fully aware of the enormity of Ḥāṭib's action. However, he decided to pardon him because of his past service to Islam. Furthermore, he instructed his companions to remind themselves of Ḥāṭib's past history in the service of Islam. One slip, however serious, should not wipe away all the good service a man has given for this blessed cause.

And a Pardon for Old Enemies

When the Muslims had completed their preparations, the Prophet marched at the head of an army which was very large by Muslim standards; it was indeed the largest army ever raised under the Prophet's leadership. Some reports suggest that it was 12,000 strong, but it is perhaps more accurate to say that the Prophet had 10,000 soldiers with him. They had not marched far before they met al-ʿAbbās ibn ʿAbd al-Muṭṭalib, the Prophet's uncle. Al-ʿAbbās had all his family with him. They all came to join the Muslims. They declared their belief in God and His Messenger and joined the Muslim army.

There are reports which suggest that al-ʿAbbās had embraced Islam long before this, but these reports cannot be confirmed. What is known is that his sympathies were always with the Muslims.

Shortly afterwards, the Muslim army met two men from the Quraysh who had come to join the Prophet. Those were Abū Sufyān ibn al-Ḥārith ibn ʿAbd al-Muṭṭalib and ʿAbdullāh ibn Abū Umayyah. The two were relatives of the Prophet. Abū Sufyān had been his cousin and playmate in childhood, but when the Prophet received his message, Abū Sufyān chose to be very hostile to him and attacked him in his poetry. ʿAbdullāh ibn Abū Umayyah had been very abusive to the Prophet in the past, despite the fact that his mother was the Prophet's aunt. At one time he said to the Prophet that he would never believe in him until he had seen him climb a ladder right to the sky and return with a written testimony that he was God's Messenger, bringing with him four angels to give evidence of that. The abuse of near relatives is especially painful. Hence, the Prophet was not keen to meet either of these two men. When they approached him, he refused to receive them.

Umm Salamah, one of the Prophet's wives, tried to mediate on the Quraysh men's behalf. She said to the Prophet: "God's Messenger, they are your own cousins and kinsfolk." He replied: "I have no need of them. My cousin defamed me, and my aunt's son was the one who said what you know in Makkah."

When they were informed of what the Prophet said, they felt themselves to be in a very bad position. They did not know what to do. Abū Sufyān, who had his son with him, said: "If he will not receive me, I will take this son of mine by the hand and we will both wander through the land until we die of starvation and thirst."

ʿAlī ibn Abī Ṭālib, who was a cousin of both the Prophet and Abū Sufyān, gave the latter this sound advice. He told him to approach the Prophet directly, face to face, and use the same words as Joseph's brothers spoke to him when they recognized him: "Indeed, God has granted you a better status than ours, and we have indeed been in the wrong." ʿAlī told him that the Prophet would not like that any one else should give a better answer than his own in similar circumstances. Abū Sufyān did as he was advised and the Prophet answered with the same answer Prophet Joseph gave to his brothers: "No blame shall be attached to you this day. May God forgive you. He is indeed the most Merciful." Thus, Abū Sufyān and his relative were rehabilitated. He immediately started to use his poetic talent in the service of Islam and the advocacy of its cause.[5]

These two incidents reveal one side of the Prophet's character: he was the most loyal and forgiving of people.

On the March

The Muslim army under the Prophet's leadership started its march towards Makkah on the 10th day of Ramaḍān in the eighth year of the Islamic calendar. Muslims from various tribes joined the army in large numbers. There were, for example, 700 from the tribe of Sulaym. Some reports put the figure of Sulaym soldiers at 1,000. There were also 1,000 from the tribe of Muzaynah. Each tribe formed a unit of the army. All the Muhājirīn and the Anṣār responded to the Prophet's call and joined up. None of them was left behind. When the Prophet reached a place called ʿAsafān, not far from Madinah, he asked for a jug of water. When it was brought to him, he raised it so that he was seen by as many people as possible and drank during the day so that his companions would follow his example and not fast while travelling. He did not fast on any subsequent day until he reached Makkah.

The army continued its march until it reached a place called Marr al-Ẓahrān, not very far from Makkah, where it encamped. It was indeed remarkable that the Quraysh did not receive any intelligence until then of the Prophet's move. This is owing to the Prophet's prayer to God just before he embarked on this enterprise: "My Lord, let the Quraysh receive no news of us until we take them by surprise in their own land." Nevertheless, the Quraysh were uneasy. They realized that the Prophet was bound to take some action. They knew that he was always positive in his attitude to events. He would not stand idle while his allies were treacherously massacred. Hence they were sending people outside to gather information, but the information they received was far from accurate.

The Prophet and his army encamped at Marr al-Ẓahrān in the evening. The Prophet ordered his companions to light fires. His strategy now was to win the psychological war in the hope that that would avert a full-scale battle. Therefore, every single soldier lit a fire.

One should try to imagine 10,000 fires being lit in the valley where the Muslims encamped. Should any person be sent by the Quraysh to gather intelligence, the sight of those fires would drive him fast to warn the people of Makkah against the approaching danger. There was one man in the Muslim camp who realized that the Quraysh's cause was hopeless unless they negotiated new terms with the Prophet. That man was none other than al-ʿAbbās, the Prophet's uncle, who had joined him only a few days earlier. Al-ʿAbbās realized that the only course open to the Quraysh was to surrender and accept the Prophet's verdict, whatever it might be. Should the Quraysh do that, the Prophet would be more inclined to spare them any humiliation. Al-ʿAbbās decided to send a message to the Quraysh urging them to come forward and ask the Prophet for a peaceful accommodation.

One must differentiate here between al-ʿAbbās's decision and the letter sent by Ḥāṭib ibn Abī Baltaʿah to warn the Quraysh. That letter was sent before the army had completed its preparations in order to march. The Quraysh would have had adequate time to prepare for a full-scale battle. Now the situation was different. The Prophet did not mind the Quraysh knowing that his aim was Makkah; that was the reason for the lighting of all those fires. Moreover, al-ʿAbbās's advice was sure to be well received, since only a few days earlier he had been on the friendliest of terms with all the chiefs of the Quraysh. It was almost certain that the Quraysh would act on al-ʿAbbās's advice. This is al-ʿAbbās's own account of the events of that night:

> When God's Messenger (peace be upon him) encamped at Marr al-Ẓahrān, I felt sad for the people of Makkah. I thought that if God's Messenger were to enter Makkah by force, before the Quraysh came forward to seek a peaceful accommodation with him, it would be the end of the Quraysh for the rest of time. I, therefore, mounted the Prophet's own mule and went as far as the valley of Arāk [which was known by this name

because Arāk trees were plentiful there]. I thought that I might find some woodman or shepherd or some other person whom I might ask to go to Makkah and tell its people of the location where the Prophet had encamped and give them my advice to come forward and seek security for their city before he entered it by force. It was God's will that Abū Sufyān ibn Ḥarb, the leader of the Quraysh, went out that night in the company of Ḥakīm ibn Ḥizām and Budayl ibn Warqā', to gather intelligence and to try to find some traveller who might have some news or some other information. I was still going on my way, riding the Prophet's mule, when I heard a conversation between Abū Sufyān and Budayl ibn Warqā'. Abū Sufyān said: "I have never seen such fire and such a great army." Budayl ibn Warqā' answered him: "This must be the tribe of Khuzāʿah with the fire of war urging them from within." [This was a reference to the raid launched on the Khuzāʿah, the Prophet's allies, which started all these events. The Khuzāʿah was expected to seek revenge against the Quraysh and its allies, the Bakr.] Abū Sufyān rejoined: "The Khuzāʿah are far too small to be able to raise such an army and to have such fires."

I recognized Abū Sufyān by his voice, and called him by his other nickname, Abū Ḥanẓalah. He recognized me and said: "Abū al-Faḍl? What brings you here?" I replied: "Matters are grave indeed, Abū Sufyān. This is God's Messenger (peace be upon him) with his people. The Quraysh are doomed indeed." He said: "What can we do, my dear friend?" I said: "I am sure that if he were to take you captive, he would have you beheaded. Mount behind me on this mule and I will take you to God's Messenger and ensure your safety."

Let Me Kill God's Enemy

Thus Abū Sufyān was now heading towards a face-to-face meeting with the Prophet, the man he was trying with all his power to defeat. He realized that his was the weaker position by far. Al-ʿAbbās's narrative continues:

> He mounted behind me while his two companions went back. Every time I passed a group of Muslims by their fires they wondered who was moving across their positions. Each time they let us pass when they recognized that I was riding the Prophet's mule. I then passed by the fire of ʿUmar ibn al-Khaṭṭāb and he said: "Who is it?" and came forward. When he realized that Abū Sufyān was riding behind me, he said: "Abū Sufyān, God's enemy. Praise be to God, Who has brought you here with no treaty or promise to save you." He ran towards the Prophet's tent. The mule also started to run and it passed him by a short distance. I dismounted quickly and entered the Prophet's tent. ʿUmar came in right behind me and said: "Messenger of God, this is Abū Sufyān, God's enemy. God has handed him to us with no treaty or agreement to spare him. Allow me to chop his head off." I interposed: "Messenger of God, I have extended protection to him." I then sat down to speak to the Prophet and was determined not to allow anyone else to spoil my aim.

Apparently, there was some heated discussion between al-ʿAbbās and ʿUmar concerning the fate of Abū Sufyān, with ʿUmar insisting that he should be executed. Al-ʿAbbās, who was very new to the Muslim society and did not recognize how Islam radically reshaped the loyalties of its followers, said to ʿUmar: "I swear, ʿUmar, that had Abū Sufyān been a man from ʿAdiy [ʿUmar's own clan in the Quraysh], you would have said something else. You know, however, that he belongs to the clan of ʿAbd Manāf."

ʿUmar's reply was that of a person whose ties and loyalties have been totally remoulded by Islam: "Do not jump to any conclusions, al-ʿAbbās. When you embraced Islam I was happier than I would have been had al-Khaṭṭāb [ʿUmar's own father] embraced Islam. This is only because I know that the Prophet is more pleased with you being a Muslim than he would have been with al-Khaṭṭāb becoming a Muslim."

When the discussion became prolonged, with both al-ʿAbbās and ʿUmar insisting on their respective views, the Prophet ordered his uncle to take Abū Sufyān to his tent, where he was to stay that night, and to bring him back to him in the morning.

Abū Sufyān stayed with al-ʿAbbās that night. At dawn, when the Muslim soldiers started making ablutions in preparation for their prayers, Abū Sufyān shivered with fear. He asked al-ʿAbbās what they were doing. Al-ʿAbbās explained that they were preparing for prayers. When they prayed, led by the Prophet, Abū Sufyān watched in amazement as he saw all the Muslims bowing in prayers when the Prophet bowed, and prostrating themselves when he prostrated himself. He said to his interlocuter: "Al-ʿAbbās, they are always doing his bidding?" Al-ʿAbbās answered: "Yes, indeed. Were he to bid them to stop eating and drinking, they would obey him."

One report suggests that when the Prophet made his ablutions, many a Muslim tried to catch the drops of water which dripped off his face and hands and rub their own faces with it. Abū Sufyān remarked to al-ʿAbbās: "I have never seen any king or emperor being treated like this."

That night must have been highly momentous in shaping Abū Sufyān's decision on what course to follow in the next few decisive hours. He must have reflected on his earlier mission to Madinah, which was a complete failure. That trip, however, gave him an insight into the feelings of the Muslim community towards the Quraysh. The very people whom he had reason to believe would be concerned about the fate of the Quraysh were not prepared to lift a finger in order to help them escape punishment for their unwarranted treacherous act. Now he saw with his own eyes, and heard with his own ears, that the Muslims were in no mood to compromise. His head was demanded as an initial payment of the price of the Quraysh's treachery. On the other hand, Abū Sufyān witnessed some aspects of the ties which united the Muslim community. He saw that the Muslims were very happy with their new faith and recognized that God had bestowed on them His grace when He sent Muhammad with His message to them. None of them had any doubts about the justice of their cause. Moreover, love was the predominant sentiment in the Muslim camp. All the Muslims loved one another, and the Prophet was dearer to any one of them than his own parents or children. Indeed, they loved the Prophet more than they loved themselves.

Second Meeting with the Prophet

To Abū Sufyān, such feelings were perhaps incomprehensible, but they were very real indeed. Their significance, however, stared him in the face. He realized that the Quraysh were no match for the Muslims in spirit or in material force. All these thoughts must have been present in Abū Sufyān's mind as he was taken the following morning by al-ʿAbbās for his second meeting with the Prophet.

The first question the Prophet put to Abū Sufyān, according to al-ʿAbbās's own account of their conversation was: "Abū Sufyān, is it not time for you to realize that there is no deity other than God?"

Abū Sufyān's reply was both conciliatory and to the point: "How forbearing, generous and kind you are! By God, had there been any deity alongside God, he would have been of some use to me by now."

Since this was the first essential of Islam, the Prophet's second question was aimed at establishing the second: "Is it not time for you to realize that I am God's Messenger?"

Again Abū Sufyān's answer was both frank and direct: "How forbearing, generous and kind you are! On this point, I still have some doubts."

Abū Sufyān summed up, in this answer, the reason for much of the hostility with which Islam was received by the Quraysh. Their leaders could not bring themselves to accept the fact that God might choose one of His servants to deliver His message to mankind. It was obvious that any person chosen for this task would command a position of great honour throughout his life and for the rest of time. Hence they begrudged any person such an honour. This is perfectly understandable if people choose to apply their own standards to judge God's actions, but no man may question God's actions by any standards. In their tribal society, which gave infinitely greater importance to honour, it was only natural that those who competed for honours – namely the Quraysh chiefs – would take some time before they accepted the fact that someone else was chosen by God to deliver His message. Abū Sufyān was one of those, and his reluctance to accept that Muhammad was God's Messenger was the cause of many of the battles recounted in this record of the Prophet's life.

Al-ʿAbbās realized the sort of thoughts and feelings which were in Abū Sufyān's mind. He wanted to remind him that his position was untenable unless he accepted the facts as they were. He said to him: "Come on, man. Declare your acceptance of Islam and make it clear that you believe that there is no deity but God and that Muhammad is God's Messenger, before you are beheaded."

Abū Sufyān was grateful for that reminder and he made the declaration which brought him into the fold of Islam. Thus the Quraysh's leader became a Muslim and it was left to him to try to secure a peaceful outcome of the confrontation. It was clear to him that he must play his role well in order to spare his people a military defeat. The Prophet, however, made it clear that he still viewed the Quraysh's treachery very seriously, but he would rather see a peaceful end to the conflict.

Al-ʿAbbās was still playing the role of mediator. He wanted Abū Sufyān to go back with something for the Quraysh and something for himself, in order to ensure that there would be no going back on what had already been achieved. Al-ʿAbbās pointed out to the Prophet that Abū Sufyān was a man who coveted honour. It was bound to be very useful if he was seen to go back to his people with honour. The Prophet accepted al-ʿAbbās's plea and said: "He who enters Abū Sufyān's home is safe."

This was a special treatment of Abū Sufyān, making his home a place where anyone from Makkah could be safe. Abū Sufyān, however, wanted to ensure the safety of all the Quraysh. He said: "How many people can be accommodated in my home?" The Prophet then said: "And he who enters the Kaʿbah is safe."

Abū Sufyān again expressed his view that the Kaʿbah could not accommodate very many people. The Prophet added: "And he who enters the mosque is safe." Abū Sufyān again asked: "How many can be accommodated in the mosque?" The Prophet added: "And he who stays in his home, with his door locked, is safe."

Abū Sufyān was pleased and said: "This is certainly more than sufficient." He was now ready to go back to his people to inform them of the results of his negotiations. The Prophet, however, wanted to ensure that Abū Sufyān would have no second thoughts about the Quraysh's surrender. He wanted him to go back with the clear view that any military confrontation was bound to result in much bloodshed and a humiliating defeat for the Quraysh. He, therefore, asked his uncle, al-ʿAbbās, to stand with Abū Sufyān at the bottom of the valley to watch the Muslim army as it resumed its march towards Makkah. In other words, he wanted Abū Sufyān to have a very clear view of the Muslims' strength.[6]

A Special Parade

As Abū Sufyān and al-ʿAbbās stood at the bottom of the valley to watch the Muslim army marching, Abū Sufyān was highly impressed by their strength. The units and divisions were made according to tribes. Each tribe constituted its own division. As they passed by, Abū Sufyān asked al-ʿAbbās about every tribe. When al-ʿAbbās answered: this is Sulaym or Muzaynah, or some other tribe, Abū Sufyān would say that he was not concerned about Sulaym or Muzaynah, or any tribe al-ʿAbbās named. Still, the numerical strength was there to see. At the rear marched the Prophet himself at the head of his 'green battalion' composed of the Muhājirīn and the Anṣār. They were all wearing their armour. Only their eyes were visible through their head armour.

Abū Sufyān asked: "Al-ʿAbbās, who are these?" He answered: "This is God's Messenger at the head of the Muhājirīn and the Anṣār." Abū Sufyān rejoined: "None can stand up to the force of this battalion. Abū al-Faḍl, your nephew has certainly acquired a great kingdom!" Al-ʿAbbās reminded him of the facts: "Abū Sufyān, he is a Prophet, not a king." Abū Sufyān replied: "Oh yes, indeed."

When the army had marched, al-ʿAbbās advised Abū Sufyān to make haste and go to his people with the Prophet's message. Abū Sufyān was overwhelmed by what he saw in the Muslim camp. He realized that the Muslim army was like a hurricane which would sweep everything before it, should anything try to resist it. He had no doubt in his mind that there was only one way to save the Quraysh: namely, surrender. Realizing that there was no time to waste, he proceeded as fast as he could.

Back in Makkah, people were restless, having heard during the night from Abū Sufyān's two companions that the Muslim army was approaching. They were gathered in groups all over the place when Abū Sufyān arrived. As they saw him, they ran to him to enquire what news he brought. Abū Sufyān had no time for long explanations. He wanted everyone to understand fully that the fall of Makkah was imminent and that resistance was of no avail. He shouted as loud as he could: "People of Quraysh, Muhammad is approaching at the head of an army for which you are no match. He who enters Abū Sufyān's house is safe..."

Hind bint ʿUtbah, Abū Sufyān's own wife, was stunned as she heard his words. She was a woman who had thus far harboured an unabating grudge against the Prophet and the Muslims ever since her father, brother and uncle were killed at Badr. As long as the two camps continued in their hostility, she would remain prominent among those who advocated a very hard line against the Muslims. She rushed to Abū Sufyān, took hold of his moustache and said: "Kill this good-for-nothing fat man. Confound you as a leader."

Abū Sufyān was not to be distracted from what he considered to be his most important duty which made him the saviour of Makkah. He said to his people: "Do not let this woman delude you. You are going to face something for which you are no match. He who goes into Abū Sufyān's house is safe..." He was interrupted here by people saying to him: "Confound you! Of what avail would your house be to us?" He continued: "He who enters the mosque is safe, and he who stays in his own home, with his door locked, will be safe."[7]

The message was absolutely clear. Everyone in Makkah realized its validity. People, therefore, dispersed. Some went to the mosque, the majority went to their homes, while a few went to Abū Sufyān's home. An air of fear spread through Makkah. The fighters who were held in awe by all the Arabs, before the advent of Islam, were not to be seen. They remained behind closed doors, while those inside the mosque watched with fear in their hearts.

Entry in Four Columns

As his army reached the outskirts of Makkah, the Prophet split it into four divisions, each entering Makkah from one side so that the whole city would be in their grip at the same time. Saʿd ibn ʿUbādah and his son Qays ibn Saʿd were at the head of the division entering from the east. Abū ʿUbaydah ʿĀmir ibn al-Jarrāḥ was leading the division entering from the west, with the Prophet himself in that division. Al-Zubayr ibn al-ʿAwwām led the Muhājirīn and the Anṣār as they entered from the north, where they were to raise the banner of the Muslims at al-Ḥajūn. Khālid ibn al-Walīd commanded the forces entering Makkah from the south. All commanders were under strict orders not to start fighting unless they were attacked. The Prophet was very keen not to shed blood in Makkah – not only because Makkah was his home town and its people were his own tribe, but also because Makkah was, and still remains, a sacred city where all creatures should be safe.

It must have been a great moment for every single soldier in that army, particularly for those who had accepted Islam in its early years and taken part in its long struggle ever since those days when the Muslims were a small force taken lightly by most people around them until they had gained their new position of supremacy in Arabia. Saʿd ibn ʿUbādah, the chief of the Anṣār, was one such man. At that moment when he was entering Makkah at the head of one of the four divisions of the Muslim army, he must have had images of those days of long struggle against the Quraysh, which did everything in its power to suppress Islam. He must have felt that it was now time for revenge against those who forced the Prophet to seek shelter away from his home town. Those who were not prepared to listen to God's Messenger as he warned them against incurring God's anger and called on them to accept the faith which was certain to bring them happiness in this life and in the life to come must be, Saʿd felt, prepared to reap the fruits of their misdeeds. Hence, he shouted:

"This is the day of the great clash. This is the day when the sanctuary [meaning Makkah] is overrun."

This was reported to the Prophet, who feared that Saʿd might be so carried away by the occasion that he would start killing the Quraysh people. The Prophet was keen not to shed a drop of blood, if that was at all possible, so he replaced Saʿd at the command of that division with his own son, Qays ibn Saʿd.

The four divisions of the Muslim forces marched into Makkah. The Prophet himself was overwhelmed by the great favour God granted him. Only eight years ago he had had to flee from this very city, with a great reward on his head. Now, his forces were entering the same city, the most powerful in Arabia, and meeting no resistance. He bowed his head very low as he entered. It was something unparalleled in history. No conqueror would march into his enemy's capital showing humility. Conquerors would be elated with their achievements, drunk with their feeling of power. The Prophet, on the other hand, felt that it was all achieved by the grace of God. Hence he was very thankful and he manifested his gratitude. He bowed until his head nearly touched the back of his she-camel, reciting all the time the *Sūrah* entitled *al-Fatḥ* or The Conquest.

One division of the Muslim army, which was commanded by Khālid ibn al-Walīd, was attacked by a group of Quraysh people who felt that they could not allow the city to fall without a fight. Khālid had to reply in kind. Those Makkans, however, were no match for his division. Over 20 Quraysh men were killed for the loss of two Muslim soldiers.

When the Prophet heard the news, he was very angry. He said: "Have I not given clear orders to all units not to fight?" He was told that Khālid was attacked by the Makkans first and had to fight back. The Prophet said: "Whatever God brings is good."[8]

Makkah: The Islamic City

The Prophet declined to use any house in Makkah. A tent was put up for him in al-Ḥajūn. When the authority of the Muslim army was fully established in Makkah, the Prophet went straight to the Kaʿbah, riding his she-camel. When he arrived there, he touched the black stone with a short stick he was carrying and raised his voice, saying: *Allah-u-Akbar*, which means "God is most supreme." The Muslims repeated what he said and their shouting resounded all over Makkah. The Prophet started his *ṭawāf* on his she-camel, touching the Black Stone with his stick every time he finished one round. When he had completed his seven rounds, he dismounted and prayed two *rakʿahs* at Maqām Ibrahīm, which was the place used by the Prophet Abraham for worship after he had built the Kaʿbah. He moved on to Zamzam, where he drank some water and renewed his ablutions. The Muslims around him were competing to gather the drops of water from his face and hands. Those of the unbelievers who were present were amazed. They exclaimed: "We have never heard of a king enjoying any comparable measure of love from his people!"

The Prophet then called in ʿUthmān ibn Ṭalḥah, who kept the keys of the Kaʿbah. ʿUthmān opened the Kaʿbah for the Prophet, who went inside and prayed two *rakʿahs*. When he had finished, he stood at the door of the Kaʿbah and made a long speech clarifying a number of rulings. He opened his speech by praising God for His blessings:

> There is no deity other than God, who has fulfilled His promise, supported His servant and defeated the confederate tribes on His own. No practice of pride or privilege nor any revenge or claim to any property is valid except that of the care of the Kaʿbah and the provision of drinking water to pilgrims. People of Quraysh, God has taken away from you the passionate pride of ignorance which made you attach great value and honour to your ancestors and value them highly. All people are the descendants of Adam, and Adam was created from clay.

He then recited the Qur'ānic verse: "Mankind, We have created you all from one male and one female so that you may know one another. The most honourable among you is the most God-fearing." (49: 13)

He then addressed the Quraysh and asked them: "What sort of judgement do you think I am going to pass against you?" They replied:

"A benevolent one. You are an honourable brother and the son of an honourable brother of ours." He said: "You may go free. You are all pardoned."[9]

ʿAlī, the Prophet's cousin, came to him with the key of the Kaʿbah in his hand and made this request: "Messenger of God, give us the privilege of looking after the Kaʿbah in addition to our present one of providing drinking water for pilgrims." The Prophet refused and called ʿUthmān ibn Ṭalḥah. He handed him his key back and said: "This is a day of honesty, when promises are honoured."

The pardon granted by the Prophet to the people of Makkah was a general pardon which included all those who fought against him in the battles which had taken place between the Quraysh and the Muslims. Before entering Makkah, the Prophet had given special orders to the commanders of all four divisions that certain people he named were to be killed, even if they were found hiding under the coverings of the Kaʿbah itself. It is well known that the Kaʿbah has a special sanctity which means that any human being or animal is not to be harmed within its precincts. Hence, for the Prophet to issue such orders meant that those people had committed certain crimes which could not be pardoned. Indeed, not even the sanctity of the Kaʿbah was a reason for delaying the administration of their punishment. Those people, however, met different ends.

The Death List

One of them was ʿAbdullāh ibn Khaṭal. He used to be a Muslim. The Prophet once sent him to collect *zakāt* from people who lived far away. He travelled with another man and a servant of his who was a Muslim. At one stage on the way they stopped. He gave the servant orders to slaughter a big goat and prepare food while he himself went to sleep. When he woke up, he discovered that the servant had not done anything. He killed his servant and, fearing the Prophet's punishment, reverted to idolatry. He also had two slave girls who used to sing for him and for his companions songs full of abuse of the Prophet. The Prophet's instructions specified that the two slave girls should also be killed. The man was killed as he was actually holding on to the coverings of the Ka'bah. Abū Barzah al-Aslamī and Saīd ibn Ḥurayth al-Makhzūmī killed him along with one of his slave girls. The other managed to flee until someone sought a special pardon for her from the Prophet, which he granted.

Al-Ḥuwayrith ibn Nuqaydh ibn Wahb was another such person. He used to do his utmost to cause bodily harm to the Prophet when he was in Makkah. Moreover, it is reported that when al-'Abbās, the Prophet's uncle, took Fāṭimah and Umm Kulthūm, the Prophet's daughters, to Madinah to join their father in the early days after the Prophet's emigration to Madinah, this man deliberately caused the camel they were riding to jump and they fell off. It was 'Alī ibn Abī Ṭālib who killed him.

Another person was Miqyas ibn Hubābah, whose brother, Hishām, was killed in the expedition against the tribe of al-Muṣṭalaq by a Muslim soldier who thought he was an idolater. Miqyas came to Madinah pretending to be a Muslim and asked to be paid blood money for the accidental killing of his brother. When he was paid he assaulted the person who had killed his brother and killed him. He then returned to Makkah to live as an idolater. When the Prophet named him among those not to be pardoned, he was actually killed as he was passing between the two hills of al-Ṣafā and al-Marwah.

Yet another person was 'Abdullāh ibn Sa'd ibn Abī Sarḥ, who had adopted Islam and was employed by the Prophet to write the Qur'ān as its verses were revealed. He later turned away from Islam and went to Makkah to live as an idolater. When he realized that he had been named by the Prophet among those sentenced to death, he sought refuge in the house of 'Uthmān ibn 'Affān, who was his brother having been breastfed with him by the same woman. When the Prophet called on the people of Makkah to embrace Islam and to pledge loyalty to him, 'Uthmān brought 'Abdullāh ibn Sa'd to the Prophet and requested him to accept 'Abdullāh's pledge of loyalty. It is said that the Prophet raised his eyes to him and stopped short of accepting 'Abdullāh's pledge. It was repeated three times, and finally the Prophet accepted that. When he left with 'Uthmān, it is said that the Prophet asked those of his companions who were around him: "Was there not among you a wise man to kill that person when you saw me declining to accept his pledge?" They replied: "How could we make sure of what was in your mind without you giving us a signal with your eye?" The Prophet said: "It is not for a Prophet to make such signals."

ʿAbdullāh ibn Saʿd ibn Abū Sarḥ, however, became a good Muslim and was assigned some missions by ʿUmar. In the reign of ʿUthmān he was among the commanders of Muslim armies engaged in the conquest of North Africa.

A woman called Sarah, who used to cause the Prophet considerable harm when he was in Makkah, was also among those condemned by him. Some people, however, sought a special pardon for her and the Prophet granted that. She lived until the time of ʿUmar ibn al-Khaṭṭāb, when she was killed in a riding accident.[10]

Purging the Heart of an Old Foe

Another man on the death list was ʿIkrimah ibn Abī Jahl. ʿIkrimah's father had been the worst enemy of Islam ever since its very early days. Abū Jahl continued to do his utmost to harm the cause of Islam until he was killed at the Battle of Badr. His son, ʿIkrimah, was among the leading figures in the Quraysh and continued to be very hostile to the Prophet's message. When the Muslim army entered Makkah, he fled to Yemen. His wife, Umm Ḥakīm bint al-Ḥārith, became a Muslim. She went to the Prophet and asked him to pardon ʿIkrimah and grant him safety. He granted her request. She then followed him to Yemen and brought him back to the Prophet when he adopted Islam.

It is also reported that when ʿIkrimah fled, he managed to get on a boat. The boat was soon passing through very heavy seas which threatened to capsize it. Everyone on board realized that there was nothing they could do to save themselves, unless they sought God's help. Some of them said to the others: "Purge your hearts of any false concepts. Your idols cannot give you any help whatsoever in this situation." ʿIkrimah thought to himself: "If nothing but pure faith can save me in the sea, nothing else can save me on dry land." Then he made this pledge: "My Lord, I pledge to You that if You save me from what I am passing through now, I will go to Muhammad and put my hand in his hand, and I shall certainly find him benevolent and forgiving." He survived that ordeal, went to the Prophet and declared himself to be a Muslim.

ʿIkrimah was certainly sincere in his pledge. He subsequently did everything in his power to promote the cause of Islam. He was one of the commanders sent by Abū Bakr to fight those who rebelled against the Muslim state. He moved on from one battle to another in defence of the cause of Islam to compensate for his fighting Islam before the fall of Makkah.[11]

Umm Hāni' was a cousin of the Prophet. She was the daughter of Abū Ṭālib, his uncle. She was married to Hubayrah ibn Abī Wahb of the Makhzūm clan. She reported that when the Prophet encamped on the outskirts of Makkah, two men related to her husband sought refuge in her house. They were al-Ḥārith ibn Hishām and Zuhayr ibn Abū Umayyah. Her brother ʿAlī followed them into her house, threatening to kill them. She locked them in and went straight to the Prophet in his camp. She found him having full ablutions (that is, a complete bath) using water in a bowl with traces of dough in it. His daughter Fāṭimah was holding his robe with her hands stretched out to provide a screen for him. When he had finished his ablutions he took the robe and covered himself. He then prayed eight *rakʿahs*, stopping between each pair. According to Umm Hāni', it was mid-morning and his prayers were very short. When he had finished his prayers, he welcomed Umm Hāni' and asked her if she wanted anything from him. She told him about the two men and that she had extended protection to them. He said to her: "We will protect those to whom you have extended protection and we will ensure their safety as you have promised them safety. He [i.e. ʿAlī] must not kill them."[12]

Scholars differ as to the prayers of the Prophet at that time. Many of them think they were the mid-morning *Sunnah* known as *Ḍuḥā*. It is perhaps more accurate to say that they were the *Sunnah* of victory. There are a number of reports about what the Prophet did when he went for his *ṭawāf* in the Kaʿbah. One report suggests that when he entered the Kaʿbah he found there a number of pictures of angels and a picture showing Abraham drawing lots. Referring to the unbelievers, the Prophet said: "Confound them. They have made our great man draw lots. What has he got to do with drawing lots?"

He then recited the Qur'ānic verse: "Abraham was neither a Jew nor a Christian, but a man of pure faith who submitted himself to God. Never was he an unbeliever." (3: 67) The Prophet then ordered all those pictures to be rubbed out. Another report suggests that the Prophet ordered the pictures to be removed before he went into the Kaʿbah. ʿUmar used a wet robe to rub them out. When the Prophet went into the Kaʿbah, none of those pictures remained.[13]

Flimsy Idols

One report suggests that when the Prophet entered Makkah, there were 360 idols on and around the Kaʿbah. He had a stick in his hand and he pointed it at those idols. If he touched one idol in the back with his stick, the idol fell on its face; and if he touched it with his stick in the front, it fell on its back. The Prophet kept repeating: "The truth is triumphant; falsehood is vanquished. Falsehood will always be vanquished."[14]

These reports combine to confirm that the Prophet's main preoccupation as he entered Makkah was to remove all signs of idolatry and replace them with signs of monotheism in its purest form – that is, the worship of God alone.

Notes

1. Ibn Hishām, *al-Sīrah al-Nabawiyyah*, Dār al-Qalam, Beirut, Vol. 4, pp. 31-37. Also, al-Wāqidī, *Kitāb al-Maghāzī*, Oxford University Press, 1996, Vol.2, pp. 784-792.
2. Ibn Hishām, op.cit., Vol. 4, pp. 37-39. Also, al-Wāqidī, op.cit., pp. 792-795.
3. Ibn Hishām, op.cit., pp. 39-40.
4. Ibid., pp. 40-41. Also, al-Wāqidī, op.cit., pp. 797-798.
5. Ibn Hishām, op.cit., pp. 42-43.
6. Ibid., pp. 44-46.
7. Ibid., pp. 46-47.
8. Ibid., pp. 70-72. Also, al-Wāqidī, op.cit., Vol. 2, pp. 825-826.
9. Ibn Hishām, op.cit., pp. 54-55.
10. Ibid., pp. 51-53.
11. Al-Wāqidī, op.cit., pp. 850-853.
12. Ibn Hishām, op.cit., pp. 53-54.
13. Ibid., p. 55.
14. Ibid., p. 59.

35

A Conquest of Hearts

HISTORY BOOKS RELATE the events which led to the surrender of Makkah to the Prophet in a chapter entitled 'The Conquest of Makkah'. The word 'conquest' suggests a hard military battle, yet there was very little fighting to speak of in that particular conquest. Indeed, it is more appropriate to speak of the conquest of the people of Makkah. That was the real objective of the campaign.

What that campaign achieved was unparalleled in history. The story was that of the homecoming of a person who was rejected by his own people, driven out of his home town with a rich reward on his head, but was able to flee and establish a base elsewhere. He then acquired power and moved gradually to a position of overall supremacy in the land surrounding the area from which he was driven out. Would not that person entertain visions of what sort of vengeance he would finally inflict on those who drove him out of his home town once they had fallen into his hands? History books are full of reports and stories of atrocities committed by conquerors after subjugating their old enemies. Such atrocities were never the monopoly of one race of humankind in any period. The process begins immediately after victory has been achieved: a period of lawlessness in which everything of value is looted; killings, rape and theft become perfectly acceptable when committed by the victors; summary execution of war criminals; courts formed for war crimes committed by the vanquished, but not by the victor ... the list is endless. The ferocity of all such actions is much greater when personal grudges are involved.

Yet the idea of vengeance was far from the Prophet's mind. Indeed, his thoughts moved in the opposite direction. He was thinking hard about how to reduce casualties, how to preserve the lives of the people of Makkah and how to achieve victory without bloodshed. Two years earlier, when the Prophet and his companions had tried to visit Makkah for offering an *ʿUmrah*, and when he had realized that the Quraysh were not going to allow him inside Makkah, he had declared his readiness to accept any formula which ensured that no blood was shed. One would have thought, however, that the fact that the Quraysh violated the peace agreement which was made between the two sides at al-Ḥudaybiyah would have exhausted the patience of the Prophet and his companions to the extent that they would be in no mood to forgive the Quraysh's treachery. The Prophet was not a person to leave matters unresolved when they called for decisive action. He would not overlook hostile actions if that would result in giving the enemy a feeling that the Muslims were weak. Nor would he resort to the use of force where a kind gesture would be sure to bring better results. Hence, the Prophet was certain that the Quraysh should be brought face to face with the consequences of their treachery. The price they would be made to pay, however, would depend on how they viewed that price in that particular situation.

Avoiding Bloodshed

One thing which was abundantly clear right from the start was that the Prophet wanted to avoid bloodshed as much as he could. As his army began to prepare, he prayed God to enable him to take the Quraysh by surprise in their own land. The purpose of that prayer was not the launching of a surprise attack which would have resulted in mass killings among the Quraysh in return for very few casualties among the Muslims. Rather, the Prophet wanted to face the Quraysh with a situation in which they would feel themselves no match for him. In such a situation, they might choose not to put up any resistance and victory for the Muslims would be achieved without bloodshed.

This was abundantly clear when Abū Sufyān, the Quraysh's leader, was brought to the Prophet. Had Prophet Muhammad been an ordinary commander or leader of any victorious army or nation, Abū Sufyān would have paid dearly for his past hostility to the cause of Islam, which had cost the Muslims over the years many martyrs and several war campaigns. Instead, Abū Sufyān was pardoned and sent back to his people with a position of honour. His house was made a haven of safety for anyone who wished to stay there.

When the Prophet heard that one of his commanders, Saʿd ibn ʿUbādah, was threatening revenge, he replaced him with his son. He made it absolutely clear to all his commanders and his soldiers that they were not to fight unless attacked. But who were those people whose lives the Prophet was keen to spare? They were indeed the very people who turned him out of their city after repeatedly plotting to destroy his life. When he called on them to believe in God they answered, as the Qur'ān tells us: "Our hearts are insulated against what you are calling on us to believe in, our ears are sealed, and a heavy curtain is drawn between you and us." They stopped at nothing in their hostility to him personally and to his cause. They accused him of being a liar, a sorcerer and a madman. They schemed against him and urged others to be hostile to him and to his companions. They forged alliances to meet his peaceful call with the force of arms. When he gained complete victory and all of them were at his mercy, he was much more merciful to them than they dared hope. At the height of his victory, the Prophet did not forget for a single moment the fact that he was a Prophet and that his message came first. Those very people were there to be won over to the cause of Islam, and that was his top priority. What could win them over more than a general pardon, which he readily gave? All that was required of anyone to be safe was to stay at home.

Even the Most Hostile

Even those individuals whom the Prophet sentenced to death in any circumstances were not all killed. Any one of them who came to him, in any way, regretting his earlier misdeeds was given a free pardon. One must not forget that those people were sentenced to death because they had committed unpardonable crimes. But in spite of those crimes, a pardon was not difficult to arrange once they showed their willingness to live with the new situation.

To appreciate the attitude of the Prophet fully, it is worth reflecting on the following incident. As the Prophet was going round the Kaʿbah in his *ṭawāf*, a man from the Quraysh called Fuḍālah ibn ʿUmayr was watching him with a burning grudge in his heart. He thought to himself: "Why do I not kill Muhammad now that he feels safe? I do not care what happens to me afterwards if I can avenge our defeat?" With this thought in mind, Fuḍālah manoeuvred himself into a position which enabled him to walk right behind the Prophet. The Prophet suddenly turned to him and said: "Is that Fuḍālah?" The man answered, "Yes, it is Fuḍālah, Messenger of God." The Prophet asked him again: "What have you been saying to yourself?" Fuḍālah answered: "Nothing. I was only praising God." The Prophet laughed and said: "Seek God's forgiveness." He put his hand on Fuḍālah's chest and pressed it a little until he calmed down. Fuḍālah used to say later: "I swear by God that when he lifted his hand off my chest, there was no one on earth dearer to me than he was."

Apparently, Fuḍālah used to be a playboy. On the way home, he passed a woman with whom he had an illegitimate relationship. She invited him in, but he refused and told her that he was now a Muslim. He accepted the faith and believed in God alone, and renounced idolatrous worship.[1]

This symbolizes the Prophet's attitude. It was an attitude based on giving a complete, total pardon which erased all hostilities and all bad feelings. In this way, the Prophet won over the hearts of the Quraysh. It was only a matter of hours or days before they started to declare their acceptance of Islam. The maxim on which the Prophet's attitude was based is best expressed by the Qur'ānic verse: "A good deed and a bad one can never be alike. Repel the latter with the one which is best and you will find that the person with whom you have a long hostility behaving to you as an intimate friend." (41: 34) The Prophet's attitude pulled down all those barriers which stood between the Quraysh and Islam. The conquest of the hearts of the Quraysh was absolutely complete.

Every Individual Is Important

The Prophet was very eager to win every heart in Makkah. As already seen, he pardoned the majority of those people whom he had earlier sentenced to death for their unpardonable crimes. Indeed, he was keen to win over the very person who was contemplating his assassination. The Prophet's actions in Makkah suggest that he would have been prepared to sit with every individual to explain the message of Islam to him personally and show him the benefits of Islamic life. No military commander in the position of the Prophet, at the moment of his complete victory over his most hostile enemy, would have bothered himself about what might have happened to any individual soldier, officer or commander of the enemy army. But the Prophet cared for every single one, because he treated them as human beings to whom God's message was addressed.

Ṣafwān ibn Umayyah was one of the young generation of the Quraysh leaders. He was head of the clan of Jumaḥ. He nursed a deep grudge against the Prophet and the Muslims. At the Battle of Badr, Ṣafwān had lost his father and brother. At the Battle of Uḥud, he had lost his uncle. In order to have a good idea of how Ṣafwān felt his losses and nursed his grudges, it may be useful to remind ourselves of an incident which took place shortly after the Battle of Badr and which was related fully in its appropriate place (Chapter 18).

Ṣafwān sat down with an intimate friend of his called ʿUmayr ibn Wahb, speaking of their bereavement and mourning those who were killed at Badr. ʿUmayr, a young man full of enthusiasm, said to Ṣafwān: "Had it not been for the fact that I have young children who have no one to support them if I am killed and the fact that I am heavily in debt, I would have gone to Madinah and killed Muhammad. I have a good pretext to go near him. I have a brother whom the Muslims have taken prisoner and I would pretend that I want to negotiate his ransom." Ṣafwān jumped at the chance of having Muhammad killed in revenge for his father and brother. He pledged his word of honour to ʿUmayr that he would settle all his debts and look after his children as if they were his own if ʿUmayr would go to Madinah and try to kill Muhammad. This was all agreed in absolute secrecy.

Carrying out his plan, ʿUmayr was in Madinah in a few days, entering the mosque to meet the Prophet. When he mentioned his pretext for being there, the Prophet related to him word for word his secret conversation with Ṣafwān. ʿUmayr was overwhelmed and declared that no one but a messenger from God could have known his secret. He accepted Islam, remained in Madinah and fought with the Muslims in all subsequent major battles. Needless to say, Ṣafwān was more than furious when he heard of his friend's conversion to Islam.

ʿUmayr continued to wish his old friend well. When the Muslim army entered Makkah, his thoughts went to Ṣafwān, whom he hoped to find in a state of mind which would help him accept Islam. He was soon to be disappointed. When he enquired about his friend, he was told that he had made his way to Jeddah, where he planned to take a boat to Yemen. At that time, the Arabs viewed travelling by sea as extremely dangerous. But what was more dangerous for Ṣafwān in ʿUmayr's view was to remain hostile to Islam and to allow his personal grudges to blind him to its truth. ʿUmayr felt that he had to do his utmost to save his friend. He went straight to the Prophet and said: "Messenger of God, Ṣafwān ibn Umayyah is the chief of his clan. He has fled to save himself from you. However, he plans to risk himself in the sea. Could you please give me a guarantee of his safety, may God shower His blessings on you?" The Prophet granted ʿUmayr his request. ʿUmayr then asked him for a sign which he could give to Ṣafwān as a guarantee of his safety, and the Prophet gave him his own turban which he had on his head at the time when he entered Makkah.

Travelling at full speed, ʿUmayr managed to catch up with Ṣafwān just as he was boarding a boat. He spoke to him passionately: "Ṣafwān, may both my parents be sacrificed for your sake. [This was a phrase of endearment which was not meant literally.] Take care before you kill yourself. I have brought you a guarantee of safety from God's Messenger." Ṣafwān spoke in a defiant manner: "Leave me alone and do not speak to me, you liar." ʿUmayr, however, was not to be deterred. He continued with his passionate appeal: "Ṣafwān, I have come here after I have spoken to the man who is the best, the kindest, the most gracious and the most benevolent of all people. He is your cousin. You know you can share in his honour, power and kingdom." Needless to say, ʿUmayr was appealing to those feelings which were paramount in the mind of any noble Arab who had not yet accepted the message of Islam. Ṣafwān relented a little and said: "I fear for my life." ʿUmayr reassured him: "He is much too kind and clement to all people for you to fear for your life."

Realizing that travelling to Yemen did not offer him any great prospects and sensing the truth in what ʿUmayr had said, and that he truly had his interest at heart, Ṣafwān was persuaded that it was far better for him to go back with his old friend. ʿUmayr took him straight to the Prophet.

After ʿUmayr had greeted the Prophet, Ṣafwān said: "This man claims that you have guaranteed my safety." The Prophet answered: "He is telling the truth." Ṣafwān said: "Allow me, then, a period of two months to think my position over." The Prophet replied: "You have four months to think it over and make your own free choice."[2] Thus Ṣafwān ibn Umayyah was free to go about Makkah in absolute safety and under no obligation to join Islam. This was a personal gesture by the Prophet to let a sensible man make his own free choice. How this treatment was instrumental in winning Ṣafwān over to Islam will be illustrated later.

Makkah the Solid Base for Islam

The Prophet's attitude towards such individual cases was appropriate to the overall objective he had set for himself with regard to

Makkah – namely, that Makkah should become a solid base of Islam. The change over was to be complete. The city which housed the most ancient temple built for worshipping God alone must always remain a cornerstone in the structure of Islam and a base in which Muslims would always enjoy total security. For Makkah to be a Muslim city was to establish a strong link between Islam and former Divine religions and to make this link felt by every Muslim in every age. On the other hand, for Makkah to remain an un-Islamic city was unthinkable.

The Prophet was, therefore, working for a definite and most honourable aim. Moreover, he realized that God wanted him to win Makkah over, rather than to defeat the Quraysh in a military confrontation. It is generally agreed by Muslim scholars that two years earlier, at the time when the Prophet concluded the peace agreement at al-Ḥudaybiyah, he was acting on clear and direct instructions from God. For a certainty, God told the Muslims, shortly after the peace agreement was concluded against the express wishes of most of them, that had there been a confrontation between them and the unbelievers of Makkah, they would certainly have scored a remarkable victory. In the *Sūrah* which comments on the events of al-Ḥudaybiyah, God says: "Had the unbelievers fought against you, they would indeed have turned their backs in flight, and would have found none to protect them and none to bring them succour." (48: 22) What this meant in effect was that God was able to bring about the fall of Makkah into the hands of the Muslims two years earlier. All that was required was for the Prophet and the Muslims to stick to their rightful demands to be allowed to worship at the Kaʿbah. The Quraysh was bound to prevent them and an armed clash would then have been inevitable. That would have resulted, as God clearly states, in a total defeat for the Makkans. Nevertheless, God preferred to leave the unbelievers to rule in Makkah for another two years in order to bring about a far better result.

Considering these events with hindsight, one can appreciate the great wisdom which accompanied the Prophet's actions at al-Ḥudaybiyah and subsequently until the fall of Makkah into the hands of the Muslims. Had there been a military confrontation two years earlier, it would have left too many grudges for any real peace to be established between the Quraysh and the Muslims. Such a conquest would have been a conquest of a city, but not a conquest of hearts. What the Prophet achieved two years later was a conquest which brought about the total transformation of Makkah, from a city which was profoundly hostile to Islam to the city which has continued to be ever since, and will continue to be for ever, the solid base of Islam. That sort of victory could have been achieved only with the remarkable attitude shown by the Prophet to his old enemies: an attitude of clemency, love, mercy and a profound desire to show these old enemies the way to their own happiness. No ordinary human being could have behaved in such a manner at such a time, after such a long history of hostility. Muhammad was able to do so, because he was God's Messenger and Prophet.

Substituting Love for Hostility

To have a complete picture of what happened in those days in Makkah, it is important to consider how effective the Prophet's method was in achieving his purpose of winning the hearts of his former enemies.

For the previous 20 years or so, no one in Makkah, not even the most hostile and sworn enemy of Islam, could have denied that the Prophet treated all people with kindness and was keen to replace any hostility any person harboured towards Islam with friendship and loyality. It was equally true, however, that no one could have dreamed that the Prophet would have extended such a measure of unparalleled kind treatment to the people of Makkah. For 20 years, those people had nurtured an unabating hostility towards Islam, making every effort to suppress it and plotting time after time to kill the Prophet. For them to be pardoned *en masse* was beyond their wildest dreams. They certainly hoped that Muhammad would not scourge them with his vengeance, but that he spared their lives, guaranteed their safety, protected their properties and loved their children was far more than they had dared hope.

What the Prophet's treatment achieved was an instant change of attitude by every person in Makkah. Worry and fear for their own lives, families and children disappeared, to be replaced by a new look at Islam. It was not to be expected that people would immediately forget their past hostility, but it was reasonable to expect them to ask themselves: how did Islam change those Arabs who responded to the call of the Prophet? How did they achieve such an unparalleled degree of discipline? Why did they attach greater value to enforcing the commands of the Prophet than to looting a wealthy city which had fallen to them after a long history of hostility?

The people of Makkah looked at the Muslims as they prayed in congregation and admired their discipline and their dedication. They looked at the new bonds which Islam had cemented within the Muslim community and realized that pure love, for God's sake, was the bond which replaced all past loyalties in order to forge out of those Arab tribes a single community, united by its dedication to the cause of Islam.

Moreover, the people of Makkah were able to listen to the Qur'ān and consider the meaning of its verses objectively for the first time in their history. In the past, they used to make fun of the Qur'ān and told one another not to listen to it. Now that they were free from those chains which had restricted their thinking and fettered their minds, they were able to appreciate how profound and sublime the faith of Islam was in comparison to their pagan beliefs which made them worship idols made of stone and gold.

The Influence of a Unique Example

One can imagine that a great debate was taking place in the homes and meeting places of the Quraysh people in the days following the fall of their city to the Prophet. Those of the Quraysh leaders who were able to detach themselves from their past hostility to Islam and to look at it in the new light offered to them were quick to see that the best way to remedy their past wrong was to accept Islam and join the new call which was promising to change the whole world. Those who had relatives or friends among the Muslims, especially those of the Quraysh who had emigrated with the Prophet, were also in contact with them and were able to learn more about Islam.

Hence, many people started to come to the Prophet to declare their adoption of Islam. It was an individual process at first, but in a few days, the majority of the people of Makkah wanted to become Muslims. The Prophet, therefore, sat at the hill of al-Ṣafā, near the Kaʿbah, to accept their pledges of embracing Islam. Beneath him, ʿUmar ibn al-Khaṭṭāb was accepting the pledges of the Makkah people on behalf of the Prophet. They pledged to obey God and the Prophet as best as they could. No one was forced to come, but people realized that they had been in the wrong for too long, and that the wise course was for them to acknowledge their mistake and make amends. Some people wanted their pledges of loyalty to include a covenant to emigrate from Makkah in order to join the Prophet. Mujāshiʿ ibn Masʿūd, one of the Muhājirīn, brought his brother, Mujālid, to the Prophet and said: "Messenger of God, I have brought my brother so that you will accept his pledge to emigrate with the Muhājirīn."

The Prophet answered: "Emigration is now a thing of the past. Those who have emigrated, [that is, the Muhājirīn] have taken all its reward." Mujāshiʿ asked him: "What sort of pledge would you then accept from him?" He said: "I accept his pledge to embrace Islam, to be a true believer and to struggle for the cause of God."[3]

The Prophet made it clear to the people of Makkah that those who had emigrated with him – that is, the Muhājirīn – achieved a standard which could not be achieved by anyone else. They had left their home town in support of their faith when the cause of Islam was weak and threatened on all sides. Now that Islam was strong and people were joining it in large numbers every day, it was not possible for any new Muslim to achieve that standard. However, people could struggle and work hard for their faith so that more people might come to know of it and accept it.

When the Prophet had accepted the pledges of the men of Makkah to follow Islam, he met the Makkan women and accepted their pledges. The pledges of the women were a little more detailed. They had to pledge "not to ascribe divinity to anyone other than God, not to steal or commit adultery, not to kill their children and not to claim falsely that a child belongs to a certain father when it does not, and not to disobey the Prophet in anything reasonable he orders them."

In order to appreciate how relaxed the atmosphere in Makkah was when the Prophet accepted those pledges, and to be certain that these pledges were given freely, without any degree of coercion, one can quote this incident. Hind bint ʿUtbah was the wife of Abū Sufyān, the leader of Makkah. She was a passionate woman who nurtured unabated grudges against the Prophet and the Muslims. She had lost her father and brother at the Battle of Badr, and took revenge by arranging the killing of the Prophet's uncle at the Battle of Uḥud. When he was killed, she disfigured him, opened his stomach, took out his liver and tried to eat it raw. Now she came to the Prophet to pledge her loyalty to Islam. However, she hid her face so that he would not recognize her. She feared that he might want to avenge his uncle's death. Nevertheless, the atmosphere was relaxed and she was able to comment on every item in the pledge required of women.

When the Prophet said to the Makkan women: "Pledge to me that you will not ascribe Divinity to anyone other than God," Hind said: "You are certainly asking us to give you more than you asked the men." He continued: "And not to steal." Hind said: "I used to take some money from Abū Sufyān, little by little behind his back. I did not know whether that was permissible or not." Abū Sufyān, her husband, who was present, said: "Whatever you have taken in the past is yours." The Prophet said: "Then you are Hind bint ʿUtbah?" She answered: "Yes, indeed. Forgive the past, may God forgive you." The Prophet continued outlining the terms of the pledge: "And not to commit adultery." Hind said: "Messenger of God, would an honourable woman be an adulteress?"

When the Prophet mentioned the next item of the pledge: "And not to kill your children," she said: "We reared them from when they were young until they grew up, and then you and your companions killed them at Badr.' (ʿUmar ibn al-Khaṭṭāb chuckled merrily at this comment.)[4]

The Prophet then continued with the other terms of the pledge and instructed ʿUmar to accept their pledges. The Prophet never shook hands with a woman who was not his wife or a member of his immediate family.

The Prophet stayed nearly 20 days in Makkah, setting its affairs on a proper Islamic course. He wanted the city's change of character to be complete. He also took care to remove all appearances of idolatry from every place in Makkah. Already mentioned is the fact that he ordered the removal of all the idols in and around the Kaʿbah. Now he ordered that no one in Makkah should keep an idol in his home.[5] It was the habit of the people of Makkah to have in their homes idols which they would touch whenever they went out or came back, seeking their blessings. The people of Makkah carried out that order and all idols were broken. Hind bint ʿUtbah took an axe with which to break her idol. As she did so, she said: "We were deceived by you."[6]

The Prophet also sent several expeditions to the surrounding area to remove and break all the idols. Khālid ibn al-Walīd was dispatched at the head of a detachment of 30 horsemen to the valley of Nakhlah to destroy the idol known as 'al-ʿUzzā', the largest idol in the whole district. Khālid carried out the Prophet's orders and destroyed the home where the idol was kept. Its custodian was shouting at the top of his voice: "Al-ʿUzzā, show them your anger." But al-ʿUzzā was nothing more than a statue.[7]

ʿAmr ibn al-ʿĀṣ was sent with a detachment of Muslim forces to Hudhayl, where he destroyed its idol Suwāʿ. Its guard asked ʿAmr when he saw him approaching: "What do you want?" ʿAmr told him that he wanted to destroy Suwāʿ and the guardian tried to persuade him not to do so for his own safety. ʿAmr said to him: "You are still as ignorant as ever."[8]

Saʿīd ibn Zayd was sent to destroy another main idol, Manāt, which was worshipped by the tribes of Madinah before they became Muslims. Thus, the marks of idolatry were removed from Makkah and the surrounding area, and the majority of the people of Makkah became Muslims.[9]

The Quraysh had been the main tribe standing firm against Islam. Now that it had surrendered, would the forces hostile to Islam accept the Quraysh's defeat as their own? Or would they try to group and marshal their forces in order to stop the tide of Islam?

NOTES

1. Ibn Hishām, *al-Sīrah al-Nabawiyyah*, Dār al-Qalam, Beirut, Vol. 4, pp. 59-60.
2. Ibid., p. 60. Also al-Wāqidī, *Kitāb al-Maghāzī*, Oxford University Press, 1996, Vol. 2, pp. 853-854.
3. Ibn Kathīr, *al-Bidāyah wal-Nihāyah*, Maktabat al-Maʿārif, Beirut, Vol. 1, p. 320.
4. Ibid., pp. 319-320.
5. Ibn Sayyid al-Nās, *ʿUyūn al-Athar*, Dār al-Turāth, Madinah, 1996, p. 243.
6. Amīn Duwaydār, *Ṣuwar Min Ḥayāt al-Rasūl*, Dār al-Maʿārif, 4th edition, Cairo, p. 544.
7. Ibn Sayyid al-Nās, op.cit., p. 249.
8. Ibid.
9. Ibid., pp. 249-250.

36

Grouping for a Final Assault

MAKKAH'S FALL TO the Muslims was a great blow for all the unbelievers in Arabia. None of them could have imagined that the structure of disbelief had so rotted away from inside that it could no longer withstand a determined attack. In such a prolonged confrontation as took place in Arabia at that time, it was not to be imagined that once Makkah had fallen to the Muslims, all the unbelievers would lay down their arms. There were still major tribes in Arabia which maintained their stand in opposition to Islam. To them, the situation was not over yet, despite the fall of Makkah. They felt that they could muster a force large enough to defeat the Muslims.

One such major tribe was the Hawāzin, who lived in a mountainous area close to Ṭā'if. Ṭā'if itself was the most fertile area in Arabia and was where the idol called al-Lāt, the second largest idol of the Arabs after Hubal, was worshipped. Ṭā'if was also the home town of another major tribe called the Thaqīf.

Notables of the two tribes met for consultations. Their main worry was that Muhammad would inevitably turn against them now that he had overcome the Quraysh. They felt that their very identity was threatened. Muhammad was sure to change their religion, destroy their idols and impose his authority on them. None of this was a welcome prospect as far as they were concerned. Hence, they decided to take the initiative against the Muslims before the latter had had time to march towards them.

Hawāzin was the most active partner in this unholy alliance. Its leader, Mālik ibn ʿAwf, was a young man of immense courage. He tried hard to gather all the clans for this final assault. Several tribes joined in – the Nasr, Jusham, Saʿd ibn Bakr and groups of Hilāl. The notable absentees were the tribes of the Kaʿb and the Kilab. The allied forces of those tribes agreed to give the overall command to Mālik, as they admired his enthusiasm. But Mālik's enthusiasm was not coupled with any practical wisdom. This is evident from the following conversation between Mālik and an old man from Jusham called Durayd ibn al-Ṣummah, who was the sage of his tribe. Had Durayd been 20 years younger, he would in all probability have been the commander. Now that he was very old, his contribution was merely to give advice.

When the forces of Hawāzin and their allies encamped at a valley called Awṭās, Durayd said to Mālik: "You have now assumed the leadership of your people. This is a day which will have a bearing on the future. I hear noises of domestic animals, such as sheep and donkeys, and I hear young children crying. Can you tell me why that is?"

Mālik replied: "I have asked the people to bring their property and their families with them. I want every soldier to know that his family and his wealth is right behind him so that he fights hard to protect them."

Durayd said disapprovingly: "You are no more than a shepherd. What would stop a fighter fleeing from the battle? If you are winning, no one will be of use to you except a man who can carry a sword or a spear. If you are losing, you will bring on your people the greatest scandal of all, and they will lose all their property." Durayd then asked about the Kaʿb and the Kilab, and when he was told that they were not joining in, he said: "Courage and determination are absent. They would not have been absent if the score was one of glory. I would have preferred you to follow their example." He then asked about the Hawāzin dignatories who were taking part, and when the names of the two brothers, ʿAmr and ʿAwf, were mentioned, he said:

"They are of no great use and their absence would not have caused any great harm." He then addressed Mālik with this sound advice: "Mālik, you cannot achieve much by bringing the whole of the Hawāzin to the battlefield. You would be better advised to put them in their well-protected areas before meeting the Muslims on your horses. If you win, your people will join you. If you lose, you will have saved your families and your property."

Mālik, however, was driven by his enthusiasm and he did not want Durayd to win any praise for his opinion. He said to him: "By God, I would not do that. You have aged, and so has your reason." He then addressed his people: "People of Hawāzin, you will either follow my orders or I shall fall on this sword of mine until it pierces right through me." They pledged that they would obey him and Durayd said: "This is a battle which I have neither witnessed nor missed." Thus, the Hawāzin marched with their women and children and all their wealth for their decisive meeting with the Muslims.

Preparing to Meet the Enemy

Back in Makkah, the Prophet heard that the Hawāzin were preparing to fight the Muslims. He, therefore, sent ʿAbdullāh ibn Abī Ḥadrad, from the tribe of the Aslam, to gather information. He instructed him to go right into their camp and pretend to be one of them until he had gathered detailed information about them. The man went and did as the Prophet said. He even spoke to Mālik and made sure of the plans of the Hawāzin. He went back to report to the Prophet what he had learnt. He told him the Hawāzin were planning to march to a valley called Ḥunayn. When the Prophet heard all this, he smiled and said: "This will be a prize for the Muslims, God willing."

The Prophet started his preparations to meet the Hawāzin in battle. He asked the people of Makkah, including those who had not become Muslims, to help him with his preparations. He specifically asked Ṣafwān ibn Umayyah to lend him some arms which he heard that Ṣafwān had.

Ṣafwān asked: "Do you want to take those arms by force, Muhammad?" The Prophet answered: "No. We want to borrow them, and we guarantee to return them to you." Ṣafwān then agreed and gave him 100 shields with their accompanying arms. This is yet another instance of cooperation with unbelievers for a definite purpose.

When the Muslims had completed their preparations, the Prophet left Makkah at the head of his army on Saturday the 6th of Shawwāl (28 January AD 630). His army now numbered 12,000. There were 10,000 with him when he left Madinah marching towards Makkah. Now, the Muslim army was swelled by 2,000 from among the people of Makkah, some of them still non-Muslims. It was a large army by Muslim standards. One must remember that two years earlier, when the Prophet came to Makkah for his *ʿUmrah*, only 1,400 people were with him. That was the time when he concluded his peace agreement with the Quraysh at al-Ḥudaybiyah. The same number had fought with him the major Battle of Khaybar against the Jews a few months later. It was not surprising that many people would have looked at that large Muslim army and thought that nothing would stand up to it. That was indeed a natural feeling after the ease with which Makkah had fallen to the Muslims. The majority of the believers in Islam felt that idolatry was in its last throes. It could not put up any resistance worth mentioning. The newcomers to Islam were full of euphoria as they saw the Muslim army moving to meet the unbelievers. For once, it seemed, the Muslims were a little too relaxed before an enormous task, but why should they not be? They used to be very few in number, yet were able to win major battles. Now they looked at their size and felt that numerical strength was no longer lacking. In previous conflicts, the smaller forces had been those of the Muslims. This time, however, they felt that the size of the enemy army was irrelevant. Theirs was a large army and they would not be overrun on account of their inferior numbers.

The Prophet and the Muslim army reached the valley of Ḥunayn on Tuesday evening 10th of Shawwāl. Reports suggest that it was the Prophet's plan to take his enemy by surprise before the light of day, when they would still be asleep. He, therefore, mobilized his forces in ranks, assigned flags and banners, appointed commanders mostly from among the Muhājirīn and the Anṣār, and gave the command of his horsemen to Khālid ibn al-Walīd. Having done that, he ordered his army to move.

A Plan to Defeat the Muslims

Mālik ibn ʿAwf, the commander of the enemy forces, had already encamped in the valley of Ḥunayn, a sloping valley whose very steep, hilly entrance had several narrow points. It opened up further on. Mālik wanted to utilize the strategic advantage afforded by that entrance. He, therefore, placed some detachments of his forces at the top of each narrow point and mobilized large numbers of his forces on the sides, keeping some of them absolutely unobserved. The Hawāzin were renowned for their marksmanship with arrows. Mālik also wanted to make use of that skill to score a clear advantage. He placed some of his best marksmen at high points close to those straight and narrow areas. He ordered them to pour their arrows over the Muslims once they saw them there. He hoped that that would cause chaos among the Muslim army, and then the rest of his forces would launch a full-scale attack against them.

This seemed to be Mālik's plan. It seems also that he was well aware of the moves of the Muslims. Without such intelligence, it would have been difficult for him to make such an effective plan. He must have sent spies to gather intelligence of the Prophet's moves. On the other hand, there might have been some people from Makkah who still harboured grudges against Islam and wanted the Hawāzin to triumph.

As the Muslim army moved with the first rays of light, hardly able to see its way, they were unaware that their enemies had taken their positions and were ready to meet them as they approached. The horsemen, under the command of Khālid ibn al-Walīd, marched at the front, followed by the infantry battalions, and at the end marched the Prophet on his white mule, wearing his body armour which consisted of two shields. With him were some of the leading figures of his companions. His uncle, al-ʿAbbās, and quite a few of his relatives. As soon as the front forces reached the entrance to the valley, they were surprised by a heavy shower of arrows aimed at them from all angles. They could hardly tell where the arrows came from. They suddenly found themselves in a very difficult situation which necessitated retreat. Their retreat, however, was disorderly. The unbelievers did not waste time; they attacked the Muslims as they retreated, bringing in large forces with mounted and infantry units. The Muslim army was soon in absolute chaos with soldiers moving everywhere, most of them trying to flee. There was a terrible scramble and the Muslim soldiers were soon overwhelmed.

Mālik ibn ʿAwf had ordered his soldiers to concentrate their efforts and to launch their attack as if they were one man. He also told them to break the sheaths of their swords – a gesture signalling determination to fight to the end – and to have their cattle and women behind them. At that point in the battle, the Hawāzin and the Thaqīf forces were following Mālik's orders to the letter.

Many people from Makkah, some of them still unbelievers, went with the Muslim army. Among them was Ṣafwān ibn Umayyah, whom the Prophet had allowed a period of four months to think about Islam and define his position towards it. When the Muslim army was in this state of chaos, a man from the Quraysh said to Ṣafwān: "I am bringing you the happy news of the defeat of Muhammad and his companions. By God, they will never be able to make amends for this defeat." Ṣafwān answered angrily: "You describe the victory of the Bedouin Arabs as happy news. I would much sooner be under the leadership of a man from the Quraysh than under the leadership of a Bedouin."

Rallying the Troops

When the Prophet saw his soldiers in such disorder, he shouted to them: "Where are you going, people? Come back to me. I am God's Messenger. I am Muhammad ibn ʿAbdullāh." Few people took heed. Perhaps they did not hear the Prophet shouting. They cared for nothing around them. Soon the Prophet was in a vulnerable position. Only a small group of the Muhājirīn and the Anṣār and a few individuals of his own household remained steadfast with him. Among these was al-ʿAbbās ibn ʿAbd al-Muṭṭalib, who was known for his loud voice. The Prophet instructed him to shout to the Anṣār and the Muhājirīn to come back. Al-ʿAbbās then started to shout: "You, Anṣār, who had welcomed your Prophet and supported him. You, Muhājirīn, who pledged to sacrifice your lives. Come back to God's Messenger." As soon as any one of the Muhājirīn or the Anṣār heard this shouting, he turned back and walked towards the voice of al-ʿAbbās, saying: "Here I come. Here I come." If any of them was impeded in his move towards the Prophet, he would dismount in order to move quickly to join the Prophet.

In the meantime, the Prophet continued to move towards the enemy with those surrounding him. Indeed, he moved dangerously close to them. He was completely exposed to their swords and spears. It may seem strange that the commander of the army should so expose himself. The attitude of the Prophet, however, revealed the strength of his faith. There was absolutely no trace whatsoever of panic on his part. His conviction in the truth of his message and the nature of his role was never shaken. This is absolutely clear in his shouting to his people: "I am God's Messenger." Moreover, the Prophet had been told by God in the Qur'ān that God was responsible for his security. His drawing close to the enemy must be viewed in that light. He was absolutely confident that God's promise would come true. Hence he must not fear for his life.

The Prophet took some dust in his hand and threw it at the enemy army, saying: "Your faces are blackened." As a small group of the Muhājirīn and the Anṣār gathered around the Prophet, events started to turn. That group was able to withstand the pressure of the enemy attack. As it grew larger, with more people coming back, it was able first to hold the enemy and then to turn the pressure against it. By that time, it was broad daylight and they were able to see the position of their enemy. They launched a determined counterattack and soon chaos overtook the enemy forces. The Muslims chased them everywhere, killing some and capturing others. A large number fled. Among those who fled was Mālik ibn ʿAwf, who managed to get to Ṭā'if, where he was admitted into its fortress. He left behind all the cattle and the property which he had ordered his tribesmen to bring to the battlefield. All that became the property of the Muslims. It was by far the greatest loot the Muslims had ever laid their hands on. Moreover, they captured all the women and children the Hawāzin soldiers had brought with them.

It is said that when the Prophet threw the dust on the army of the Hawāzin and the Thaqīf, every enemy soldier felt dust in his eyes. That was the turning point for them, when they started to be confused and disorderly.[1]

An Appropriate Look at Events

The events of this encounter are mentioned briefly in the Qur'ān:

> On the day of Ḥunayn, when you were pleased at your numerical power, you found out that it was of no avail to you. The vast expanse of the earth seemed to you very narrow and you began to flee. Then God sent down His reassurance and tranquillity on His Messenger and on the believers, and He dispatched soldiers whom you did not see and inflicted suffering on the unbelievers. That is the rightful reward for those who reject the faith. (9: 25-26)

These two verses give an important message: numerical strength is of little importance if the other elements necessary for victory are overlooked or neglected. It is important for Muslims to be on their guard against any complacency in their attitude.

The Prophet was eager that the Muslims would always observe their moral code in war. He is reported to have passed a woman from the enemy killed by the forces under the command of Khālid ibn al-Walīd. He immediately dispatched a message to Khālid ordering him not to kill any child, woman or elderly man. It was not for the Muslims to kill women.[2]

When the battle was over, the Prophet ordered all the cattle, property and prisoners taken by the Muslims to be gathered together and dispatched to a valley called al-Jiʿrānah, a short distance from

Makkah. He appointed Masʿūd ibn ʿAmr al-Ghifārī to be in charge of the spoils of war. He intended to distribute them later. Meanwhile, the Muslim army still had an important task to finish.[3]

For the first time in several years, the Muslims stood at the brink of defeat in Ḥunayn. This followed immediately after their conquest of Makkah. For any army to suffer a defeat after its greatest victory can only be described as a setback of mammoth proportions. That initial defeat, however, provides an important lesson for Muslims everywhere and in every age.

Every Muslim should realize that victory comes from God, not from numerical strength or force of arms. God states in the Qur'ān on two different occasions that "Victory is granted only by God." (3: 126 and 8: 10) Muslims, then, must heed this and work for victory on the basis of that understanding; they do not claim that victory can be achieved only by believing in God and the message of Muhammad. Victory is a prize to be sought by hard work. But unless that hard work is coupled with faith, God leaves the combatants to their own devices. When Muslims fight unbelievers, the Muslims must rely on their faith as much as they rely on their arms, if not more. They must be aware that they fight for God's cause, and as such they should sacrifice for it everything they are called upon to sacrifice. At no time does a Muslim go to war thinking that he is going to achieve an easy victory. He is not after material gain. What he is after is to remove certain impediments from the path of the Islamic message. It is for God's cause that he fights, and his aim is to ensure that people are free to listen to God's call and to believe in it if they so desire. At Ḥunayn, the Muslims lost sight momentarily of their true objective. They also lost sight of the real cause of their past victories. That cause was that they had the proper perspective on their own situation and realized that they were fighting the battle of Islam, for the sake of Islam, ready to sacrifice for it whatever was necessary in order to achieve victory. When they lost sight of this, it was easy for their enemy to take them by surprise and cause chaos in their ranks.

It was sufficient for the Hawāzin to be able to force the Muslims to retreat a little and for that retreat to herald a major debacle which most certainly would have been the result of the Battle of Ḥunayn, had it not been for the Prophet's own determination and clear vision. Many historians put the blame for the initial setback suffered by the Muslims at Ḥunayn on the new elements that swelled their ranks. Those were people from Makkah who had just embraced Islam, indeed some of them still had not. They say that those people joined the army hoping to share in the loot. But when the chaos overtook the Muslim army, it was not only they who fled. Reports suggest that at one time only ten people remained with the Prophet. When al-ʿAbbās, his uncle, at the Prophet's instruction, started to call the Muhājirīn and the Anṣār to come back, reports suggest that around 100 of them soon gathered around the Prophet.[4] This means that he was for some time fighting with only about 100 soldiers. The bulk of the Muhājirīn and the Anṣār were overtaken by the chaos. It was necessary to remind them of their position before they rallied to the Prophet. Hence, the setback cannot be explained away by lack of courage on the part of the new soldiers. The Qur'ānic admonition to the Muslims in its comment on the events of Ḥunayn suggests that they all shared responsibility.

One need not seek easy explanations in order to present the companions of the Prophet as free of all blame, or as having no share in the mistakes of that day. It does not help the cause of Islam in future generations to do so. The companions of the Prophet were the best Muslims; that is an absolute fact. They served the cause of Islam in such a way as to provide the best ideals for all Muslims in all generations to follow. But they must not be shown in such a light as to raise them above the level of human beings. If they are viewed as superhuman, they cease to be an example for future Muslim generations. If, on the other hand, one says that even the companions of the Prophet suffered when a feeling of complacency crept in, future generations will understand that they cannot afford to allow complacency to creep into them. Otherwise, they will suffer defeat after defeat. It is important for all Muslim generations to recognize that God will grant them victory if they themselves fulfil the requirements of victory. These include the pure motive of serving the cause of God, exerting their best efforts, coupled with a determination to make whatever sacrifice is necessary and to rely on God and trust in Him.

A Second Battle

When the scales were turned against the Hawāzin and victory was claimed totally by the Muslims, most of the Hawāzin soldiers, including their commander Mālik ibn ʿAwf, went to Ṭā'if, where they joined the Thaqīf in their forts. A battalion went to the valley called Awṭās. The latter group represented the most immediate threat. It was necessary, therefore, to neutralize that threat. The Prophet sent a unit of his forces under the command of ʿUbayd Abū ʿĀmir al-Ashʿarī. A battle erupted between the two sides and it soon appeared that the battle would be resolved in the Muslims' favour. Some detailed reports of that battle exist which suggest that Abū ʿĀmir himself fought ten brothers of the enemy soldiers, one after the other. Every time one of them stood up to the Muslim commander, the latter called on him to accept Islam. When he did not respond, Abū ʿĀmir said: "My Lord, be witness to his rejection." Then Abū ʿĀmir killed him. He killed nine of the ten brothers in this way, calling on them one by one to accept Islam, and praying God to be his witness when they did not respond. When he clashed with the tenth, again he called on him to accept Islam. The man did not respond. Then Abū ʿĀmir said: "My Lord, be witness to his rejection." The man said: "My Lord, do not be witness." Abū ʿĀmir let him go. It was not long after this battle that the man accepted Islam and became a good Muslim. When the Prophet saw him, he said: "This man is the one left by Abū ʿĀmir."

Abū ʿĀmir himself was killed in this battle. Two enemy soldiers attacked him together; one of them hit him in the chest and the other hit him in the knees. A cousin of his, ʿAbdullāh ibn Qays, who is better known in history books as Abū Mūsā al-Ashʿarī, took command of the Muslim battalion. Apparently, the first hit suffered by Abū ʿĀmir was not fatal. Abū Mūsā reports that he went to his cousin when he was hit and asked him who had hit him. Abū ʿĀmir pointed the man out and Abū Mūsā chased him. He tried to escape, but Abū Mūsā said to him tauntingly: "Are you not ashamed of yourself fleeing away? Why don't you show your courage and stand up to me?" The man turned back and Abū Mūsā was able to kill him. He went back to Abū ʿĀmir and said to him: "God has killed the man who hit you." Abū ʿĀmir asked him to pull the spear out of his knee. When he did so, blood gushed forth. Abū ʿĀmir realized that this wound was fatal. He, therefore, asked Abū Mūsā to convey his greetings to the Prophet and ask him to pray for his soul. He appointed him commander. Abū Mūsā and his soldiers fought the unbelievers until they inflicted a heavy defeat on them.

Soon afterwards, Abū ʿĀmir died and the Muslim battalion went back to the Prophet. Abū Mūsā found the Prophet sitting on a bed of sand which had left its mark on his back and sides. Abū Mūsā gave him a report on the battle and conveyed to him the message of Abū ʿĀmir and his request to the Prophet to pray for him. The Prophet asked for water to be brought in, and had ordinary ablutions. He lifted his arms and prayed to God: "My Lord, forgive ʿUbayd Abū ʿĀmir. My Lord, place him on the Day of Judgement ahead of many of Your creation."

Abū Mūsā said to the Prophet: "And pray to God to forgive me as well, please." The Prophet said: "My Lord, forgive ʿAbdullāh ibn Qays his sins and assign to him an honourable entrance [to heaven] on the Day of Judgement."[5]

The Battle of Awṭās was a follow-up to the Battle of Ḥunayn. It was necessary because, if the Prophet had left that force of unbelievers intact in the place where they encamped, it would have represented a serious threat to Islam. The Prophet realized that it was important for him to break all resistance put up by the unbelievers. Hence he did not hesitate to meet them on the battleground they had chosen.

After the Prophet and the Muslims achieved victory over the Hawāzin at the Battle of Ḥunayn, and after the follow-up engagement at Awṭās which ended in yet another defeat for the unbelievers, the main concentration of forces hostile to Islam which represented a threat to the Muslims was at Ṭā'if, where the tribe of Thaqīf had their fortified dwellings. The Prophet's approach was always a very serious one. He would not leave the Thaqīf to continue their hostility to Islam without trying to subdue them. He therefore ordered his army to march towards Ṭā'if.

The Siege of Ṭā'if

Ṭā'if was a fortified city whose inhabitants were well trained to withstand any siege. The Thaqīf had prepared themselves for a long siege and took into their forts enough provisions to last them a long time. They had made up their minds not to succumb to the forces of Islam as long as they could put up any effective resistance.

The Muslim army arrived at Ṭā'if to find its people well protected in their forts. It was the Prophet's plan not to rush his army into battle, in the hope that the Thaqīf would reconsider their position and decide to give up. As soon as the Muslim army drew near to the forts, a shower of arrows poured over them. A few soldiers were killed and a number of others were injured. The Muslim army was then forced to draw back a little so that it could not be hit. The army took its positions and a siege was imposed on Ṭā'if. It continued for over 20 days.

During this period, the Muslims tried hard to draw the unbelievers out of their fortifications. Their attempts were unsuccessful. The Muslims first asked the Thaqīf to send down some of its best soldiers for individual duels, but the Thaqīf declined. The Muslims taunted them and accused them of cowardice, but that did not influence the Thaqīf's position. The Muslims then tried to hit them with stones, but all that was to little effect. A number of Muslims utilized a primitive form of tank, made of wood, in order to reach the wall of Ṭā'if's fort, hoping to make a hole in it, but the Thaqīf replied by throwing over them pieces of red-hot iron and this forced the Muslim soldiers to come out of their tank. As they did so, the Thaqīf shot their arrows and killed a number of Muslims. The Muslims then tried to cut the Thaqīf's vines. This worried the Thaqīf and they appealed to the Prophet not to do so for the sake of God and kinship. He responded by ordering his soldiers to stop cutting any vine.

All the Muslims' attempts could not make any headway. The unbelievers of the Thaqīf were still in their forts, which remained immune to any attack. The Prophet then caused it to be proclaimed that if any slave who belonged to the Thaqīf deserted and joined the Muslims, he was to be set free immediately. Some 20 slaves managed to come out, and the Prophet granted them their freedom. From those slaves, the Prophet learnt that the Thaqīf had enough provisions to last them for a year. They were able to withstand the Muslim siege for that length of time. They remained resolved to continue their defiance as long as their provisions were sufficient to meet their needs. They would then fight to the last man.

The Prophet then realized that it was time to reconsider his position. It seemed that prolonging the siege would be of little use. He consulted some of his companions about the situation. Nawfal ibn Muʿāwiyah al-Di'lī said to him: "They are just like a fox in a hole. If you exhaust the fox's patience, you will get it out. If you leave it alone, it can cause you no harm."

The Prophet realized that Nawfal's description was very accurate. Moreover, the consecrated months were about to begin. He was, therefore, more inclined to leave the Thaqīf alone for the time being. He hoped that they would soon realize that Islam was the religion of truth, and come to him voluntarily to declare their acceptance of Islam. He ordered his army to leave Ṭā'if and move back to Makkah.[6]

One must remember here an incident which took place some 11 years earlier. The Prophet had gone to Ṭā'if seeking support against the Quraysh. The attitude of the Thaqīf was then very hostile: they ordered their children and slaves to abuse the Prophet; they hurled stones at him and chased him around until he had to seek shelter in an orchard which belonged to one of the leaders of Makkah, who himself was very hostile to him. At that point, the Angel Gabriel came to him to say: "Muhammad, your Lord has sent me to give you His greetings and to tell you that He heard what you said to those people and their answers to you. I will close in these two mountains over them if you wish me to do so."

The Prophet answered: "I would rather leave them a while in the hope that God will make their offspring people who worship Him alone and do not ascribe Divinity to anyone other than Him."

Now the Prophet still hoped that the Thaqīf would come round. One of his companions suggested that he should pray to God to destroy them, but the Prophet prayed for them in these words: "My Lord, guide the Thaqīf to the truth and relieve us of their burden."[7] We will see later on that the Prophet's prayers were answered.

Notes

1. Ibn Hishām, *al-Sīrah al-Nabawiyyah*, Dār al-Qalam, Beirut, Vol. 4, pp. 80-101. Also, al-Wāqidī, *Kitāb al-Maghāzī*, Oxford University Press, 1996, Vol. 3, pp. 885-918; and Ibn Kathīr, *al-Bidāyah wal-Nihāyah*, Maktabat al-Ma'ārif, Beirut, Vol. 1, pp. 322-325.
2. Ibn Hishām, op.cit., p. 100.
3. Ibid., p. 101.
4. Ibid., p. 87.
5. Al-Wāqidī, op.cit., pp. 914-916.
6. Ibn Sayyid al-Nās, *'Uyūn al-Athar*, Dār al-Turāth, Madinah, 1996, pp. 270-271. Also, al-Wāqidī, op.cit., pp. 922-937.
7. Ibn Hishām, op.cit., p. 131. Also, al-Wāqidī, op.cit., p. 937.

37

Generous Gifts to Old Foes

REALIZING THAT A continued siege of Ṭā'if would not bring about the desired results, the Prophet ordered his troops to decamp. The Thaqīf were unlikely to try to stage a military operation against the Muslims. Even if they did, that would mean abandoning their fortified city, when it would be easier for the Muslims to inflict on them a telling defeat. The Prophet, however, hoped that if the Thaqīf were left alone for a while, they might start to reconsider their position. The wiser men might begin to think about Islam in a new light.

Moreover, some elements in the Muslim army were probably feeling weary after this long campaign. Besides, some might have been eager to receive their share of the booty the Muslims had gained from the Hawāzin. The departure from Ṭā'if to Makkah signalled the approach of the division of that booty. The Prophet had sent all the cattle and other property which the Muslim army had gained to al-Jiʿirrānah. Now he was heading there himself to divide the spoils of war among his companions, as is customary in Islam. The Muslims had indeed gained great wealth from the Hawāzin. The women and children now travelling with their army as captives numbered 6,000. There were reported to be 24,000 camels and 40,000 sheep in addition to 4,000 ounces of silver.[1]

Appeal by the Captives

When the Prophet reached al-Jiʿirrānah, he was soon joined there by a delegation from the Hawāzin. Many Hawāzin people were now Muslims. The delegation said to him: "Messenger of God, we are your people and your own clan. You know the sort of disaster which has befallen us. We appeal to you to show mercy to us, may God bestow His grace on you." Their spokesman, Zuhayr ibn Ṣarad, said to the Prophet: "Messenger of God, those women who have fallen captive to you include some who are your aunts and some who were your wet nurses when you were young. Had we been in such a relationship with the King of Ghassān in Syria or the King of al-Manādhirah in Iraq, and had this sort of disaster befallen us at their hands, we would still have hoped that they would show leniency towards us. You, God's Messenger, are the best to return kindness." (The reference to the Prophet's aunts from the Hawāzin is a reference to the fact that as an infant, the Prophet was looked after by Ḥalīmah, a wet nurse from Saʿd, a clan of the Hawāzin.)

The Prophet asked them which they loved better, their women and children or their wealth. They answered: "Messenger of God, are you giving us a choice between our families and our wealth? Our women and children are certainly dearer to us."

The Prophet said to them: "My own share and the share of my clan, the ʿAbd al-Muṭṭalib, are yours. When I have finished the congregational prayers, stand up and say: 'We appeal by God's Messenger to the Muslims, and we appeal by the Muslims to God's Messenger, to release our women and children.' When you do that I will give you what I can and I will ask others to give you what they can as well."

When the Prophet had finished his mid-day prayers, with all the Muslims praying with him, the delegation from the Hawāzin stood up and said what the Prophet had told them to say. The Prophet explained to the Muslims that the Hawāzin had repented of their previous attitude and had become Muslims. He also said to the Hawāzin people: "My own share and the share of the clan of ʿAbd al-Muṭṭalib are yours."

The Muhājirīn said: "Our shares belong to God's Messenger." The Anṣār said likewise. Al-Aqraʿ ibn Ḥābis, the chief of the Tamīm tribe, said: "As for me and my tribe, we decline." The same attitude was expressed by ʿUyaynah ibn Ḥiṣn, the chief of the Fazārah tribe, and al-ʿAbbās ibn Mirdās, the chief of the tribe of Sulaym. People from Sulaym, however, turned him down and said: "Indeed, our shares belong to God's Messenger." Al-ʿAbbās ibn Mirdās was unhappy with his people. He said to them. "You have let me down."

This created a situation where some women and children from the Hawāzin were still in captivity. According to the general rules and traditions of the time, they would have been enslaved. The Prophet did not like that at all. For one thing, he disliked slavery. For another, he was keen that the Hawāzin should be an asset to Islam. They should not have any cause for complaint against the Muslims. He, therefore, announced to the Muslims: "He of you who wants to hold to his right will be given instead of what he has now six shares of the first spoils of war we gain."[2] This was rich compensation, and all those who refused to give up their shares in the captive women and children from the Hawāzin were happy with the exchange.

Thus, all the women and children from the Hawāzin were freed and returned to their people. That gesture went a long way to reconcile the Hawāzin and encouraged them in their new determination to be Muslims.

Replacing Old Hostility

It has already been mentioned that the Battle of Ḥunayn resulted in huge gains of camels, sheep and silver for the Muslims. All these spoils of war were now at al-Jiʿirrānah awaiting the Prophet's arrival with his Muslim army.

Those who were in the Muslim army besieging Ṭā'if were looking forward to the time when it would be shared out. The release of the Hawāzin captives, however, made many of them, especially among those who belonged to Bedouin tribes or had only recently embraced Islam, fear that the wealth of the Hawāzin might yet be returned to them. Some of them came to the Prophet and asked him insistently to divide the spoils of war. The Prophet had certain ideas about the division of the property. One has to remember that only a few weeks earlier, Makkah had fallen to the Muslims. Although many Makkans had adopted Islam, it was not to be expected that 20 years of hostility would be replaced by love and compassion overnight. Hence, he felt that the wealth he had gained at Ḥunayn provided him with a chance to help this process of removing the traces of former hostility.

Abū Sufyān ibn Ḥarb, the Makkan chief who had led the Quraysh for several years in its attempts to suppress Islam and had accepted Islam only recently, came to the Prophet when all the silver – more than 4,000 ounces – that was gained at Ḥunayn was put in front of him. Abū Sufyān looked at it and said: "Messenger of God, you have become the richest among the Quraysh." The Prophet smiled. Abū Sufyān continued: "Give me some of this, Messenger of God." The Prophet turned to Bilāl who quite often acted as his treasurer and said: "Bilāl, weigh 40 ounces of silver for Abū Sufyān and give him 100 camels." Abū Sufyān was gratified, but wanted to gain more. He said to the Prophet: "What about my son, Yazīd?" The Prophet said to Bilāl: "Weigh for Yazīd 40 ounces of silver and give him 100 camels." Abū Sufyān then said: "And my son Muʿāwiyah, Messenger of God." The Prophet again told Bilāl to weigh 40 ounces of silver for Muʿāwiyah and to give him 100 camels.

Abū Sufyān was overwhelmed. He said to the Prophet: "You are indeed very generous. May my parents be sacrificed for your sake. I fought you and you were the most honourable of foes, and I have made peace with you and you have proved to be the best of friends. May God reward you with His best blessings."[3]

The Prophet also gave a number of other people 100 camels each: Ḥakīm ibn Ḥizām, al-Ḥārith ibn Kildah, ʿAlqamah ibn ʿAllādhah, al-ʿAlāʾ ibn Ḥārithah, al-Ḥārith ibn Hishām, Jubayr ibn Muṭʿim, Suhayl ibn ʿAmr, Ḥuwayṭib ibn ʿAbd al-ʿUzzā, ʿUyaynah ibn Ḥiṣn and al-Aqraʿ ibn Ḥābis.[4] He was also reported to have given Ṣafwān ibn Umayyah 100 camels. Indeed, he gave him 300 camels in three successive instalments. He looked at him and saw him looking at a piece of land where some cattle and sheep were kept. The Prophet asked him: "Do you like this piece of land, Abū Wahb?" Ṣafwān said: "Yes, indeed." The Prophet said: "It is yours, with all that is in it." Ṣafwān said: "Kings do not make such gifts willingly. No one can give so generously except a Prophet. I declare that there is no deity other than God, and that you are God's Messenger."[5]

The Prophet also gave al-ʿAbbās ibn Mirdās a number of camels which did not amount to 100. He did not like that. Since he was a gifted poet, al-ʿAbbās expressed his feelings in a few lines of poetry. The Prophet then increased his gift to make him equal with the others. One notes here that al-ʿAbbās ibn Mirdās was a Muslim before the conquest of Makkah. This is perhaps the reason for the Prophet giving him less than the others because those who were given large gifts were recent converts, or dignitaries who had not yet become Muslims.

Gifts to Transform Hearts

The word was soon heard all over the place that Muhammad was giving large gifts to tribal chiefs. People from every tribe and clan raced to take their share. Everyone wanted something special for himself. Bedouins surrounded the Prophet and said to him: "Messenger of God, divide our booty among us."[6] There were several of them and they pressed him hard. He moved close to a tree, and part of his robes fell off him. He said to them: "Give me back my robe, you people. By Him who holds my soul in His hand, if I had as many cattle as the trees in Tihāmah [a large area of Arabia], I would have shared it out among you, not begrudging you any of it. You would not have found me miserly, or cowardly, or a liar." He then took a hair off a camel and held it up between his two fingers and said: "Nothing of your booty belongs to me, not even this hair, apart from one-fifth of it. This one-fifth is given back to you."[7] This, as we have seen, was a reference to the Divine rule that any spoils of war which are gained by Muslims are divided into two sections: one-fifth belongs to the state and the remainder is shared out among the soldiers.

What this division of the spoils of war meant was that those who were yesterday's enemies, and those who were absolutely useless in the initial stage of the Battle of Ḥunayn, fleeing in front of the Hawāzin, were given the largest shares. The Prophet viewed material wealth as petty. It did not deserve to be given much thought. Yet it was important to gain such people for Islam if Islam was to be established firmly in the rest of Arabia. They must not remain shaky. The Prophet realized that many people are won over to the camp of truth only through material gain. They did not belong to that class of the Muhājirīn and the Anṣār, who believed in the cause of Islam and were always ready to defend it with their lives. Such people needed encouragement and a feeling that they would not lose materially if they were to join the camp of Islam. How else would a man like Abū Sufyān, who until yesterday was a sworn enemy of Islam, be genuinely reconciled to its message and be expected to defend it, if he was not reassured that what he had lost in position he had recovered in wealth? This division of the spoils of war was meant to gain for the cause of Islam people of influence and high position in order to ensure that Islam did not remain confined to Madinah or to the elite in Arabia – namely, the Muhājirīn and the Anṣār. It was an exercise in winning hearts. Ṣafwān ibn Umayyah remarked later on: "God's Messenger was the most hateful person to me, but he continued to give me of the spoils of the Battle of Ḥunayn until he was dearer to me than any creature on the face of the earth."[8] If giving such gifts meant such a transformation of feelings and passions, then it was indeed done for a good purpose. A person like Ṣafwān ibn Umayyah, with his influence among his people, was an important gain for Islam. To buy his genuine loyalty was certainly cheap at the price.

Yet the purpose behind such division was not immediately apparent to most people, despite the fact that God has made 'those whose hearts are to be won over' one of the eight groups to whom *zakāt* can be given. Some people made very offensive remarks about this distribution of the spoils of war. One person said: "This is a division devoid of justice. It was not done for the sake of God."

The Prophet was very angry when he was told of this. He said: "Who is fair if God and His Messenger are not? May God have mercy on Moses. Worse abuse was showered on him and he tolerated it patiently."[9]

The remainder of the spoils of war was divided among his soldiers. A fighter on foot received four camels and 40 sheep. A horseman received three times as much, as this was customary in sharing out spoils of war. Yet the large gifts made to yesterday's foes caused more friction.[10]

It should be remembered that those gifts were made in public. There were no secret deals. It was, therefore, inevitable that they would give rise to different reactions from different people. What was obvious was that no one among the Anṣār, be he a chief or an ordinary member of his clan, was given any special gift. Such an omission could not have been the result of forgetfulness on the part of the Prophet. The Anṣārī chiefs were very close to him. Hence, it was not surprising that some of them should feel aggrieved. There were even whispers of dissatisfaction among them. Abū Saʿīd al-Khudrī, a young companion of the Prophet who belonged to the Anṣār, reports: "When God's Messenger gave away those generous gifts to people in the Quraysh and in other Arabian tribes while no such gifts were given to anyone from the Anṣār, the Anṣār felt hard done by. Remarks of dissatisfaction were frequently uttered. Some of them said: 'Indeed, God's Messenger has met his people,' meaning that he had forgotten his loyal supporters."

Dissatisfied Supporters

Saʿd ibn ʿUbādah, the chief of the Anṣār, went to the Prophet and said to him: "Messenger of God, these clans of the Anṣār have taken your action to heart." The Prophet asked: "What action?" Saʿd said: "The way you have distributed those spoils of war among your own people and the other Arabian tribes. No such gifts were made to any person among the Anṣār." The Prophet wanted to gauge those feelings, so he put this direct question to Saʿd: "What is your own stand?" Saʿd answered: "I am only one of my people." The Prophet, therefore, told him to ask all his people to assemble in a nearby place and to let him know when they had assembled. When all of them were gathered, Saʿd came to the Prophet and said: "Messenger of God, the Anṣār have assembled where you have instructed me to gather them for you."

The Prophet went out to them and addressed them, starting by praising God and glorifying Him as He should be glorified. He then said to them: "People of the Anṣār, what is this which has been reported to me that you have been saying? And what are you aggrieved about? Did I not come to you when you were astray, and God has guided you to the right path? Did I not find you poor, and God has given you of His riches? Did I not come to you when you were at war, and God has united your hearts?" They answered: "Indeed. We have been graced with great bounties by God and His Messenger."

The Prophet then asked them: "Why do you not answer me, people of the Anṣār?" They said: "How shall we answer you, Messenger of God? We are greatly indebted to God and to His Messenger." The Prophet said to them:

> You can, if you wish, say what is true and what people will believe: 'You came to us when people denied your message, and we have accepted it. You were rejected, without support and shouldering a heavy burden when you came to us, and we have given you welcome and support, and have also lightened your burden.' People of the Anṣār, are you aggrieved at a trifle of this world which I have given out to certain people in order to win their hearts over to Islam and left you to rely on your faith? Are you not satisfied, people of the Anṣār, that other people should go to their quarters with sheep and camels while you go back to your own quarters with God's Messenger? By Him who holds Muhammad's soul in His hand, had it not been for my emigration I would have been one of the Anṣār. If all people went one way and the Anṣār went another way, I would take the way of the Anṣār. My Lord, shower your mercy on the Anṣār, and the Anṣār's children and the children of their children.

As they heard the Prophet's words, tears sprang to their eyes. They were so touched that their beards were wet with tears. They said: "We are satisfied with God's Messenger as our share."[11]

This is yet another lesson learnt from the Prophet. It shows how remarkable the difference is between Islam as a message and any other theory or philosophy: had the Anṣār been the supporters or advocates of any creed or philosophy, and had they sacrificed for it what they had willingly sacrificed for Islam, they might have been in revolt against the Prophet for denying them what would have seemed to all people to be their rightful reward. After all, they were the people who had given willingly, time after time, all the sacrifice they were called upon to give in order to achieve what had finally been achieved with the conquest of Makkah and the victory at Ḥunayn. Yet at that very moment of triumph they were denied the fruits of their efforts – or so it might have seemed to anyone who took a narrow view of things.

Yet the Anṣār were denied nothing. At no time was material reward a part of the bargain which they had made with the Prophet when they pledged their support to him at ʿAqabah, some nine or ten years earlier. At that time, they asked the Prophet what reward they were to expect for giving him all the support he needed, even if it meant fighting against the whole world. His answer was: "Heaven." He did not promise them anything in this world. Hence, they were not to expect anything.

Some people may nevertheless argue that although the Anṣār did not expect anything, now that riches were at the Prophet's disposal, a token of appreciation might not have gone amiss. That again is a narrow view of the nature of the role of the advocates of Islam. They are always called on to show that whatever effort they exert in support of Islam, their pure motive is to win God's pleasure. They look forward to no other gain.

A Mere Trifle

It is worth reflecting a little on the Prophet's description of those large gifts he made to those dignitaries of the Quraysh and other Arabian tribes. A camel represented wealth to the Arabs at that time. Compared with today, a camel was much more valuable than a luxury motor car. One may spend a great deal of money on car maintenance, while a camel can eat any dry plants, which cost nothing to grow. Moreover, the female camel produces milk which is highly nourishing. She bears offspring and she can be slaughtered for food. One hundred camels to each of those Arab chiefs was, then, very great wealth. Yet it was such great wealth which the Prophet describes as 'a trifle of this world'. This description fits perfectly with the Islamic view of the role of the advocates of Islam, their motives and ambitions. They seek only the pleasure of God. This cannot be combined with any other motive. Hence, they are called on to give their all in this life while expecting nothing. Their reward comes in the Hereafter.

This view has been expressed very vividly by the Prophet in connection with one individual. Al-Bukhārī relates, on the authority of ʿAmr ibn Taghlib: "The Prophet made large gifts to some people while denying others. Some of them felt aggrieved. He said: 'I give out gifts to certain people because I fear that they may be shaken. Others I trust to what God has placed in their hearts of goodness and riches. Among the latter is ʿAmr ibn Taghlib'." ʿAmr comments: "I would not exchange the Prophet's statement for the world."

The final word in this connection is that the Prophet's action was a lesson for all advocates of Islam in all generations. They must expect no reward in this life.

When the Prophet had finished the business of sharing out the spoils of war, he entered into the state of consecration in order to offer an *ʿUmrah*. There was soon something else to satisfy the Anṣār. When the Prophet had done his *ʿUmrah* and no more trouble lay ahead, the Anṣār whispered to one another: "Now that God has given His Messenger his own land and his own city, do you think that he will settle here?"

At that moment, the Prophet was praying to God at the top of the hill of al-Ṣafā. When he had finished his prayers, he asked the Anṣār what they had said. At first, they would not tell him. When he insisted, they expressed their fears that he might wish to settle in Makkah. He answered: "Far be it from me. My life is with you and my death will be among you." They were very happy with this reassurance. This showed that the ties between the Muhājirīn and Madinah were too strong and profound to be outweighed by nostalgic memories of the dearest of homelands.[12]

Since the people of Makkah had converted only recently to Islam, the Prophet appointed his companion, Muʿādh ibn Jabal, one of the Anṣār, to teach them the Qur'ān and the *Sunnah*. He also appointed ʿAttāb ibn Usayd as governor of Makkah. ʿAttāb was a young man, only 20 years old, but he had already shown qualities of leadership. He was courageous, endowed with native intelligence and he did not view his position as a means to gain any riches. The Prophet had fixed his salary at a mere one dirham per day. ʿAttāb, however, was very happy with it. He said to the people: "He who feels hungry when he is given one dirham, let him remain hungry forever. The Prophet has given me one dirham per day, which means that I need nothing from anyone else."[13]

The Prophet then went back to Madinah with the Muhājirīn and the Anṣār.

Notes

1. Ibn Sayyid al-Nās, *Uyūn al-Athar*, Dār al-Turāth, Madinah, 1996, p. 260.
2. Ibn Hishām, *al-Sīrah al-Nabawiyyah*, Dār al-Qalam, Beirut, Vol. 1, pp. 131-132.
3. Al-Wāqidī, *Kitāb al-Maghāzī*, Oxford University Press, 1996, Vol. 1, pp. 944-945.
4. Ibn Hishām, op.cit., pp. 135-136. Also al-Wāqidī, op.cit., pp. 945-946; and Ibn Sayyid al-Nās, op.cit., p. 260.
5. Al-Wāqidī, op.cit., p. 946.
6. Ibid., pp. 946-947. Also, Ibn Hishām, op.cit., pp. 136-137; and Ibn Sayyid al-Nās, op.cit., p. 260.
7. Ibn Hishām, op.cit., pp. 134-135. Also, al-Wāqidī, op.cit., pp. 942-943.
8. Ibn Kathīr, *al-Bidāyah wal-Nihāyah*, Maktabat al-Maʿārif, Beirut, Vol. 1, p. 360.
9. Al-Wāqidī, op.cit., p. 949.
10. Ibid., p. 949.
11. Ibn Hishām, op.cit., pp. 141-143. Also, Ibn Sayyid al-Nās, op.cit., pp. 261-262.
12. Ibn Hishām, op.cit., p. 59.
13. Ibid., p. 143.

38

Men of Distinction

THE PROPHET AND his companions were on their way back home to Madinah after nearly three months' absence. This was the month of Dhul-Ḥijjah, the last month in the eighth year of the Prophet's settlement in Madinah. He had started his journey in Ramaḍān of that year. Those were three months that changed the situation in Arabia beyond recognition. Makkah, which was the focal point for all forces and tribes opposed to Islam in Arabia, was fast becoming a solid base of the Divine faith. The major tribe of the Hawāzin, which took over the banner of opposition of Islam, also came into the fold. Ṭā'if was abandoned by the Muslims to sort out its affairs because, as the new situation took shape, the Thaqīf, the major Arabian tribe whose centre was there, was reduced to insignificance. There was no longer any tribe or grouping in Arabia which could challenge the supremacy of the Muslims.

The Prophet's arrival in Madinah this time was very different from his first journey there eight years earlier. In both cases he was coming to Madinah from the city in which he was born and in which he lived for over 50 years of his life. The first time he had come with Abū Bakr, his only companion on that journey. He was chased by all the Arabs and had a large reward on his head. He was a stranger in his new place, beginning a new life with prospects which were totally unknown. He was well received by the people of Madinah, who gave him unconditional support and stood by him against friend and foe, following his guidance and accepting his authority without question. Now, eight years later, he was returning to Madinah as the undisputed master of the whole of Arabia. That dramatic change in fortunes did not bring about any change in the Prophet's personality. If anything, he showed greater kindness to his companions and greater modesty as he praised God for what He had given him.

ʿAdiy ibn Ḥātim

After the Prophet and his companions had settled back in Madinah, they stayed there for six months, which was a period of consolidation after the great gains they had achieved for Islam. Those six months were largely a peaceful period in which the Prophet sent only a few small expeditions which were meant either to motivate certain tribes to come forward and join the Islamic camp more speedily, or to destroy certain famous idols. One such idol, called al-Fuls, was worshipped by the tribe of Ṭayy. An expedition of 150 men from the Anṣār marched in the month of Rabīʿ al-Awwāl, three months after the Prophet's return to Madinah, under the command of ʿAlī ibn Abī Ṭālib, towards the Ṭayy's quarters. They were able to destroy that idol and burn it, and to capture a number of people, including some women, as well as some cattle and silver. Among those who were captured was a woman called Sufānah bint Ḥātim.[1] Her father gained a great reputation as the most generous man in Arabia. His son, ʿAdiy, was the leader of his people. He managed to flee before the arrival of the Muslim expedition. His own account of his flight and subsequent events is well worth quoting:

> Perhaps no one in Arabia hated God's Messenger as I did. I was a man of noble birth, Christian by religion, and I enforced the rule which gave me one quarter of all spoils of war gained by my tribe. [This was done by tribal chiefs who enjoyed undisputed authority among their people.] This meant that I had my religion for myself and I was truly a king of my people. When I heard about the Prophet, I hated him. I told my shepherd, who was a good Bedouin: "Prepare me a few strong

camels, good for travelling, and keep them at hand. If you hear that an army dispatched by Muhammad comes near our place, let me know immediately."

Soon afterwards, my shepherd came to me and said: "ʿAdiy, whatever you intended to do when Muhammad's horsemen arrive, start doing it now. I have seen certain flags, and upon enquiry I was told that it was an army belonging to Muhammad."

I told him to get the camels ready and I moved out with my women and children, having made up my mind to join my Christian co-religionists in Syria. However, I left behind in our quarters a sister of mine. I settled in Syria after my arrival there. Shortly after my departure, the forces of the Prophet attacked our quarters and took my sister prisoner along with others. They were all taken to the Prophet. He was also informed of my flight to Syria. My sister was kept in a confined place at the doorstep of the mosque, where other captives were also kept. She was a woman of sound mind. One day, as the Prophet passed by her, she addressed him: "Messenger of God, my parents are dead and my guardian has disappeared. Be generous to me, may God be generous to you." He asked her who her guardian was and she said: "ʿAdiy ibn Ḥātim." He said: "The one who has fled from God and His Messenger?"

Sufānah takes up the story:

The Prophet left me in my place after he said that. On the following day he passed by me and I repeated what I had said to him the day before. He also repeated the same words he had said to me. Another day passed and the Prophet went by me, but I had already despaired. A man walking behind him, however, gave me a signal to speak to him. I did so and made my request to him to be generous to me. God's Messenger said: "I set you free. Do not, however, leave hastily until some trustworthy people from your own folk come along and you are sure that they will take you home. When such people come along, let me know." I enquired about the man who gave me that signal and I was told that he was ʿAlī ibn Abī Ṭālib. I stayed in Madinah until a caravan from the tribe of Baliyy or Quḍāʿah came along. I had made up my mind to go and join my brother in Syria. When I heard of this caravan, I went to the Prophet and said: "Messenger of God, a group of my people whom I believe to be trustworthy have arrived." The Prophet gave me good clothes and a camel as well as some money. I travelled with them until I arrived in Syria.

The narrative is resumed by ʿAdiy:

I was sitting with my family when a woman was approaching us, gazing at me. I thought: "Ḥātim's daughter!" When she was nearer, I recognized her. When she arrived, she started abusing me for leaving her behind: "You uncompassionate, unkind man. You took all your women and children and left your own sister behind." I said: "Dear sister, do not abuse me. I have no excuse. I have certainly done what you have said." She joined us and stayed with me. I realized that she was a sagacious, far-sighted woman. One day I asked her about the Prophet. She said: "I think you would be well advised to join him as soon as you can. If the man is truly a Prophet, the earlier you join him, the better for you. If he is only a king, you will not suffer any harm if you join him, considering your position and personality." I said: "This is certainly sound advice."

Soon afterwards, I travelled all the way to Madinah. I went to see the Prophet in his mosque. When I greeted him, he asked me my name, and I said: "ʿAdiy ibn Ḥātim." He then stood up and took me to his home. As we walked to his place, an elderly, weak woman stopped him. He stood with her for a long while as she explained what she wanted. I thought to myself: "He is certainly not a king."

He then took me into his rooms, gave me a cushion and said: "Sit on this." I said: "No, you sit on it." He said: "It is yours." I sat down on the cushion and he sat on the floor. Again I thought to myself: "He is certainly not a king."

> He then said to me: "Tell me, ʿAdiy ibn Ḥātim, have you not been a Rekūsī [a follower of a creed which was in between Christianity and the religion of the followers of Zachariah]. I answered in the affirmative. He then asked me: "But you nevertheless took for yourself one-quarter of the spoils of war gained by your people?" I again answered in the affirmative. He said: "But that was forbidden according to your religion." I said: "It was indeed." I knew then that he was a Prophet sent by God, for he knew what nobody else did.
>
> The Prophet then said to me: "ʿAdiy, you may be reluctant to embrace this religion because you see that its followers are poor. By God, it will be only a little while before they will have money in such abundance that there will be nobody to take it. You may stop short because their enemies are numerous, while they are few. By God, in a little while you will hear of a woman travelling by herself on her camel from Qādisiyyah [in Iraq] until she has visited the mosque in Makkah, fearing nothing. Again, you may be reluctant to accept Islam because you see that power and kingdoms belong to other people. By God, little time will lapse before you hear that the white palaces in the land of Babylon have surrendered to them." When I heard his words, I declared my acceptance of Islam.

Later, ʿAdiy used to say: "Two prophecies have passed, and one has not been fulfilled yet. I swear by God that it will be. I have seen with my own eyes the white palaces of Babylon falling to the Muslims, and I have seen women travelling alone from Qādisiyyah to offer the pilgrimage in Makkah fearing no one. By God, a third prophecy will be fulfilled and money will be offered in abundance and no one will take it."[2]

That third prophecy was certainly fulfilled in the following decades during the time of ʿUmar ibn al-Khaṭṭāb, the second Caliph. It is authentically reported that Muʿādh ibn Jabal was appointed a ruler of Yemen. He sent some of the alms collected in Yemen to ʿUmar. ʿUmar objected to this and wrote: "I have not sent you to be a tax collector. I have asked you to take *zakāt* from the rich and pay it to the poor people of Yemen." Muʿādh wrote back: "I have not sent you a thing which I could find someone to take." The following year, Muʿādh sent him half the alms collected in Yemen. A similar exchange took place between them. In the third year, Muʿādh sent ʿUmar all the alms he collected and when ʿUmar objected, Muʿādh wrote back: "I could not find anyone to take any *zakāt*." Historians have recorded that during the time of ʿUmar ibn ʿAbd al-ʿAzīz, people went out into the marketplace with their *zakāt* and could find no one to take it.[3]

The Poets

One group of people was given special importance by the Prophet as he continued to convey his message to the population in Arabia and humanity at large. Those were the poets. At that time, poets occupied a position of distinction in Arabia. In a nation which was known for its illiteracy and, paradoxically, for its eloquence, poets were a very highly valued breed. A tribe who could not have a fine poet was deprived of advocating its cause on the wider stage of Arabia. A poet was the mouthpiece of his people. He sang their praises and attacked their opponents, pouring on them abuse which could, quite often, cause them to be held in contempt by the rest of the Arabs. Historians draw a comparison between the role played by poets in that society and the role played by radio or television stations in our modern societies. The poet was perhaps the only form of 'mass media' in that society where those who could read and write were remarkably few.

As the war between Islam and idolatry continued over many years, poets played an important role in it. The unbelievers had a number of poets always abusing the Prophet and his companions, and speaking ill of Islam as a faith. The Muslim camp also had its poets. Most distinguished among these were Ḥassān ibn Thābit, who earned himself the title 'the Prophet's poet', Kaʿb ibn Mālik and ʿAbdullāh ibn Rawāḥah.

Many poets responded favourably to the call of Islam when it was communicated to them. Those who were immersed in the battle of words, as well as the battle of swords, were much less forthcoming. This is perfectly understandable, since they were acting as the mouthpiece of 'unfaith'. They had to think over their position and to make a reasoned choice between Islam and their pagan beliefs. Every time something happened between the two camps, they had to comment on it with a poem, arguing their case and making whatever propaganda they could. Hence, they were much more deeply involved in the battle than any ordinary soldier. The collapse of the Quraysh and its surrender to Islam presented those poets, as individuals, with a dilemma. They could not switch allegiance suddenly. Hence, many of them fled. ʿAbdullāh ibn al-Zibaʿrā, one of the Quraysh's finest poets and its spokesman for many years, fled to Najrān. Ḥassān attacked him with one line of poetry, and that was sufficient for him to reflect on his position much more deeply and realize that he had to succumb to Islam, the word of truth. He came back and met the Prophet, declaring his repentance in four lines of his best poetry. The Prophet, as usual, pardoned him.

Kaʿb ibn Zuhayr

One such poet was Kaʿb ibn Zuhayr, who belonged to a family with a long line of poets and argued the case of the Quraysh in his poetry over many years. His brother, Bujayr ibn Zuhayr, also a fine poet, was a Muslim. Their father, Zuhayr ibn Abī Sulmā, is still studied in schools and universities all over the Arab world as one of the finest poets of the pre-Islamic era. After the fall of Makkah to the Muslims, Kaʿb was in hiding. He managed to send his brother, Bujayr, a message in five lines of poetry requesting his advice over his own position and speaking of his bewilderment over switching loyalties and following Islam, which meant that he would have to adopt moral values which were unknown to his parents. This was an important point with unbelievers, who found the break with tradition too much of a difficulty. In his short poem, Kaʿb describes the Prophet as 'the trustworthy.'

When Bujayr received this message, he felt that he could not conceal it from the Prophet. He, therefore, went to the Prophet and recited the poem to him. The Prophet is reported to have said in comment about his own description: "He has told the truth, although he is a confirmed liar. I am certainly trustworthy." He also commented: "Certainly, the moral values of Islam were not known to his parents." There is no authentic report, however, of any comment by the Prophet on Kaʿb's position. It is known that his brother, Bujayr, wrote him a mixed answer of poetry and prose. Both were to the same effect. Bujayr explained that the Prophet killed some of those who poured abuse on him in the past. Those who were still alive had to flee and hide. He advised his brother that the only way to safety is to come with speed to the Prophet and to declare his repentance. "The Prophet has never killed any person who came to him repenting of his past mistakes", Bujayr said. "If you do not wish to do so, your only alternative is to flee." In his poetry, Bujayr reminded his brother of the Day of Judgement and that no one would escape punishment then unless he believed in God. He declared that he himself was a believer and that the religion of his forefathers meant nothing to him.

When Kaʿb received his brother's message, he felt that he was in a desperate position. He did not know what to do. He consulted some of those who were close to him, but they all told him that he would soon be killed. Everybody seemed to expect that fate for him. That, however, caused him to reflect more and more about his brother's message. He thought deeply about that quality of the Prophet which we have seen in action time after time. The Prophet never killed anyone who declared his repentance of his past hostility to Islam, no matter how grievous the crimes against Islam he had committed in his past. Names like Waḥshī, who had killed Ḥamzah, the Prophet's own uncle, and Hind, who disfigured him, come readily to mind. When each of them came to the Prophet declaring repentance, the Prophet forgave them. Kaʿb must have heard of them, and of others in similar positions. He then realized that the only way to safety was to take the well-beaten track to Madinah and to apologize to the Prophet. This, in turn, caused him to reflect about the true message of Islam. A man of his intellectual talent needed only to reflect objectively in order to realize that Islam was the word of truth. When he had done that, the way ahead was very clear before him.

Ka'b ibn Zuhayr travelled secretly and managed to enter Madinah unnoticed. He went straight to the home of a man from the tribe of Juhaynah who was an old friend of his. This man was, of course, a Muslim. The following day, Ka'b went to the mosque with his Muslim friend and joined the dawn prayers. When the prayers were finished, his friend pointed the Prophet out to him and told him to go and speak to him. Ka'b moved across until he sat opposite the Prophet and said to him: "Messenger of God, Ka'b ibn Zuhayr has repented of everything that he did or said against Islam in the past. Would you accept him and forgive him if he came to you and declared his repentance?" The Prophet answered in the affirmative. He then said: "Messenger of God, I am Ka'b ibn Zuhayr." At this moment, a man from the Anṣār jumped up and said to the Prophet: "Messenger of God, allow me to kill this enemy of God." The Prophet said to him: "Leave him alone. He has come here a repentant man, motivated by his new faith."

Thus, Ka'b was admitted into the Islamic fold. He represented an important gain for the call of Islam. He recited to the Prophet a long poem which he had composed. The poem follows the traditional method of the poetry of the time, starting with a few lines expressing love to an unknown woman given the name of Su'ād. In his poem, Ka'b expressed his apology for his past attitude and described his fear when he was in hiding, and the fact that many people considered that he would inevitably be killed. He also expressed his hope that he would be pardoned and he praised the Prophet and his companions, especially the Muhājirīn.

The poem does not include any praise of the Anṣār. Some reports suggest that Ka'b recited this poem to the Prophet a few days later, and that the omission of the Anṣār was due to the fact that one of their number was quick to suggest to the Prophet that Ka'b should be killed.[4] It is perhaps more accurate to say that, in keeping with the traditions of the time, Ka'b recited his poem to the Prophet at that first meeting. That he did not include any praise of the Anṣār was due to the fact that Ka'b did not know much about them. He praised the Muhājirīn because they were his own people who had supported the Prophet ever since the early days of Islam. Shortly afterwards, Ka'b composed a fine poem praising the Anṣār, after having learnt fully the true nature of their role in serving the cause of Islam.

The stories of Ka'b ibn Zuhayr and Ḥātim ibn 'Adiy serve to give a clear idea of the sort of progress Islam was making in winning the hearts of important individuals, as distinct from the progress it was making on the battlefield and in international relations. This latter form of progress is the one to which we shall turn our attention presently.

Notes

1. Ibn Sayyid al-Nās, *'Uyūn al-Athar*, Dār al-Turāth, Madinah, 1996, p. 278. Also, al-Wāqidī, *Kitāb al-Maghāzī*, Oxford University Press, 1996, Vol. 1, pp. 984-989.
2. Ibn Hishām, *al-Sīrah al-Nabawiyyah*, Dār al-Qalam, Beirut, Vol. 1, pp. 225-228.
3. Ibn Kathīr, *al-Bidāyah wal-Nihāyah*, Maktabat al-Ma'ārif, Beirut, Vol. 6, p. 239.
4. Ibn Hishām, op.cit., pp. 144-158.

39

Trouble Looming at International Borders

THE LAST FEW months of the eighth year of the Islamic calendar, which begins with the Prophet's settlement in Madinah, brought about a total change in the map of Arabia which was bound to have an effect on the whole region. It may be useful to remind ourselves that the authority of the Byzantine Empire extended to the area which today forms Palestine and Jordan. These areas, as well as southern Syria, were under the rule of an Arab governor from the tribe of Ghassān who exercised his limited authority as an agent of the Byzantine Emperor. It is a well-known fact of history that changes of a radical nature in one country are bound to affect neighbouring countries. Hence, it is only natural that the Byzantine Empire should keep a close eye on what was happening in Arabia.

Before the advent of Islam, the emperors of Byzantium looked at Arabia as a vast desert which could present no trouble to their Empire. It was thinly populated by tribes who were often at loggerheads with one another. These tribes were not expected to present a threat of any kind to one of the two superpowers of the day. Internal feuding among these tribes was the surest of guarantees against any trouble emanating from their area. This was perhaps a major reason for the emperors of Byzantium not to try to extend their rule over Arabia itself; there was little to tempt them to do so.

The Arabs themselves lived in awe of their great neighbour. They tried not to meddle with the affairs of the Byzantine Empire or its semi-autonomous regions closest to them. They were happy to have the reassurance that the Emperor in Byzantium did not concern himself unduly with their own affairs.

All this underwent a radical change over a period of a few years. When Islam moved to Madinah and established its small state there, this might have looked to the ruler in Byzantium as one of the numerous insignificant developments which constantly took place in that area of tribal warfare. That ruler, however, might have felt the need to take a closer look at what was happening in the heart of Arabia a few years later, when Islam scored one success after another against its enemies. Whether he did take such a look or not, he was soon to be disturbed by a strong knock on his own door in the form of an emissary from the Prophet calling on the then greatest ruler on earth to submit himself to God and to accept the authority of God's Messenger. The first contact between the Muslim state and the Byzantine Empire was described in detail earlier on, as was the Battle of Mu'tah, the first military encounter between the new Islamic state and the Byzantine Empire. Although that battle ended in a military defeat, in the technical sense, for the Muslims, it must have been an unpleasant jolt to the Byzantine Emperor. A force of 3,000 Muslims was able to cause enormous trouble to a Byzantine army at least 50 times bigger, and to inflict heavy losses on it.

Close Monitoring of Arabian Affairs

When the Byzantine Emperor looked at Arabia some 18 months later, the political map looked very different to him. There was no longer any war going on in Arabia. All resistance to the new message of Islam there had collapsed. Makkah itself, for so long the focus of opposition to the Prophet and his message, had now confirmed its loyalty to him. The new faith was making inroads into Makkan society at a great rate. All other major tribes of Arabia, such as the Hawāzin and the Thaqīf, were forced to admit their helplessness against the rising tide of Islam. The Hawāzin were quick to try their luck against Islam after the fall of Makkah, and that helped them to recognize their error and to remedy it by declaring their acceptance of the new faith. The Thaqīf, on the other hand, were so helpless that the Prophet decided that there was no point in maintaining their siege. It was only a matter of time before they were bound to come into the fold. Moreover, the Jews in Arabia no longer represented any threat of any kind to Islam. Looking at the Arabian scene at the end of the eighth year of the Prophet's settlement in Madinah, the Byzantine Emperor would have been startled to realize that all Arabia was now loyal to the Prophet.

The first four months of the ninth year of the Islamic calendar were relatively quiet. The Prophet, however, was soon to hear that the Byzantines were raising a large force to attack the Muslim state and try to inflict on it a heavy defeat which, they hoped, would cut it down to size. The Prophet verified the information and soon found out that it was accurate. It was mostly communicated by Coptic traders who came to Arabia to sell their goods.

There were several indications which suggested that the Byzantines showed great interest in what was taking place in the Muslim state. For one thing, a companion of the Prophet who was boycotted by the Muslim community because of his failure to join the Muslim army on the expedition of Tabūk, without any valid reason for his failure, was contacted by the Ghassānī ruler, who was an agent of the Byzantine Emperor, offering him asylum and a good position. This will be discussed in more detail in the next chapter, but the point here is that the case of that companion of the Prophet was a very localized case and the ruler of the Ghassān would not have heard of it unless he had constant contact with some elements in Madinah. These elements must have belonged to the group of hypocrites who pretended to be Muslims. That was a false pretence, but there were quite a few such people in Madinah. They were largely people who were too cowardly to acknowledge their lack of faith and felt that their pretending to be Muslims could serve certain interests of theirs.

Another example of the interest shown by the Byzantine Empire in the affairs of the Muslim state is the case of Abū ʿĀmir al-Rāhib. Abū ʿĀmir was a man of high standing in Madinah before the arrival of Islam there. He had expected that a prophet was bound to come soon and harboured the aspiration that he would be the chosen Prophet. When he realized that his aspiration was not to be fulfilled after the arrival of the Prophet in Madinah, he defected to the Quraysh. Later, he defected to Byzantium and tried to raise support there against the Prophet. Apparently, the Byzantine Emperor received him well and promised him support. Abū ʿĀmir then established contact with some of the hypocrites in Madinah, promising them to raise an army to fight the Prophet at the appropriate time. He encouraged them to establish headquarters which could be used by his emissaries to them and could serve in the meantime as an outpost for his people.

A Mosque for Intrigue

Having gained experience in scheming against the Muslim state, the hypocrites in Madinah thought of the devilish idea of building a mosque and inviting the Prophet to pray there. They chose a site close to the Mosque of Qubā', which was built by the Prophet as he made his first journey to Madinah. Qubā' was a few kilometres from Madinah, and building a mosque for the hypocrites there would serve the dual purpose of giving credence to their pretence to be good Muslims and at the same time allowing them to stay away from the watchful eyes of the closest companions of the Prophet. When they had completed their building work, they came to the Prophet as he was preparing to go on his expedition to Tabūk and said to him: "Messenger of God, we have built a mosque for the poor and the weak. It is easy for the people away from Madinah to use on rainy nights. We would be grateful if you would come and offer your prayers there." They used this stratagem in order to win the Prophet's sanction for their efforts. The Prophet said to them: "You see that we are preparing for a long journey, and we are busy with our preparations. When we come back, God willing, we will visit your place and pray there."

On his way back from Tabūk, the Prophet was informed by God that those hypocrites intended to use their mosque only to spread unfaith and to sow the seeds of division within the ranks of the believers. They also wanted it to be an outpost for those who fought against God and His Messenger. The Prophet, therefore, sent some of his companions to destroy that mosque before his arrival in Madinah. The whole incident is related in the Qur'ān (verses 107-110 of *Sūrah* 9, Repentance, which is largely devoted to revealing the truth about the hypocrites).[1]

There were other indications which confirmed that the Byzantine Empire maintained a close watch on what was happening in the Muslim state and in Arabia generally. It was natural, therefore, that the Prophet should take seriously the report that the Byzantines were mobilizing to attack the Muslim state. As has already been seen, the Prophet always adopted the strategy of attack as the best form of defence. That applied when his wars were mostly against Arabian tribes of large or limited capabilities. Could the same strategy be effective against the greater of the two superpowers of the time?

The Best Form of Defence

When intelligence reached the Prophet that the Byzantines were mobilizing to attack the Muslim state in Arabia, he was further informed that the Byzantine troops were being raised in Syria. The Emperor had given his soldiers their salaries and allowances for a year in advance. The Arab tribes of Lakhm, Judhām, 'Āmilah and Ghassān also mobilized to join the Byzantine army. Their forces moved into the plains of Balqā' in Palestine.[2] The choice which the Prophet faced was, according to historians, that he could either allow the Byzantines to penetrate into the desert of Arabia before meeting up with them at a place of his own choosing, or alternatively he could start by launching an attack against them. The first alternative was the easier one for the Muslims. However, it involved the risk of losing the loyalty of a number of tribes in northern Arabia, which had only recently entered into an alliance with the Muslims. Hence, the Prophet chose the second alternative.

That was not an easy choice. One can only imagine the dilemma of any small or medium-sized state of today's world finding itself in a position where it has to choose to launch an attack on the United States, or alternatively allow that superpower to attack it.

The Muslim state was in such a position barely four months after Arabia had become united under the leadership of the Prophet. Needless to say, the Prophet himself did not fear the consequences of challenging the authority of the Byzantine Empire. He trusted to God to bring about the desirable victory. When he made up his mind to go on the attack, the Prophet was simply continuing his policy that attack was the best form of defence. Moreover, it was only proper to trust to the power of God, Who had never let him down.

One must remember that it is not easy to get rid of well-established notions. Although the majority of the Arabs were now Muslims, they had until very recently held the Byzantines in awe. They could not have imagined themselves in opposition to the Byzantine Emperor. How could they now view the prospect of challenging Byzantium and its mighty forces?

The call to arms was announced in the month of Rajab, which happened to fall at the height of summer when the weather was extremely hot and travelling in the desert was almost unbearable. At that time of year people simply wanted to remain at home and do very little work. The prospect of going on a journey of up to 1,000 kilometres on camel back was not one which anyone could look forward to. Nevertheless, it had to be done. The Muslim state was facing an emergency, and emergencies impose their own rules. The call to arms was spread all over Arabia, so that all new Muslims could join up.

For the first time in his history, the Prophet specified his destination. In the past, whenever he intended to attack any people, the Prophet would not specify the particular place he was going to, or the particular tribe he intended to attack, hoping to take his enemies by surprise. This time, the difficulties presented by the journey made him inform the Muslims exactly where they were going, so that everyone could prepare himself as best he could for the difficult task ahead. Obviously, it would have been an ideal situation if every Muslim soldier could have his own camel to ride. That, however, was not easy to arrange. Most people lacked any means of transport. It was imperative that the mobilization should be a mobilization of all resources. Money, horses and camels were badly needed as well as soldiers.

Donations for the War Effort

The Prophet addressed the believers and encouraged them to respond to the call to *jihād*. He also reminded them of the importance of spending their money for the cause of God. He encouraged the rich to spend generously. The emergency the Muslim state was facing necessitated pooling all resources. Once again, the best response came from those companions of the Prophet who had always shown themselves to be in the forefront to meet any emergency. ʿAbd al-Raḥmān ibn ʿAwf donated 200 ounces of silver. Al-ʿAbbās ibn ʿAbd al-Muṭṭalib, the Prophet's uncle, gave a large donation, said to be 90,000 dirhams, or 9,000 dinars. Ṭalḥah ibn ʿUbaydellāh, Saʿd ibn ʿUbādah and Muhammad ibn Maslamah all donated generously. ʿUmar ibn al-Khaṭṭāb divided all his property into two halves and brought in one half as a donation. Abū Bakr brought in all his property. When the Prophet asked him what he had kept for his family, Abū Bakr answered: "God and His Messenger."

The largest donation of all, however, was made by ʿUthmān ibn ʿAffān. When the Prophet made his speech encouraging his companions to donate generously, ʿUthmān said: "My commitment is to provide 100 camels with all their equipment." As the Prophet descended one step from the pulpit, ʿUthmān made a further commitment of 100 camels, fully equipped for the journey. The Prophet came one step further down and ʿUthmān increased his commitment to 300 camels, fully equipped. The Prophet was so deeply touched by the donation made by ʿUthmān that he waved with his hand to express his admiration. He also said: "ʿUthmān will not suffer in consequence of anything he does in future." What this meant was that ʿUthmān's reward for his most generous donation was bound to outweigh any sin he might commit in future years. It also suggests that a person motivated by his deep faith to donate so generously could not be shaken, no matter what happens to him. Both facts were true of 'Uthmān. 'Uthmān also made a further financial donation which cannot be easily determined. According to certain reports, it was 1,000 dinars. Other reports put the figure at 10,000 dinars. Whichever amount it was, it was certainly a very generous donation which showed his unequalled generosity and willingness to help the Islamic cause as much as he could. The Prophet said on this occasion: "The one who has equipped the 'hardship army' has been forgiven his past sins by God."

'The hardship army' was the title given by the Muslims and historians to that expedition when the Muslims moved to meet the forces of the Byzantine Empire. Nothing describes that expedition more aptly than this title. It was an expedition beset by hardships from the very first moment. It, therefore, presented a difficult test for the believers.

All believers shared in the mobilization. Women sent in their jewellery to help equip the fighters with arms and transport. Everyone gave what he or she could give. If any believer had a camel to spare, he would give it to one or two of those who responded to the call to arms but did not have any means of transport, to share it between them. The believers realized that they had a difficult task ahead and they had to show that they could always be relied upon to respond well to the challenge facing them.[3]

A Test for the Faithful

It has already been mentioned that the Prophet specified the objective of the mission he was undertaking. One reason for breaking his very useful habit of keeping his destination a secret was that knowing the difficulty of the task ahead was bound to deter many a hypocrite from joining the army. Past experience showed that whenever those who were weak in faith or were hypocrites joined a Muslim army in any expedition, matters went wrong in one way or another. The Prophet wanted only those who were dedicated to the cause of Islam and willing to make whatever sacrifice was required of them to go with him. Only those people were useful soldiers when the going was bound to be hard. When the call to arms was made and those hypocrites realized what was required of the believers, they found themselves in a difficult spot. What position should they take? Should they demonstrate their reluctance, thereby giving themselves away and making their lack of faith well known? Or should they join in that army and undertake a journey which could be very difficult indeed?

In *Sūrah* 9 of the Qur'ān, Repentance, a lengthy passage is devoted to describe the attitude of the hypocrites. One should remember here that these were people who pretended to be in the Muslim camp, but were not true Muslims. The task of facing the Byzantine Empire in war was far too awesome for them to contemplate. It should be pointed out that in comparison to the Byzantine Empire the Muslim state was only a small, underdeveloped country suffering a shortage of everything needed in war: arms, material resources and men. It was not surprising, therefore, that most of the hypocrites decided to give that expedition a miss. They certainly had to seek excuses for not joining the Muslim army. Their excuses were mostly absurd. Some of them said that the hot summer was not suitable for war, and advised the Muslims not to go to war in the summer. The Qur'ān replies to this: "The fire of Hell is much hotter."

Absurdity Knows No Limits

The most absurd excuse, however, was that given by a man called al-Jadd ibn Qays. The Prophet met him one day as mobilization was going on and said to him: "How do you fancy fighting the Byzantines this year." Al-Jadd said: "I would rather you excuse me and not put me to such a severe test. My people know very well that no man is more infatuated by women than I am. I fear that if I see the Byzantine women and their beauty I may not be able to resist the temptation."

The Prophet left him after saying: "I excuse you." This particular incident is referred to in the Qur'ān as *Sūrah* 9 discusses the attitude of the hypocrites.

The hypocrites did not seek excuses only for themselves. They tried to discourage the believers from joining the army and to portray the impending encounter with the Byzantines as one of great danger. They spoke ill of the Prophet and tried to show that the decision to fight the Byzantines was not the result of proper and careful planning and consideration. Some of them said to the believers: "Muhammad wants to fight the Byzantines despite the lack of resources, the hot weather and the long distance separating them from us. Does he imagine that fighting the Byzantines will be as simple as inter-tribal warfare among the Arabs? It is easy to imagine his companions being driven in chains tomorrow by the Byzantines."

This is not a surprising attitude by people who were weak of faith when they considered the Byzantine Empire in the same light as most people view the super-powers of today. The prospect of any small country declaring war on the stronger of the two super-powers is not easy to contemplate in purely human terms. The hypocrites, however, did not reckon with faith as the prime motivator of the believers. Their leader, ʿAbdullāh ibn Ubayy, took all the steps which gave the impression that the hypocrites were joining the Muslim army. He chose a place for his supporters to encamp at. There were many of them pretending to be ready to go with the Muslim army. When the time came, however, and the Muslims marched northwards, ʿAbdullāh ibn Ubayy and his followers stayed behind, just as they did at the Battle of Uḥud.[4]

A highly contrasting attitude was shown by some of the believers whose poverty did not enable them to arrange transport for themselves. There were seven people, mostly from the Anṣār, who could not manage to get any camel or horse to travel with the Prophet and the Muslim army. They, therefore, went to the Prophet to explain their situation and request him to give them some transport. The Prophet explained that he had nothing available. All the horses and camels were allotted to other people and many camels were already shared by two or more people. The seven men realized that they were missing a valuable chance of going on a campaign with the Prophet. They went back to their homes with tears in their eyes. Again, this particular incident is mentioned in the Qur'ān where it absolves them of all blame for not joining the army. It was not to be expected that any person could walk all the way to Syria, which was over 1,000 kilometres away. Even if some people were prepared to walk, the army could not afford to move at walking pace.

Two of the seven men, ʿAbd al-Raḥmān ibn Kaʿb and ʿAbdullāh ibn Mughaffal, were still in tears when they met a man called Yāmīn ibn ʿUmayr. He asked them why they were crying and they told him that they were prevented from joining the army by their poverty and the fact that the Prophet did not have any spare camels to give them. He offered them a camel of his own to share between them and they were thus able to join.

Certain reports suggest that the Prophet subsequently received some camels and was able to give them to those men. So their desire to join the Prophet on that expedition was doubly gratified. It must be mentioned here that there was no question about the feelings of those people. They genuinely wanted to go with the Prophet, and the prospect of fighting the Byzantine army did not alarm them in any way, as it alarmed the hypocrites.[5]

Undermining the Army's Morale

The hypocrites were able to mix with Muslim society with ease. To all appearances, they were Muslims. Only at a time when true feelings were tested was the reality of their lack of faith apparent. When a genuine Muslim discovered that a friend of his, or someone with whom he had some social or business relationship, was not truly a Muslim, he made his loyalty to Islam absolutely clear. A man called Makhshan ibn Ḥumayyir was with a group of people when they started to speak about the awesome prospect of fighting the Byzantines. They spoke about the military prowess of the Byzantines and suggested that the Muslims would come out of their impending encounter with a result totally different from the victories they used to score against other Arab tribes. Makhshan made his feelings known to them: "What an enormity you have uttered! I wish to God that He would accept that each one of us be given a hundred lashes and be absolved of the consequences of what you have said, without it being mentioned in the Qur'ān."

The Prophet was informed by God of what those people had said. He sent one of his old companions, ʿAmmār ibn Yāsir, to ask them about it. He told them that if they denied saying anything, he would tell them exactly what they had said. When ʿAmmār did that, they came to the Prophet to apologize. One of their number, Wadīʿah ibn Thābit, spoke to the Prophet without dismounting from his camel: "Messenger of God, we were only joking and jesting." His words are also quoted in the Qur'ān. Makhshan ibn Ḥumayyir apologized to the Prophet, and he was the only one to be pardoned of those involved in that incident. He changed his name to ʿAbd al-Raḥmān and prayed to God to grant him martyrdom by being killed in a place where his body would not be found. God answered his prayers and he was killed at the Battle of Yamāmah, but no trace of him was ever found.[6]

The expedition of Tabūk is the name Muslim historians give to that campaign which was envisaged to culminate in a military conflict between the Muslims and the Byzantine Empire, which would perhaps be taking place in the southern parts of Syria or Palestine. The expedition of Tabūk was full of invaluable lessons for the advocates of Islam in all generations and societies. It posed a very hard test which could have been passed only by a person whose faith was his prime motivator. Anyone who harboured doubts about the truth of Islam was certain to fail that test. That expedition showed clearly who were the true believers who could be relied upon in times of difficulty. Their response was highly gratifying to the Prophet. The hypocrites, on the other hand, sought all sorts of excuses to relieve themselves of the task of keeping up appearances. So, when the army started its march, ʿAbdullāh ibn Ubayy and most of his fellow hypocrites stayed behind. The army left Madinah in the height of summer. The excessive desert heat, added to the great distance the army was supposed to traverse, combined to make its march exceedingly difficult. Yet the believers did not hesitate to join the army. There were 30,000 of them, which made that army the largest ever during the Prophet's time.[7]

Good Believers Staying Behind

There were some people who had genuine reasons to stay behind, and there were some who were asked by the Prophet to do so. Historians differ as to whom the Prophet asked to deputize for him in Madinah. Some of them mention Muhammad ibn Maslamah of the Anṣār; others suggest that it was Sibāʿ ibn ʿArfaṭah who was given that task. ʿAlī ibn Abī Ṭālib, the Prophet's cousin and one of the earliest to adopt Islam, also stayed behind. The Prophet asked him to look after his family during his absence. The hypocrites slandered ʿAlī and started to whisper that the Prophet did not like his presence and wished to be relieved of his company. When this rumour was circulated in Madinah, ʿAlī carried his arms and followed the army at high speed. He caught up with them at their first encampment, a short distance from Madinah. He told the Prophet what the hypocrites were saying. The Prophet said: "They are telling lies. I have asked you to stay in order to look after those I left behind. Go back, then, and take care of my family and yours. Are you not satisfied, ʿAlī, to be with me in the same relationship as Aaron was with Moses? The only difference is that there can be no Prophet after me." ʿAlī then went back to Madinah and the Prophet proceeded with his expedition.[8]

Four people whose faith was not to be doubted were still in Madinah when the army moved on – Kaʿb ibn Mālik, Murārah ibn al-Rabīʿ, Hilāl ibn Umayyah and Abū Khaythamah. They were all known to be true believers. Nevertheless, they were still in Madinah when the army was on its way. The first three were to have very special treatment which will be discussed in due course. Abū Khaythamah, whose name was Mālik ibn Qays, had a different story.

A few days after the army had moved, Abū Khaythamah came back home to rest on a day when it was extremely hot. He had two wives. At home, there were all the comforts one needed on such a hot day. Each of his two wives had prepared her sitting place in a well-shaded area of the yard. Each had prepared food and cold water for her husband. Both were awaiting his arrival.

When Abū Khaythamah came in, he looked at his two wives and what they had prepared for him. The thought of the Prophet moving along on his journey was before his eyes. He said to his wives: "God's Messenger (peace be upon him) is suffering the burning sun and the stormy wind, while I, Abū Khaythamah, enjoy the cool shade and the delicious food in the company of two pretty women in my own home? This is not fair. By God, I will not enter either of your two places until I have caught up with God's Messenger. Prepare some food for me to keep me going on my journey." When the food was prepared, he mounted his camel and went as fast as he could. He did not manage to catch up with the army until it arrived at Tabūk.

On his way, Abū Khaythamah met ʿUmayr ibn Wahb, who was also travelling fast to catch up with the army. Apparently, ʿUmayr, who was frequently sent on different errands by the Prophet and acted as his ambassador to rulers of other countries, had some good reason for his delay. The two travelled together until they were close to Tabūk. Abū Khaythamah then said to ʿUmayr: "I have perpetrated something bad. It may be advisable for you to slow down a little until I catch up with the Prophet, peace be upon him."

ʿUmayr slowed down and Abū Khaythamah continued to travel at speed. When his figure was visible to the army encamping at Tabūk, some of the companions of the Prophet drew his attention to that person travelling alone. The Prophet said: "Let it be Abū Khaythamah." When the man drew nearer, they said: "Messenger of God, it is indeed Abū Khaythamah."

When he reached the place where the Prophet was, he dismounted and greeted the Prophet. The Prophet spoke to him a phrase which implied warning. Interpreters suggest that it meant that he, Abū Khaythamah, brought himself very close to destruction. Abū Khaythamah related his story and the Prophet prayed to God to forgive him.

This was an example of how faith motivated people. Abū Khaythamah did not forget the Prophet and the situation he was in at a time when his own situation should have reduced everything else to insignificance. He realized that his place was with the Prophet and the Muslim army. When comforts beckoned, he was mindful of the discomfort his fellow Muslims were suffering. He had been slow to respond to the call of arms, but he did not allow his own comfort and enjoyment to distract him from his duty for long. When the full dimensions of the situation were clear before him, he wasted no time in rectifying this omission.[9]

The Prophet accepted Abū Khaythamah's apology and pardoned him. He even prayed to God to forgive him. This is the normal Islamic attitude. Any slip, error or sin is easily forgiven provided that the perpetrator turns to God in repentance and is sincere in his resolve not to sink back into error again. Islam realizes that human beings are subject to all sorts of temptations and can easily be turned away from the path of faith. What is needed is an assured welcome when a stray sheep comes back into the flock. Without such a chance we all would have been doomed, because we are always making mistakes and yielding to temptation.

This is a perfectly logical attitude of the religion of Islam, which welcomes every new Muslim with open arms. No matter how great one's past mistakes, how grave one's sins, the moment one accepts Islam is considered a new birth. One turns over a new leaf in one's own life and is, to all intents and purposes, a new person. This attitude is extended to Muslims who weaken before temptation. When they repent sincerely, they are assured of forgiveness. Needless to say, this applies to all Muslim men and women.

The Going is Tough, the Means Scarce

As has been seen, the expedition of Tabūk presented a challenge to every single man to give credence to his claim to belong to the Muslim nation. To do that he had to pass a number of tests, the first of which was when the Muslims were called upon by the Prophet to put in all their resources in order to raise a large and properly equipped army to take on the much larger forces of the Byzantine Empire. We have seen how the true believers responded to that call, but what can a poor man do in such circumstances? When the going gets tough and the means are scarce, how can a man with no money buy a camel, or a share of a camel, in order to join the campaign of the believers? *Jihād*, or struggle for the cause of God, demands sacrifice of either body or money or both. In the circumstances just before the expedition of Tabūk, a man with no money could do nothing. Yet there were examples of a high standard of faith attained by some of those very poor people.

ʿUlbah ibn Zayd was one such poor person. He yearned to go with the Muslim army, but could not find the means to do so. One night, he was alone in his home. He woke up and prayed for a long while. He reflected on the situation and tears sprang to his eyes. Then he addressed God with this emotional prayer: "My Lord, You have commanded us to go on *jihād* and You have encouraged us not to abandon this duty. Yet You have not given me what I need in order to be able to go on this campaign. Your Messenger cannot give me any means of transport. I therefore give in charity to every Muslim any right which I hold against him for a wrong he had done to me, whether in matters of money or self or honour."

The following morning, the man joined the dawn prayers as he always did. The Prophet asked: "Where is the man who was charitable last night?" Nobody answered. The Prophet repeated the question and said: "Let this man stand up." ʿUlbah stood up and explained to the Prophet what he had done. The Prophet said: "By Him who holds my soul in His hand, this has been credited to you as *zakāt* accepted by God."[10]

This is a case of a man who would dearly have loved to join the Muslim campaign. What he wanted was the chance to scale the height of sacrifice and lay down his life in the service of God's cause. He was unable to do so because of his poverty. However, he was rich in spirit. He felt that the least he could do was to forgo, for the sake of God, any right he held against any Muslim who might not have been in similarly difficult circumstances.

Unable to Keep Pace

The Prophet was fully aware of the magnitude of the problem of hypocrisy. He, therefore, wanted the challenge posed by the campaign to be a continuous one. That would give him and the Muslim community a better chance of knowing those elements in their midst who did not harbour any good feelings towards Islam, the Prophet or the Muslim community. As we have said repeatedly, the going was very tough indeed. It was only natural, therefore, that among those 30,000 who were in the army, there would be some who might not be able to keep pace with the rest. Every time a man fell behind, his case was reported to the Prophet. Every time the Prophet gave the same answer: "Leave him alone. If he is good, God will see to it that he will catch up with you. If he is otherwise, good riddance." The Prophet wanted to emphasize to all his companions that he would wait for no one. He who cared to be with the Prophet should not allow himself to be distracted by anything, not even his camel tiring.

At one stage of the journey, a man of no lesser standing in the Muslim community than Abū Dharr, one of the Muhājirīn and one of the first to accept Islam, was falling behind. His camel was no longer able to keep pace with the army. Abū Dharr tried hard to make his camel move faster. All his efforts were to no avail. Some of his fellow Muslims went to the Prophet and reported that Abū Dharr had fallen behind. The Prophet repeated the same answer: "Leave him alone. If he is good, God will see to it that he will catch up with you. If he is otherwise, good riddance."

Abū Dharr gave his camel every chance to pick up strength. He then realized that it was useless: the camel was absolutely exhausted. Feeling that there was no alternative, Abū Dharr dismounted, took his belongings off his camel and walked at a fast pace, hoping to catch up with the Prophet.

Soon, the Prophet stopped for a short while to allow the army a little rest. This stop gave Abū Dharr the chance to catch up. Someone standing near the Prophet pointed to the direction from which Abū Dharr was coming and said: "Messenger of God, there is a man walking alone in our trail." The Prophet said, "Let it be Abū Dharr." When the man drew nearer, they said: "Messenger of God, it is indeed Abū Dharr." The Prophet said: "May God have mercy on Abū Dharr: he walks alone, dies alone and will be resurrected alone."[11]

Here is another example of yet another companion of the Prophet scaling the unscaleable, motivated only by his faith. No army would punish a soldier for staying behind if his means of transport goes out of action in the middle of nowhere. Perhaps, if Abū Dharr had given his camel a day's rest, the camel would have been able to catch up with the army the following day. That was too long for Abū Dharr to wait. Rather than stay behind, he continued his march on foot.

It is perhaps appropriate to mention here that the Prophet's prophecy about Abū Dhārr's death came true. When he was in his final illness, Abū Dharr was at a place called al-Rabadhah, not far from Madinah. However, there was no one with him at that place apart from his wife and his servant. When he realized that he was dying, Abū Dharr told them that when he died they should wash him and have him wrapped. They were to put his body out on the road. They were to wait for the first caravan to pass and to tell them that the dead man was Abū Dharr, the Prophet's companion, and seek their help in burying him. When he actually died, his wife and servant did as he had told them. Soon a group of people from Iraq passed by on their way to Makkah to do the *ʿUmrah*. With them was another companion of the Prophet called ʿAbdullāh ibn Masʿūd. They were surprised to see that there was a dead man in that place. The servant addressed them: "This is Abū Dharr, the Prophet's companion. Help me bury him please." ʿAbdullāh ibn Masʿūd was in tears as he said: "The Prophet tells the truth. You walk alone, die alone and will be resurrected alone." He dismounted with his companions and buried Abū Dharr. ʿAbdullāh also told his fellow travellers about what the Prophet had said in connection with Abū Dharr during the expedition of Tabūk.[12]

Where Are the Byzantines?

The army marched on in those most difficult circumstances. There was no chance that anyone would contemplate going back, but the prospect of taking on the Byzantine forces in battle was drawing ever nearer. Genuine believers, however, did not mind that prospect. It could bring them one of two eventualities: victory over the Byzantines or martyrdom for the cause of God.

Today Tabūk is a relatively short distance within the northern borders of Saudi Arabia. At the time it was very close to the borders of the Byzantine Empire. When the Muslim army arrived there it encamped, ready to take on the might of the Byzantines. According to the information received by the Prophet, the encounter should have taken place in those parts. The Muslims, however, found no traces of any Byzantine forces.[13]

There are two explanations for the Byzantines' failure to clash with the Muslim army. The first is that the Byzantines withdrew their forces when they heard of the strength of the Muslim army. Had there been any confrontation in Tabūk, that would have been the second clash between the two sides within a short span of time. The first was Mu'tah, when the Muslim army was only 3,000 strong. In that clash, the Byzantine forces suffered heavy casualties, although the Muslim forces could not overrun their far superior forces. Now the Muslim army was ten times stronger. Hence, the prospect of fighting the Muslims did not appeal to the Byzantine Emperor.

The other explanation is that the information received by the Prophet was not correct. The Byzantines did not prepare an army to attack the Muslims in Arabia. That information about the mobilization of Byzantine forces was given by Coptic traders from Egypt doing business in Arabia. The present author finds the first explanation nearer to the truth. The Prophet would not have raised such a large army and marched such a long distance unless he was absolutely certain of the intelligence he received. In any case, the expedition stopped at Tabūk where the presence of the Muslim army was a demonstration of the strength of the Muslim state. The expedition was extremely useful to the Muslim community. The importance of the test provided by that expedition has already been mentioned. Moreover, it gave those Muslims who had embraced Islam only recently, after the conquest of Makkah and the Battle of Ḥunayn, a chance to discover for themselves what the requirement of *jihād* meant to every Muslim. There were also certain political gains to be made.

Dūmat al-Jandal

Tabūk was not very far from Dūmat al-Jandal, where a man from the tribe of Kindah called Ukaydīr ibn ʿAbd al-Mālik, a Christian, was the ruler. The Prophet sent a detachment of his forces under the command of Khālid ibn al-Walīd to bring Ukayder to him. The Prophet told his commander: "You will find him cow-hunting."

It was a hot night at Dūmat al-Jandal. The ruler was with his wife on the roof of his palace. Bulls and cows came very close to the palace and rubbed its door and walls with their horns. His wife said to Ukayder: "Have you ever seen such a thing before?" When he answered in the negative, she encouraged him to go down and hunt. He ordered his horse to be prepared and went out with his brother and many of his servants. When they were out in the open and started to chase the bulls, Khālid ibn al-Walīd and his force arrived and were able to arrest them without difficulty. Ukayder's brother, who was called Ḥasan, was killed. Ukayder was wearing a fine robe ornamented with gold. Khālid took it off him and sent it to the Prophet. When the messenger carrying it arrived, Muslims who felt the robe were amazed at its fine quality. The Prophet said: "Do you wonder at this robe? By Him who holds my soul in His hands, the handkerchief of Saʿd ibn Muʿādh in Heaven is far better than this."

Khālid travelled back with Ukayder until he arrived at Tabūk. The Prophet spared the life of Ukayder and entered into a peace agreement with him. That required Ukayder to pay tax to the Muslim state and accept its authority. The Prophet then allowed him to go back to his town. Shortly after the Prophet went away, Ukayder violated the agreement and Khālid ibn al-Walīd was dispatched to re-establish the authority of the Muslim state there. Khālid overran Ukayder's forces and was able to kill him.[14]

The Prophet recognized that those northern parts of Arabia which were very close to the Byzantine Empire were bound to be volatile. They could always be used by the Byzantines to create problems for the Muslim state in Arabia. The expedition to Dūmat al-Jandal should therefore be viewed in that light. It was undertaken in order to establish the authority of the Muslim state in those northern parts. It was indeed part of a more comprehensive effort which included several places. At Tabūk, the Prophet met Yūḥannah ibn Ru'bah, the ruler of a place called Aylah. He also entered into a peace agreement with the Prophet. The Prophet wrote him this document:

> In the name of God, the Merciful, the Beneficent. This is a pledge of security given by God and Muhammad the Prophet, God's Messenger, to Yūḥannah ibn Ru'bah and the people of Aylah, their boats and caravans travelling in land and on sea. They are given this covenant with God and with Muhammad the Prophet which includes all those who are with them, be they of the people of Syria or the people of Yemen or sailors. If any of them commits an offence, his money does not prevent his punishment in person. It is good for whoever takes it. They are not allowed to prevent people from making use of any spring of water which they have in land or sea.[15]

A delegation from the people of Jarbā' and the people of Adhruḥ came to the Prophet and agreed to pay the Muslims a protection tax. The Prophet wrote them a document outlining the terms of their agreement, and they kept that document. These were significant steps because the agreements made by the Prophet with those people ensured that the Muslim state in Madinah feared no trouble from the northern parts of Arabia.[16]

The Prophet spent 20 days at Tabūk with the Muslim army. He then consulted his companions on whether to move on to Syria or return to Madinah. ʿUmar said to him: "Messenger of God, if you are ordered to march on, then do so." The Prophet replied: "Had I been commanded to march on, I would not have consulted anyone." ʿUmar said: "Messenger of God, the Byzantines command very large forces. There are no Muslims in Syria. You have certainly come close to them, and they are worried about your approach. It seems to me that it may be preferable to go back this year and wait for future events as they will be determined by God." The Prophet acted on ʿUmar's advice and gave his instructions for the army to go back to Madinah.[17]

A Hard Test is Concluded

Those were the events of the expedition of Tabūk which may be compared, in certain respects, to the Encounter of the Moat which had taken place four years earlier when the allied forces of the Quraysh, the Ghaṭafān and the Jews launched a pincer attack on Madinah with the aim of exterminating the Muslims. That was an encounter which set the Muslims a very hard test. No major battle took place then, but the test was enough to prove how seriously the Muslims took their religion and how much they were prepared to sacrifice for it.

The expedition of Tabūk provided another very hard test on a much wider scale. The difference between the two is that the Encounter of the Moat came at a time when the Muslim state was still confined to Madinah and the Muslim forces were well below 2,000. The expedition of Tabūk was at a time when many people were willing or eager to pretend to be Muslims in order to join in what they considered to be the heyday of Islam. It was necessary, therefore, for the Muslim community always to try to establish who was a true Muslim and who was a hypocrite.

The Prophet and the Muslim army started their return to Madinah after they had ascertained that there was no possibility of an encounter with the Byzantine forces. Needless to say, the returning army needed to replenish its stock of water on every possible occasion. The Prophet realized this and made sure that the army would not be without water. At a certain stage on the way back, the army was approaching a valley called al-Mushaqqaq. Knowing that there was only a trickling spring in that valley, the Prophet gave his instructions to all his soldiers that if any of them reached that spring before him, he must not use any water until the Prophet had arrived there.

But the main problem of the Muslim state at that time was the presence of the hypocrites. The expedition of Tabūk was a test to distinguish true believers from those who pretended to be Muslims. Although most hypocrites did not go on this expedition, a small number of them did. There were always those who deliberately disobeyed the orders of the Prophet, hoping that their disobedience would prove to others that the Prophet was only an ordinary ruler who achieved a measure of glory by skilfully exploiting favourable events and circumstances. On this particular occasion, a small group of hypocrites preceded the army and arrived at that spring before the rest. Aware that the Prophet did not wish anyone to use the water of that spring, they deliberately used all the water that was available in the small pond there, leaving only the trickling spring for the rest of the army.

When the Prophet arrived at the spring, he found no water there. He wanted to know who had arrived there first, and when he was told their names, he said: "Did I not make my instructions clear that no one should use this water?" The Prophet cursed those people and prayed to God not to have mercy on them. He then dismounted from his camel and put his hand underneath the trickling water. He kept his hand under the water for some time before taking some water and pouring it on to the spring itself. He then rubbed it with his hand and prayed to God in a low voice which was not audible to his companions. Soon, the water was gushing out in force. The entire army had all the water they needed to drink and to give their camels. They carried as much water as they could. As they were leaving, the Prophet told them that those of them who lived for a few years more would hear that that valley would be the most fertile in the whole area.[18]

A Loner is Laid to Rest

Another incident which took place on the way back from Tabūk was that reported by ʿAbdullāh ibn Masʿūd, a companion of the Prophet who was known for his profound knowledge of Islam, his thorough study of the Qur'ān and his sure knowledge of the Prophet's traditions and pronouncements. He says that one night he woke up and noticed the light of a small fire at one side of the army. He went there and found the Prophet with his two closest companions, Abū Bakr and ʿUmar. He also realized that ʿAbdullāh al-Muznī, also known as Dhul-Bijādayn, had died. The Prophet and his companions dug a grave for him and the Prophet went down and asked his two companions to lower the body of the deceased. The Prophet said to them: "Lower your brother and hand him to me." They did, and he put him in his grave lying on one side. He then prayed to God: "My Lord, I am pleased with him, be pleased with him." When ʿAbdullāh ibn Masʿūd heard this prayer of the Prophet, he wished he was the man being buried in that grave.[19]

It is perhaps proper to mention here something about this man who was honoured by the Prophet in this way. The Prophet could very easily have instructed some of his companions to dig a grave and bury the man when he died. However, he was eager to make everyone realize that he himself held the deceased man in high esteem.

ʿAbdullāh was an orphan. When his father died, he left him nothing. His uncle was his guardian and helped him lead a successful life, and ʿAbdullāh was soon wealthy. He and his family lived with their tribe in an area not far from Madinah. When the Prophet arrived there the boy, whose original name was ʿAbd al-ʿUzzā, realized the merit of Islam and wished to be a Muslim. However, he could not disobey his uncle, who made it clear that he had no interest in being a Muslim. After a few years had passed, the boy said to his uncle: "I have been waiting for you to adopt Islam, but I see that you have no intention of doing so. Allow me, then, to follow the Prophet."

His uncle was angry and told him: "By God, if you follow Muhammad, I will deprive you of everything I have given you. I will confiscate everything you have, including the garments you are wearing." The boy was not to be put off. He said to his uncle: "I am indeed following Muhammad and abandoning idolatrous worship. You may take everything I have." His uncle took all his property and carried out his threat to the letter. He even made him take off his clothes.

The boy then went to his mother and asked her to give him something to cover his body. She had a very thick garment which she gave him. He took it and managed to make his way stealthily to Madinah. When he arrived there, he cut the garment in two and wrapped one half around his body and put the other piece over his shoulders. He went straight to the mosque in the middle of the night. When the Prophet had finished his dawn prayers, he saw him and asked him his name. When he answered that his name was ʿAbd al-ʿUzzā (which meant servant of al-ʿUzzā, a famous idol), the Prophet renamed him as ʿAbdullāh, and gave him the title of Dhul-Bijādayn, which meant the man with two thick garments. He told him to keep close to him. If the Prophet had any guests, Dhul-Bijādayn was always among them. He managed to learn considerable portions of the Qur'ān over a short time. When the Prophet was about to march to Tabūk, Dhul-Bijādayn asked him to pray to God to make him a martyr. The Prophet wrapped his upper arm with some plant and said: "My Lord, do not let the unbelievers shed his blood." The man said that he did not want that. The Prophet told him that if he went out on an expedition of *jihād* and fell ill and died, then he would be a martyr. If his horse or camel threw him and he broke his neck and died, he would be a martyr. It was in the expedition of Tabūk that ʿAbdullāh Dhul-Bijādayn died.[20]

One cannot fail to notice the fact that the Prophet did care for his companions as individuals. That boy would in all probability have remained just another person, had he joined any community other than that of the Muslims at the time of the Prophet. The Prophet, however, appreciated his keen desire to be a Muslim. He realized that he had strong faith. Otherwise, he would not willingly have agreed to be deprived of all his money in order to join the Prophet and the Muslim community.

Superior Compassion

Caring for individuals was something that came naturally to the Prophet. He was God's Messenger to all mankind. He could not, then, belittle any human being, no matter how humble he was. Another incident which shows how much the Prophet cared for every individual among his companions is the one reported by Abū Ruhm Kulthūm ibn al-Ḥusayn. He had been a companion of the Prophet for some time before the expedition of Tabūk. Indeed, he was among those who pledged their readiness to sacrifice themselves at the time of al-Ḥudaybiyah, when the Prophet asked his companions to make that pledge which was to be known as 'the Pledge under the Tree'. He mentioned that during the expedition of Tabūk, he was on his camel one night close to the Prophet. Many of the Muslims were sleepy, but they marched on.

He kept dozing off and waking up suddenly, realizing that his camel was drawing nearer to that of the Prophet. He feared that if his camel drew very close, he might hurt the Prophet's leg. However, he was no longer able to stay awake. As he dozed off, his camel was very close to that of the Prophet. He woke up suddenly as he heard the Prophet expressing his pain. He apologized to the Prophet and asked him to pray for his forgiveness.

The Prophet asked him to march alongside him. He questioned him about those who did not join the army from his own tribe, the Ghifār. He mentioned their names. The Prophet then asked him about "those tall men with thin hair in their beards." Abū Ruhm mentioned that they did not join the army. The Prophet then asked about "those short people with thick black hair." Abū Ruhm said that he did not know any group of people in the Ghifār tribe who answered that description. The Prophet affirmed that there were such people and mentioned that they had some cattle near a spring called Shabakat Shadakh. Abū Ruhm then remembered that they were a group from a clan called Aslam and they were allied to the Ghifār. He mentioned that fact to the Prophet who said: "If any of those men wanted to stay behind, could he not have given a camel to a man who wanted dearly to join the army? I feel particularly sorry when anyone from the Muhājirīn, the Anṣār, the Ghifār or the Aslam stays behind when we go on an expedition in support of God's cause."[21]

The army went back the whole way and as it approached Madinah, the Prophet sent two of his companions to destroy the mosque built by the hypocrites outside the city in order to be a centre of conspiracy against Islam. Following the Prophet's order, the two men destroyed the place and set it on fire.[22]

The army was received in Madinah by all the Muslims there. Women and children were singing and chanting, feeling very happy at the return of the Prophet and his companions. When the Prophet had settled back in Madinah, the hypocrites who stayed behind came to him offering their excuses for not joining the army. Every one of them asked the Prophet to forgive him, and the Prophet readily did so.[23] There was, however, a special case which involved three individuals who stayed behind but were not among the hypocrites. Their case is discussed in the next chapter.

NOTES

1. Ibn Hishām, *al-Sīrah al-Nabawiyyah*, Dār al-Qalam, Beirut, Vol. 1, pp. 173-174
2. Al-Wāqidī, *Kitāb al-Maghāzī*, Oxford University Press, 1996, Vol. 3, p. 990.
3. Ibid., pp. 991-992. Also, Ibn Hishām, op.cit., pp. 159-161.
4. Ibn Hishām, op.cit., pp. 160-162. Also, al-Wāqidī, op.cit., pp. 995-996.
5. Ibn Hishām, op.cit., pp. 161-162. Also, al-Wāqidī, op.cit., p. 994.
6. Ibn Hishām, op.cit., pp. 168-169.
7. Al-Wāqidī, op.cit., p. 1002.
8. Ibn Hishām, op.cit., pp. 162-163.
9. Ibid., pp. 163-164.
10. Ibn Kathīr, *al-Bidāyah wal-Nihāyah*, Maktabat al-Ma'ārif, Beirut, Vol. 5, p. 5.
11. Ibn Hishām, op.cit., p. 167.
12. Ibid., p. 168.
13. Ibid., p. 170.
14. Ibid., pp. 169-170.
15. Ibid., p. 169. Also, al-Wāqidī, op.cit., pp. 1025-1030.
16. Al-Wāqidī, op.cit., p. 1031.
17. Ibid., p. 1019.
18. Ibn Hishām, op.cit., p. 171.
19. Ibid., p. 171.
20. Al-Wāqidī, op.cit., pp. 1013-1014.
21. Ibn Hishām, op.cit., pp. 172-173.
22. Ibid., pp. 173-174.
23. Ibn Sayyid al-Nās, *'Uyūn al-Athar*, Dār al-Turāth, Madinah, 1996, p. 301.

40

Failure by True Believers

IT IS NOT uncommon for a person to act out of character at a certain moment in time. He may be a model of hard work and conscientiousness, yet he falls into a state of total apathy for no apparent reason. This may last for a brief spell and the person concerned may be able to resume his life as before, or it may continue for some time and lead to wide-ranging effects and complications. It is not our purpose here to try to analyse the psychological causes which may lead a person into such a state. One only wonders what should be the attitude of an army commander if he encounters such a problem with one of his lieutenants whom he knows for certain to be a dedicated soldier?

Psychologists may provide a variety of answers, but this question is asked here only as a way of introducing the following episode in the life of the Prophet. This episode concerns such a problem faced by three true believers at the time of the expedition of Tabūk. One must remember here that the Prophet was not merely an army commander – he was a Messenger of God. God has ordered all believers in all generations to obey the Prophet in all circumstances, whatever instructions he may give. Hence, obedience to the Prophet is a mark of faith. Conversely, disobedience is a mark of hypocrisy or lack of faith.

One should remember that when the Prophet ordered his companions to get ready for an armed conflict against the Byzantines, he made it clear that no one was excused from joining the army as long as he was physically able to travel. Yet over 80 people stayed in Madinah until the Prophet and his army came back. The large majority of them were hypocrites. When the Prophet came back, they went to him and gave various reasons for staying behind, asking him to pardon them. The Prophet granted their request, but God has made it clear in the Qur'ān that they have not been pardoned by Him. Three people had a different case altogether. Here is their story, as related by one of them, Kaʿb ibn Mālik:

No False Excuses

I have never stayed behind when the Prophet went on any expedition, except that of Badr. Neither God nor the Prophet blamed anyone for staying behind at the time of Badr, because the Prophet set out from Madinah to intercept a trade caravan which belonged to the Quraysh. The battle took place without any preparation or prior planning. On the other hand, I had attended the pledge of the Anṣār to the Prophet at ʿAqabah when we made our commitment to Islam absolutely clear. I would not exchange my attendance there with taking part in the Battle of Badr, although Badr is the more famous occasion.

Nevertheless, I failed to join the army of the expedition of Tabūk. I was never in better circumstances or more physically able than I was then. At no time did I have two means of transport except on that occasion. It was the habit of the Prophet to keep his destination secret. This time, however, setting his destination so far away, and moving in an exceptionally hot climate, he made it clear to the people that he intended to attack the Byzantines. Those who joined the Prophet were in such large numbers that no register of them could have been kept.

In the circumstances, anyone who wished to stay behind might have thought that he would not be noticed, unless God chose to inform the Prophet about him by revelation. The

Prophet decided to launch that attack at a time when fruits were abundant and people preferred to stay in the shade. The Prophet and the Muslims, however, were busy getting ready for their impending task. I went out day after day to the market place in order to get my equipment, but I always came back having done nothing. I always thought that I was able to get whatever I needed in no time. Nevertheless, I continued in that condition until it was time to move. The Prophet and the army with him started their march and I had not got my preparations under way. I thought to myself: "I can still get myself ready in a day or two and should be able to catch up with them." When they had covered quite a distance, I went out to the market and came back having done nothing. This continued day after day. By this time, the army must have covered quite a long distance. I thought I must make a move now and catch up with them. I wish I had done that, but I did not. Every time I went out after the Prophet and the army had left, I was troubled by the fact that I saw only people who were known to be hypocrites or people who were physically unable to join the army. My place was not with either group. I was told that the Prophet did not mention me until he had arrived at Tabūk. He remarked once to those who were present at Tabūk: "What has happened to Kaʿb ibn Mālik?" A man from the tribe of Salamah said to him: "Messenger of God, his wealth and arrogance made him stay behind." Muʿādh ibn Jabal said to him: "What a foul remark! Messenger of God, we have known nothing bad of the man." The Prophet made no comment.

I soon heard that the Prophet and his companions had started their journey back from Tabūk. I felt very sad. To tell a lie was paramount in my mind. I started thinking about what to say to the Prophet tomorrow, after his arrival, in order to spare myself his anger. I sought the help of everyone in my household. When it was mentioned that the Prophet was soon to arrive, all thoughts of seeking false excuses disappeared from my mind. I realized that the only way to spare myself the

Prophet's anger was to tell the truth. I was determined, therefore, to say exactly what happened.

The Prophet then arrived in Madinah. It was his habit when he came back from travelling to go first to the mosque and pray two *rak'ahs* before sitting to meet the people. When he did that, those who had stayed behind went to him and stated their excuses, swearing to their truth. They were over 80 people. The Prophet accepted their statements and their oaths and prayed to God to forgive them, leaving it to God to judge them by His knowledge. I then followed and greeted the Prophet. He said: "What caused you to stay behind? Have you not brought your transport?"

I said to him: "Messenger of God, had I been speaking to anyone on the face of the earth other than you, I would have been able to avoid his anger by giving some sort of an excuse. I can make a case for myself. But I know for certain that if I were to tell you lies in order to win your pleasure, God would soon make the truth known to you and I would incur your displeasure. If, on the other hand, I tell you the truth and you are not happy with me because of it, I would hope for a better result from God. By God, I have no excuse whatsoever. I have never been more physically able or in better circumstances than I was when I stayed behind." The Prophet said to me: "You have certainly told the truth. You await God's judgement."

Thus the man of honesty and true faith made his case. He did not try to make a false case for himself. His faith made him fully aware that he could not tell the Prophet a lie. Yet the Prophet did not pray to God for his forgiveness. His sincerity and honest reply did not merit him more than an acknowledgement of his truthfulness by the Prophet. Judgement was left to God. It was not an easy position for him, nor was his attitude appreciated by all people. Some people might have thought that had he given any excuse, the Prophet would have prayed to God to forgive him and that would have been sufficient. Indeed, some members of his clan came to him and said: "We have never known you to commit a sin before this. You could certainly have given the Prophet an excuse like all those who stayed behind. You would have been spared this trouble had the Prophet prayed to God to forgive you as he would surely have done."

Harder Times Ahead

Kaʿb says:

> They continued pressing me on this to the extent that I wished to go back to the Prophet and tell him that I was lying. Before I did that, however, I asked whether anyone else said the same thing as I did. They answered that two more people said the same and were given the same answer. When I asked their names, they mentioned Murārah ibn al-Rabīʿ and Hilāl ibn Umayyah. I knew these two to be men of faith and sincere devotion. I realized that the proper attitude for me was to be in their company. I, therefore, made no further move.
>
> The Prophet ordered all his companions not to speak to us three. He made no similar instruction concerning anybody else of those who stayed behind. All people were now evading us. Their attitude was changed. It was very hard for me that I did not even know myself or the place I was in. This was no longer the town I lived in. My world had changed. We continued in this condition for 50 days.
>
> My two companions, Murārah ibn al-Rabīʿ and Hilāl ibn Umayyah, stayed at home. I was the youngest of the three. I continued to go out and attend the congregational prayers with other Muslims. I frequented all the markets, but nobody would speak to me. I would also go to the Prophet and greet him as he sat down after prayers. I would always think to myself: "Have I detected any movement on his lips suggesting that he has answered my greeting?" I would pray close to him and look at him stealthily. When I was preoccupied with my prayers he would look at me, but when I looked towards him, he would turn his face away.
>
> When this boycott by all the Muslim community seemed to have lasted too long, I climbed the wall of an orchard which

belonged to a cousin of mine named Abū Qatādah, who was very close to me. I greeted him, but he did not answer. I said to him: "Abū Qatādah, I beseech you by God to answer me: do you know that I love God and His Messenger?" He did not answer. I repeated my question three times, but he still did not answer.

I then beseeched him again, and his answer came: "God and His Messenger know better." Tears sprang to my eyes and I came down. I went to the market and as I was walking I saw a strange man, apparently from Syria, enquiring about me. People pointed me out to him. He came to me and handed me a letter from the King of Ghassān, the Arab tribe in Syria. The letter was written on a piece of silk and read: "We have learnt that your friend has imposed a boycott on you. God has not placed you in a position of humiliation. If you join us, we will endeavour to alleviate all your troubles." When I read it, I thought it to be yet another test of my sincerity. I have reached so low that an unbeliever hopes that I would willingly join him. I put the letter in an oven and burnt it. When we had spent 40 nights in that situation, a messenger from the Prophet came to me and said: "God's Messenger (peace be upon him) commands you to stay away from your wife." I asked whether that meant that I should divorce her and he answered in the negative. He told me only to stay away from her. My two companions also received the same instruction. I told my wife to go to her people's home and stay there until God had given His judgement in this matter.

Hilāl ibn Umayyah was an old man. His wife went to the Prophet and said: "Messenger of God, Hilāl ibn Umayyah is very old and has no servant. Do you mind if I continue to look after him?" He said: "That is all right, but do not let him come near you." She said: "By God, these things are far from his mind. He has not stopped crying ever since this has happened to him. I indeed fear for his eyesight." Some people in my family suggested that I should seek the Prophet's permission to let my wife look after me. I said: "I am not going to ask him that. I do not know what his answer would be, considering that I am a young man."

The Test is Over

Another ten nights passed, to complete 50 nights since the Prophet instructed the Muslims not to talk to us. At dawn after the 50th night I prayed at the top of one of our houses. I was still in that condition which I have described: the world seemed to me suffocatingly small and I did not recognize myself any more. As I sat down after dawn prayers, however, I heard a voice from the direction of Mount Silaʿ saying: "Kaʿb ibn Mālik! Rejoice!" I realized that my hardship was over, and I prostrated myself in gratitude to God.

What happened was that the Prophet informed the congregation after finishing the dawn prayer that God had pardoned us. People moved fast to give us that happy news. A man came at speed on horseback to tell me, while another from the tribe of Aslam went on top of the mountain to shout the news to me. His voice was quicker than the horse. When I heard that man's voice giving me the happiest piece of news I ever received, I gave him my two garments as a gesture of gratitude. By God, they were the only clothes I had at that time. I borrowed two garments and went quickly to the Prophet. People were meeting me in groups, saying: "Congratulations on being forgiven by God." I entered the mosque and saw the Prophet sitting with a group of people around him. Ṭalḥah ibn ʿUbaydellāh came quickly towards me, shook my hand and congratulated me. He was the only one from the Muhājirīn to do that. I will never forget Ṭalḥah's kindness.

When I greeted the Prophet, he said to me, with his face beaming with pleasure: "Rejoice, for this is your happiest day since you were born!" I asked him: "Is my pardon from you, Messenger of God, or is it from God?" He said: "It is from God." When the Prophet was pleased at something, his face would light up and look like the moon. We always recognized that.

When I sat down facing him, I said to him: "Messenger of God, I will make my repentance complete by giving away all my property in charity." The Prophet said: "Keep some of your wealth, for that is better for you." I answered that I would keep my share in Khaybar. I then added that I was forgiven only because I told the truth, and I would make my repentance complete by never telling a lie at any time in my life.

I feel that the greatest grace God has bestowed on me ever since He guided me to accept Islam is my telling the truth to the Prophet on that day. Had I invented some false excuse, I would have perished like all those who told him lies. God has described those people in the worst description ever. He says in the Qur'ān: "They will swear by God to you when you return to them so that you may leave them alone. Turn away from them, for they are an impurity. Hell is their abode as a punishment for what they used to do. They swear to you so that you may be pleased with them. If you are pleased with them, know then that God will never be pleased with the evildoers." (9: 95-96) I have never knowingly or deliberately told a lie ever since I said that to the Prophet. I pray to God to help me keep my word for the rest of my life.[1]

This is the story of those three who were left to await God's judgement, as told by one of them. Every paragraph in this story is a lesson. It also serves to provide a picture of that first Islamic society which shows the strength of its structure, its purity of faith, its clear concept of their united community and of Islamic duties, as well as its recognition that everyone must always obey the orders given him or her.

Notes

1. Ibn Hishām, *al-Sīrah al-Nabawiyyah*, Dār al-Qalam, Beirut, Vol. 1, pp. 175-181. Also, al-Wāqidī, *Kitāb al-Maghāzī*, Oxford University Press, 1996, Vol. 1, pp. 1049-1056; Ibn Kathīr, *al-Bidāyah wal-Nihāyah*, Maktabat al-Ma'ārif, Beirut, Vol. 5, pp. 23-26; Ibn Sayyid al-Nās, *'Uyūn al-Athar*, Dār al-Turāth, Madinah, 1996, pp. 301-305; Amīn Duwaydār, *Ṣuwar Min Ḥayāt al-Rasūl*, Dār al-Ma'ārif, 4th edition, Cairo, pp. 571-576.

41

A Reluctant Change of Heart

THE PROPHET WAS first of all a man working for a cause. He viewed his mission first and foremost as one of a preacher who aimed at bringing about a total change in the lives of human beings. He went to war only when war was absolutely unavoidable. It was never his first choice. However, when circumstances made war inevitable, the Prophet did not weaken. He faced that eventuality with complete trust that God, who had sent him with His message, would do with him and the message of Islam itself whatever He pleased. The Prophet then carried out his task with the determination of one who knew that the ultimate result would be eventually decided by God. The Prophet, therefore, never slackened before any task, no matter how impossible it seemed to the human mind.

Every time the Prophet went to war he was confident that victory was assured to the Muslim community provided that they fulfilled their part of their deal with God – that is to say, they fulfilled their duties towards God and purged their hearts of any weakness of faith. As a human being and a leader of a community, the Prophet always loved to emerge from any military encounter victorious. Yet as a Prophet and a man working for a cause, which was his primary position, the Prophet always preferred not to have to go to war. He was more pleased with one person accepting Islam than with any military victory. To him, success was measured by how many people were able to accept God's guidance and how far he was able to spread his message.

The siege of Ṭā'if, where the major Arab tribe, the Thaqīf, lived was discussed earlier. This took place shortly after the Prophet's conquest of Makkah. From Makkah the Prophet marched to meet the Hawāzin, the tribe which became the focus of opposition to Islam. The Hawāzin were vanquished in the Battle of Ḥunayn and later joined the ranks of the Muslims. The Prophet then besieged the Thaqīf in Ṭā'if. When the siege continued for many days without any sign of weakness on the part of the Thaqīf, the Prophet consulted Nawfal ibn Muʿāwiyah about the situation. He compared the position of the Thaqīf to that of a fox in his hole. He said to the Prophet: "If you hold on, you will achieve the result you want. If you leave them now, they can cause you no harm." That was sound advice because at the time the Thaqīf were the only major Arab tribe left in opposition to Islam. On their own, they could do very little to impede its march. Indeed, the early signs of their change of heart were forthcoming.[1]

Hardened Hearts

When the Prophet ended the siege of Ṭā'if and went back to Madinah, he was followed by ʿUrwah ibn Masʿūd, a young man who was among the chiefs of the Thaqīf. ʿUrwah caught up with the Prophet before he arrived in Madinah. He declared his acceptance of Islam and stayed in Madinah for a while. He then requested the Prophet's permission to go back to his people in order to call on them to accept Islam. The Prophet warned him that they would kill him. He recognized that the people of Thaqīf were not in a mood to listen to any sound advice. Their pride would dictate their attitude. They needed time before they could view matters in a different light. ʿUrwah said: "Messenger of God, they love me more than they love their first children."

ʿUrwah indeed enjoyed a great measure of love among his people. They obeyed him in practically all matters. It was not unreasonable for him to hope that they would obey him when he called them to Islam. Subsequent events showed, however, that he did not gauge their mood correctly. He addressed his people from a platform, making clear to them that he had become a Muslim and calling on them to follow his suit. Little did he expect violent opposition, but that was what he received. Arrows were showered on him from all sides. One arrow hit him in a dangerous position and he was killed. On his deathbed, ʿUrwah was asked how he wanted his death to be avenged. He said: "My death is an honour given to me by God, who has made me a martyr. Nothing should be done more than was done in the case of those martyrs who were killed before God's Messenger left here. Bury me alongside them." He was buried there. What he meant was that no revenge should be sought.

A few months went by and the Thaqīf were still the only major Arab tribe which stood in opposition to Islam. They realized that their position was not a comfortable one. Should there be a fresh conflict, they would stand alone against the rest of Arabia. They reflected on their position for a long while before deciding to send a representative to hold preliminary talks with the Prophet. The man they chose for the task was also one of their leaders, ʿAbd Yālīl ibn ʿAmr ibn ʿUmayr. He knew the mentality of his people well. He recognized that the Thaqīf might be seriously considering its position, but he still feared that should he go on that mission and come back with something they did not like, they might treat him in the same way as they had treated ʿUrwah. He, therefore, said to them when the approach was made to him to go on that mission: "I shall not go alone. You have to send a full delegation with me." When they considered his attitude, they felt that a delegation might be even more useful to them. Whatever they agreed with Muhammad would be a collective decision, not one taken by a single person. They agreed to send a delegation of six people. In addition to ʿAbd Yālīl, they sent on this mission two of their allies, al-Ḥakam ibn ʿAmr and Shuraḥbīl ibn Ghaylān. The other three were of the clan of Mālik: ʿUthmān ibn Abī al-ʿĀṣ, Aws ibn ʿAwf and Numayr ibn Kharashah.

The Thaqīf Delegation in Madinah

The delegation travelled towards Madinah and when they were on the outskirts, they stopped at a place called Qanāh to rest. There they met al-Mughīrah ibn Shu'bah, a man from the Thaqīf who had been a Muslim for several years. When he was informed of their mission, he was so pleased. He left them to rest there and went quickly to give the happy news to the Prophet. On his way he was met by Abū Bakr who, on hearing the news, beseeched al-Mughīrah to let him be the one to give that news to the Prophet. Al-Mughīrah gratified Abū Bakr's wish and they both went to the Prophet. Abū Bakr was the one to speak and the Prophet was certainly pleased with this news.

Al-Mughīrah went back to his people at their place of rest. He taught them how to greet God's Messenger with the Islamic greeting: 'Peace be to you.' When they met the Prophet, however, they used their pre-Islamic form of greeting, which was equivalent to 'Good day.'

Al-Mughīrah had a personal request to put to the Prophet. When he made up his mind to embrace Islam, he was travelling with a group of his people towards Ṭā'if. They stopped at a certain point to rest, and he killed them all while they were asleep. He took all their belongings and went straight to Madinah to declare his acceptance of Islam. The Prophet accepted him as a Muslim but refused to take the money and property of those people as a booty of war. He said to him: "We accept you as a Muslim, but not the money. We do not admit treachery."

Now al-Mughīrah wanted to make amends. He thought that if he had the Thaqīf's delegation as his personal guests and extended hospitality to them, he would improve his standing in their books. The Prophet, however, had different priorities. He wanted those people to know as much about Islam as possible during their stay in Madinah. He told al-Mughīrah: "I am not stopping you from being kind and hospitable to your people, but I would like them to stay where they can listen to the Qur'ān." The Prophet, therefore, wanted a tent to be put up for them next to the mosque. In that place, they would be fully aware of the change Islam brought about in the lives of people. They would see how Muslims viewed their prayers and what effect prayers generally, and congregational prayers in particular, meant to them. They would listen to the Qur'ān, which expressed the message of Islam in God's own words.

The delegation from the Thaqīf was able to observe everything they wanted to observe. One thing they noticed was that the Prophet did not mention himself when he gave sermons. He said only: "I bear witness that there is no deity other than God." He did not follow that by the second part of the first article of the faith of Islam: "I bear witness that Muhammad is God's Messenger." The Thaqīf people wondered how the Prophet wanted them to declare their belief that he was God's Messenger when he did not reiterate that fact in his sermons. When he heard what they were saying, the Prophet said: "I am the first to testify that I am God's Messenger."

The Prophet appointed Khālid ibn Sa'īd ibn al-'Āṣ to look after the delegation and to serve as an intermediary between them and the Prophet. Indeed, it was Khālid who wrote down their agreement with the Prophet when it was finally concluded. They trusted Khālid to the extent that they would not touch any food sent to them by the Prophet unless Khālid joined them and ate with them.

Bargaining Hard

The members of the Thaqīf delegation went every morning to the Prophet to speak to him, leaving behind 'Uthmān ibn Abū al-'Āṣ, the youngest among them, to guard their belongings. When they came back to have their rest, 'Uthmān went to the Prophet to put his questions about Islam and to learn the Qur'ān. He did that many times and was soon a man with sound knowledge about Islam. If he found the Prophet asleep, 'Uthman ibn Abū al-'Āṣ would go to Abū Bakr to learn from him. He did not tell his fellow delegates about his activities. However, he deservedly earned the Prophet's love. When the delegation had spoken to the Prophet several times, they became inclined towards Islam.

Kinānah ibn 'Abd Yālīl said to him one morning: "Are you going to conclude an agreement with us so that we may return to our people?" The Prophet answered: "Yes, if you accept Islam. If you do not, then there is no meeting ground between us and we cannot have a peace agreement."

Kinānah wanted to extract some concessions. He and the rest of the delegation were aware that they would have to refrain from everything God had forbidden if they were to become Muslims. They feared that their people would not readily accept such restrictions. Kinānah said to the Prophet: "We travel far and wide, and we cannot do without adultery. Can you give us a concession?" The Prophet said: "It is forbidden. God says: Do not commit adultery; for it is indeed an abomination and an evil way." (17: 32)

Kinānah then made another request, this time seeking a concession on usury. He said that all the Thaqīf earnings came from usury. The Prophet answered: "You may have only your principal loans. God says: 'Believers, fear God and give up all outstanding gains from usury, if you are truly believers'." (2: 278)

Kinānah tried some other area to extract a concession. He said: "What about wine? It is only the juice of the fruits we grow, and we cannot do without it." The Prophet said: "God has made it forbidden." He recited the Qur'ānic verse: "Believers, intoxicants, games of chance, idolatrous practices, and the divining of the future are but a loathsome evil of Satan's doing. Shun it, then, so that you may attain to a happy state." (5: 90)

That session of the negotiations ended there. The Thaqīf delegation went back for consultation. When they were alone they considered what might be the result if they went back home without accepting Islam. The prospect was not a very promising one for them. Some of them said they feared that the Prophet would be able to march into Ṭā'if, their city, in the same way as he marched into Makkah, and the Thaqīf would not be able to put up any resistance. The result of their private consultations was that they agreed to accept the Prophet's terms.

They went back to the Prophet and told him that they accepted his terms. However, they questioned him about what he proposed to do with their great idol, known as al-Lāt. The Prophet told them to destroy it. They said: "That is impossible. Should the Deity know that you want us to destroy her, she would kill all the people around her." ʿUmar ibn al-Khaṭṭāb, who was present, said to Kinānah ibn ʿAbd Yālīl, "How ignorant you are! That Deity is nothing but a stone." The Thaqīf man retorted: "We have not come to speak to you, ʿUmar."

They made a passionate appeal to the Prophet to allow them to keep al-Lāt for three years, but he would hear nothing of it. They tried to compromise by reducing that period to two years, then to one year. But he refused all such requests. They argued that they feared for their lives, because the ordinary people of the Thaqīf, the women and the children, would be terrified if they were to see al-Lāt being destroyed. They said that they feared for their own lives if that was the outcome of their mission. Their arguments were of little value. To allow that idol to remain even for one day would be a negation of the first article of the faith of Islam. The Prophet would have nothing of it. When they reduced the period to one month, he told them most emphatically that he would not accept any such request. They finally said to him: "Then you destroy her yourself. We shall never destroy her."

They still wanted to extract some concession, and they asked the Prophet to exempt them from prayers. He finally said to them: "I will relieve you of the task of destroying your idols with your own hands. As for prayers, no good religion is without prayer."

A further session of private consultations followed those negotiations between the Thaqīf and the Prophet. By this time, members of the delegation learnt more about Islam than they ever had before. They were able to see the Muslim community conducting its life according to Divine teachings. They realized how strong the bonds between Muslims were. They also recognized how clean and pure Islamic life was. Everything they saw of Islam was highly appealing to them. Moreover, the basic concept of the monotheistic faith had its own appeal. They went back to the Prophet and declared their acceptance of Islam. Thus the agreement was made, written down and concluded. The rest of the Thaqīf, the last major Arab tribe to remain idolatrous, was now on the threshold of a great change in their lives.[2]

A Pattern to Be Repeated

The Thaqīf delegation was the first of a long stream of delegations from various Arab tribes, mostly in the remote places in Arabia. There was no longer any violent resistance to Islam. The Muslim state in Madinah was the only power in the area. Hence, the message of Islam was conveyed to the people freely. They feared nothing if they listened to it and accepted it. That was a remarkable change from the early days of the Islamic state in Madinah, when every other tribe was mobilizing some forces in order to attack Madinah or to fight the Muslims. Now all tribes were seeking to be in the good books of the Muslim state.

The same pattern is repeated again and again with the delegations from various Arabian tribes coming to Madinah. The Prophet first gave the delegation a chance to listen to the Qur'ān. He realized that nothing can soften the hearts of people towards the religion of Islam better than listening to the Qur'ān. It is, after all, God's word carrying God's message.

In the negotiations between the Thaqīf and the Prophet the delegation could not determine what the reaction of their people would be. This was because the Thaqīf were a large tribe, able to mobilize a large force. Moreover, their terrain was very difficult for any attacking army, so the delegation feared that when the Thaqīf realized that they were to give up everything, they might not accept those terms. Hence the delegation's attempt to extract concessions. The Prophet, however, adopted the only attitude worthy of a man of principle: nothing can be negotiable when it comes to the basics of faith. Nothing can be made lawful when God has made it unlawful. God has forbidden people adultery, usury, intoxicants and idol worship. No one can give any concession in these matters. This is a lesson to all those who advocate the message of Islam. Once they compromise their basic principles, the compromise will stop at nothing. People will want them to compromise the very basic concept of their faith – that is, submission to God. What they should do is stick to the principles of their faith and accept no compromise whatsoever.

Al-Lāt, which was generally referred to as a female idol or a goddess, was also known by other names, such as *Ṭāghiyah*, or the Tyrant, and *Rabbah*, or the Goddess. To describe al-Lāt's importance in the pre-Islamic days in Arabia, one can say that she was the first idol by whom any Arab would swear when he wanted to affirm anything. At the request of the delegation from the Thaqīf, the Prophet said that he would be sending some of his companions shortly after they had departed to destroy al-Lāt, in order to spare them that task.[3]

The delegation also requested the Prophet to appoint for them a man to lead them in prayer, and he assigned that task to ʿUthmān ibn Abū al-ʿĀṣ, who had shown great interest in learning about Islam and memorizing the Qur'ān. As already described, ʿUthmān was the youngest of the delegation, at only 20 years of age. He came to the Prophet and told him that he kept forgetting what he learnt of the Qur'ān. The Prophet put his hand on ʿUthmān's chest and prayed to God to help him. Later, ʿUthmān reported that he did not forget any part of the Qur'ān he subsequently memorized. The Prophet told ʿUthmān to be mindful of the weakest among his congregation and to appoint a *mu'adhin*, or a man to call for prayers, who would not expect wages for that task.[4]

Return of the Thaqīf Delegation

When the Thaqīf delegation were on their way home, they discussed among themselves the best way to break the news to their people. The killing of ʿUrwah ibn Masʿūd was foremost in their minds; ʿUrwah was a man dearly loved by the Thaqīf, yet they did not hesitate to kill him when he called on them to become Muslims. The delegation was made up of only six people, and they could be easily killed if the Thaqīf were not happy with the outcome of their mission. Their consultations led them to agree to follow the advice of Kinānah ibn ʿAbd Yālīl, who said to them: "I know the Thaqīf better than anyone else. Let us keep our agreement with the Prophet secret for the present and raise before them the spectre of having to meet Muhammad and the Muslims in war. Let us tell them that Muhammad made too many demands of us and we stood firm in our refusal. Tell them that he has demanded that we destroy the idol, al-Lāt, ban intoxicants and adultery and stop dealing in usury."[5]

As the delegation drew very near to Ṭā'if, their people came out to receive them. They were shocked to see the delegation covering their heads with their clothes to signal that they were distressed, and that their mission was a total failure. People thought that their delegation had come back with nothing good.

The delegation dismounted and immediately came to the place where al-Lāt stood in order to pay her their respects. This seemed very logical to the people of the Thaqīf, who realized that the members of the delegation had not seen al-Lāt for some time. Every member of the delegation went to his home. They were soon visited by their immediate relatives and neighbours, who were eager to find out what happened in Madinah between the delegation and the Prophet. They told them: "We have met a very hard man who insists on having everything he demands. He offers no compromise whatsoever, because he realizes that he owes his present position of strength to the sword and that his power extends over all Arabia. His offer to us was too hard to accept. He wants us to destroy al-Lāt, to abolish usury and to take back only the principal of whatever loans we give to people, ban intoxicants and adultery as well as similar demands."

The Thaqīf people said: "We will never accept such conditions." The delegation then advised them to get ready, mobilize all their forces and strengthen their forts.

For two or three days, the Thaqīf were preparing for a military confrontation. In the back of their minds, however, there was a different thought. Two days ago they had still been hoping that their delegation would come back to declare that they had achieved peace with Muhammad. The fact that they had originally thought of sending a delegation to the Prophet was an indication that they did not view the prospect of fighting the Muslims as a very welcome one. They realized that the Muslims were far stronger than they were. They were now shuddering at the thought of engaging them in battle. People of the Thaqīf started saying: "We are no match for Muhammad when the rest of Arabia has submitted to him. Let the delegation go back to tell him that we accept his conditions, and let us have a peace agreement with him on his terms."

When the delegation members realized that their people were serious about that, and would rather have peace than war, they told them the truth: "We have indeed made an agreement with him, giving him what we wanted to give and stipulating our conditions. We have found him to be the most God-fearing, truthful, compassionate and sincere of all people. We believe that our mission to him was a blessing to us and to you all. Our agreement is also a blessing. Rejoice, then, with God's blessings." Their people said: "Why then have you concealed the truth from us and caused us to be so depressed by the prospect of war?" The delegation replied: "We only wanted to give you a chance to rid yourselves of your pride." People from the Thaqīf started to declare their acceptance of Islam.

Destroying a False Goddess

A few days elapsed and a delegation from Madinah sent by the Prophet arrived at Ṭā'if. The delegation was under the leadership of Khālid ibn al-Walīd and included al-Mughīrah ibn Shuʿbah. They went straight to al-Lāt to destroy it.

All the Thaqīf came to witness that event: men, women and children. The vast majority of them did not think for a moment that al-Lāt, the goddess they were worshipping until yesterday, would be destroyed. They seriously thought that she had the power to protect herself. Al-Mughīrah ibn Shuʿbah, who belonged to the Thaqīf but had accepted Islam a few years earlier, took the axe in his hand and said quietly to his fellow Muslims: "I will give you a good laugh at the Thaqīf." As he hit al-Lāt with the axe, he pretended to fall down immediately.

The people of Ṭā'if cheered loudly. They said: "Away with al-Mughīrah. He has been killed by the Rabbah." They could not conceal their pleasure when they saw him falling down. They turned to the Muslim delegation from Madinah and said to them: "Let any one of you who dares try to destroy her. You will soon realize that you cannot touch her."

At this moment, al-Mughīrah sprang to his feet and said to them: "Foul on you, Thaqīf. What is she but a heap of mud and stones? It is about time you recognized God's blessings and worshipped Him alone."

He hit the door with the axe to break it and, together with his fellow Muslims, climbed the wall of the place housing al-Lāt. They broke her up into pieces until the place was completely levelled down. The key-keeper of the place said repeatedly: "The foundation will now show its fury and they will sink down into the bottom of the earth."

Al-Mughīrah then said to Khālid: "Let me dig up her foundation." He did so and the earth underneath was turned upside down. The Muslims took off all the jewellery which was placed on al-Lāt, a great amount. The Thaqīf were bewildered as the Muslims went ahead with their task. The destruction of al-Lāt went a long way towards reassuring the Thaqīf that they had chosen the right course. They realized that al-Lāt was absolutely useless: she was nothing more than a stone statue. Hence, their acceptance of Islam proved to be genuine.[6]

When the Prophet received the jewellery and the fine garments which the Muslim delegation brought with them from their mission to destroy al-Lāt, he thanked God and praised Him for His help and kindness. A few months earlier the Prophet had received two young men from the Thaqīf who came to declare that they were Muslims. One of them, Abū Mulayḥ, was the son of ʿUrwah ibn Masʿūd. The other was his cousin, Qārib ibn al-Aswad. When they came to the Prophet, they stated to him that they did not want to have anything to do with the Thaqīf for the rest of their lives. He suggested that they should ally themselves with whomsoever they wished. They said: "We ally ourselves with God and His Messenger. The Prophet said: "And with your maternal uncle, Abū Sufyān ibn Ḥarb." They accepted that.

When the Prophet received the jewellery of al-Lāt, Abū Mulayḥ asked him to pay back his father's debts from that money. The Prophet agreed. His cousin, Qārib ibn al-Aswad, said: "And also please pay the debts of al-Aswad, Messenger of God." The Prophet said, "But al-Aswad was an unbeliever when he died." Qārib replied: "Messenger of God, but if you do, you are doing a kindness to a Muslim relative of yours [meaning himself]. The debt is mine and I have to pay it back." The Prophet ordered Abū Sufyān, who was the one who brought the jewellery and other money of al-Lāt, to pay back ʿUrwah's and al-Aswad's debts out of that money. Abū Sufyān complied.[7]

This is how the Thaqīf changed camps. It was the last major Arab tribe to surrender to the new message. When it did so, however, the change was sincere and final.

Notes

1. Ibn Sayyid al-Nās, *ʿUyūn al-Athar*, Dār al-Turāth, Madinah, 1996, Vol. 2, p. 271. Also, al-Wāqidī, *Kitāb al-Maghāzī*, Oxford University Press, 1996, Vol. 1, p. 937.
2. Ibn Hishām, *al-Sīrah al-Nabawiyyah*, Dār al-Qalam, Beirut, Vol. 1, pp. 182-184. Also, al-Wāqidī, op.cit., pp. 960-967.
3. Ibn Hishām, op.cit., pp. 184-185. Also, al-Wāqidī, op.cit., pp. 967-968.
4. Ibn Hishām, op.cit., p. 186. Also, al-Wāqidī, op.cit., pp. 968-969.
5. Al-Wāqidī, op.cit., pp. 968-969.
6. Ibid., pp. 969-972.
7. Ibn Hishām, op.cit., pp. 186-187. Also, al-Wāqidī, op.cit., pp. 969-971.

42

Arabian Relations Set on a New Basis

AN IMPORTANT EVENT which took place in the same year as the expedition of Tabūk and the negotiations with the delegation from the Thaqīf was the death of ʿAbdullāh ibn Ubayy. He fell ill in the month of Shawwāl of the ninth year of the Islamic calendar, and died 20 days later. ʿAbdullāh ibn Ubayy was the chief of the hypocrites in Madinah. He was a man of high standing among his people; indeed, he was their choice for king shortly before they came to know about Islam. When the people of Madinah began to embrace Islam, they saw no need to choose a leader since it was taken for granted that the Prophet was the only leader of the Muslim community. Over the years. ʿAbdullāh ibn Ubayy demonstrated that he did not really believe in Islam. He maintained his close relationship with the Jews of Madinah and took their side against the Prophet on more than one occasion. He deserted the Muslim army just before the start of the Battle of Uḥud. On several occasions he expressed hostile feelings towards the Prophet and the Muslims generally. He was well known to be a hypocrite.

The Hypocrite Dies

His past, however, did not prevent the Prophet from visiting him during his illness. The Prophet realized that ʿAbdullāh ibn Ubayy was dying and said to him: "I have repeatedly told you not to love the Jews." ʿAbdullāh ibn Ubayy was unrepentant. He said: "Asʿad ibn Zurārah hated them, but what benefit was that to him?"

Asʿad ibn Zurārah was one of the very early people from Madinah to embrace Islam. He died soon after Islam was established in Madinah. ʿAbdullāh ibn Ubayy then said to the Prophet: "Messenger of God, this is not the time for speaking about past events. I am dying. May I ask you to be present when they prepare me for burial. May I further ask you to give me the garment you wear next to your skin so that I may be wrapped with it. Pray for me and ask God to forgive me!" The Prophet did so.

A different report suggests that when ʿAbdullāh ibn Ubayy died, his son, who was also called ʿAbdullāh and was a good Muslim, came to the Prophet and asked him to give him his shirt to wrap his father with. The Prophet did so. ʿAbdullāh then asked the Prophet to offer the prayer for the deceased for his father and the Prophet agreed. As he got up to walk with ʿAbdullāh to offer that prayer for the dead man, ʿUmar ibn al-Khaṭṭāb held him by his robe and said: "Messenger of God, are you going to pray for him when God has enjoined you not to do so?"

The Prophet said: "God has given me the choice when He said: 'Pray for their forgiveness or do not pray for it. If you pray for their forgiveness 70 times, God will not forgive them'." (9: 80)

ʿUmar still persisted. He questioned the Prophet on his prayer for a confirmed hypocrite who was always hostile to Islam. He quoted what ʿAbdullāh ibn Ubayy had said on several occasions. The Prophet then said to him: "Let me alone, ʿUmar. I have been given a choice. If I knew that he would be forgiven should I pray for him more than 70 times, I would certainly do so."

ʿUmar later reflected that he had thrust himself in this matter in a rather impertinent way. He was happy, however, when new Qur'ānic revelations judged his attitude to be the right one. In this revelation

God instructs the Prophet never to pray for a confirmed hypocrite again: "Never pray for any one of them when he dies, and never stand at his grave." (9: 84)[1]

ʿAbdullāh ibn Ubayy died when Islam was the supreme power in Arabia. The expedition to Tabūk was the last expedition during the lifetime of the Prophet. Since Makkah declared its loyalty to Islam, it was clear that no force in Arabia could mount any resistance to Islam. It has been seen how the Thaqīf, one of the most powerful of Arabian tribes, opted voluntarily to make peace with Islam and to accept the new faith.

The Thaqīf were the last hope for the forces opposed to Islam. When they became Muslim, there was no longer any possibility of any Arabian tribe mounting a campaign against the Muslim state.

There were, of course, numerous Arabian tribes scattered all over the Peninsula which had not made their position clear in one sense or the other about Islam. None of them was powerful enough to stand up to the might of the Muslim state. They were expected to make their position clear shortly. How delegations from various tribes started arriving in Madinah to declare their loyalty and acceptance of Islam is described in the next two chapters.

At the individual level, there were still a large number of unbelievers from all Arabian tribes. It was not to be expected that people would change their faith simply because the chief of their tribe issued his orders to them to do so. Faith remains a matter for the individual. Although idols were destroyed – especially the main ones like al-Lāt and al-ʿUzzā – and despite the fact that the Kaʿbah itself was now free of all idols, there were still people in Arabia who believed in idol worship. They carried on with their old habits and practices, some of which were offensive to Islam, especially in matters of worship. Moreover, those who accepted Islam needed time to learn about their new faith and to appreciate its moral values. It was not to be expected that they would change their lifestyle overnight, or become well versed in Islam in a few days. It was time, then, for the Prophet to consolidate the gains Islam had made over the last two years by confirming Islamic habits and practices.

Abū Bakr Leads the Pilgrimage

The Prophet and the Muslim army came back from the expedition of Tabūk in the month of Ramaḍān. Two months later the Prophet sent Abū Bakr, his closest companion, to do the pilgrimage and to be the Amīr of Muslim pilgrims. Three hundred Muslims from Madinah went with Abū Bakr. The Prophet sent with him 20 camels to be slaughtered in Makkah on his behalf. He appointed Najiyyah ibn Jundub from Aslam to look after those camels.

Abū Bakr took five more camels with him as his own sacrifice. The purpose of his pilgrimage was to make the difference clear between the Islamic way of pilgrimage and that of the unbelievers. The unbelievers used to do their *ṭawāf* naked. They felt that their nudity was a sign of their consecration of the Kaʿbah. They said that if they went round the Kaʿbah stark naked they would not be wearing anything which smacked of injustice. That was absurd logic!

Notice for All Non-Muslim Arabs

When Abū Bakr had gone part of the way towards his destination, *Sūrah* 9 of the Qur'ān, entitled Repentance, was revealed. It starts with a declaration terminating all past treaties made between the Prophet and the Arabian tribes, with the exception of those tribes which were absolutely faithful to the terms of their treaties. A period of grace lasting four months was announced. It was necessary to convey that message to all Arabian tribes, most importantly those who were parties to such treaties. The approaching pilgrimage season was the proper occasion for the termination of treaties to be announced. The Prophet consulted his companions, and they suggested that he should send someone to inform Abū Bakr of the new stand in order to declare it there. The Prophet said: "Only a man from my own household should convey this on my behalf." This was in keeping with social traditions of the time.

The Prophet summoned his cousin, ʿAlī ibn Abī Ṭālib, and gave him the following instructions: "Take out this new revelation of the beginning of the *Sūrah* and declare to all people on the day of sacrifice, when they have assembled in Minā, that no unbeliever will go into Heaven, and no unbeliever may offer the pilgrimage after this year. No one is allowed to do the *ṭawāf* naked, and whoever has a covenant or a treaty with the Prophet, that treaty will be honoured for the full length of its term."

ʿAlī travelled fast on the Prophet's own she-camel, al-ʿAḍbā'. When he caught up with Abū Bakr, the latter asked him whether he was appointed a leader or was merely joining him to remain under his leadership. ʿAlī said that Abū Bakr remained the leader of that expedition. They travelled together and Abū Bakr looked after the Muslim party as they offered their pilgrimage rituals.

Choosing the grand day of pilgrimage, which is the day of sacrifice, for the announcement of the termination of all treaties previously made between the Prophet and all unbelievers was ordered by God in the second verse of the *sūrah*. It was the most natural choice, since all Arabian tribes would normally be represented by their pilgrims who were certain to convey the contents of the announcement to their peoples. Thus, all Arabia was certain to know of the termination of treaties and no one could make an excuse of ignorance.

On the appointed day – that is, on the 10th of Dhul-Ḥijjah, when all pilgrims were in Minā – ʿAlī made his declaration: "This is an address to all people. Let them all know that no unbeliever may be admitted into Heaven. No unbeliever is allowed to offer the pilgrimage after this season, and no one is allowed to do the *ṭawāf* round the Kaʿbah in the nude. Whoever has a treaty with the Prophet, that treaty will be honoured for its full term. Those who do not have a treaty with the Prophet are hereby given a four months' notice." Abū Bakr despatched several people to make the same declaration at the encampments of various tribes so that everybody would hear of it on the same day.[2]

Claiming Arabia as the Land of Islam

What this declaration amounted to was a determination to make Arabia a land of Islam, to which no other grouping might have a claim. The announcement told the unbeliever Arabs that they had to define their attitude towards Islam by either accepting it or leaving its land. They had four months to make up their minds. All the Arabs knew that Muslims honoured their pledges. A period of grace was indeed a period of grace. Everyone, therefore, was safe and secure for that period. Everyone had ample time to organize his affairs and make his arrangements. If any person did not wish to be a Muslim, he would be able to liquidate his business, recover his debts and do whatever he liked in preparation for the new relationship.

Moreover, those who had treaties with the Muslims and were faithful to the terms of their treaties were given a new confirmation that the treaty was to be honoured by the Prophet and the Muslims up to its last day. There could be no renewal. If any treaty lapsed before the end of four months, then those who had that treaty would enjoy the longer period of four months.

This applied only to the unbelievers of Arabia. It amounted to the total liquidation of idolatry from that land. It was indeed a well-considered step to make Arabia the base of the Islamic message. As for the unbelievers in other parts of the world, they could co-exist peacefully with Islam and the Muslim state. What was expected of them was not to oppose and not to fight the Muslim state or back any power which was at war with the Muslim state. Many writers and commentators have spoken on this declaration. Many have written apologetically, trying to justify that declaration by showing that Islam was pushed into this attitude. Such an apologetic stance is absolutely unnecessary.

Firstly, a campaign against polytheism is similar to a campaign to combat illiteracy. Both are noble objectives. No one who wishes mankind well may raise any objection against either. For man to worship idols of stone or gold is to sink very low into the depths of ignorance. Moreover, Islam spared no effort over a period of 22 years to make people realize what evils they brought on themselves by worshipping statues and idols. The opposition to its call was simply an opposition which served the interests of certain leaders and groups who did not care for the well-being of mankind. Now that the issues were absolutely clear, and the opposition to Islam was no longer a matter of mistaken concepts, only those who harboured no good intentions towards Muslims and Islam were expected to hold to their idolatrous beliefs. They were a source of danger which had to be stamped out.

Secondly, the experience of those 22 years had shown absolutely clearly that there could be no real co-existence between Islam and polytheism. They are two fundamentally different ways of life. Indeed, they differ on every point of detail in matters of faith, morals and social values, as well as in their economic, political and social set-up. It is not to be expected that such radically opposed concepts of life can coexist peacefully for any length of time. Every step either of them takes must be totally and completely opposed to the attitude of the other. The clash between them was inevitable at every turn.

Some people may try to exploit this event in order to accuse Islam of standing against freedom of belief. They may cite the example of a person who wishes to continue to worship idols but does not take any hostile attitude towards Islam. They may ask: why should such a person be made to leave his Arabian home and seek to live somewhere away from Arabia? They forget that the concern here is the security of the Muslim state. The past history of relations between polytheism and Islam – and indeed the experience of the generations which followed – confirm beyond any doubt that the unbelievers would spare no effort, miss no chance and collaborate with any third party in order to undermine Islam. Now that Arabia was overwhelmingly a Muslim land, it was time to make it a land purely for Islam. The unbelievers must not be allowed to conspire against Islam in its own back yard.

One must not forget that those regulations applied only to the Arabian Peninsula. At no stage in Islamic history did unbelievers outside Arabia fear any personal or religious persecution by the Muslim state, as long as they did not meddle in its affairs. Followers of other religions, such as Christians and Jews, are treated differently. They may be citizens in the Muslim state, provided that they respect the rules and laws of that state. Any act of treachery or aggression against Islam is dealt with firmly by the Muslim state. If they maintain their peace with the Muslim state, they are given the right to be protected by the state; this protection means that they are free to live, work and worship in complete security. Islam needs no preaching about tolerance; its history shows that it has always been the most tolerant of religions. Tolerance, however, does not mean allowing a confirmed enemy to live and prosper in one's own back yard, knowing for certain that he will seize the first chance to evict his enemy. That was always the attitude of the unbelievers, as history has clearly shown. A serious religion like Islam cannot tolerate that without taking a firm and positive attitude. That was represented in the declaration which ʿAlī announced on behalf of the Prophet on the grand day of pilgrimage.

Notes

1. Al-Wāqidī, *Kitāb al-Maghāzī*, Oxford University Press, 1996, Vol. 1, pp. 1057-1058.
2. Ibn Hishām, *al-Sīrah al-Nabawiyyah*, Dār al-Qalam, Beirut, Vol. 1, pp. 188-191.

43

Islam Makes its Mark on Arabia

IT IS IN the nature of things that when a new religion or a new comprehensive ideology is preached, only a small number of people respond to it at the initial stage. They are those who are endowed with the type of insight which helps them identify the evil in the life of their society and discern the benefits which the new religion is bound to give. Also few are those who actively oppose the new religion. They are normally the people who fear for their vested interests as a result of the spread of the new faith. They are, however, able to recruit for such opposition the people who are immediately under their control, or follow their lead. The majority of people remain neutral. They prefer to adopt an attitude of 'wait and see'. They do not like to jeopardize their relations with either camp.

Before the advent of Islam, all Arabian tribes acknowledged that the Quraysh enjoyed the highest position of honour and authority in Arabia. When they saw the Quraysh taking a position of active hostility towards Islam, the faith preached by the Prophet Muhammad, all Arabian tribes, with the exception of the Aws and the Khazraj in Madinah, either joined the Quraysh in their hostility to the new faith or remained neutral. This last group of neutral tribes did not even bother to examine the faith of Islam. The merits of the cause did not matter to them. They did not feel that there was anything wrong with the way they lived that should be changed by Islam.

Nor did they aspire to play any important role in improving the quality of human life in order to embrace the cause of Islam. They simply adopted an attitude of 'wait and see'. Should Islam triumph, they were prepared to think seriously about joining its camp. If it were to be defeated, they would have taken appropriate precautions to remain in the Quraysh's good books.

After returning from the expedition of Tabūk, the Prophet sent his closest companion, Abū Bakr, to lead the pilgrimage and his cousin, ʿAlī, to claim total and religious authority over Makkah so that no unbeliever was able to offer pilgrimage according to the old practices of ignorance. The time had come for all Arabian tribes to realize that there was no longer any power in Arabia to challenge the authority of the Islamic state in Madinah. Even the last of the major Arab tribes, the Thaqīf, had given up the struggle against the tide of Islam. They were now followers of the Prophet. Hence, it was only to be expected that the Arabian tribes should start to review their position.

Delegations followed one another to Madinah, either to enquire about the essential elements of the faith of Islam or to pledge their loyalty to the Prophet and declare their belief in God's oneness and the message of Muhammad. There were, however, certain delegations which had some other purposes. Only the visits of delegations which had a special significance in one way or another will be described here.

A Drive for Power

One of the earliest delegations to arrive in Madinah was that of the tribe of ʿĀmir. This delegation included two men who did not have the smallest particle of faith, ʿĀmir ibn al-Ṭufayl and Arbad ibn Qays. The latter was famous all over Arabia for his physical power and fearlessness. The rest of the delegation realized that ʿĀmir ibn al-Ṭufayl did not harbour any good intentions towards the Prophet. Some of them tried to counsel him against doing anything foolish. They told him that the majority of the Arabs were now Muslims. It was only wise and expedient that their own tribe should follow suit.

ʿĀmir said to those who gave him that advice: "I have pledged to myself that I will not stop until I have forced the Arabs to accept my authority. Would I now be the one to accept the authority of this man from the Quraysh?"

The rest of the delegation had a different attitude. When they met the Prophet they said to him: "You are our master and the one who has power over us."

The Prophet said: "Watch what you say and do not let Satan fool you. The master is God." By this the Prophet meant that they should not place him in the position of any tribal chief, or indeed in the place of a king. He derived his authority from the fact that he was a Prophet and a Messenger of God. They were to address him acknowledging that fact. ʿĀmir ibn al-Ṭufayl, however, had a different objective. He said to his friend, Arbad ibn Qays: "When we sit with that man, I will try to distract him to give you a chance to hit him with your sword."

When they met the Prophet and discussed with him the purpose of their visit, ʿĀmir told him that he wanted to speak to him privately. The Prophet said: "Not until you have declared that you believe in God's oneness." ʿĀmir repeated his request again, and the Prophet reiterated that condition. As that discussion went on between the Prophet and ʿĀmir, the latter waited for his friend, Arbad, to hit the Prophet with his sword. Arbad made no move. ʿĀmir then said to the Prophet: "I will offer you one of three possibilities: you rule over the town people and I over the desert people; or I will be your successor; or I will raise the Ghaṭafān against you, mobilizing thousands of horsemen." The Prophet rejected all three and the delegation soon left.

ʿĀmir said to Arbad, the brave, fearless fighter who was supposed to kill the Prophet: "Confound you, Arbad. Why have you not done as I told you? I never feared a man on the face of the earth as I used to fear you. By God, I will never have any fear of you henceforth." Arbad said: "Do not blame me. Every time I was about to do as you said, I saw you in between him and me. If I lifted my sword I would have hit you. Would you have liked me to hit you with my sword?"

As they left, the Prophet prayed to God to spare him the designs of ʿĀmir ibn al-Ṭufayl. When the delegation were on their way back, ʿĀmir contracted some illness in his neck and quickly died as he was being nursed in the house of a woman from the tribe of Salūl.

When the remaining delegation arrived back at their dwellings, their people came to them to enquire about their mission. They spoke to Arbad and asked him what the Prophet said to him. His answer was: "He asked me to worship someone whom I would love to have in front of me now so that I could hit him with my arrows and kill him." Only a day or two later he left home leading a camel. Soon a thunderstorm was building up and he was hit by a thunderbolt which burnt him together with his camel.[1]

A Friendly Delegation

A delegation with a different attitude was that of the tribe of ʿAbd al-Qays. When they arrived, the Prophet asked them which tribe they came from. They answered: "We are from Rabīʿah." That was the name of the main tribe of which the ʿAbd al-Qays formed a clan. The Prophet said to them: "Welcome to a delegation who will suffer no humiliation and have no regrets."

Their attitude was one of loyalty to the Prophet right from the beginning. It is reported that the Prophet was talking to his companions earlier and said to them: "A group of travellers will come from this direction and they are the best people from the east."

ʿUmar went out in that direction to receive them. He met a group of 13 travellers who told him that they belonged to the tribe of ʿAbd al-Qays. When he asked whether they had come for trade, they answered in the negative. He told them that the Prophet had spoken highly of them a short while earlier. He walked with them until they arrived at the spot where the Prophet was. ʿUmar pointed him out to them and they quickly dismounted and went directly towards him. Some of them walked, some ran. They kissed the Prophet's hand. One man, known as al-Ashajj – that is, 'the man with a cut in his forehead' – was left behind. He took care of their camels and put on clean clothes before coming towards the Prophet and kissing his hand. The Prophet said to him: "You have two qualities which God and His Messenger love, patience and forbearance." The man asked the Prophet whether they were acquired by him or God had made him so. The Prophet answered that he was born with them. The man said: "Praise be to God, who has created me with those two qualities loved by God and His Messenger."

The delegation had no doubts about what course to take. They were Muslims before they came. They asked the Prophet to teach them something which was sufficient for them to conduct their lives on Islamic principles and to ensure that God would be pleased with them and admit them into heaven. The Prophet said: "I command you to do four things and forbid you four others. I command you to believe in God alone. Do you know what believing in God means? It is to declare that there is no deity other than God and that Muhammad is God's Messenger, to attend regularly to prayers, to pay the purifying alms [that is, *zakāt*], to fast in the month of Ramaḍān, and to give one fifth of the spoils of war to the Islamic state." He also forbade them the use of four types of containers which were used to make intoxicant drinks. One of them was called *naqīr*. They were certain that it was not known in the heartland of Arabia (their tribe lived in the eastern area which used to be called Bahrain). When the Prophet mentioned it, they asked him whether he knew what it was. He said: "It is made of the trunk of a tree in which you open a hole. You put dates in it, pour water over it and boil it. When it has cooled, you drink it. It has such an effect on you that one of you may hit his cousin with his sword." The Prophet mentioned this because he knew that the delegation included a man who had been hit with the sword by his cousin. He was trying to hide his injury from the Prophet.

The delegation also included a man called al-Jārūd ibn Bishr, who was a Christian. He said to the Prophet: "Messenger of God, I have been following a religion which I am now abandoning in order to follow your faith. Do you guarantee me your faith?" The Prophet said: "Yes indeed. I guarantee you that what I am calling you to believe in is better than your present faith."

The man declared his acceptance of Islam. He proved that he was firm in his faith. After the Prophet's death, many of his people reverted to their pagan religion. He, however, stood firm and addressed his people: "I declare that there is no deity except God, the One God who has no partners, and I declare that Muhammad is His servant and Messenger. He who does not believe in that is an unbeliever."[2]

Dialogue with a Wise Bedouin

Ḍammām ibn Thaʿlaba, a Bedouin from the tribe of Saʿd ibn Bakr, was a man with a straightforward approach. The companions of the Prophet were delighted with any wise Bedouin who came to the Prophet and put his questions to him. Such questions were normally of great value because the Prophet realized that he had to give his interlocutor satisfying answers which combined a direct approach and a precise mode of expression. Ḍammām was a unique example of such people. When he arrived in Madinah, he went straight to the mosque and dismounted from his camel at the doorstep. He tied up his camel and went in to find the Prophet sitting there with a number of his companions. The Prophet's companions looked up to find out who was that rough man with thick hair approaching them. As he drew close to them, he said: "Which of you is the son of ʿAbd al-Muṭṭalib?" ʿAbd al-Muṭṭalib was the Prophet's grandfather. It was customary in Arabia to address a man as the son of his grandfather.

The Prophet answered him: "I am his son." Then there followed this remarkable conversation between the man and the Prophet:

Ḍammām:	Muhammad!
The Prophet:	Yes.
Ḍammām:	Son of ʿAbd al-Muṭṭalib, I am going to put some questions to you but I will be hard on you. Do not be angry with me.
The Prophet:	I shall not be angry. You may ask whatever you wish.
Ḍammām:	I appeal to you by your God, the God of whoever lived before your time and the God of all those who will live after you: is it God who has sent you as a messenger to us?

The Prophet: It is certainly so.

Ḍammām: I appeal to you by God, your God and the God of those who lived before you and the God of those who will live after you: is it God who has commanded you to tell us that we must worship Him alone, without associating any partners with Him, and to disown those partners worshipped by our forefathers?

The Prophet: Yes indeed.

Ḍammām: I appeal to you by God, your God and the God of those who lived before you and the God of those who will live after you: has God ordered you that we must pray those five prayers every day?

The Prophet: Yes.

Ḍammām: I appeal to you by God: has God ordered you to take a portion of the money of the rich among us in order to pay it to our poor?

The Prophet: Yes indeed.

Ḍammām: I appeal to you by God: has God ordered you and us to fast this month in every 12 months?

The Prophet: Yes indeed.

Ḍammām: I appeal to you by God: has God ordered you that those of us who can afford it must make the pilgrimage to the House?

The Prophet: Yes indeed.

Ḍammām: I declare that there is no deity save God and I also declare that Muhammad is God's Messenger. I will certainly fulfil those duties and refrain from what you have forbidden me. I will not add anything to them and I will omit nothing from them.

Ḍammām went straight back to his camel and rode away. The Prophet said to his companions: "If that man with two plaits of hair honours his pledge, he will be admitted into Heaven." ʿUmar ibn al-Khaṭṭāb later commented: "I have never seen anyone who put his questions more precisely and concisely than Ḍammām ibn Thaʿalabah."

Ḍammām went straight to his people. When they saw him, they gathered round him to listen to the outcome of his mission. His first words were: "Al-Lāt and al-ʿUzzā are worthless." To start by declaring that the two main idols worshipped in Arabia were worthless was a shock to his people. They counselled him against using such words, lest the two idols punish him. They told him that he might be struck by leprosy or madness. He said: "They certainly cannot do anybody any harm or good. God has sent a Messenger and revealed to him His teachings in order to save you from your erring ways. I declare that there is no deity save God, the one God Who has no partners, and I declare that Muhammad is God's servant and Messenger. I have come back to you with the details of what God has ordered you and what He has forbidden you."

By evening, all the people of the tribe of Saʿd ibn Bakr, men and women, were Muslims. Ibn ʿAbbās declares that Ḍammām ibn Thaʿalabah was the best delegate who ever came to the Prophet.[3]

That was a successful mission by a man who sought the truth and abided by it when he learnt it. He approached his mission squarely, dealt with it fairly and acted on its results responsibly.

A Delegation Including a Liar

Another delegation arrived in Madinah sent by the tribe of Ḥanīfah from Yamāmah, a remote area of Arabia. That was a large delegation which included a man called Musaylamah. Apparently, Musaylamah was a man of ambition; he used to say to his people that if Muhammad could make him his successor, he would follow him. The Prophet never gave such a position to anyone.

When the delegation arrived in Madinah, they left Musaylamah to guard their camels and property and went to the Prophet. After their detailed discussions with the Prophet, they accepted Islam and pledged their loyalty to him. They also told him of Musaylamah being left to guard their property. The Prophet ordered that he should be given his share of gifts in equal measure to what he had given to every member of the delegation. He also commented: "The man is none the worse for being in his position." By this the Prophet meant that it was not a dishonour for the man to be left behind in order to guard the property of his people.

When the delegation went back to their quarters in Yamāmah, Musaylamah claimed that he was a Prophet. He told his people that he was given an equal share of prophethood with Muhammad. He said to the members of the delegation: "Did he not tell you when you mentioned me to him that I was none the worse for being left behind? He certainly did know that I was his partner."

Musaylamah also claimed to have received revelations from God. He used to repeat a few rhyming phrases which were indeed laughable. He told his people that he cancelled the prohibition of intoxicants and adultery. He also told them not to pray. He continued, however, to speak of the Prophet as a Messenger of God. He simply wanted to be treated on an equal footing. His tribesmen followed him.

Another report suggests that Musaylamah met the Prophet before the Ḥanīfah delegation went back. He apparently asked the Prophet to give him some position of honour. The Prophet told him that he would not give him even a piece of wood. He told him that he could not run away from God's will. The Prophet also mentioned to him that he had a certain dream and he supposed that he was the man concerned with that dream.

Ibn ʿAbbās reports that he enquired about that statement of the Prophet about his dream, and that Abū Hurayrah, another companion of the Prophet, told him that God's Messenger said: "As I was asleep, I saw myself wearing two gold bracelets on my hand. [Gold is forbidden to Muslim men.] I was troubled to see them on my hand. On inspiration in my dream, I blew them and they flew into the air. I interpreted them as two liars who would make their claims at a later stage. Here they are now. One of them is the one from ʿAns, in Ṣanā'. The other is Musaylamah, the liar from Yamāmah." (This *ḥadīth* is related by al-Bukhārī and Muslim.)

Musaylamah managed to gather a large force around him. A battle raged between him and the forces of Islam after the Prophet's death, in which he was killed. He certainly caused a great deal of trouble for a period of time shortly before the Prophet passed away, and in the early days of the reign of Abū Bakr.[4]

Christian Consultations at Najrān

In the south of Arabia, and a short distance to the north of the Yemen, lies the city of Najrān. At the time of the Prophet, Najrān and its surrounding area was a Christian valley. It had a Bishop called Abū Ḥārithah ibn ʿAlqamah from the tribe of Bakr ibn Wā'il. He was considered an authority on the Christian faith. He was in touch with Byzantine emperors who respected him, sent him financial aid and helped build a number of churches in the area.

When the conflict in Arabia moved strongly in favour of the Muslims, the Prophet sent a letter to the Bishop of Najrān which read: "In the name of the God worshipped by Abraham, Isaac and Jacob. I call on you to worship God alone and not to worship anyone alongside Him, and I call on you to give your loyalty only to God rather than to any of His servants. Should you refuse, you have to pay *jizyah* [a tax denoting loyalty and entitling the people who pay it to be protected by the Muslim state.] Should you also refuse that, I will declare war against you."

When the Bishop read that letter from the Prophet, he felt that the matter was very serious indeed. He was very much perturbed. He summoned a man called Shuraḥbīl ibn Wadāʿah, a man of sound judgement who was always called for consultation whenever a problem arose. None of the important people of Najrān was called before him. When he arrived, the Bishop gave him the Prophet's letter to read, then he asked him: "Abū Maryam, what do you say?"

Shuraḥbīl answered: "You know what God has promised Abraham about sending a Messenger from the children of Ishmael. You cannot rule out the fact that this man may be that Messenger. I have no opinion or judgement concerning prophethood. Had it been a matter of this world, I would have given you my opinion and I would have considered it carefully."

The Bishop asked him to sit aside. He then called in other people for consultation: ʿAbdullāh ibn Shuraḥbīl from the tribe of Asbaḥ and Jabbār ibn Fayḍ from the tribe of al-Ḥārith. Their opinion was exactly the same as that of Shuraḥbīl ibn Wadāʿah. When the Bishop considered that, he decided to call a public meeting. Church bells rang to announce to the people that a serious matter needed to be considered. People from all over the valley assembled to find out what was happening. There were 73 villages in that valley which could raise over 100,000 fighters. The Bishop read the Prophet's letter to the meeting and asked them for their opinion. They agreed to send a delegation of 60 people to Madinah, headed by the three men first consulted and including leading figures who held official positions, in order to get first-hand information about the Prophet.

When the delegation arrived in Madinah they changed into their best garments, which were made of silk. They also put on gold rings. They greeted the Prophet, but he did not reply. They tried to speak to him, but he would not answer. Amazed at his behaviour, they went about looking for two of the Prophet's companions, ʿUthmān ibn ʿAffān and ʿAbd al-Raḥmān ibn ʿAwf, who were well known to them. Both were traders who used to have some business with Najrān. They found them in the company of a number of Muslims from the Muhājirīn and the Anṣār. They told them that the Prophet wrote them a letter and they came in response, but he would neither reply to their greetings nor speak to them. They asked them whether they should return home. ʿUthmān and ʿAbd al-Raḥmān asked ʿAlī ibn Abī Ṭālib, the Prophet's cousin and son-in-law, what he felt about this. ʿAlī answered: "I feel that they should take off those garments and gold rings, and change back into their travelling clothes before coming to the Prophet again."

The Najrān Delegation with the Prophet

When they acted on ʿAlī's suggestion, the Prophet returned their greetings, and spoke to them in his friendly manner. Their discussion with the Prophet in the mosque took quite a long time. When it was time for their evening prayer, they prepared to pray, but some of the Prophet's followers wanted to prevent them from doing so. The Prophet ordered them to let the Najrān people offer their normal prayer. The discussion was resumed afterwards and it took a long while. They eventually asked the Prophet: "What do you say about Jesus? Since we are Christians, we would love to know your opinion so that we may be able to tell our people."

The Prophet said, "I have nothing to say about him today. You have to stay until I can tell you what will be said to me about Jesus, peace be upon him." Next morning, the Prophet received fresh Qur'ānic revelations which stated: "Jesus, in God's view, is the same as Adam, whom He had created from dust and said to him: 'Be', and he was there. This is the truth from your Lord. Be not, therefore, one of the doubters. Should anyone argue with you about him after what has been given to you of true knowledge, say to them: let us call in our children and your children, our women and your women, and ourselves and yourselves. Let us then all pray God and ask that God's curse overwhelm the liars." (3: 59-61)

When the Prophet told the Najrān delegation the following day what information he had received about Jesus, they refused to accept it. The Prophet then offered them the challenge which was outlined in the Qur'ānic verses quoted above. It was a serious challenge. It meant for the Najrān people that they risked being cursed by a Prophet and a Messenger of God. Such a prospect was not to be trifled with.

The following morning the Prophet came, bringing with him his two grandchildren, Ḥasan and Ḥusayn. His daughter, Fāṭimah, was walking behind him. He also had several wives at that time. When the Najrān people saw them, Shuraḥbīl ibn Wadāʿah felt that the matter was coming to a head. He said to his fellow leaders of the delegation, ʿAbdullāh ibn Shuraḥbīl and Jabbār ibn Fayḍ:

> The two of you know that our valley would not accept any opinion other than mine. I feel that the matter is very serious indeed. Should this man be a king, and should we be the first of the Arabs to reject his authority and challenge him, he will always harbour a grudge against us. He will not stop until he has overwhelmed us. We are not very far away from his land. If he is truly a Prophet and a Messenger of God, and we exchange curses with him, doom will befall us until the last hair and the last nail.

The two men rejoined: "What do you say, then? You do not have an easy way out there." Shuraḥbīl said: "My opinion is that we accept his judgement. I can see in him a man who is a model of fairness and justice." The two men accepted Shuraḥbīl's idea.

When Shuraḥbīl was face to face with the Prophet, he said to him: "I have come upon something better than exchanging curses with you." When the Prophet asked him what that was, Shuraḥbīl answered: "I will give you the whole day till the evening, and the whole night till the morning, to give your verdict in our case. Whatever you judge is acceptable." The Prophet said to him: "There may be some people back home who would blame you for this." Shuraḥbīl suggested that the Prophet should ask his two companions about his standing among his people. They told the Prophet that the whole valley accepted nobody's opinion except that of Shuraḥbīl. The Prophet remarked: "Well-judged by someone who rejects the faith."

Najrān's offer to accept the Prophet's judgement without question, giving him 24 hours to make it known to them, meant that they wanted a peace treaty with the Prophet, and left it to him to specify the terms of that treaty, promising to accept those terms whatever they were. They relied on what they knew of his absolute fairness.

A Treaty with Najrān

The following day they went to the Prophet, who caused the terms of the peace agreement to be written down for them. The agreed provisions were as follows:

> In the name of God, the Merciful, the Beneficent. This is what Muhammad, the Prophet and God's Messenger, has written down for the people of Najrān when he has the authority over all their fruits, gold, silver, crops and slaves. He has benevolently left them all that in return for 2,000 *ḥullas* every year, 1,000 to be given in the month of Rajab and 1,000 in the month of Ṣafar. Each *ḥulla* is equal to one ounce [a measure equal to 4 dirhams]. The Najrān are also required to provide accommodation and expenses for my messengers, for up to 20 days. None of my messengers shall be kept in Najrān more than one month. They are also required to give, as a loan, 30

> shields, 30 horses and 30 camels, in case of any disorder and treachery in Yemen. If anything is lost of the shields, horses or camels they loan to my messenger, it will remain owing by my messenger until it is given back. Najrān has the protection of God and the pledges of Muhammad, the Prophet, to protect their lives, faith, land, property, those who are absent and those who are present, and their clan and allies. They need not change anything of their past customs. No right of theirs or their religion shall be altered. No bishop, monk or church guard shall be removed from his position. Whatever they have is theirs, no matter how big or small. They are not held in suspicion and they shall suffer no vengeance killing. They are not required to be mobilized and no army shall trespass on their land. If any of them requests that any right of his should be given to him, justice shall be administered among them. He who takes usury on past loans is not under my protection. No person in Najrān is answerable for an injustice committed by another.

These were the main provisions of the peace agreement which was witnessed by Abū Sufyān ibn Ḥarb, Ghaylān ibn ʿAmr, Mālik ibn ʿAwf, al-Aqraʿ ibn Ḥābis and al-Mughīrah ibn Shuʿbah. When this was done, the Najrān delegation returned home. They were met on the way by the Bishop and the notables of Najrān who had travelled for one night in order to meet them. Alongside the Bishop was Bishr ibn Muʿāwiyah, also known as Abū ʿAlqamah, who was his half-brother and cousin. The Bishop was handed the written peace treaty. As he was reading it, with Abū ʿAlqamah on his she-camel alongside him, the camel slipped. In his anger, Bishr said: "Confound that man", meaning the Prophet.

The Bishop said to him: "You have indeed confounded a Prophet sent by God." Bishr replied: "Indeed! By God, I shall not get my camel to relax until I have gone to him." He directed his she-camel towards Madinah and proceeded to go.

The Bishop caught up with him and said: "Please understand me. I said this only so that the Arabs would know it. I fear they may say that we have been naïve, or that we have given this man what no other tribe has given him, while we are the strongest and the most powerful among them."

Bishr said to him: "By God, I shall never forgive you for what you have said." He drove his camel fast, leaving the Bishop behind. He went straight to the Prophet and declared his acceptance of Islam. He stayed in Madinah until he died as a martyr in one of the battles, fighting for the cause of Islam.

The delegation then went to the city of Najrān, where they were received by the rest of the people. A short while later, they visited a monk called Ibn Abī Shammar al-Zubaydī. He was at the top of his monastery. They gave him an account of the contacts between Najrān and the Prophet, since the Prophet first wrote to the Bishop. They also told him of what caused Bishr, the Bishop's brother, to leave for Madinah after the Bishop had stated that Muhammad was a Prophet. The monk was excited and wanted to get down. He said to them: "Unless you let me out, I will throw myself from the top of this monastery." He carried a present and went to the Prophet. His present included a garment which continued to be worn by caliphs long after the Prophet had passed away. The monk stayed in Madinah for some time, listening to the Qur'ānic revelations, learning about Islamic practices, obligations and punishments for crimes and sins. However, he did not declare his acceptance of Islam. He sought the Prophet's permission to go back home and said: "I have some business to do, and I shall come back, God willing." However, he did not go back to Madinah during the lifetime of the Prophet.[5]

It is useful to mention here that should a follower of an earlier religion state that Muhammad is a Prophet or a Messenger of God, his statement does not bring him into the fold of Islam. This statement is not sufficient to make him a Muslim. What it signifies is that the man knows that Muhammad is a Messenger of God, but to be a Muslim is much more than mere knowledge, even when it is expressed in words and statements. To be a Muslim is to believe in God's oneness and in the message of Muhammad and to accept that in practice, making obedience to God and to the Prophet, in public and in private, one's way of life.

The story of the Najrān people is not complete unless one also mentions a later episode, when the Prophet sent his military commander, Khālid ibn al-Walīd, to the tribe of al-Ḥārith ibn Kaʿb, in Najrān. The Prophet ordered Khālid to call on those people to accept Islam and to give them a period of three days to make up their minds. If they accepted Islam, Khālid was to accept that from them. If they refused, he would fight them. When Khālid arrived there, he sent his emissaries all over the place, calling on the people to accept Islam. They did so without much hesitation. Khālid stayed there for some time to teach the people how to live according to Islam. He wrote to the Prophet about the results of his mission, and the Prophet wrote back asking him to return to Madinah bringing a delegation from that tribe. When they arrived in Madinah and spoke to the Prophet, he asked them: "How did you achieve your victories in pre-Islamic days?" They said: "We used to stick together and allow nothing to divide us into groups. We also never started any injustice." The Prophet said: "You are telling the truth." He appointed Qubays ibn al-Ḥusayn as a leader of that tribe.[6]

Notes

1. Ibn Hishām, *al-Sīrah al-Nabawiyyah*, Dār al-Qalam, Beirut, Vol. 1, pp. 213-215. Also, Ibn Kathīr, *al-Bidāyah wal-Nihāyah*, Maktabat al-Maʿārif, Beirut, Vol. 1, pp. 56-60.
2. Ibn Hishām, op.cit., pp. 221-222. Also, Ibn Kathīr, op.cit., pp. 46-48.
3. Ibn Hishām, op.cit., pp. 219-221. Also, Ibn Kathīr, op.cit., pp. 60-62.
4. Ibn Hishām, op.cit., pp. 222-223. Also, Ibn Kathīr, op.cit., Vol. 5, pp. 48-52.
5. Ibn Kathīr, op.cit., pp. 52-56.
6. Ibn Sayyid al-Nās, *ʿUyūn al-Athar*, Dār al-Turāth, Madinah, 1996, p. 327.

44

The Peaceful World of Muslim Arabia

A Delegation from Tujīb

Yemen is in the farthest southern corner of Arabia. At the time of the Prophet, the people of Yemen began to know about Islam and to respond favourably to it even before the conquest of Makkah. The Prophet even sent one of his companions, Muʿādh ibn Jabal, to teach the people of Yemen about Islam and how to recite the Qur'ān. In the ninth year of the Prophet's settlement in Madinah – that is, a few months after the conquest of Makkah – a delegation from a clan called the Tujīb from Yemen travelled to Madinah. The Tujīb were a branch of the Sakūn tribe which was, in turn, a branch of the Kindah, the predominant tribe in Yemen. The delegation included 13 men who carried with them their *zakāt*, having collected it in the manner God had ordained. The Prophet welcomed them and was very pleased to see them. He saw to it that their stay was comfortable.

In one of their meetings with the Prophet, they said to him: "Messenger of God, we have carried with us that portion of our property which is due to God", meaning their *Zakāt*. The Prophet said: "Take it back with you and distribute it among your poor."

They replied: "Messenger of God, we have brought with us only what is in excess of the needs of our poor."

Abū Bakr, the closest companion to the Prophet, remarked: "Messenger of God, no Arab clan has come with anything similar to what this clan of Tujīb has brought." The Prophet said: "Right guidance belongs to God. When He wants good to come to a certain person, He makes his heart susceptible to faith."

The delegation made certain requests of the Prophet and he saw to it that their requests were met. They further asked him about the Qur'ān and the *Sunnah*, requesting him to teach them what was beneficial to them in their worship. The Prophet was impressed with them and ordered Bilāl to be particularly hospitable to them. They stayed for a few days before they decided to leave. Their stay was rather shorter than that of other delegations. When they were questioned about their hurried return, they said: "We want to go back to our people in order to tell them that we have met God's Messenger and report to them on what has taken place between him and us."

Rich at Heart

They went to the Prophet to bid him farewell and he instructed Bilāl to give them a more valuable gift than was normally the case with other delegations. The Prophet also asked them whether there was anyone else in their delegation whom he had not yet seen. They answered that they had left behind a young man, the youngest among them, to guard their camels and luggage. The Prophet instructed them to send the young man to him.

They went back to their camp and said to their fellow delegate: "Go to God's Messenger and finish your business with him. We have finished our business with him and bidden him farewell."

The young man went to the Prophet and said to him: "Messenger of God, I am a man from the clan of Abdhah [another name for Tujīb] and one of the delegation who has just visited you and whose requests you kindly attended to. Will you please grant my request, Messenger of God?"

When the Prophet asked him what he wanted, the man said: "My request is unlike those of my friends, although they have come to you keen to be good Muslims and have brought their *Zakāt* with them. I, however, have come from my homeland only to request you to pray God, the Almighty, to forgive me and have mercy on me and to make me rich at heart."

The Prophet was pleased with the young man and turned to him attentively and prayed: "My Lord, forgive him and have mercy on him and make him rich at heart." He also ordered that the young man be given a gift similar to the gifts of his fellow delegates. He then returned to his companions and they travelled back home.[1]

The same people met the Prophet a year later in Minā when he did his pilgrimage. They introduced themselves to him, and the Prophet immediately asked them: "What has become of the boy who came to me with you?" They said: "Messenger of God, we have never seen anyone like him. Indeed, we have not been told of anyone who is more content than this boy with what God gives him. Should any group of people have the whole world at their disposal and divide it between them, he would not turn his face towards them." The Prophet said: "Praise be to God. I hope that he will die altogether."

Amazed at this prayer by the Prophet, one of them said: "Messenger of God, does not every one of us die altogether?" The Prophet said: "A person's concerns, desires and preoccupations wander about in all the valleys of his life. His time of death may come when he is in any one of these valleys. God, infinite as He is in His glory, does not care in which of them he perishes."

That young man was a person who had the insight to discover that the riches of this world count for little. He hoped for what is certainly greater than this world – that is, to be content with whatever he has and to look to the hereafter, where those who are saved enjoy happiness which cannot be compared with anything in this world. In short, he hoped to be rich at heart. Since the Prophet prayed for him to be granted his desire, God answered that prayer and the man was a model of a person who cared nothing for the riches of this world.

Some of his people remarked: "That boy continued to live among us as one of the best people. He was the most content of people and he cared nothing for any luxury of this world. When God's Messenger passed away, certain groups of the people of Yemen deserted the faith of Islam and reverted to their erring ways. He addressed his people, reminding them of God and their faith, so that none of them reverted to unbelief."

Abū Bakr, the first ruler of the Muslim state after the Prophet, remembered him. He kept enquiring after him until he learnt of what he did. Abū Bakr wrote to his governor of Yemen, Ziyād ibn Labīd, recommending the young man to him and instructing him to look after him.

That was the case of a man whose name has been forgotten. It seems that one aspect of the richness at heart God has given this man is the fact that he is not mentioned by name. What he did is well recorded, because his action serves as an example for all generations of Muslims. Fame is one aspect of the richness of this world. The man wanted nothing of that richness. Hence, his name is forgotten. When God answers a prayer from the Prophet, it is answered in the most perfect manner. Rich at heart that man certainly was.

A Young Leader for Saʿd Hadhīm

A similar case was that of a man who arrived in Madinah as a member of the delegation of a clan called Saʿd Hadhīm, a branch of the tribe of Quḍāʿah. One member of that delegation reports:

> I have travelled in my people's delegation to meet God's Messenger when he had subdued all the land and triumphed over all the Arabs. At that time, people were of two types: those who embraced Islam willingly, and those who were scared by the sword. We encamped on the outskirts of Madinah, and went towards the mosque. When we arrived at the door, we found God's Messenger offering the normal prayer for a deceased person at the mosque. We stood to one side and did not join the prayer, waiting to meet God's Messenger and pledge our loyalty to him.
>
> When the prayer was over, the Prophet looked at us and asked us to come forward. He asked who we were and whether

we were Muslims. When we answered in the affirmative he said: "Why have you not prayed for your deceased brother?" We said: "Messenger of God, we thought that we could not do that until we have given you our pledges." The Prophet said: "Wherever you embrace Islam, you are Muslims." We declared our acceptance of the faith of Islam and made our pledges to the Prophet.

When it was time for us to depart, we went back to the place where we encamped. We had left there the youngest among us to guard our property. The Prophet sent someone to call us back and we returned. Our young fellow came forward and pledged his loyalty and declared that he was a Muslim. We said: "Messenger of God, he is the youngest among us and he serves us." The Prophet said: "The youngest of the people is their servant, may God bless him." He was indeed the best among us, and he read the Qur'ān better than any one of us because of the Prophet's prayer for him.

The Prophet made that young man our leader. He always led us in prayer. When it was time for us to leave, the Prophet ordered Bilāl to give every one of us a gift, which was a few ounces of silver. We went back to our people and God was kind to them and guided them to accept Islam.[2]

The Year of Delegations

History books which report the events that took place during the lifetime of Prophet Muhammad (peace be upon him) call the ninth year after the settlement of the Prophet in Madinah the 'year of delegations', to denote the fact that numerous delegations arrived from all over Arabia pledging loyalty to Islam and the Prophet. The lessons that can be learnt from those delegations and their conversations with the Prophet are many and varied. Some came to try to find out what was going on in Madinah and what was the true nature of the new faith. Some represented tribes who were already Muslims. The overwhelming majority of those delegations went back after declaring that they had accepted Islam. It was not to be expected that their type of life and their old habits would change overnight. When the Prophet passed away, many of those tribes had not learnt enough about Islam to continue to honour their commitment to it. This explains why some of them went back on their pledges after the Prophet's death. It is worth studying the missions of three of those delegations who were not shaken when the Prophet's life on earth ended.

It is useful to point out here that these events are not related in any chronological order. Muslim historians do not document the exact time of the arrival of each delegation in Madinah. This is not surprising, considering the fact that before Islam, the Arabs were generally illiterate. Moreover, historians and Muslim scholars were concerned most with the events as they happened and the lessons which could be learnt from them.

The Hamdān Delegation

One of these delegations came from the tribe of Hamdān in Yemen. It is authentically reported by al-Barā', a companion of the Prophet, that God's Messenger sent Khālid ibn al-Walīd to the people of Yemen calling on them to accept Islam. Al-Barā' says:

> I was one of those who went with Khālid. We spent six months calling on them to accept Islam, but the people there did not give any favourable response to Khālid.
>
> The Prophet then sent for ʿAlī ibn Abī Ṭālib and asked him to travel to Yemen and send Khālid back to Madinah. The Prophet allowed any one of Khālid's soldiers to remain with ʿAlī. I was one of those who stayed on. When we drew close to those people, they came out to meet us. ʿAlī led us in prayer, having ordered us to form only one row. When the prayer had finished, he stood up and read the Prophet's letter to the people of Hamdān. All of them declared their acceptance of Islam. ʿAlī wrote reporting to the Prophet that Hamdān had accepted the faith of Islam. When the letter was read to the Prophet, he prostrated himself, thanking God for His grace. When he lifted his head, he said: "Peace be to Hamdān. Peace be to Hamdān."

> They sent a delegation to the Prophet which included Mālik ibn al-Namṭ, Mālik ibn Ayfaʿ, Ḍammām ibn Mālik and ʿAmr ibn Mālik. They met the Prophet shortly after his arrival back from Tabūk. They had their best clothes on. Mālik ibn al-Namṭ recited a few lines of poetry praising the Prophet. They spoke well in front of the Prophet. He granted them all their requests, putting it all in writing. He appointed Mālik ibn al-Namṭ their leader.[3]

Another delegation was that of the tribe of Bali, who were met by their fellow tribesman, Ruwayfiʿ ibn Thābit, a companion of the Prophet. They stayed in his home. Ruwayfiʿ took them to the Prophet and after greeting him, he said: "These are my people."

The Prophet said: "Welcome to you and to your people." When they had finished their discussions with the Prophet, they declared their acceptance of the faith of Islam. The Prophet said to them: "Praise be to God, who has guided you to accept Islam. Any one of your tribe who dies believing in a religion other than Islam will go to Hell."

The delegation was led by a man called Abū al-Ḍubayb, who was renowned for his hospitality. He said to the Prophet: "Messenger of God, I like to be hospitable to my guests. Will I have any reward for that?" The Prophet said: "Yes indeed. Any favour you do to any man, rich or poor, is counted as a charity." He then asked about the duration of hospitality one should offer to guests. The Prophet said: "Three days. If it goes on for longer, it is a charity. It is not lawful for the guest to stay with you afterwards and embarrass you."

Abū al-Ḍubayb continued his question: "Messenger of God, what do you say about a stray sheep which I may find in the desert?" The Prophet replied: "It belongs to you or to your brother or to the wolf." The man said: "What about the camel?" The Prophet answered: "Why do you want to bother with him? Leave him until he is found by his owner."

Ruwayfiʿ ibn Thābit reports: "The people then left the Prophet and came back to my home. Shortly afterwards, the Prophet himself came to my place, carrying some dates. He said to me: 'Make use of these dates.' They ate them and other things, spending only three days with me. They then bade farewell to the Prophet and he gave them some gifts before they returned to their people."

It is worth pointing out here that the Prophet gave two different rulings in the cases of different stray animals, depending on the nature of each. In the case of a stray sheep, it is sure to end up eaten by a wild animal unless it is claimed by someone. Hence, the person who takes it is supposed to hold it for some time in order to give it to its owner, should he be known. If it remains unclaimed, the person who found it may benefit from it. He is required to compensate the owner if he becomes known later. A camel, on the other hand, is expected to survive for some time in the desert, sufficient to give his owner a chance to find him.[4]

Twenty Characteristics of Faith

The third delegation was that of the tribe of Azd Suwayd ibn al-Ḥārith. A member of that delegation reports:

> I was one of seven men who were sent as a delegation from our tribe to the Prophet. When we entered the mosque and spoke to him, he was pleased with our appearance. He asked us what we were. We said: "We are believers." The Prophet smiled and said: "Every statement must have a substance. What is the substance of your statement and your beliefs?" Our answer was: "Fifteen characteristics, five of which we were ordered to believe in by your messengers, and five we were ordered by them to implement, and five were part of our moral code, prior to Islam, which we still maintain unless you reject any of them." The Prophet asked: "What are the five in which my messengers have ordered you to believe?" We said: "They have ordered us to believe in God, His angels, His books, His messengers and in resurrection after death."
>
> The Prophet asked: "What are the five that my messengers have ordered you to implement?" We said: "They have ordered us to declare that there is no deity other than God, to attend regularly to our prayers, to pay *Zakāt*, fast in the month of

Ramaḍān and offer pilgrimage to the House if we are able to do so."

The Prophet then asked us: "And what are the five which you have adopted in pre-Islamic days?" Our answer was: "To be thankful in times of plenty and to be patient in times of trial, and to accept the turns of fate, and to show our commitment and dedication when we meet the enemy, and not to express pleasure at misfortunes befalling our enemy." The Prophet commented: "These people are wise and learned. Indeed, they are so wise that they approach the degree of Prophets." He then said: "I am adding five more qualities so that you have 20 in all. If you are truly as you have described, then do not accumulate what you cannot eat, do not build houses you shall not use for living, do not compete for something you are leaving behind tomorrow, have fear of God, to Whom you shall return and be accountable, and look forward to what you are certainly facing and that in which you shall remain for ever."[5]

Two-Man Delegation from Jurash

Another report of the delegation of the Azd names Ṣurad ibn ʿAbdullāh as their leader. The Prophet appointed him chief of those of his tribe who had become Muslims. He also commanded him that he and his fellow Muslims should fight those who were still unbelievers in the tribes of Yemen. Ṣurad did as the Prophet ordered and marched at the head of a force of Muslims until he arrived at the town of Jurash, which was well fortified. Several tribes stayed in that town. They fortified themselves in it when they heard that the Muslims were marching towards them. Ṣurad besieged the town for about a month, but he could make no headway. He retreated, marching back to a mountain called Shakr. The people of Jurash thought that his retreat was an acknowledgement of defeat. They chased him and when they were close to him, he turned and fought them hard.

The people of Jurash had sent two men to the Prophet to find out about Islam. As the two men were sitting with the Prophet one afternoon, the Prophet asked: "In which land is Shakr?" The two men said: "Messenger of God, there is a mountain in our land called Kashr." That was the name the people of Jurash gave to that mountain. The Prophet said: "It is not Kashr; it is Shakr." The two men asked why the Prophet mentioned it. He replied: "Sacrifice to God is being slaughtered there now."

The two men sat with Abū Bakr and ʿUthmān, who told them: "Listen. The Prophet is giving you the sad news that your people are being killed. Go to him and ask him to pray to God to lift that disaster from your people."

The two men did as they were told, and the Prophet prayed for their people. The two men went back home to discover that their people were indeed attacked at that particular time on that particular day. That was enough for the people of Jurash to accept Islam and to send a delegation to the Prophet declaring their loyalty. The Prophet assigned them a certain area around their town as a protected area.[6]

Persisting Ignorance

The delegation of the tribe of Fazārah included fewer than 20 who arrived in Madinah shortly after the Prophet's arrival from his expedition to Tabūk. Their land was suffering from a shortage of rain which left its mark on them and on their camels. It appeared that they were willing to accept Islam, but they did not have a correct understanding of the teachings of Islam and the role of God's Messenger. When the Prophet asked them about conditions in their part of the world, one of them said: "Messenger of God, our land has been hit by drought, our cattle have been dying, our valley has become barren and our children have been suffering from hunger. Pray your Lord to save us, and intercede on our behalf with your Lord, and let Him intercede with you on our behalf."

This shows how ignorant they were of the true nature of prophethood and the role of God's Messenger. The Prophet never claimed to have any capacity other than that of a human being entrusted with the conveyance of God's message to mankind. That did not give him any sort of partnership with God to warrant that

God should intercede with him. God does not need to resort to anyone in order to accomplish what He wills. The Prophet was therefore angry that he should be addressed in this way. He did not want to take the man to task, for he knew that he meant well. He simply wanted to make the man understand his position in relation to God. He said: "Glory be to God. Mind how you speak. I may intercede with my Lord, the Almighty. But with whom does our Lord intercede? There is no deity other than Him, the Supreme, whose throne encompasses the heavens and the earth, both of which submit to Him, acknowledging His power and majesty."

The Prophet then gave them the happy news that rain would reach their land soon. He said: "God, the Almighty, laughs as He looks at your hardship and its impending end." The Bedouin said: "Messenger of God, does our Lord, the Almighty, laugh?" When the Prophet answered in the affirmative the Bedouin said: "We shall certainly have something good from a Lord who laughs."

The Prophet smiled at his comment. He then went up to the pulpit and lifted his hands and prayed. Part of his prayer ran as follows: "Our Lord, give rain to Your land and Your cattle, spread Your mercy and revive Your dead land. Our Lord, give us rain which brings us good, healthy drinking water, coming soon and in plenty, bringing benefit and no harm. Our Lord, give us a drink of mercy, not a drink of suffering, destruction, drowning or wastage. Our Lord, give us a reviving drink and grant us victory over our enemies."[7]

Super Food for Guests

Another delegation was that of the tribe of Bahrā', a branch of the major tribe of Quḍā'ah, who came from Yemen. The delegation included 13 men who went straight to the house of al-Miqdād. Welcoming them, al-Miqdād brought a tray of the best food available in Madinah at that time. He was very generous to his guests. The food was prepared for the family just before they arrived. Al-Miqdād served his guests before his family could eat. Al-Miqdād's wife Ḍubā'ah reports:

The tray came back to us after the guests had eaten, and some of the food was left on it. I put it in a small plate and sent it to God's Messenger with my servant, Sidrah. She found him at the home of Umm Salamah, his wife. The Prophet asked her: "Has Ḍubāʿah sent this?" She answered in the affirmative and the Prophet asked her to put the plate down. He enquired about al-Miqdād's guests and she told him that they were staying with us. The Prophet and all those who were in the house ate as much of the food as they wanted. Sidrah also ate with them. The Prophet then told her to take what was left to our guests. Sidrah brought the plate back.

We served the same plate for our guests every day as long as they stayed with us. They ate their fill and it never diminished. The people were amazed and said to al-Miqdād: "Abū Maʿbad, you are giving us of the most delicious food. We cannot afford that except once every now and then. We have been told that food is scarce in your city, but we see that you are giving us our fill." Al-Miqdād told them that he had sent the plate to God's Messenger, who had eaten part of it and returned it. The blessing was due to the fact that the Prophet's fingers had touched that food. The people said: "We bear witness that he is God's Messenger." They were even more reassured that they had come for the right purpose and accepted the right religion. That was what the Prophet wanted.

The delegation stayed several days longer, learning their religious duties. They then came to the Prophet to bid him farewell, and he ordered that they should be given gifts. They took them and went back home.[8]

The Murrah Delegation

Another 13-man delegation was that of the tribe of Murrah, headed by al-Ḥārith ibn ʿAwf. That was a branch of the Quraysh which several generations earlier had the same grandfather as the Prophet. They wanted to stress that fact to him. They said: "Messenger of God, we are your own people and your own clan. We descend from Lu'ayy ibn Ghālib."

The Prophet answered with a smile. He then asked al-Ḥārith where he had left his family and tribe. Al-Ḥārith answered that he had left them at Silaḥ and the surrounding area. The Prophet enquired about the conditions of that area. The man answered: "We are indeed suffering from drought: pray to God for us." The Prophet prayed: "My Lord, give them rain."

They stayed a few days before coming to bid farewell to the Prophet. He ordered Bilāl to give them gifts. He gave each one of them ten ounces of silver, and he increased the share of al-Ḥārith, who received 12 ounces.

When they arrived in their land, they found that there had been a lot of rain. They enquired when the rain had started, and discovered that it had started on the very day when the Prophet prayed for them. Their land was subsequently more fertile than it had ever been.[9]

Hungry Men Feed the Beasts

A ten-man delegation from the tribe of Khawlān arrived in Madinah in the month of Shaʿban of the tenth year of the Prophet's settlement in that city. They said to the Prophet: "Messenger of God, we come as representatives of our people whom we have left behind. We believe in God, the Almighty, and we accept the message of His Messenger. We have travelled on our camels to come to you, traversing hills and valleys. We acknowledge the favours of God and His Messenger. We have come to visit you."

The Prophet said to them: "As for what you have mentioned of traversing the land to come to see me, you are credited with a good action for every step made by the camel of every one of you. As for your saying that you have come to visit me, he who visits me in Madinah shall be in my camp on the Day of Judgement." They said: "Messenger of God, this, then, is the journey which can never be regretted."

The Prophet asked them about their idol whom they previously worshipped, which was known as ʿAmm Anas. They said: "We give you the happy news that we have replaced it with your message. Some elderly people in our tribe still pay homage to it. When we go back, we shall destroy it, God willing. We have certainly been deceived by it."

The Prophet asked them about the most terrible case of their delusion by that idol. They narrated this story:

> We passed through a very bad period of drought. It was so hard that we ate whatever wastage we could pick up anywhere. We then raised all the money we could and bought 100 oxen. We slaughtered them all one morning as a sacrifice for our idol, ʿAmm Anas. We left them all for the wild beasts to eat. We needed that meat much more than the beasts. We had rain straight away, and the rain continued until the grass was several feet high. We were saying to each other: ʿAmm Anas has bestowed his bounty upon us.

They also told him they used to give a share of their cattle and harvests to their idol and a share to God. "When we planted our seeds, we reserved the middle of our fertile land for ʿAmm Anas and we reserved another area for God. Should the wind blow in such a way as to make the area we reserved for God yield richer crops we substituted our reserved lands and gave ʿAmm Anas the better crops. Should the wind blow differently, what we reserved for ʿAmm Anas remained its."

The Prophet told them that God had told him of this in His Qur'ānic revelations (*Sūrah* 6, verse 136). They also told the Prophet that when they went to ʿAmm Anas for arbitration in their dispute, the idol spoke to them. The Prophet told them that whatever they heard was the voice of Satan.

The delegation asked the Prophet about their religious duties and the Prophet explained those to them. He also ordered them to honour their promises and pledges, to give back what was deposited with them for safe keeping and to be good neighbours to whoever comes in to their neighbourhood, and not to be unjust to anyone. He said: "Injustice engulfs you with darkness over darkness on the Day of Judgement."

Having stayed for several days in Madinah, they bade the Prophet farewell and he ordered that they should be given gifts. They went back to their people and when they arrived they destroyed that idol before doing anything else.[10]

Rejecting a Post of Leadership

The delegations which continued to arrive in Madinah were the best proof of how Islam appeals to people when they have a chance to consider its teachings in a relaxed atmosphere and with open minds. Although most Arabian tribes had heard about Islam as a result of its long struggle against the Quraysh and polytheism, they could not form an objective view of its message until the Prophet sent many of his companions on informative missions to explain the message of Islam to all tribes and call on them to accept it. The account given here of these delegations is by no means exhaustive; it is meant only to give a picture of the change which was overcoming the whole of Arabia.

The story of the delegation from Ṣudā' in Yemen came in fulfilment of a promise given by one of their number to the Prophet some time earlier. After the conquest of Makkah and the conclusion of the work done by the Prophet in that area in the following months, the Prophet was preparing to go back to Madinah. However, he sent a number of detachments of his army to various parts of Arabia. One of these detachments was commanded by Qays ibn Sa'd ibn 'Ubādah, the son of the chief of the Anṣār. The detachment, 400-men strong, encamped at Qanāh in preparation to start their mission against the tribe of Ṣudā'. It so happened that a man from the same tribe was in Makkah at that time. He learnt about that force, went straight to the Prophet and said to him: "Messenger of God, I have come to you as a representative of my own people. Do not send this army to us, and I guarantee you that my people will respond favourably to your message." The Prophet issued his orders to that force not to go ahead.

Some reports mention that the man was called Ziyād ibn al-Ḥārith. He left Makkah and went back to his people, and started to call on them to accept Islam. He explained to them that it was in their interest to make their peace with the Prophet and the Muslim state. Some time later, Ziyād went to Madinah at the head of a 15-man delegation from his tribe. Sa'd ibn 'Ubādah, the chief of the Anṣār, asked the Prophet to allow him to be their host. He was a very hospitable host and the delegation wes warmly welcomed in his home. When they met the Prophet, they declared that they accepted Islam and pledged their loyalty to him. They also told him: "We will work for the cause of Islam among our people."

The Prophet said to Ziyād: "Brother of Ṣudā', you are certainly obeyed by your people." Ziyād replied: "Messenger of God, this is by the grace of God, and by the blessing of His Messenger." When the delegation went back to their people, they were able to spread Islam among them. A year later, 100 from Ṣudā' joined the Prophet in his farewell pilgrimage.

It is worth mentioning here that Ziyād accompanied the Prophet on one of his journeys. The Prophet travelled by night on that particular occasion. Ziyād reports:

> I was endowed with physical strength, and I was able to travel alongside the Prophet when his other companions could not keep pace with him. When it was dawn, the Prophet asked me to make the call to prayers [*adhān*]. I made that call without dismounting. We continued our journey for a certain time before encamping. The Prophet went away from us to relieve himself and came back. He asked me whether I had any water and I told him that I had a little. He asked me to pour it into a container and I did so. His companions were coming from all directions. He put his hand in the container and I saw, in between every two fingers, a spring gushing forth. He said: "Brother of Ṣudā'; had it not been for the fact that I feel too shy in the presence of my Lord, praised be He, we would have had enough to drink and give others to drink."
>
> He then performed his ablutions and said to me: "Announce among my companions that whoever wants to have ablution, let him come and have some water." When I did so, they all came and performed their ablutions. Bilāl wanted to announce the congregational prayer [*iqāmah*], but the Prophet

told him that since I made the call for prayer, I should make that as well. I made the announcement and the Prophet led us in prayer.

Some time earlier I had asked the Prophet to make me the leader of my people and to cause that to be put in writing. He had done so. When we had finished our prayers, a man came forward to complain against the leader of his tribe. He said: "Messenger of God, he tries to avenge certain hostilities which existed between him and us before our acceptance of Islam."

The Prophet said: "Nothing good comes to a Muslim from ruling over others."

Another man came forward and asked the Prophet to give him some money from *Zakāt*. The Prophet said to him: "God has not assigned the distribution of *Zakāt* either to an angel of high position or to a man who combines the positions of Prophet and Messenger. He has divided it among eight categories of people. If you belong to these categories, I will give you some. If you are in no need of it and you take it, it is then a headache and a sickness in your stomach."

I thought to myself that I had asked the Prophet two unnecessary things when I requested him to make me the leader of my people and asked him to give me some money from *Zakāt* when I am not in need of it. I, therefore, said to him: "Messenger of God, these are the two letters you have written me. Please take them back." When the Prophet asked me the reason I said to him: "I have just heard you saying that nothing good comes to a Muslim man from ruling over others, and I am a Muslim. I also heard you saying that to be paid from *Zakāt* when one is in no need of it, leads to a headache and a sickness in the stomach, and I do not really need it." The Prophet said: "What I have said is correct." He asked me to recommend to him a man from my tribe who could be made governor, and I recommended someone whom he appointed.

I then put my request to the Prophet: "Messenger of God, we have a well which is sufficient for our needs in winter, but in summer its water becomes scarce and we go all over the

> place to seek water. The Muslims among us today are still a minority, and we fear others. Will you please pray to God for us to make our well sufficient for us?" The Prophet asked me to give him seven little stones, and I did so. He rubbed the stones in his hand, and gave them back to me and said: "When you go back, throw these stones one by one into your well, mentioning the name of God as you do so." I did as he told me and our well has been overflowing with water ever since.[11]

The Muḥārib Delegation

Another late delegation was that of the tribe of Muḥārib, who arrived in the year when the Prophet offered his farewell pilgrimage – that is, the tenth year of his emigration to Madinah. The Prophet had some previous contacts with that tribe. At the time when he was still in Makkah, he approached pilgrims from tribes other than the Quraysh, explaining to them the principles of Islam and calling on them to believe in it. He did this when he realized that the Quraysh's hostility to Islam was, at least for the time being, insurmountable. Most of those tribes the Prophet approached did not respond favourably. One of them was Muḥārib, who gave him the harshest reply of all. Now, however, a ten-man delegation from Muḥārib arrived in Madinah to learn about Islam. They stayed for several days and Bilāl brought them their lunch and their dinner every day.

One day, the Muḥārib delegation had a session with the Prophet extending from *ẓuhr* to *ʿaṣr* – that is, from midday until mid-afternoon. One man in the delegation attracted the Prophet's attention. He fixed his eyes on him. This man said to the Prophet: "Messenger of God, you seem to recognize me. The Prophet answered: "I have seen you before." The man said: "You certainly have. You spoke to me and I replied to you most rudely when you approached the various tribes at ʿUkāẓ." The Prophet said: "That was so."

The man said apologetically: "Messenger of God, none among my fellow tribesmen at the time was as severe in his reply to you as I was. None rejected Islam more than I did. I now, however, praise God and thank Him for keeping me alive until this day in order to declare that I believe in you. Those companions of mine have all died maintaining their past faith." The Prophet said: "Hearts are in the hand of God, who is infinite in His glory." The man said: "Messenger of God, pray to God to forgive me my rudeness to you." The Prophet answered: "When anyone accepts Islam, his slate is wiped clean." The delegation from Muḥārib declared their acceptance of Islam before they started their journey home.[12]

The Land of Islam

The delegations which arrived in Madinah from various parts of Arabia all had different missions. Some of them merely wanted to gather some information about Islam and the nature of the society it had established. Others came to pledge their loyalty without committing themselves to being Muslims. Others still came to declare that they had accepted the faith of Islam and to tell the Prophet that he could rely on their support. The Prophet received all those delegations warmly. There was no question of coercing or pressurizing any group of people, or indeed any individual, to accept Islam. It was sufficient from the Islamic point of view for any tribe or community to declare its willingness to live in peace with Islam, not impeding its progress or scheming against it, to maintain the friendliest of relations with the Muslim community.

The Prophet was generous to all those delegations, whether they eventually accepted Islam or not. He ordered gifts to be given to them to the extent that every member of every delegation was given a personal gift. The Prophet's hospitality was extended to all. Those delegations who accepted Islam were assured that they were part of the Muslim community, enjoying all the rights of Muslims. With each such delegation, the Prophet sent one or more of his companions to teach them the essentials of their new faith and to help them lead an Islamic life.

Some of these delegations behaved in the manner to be expected only from uncultured Bedouins. The Prophet overlooked their rough manners and rudeness and did not allow these to interfere with his relations with them. They were people whom he loved dearly to win over to Islam, just as he loved dearly to win every person to his faith. Some delegations tried to exact concessions, or to make compromises over certain aspects of the faith of Islam. The Prophet would have none of that. He viewed his task as that of an honest messenger who had to convey his message full, complete and intact. It was not for him to change any of its principles, or indeed any of its details.

Those delegations continued to arrive, one after another, throughout the tenth year of the Prophet's settlement in Madinah. Hence, that year was generally a year of peace which the Muslim society in Madinah had not experienced before. At the same time it was a year full of activity. The work of consolidation continued throughout. One must remember that the majority of Muslims now were new converts who had not had enough training or education in their new faith. They had not lived through its 22 years of struggle and were not called upon to give the sacrifices that early Muslims had to give. Hence, they needed to learn more about Islam and they needed help in remoulding their lives in an Islamic fashion.

Hard Fighters Accept the Faith

The net result of that year was indeed that the whole of Arabia was now more or less loyal to Islam. Any tribe which contemplated standing up to the tide of Islam after the main centres of opposition to it had collapsed was simply contemplating an act which required a great deal of bravado. Its efforts, however, were bound to end in total failure. Nevertheless, the peaceful days of the tenth year of the Prophet's settlement in Madinah were disturbed by a certain tribe in Yemen boasting that it could do what no other tribe in Arabia, big or small, could. That tribe, al-Ḥārith ibn Kaʿb, lived in a certain part of Najrān. The Prophet sent a force of his companions under the leadership of his commander Khālid ibn al-Walīd, to subdue them. He made his instructions to Khālid very clear, ordering him to call on those people for three days to accept Islam before fighting them. If they responded favourably, Khālid was to accept their pledges. If their response was negative, he was to fight them.

When Khālid arrived in their area, he sent his men in all directions calling on the people of that tribe to accept Islam. They made it clear to the people of al-Ḥārith ibn Kaʿb that if they were keen to avoid war and to avoid being killed, then their only chance was to accept Islam. Their response was favourable. Khālid and his men stayed there teaching them the principles of Islam, the Qur'ān and the *Sunnah*. This he did in fulfilment of his instructions.

Khālid later sent a message to the Prophet in which he said:

> You, Messenger of God (peace be to you), have sent me to the tribe of al-Ḥārith ibn Kaʿb and commanded me not to fight them for three days during which I should call on them to accept Islam. If they do, I am to stay here, accept their pledges, and educate them in the faith of Islam and teach them God's Book and the *Sunnah* of His Messenger. If they refuse, I am to fight them. When I arrived here, I did as God's Messenger (peace be upon him) has commanded me. I sent my men to say to them: 'Banī al-Ḥārith, accept Islam and you will be safe.' They have accepted Islam without fighting. I am staying with them, telling them to do what God has commanded them to do, and to refrain from what God has forbidden them. I am teaching them the principles of Islam and the *Sunnah* of the Prophet (peace be upon him) until I receive instructions from God's Messenger. Peace and God's mercy and blessings be to you, Messenger of God.

The Prophet sent Khālid the following reply:

> In the name of God, the Merciful, the Beneficent. From Muhammad, the Prophet, the Messenger of God, to Khālid ibn al-Walīd. Peace be to you. I praise God; there is no deity other than Him. I have received your letter sent with your messenger in which you give me the news that the tribe of al-Ḥārith ibn Kaʿb have accepted Islam without a need for you to fight them. You have also told me that they have responded to your call and declared their belief that there is no deity other than God and that Muhammad is God's servant and

> Messenger. Thus God has given them His guidance. Give them then glad tidings and warn them against sin. You may come back and let a delegation from them come with you. Peace be to you and God's mercy and blessings.

Khālid returned with a delegation from the tribe of al-Ḥārith which included a number of their leading figures. When they met the Prophet they said to him: "We bear witness that you are God's Messenger and that there is no deity other than God." The Prophet said: "I, too, bear witness that there is no deity other than God and that I am God's Messenger." He, then, put to them the question: "Are you the ones who fight hard when they are checked?" Nobody replied. He repeated his question three more times before one of them, Yazīd ibn ʿAbd al-Mudān said to him: "Yes, Messenger of God, we are the ones you have described." He repeated his answer four times. The Prophet said: "Had it not been for the fact that Khālid has written to me that you have accepted Islam, I would have laid your heads under your feet." Yazīd said: "For this, we are not thankful to either you or to Khālid." The Prophet asked him: "To whom are you thankful, then?" He said: "We are thankful to God who has guided us through you, Messenger of God." The Prophet confirmed that the man's answer expresses the truth. The Prophet then asked them what helped them win their battles in pre-Islamic days. Their answer was that they were able to achieve victory because they were always united and they never started with aggression.[13]

The Last Delegation

The last of all delegations was that of the tribe of al-Nakhaʿ. They arrived in Madinah in the middle of Muḥarram of the eleventh year of the Prophet's emigration. That was nearly two months before the Prophet's death. Their delegation was the largest of all. It included 200 men and they stayed at the guest house in Madinah. They were already Muslims, since they had pledged their acceptance of Islam to Muʿādh ibn Jabal, the man the Prophet had appointed governor of Yemen. In other words, their mission was not that of learning about Islam. Rather, it was a trip undertaken to meet the Prophet and acquire the status of companionship with him.

One man in that delegation, Zurārah ibn ʿAmr, related a strange dream to the Prophet. He told him that he saw a female donkey which he left back home giving birth to a goat which was black and red in colour. The Prophet asked him whether he had left a maiden slave of his pregnant. When he answered in the affirmative, the Prophet told him that she had given birth to a boy who was Zurārah's own son. Zurārah asked the Prophet why the goat looked so strange in colour. The Prophet told him to come closer to him. When he did, the Prophet asked him in a whisper: "Do you have a whiteness in your skin which you hide from people?" The man said: "By Him who has sent you with the truth, no one has ever seen it and no one knows of it except you." The Prophet said: "That explains it for you."

Zurārah said: "Messenger of God, I also saw an ugly old woman coming out of the earth." The Prophet replied: "That is what is left of this world." Zurārah continued: "And I also saw a fire coming out of the earth separating me from a son of mine called ʿAmr. It spoke, saying: 'Fire, fire. A man with eyes and a blind man. Feed me and I will eat you all with your families and property'." The Prophet said: "This is a state of strife which takes place at a later time." Zurārah asked the Prophet what he meant by strife and he answered: "People will kill their leader, and a grinding conflict will take place between them. The one who does wrong thinks that he is doing well. A believer feels that to shed the blood of another believer is more satisfying than a drink of water. Should your son die before you, you will see it, and should you die before him, he will see it."

The man asked the Prophet to pray to God that he should not see that strife, and the Prophet prayed: "My Lord, let him not see it." The man died and his son was a participant in the strife which led to the murder of ʿUthmān, the third Caliph.[14]

A Special Position for Yemen

As already mentioned, the last two tribes of al-Ḥārith ibn Kaʿb and al-Nakhaʿ were from Yemen. The Prophet seems to have given a great deal of attention to Yemen in those years; he apparently felt that it was an area of great importance. He sent several messengers there with different tasks. Khālid was a military messenger. The Prophet also sent ʿAlī, his cousin, to consolidate the work done by Khālid.[15] In addition, he sent two civilian messengers, Abū Mūsā al-Ashʿarī and Muʿādh ibn Jabal. They were appointed governors, dividing Yemen between them. The Prophet told them that they should make things easy, not difficult, for the people. They were also to encourage people with hope and not to discourage them with pessimism. Moreover, the Prophet told them always to be on good terms with each other and not to be in dispute.

When Muʿādh ibn Jabal was about to leave Madinah to take up his assignment as governor of certain parts of Yemen, the Prophet went out with him giving him his instructions. Muʿādh was on his camel and the Prophet was walking alongside him. The Prophet said to him:

> You will be among people who had received earlier revelations. When you are there, call on them to believe that there is no deity other than God and that Muhammad is God's Messenger. Should they accept this from you, tell them that God has imposed on them the duty of praying five times daily. If they accept this from you, tell them that God has imposed on them the duty of paying *Zakāt* which is to be taken from the rich among them and paid to their poor. If they accept this from you, never touch their good money. Guard against a supplication of complaint against you by a person suffering injustice, for such a supplication goes directly to God.

The Prophet then said to him: "Muʿādh, you may not meet me again after this year. You may pass by this mosque of mine and by my grave." Muʿādh was in tears. The Prophet said to him: "Do not weep, Muʿādh. There is a time for weeping. Weeping is from the Devil."

The Prophet then looked towards Madinah and said: "The people closest to me are the God-fearing, whoever they are and wherever they are."[16]

These words of the Prophet pointed to forthcoming events. They were also the words of a Messenger of God who felt that his mission was approaching its completion.

Notes

1. Ibn Qayyim al-Jawziyyah, *Zād al-Maʿād fī Hadi Khayr al-ʿIbād*, Mu'assat al-Risālah, Beirut, 1986, Vol. 3, pp. 650-652. Also, Ibn Sayyid al-Nās, *ʿUyūn al-Athar*, Dār al-Turāth, Madinah, 1996, pp. 329-330.
2. Ibn Qayyim al-Jawziyyah, op.cit., pp. 652-653. Also, Ibn Sayyid al-Nās, op.cit., pp. 331-332.
3. Ibn Hishām, *al-Sīrah al-Nabawiyyah*, Dār al-Qalam, Beirut, Vol. 1, pp. 643-646. Also, Ibn Qayyim al-Jawziyyah, op.cit., pp. 622-723; Ibn Kathīr, *al-Bidāyah wal-Nihāyah*, Maktabat al-Maʿārif, Beirut, Vol. 1, pp. 104-108.
4. Ibn Sayyid al-Nās, op.cit., pp. 335-336. Also, Ibn Qayyim al-Jawziyyah, op.cit., pp. 657-658.
5. Ibn Kathīr, op.cit., p. 94. Also, Ibn Qayyim al-Jawziyyah, op.cit., pp. 672-673.
6. Ibn Hishām, op.cit., pp. 233-235. Also, Ibn Sayyid al-Nās, op.cit., pp. 324-325.
7. Ibn Sayyid al-Nās, op.cit., pp. 332-333. Also, Ibn Qayyim al-Jawziyyah, op.cit., pp. 653-654.
8. Ibn Sayyid al-Nās, op.cit., pp. 334-335. Also, Ibn Qayyim al-Jawziyyah, op.cit., pp. 655-656.
9. Ibn Kathīr, op.cit., p. 89. Also, Ibn Sayyid al-Nās, op.cit., p. 336; Ibn Qayyim al-Jawziyyah, op.cit., pp. 661-662.
10. Ibn Sayyid al-Nās, op.cit., pp. 336-337. Also, Ibn Qayyim al-Jawziyyah, op.cit., pp. 662-663.
11. Ibn Sayyid al-Nās, op.cit., pp. 338-340. Also, Ibn Qayyim al-Jawziyyah, op.cit., pp. 664-666.
12. Ibn Kathīr, op.cit., p. 89. Also, Ibn Sayyid al-Nās, op.cit., p. 338; Ibn Qayyim al-Jawziyyah, op.cit., pp. 663-664.
13. Ibn Sayyid al-Nās, op.cit., pp. 342-344. Also, Ibn Qayyim al-Jawziyyah, op.cit., pp. 686-687.
14. Ibn Hishām, op.cit., pp. 239-241.
15. Ibn Kathīr, op.cit., p. 104.
16. Ibid., pp. 99-100.

45

Mission Completed

WHEN THE TIME of pilgrimage drew near, the Prophet caused it to be known all over Arabia that he intended to offer the pilgrimage. It is well known that pilgrimage to the Kaʿbah has always been a religious ritual ever since Prophets Abraham and Ishmael (peace be upon them) raised that construction which was, according to the Qur'ān, the first house of worship ever to be built. Although distortion crept into the religious beliefs of the people of Arabia over the centuries to the extent that they worshipped idols and statues in place of, or in association with, God, they continued to do the pilgrimage as a religious duty, albeit in a corrupted form. Many habits were included in pilgrimage which cannot be acceptable to God, to say the least. Examples of these were the fact that the Quraysh considered themselves to be privileged over all Arabs and did not share in certain parts of pilgrimage because they were exempt from them, being the custodians of the Kaʿbah. They also imposed on pilgrims from outside Makkah to do the *ṭawāf* either wearing garments made in Makkah or in the nude. There were other forms and traces of polytheism in the rituals offered by the Arabs in their pilgrimage before the victory of Islam. As has been seen, the Prophet had dispatched his companion, Abū Bakr, to put a stop to all those aspects in the preceding year. Now it was time for the Prophet to make clear to the Muslims the duties of

Islamic pilgrimage as a major act of worship which earned the pilgrim forgiveness of his or her past sins.

For this reason, the Prophet caused it to be known that he welcomed anyone who wished to offer the pilgrimage with him. People started to come to Madinah from all over Arabia to join in this great Islamic worship. Moreover, a pilgrimage was the one act of worship which the Muslims had not yet seen the Prophet doing. Since every act of Islamic worship serves social, national and human purposes in addition to its spiritual and personal importance, it was necessary that the Muslims should learn how to offer pilgrimage directly from the Prophet. Furthermore, pilgrimage is an important part of the religion of Islam. Hence, the message of Islam would not have been conveyed complete unless the Prophet himself offered and taught Muslims how to offer pilgrimage.

Joining the Prophet on Pilgrimage

It was not surprising that people started to arrive in Madinah from all over Arabia shortly after the announcement was made that the Prophet intended to offer his pilgrimage. Every day, Madinah welcomed people from far and wide. Jābir ibn ʿAbdullāh, the Prophet's companion, supplied the most detailed and authentic account of the Prophet's pilgrimage. He recorded that when the procession of pilgrimage started from Madinah, he could not see its end either to the front or the back, or to the right or the left. Estimates of the number of people who joined the Prophet on his trip of pilgrimage from Madinah vary from 90,000 to 130,000. A similar number were waiting for him in Makkah to join him there.

When the Prophet completed his preparations for his blessed journey, he left Madinah at noon on Saturday the 25th of Dhul-Qaʿdah in the tenth year of the Islamic calendar, which makes the Prophet's emigration to Madinah its starting date. With him were all his wives and members of his household, the Muhājirīn and the Anṣār, as well as all those who came to join him from all Arab tribes. He had with him 100 camels which he intended to slaughter as a sacrifice. When he arrived at Dhul Ḥulayfah, which is now better known as Abyār ʿAlī, a place about 10 kilometres from Madinah, he offered *ʿaṣr* prayer, shortening it to two *rakʿahs*, since he was travelling. He entered into the state of consecration, wearing two white pieces of cloth, wrapping one round his waist to cover his body from the waist to well below his knees and throwing the other over his shoulders. He made his intention to offer the pilgrimage and the *ʿUmrah* combined – that is, he chose the *qirān* method of *iḥrām*, since he had brought his sacrificial animals with him.

When he mounted his she-camel to resume his journey, he started repeating the following form of *talbiyah: Labbayk Allāhumma labbayk. Labbayka Lā sharīka laka labbayk. Inna al-ḥamda wal-niʿmata laka wal-mulk. Lā sharīka lak.* This may be translated into English as follows: "I respond to Your call, my Lord. I respond to You: there is no deity other than You. All praise, grace and sovereignty belong to You. You have no partners." This epitomizes the worship of pilgrimage which enhances the notion of total submission to God and dedication to His cause. All the Muslims repeated the same sentences, asserting their submission and dedication to God. All the people in that noble procession were yearning to see the Kaʿbah and offer pilgrimage pure and complete, in the Islamic way. Every time they had to go uphill or descend a valley, encamp for rest or prayer, and every time a change of scene took place, they repeated that form of *talbiyah* which asserted their total belief in the oneness of God.

The noble procession continued its peaceful march. It was a procession which spread a feeling of security and reassurance to all around it. Its slogan was one of peace and security. Not a single person in that procession harboured any ill feelings towards anyone. None of them carried a weapon of any sort. None harmed an animal, frightened a bird, cut down a tree or destroyed any plant. It was, in short, a procession of love.

It was a peaceful march of a peaceful procession which spread a feeling of kindness, peace and security all around. Everywhere animals, birds and trees were at peace. The procession was at peace with all people and with all creatures. Its objective was one of love and solidarity. Its mark was one of true brotherhood and absolute equality. No worldly considerations distinguished any group in that procession over any other group. It was a dedicated procession in which there was no place for carnal desires, futile arguments, social distinction or quarrelling. It was a demonstration of love and brotherhood established on the solid basis of fearing to incur God's anger and seeking to earn His pleasure.

The journey took several days. The procession arrived in Makkah at sunset of the fourth day of Dhul-Ḥijjah. The Prophet stayed the night at Dhū Ṭuwā, on the outskirts of Makkah. In the morning he had a bath and entered Makkah in daylight. When the Prophet arrived at the Kaʿbah and saw the holy place, he lifted his hands and prayed to God to multiply the honour and sanctity of the House, and to honour and reward everyone who honours the House by offering pilgrimage or *ʿUmrah*. The Prophet entered the mosque and began his *ṭawāf* round the Kaʿbah, mounted on his she-camel. When he had finished his *ṭawāf* he offered a prayer of two *rakʿahs* behind the position known as Maqām Ibrahīm. Mounting his she-camel, he then proceeded to do the walk, *saʿī*, between the two hills of al-Ṣafā and al-Marwah. When he had finished that, he gave his orders to the Muslims with him who had not brought their sacrificial animals with them to release themselves from consecration, or *iḥrām*, until the time for pilgrimage was due. The Prophet and his companions stayed in Makkah until the 8th of Dhul-Ḥijjah, the time when the duties of the pilgrimage were due.

It is not our intention to give a detailed account of how the Prophet offered every duty of pilgrimage. That is more of a specialized study. The task of the biographer is to relate every major event in the life of the person whose biography he is writing to the main line of his life and the goals he sets out to achieve. He needs only to concentrate on those details which influence his decisions in major events.

In the case of the Prophet, however, every detail is important. Since pilgrimage is a main act of worship, the way the Prophet did every detail of it forms part of his guidance and should, therefore, be recorded and studied. The place of such study, however, is not his biography. It should be pursued in the works which document the Prophet's actions and sayings, relate them to one another and deduce whether a certain action is obligatory, recommended, permissible, discouraged or prohibited.

A Definitive Speech

Starting from Makkah on the eighth day of Dhul-Ḥijjah, the Prophet at midday mounted his she-camel and went to Minā, where he spent the night. In the morning, he prayed *fajr* in Minā before leaving for ʿArafāt after sunrise. At ʿArafāt he delivered his major speech, still mounting his she-camel. A man with a loud voice, called Rabīʿah ibn Umayyah ibn Khalaf, stood next to the Prophet's camel, repeating every sentence the Prophet said so that all those who were with the Prophet heard everything. The Prophet's speech that day was the highlight of his pilgrimage, outlining the nature of Islamic society. As usual, his speech began with the praise and glorification of God. The Prophet then went on to say: "People, listen to me as I explain to you, for I do not know whether I will ever meet you again in this place after this year. People, do you know in what month, day and city you are?"

They said: "We are on a sacred day, in a sacred month, in a sacred city." He said: "Know, then, that your blood, property and honour are forbidden you till you meet your Lord in the same way as the sanctity of this day of yours, in this month of yours, in this city of yours. You will certainly meet your Lord and He will certainly question you about what you do. Have I delivered my message?" They answered: "Yes." He said:

> My Lord, bear witness. He who holds something belonging to another for safekeeping must give it back to the person to whom it belongs. All usury transactions which have been made in the past days of ignorance are hereby abrogated. You may claim only your capital, neither inflicting nor suffering any injustice. God has decreed that no usury is permissible. The first usury transactions I abrogate are those of my uncle, al-ʿAbbās ibn ʿAbd al-Muṭṭalib. All cases of vengeance killings are hereby waived. The first case of killing I thus waive is that of ʿĀmir ibn Rabīʿah ibn al-Ḥārith. Have I delivered my message?

They said: "You have." He said:

> My Lord, bear witness. People, the postponement of sacred months is an excess of disbelief, a means by which those who disbelieve are led astray. They declare this postponement to be permissible in one year and forbidden in another, in order to conform outwardly to the number of months which God has made sacred, and thus they make allowable what God has forbidden. Time has now been set back in its original fashion which it had when God created the heavens and the earth. The number of months, in the sight of God, is twelve, out of which four are sacred, three consecutive ones and a single one: Dhul-Qaʿdah, Dhul-Ḥijjah, Muḥarram and Rajab, which falls between Jumādā and Shaʿbān. This is the ever-true law of God. Do not, then, sin against yourselves with regard to these months. When I am gone, do not revert to disbelief, killing one another. Have I delivered my message?

They answered: "You certainly have." Continuing his speech he said:

> My Lord, be my witness. People, you have an obligation towards your womenfolk and they have an obligation towards you. It is their duty not to allow into your homes anyone whom you dislike without your permission. Should they do that, God has permitted you to desert them in bed, then to beat them without any severity. Should they desist, they have the right to be provided with food and clothing, in fairness. Your womenfolk are in your custody; they are helpless. You have taken them on the basis of a pledge to God, and they are lawful to you with God's word. Fear God, then, in your treatment of women, and be kind to them. Have I delivered my message?

They replied: "Yes, indeed." He said: "My Lord, be my witness. People, the believers are brothers. It is illegal for anyone to take the property of his brother unless it is given without any coercion. People, your Lord is one and your father is one. All of you are the children of

Adam, and Adam was created from dust. The most noble among you is the most God-fearing. No Arab enjoys any privilege over a non-Arab except through the fear of God. Have I delivered my message?"

They answered: "Yes, you most certainly have." He said: "My Lord, be my witness. People, Satan has given up any hope of being worshipped in this land of yours. He is satisfied, however, to be obeyed in matters which you consider trivial. Guard yourselves against him, lest he corrupts your faith. I have left with you what should keep you safe from going astray should you hold fast to it. It is something clear and simple: God's Book and the *Sunnah* of His Prophet. You will be questioned about me. What will you say?" They said: "We bear witness that you have delivered your message complete and you have discharged your mission and given good counsel."

The Prophet pointed his forefinger at the sky and lowered it to point to the people, saying all the time: "My Lord, bear witness. My Lord, bear witness." The Prophet then said: "Let those who are present communicate what I have said to those who are not with us today. It may happen that those who come to know of it in this way may understand it better than some of those who have listened to it." Thus the Prophet concluded his major speech.[1]

Five Principles

This memorable speech outlines five basic principles of the Islamic programme of action. Two of these work on the level of the individual and three relate to the structure of Islamic society. Islam moulds the character of the Muslim on the basis of two fundamental principles. First, Islam severs all ties which a Muslim has with Ignorance, or *Jāhiliyyah*, its idols, practices, financial dealings, usury transactions and so on, because the adoption of the religion of Islam means a start of a new life for a Muslim which is completely divorced from the erroneous ways of the past.

The second principle is to guard against all forms of sin. The effects of sin are far more serious than the danger presented by any enemy in battle. All catastrophes in this life are caused by our sins, which also lead us to suffer in the hereafter. The Prophet also made it clear that he did not mean by sin the sinking back into idolatrous worship. Any intelligent person who comes to know of the faith based on God's oneness will never degrade himself to the extent of willingly accepting and claiming that God has partners. Yet the Evil One does not give up his attempts to seduce people into committing sins in order to lead them further astray.

The Prophet has also outlined three basic principles on which Islamic society is founded. The first is the tie of Islamic brotherhood which moulds the proper relationship between all Muslims. It is this brotherhood which makes every Muslim a patron of every other Muslim, giving him whatever help he can.

The second principle is supporting the weak so that their weakness does not make the whole society vulnerable. One should note in particular how the Prophet stressed the importance of being kind to women, since they are the weaker element in society.

The third principle is the cooperation between an Islamic government and the members of an Islamic society to achieve the proper implementation of Islamic law which works for the removal of all evil from society and its replacement with what is good.

The total sum of these five principles is to translate the Qur'ān and the *Sunnah* into practice. Hence, the Prophet did not forget to enjoin his companions to hold fast to them and implement them in their lives. Short as it was, the Prophet's speech included all the principles which are needed for the moulding of the perfect believer in Islam and the perfect Muslim society. Hence, the Prophet was keen to impress on his followers that he had delivered his message and discharged his mission. He repeatedly prayed to God to be his witness.

The Prophet's pilgrimage was his only performance of this religious duty since it was decreed by God. When he completed that pilgrimage, the Muslims were able to follow his practical guidance in all aspects of Islam. There were several indications which suggested that the Prophet's mission was approaching its end. So far, the Muslims were used to the fact that God's Messenger lived among them as one of them, receiving guidance directly from God, explaining to them the right course to follow in any problem they might have. To them, the prospect of continuing an Islamic life without the Prophet was something they could not contemplate. Yet the Prophet realized that that was inevitable. He, therefore, painstakingly tried to prepare them for that eventuality.

Indicating the Inevitable

We have seen how the Prophet bade farewell to his companion, Muʿādh ibn Jabal, whom he appointed as governor of Yemen: when Muʿādh was on the point of departure from Madinah, the Prophet told him that he might not see him again, though he might pass by his mosque and his grave. That piece of warning came only a short while before the Prophet embarked on his journey of pilgrimage. When he delivered his very important speech on the day when all pilgrims must be in attendance at ʿArafāt, he started by saying to his companions: "Listen to me, for I do not know whether I will ever meet you again in this place after this year."

That speech of the Prophet which highlighted the main principles of Islam and the foundation of Islamic society, was a farewell speech stressing the values in violation of which no Islamic society can retain its Islamic character. After every point the Prophet made in his speech, he asked his companions: "Have I delivered my message?" This was the attitude of a man, a Prophet, who understood well the value of his message and was keen to deliver it complete to the people so that they might implement it in practical life. When they declared that he certainly had delivered his message, the Prophet repeatedly asked God to be his witness to that.

If the message was duly delivered, and if that message, or the faith it represented, was complete, then the mission of the Prophet was over. Hence, when the Prophet recited to his companions during his pilgrimage the verse which was revealed to him – "This day I have completed your religion for you, and perfected My grace to you and approved Islam as your religion" – the significance was absolutely clear. ʿUmar ibn al-Khaṭṭāb, who was perhaps the companion of the Prophet endowed with the keenest perception, was in tears when he listened to the Prophet reciting this verse. Asked by his colleagues why he was crying, he answered: "Nothing comes after perfection but imperfection."[2] One can imagine that he sensed that the Prophet's life was drawing to a close.

Indeed, several statements of the Prophet and relevant incidents suggested to those who had keen insight that a great and noble life was approaching its end. When the Prophet went for stoning at ʿAqabah,[3] he said to the great crowd of pilgrims surrounding him: "Learn from me your rites, for I may never offer the pilgrimage again after this year."[4]

Moreover, the *Sūrah* entitled 'Victory' was revealed to the Prophet on the second day of his stay at Minā. It may be rendered in English as follows: "When God's help and victory come, and you see people embracing God's faith in groups, glorify your Lord and praise Him and ask His forgiveness, for He is much-forgiving." Two of the most learned companions of the Prophet, ʿUmar ibn al-Khaṭṭāb and ʿAbdullāh ibn ʿAbbās, the Prophet's cousin, realized that the revelation of the *sūrah* was an announcement to the Prophet that his time on earth would soon be over.[5]

Another indication of the approaching event took place earlier that year. In Ramaḍān, the Prophet used to stay in his mosque for ten days which he dedicated totally to worship. Every year he received the Angel Gabriel in the month of Ramaḍān and they recited the Qur'ān. This time, the Prophet stayed in his mosque for 20 days in Ramaḍān and the two of them recited the full text of the Qur'ān twice.[6]

When we look at the situation in Arabia at the time when the Prophet offered his pilgrimage, we find that he was able to establish a solid base for Islam from which it could spread its message to the rest of mankind. The Prophet was keen to indicate to his companions that Arabia must always remain the base of Islam. It is by the grace of God that it has continued to be so ever since. By the time all these indications were pointing to the approaching end of the Prophet's mission, the whole of Arabia was loyal to Islam. While it was true that many parts of the Arabian Peninsula underwent that great transformation from its old pagan faith to Islam, the most monotheistic of all religions, the Prophet realized that a change in reverse was highly unlikely. Certain factors and circumstances may lead to a renunciation of Islam, as indeed happened after the Prophet's death, but such challenges were bound to end in failure. Once the straightforward faith, based on God's oneness, took its hold in the hearts of people, it could never be easily renounced.

The Prophet's mission was approaching its end because the message of Islam embodied in God's revelations was conveyed by him to the Arabs, and through them to the rest of mankind. The establishment of the geographical base of Islam in Arabia ensured that Islam was to remain for ever an active force in man's world. Hence, the task of the Messenger was completely fulfilled.

After the Pilgrimage

When the Prophet had completed his pilgrimage, it was time for him to go back to Madinah. He returned with the Muhājirīn and the Anṣār, while people from other tribes went to their various places. The fact that he had delivered his message did not mean that the Prophet was to lead a comfortable and luxurious life. He went to Madinah in order to resume his duty as an advocate of Islam who called on people to embrace it. He went back to teach that the duty of striving for God's cause, i.e. *jihād,* does not end until the last breath of life.

If we imagine an ordinary leader returning to his capital after undertaking a journey which reassured him that the unity which he managed to achieve in his formerly badly divided country was absolutely solid, and the philosophy he has been preaching has taken its hold on the minds and hearts of his people, we are certain to have in mind a happy picture of a happy leader. He would certainly look at his past efforts, crowned with that unity, with satisfaction. We can also be certain that his first priority would be to consolidate that achievement before setting himself any further objectives.

When the Prophet returned to Madinah after his journey of pilgrimage, he was in a far better situation than that of our imaginary leader. He had certainly established a very solid base for Islam. Yet he recognized that the new faith needed time to deepen its roots in the life of Arabian society. Hence, a consolidation effort was needed.

The Prophet, however, was no ordinary national leader. Indeed, he was not a national leader at all. He was a Messenger of God and the head of a state which prided itself on having an ideological foundation. Considerations of race, nation, language or colour were not given any value in that state. At the same time, the Prophet realized that his message was not aimed at any particular nation. It was God's message to mankind. Hence, all people were addressed by that message. The Muslim nation, whether Arab or not, is placed in trust of that message, and it is responsible for making it known to all people. While compulsion is totally rejected as a means of converting people to Islam, informing others of the message God wants them to adopt and implement remains a duty of the Muslim nation.

This is the fundamental factor which made the Prophet's return to Madinah after his pilgrimage totally different from the return of a highly successful leader from a journey in which he takes stock of his achievements. The Prophet realized that a state founded on faith will always be exposed to a threat from any major power which finds that faith a threat to its supremacy. The danger was certain to be much greater, considering the fact that there were common borders between the Muslim state and the Byzantine Empire. Hence, he wanted to demonstrate to that empire that the old image of a weak tribal society in Arabia had been shattered for ever.

For a few weeks after the Prophet's return to Madinah, the Muslims lived in peace. That was a period of calm the like of which had not been seen in Arabia for many years. Soon, however, that air of peace was shattered. Farwah ibn ʿUmar al-Juthamī was governor of Maʿān, in the south of the present-day Jordan, appointed by the Byzantine Emperor. Farwah, however, received the message of Islam and recognized its truthfulness. He sent a message to the Prophet informing him of his acceptance of Islam. His action, however, infuriated the Byzantine Emperor, who ordered an army to subdue Farwah and arrest him. The Byzantine army did just that, and soon Farwah found himself in prison. After a summary trial, he was sentenced to death. Shortly afterwards, he was executed near a spring known as ʿAfrā' in Palestine. He was crucified and left on the cross for a long time in order to dissuade others from following his example. It is reported that when he was about to be executed, his final words were an appeal to those who were present to convey to the Muslims that he sacrificed his life willingly for the cause of Islam.[7]

The Choice of an Army Commander

The Prophet viewed the execution of Farwah as an act of provocation which could not be allowed to pass without the Muslim state making its presence felt. He, therefore, ordered that an army be raised under the command of Usāmah ibn Zayd ibn Ḥārithah, a youth of 17 whom the Prophet loved dearly. The Prophet's choice of commander served several purposes. For one thing, Usāmah was a talented young man. There was bound to be in his army a large number of capable soldiers, much older than him and highly qualified to be commanders themselves. The Prophet wanted it to be known that under Islam, seniority of age or position counted for nothing. Ability was the only criterion which distinguished people.

Moreover, Usāmah's father, Zayd ibn Ḥārithah, was formerly a slave owned by the Prophet's first wife, Khadījah. When she was married to the Prophet, 15 years before he received his first revelations, she gave him Zayd as a gift. He set him free, but Zayd stayed with him until he was killed in the first encounter between the Muslim state and the Byzantine Empire. He was the first commander of the Muslim army which fought that battle. The choice of Usāmah as the commander of the army on this occasion was a fresh demonstration that under Islam a son of a former slave was worthy of being commander of an army in which many people of noble birth were ordinary soldiers. Indeed, a great number of the Prophet's companions, from the Muhājirīn and the Anṣār, volunteered to take part in that expedition. Although the hard core of the Muslim nation – that is the Muhājirīn and the Anṣār, who had moulded their lives in accordance with Islam – were fully aware that the old distinctions between master and slave, aristocracy and commoners, were totally destroyed by Islam, a fresh, practical demonstration of their destruction was needed in order to instil the notion of equality of all Muslims in the minds of those who had only recently adopted Islam. For Usāmah to be a commander of an army in which the most senior of the Prophet's companions were soldiers was one such practical demonstration.

It has already been mentioned that Usāmah's father was the first commander of the Muslim army which fought the first encounter between the Muslim state and the Byzantine Empire. By his choice of commander, the Prophet perhaps wanted to pass a message to the Byzantines that the Muslim state wanted to avenge its military defeat in that encounter.

Yet the fact that Usāmah was so young led a number of the companions of the Prophet to question his appointment. The Prophet was informed of this when he was ill. He went out to the mosque with a band round his head and addressed the people. After praising God and glorifying Him, he said: "People, let this army of Usāmah fulfil its mission. I know you are questioning his appointment as you had questioned the appointment of his father as commander. He [Usāmah] is a worthy commander, as his father was also worthy of his command."

The Prophet gave Usāmah very clear instructions. He was to take his army into the heartland of Palestine, reaching the area of al-Balqā' and Darūm. This meant that Usāmah's mission was one of a demonstration of strength, aiming at making the Byzantine rulers think twice before embarking on any provocative adventure against the Muslim state. Another purpose was to reassure the Arabian tribes in the border area that the Muslim state did not look at its mighty neighbour with any feeling of awe. They were to be reassured that by embracing Islam, they did not expose themselves to any great danger from the Byzantine Empire.

It was only a matter of a few days until the army was raised. All the earlier Muhājirīn and many of the Anṣār volunteered to join. Among Usāmah's soldiers were such great figures as Abū Bakr and ʿUmar ibn al-Khaṭṭāb. Usāmah's army encamped at a place called al-

Jurf, a few miles from Madinah, waiting for the volunteers to get ready. Its departure, however, was delayed by an unexpected and unwelcome event.[8]

Notes

1. For details of the Prophet's journey to Makkah and the original text of his farewell speech see: Ibn Hishām, *al-Sīrah al-Nabawiyyah*, Dār al-Qalam, Beirut, Vol. 1, pp. 248-253; Ibn Kathīr, *al-Bidāyah wal-Nihāyah*, Maktabat al-Maʿārif, Beirut, Vol. 1, pp. 109-202; al-Wāqidī, *Kitāb al-Maghāzī*, Oxford University Press, 1996, Vol. 1, pp. 1088-1113; and Amīn Duwaydār, *Ṣuwar Min Ḥayāt al-Rasūl*, Dār al-Maʿārif, 4th edition, Cairo, pp. 586-593.
2. Ibn Kathīr, op.cit., p. 215.
3. Stoning is one of the symbolic rites of pilgrimage. A pilgrim throws seven little stones at three places close to each other to commemorate Prophet Abraham, who stoned Satan when he tried to dissuade him from complying with God's command to sacrifice his son, Ishmael.
4. Ibn Kathīr, op.cit., p. 187.
5. Ibid., p. 215.
6. Ibid., p. 223.
7. Ibn Sayyid al-Nās, *ʿUyūn al-Athar*, Dār al-Turāth, Madinah, 1996, pp. 326-327.
8. Ibid., pp. 369-370. Also, al-Wāqidī, op.cit., pp. 1117-1120; and Ibn Kathīr, op.cit., p. 222.

46

The Curtain Falls

IN HIS GREAT speech on the day of ʿArafāt, during his pilgrimage, the Prophet recited to the Muslims the third verse of *Sūrah* 5, The Repast, which says: "This day I have completed your religion for you, perfected My grace on you, and approved Islam as your religion." Indeed, that verse was the last to be revealed. One or two of the Prophet's companions, endowed with keen insight, recognized that it was an announcement of the completion of the Prophet's mission. They realized that when perfection has been achieved, only imperfection can creep in. No one, however, could imagine that the Prophet's life was approaching its end. But the Prophet was a human being, distinguished only by the fact that God had chosen him to convey His message to mankind. When the message has been delivered, his role is fulfilled.

Late in the month of Ṣafar, the second month in the Islamic calendar, of the eleventh year of the Islamic era, the Prophet asked Abū Muwayhibah, a servant of his, to accompany him one night to the graveyard of Madinah known as Baqīʿ al-Gharqad. He stood there praying to God to forgive those who were buried in that graveyard, as they had served Islam during their lives. It was an act which showed the Prophet's love and compassion for those who recognized the truth of Islam and moulded their lives according to it.[1]

The Prophet's Illness

In the morning, the Prophet found his wife ʿĀ'ishah complaining of a headache, but he told her that he also had a very bad headache. Following his habit, the Prophet visited all his wives that day, but he was in pain. Indeed, his illness was getting worse. When he was in Maymūnah's home, he felt too weak to carry on with his round. He, therefore, sought his wives' permission to be nursed in ʿĀ'ishah's home. They all agreed. This showed how the Prophet maintained an exceptional standard of fairness in his treatment of his wives. When they agreed that he might stay in ʿĀ'ishah's home, he went there supported by two of his cousins.

The Prophet's illness continued to get worse and he became feverish. He asked to be given a cold bath. He said to his immediate relatives: "Pour on me seven containers of water gathered from several wells.' ʿĀ'ishah reported that they made him sit in a tub which belonged to Ḥafṣah, another of his wives, and they poured the water on him until he asked them to stop. When he felt that his temperature had gone down, he asked his cousin, al-Faḍl ibn al-ʿAbbās, to take his hand and walk him to the mosque. He sat on the pulpit with a band round his head. He asked him to call the people. They came to listen to the man who had been teaching them what to do in every situation they faced. His address to them was one which stressed that injustice was not admissible in Islam in any way. He put that message in the clearest of forms: "I praise God, the One other than whom there is no deity. If I have ever beaten any of you on his back, let him come and avenge himself by beating me on my back. If I ever abused anyone, let him come and abuse me. To dispute is not part of my nature, nor does it appeal to me. The one of you who is dearest to me is the one who has a right against me and claims it. By so doing, he releases me, and I will be able to meet God with nothing held against me by any person."

There are more detailed reports of this and other addresses the Prophet made to the people in his illness. Their authenticity is not established absolutely. Their import, however, is in line with the Prophet's priorities. He was always eager to stress that justice was the main characteristic of Islamic society.

The Prophet stayed indoors as his health gradually deteriorated. On those few occasions when he felt a little better, he went out to the mosque to cast a glance on the community he had moulded and the people he loved. Abū Saʿīd al-Khudrī, the Prophet's companion, reports that the Prophet sat one day on the pulpit and said: "A servant of God has been given the choice of taking whatever he wished in this world or being with God. He chose the latter."

Abū Bakr was in tears as he said: "We sacrifice our parents for your sake, Messenger of God." The people were amazed as they heard Abū Bakr, an old man by then, making this remark when the Prophet was simply telling them of a choice made by a servant of God. Abū Bakr, however, was the one who recognized that the Prophet meant himself when he referred to that servant of God who was given the choice. The Prophet then said: "The one who has done me the greatest favour in his companionship and out of his wealth is Abū Bakr. Were I to choose a special friend, I would have chosen Abū Bakr. However, I opt for a relationship of Islamic brotherhood with him until God unites us all with Him."[2]

Those brief moments when the Prophet felt better made some of his companions feel that his complaint was only temporary. They were sure that he would soon be resuming his struggle for God's cause, and continue to take good care of the Muslim community. One day, his cousin and son-in-law, ʿAlī ibn Abī Ṭālib, visited him. When he left, people asked him how the Prophet felt that morning. He said: "I think that he has recovered, praise be to God."

His uncle, al-ʿAbbās, took him aside and said: "Cannot you realize? In three days it will all be over. I feel that God's Messenger will soon die as a result of this illness. I have seen men from the ʿAbd al-Muṭṭalib household when they were about to die. I would like you to go to God's Messenger to ask him who will be in charge when he has gone. Should it be one of us we would know, and if he is of a different clan, the Prophet might put in a word on our behalf."

ʿAlī said to his uncle, who was also the Prophet's uncle: "If we were to ask God's Messenger and if he were to deny us authority after him, people would never give it to us in future. By God, I would never ask it of the Prophet."[3]

It was clear that al-ʿAbbās referred to the political authority. He was certain that the Prophet was on his deathbed. He had seen many of his relatives when they were about to die, and he recognized that the Prophet was in the same state. Since he was the eldest and most distinguished man in the Hāshimite clan, to which the Prophet belonged, he wanted to know who would be the ruler after the Prophet. It was only natural that al-ʿAbbās should approach ʿAlī in this connection. ʿAlī was the first Hāshimite to accept Islam. Moreover, he was a man of high qualities, loved by people, close to the Prophet and a great servant of the Islamic cause. Hence, he was the natural Hāshimite candidate for the top post if the Prophet were to die. ʿAlī, however, did not wish to approach the Prophet in order that the Muslim nation could make its choice in the normal way. Moreover, ʿAlī's answer to his uncle showed his keen awareness of the Islamic view with regard to Islamic government. His Islamic instinct must have told him that no single family or clan was to enjoy any perpetual position of authority, not even the Prophet's own.

Expecting the Inevitable

The atmosphere in Madinah in those final days of the month of Ṣafar and the early days of Rabīʿ al-Awwal of the eleventh year of the Islamic era was a sad one. The Prophet was ill and showed no sign of any improvement in his health. Moreover, there was the added element of expectation, since a Muslim army was being raised for a confrontation with the Byzantine Empire. Every Muslim in Madinah loved the Prophet more than he loved his own children, or indeed himself. It is such a degree of love which faith demands of the believers. Hence, to see him ill and in pain was a very distressing sight for everyone. His illness was getting worse. He suffered a great deal, and those who were around him were very sad to see him suffering. His only surviving daughter, Faṭimah, was very unhappy to see it. She remarked: "How poorly and distressed my father is!" Hearing her, the Prophet said: "Your father will have no distress after this day."[4]

The army raised for an expedition against the Byzantines delayed its departure because of the Prophet's illness. When they heard that there was no improvement in his condition, Usāmah, the army commander, and a number of his soldiers came down to see the Prophet. When they were admitted into his room, they found him unable to speak. Later, Usāmah said that the Prophet raised his hand to heaven and put it on him, so he realized that the Prophet was praying for him.

The Prophet, however, continued to go out into the mosque and speak to the people whenever he had the strength to do so. One day he sat on the pulpit, with a band round his head, and people surrounding him. The first thing he said was that he blessed the people killed at the Battle of Uḥud, which witnessed the first military defeat suffered by the Muslims. He prayed for them at length and repeated his prayers for their forgiveness. He also ordered that all the doors which opened directly from people's houses into the mosque be closed down, with the exception of the door which opened from Abū Bakr's home. The Prophet's reason was that Abū Bakr was his closest companion and the one who had given his all for the service of Islam and the service of the Prophet.

Once he also commended the Anṣār and asked the Muhājirīn to take care of them. He said that the Anṣār would not increase in number as people do: "They have been my dedicated supporters who have given me refuge and support. Be kind to those who are good among them and forgive those who commit errors."[5]

It seems that the Prophet sometimes lost consciousness because of his illness. One day there were a number of women in his home, including some of his wives, as well as his uncle al-ʿAbbās. After a discussion of his condition they were agreed to give him some medicine in one of his cheeks. When the Prophet regained consciousness he asked them who had done that to him. They told him that it was his uncle giving him a medicine which was brought from Abyssinia. When he enquired why they had done that to him, al-ʿAbbās said that they feared that he was suffering from pleurisy. He answered: "This is an illness which God would not inflict on me."[6]

Abū Bakr to Lead the Prayer

The Prophet continued to lead the believers in prayers despite his illness. As his condition worsened, however, he was unable to continue to do so. He, therefore gave his order that Abū Bakr should lead the prayers. ʿĀ'ishah, the Prophet's wife and Abū Bakr's daughter, did not like her father to take that task. She feared that people would associate her father's leading the prayer with the Prophet's illness. She said to the Prophet: "Abū Bakr is a soft man. When he stands in your position he may feel it too hard on him." The Prophet said: "Tell Abū Bakr to lead the prayers!"

ʿĀ'ishah repeated her objection and the Prophet was angry with her. He said to her: "You women are Joseph's companions [referring to the incident when certain women dealt cunningly with the Prophet Joseph]. Let Abū Bakr lead the prayers."

Abū Bakr led the prayers 17 times, which meant three and a half days. Those were days when the Prophet was very ill. He is authentically reported to have said: "I suffer as much as two of you put together." Yet despite the severity of his illness, the Prophet continued to be alert, his mind always intact, and he continued to show his keenness to establish the main principles of Islam deep in the hearts of his followers. He continued to remind them of the basic principles of his message.[7]

The worst thing the Prophet feared for his nation was that they should come to attach undue importance and give unwarranted reverence to people or graves or anything else, as followers of other religions have done and still do. He wanted his nation always to maintain its firm belief in the oneness of God, worshipping Him alone. Even when he was in the throes of death, he continued to warn the Muslims against this danger. Both ʿĀ'ishah and Ibn ʿAbbās report: "When God's Messenger (peace be upon him) was in his illness, he used to put a shirt on his face. If he was breathless, he took it off. One day he said: 'Confound the Jews and the Christians for having made the graves of their Prophets places of worship'." That was a clear warning for the Muslims against making the grave of anyone a shrine to which homage is paid.[8]

Another evil which the Prophet continued to warn his followers against was following one's caprice or looking on others with contempt. Those who follow their caprice are bound to neglect their prayers, and those who are contemptuous of others are bound to treat their servants, employees and slaves badly. A nation which gives way to such evils is not worthy of life, nor can it contribute anything useful to life. It is bound to be neglected by God in punishment for its offences. Such neglect brings humiliation in this world and suffering in the Hereafter. The Prophet's fear that his Islamic nation should suffer such evils caused him to repeat warnings against them time after time. On his deathbed, the Prophet continued to draw the attention of the Muslims to the main aspects of good conduct. Anas ibn Mālik reports that on his deathbed the Prophet continued to emphasize the importance of prayers and extending good treatment to slaves. Other reports confirm this, pointing out that the Prophet continued to advise the Muslims with these words: "Attend to prayers; attend to prayers. Do not charge those whom your right hands possess [i.e. your slaves] with what they cannot bear. Fear God in your treatment of women."[9]

Prayer and Reassurance

Sometimes the Prophet was very keen to attend the congregational prayers and to see his followers in their worship. He would come out of his room and join them. Ibn ʿAbbās reports that one morning the Prophet came out for the dawn prayers when Abū Bakr had already started. Abū Bakr wanted to leave the leadership of the prayers to the Prophet and join the ranks of the Muslims. The Prophet, however, signalled him to stay in his position. He sat to the left of Abū Bakr and took over the leadership of the prayers, beginning his recitation at the point where Abū Bakr stopped. This meant that Abū Bakr was being led in prayer by the Prophet while he, Abū Bakr, continued to lead the congregational prayers.[10]

It seems that God wanted to reassure His Messenger that his nation was very firm in its belief in the message of Islam. He enabled him to look at them in their dawn prayer on the Monday when his death occurred. When they had stood in their rows, fully engaged in their worship, and Abū Bakr was reciting the Qur'ān in his melodious voice, the Prophet came out of ʿĀ'ishah's room and looked at them. When they saw him coming out, they were overjoyed. They started to move in their prayers so that they might enable him to pass. He, however, signalled them to stay in their positions. He was so happy looking at them in their prayers. Anas ibn Mālik reports: "I have never seen God's Messenger in a better shape than at that time."[11]

The Final Moments

The Prophet's appearance in that prayer gave the Muslims a false impression that he was much better. They thought that he was on his way to complete recovery. That took place on Monday the 12th of Rabīʿ al-Awwal in the eleventh year of the Islamic era. Happy in these hopes, people dispersed to attend to their affairs. Even Abū Bakr sought and obtained the Prophet's permission to visit those of his family who lived on the outskirts of Madinah. However, those were forlorn hopes, which were soon to be dashed. ʿĀ'ishah reports:

> On that day when God's Messenger went into the mosque he came back and laid down, putting his head in my lap. A man from Abū Bakr's household [ʿĀ'ishah's own family] came in carrying a green *miswāk* [a stick which Arabs used as a toothbrush] in his hand. God's Messenger looked at him and I realized that he wanted that *miswāk*. I asked him whether he wanted me to give it to him and he answered in the affirmative. I took it and chewed it a little to make it soft before giving it to the Prophet. He cleaned his teeth with it very strongly and in such a way as I had never seen him do it before. He then put it down. I felt his head getting heavier in my lap. I looked at his face and noticed that his eyes were staring hard. He said in a faint voice: "The Highest Company in Heaven." I said: "By Him who has sent you with the truth, you have been given a choice and you have made your choice." God's messenger (peace be upon him) then passed away.

ʿĀ'ishah is also quoted as saying: "God's Messenger (peace be upon him) died with his head between my chest and my neck, on my day [meaning that it was her turn, since the Prophet used to spend one day with each of his wives]. I have done no injustice to anyone in that."[12]

The Stunning News

The tragic news was soon known and people were stunned. The believers felt that the whole city of Madinah sank into total darkness. They were like young children losing their parents. They did not know what to do. Despite the repeated hints by the Prophet of his impending death and the fact that the Qur'ān mentions that possibility clearly, to lose him was, for his companions, something they could not imagine or visualize. He lived among them as one who was dearer to them than their souls. He was the sun of their lives. His death meant that they had to live in absolute darkness. For the Prophet to be withdrawn from their lives meant to them a vacuum which could never be filled. It was an event which they could not imagine or comprehend. Some of them were physically paralysed, others were dumb, others still made statements which they could not have thought out properly.

ʿUmar ibn al-Khaṭṭāb himself, whose opinions had been confirmed by the Qur'ān on more than one occasion, could not make a proper judgement. He stood up to address the people and said: "Some hypocrites are alleging that God's Messenger (peace be upon him) has died. God's Messenger has not died. He has gone to his Lord as Moses had done before and was away from his people for 40 nights. He then returned after people had said that he had died. I swear that God's Messenger (peace be upon him) shall return and chop off the hands and legs of those who allege that he has died."

The Realization

As ʿUmar was making his speech, Abū Bakr arrived, having been summoned when the tragic event took place. He paid no attention to anything going on around him until he went into the room of his daughter ʿĀ'ishah, the Prophet's wife. The Prophet was at one side, covered by a Yemeni robe. Abū Bakr went straight to him and uncovered his face, knelt down and kissed him, saying: "My father and my mother may be sacrificed for your sake. The one death that God has decreed that you shall experience, you have now had. You shall never die again."

He covered the Prophet's face and went out to find ʿUmar still speaking to the people. Abū Bakr said to him: "Listen to me." ʿUmar, however, went on speaking. Abū Bakr, therefore, started to speak to the people. When they realized that it was Abū Bakr, they turned to him and left ʿUmar. Abū Bakr began by praising God and thanking Him for His grace. He then said: "People, if any of you has been worshipping Muhammad, let him know that Muhammad is dead. He who worships God knows that God is always alive; He never dies." He then recited a verse of the Qur'ān which may be translated as follows: "Muhammad is but a messenger before whom other messengers have passed. Should he die or be slain, would you turn back on your heels? He who turns back on his heels shall do God no harm. God shall reward those who give thanks to Him." (3: 144)

When people heard Abū Bakr reciting that verse of the Qur'ān, they seemed as if they had never heard it before. They had indeed heard it repeatedly, and they repeated it then.

ʿUmar said: "When I heard Abū Bakr reciting that verse I was stunned and perplexed. I fell down to the ground, feeling that my legs could not support me. I realized, however, that God's Messenger was dead."[13]

Some years later, ʿUmar explained to Ibn ʿAbbās as the two were walking together why he said what he said on that day. He told him that reading the Qur'ānic verse – "We have made you a middle nation so that you may bear witness against mankind and the Prophet may bear witness against you" (2: 143) – he thought that the Prophet would remain alive in order to witness the actions of his nation for as long as human life continues.

It is only understandable that people should be stunned by the news of the Prophet's death. It was also to be expected that Abū Bakr, the first man to accept Islam and the closest to the Prophet of all his companions, should be the one who reminded the Muslim community of the very basic fact that God's Messenger was an ordinary human being and that he would ultimately die as every human being would die.[14]

The Final Preparations

The next thing to be done was to prepare the Prophet's body for burial. His body needed to be washed like every dead person. ʿAlī ibn Abī Ṭālib, the Prophet's cousin, and al-ʿAbbās's two sons, al-Faḍl and Qutham, as well as Usāmah ibn Zaid and Shaqrān, the Prophet's servant, were given that task. Aws ibn Khawlī, a man from the Anṣār, appealed to ʿAlī to let him also attend. ʿAlī supported the Prophet's body on his chest, al-ʿAbbās and his two sons helped him turn the Prophet's body while Usāmah and Shaqrān poured the water and ʿAlī washed him.

ʿĀ'ishah reports that when they were about to start washing the Prophet's body, they did not know whether to take off his clothes or to wash him with his clothes on. They were in disagreement when they were overtaken by sleep. All of them sat down and dozed off. They heard a voice telling them to wash the Prophet's body with his clothes on, so this was how they did it. They poured the water over his shirt and rubbed his body holding his shirt. They did not insert their hands underneath his shirt.

When they had finished washing him, they wrapped him in three robes. There were several suggestions concerning where to bury the Prophet. Some people suggested that he should be buried in his mosque. Others suggested that he should be buried alongside his companions. Abū Bakr, however, told them that he heard the Prophet say: "Every Prophet was buried in the place where he died." That settled the matter. The bed on which the Prophet died was removed and his grave was dug there. He was buried on Wednesday night, in ʿĀ'ishah's room. This is the spot where his grave remains.

After the Prophet was wrapped for burial, he was put on his bed. Abū Bakr and ʿUmar entered the room and said: "Peace be upon you, Messenger of God, with God's mercy and blessing." A number of the Muhājirīn and the Anṣār went in with them, as many as the room could accommodate. They spoke the same greetings and stood up in rows to offer the prayer for the deceased, the *janāzah* prayer. No one led the prayer as an Imām. Abū Bakr and ʿUmar, however, were in the first row next to the Prophet. They said:

> Our Lord, we bear witness that he has conveyed to us what has been revealed to him, given good counsel to his nation, struggled for God's cause until God has given triumph to His religion at his hands, and until God's words were complete. People believed in Him alone without partners. Our Lord, place us with those who follow the word revealed to him, and join us to him so that he recognizes us and You make us known to him. For he was compassionate and merciful to those who believed.

When they had finished they left the room to allow another group of the Muslims to go in and offer the *janāzah* prayer for the Prophet. They were followed by other groups as the room could accommodate them. When all men had offered their prayers, women went in also in groups to do the same. Children then followed in groups. However, there was no congregational prayer for the deceased. Everyone prayed on his own. This took the whole of Tuesday and the Prophet was buried on Wednesday.[15]

Thus the Prophet's life ended. His message, however, remains alive. It will remain intact for the rest of time as God has guaranteed its preservation in its original form. May God reward the Prophet Muhammad, His last Messenger, and grant him peace and blessings.

Notes

1. Ibn Kathīr, *al-Bidāyah wal-Nihāyah*, Maktabat al-Maʿārif, Beirut, Vol. 1, p. 224. Also, Ibn Sayyid al-Nās, *ʿUyūn al-Athar*, Dār al-Turāth, Madinah, 1996, p. 445.
2. Ibn Sayyid al-Nās, op.cit., pp. 445-446. Also, Ibn Kathīr, op.cit., pp. 224-229.

3. Ibn Hishām, *al-Sīrah al-Nabawiyyah*, Dār al-Qalam, Beirut, Vol. 1, p. 304.
4. Al-Bukhārī, *Al-Tārīkh al-Kabīr*, Vol. 16, Jamʿiyyat Dā'irat al-Maʿārif al-ʿUthmāniyyah, Hyderabad, India, 1960, pp. 283-284.
5. Ibn Hishām, op.cit., p. 300. Also, Ibn Sayyid al-Nās, op.cit., p. 447.
6. Ibn Hishām, op.cit., pp. 300-301.
7. Ibn Sayyid al-Nās, op.cit., p. 447. Also, Ibn Kathīr, op.cit., pp. 231-232.
8. Ibn Kathīr, op.cit., p. 230 and p. 238.
9. Ibid., p. 238.
10. Ibid., p. 234.
11. Ibid., p. 235.
12. Ibn Hishām, op.cit., pp. 304-305. Also, Ibn Kathīr, op.cit., pp. 239-240.
13. Ibn Hishām, op.cit., pp. 305-306. Also, Ibn Kathīr, op.cit., pp. 241-244.
14. Ibn Hishām, op.cit., p. 312.
15. Ibn Kathīr, op.cit., pp. 260-265.

Bibliography

Arabic

Classical Works

Al-Baghawī, Ḥusayn ibn Masʿūd, *Al-Anwāar fi Shamā'il al-Nabiyy al-Mukhtār,* "Focus on the Manners and Character of the Chosen Prophet," Beirut, Dār al-Ḍiyā', 1989

Al-Bukhārī, Muhammad ibn Ismāʿīl, *Al-Jāmiʿ al-Ṣaḥīḥ*, "The Authentic, Comprehensive Compilation," with commentary by Ibn Ḥajar under the title, *Fatḥ al-Bārī*, various editions.

Al-Suhaylī, ʿAbd al-Raḥmān ibn ʿAbdullāh, *Al-Rawḍ al-Unuf*, "The Sublime Garden," Cairo, Dār al-Ḍiyā'

Al-Wāqidī, Muhammad ibn ʿUmar, *Kitāb al-Maghāzī*, "The Expeditions," Beirut, ʿĀlam al-Kutub, 1984

Ibn al-Zubayr, ʿUrwah, *Maghāzī Rasūl Allah*, "The Expeditions of God's Messenger," Riyadh, Arab Education Council of the Gulf States, 1981

Ibn ʿAbd al-Wahhāb, Muhammad, *Mukhtaṣar Sīrat al-Rasūl*, "A Concise History of God's Messenger," Riyadh, Imam Muhammad ibn Saud University Press

Ibn Hishām, ʿAbd al-Malik, *Al-Sīrah al-Nabawiyyah*, "Life of the Prophet," Cairo, Mustafa al-Bābī al-Ḥalabī Publications, 1955

Ibn Qayyim al-Jawziyyah, *Zād al-Maʿād fī Hadi Khayr al-ʿIbād*, "The Guidance of God's Best Servant," Beirut, Al-Risālah Foundation, 1979

Ibn Sayyid al-Nās, Muhammad ibn Muhammad, *ʿUyūn al-Athar fī Funūn al-Maghāzī wal-Shamā'il wal-Siyar,* "Highlights of the Prophet's Expeditions, Character and Life," Beirut, Dār al-Ma'rifah

Recent Works

Al-Būṭī, Muhammad Saʿīd, *Fiqh al-Sīrah*, "A Scholarly Study of the Prophet's Life," Damascus, 1975

Darwazah, Muhammad ʿIzzat, *Sīrat al-Rasūl*, "The Life of God's Messenger," Cairo, ʿĪsā al-Bābī al-Ḥalabī, 1965

Duwaydār, Amīn, *Ṣuwar Min Ḥayāt al-Rasūl*, "Glimpses of the Life of God's Messenger," Cairo, Dār al-Maʿārif, 1953

Al-Ghaḍbān, Muhammad Munīr, *Al-Minhāj al-Ḥarakī lil-Sīrah al-Nabawiyyah*, "The Method of Action in the Prophet's History," Zarqā, Al-Manār, 1984

Al-Ghazālī, Muhammad, *Fiqh al-Sīrah*, "A Scholarly Study of the Prophet's Life," Cairo, ʿĀlam al-Maʿrifah, 1955

Al-Guindi, Anwar, *Al-Islam wa Ḥarakat al-Tarīkh*, "Islam and the Turn of History," Cairo, al-Risālah, 1968

Khalīl, ʿImād al-Dīn, *Dirāsah fī al-Sīrah*, "A Study of the Prophet's Life," Beirut, Al-Risālah and Dār al-Nafā'is, 1987

Khaṭṭāb, Maḥmūd Shīt, *Al-Rasūl al-Qā'id*. "God's Messenger as a Military Commander," Baghdad, Maktabat al-Ḥayāt and Maktabat al-Nahḍah, 1960

Al-Nadwī, Abū al-Ḥasan ʿAlī al-Ḥasanī, *Al-Sīrah al-Nabawiyyah*, "The Prophet's Life," Jeddah, Dār al-Shurūq, 1977

Al-Nadwī, Sulaymān, *Al-Sīrah al-Nabawiyyah*, "The Prophet's Life," Damascus, Dār al-Fatḥ and Al-Maktab al-Islāmī, 1963

Qalʿajī, Muhammad Rawās, *Al-Tafsīr al-Siyāsī lil-Sīrah al-Nabawiyyah*, "A Political Interpretation of the Prophet's History, Beirut, Dār al-Salām, 1979

Quṭb, Sayyid, *Fī Ẓilāl al-Qur'ān*, "In the Shade of the Qur'ān," 10th edition, Beirut, Dār al-Shurūq, 1982

Al-Sibā'ī, Muṣṭafā, *Al-Sīrah al-Nabawiyyah*, "The Prophet's Life," 4th edition, Beirut, Al-Maktab al-Islāmī, 1977

'Uthmān, Muhammad Fatḥī, *Dawlat al-Fikrah*, "The Ideological State," Kuwait, Al-Dār al-Kuwaitiyah, 1968

Works in English

'Abdul Hakim, Khalifa, *The Prophet and His Message*, Lahore, Institute of Islamic Culture, 1972

Ahmad, Fazl, *Muhammad, the Holy Prophet,* "Heroes of Islam Series", Lahore, Ashraf, 1960

Ahmad, Syed Khan Bahadur, *Essays of the Life of Mohammed and Subjects Subsidiary Thereto,* Vol. 1, London, Trubner, 1870

Ali, Syed Ameer, *A Critical Examination of the Life and Teachings of Mohammed,* London, William, 1873

———, *The Spirit of Islam, A History of the Evolution and Ideals of Islam with a Life of the Prophet,* amplified and revised ed., London, Chatto & Windus, 1964

Amin, Muhammad (ed.), *The Sayings of the Prophet Muhammad,* Lahore, Lion Press, 1960

Amin, Muhammad, *Wisdom of Prophet Muhammad*, Lahore, Lion Press, 1960

Andrae, Tor, *Mohammed: The Man and His Faith*, translated by Theophil Menzel, New York, Barnes & Noble, 1957

Azzam, Abdel Rahman, *The Eternal Message of Muhammad*, translated by Caesar E. Farah, New York, Devin-Adair Co., 1964

Bodley, Ronald Victor Courtenay, *The Messenger: The Life of Muhammad,* Garden City, New York, Doubleday & Co., 1946

Bosworth-Smith, R., *Mohammed and Mohammedanism*, London, Murray, 1889

Carlyle, Thomas, *On Heroes, Hero Worship, and the Heroic in History*, Berkeley, University of California Press, 1993

Draz, Muhammad Abd Allah, *Islam, The Straight Path*, edited by Kenneth Morgan, New York, The Ronald Press, 1958

Essad Bey, *Mohammed: A Biography*, translated by Helmut L. Ripperger, New York and Toronto, Longmans, Green & Co., 1936

Galwash, A.A., "The Life of Prophet Mohammad," *The Religion of Islam*, 5th ed., Cairo, Imprimerie Misr, 1958

Al-Ghazālī, Abū Hamid Muhammad, *Ihya' Ulum al-Din*, Book XX, edited and translated by L. Zolondek, Leiden, E.J. Brill, 1963

Gibb, H.A.R., *Mohammedanism, An Historical Survey*, London, Oxford University Press, 1953

Glubb, Sir John Bagot, *The Life and Times of Muhammad*, London, Hodder & Stoughton, and New York, Stein & Day, 1970

Guillaume, Alfred, *New Light on the Life of Muhammad*, Manchester, Manchester University Press, 1960

Gulick, Robert, *Muhammad, the Educator*, Lahore, Institute of Islamic Culture, 1953

Haykal, Muhammad Hussein, *The Life of Muhammad*, translated by Ismail Al-Faruqi, London, Shorouk International, 1983

Hilliard, Frederick Hadaway, *The Buddha, the Prophet, and the Christ*, London and New York, C. Allen & Unwin and Macmillan, 1956

Hosain, Sayid Safdar, *The Early History of Islam: An Impartial Review of the Early Islamic Period Compiled from Authentic Sources*, Karachi, Mushtaq Ali K. Laddhani, 1971

Husain, Athar, *Prophet Muhammad and His Mission*, Bombay and New York, Asia Publishing House, 1967

Ibn Hisham, ʿAbd al-Malik, *The Life of Muhammad: A Translation of Ibn Ishaq's Sirat Rasul Allah*, London and New York, Oxford University Press, 1955

Ibn Sa'd, Muhammad, *Kitab al-Tabaqat al-Kabir*, translated by A. Moinul Haq assisted by H.K. Ghazanfar, Karachi, Pakistan Historical Society, 1967

Imamuddin, A.M., *A Political History of Muslims: Prophet and Pious Caliphs,* Dacca, Najmah, 1967

Iqbal, Afzal, *Diplomacy in Islam: An Essay on the Art of Negotiations as Conceived and Developed by the Prophet of Islam*, Lahore, Institute of Islamic Culture, 1962

Jeffery, Arthur, *Islam: Muhammad and His Religion*, New York, Liberal Arts Press, 1958

Johnstone, P. Delacy, *Muhammad and His Power*, New York, Charles Scribner's Sons, 1901

Khan, Inamullah, *Maxims of Mohummud*, Karachi, Umma Publishing House, 1965

Lane-Pool, Stanley, *The Prophet and Islam*, abridged from 1879 edition, Lahore, National Book Society, 1964

Liu Chai-Lien, *The Arabian Prophet: A Life of Mohammed from Chinese and Arabic Sources*, translated by Isaac Mason, Shanghai, Commercial Press Ltd., 1921

Margoliouth, D.S., *Mohammed and the Rise of Islam*, London, G.P. Putnam's Sons, 1905

Mohy-ud-Din, Ata, *The Arabian Prophet: His Message and Achievements*, Karachi, Ferozsons, 1955

Muir, Sir William, *The Life of Mohammad from Original Sources*, a new and revized edition by T.H. Weir, Edinburgh, J. Grant, 1923

Pike, Edgar Royston, *Mohammed, Prophet of the Religion of Islam*, 2nd ed., London, Weidenfeld, 1968

Quṭb, Sayyid, *In the Shade of the Qur'ān*, Leicester, The Islamic Foundation, Vols. I–V (1999–2002) so far Published.

Sarwar, Hafiz Ghulam, *Muhammad the Holy Prophet*, Lahore, Sh. Muhammad Ashraf, 1964

Siddiqui, Abdul Hameed, *The Life of Muhammad*, Lahore, Islamic Publications, 1969

Stobart, James William Hampson, *Islam and its Founder*, London, Society for Promoting Christian Knowledge; and New York, Pott, Young & Co., 1877

Suhrawardy, Sir Abdullah al-Mamun, *The Sayings of Muhammad*, London, J. Murray, 1954

Watt, William Montgomery, *Muhammad at Mecca*, Oxford, Clarendon Press, 1960

———, *Muhammad at Medina*, Oxford, Clarendon Press, 1966

———, *Prophet and Statesman*, London, Oxford University Press, 1961

Wessels, Antonie, *A Modern Arabic Biography of Muhammad: A Critical Study of Muhammad Husayn Haykal's Hayat Muhammad*, Leiden, E.J. Brill, 1972

Widengren, George, *Muhammad, the Apostle of God, and His Ascension*, Uppsala, Lundequistska Bokhandeln, 1955

Index

B

I

J

N

R

S

T

U

V